Mikayel S. Giurjian
His Life and Work

Mikayel S. Giurjian, c. 1960.

Harutiun Mekeryan

Mikayel S. Giurjian
His Life and Work

Edited and translated by

Vatche Ghazarian

Mayreni
2005

Library of Congress Control Number: 2005927894

Mekeryan, Harutiun
Mikayel S. Giurjian: His Life and Work

For information:
Mayreni Publishing, P.O. Box 5881, Monterey, CA 93944, U.S.A.

ISBN: 1-931834-12-1
ISBN: 978-1-931834-12-4

MAYRENI PUBLISHING 2005

This publication was made possible by a generous grant from

The Dolores Zohrab Liebmann Fund

Dedication

I dedicate this book to the memory of my deported parents:
Hagop Harutiun Mekeryan (1887–1959)
and
Mariam Hagop Mekeryan, née Tavitian (1895–1979)

Acknowledgments

The author extends his gratitude to the Dolores Zohrab Liebmann Fund for financing the publication of this monograph, and by doing so, helping save Mikayel Giurjian's work from oblivion.

The author is most thankful to his close friend Yervant Azadian who, as the trustee of Giurjian's archive, graciously wrote the foreword entitled, "Restoring Giurjian's Literary Heritage."

A word of appreciation also to the translator, Dr. Vatche Ghazarian, for his meticulous approach.

Contents

Restoring Giurjian's Literary Heritage

A sincere confession is in order. When I first began reading in the media an elaborate study on Mikayel S. Giurjian's literary legacy, I was overcome by feelings of jealousy and a sense of being robbed. I was a close associate of Giurjian during his last years, and he had bequeathed his personal archive and library to me, assuming that I would maintain and assess his literary heritage to the best of my ability. And here, a stranger was intruding in our intimacy and daring to make an evaluative attempt, as if robbing me of a proprietory right.

However, as I familiarized myself with the meticulous and devoted work of the stranger, Harutiun Mekeryan, a feeling of embarrassment began to sink in, as I came to realize that I had been late in fulfilling the mission with which Giurjian had entrusted me. Gradually embarrassment turned into admiration, not because I found in Mekeryan a person who shared my appreciation for Giurjian's work, but because a consumate philologist was analyzing the writer's heritage thoroughly and in a scholarly manner. Mekeryan was deciphering and evaluating it as only a skilled scholar of our literature in Armenia is trained to do, with regard to our classical writers.

Leaving behind emotional considerations, the restoration and publication of Giurjian's novel, *Mardig Agha,* along with Mekeryan's study, provided me with the opportunity to collaborate with him. Earlier, the publication of *Mardig Agha* was left incomplete, because of the unprecedented storm the novel had stirred when it was first published as a serial in Arpiarian's *Nor Geank* in London.

The partial publication of the novel had naturally left the door open for misjudgments and, even, ill judgment. A critic like Oshagan, otherwise an admirer of Giurjian's aesthetic taste and broad literary concepts, had considered the novel incomplete because of the structural flaws of the second part. Mekeryan, however, thanks to his meticulous and diligent work, was able to gather and piece together the scattered portions of the novel—its incomplete published sections and unpublished hard-to-read manuscripts—to reveal the full profile of the novel and, finally, present it to the assessment of readers and literary historians alike.

When Giurjian was still alive, every time I prodded him to prepare the complete manuscript of *Mardig Agha* for publication, he would refer, with a mixture of seriousness and fun, to the national and partisan storm the work had caused and the physical threats he had received earlier. His fear was validated when his close literary associate, Arpiar Arpiarian, was assassinated in 1908 and by the attack Vahan Tekeyan suffered in 1916, which left him with an orphaned eye. These acts deepened Giurjian's fear that within the Armenian community there were people who might react to the power of words with brute force. At Guirjian's death, caused by an accident, the novel had remained incomplete for sixty-six full years, depriving readers of the pleasures of its complete version along with the opportunity to assess it. Thanks to Mekeryan, on the centennial of the completion of the novel, *Mardig Agha* was published in its entirety. Now, standing firm on the facts of world literature, we can assert that the novel was not only a masterpiece in Mikayel Giurjian's literature, but also in Armenian satirical literature. With the complete novel published, Giurjian's literary profile emerged under a new light.

Unfortunately, the fate of *Mardig Agha* loomed over Giurjian's entire collection. Despite numerous works, a multifaceted literary profile, and his continuous presence on the literary-theatrical-national stage, his literature has been forsaken.

In an ironic turn of events, Giurjian was even "deprived" of the "fate" of martyred writers. Indeed, in the aftermath of the Genocide, the Friends of Martyred Writers, in their zeal to bring justice to those writers who had been martyred, published their selected works. Giurjian suffered because he was not a martyred writer. The irony of fate was that although those writers were physically martyred, their literature was partially redeemed, whereas Giurjian survived physically, while his valuable literary accomplishments traveled the road of martyrdom. The work Mekeryan initiated emancipates Giurjian's literature from martyrdom and elevates it to the level he deserves within Armenian and world literature.

Mekeryan has written a monograph entitled, *Mikayel S. Giurjian: His Life and Work*. This work is not reminiscent of what Henri Troyat did when he outlined Tolstoy, Turgenev, and other Russian writers with factual and fictional definitions, nor did Mekeryan follow the footsteps of Chobanian who immortalized, with pulsating sensitivity, the last days of the dying poet, Turian. Mekeryan takes a more pragmatic approach, believing and suggesting that the complete restoration of Giurjian's heritage will provide Armenian literature and critics with a completed universe of data from which to fairly review and reclassify the wronged writer.

Giurjian himself, during the last decade of his life, revolted against the indifference his monumental contribution experienced. He tried, with the haste of a traveler running late to catch a train, to save a portion of his works from oblivion. But when he died suddenly and I was left as his literary heir, I felt obliged to transfer the archives entrusted to me to the Museum of Literature and Art in Armenia in order to save them. I hoped that a caring hand someday would revive his valuable literary heritage.

The scheme Mekeryan has used in this volume was beyond my imagination and even beyond Giurjian's recollections that had begun to fade in his last years.

During my conversations with the aging author, although he always demonstrated to me a real taste of his literary spirit, he failed to impress those around him with the multifaceted and incredible volume of his creations. In Mekeryan's monograph, different dimensions of the writer are demarcated, revealing the full profile of the literary critic and the scholar of literary history. All the facets of Giurjian's profile fall into place here.

Mekeryan expands our knowledge of Giurjian's labor by defining the impressive literary fruit harvested from Giurjian's pen. In other words, this book focuses on Giurjian's work. It is the first completed endeavor on the topic. At the same time, the profoundness of Giurjian's contribution and literary talent remains a challenge to measure.

Mekeryan's unreserved admiration for Giurjian's work is very moving; his love for the writer is unquestionable; and his commitment, in particular, is pure as he dares to fill a gap in Armenian literary history that can no longer be ignored.

Mekeryan's admiration for Giurjian does not blunt his senses as a literary critic. He feels free also to point out the weaknesses in Giurjian's works.

I have always entertained the presumption to have a good command of Giurjian and his work, loving both with unreserved admiration. But this monograph by Mekeryan has made Giurjian more familiar and more likable even to me; that is, of course, assuming there was room left in my complete love and admiration.

In civilized countries, the archives of writers have fared better: national libraries, museums, or personal collections host them, leaving little room for hazards and plenty of opportunity for investigation and research. Specialists simply go to these centers to conduct their research. In the Armenian case, too often, works—together with the writers—have been martyred. This loss has narrowed the confines of research, and often resulted in scattering a writer's heritage throughout the world, owing to the wanderings of the writer during his lifetime.

Researchers of Armenian literary talent often confront insurmountable barriers. Giurjian's literary heritage is scattered throughout the literary and social media of his times, from Constantinople to Tbilisi and from Cairo to

Europe—the possibility for the researcher to miss something remains ever present. But Mekeryan did not despair before this challenge. Instead, he patiently gathered the materials he intended to study. By the time he initiated his research, he had collected an impressive body of works by Giurjian, and with the patience of a conscientious philologist, he classified the material into separate chapters in order to develop a complete mosaic.

After his brief introduction, the author designates a chapter to the evaluation of Giurjian's contemporaries and literary critics. Mekeryan follows this with a chapter on Giurjian's life, including many previously unpublished and interesting new facts. He then dedicates a chapter to Giurjian's two satirical novels, *Mardig Agha* and *New School*—the first was published incomplete; the second never went to print. Mekeryan continues by discussing Giurjian's plays, then discusses the author's novellas, short stories, and literary sketches. Giurjian the poet is yet another revelation, and Giurjian the journalist presents one of the most interesting facets of the writer.

The works Giurjian translated deserve credit as well. Mekeryan focuses on Giurjian's work as a critic and dedicates a separate section to him as the ingenious coiner of new words, which is a rare phenomenon in the history of Armenian literature.

The volume concludes, appropriately, with an epilogue. Each of these chapters deserves reflection on its own, because Mekeryan has included so much in each: so rich are they that it will be impossible to reflect upon them without pleasure.

Despite his admiration, Harutiun Mekeryan does not go overboard in his judgment of Giurjian's literature. Rather, he sees his role as discovering and introducing the writer's works, in the belief that the discovery and publication of them will secure a fair evaluation of Giurjian's talent by contemporary and future critics. Collecting the evaluations by Giurjian's great contemporaries reflects part of this effort.

Mekeryan bases his evaluation of Giurjian's works on source materials and not on published articles or analyses. At first, he gathered sources from dust-covered archives, letters, and media in order to synthesize them later and position his discoveries within a panoramic picture. The style of his work is reminiscent of that of Manug Apeghian who, while composing his study, *History of Armenian Ancient Literature*, excavated the sources and subjected them to literary evaluations at the same time.

Mekeryan's work is the first monograph dedicated to Giurjian's literary legacy. Even individual articles and studies on Giurjian are rare in the Armenian media. This volume lays the foundation for *Giurjianology*.

Charents, in illustratively assessing Tumanian's work, stated that Tumanian toasted with Homer, Goethe, and other great people. The same image applies to Giurjian, too. He not only toasted with great world writers such as Corneille, Racine, Balzac, and Daudet, but also he was a close friend of many great Armenian contemporaries, such as Tekeyan, Indra, Arpiarian, Odian, Yeghia Demirjibashian, Oshagan, Pashalian, and Gamsaragan. If we consider the diversity of talents and the unique natures each of these great Armenians possessed, and if we consider that they were unable to find common ground with each other—for example, with his love for life and drinking, Odian was the opposite of self-contained, austere Tekeyan; in the intensity of his metaphysical hallucinations, Yeghia was hardly a match for Arpiarian who kept his finger on the pulse of *The Day's Life*—Giurjian found common ground with all of them: he drank with Odian, became sobered with Tekeyan, and shared Indra's grief over the mystery of the cypress trees. He was a man of bohemian lifestyle and noble mind. People loved him sincerely and appreciated the diversity of his talent.

The dark genius of Armenian literature, Indra, wrote in a letter to Giurjian: "Your mastery surpasses all." Dikran Gamsaragan declared Giurjian "a true talent." The master of Armenian satire, Yervant Odian, summarized Giurjian's satirical giftedness as follows: "Mikayel Giurjian was a permanent contributor to the newspaper; he flooded the pages of *Azad Pem* with his boundless wit, sharp mind, and sparkling and unparalleled zeal." Oshagan, the stringent critic, who was more inclined to "flatten" than praise, offered the following appraisal of Giurjian with his stingy pen: "Mikayel Giurjian comes into view with all the liveliness, interests, and aspirations of his generation. And like the most talented of them, he almost always remains at the brink of his intentions." Had Oshagan known what Mekeryan knows about Giurjian, he would certainly have moved him from the edge to a more central position in contemporary literature.

Mekeryan also cites testimonies from Teotig, Pashalian, Tekeyan, Sarukhan, and others, and even includes comments from non-Armenian authors who read Giurjian's works in French. By doing so, he paints a panoramic picture of Giurjian's work. In addition, Mekeryan does not limit himself to gathering the praises addressed to Giurjian; he criticizes authors such as Meruzhan Barsamian and Kurken Mkhitarian, who in the works they dedicated to the history of literature either mistreated or completely ignored Giurjian's contribution.

A Life's Outline

Mekeryan believes that the discovery of a writer or an artist is the sum of the merits that have been stored over generations and often fermented by the environment's influence on genes. For example, Leopold Mozart, a rigid musician, gave birth to Wolfgang Amadeus Mozart's genius, and each of Bach's twenty sons carried in them a strain of their father's universally resonant sparkle. Among Armenians, Shahnur owes much to his folklorist uncle, Teotig.

This is the context in which Mekeryan approachs Giurjian's life. He dissects the facets of the author's family heritage: the journalistic side of his father, Sahag Effendi; the attempts his uncle, Arshag Altunian, made in writing novels (*The Poor Man's Honor*); and finally his mother's wit and metaphoric expressions. All of these combine to form the subsoil of Giurjian's literature.

Mekeryan emphasizes Giurjian's sudden emergence as a consummate writer. Indeed, at the age of nineteen or twenty, his composition of such a perfect novel as *Mardig Agha* was testimony to a precocious talent. Mekeryan cites Giurjian's contemporaries as evidence of those who were caught by surprise that they had not witnessed Giurjian's talent grow, because he made such an abrupt debut as a polished mind and literary talent rarely encountered. This phenomenon belongs to poetry in general: Medzarents and Turian in Armenian literature; Shelley, Keats, and Lord Byron in English literature. With regard to the novel, for example, it is said that Balzac's literary genius achieved maturity once after his fortieth birthday.

Giurjian's friendship with Tekeyan, Arpiarian, Demirjibashian, Indra, Shirvanzaté, Gamsaragan, Pashalian, Reteos Berberian (his teacher), and others is an inseparable part of his biography. The fire that fueled Giurjian's literature was, undoubtedly, his boundless love of life. As a young man, he made the following entry in his diary: "I killed death. Instead of death killing me, I killed death. I did well, didn't I? I do not want anything related to death in me."

This struggle against death was a constant theme in Giurjian's life and work. For instance, in a short story entitled *March*, an aging couple superstitiously believes the month of March to be deadly and by repelling it, year in and year out, they believe to have gained another year to live. I have witnessed the revision of the story. Originally, Giurjian attributed the shriveled features of the old couple to eighty-plus years. When revising it, Giurjian himself had left his eighty-fifth year behind. Feeling his own mortality close, with a strike of his pen he raised the old couple's age to ninety, believing that he had repelled death by several more years by doing so. My last evening conversation with Giurjian also touched upon the theme of death. He said he had left behind all kinds of ailments and disasters, and he was curious about what would cause his demise.

The following morning, he died, the victim of a tram accident. I don't think he had counted on such a fate.

Giurjian turned his life into literature and his literature into life; he believed both were immortal.

Mekeryan comes up with a unique approach in constructing Giurjian's biography. He interlaces the author's life with the major developments of his time, especially those that influenced his thoughts, emotions, and literary production. Through memoirs and citations from articles, Mekeryan vividly revives the era in which Giurjian lived. Giurjian was the chronicler of his era, living on the margins of partisan confrontations.

The full discovery of the pseudonyms Giurjian used is not a minor achievement. Karekin Levonian's *Dictionary of Armenian Pseudonyms* and Father Arsen Pakraduni's *Armenian Bibliography and Encyclopedia of Armenian Life* did not satisfy Mekeryan in unearthing Giurjian's pseudonyms. Relying instead on primary sources, he was able to complete possibly the whole gamut of pseudonyms used: Hamshirag A., Zarmayr, Baruyr, Arsen Molar, Bedros Akatan, Bond, Srjep, etc.

Giurjian not only liked to adorn himself with pseudonyms, but he also found pleasure in dealing with others' pseudonyms. He related that once Vahram Papazian visited Egypt to stage a play with local actors, reserving the major role for himself. One of the actresses was a wealthy Armenian lady whose precious ring Papazian snatched during the performance, touching off a scandal in the community. Years later, Papazian visited Egypt again, this time with an Italian theatrical group, disguised under the name Vahram Bardi. Charmed by the pseudonym, Giurjian wrote a critical essay, adding in its concluding part: "Yes, Vahram owes[1] … a ring to the Egyptian Armenian community."

The Place of the Satirical Novel, *Mardig Agha,* in Literature

The fact that the satirical novel *Mardig Agha* has not been published in full in the Armenian media, nor as a complete book, has had adverse impact on the recognition of Giurjian's talent. This unfortunate circumstance has always kept his ability lagging behind his potential. The satirical novel has not been evaluated adequately in order to clarify Giurjian's true status in Armenian literature.

Perhaps this fact troubled Harutiun Mekeryan, the erudite specialist of Armenian literature, more than it caused anguish to Giurjian. Therefore, to rectify this condition, Mekeryan tried to remedy the injustice. The remedy would have not been possible through praising Giurjian's talent or blaming the critics for their indifference; rather, what was necessary was entrusting the novel, in its entirety, to the judgment of history. Therefore, a century after the creation of the novel, Mekeryan wrote: "We are pleased that our dream of many years has finally come true and that we have succeeded in publishing the continuation of the novel, *Mardig Agha*. We were able to gather, interpret, and edit copies of the manuscripts of unpublished chapters, and present the satirical novel in its full text to the readers in 1999."

This is not as a modest an achievement as Mekeryan admits to. In fact, it is a responsible and commendable realization that has breathed new life into Giurjian's literature by providing both critics and readers with the opportunity to see the real features of the wronged author under a new light; and, having done so, to pronounce a more positive verdict upon his rich heritage.

Giurjian excelled in every genre he applied himself to, thanks to his profound aesthetic sense. Nevertheless, *Mardig Agha* remains his masterpiece.

Despite the great admiration Mekeryan holds for Giurjian and his legacy, he does not lose his balance when dealing with Giurjian's deficient works. For instance, Giurjian's biographies mention a second novel, *New School.* The fact that Giurjian never completed it led literary historians to speculations, and it generated a mystique to the effect that its publication would have been an additional contribution upon which to build Giurjian's literary merits. It is a fact, though, that Giurjian never revised nor completed the work. I have to confess that as the beneficiary of Giurjian's manuscripts, I have not had the opportunity to look into the novel in full, because of the haste with which I sent his archive to Armenia for safekeeping. Mekeryan was perhaps the first person, other than the author, who looked at the manuscript. After a thorough examination he decided that "*New School* is not on the level of *Mardig Agha*." Consequently, Mekeryan avoided the temptation to edit and subsequently publish the book.

New School reflects the clash between the romantic and realist literary schools, without necessarily reflecting the fire of creation or the craft of literary composition.

Conversely, *Mardig Agha* announced Giurjian's tumultuous entry into the field of Armenian literature at a time when he was barely twenty years old. During historic critical moments, writers—whether satirists, novelists, or poets—make irreproachable discoveries from nations' characters. For example, it is said that in 1453, when Sultan Fatih besieged Constantinople, the Byzantine palatines were debating how many angels could stand on the tip of a pin. Or, in the case of Armenians, Tigran the Great exclaimed in view of the approaching Roman army: "If the approaching people are delegates, they are too many; but if they are soldiers, too few!" The Romans, however, approached and destroyed the first ever and last Armenian empire. These happenings might not correspond with historic truths; nevertheless, they precisely and truthfully characterize the period and situations. It is possible to see a direct link that stretches from Tigran the Great's boastful statement to Yervant Odian's *Panchuni* and Giurjian's *Mardig Agha*. Even Cervantes's *Don Quixote*, in its boundless satire, characterizes the dismal period of the decline of the age of chivalry.

Mardig Agha is the satirical chronology of Armenian society's developments. The 1894–1896 massacres under Sultan Abdülhamid touched off a mass migration toward Egypt and elsewhere. These human masses, uprooted from their lands, desperately tried to adapt to new and strange circumstances. Demonstrating human and national attributes typical to crisis periods, these events provided the focus for Giurjian's extraordinary talent.

The powerful novel made two important statements. First, it shook the contemporary society from its foundation by creating a major scandal. Second, it heralded the appearance of an established novelist.

Odian, Pashalian, Bartevian, and others offered many testimonies about the novel, but the best description of Giurjian's talent comes from an excerpt from a letter by Indra: "You never demonstrated the apprenticeship or rawness of a beginner as I did in the arena, and it was on the occasion of your first writing (signed Zarmayr Sahagian) that Yeghia Demirjibashian told me in Geneva that you were, already, an accomplished master. I had the opportunity to read *Mardig Agha* in the issues of *Nor Geank*, and I can testify that it is barely worth less than any of the recent works that carry your signature, and I cannot think of a truly able person, except you, whose literary life has been free of the weakness of revealing the story of his *progress*."

Other Elements of Giurjian's Talent and Labor

Giurjian spent most of his days befriending the great writers of his time, enriching his talent through their works and, unconsciously, approaching their heights. Having had the opportunity to periodically flip through the mostly French books Giurjian bequeathed to me, I discovered that he penned in the margins of these books words of admiration, comments, or noteworthy phrases, as if planning to use his scribbles as raw material for his prose or poetry.

All of these thoughts, inspirations, and scintillations passed through Giurjian's prism and then were expressed in his short stories, sketches, or poems.

Mekeryan's study dedicates a chapter to prosaic works of the genre. He critically examined *The Scribe's Dream, The Café, What the Angel Saw, New Dress, March, Runaway Horses,* and other works. *The Scribe's Dream* was first published in French and met with critical acclaim. On the occasion of the publication of its Armenian version, Indra wrote to Giurjian: "*The Scribe's Dream* made me cry; it is a gem." Indeed, these are works endowed with rich Oriental colors, the scents of spices, and an unusual talent for observation. After classifying and analyzing every thing, Mekeryan refers to Giurjian, saying: "This is why one can place him in the company of Goethe, Schiller, Hugo, Tolstoy, and Dostoyevsky."

Giurjian the Poet

Giurjian's thoughts seemed to always flow with poetic images. Even in his prose, his tendency to compose with metaphoric thought is present. Giurjian sporadically paused even in *Mardig Agha,* which is a novel and belongs to the prosaic genre, to describe nature's lyrical scenery. To a certain extent, his poetry reflects, in Armenian literature, the atmosphere of Baudelaire, Verlaine, and Rimbaud from the symbolist school of literature.

Over and above his rhymed poems, which are thoroughly discussed by Mekeryan, Giurjian caught readers by surprise when in his advanced age he published a book of free verse, *To the Adored, from the Bottom of My Heart,* that was filled with the tender pulsation of adolescent love.

Giurjian as Publicist

Giurjian contributed to many publications, extending from Constantinople to Egypt, Bulgaria, France, the United States, Lebanon, and elsewhere. Relentless in his search, Mekeryan found and mentioned in his monograph the names of all of these publications, and he often reflected upon Giurjian's important articles and presents excerpts from them.

Giurjian's pen cut into our national ego like a sharp lance. He analyzed many facets of Armenian life, and like the responsible and knowledgeable thinker he was, he always discussed issues and phenomena, pointing out, at times, our sensitivities and ethnic pride.

Years before Shahnur, he dared to antagonize our presumptions and describe the mindset of our nation realistically and truthfully. For instance, in an article entitled "The Armenian's Mind," he wrote: "The Armenian mind, in its general and essential lines, is more imitating than creative, more receptive than productive, more analytical than synthetic. The primary characteristic of the Armenian mind is appropriation. Due to the unfavorable conditions our nation has been destined to from the beginning, the Armenian mind has not been able to freely develop or the seeds of creative forces to flourish."

Giurjian often came up with similar courageous statements. By depicting flaws in the Armenians' character, he strived to see the national collective will strengthened. In another article, he suddenly burst out: "We have to be collectivist more than ever, pan-national as never before, give up our individualism, and belong to the race, allow ourselves to be driven by its infallible instinct and palpitate with its boundless love."

It is evident that the sensitive poet of lyric personal emotions knew also the value and weight of collective power when using his journalistic pen.

Translated Literature

The huge stock of translated literature has had an important impact upon the formation and fruition of modern Armenian literature. The translators of the nineteenth century intended to make international, and, in particular, French literature accessible to Armenian readers. Mekeryan, in his monograph, presents a list of these translated works, most of which were in line with popular taste. Toward the end of the nineteenth century, however, literature in translation was refined and poetry and works of finer literary taste were added. Just as our Golden Age brought the literature of the ancient world to our people, so did the nineteenth century with regard to contemporary literature.

Mekeryan reserves a special place for Giurjian within the field of translated literature.

Giurjian had already provided evidence of an amphibious literature by publishing his first poetic works in French, and having published his most renowned oriental sketches in two languages. Therefore, to him, crossing from one language to another, or analyzing the literature of one language in another language, was second nature. Mekeryan, in his monograph, chose translations from Baudelaire, Verlaine, Lamartine, Ronsard, and other

French writers, and compared them with the translations of other Armenian writers, in order to prove Giurjian's skill and competence in this field. By doing so, Mekeryan demonstrated Giurjian's linguistic and literary skills, particularly when he compared Giurjian's translations from French with translation of the same works into English, such as Baudelaire's *The Cracked Bell* and Lamartine's *The Lake.* At the same time, Mekeryan exposed the characteristics and poetic rules of each language.

One of the most interesting chapters of the book is the chapter dedicated to Giurjian's translational art. However, I have to say that the sections covering Giurjian's prosaic and poetic translations are unbalanced. For example, the section reserved for Alfonse Daudet's satirical novel, *Tartarin of Tarascon*, could have been more elaborate. Indeed, the translation of Daudet's novel is a masterpiece in itself, especially with regard to the psychological penetration, the coinage of appropriate words, and the truthful transfer of the fine humor. Daudet had left Paris to retire to his provincial home and felt free to voice sharp judgments about the lifestyle and mentalities of Parisians and big cities in general, through allegoric works and, in particular, through his *Letters from My Mill. Tartarin* was his great contribution to world satire. In the preface Giurjian wrote for Odian's *Panchuni* by Aleksandr Sarukhan's caricatures, he stated that Daudet's satirical novel is of the same caliber as Dickens's *Pickwick Papers* and Cervantes's *Don Quixote.* Giurjian translated *Tartarin* with the same verve, maintaining not only its spirit, but also its taste and scent.

In the epilogue attached to the complete publication of *Mardig Agha* (which was supposed to be the prologue), I mentioned that had Daudet known the Armenian language and been acquainted with Giurjian's translation, he would have wished, to begin with, to have had his work written in Armenian, because thanks to Giurjian's talent, Daudet's talent was reflected so truthfully.

Giurjian the Literary Critic

Those who are only marginally familiar with Giurjian's critical works may, perhaps, be tempted to marginalize their importance. The same applies to many others, because Giurjian's profound critical works are not collected in one volume. Here, too, Mekeryan searched the media and gathered a rich stock of the author's critical works, in order to assert that Giurjian was an authority in this field as well.

Giurjian analyzed and assessed certain contemporary writers, and he argued with influential critics in defense of true values. For example, he describes Yeghia Demirjibashian's best pages and spirituality as composed "with an intense dash… inspiration, one drop of blood and self-gushing abundance." In a different instance, he refutes Oshagan's verdict about Indra, writing: "I find him stunningly and outrageously unfair toward Diran Chrakian who, in his opinion and the opinion of many others like me, which will also be shared by future generations, was the greatest Armenian genius, our most 'universal' genius in a European sense, and our greatest artist-poet-thinker."

Making generalizations about Armenian literature, Giurjian laments the lack of memoirs, a genre that is fortunately witnessing a renaissance particularly in American literature. He considers Arpiarian's *Obituaries* and *The Day's Life*, and Odian's *Twelve Years Outside Constantinople*, successful examples in this regard.

The Miracle of Coining Words

In Armenian literature, Mikayel Giurjian is one of the most aesthetic writers, if not the most aesthetic, not only in terms of content, but also, and in particular, with regard to his ability for artistic processing, linguistic flexibility, and his exceptional gift in preserving the inner soul of words.

Giurjian's language is juicy and picturesque. Puns and word coinage, in particular, pleased him.

Writers establish the linguistic standards of literature, the media, the stage, and even daily conversation. It is they who give life to new words.

Mekeryan's monograph would have been incomplete if he had not included Giurjian's exemplary contribution to this field.

The gift of providing casual words with new connotation, and creating newly coined words, requires a profound knowledge of our language and particularly a familiarity with classical Armenian, which enables correct etymological endeavors and coinage of new meaningful words.

The writers of the Soviet era were deprived of this linguistic potential, because by adopting a new orthography, they could not recognize the profiles and roots of words. Consequently, they could not create new words by adding suffixes or prefixes, or turning simple words into compounds. Even the most graceful writers—when unfamiliar with Ancient Armenian or classical orthography—were captives of a language that was superficial and, often, lacking in character.

The lack of new word coinage leads one to adopt new words, thus impoverishing our language. Giurjian's literature offers guidance to all writers who aspire to use finer language and add an artistic grace to their language and style. Mekeryan presents numerous samples of Giurjian's linguistic inventions.

Baruyr Sevag was a rare Soviet Armenian writer who appreciated and implemented the artistic value of language in poetry. According to Mahari, Sevag created his own language in which he wrote his poem, *Unsilenceable Bellfry.* This phenomenon remains unduplicated in Armenian literature.

Mekeryan discovered the principle behind Sevag's success and cited the very words of Sevag, which are appropriate to repeat here. In an article entitled "Let's Protect and Enrich Our Mother Language" [Bahbanenk yev harsdatsnenk mayrenin], Sevag stated: "The Armenian language, for example, has an advantage that few other languages of the world have: the ease and flexibility of coining words. And if any language, even a language richer and more flexible than the Armenian, ought to borrow words because of the scarcity of possibilities for coinage, then a language like the Armenian ought to Armenianize such a word, because, as a general rule, the foreign word says much less to Armenians than the successful coinage of a word in their mother tongue."

Today, in Armenia, people adore Sevag's labor and memory, but many intellectuals, despite adoring him, adamantly keep our language in a straitjacket that has impoverishing effects.

* * *

By writing his academic oeuvre, Mekeryan has attained several achievements. First, he made a significant contribution to the history of Armenian literature by filling in a huge gap. Second, he restored the profile of Giurjian's literary heritage. Third, he prepared a guidebook for *Giurjianology,* and in doing so, enriched our literature with the full power of the writer. Fourth, he partially remedied the anguish Giurjian felt until his departure from this world that he had been wronged and neglected. Fifth, he provides a scheme for the academic and scholarly publication of Giurjian's works, establishing the author's place in the history of Armenian classic literature.

* * *

Giurjian was always charmed by the red trees that bloomed in Egypt at the beginning of summer. The trees brightened the parks and sidewalks with flowers. Intoxicated with their charm, Giurjian walked down the streets with his big shoes as an eternal traveler on these paths. The trees are called "flamboyant" in French, and Giurjian brilliantly translated them into Armenian as "vareni" [burning tree, in a sense]. He liked the trees so much that he wished one was planted on his grave site. Years after his death, when I visited the Armenian cemetery of Heliopolis in Egypt, and I saw, next to gorgeous mausoleums, his grave—as forlorn as the destiny of Armenian literature—I wrote, "Who Will Plant a Flamboyant?" on Giurjian's mound.

With his seminal work, Harutiun Mekeryan comes to symbolically plant that flamboyant.

Yervant Azadian

Mikayel S. Giurjian, c. 1907.

Foreword

Although well known to Armenian intellectuals, Mikayel Giurjian's name is still unfamiliar to the public—this despite the fact that his prose and dramatic works have earned him a unique place in the history of modern Armenian literature. Exemplified by his cultural, civic, and patriotic activities, from the last decade of the nineteenth century into the sixth decade of the twentieth century, Giurjian remained true to his beliefs. As a writer, he produced prose and verse, plays and novels. In addition, he worked as an editor and a translator. His life crisscrossed several literary generations. Throughout his career he remained faithful to the fundamentals of literary realism and he always employed his satirical talent from a noble, avant-garde, and honorable vantage point.

Productive and multifaceted, Giurjian wrote the following works: *Mardig Agha*, a satirical novel; *Charshêlê Artin Agha*, a comedy co-authored with Yervant Odian; *The Salvation* [Prgankê], a drama co-authored with Dikran Gamsaragan; *Heroic Play* [Herosakhagh], a comedy on Armenian national themes co-authored with Yervant Odian; *Twenty Years Later…* [Ksan dari yedk…], a comedy; *The Name Day Night* [Anunin kisherê]; *New Dress* [Nor lat]; *The Lie True, the Insane Sane* [Sudê irav, khentê khelok]; *Drtad and Dajad* [Drtad yev Dajad]; and *The Ineffaceable Tome* [Anchncheli madeanê], short stories and novellas that depicted Armenian family and national life; *The Scribe's Dream* [Keatibin yerazê] and *The Café* [Srjaranê], images of the Orient; *To the Adored, from the Bottom of My Heart* [I khorots srdi khosk ênt bashdelvuyn], a collection of free verse; and a great number of chronicles, editorials, critiques, articles, and translations of both prose and verse.

Reading the works of Giurjian, who knew how to narrate and describe artfully, brings great pleasure. He emerged during the realist period of Armenian literature, and he presented life with a demanding meticulousness. He described events and people with a profound feeling that mixed human sorrow and smiles with cutting humor. Gifted in the art of masterful observation and analysis, and knowing well the transcendent social significance of satire, he played an instrumental role in popularizing the literature of his day.

He participated in the foundation and development of Armenian realist literature. His contributions have served to immortalize his name. His concerns for national education as well as other pressing issues of his time became the theme and substance of his writings, which he penned diligently and published prolifically in contemporary Armenian newspapers of many countries. Giurjian's works are appealing and inspiring. They are woven with a delicate style and scrupulously crafted with pure and fluid language.

This monograph is intended to present the literary heritage of Mikayel Giurjian—his prose, verse, dramatic works, journalism, theoretical-aesthetical articles, book reviews, and translations, as well as his biography, civic activity, and literary connections. It will acquaint the literary community and critics with this unappreciated yet exceptionally talented author of Armenian literature; and in doing so, define his rightful place in modern Armenian literature.

This monograph is the first extensive study dedicated to Mikayel Giurjian and his work. The author of this monograph thus can make no pretense of claiming that this work is flawless or exhaustive. The author studied Giurjian's work over many years and compiled an unpublished anthology that includes books Giurjian published in many countries and articles found scattered throughout Armenian newspapers and periodicals deposited at libraries in Armenia and Los Angeles. The author also studied Giurjian's personal archive located at the Museum of Literature and Art of Armenia, which includes letters, manuscripts, and journals in which Giurjian penned his feelings and travel impressions, made personal notes, and jotted literary contemplations.

While studying the life and literary heritage of Giurjian, the author deciphered, edited, and published the manuscripts he found in Armenia: *"The National Activist," or the Greatness and Fall of Iknadios Rupinian* ["Azkayinjin" gam medzutiun yev angum baron Iknadios Rupiniani], a comedy in three acts; and *Mardig Agha*, Giurjian's famous satirical novel. These works were published in 1999, in celebration of the 120th anniversary of Giurjian's birthday. They were funded by Harutiun Simonian, an Armenian diasporan patron of the literary arts, and published under the auspices of the Museum of Literature and Arts of Armenia. Giurjian's unpublished handwritten satirical novel, *New School* [Nor tbrots], was deciphered and annotated.

Arpiar Arpiarian, Yeghia Demirjibashian, Krikor Zohrab, Dikran Gamsaragan, Levon Pashalian, Yervant Odian, Yervant Srmakeshkhanlian, Arshag Chobanian, Vahan Tekeyan, Teotig, Hagop Oshagan, Suren Bartevian, Simon Simonian, Yervant Azadian, Aleksandr Sarukhan, and Hmayag Kranian are among the Armenian men of letters and arts who have highly praised Giurjian's talent.

This is the first book on Giurjian in which readers will find an analysis of the writer's aesthetic creations and a discussion of their special characteristics. Indeed, while traveling the road paved by Hagop Baronian and the writers of the 1880s, Giurjian furthered the progress of Armenian literature as a novelist and prose writer, particularly through his use of satire in which archetypal characters are rendered with realistic depth and brought alive through the power of revealing universal traits.

Mikayel S. Giurjian, by Krikor Keusseyan, c. 1961.

MIKAYEL GIURJIAN AS ASSESSED IN ARMENIAN LITERATURE

Mikayel Giurjian was the contemporary of Arpiar Arpiarian, Krikor Zohrab, Yeghia Demirjibashian, Dikran Gamsaragan, Levon Pashalian, Yervant Odian, Yervant Srmakeshkhanlian, Onnig Chifté-Saraf, Diran Chrakian, Arshag Chobanian, Vahan Tekeyan, Vahan Malezian, Teotig, and many others who enriched modern Armenian literature. These writers commended the merits of Giurjian's works of realism. They highly appreciated his insightful analysis in matters of literary criticism, and admired his satirical talent and skilled craft.

Diran Chrakian (a.k.a. Indra), a Western Armenian poet, wrote in a letter to Giurjian dated November 29, 1912: "I, who search for your name, as soon as I receive the *Armenian Literature* [Hay kraganutiun] of Smyrna, and whenever I see the *Lusaper-Arev* [Light-bearing Sun] look to see if you are there or not, do not have this heed and anxiety, this longing, this urge for the works of any other writer. This is not only a product of the special bond I have with you, but especially because, as a matter of fact, no one is more masterful than you. There are a few people whose writings I definitely read—Odian, Kechian, Levon Mgrdichian, and also Hovhannes Setian—because they, too, are unmatched among their kind—especially Odian, and Kechian, when the latter writes one of his great editorials. But the longing with which I read you is different; or rather, the feeling that makes me search for an article of yours is a true longing, whereas the feeling that makes me interested in others' writings is an assurance of satisfaction. ... I wanted to say, my dear Mikayel, that I read you before all others, which means that sometimes I want to *especially* read *only* you."[2]

Dikran Gamsaragan wrote in his autobiography: "... I have a play in hand,[3] which I hope 'to make stand' next year on the Armenian stage of Constantinople, with the collaboration of Mikayel Giurjian whose real talent is familiar to you."[4]

Teotig wrote in connection with Yervant Odian's death: "... Your old, close friends have forever gone before you—Arpiar, Kelegian, Zohrab, and Bartevian. The only survivors of your brilliant phalanx are Shahnazar, Pashalian, Gamsaragan, Tekeyan, and Giurjian, who are upon your passing obliged to revive you through your works that are scattered yet complete, like your life."[5]

In a letter addressed from Constantinople to Vahan Malezian on February 24, 1909, Meruzhan Barsamian, a Western Armenian poet and editor, referred to the authors of the play *The Salvation* as noble writers. He said: "… O this political life, this political strife. What aesthetician's ear would still insist on wanting to hear? I prepared a literary study, *The Influence of Political Life on Our Writers* [Kaghakagan geankin aztetsutiunê mer kroghnerun vra], which I want to publish, and whose appearance may possibly generate coolness between myself and some writers I call friends. I have to say that I cannot look upon these events indifferently. We are literarily dead. This is painful, isn't it? Where is the play of Gamsaragan and Giurjian? I imagine that it should be a good one. Both of them, noble writers, lacking no talent necessary to occupy the loftiest places in the literary salon."[6]

Hagop Oshagan, who was very stringent in matters of literary criticism,[7] appreciated Giurjian's "sharp talent," which he said was "beyond doubt." Oshagan wrote: "Like all the leaders of his generation, he signed his name to free and metric poems wherein meticulousness and form are more dominant than feelings and creation. Numerous are his journalistic writings on current issues. Mikayel Giurjian comes into view with all the liveliness, interests, and aspirations of his generation. And like the most talented of them, he almost always remains at the brink of his intentions."[8]

One can cite numerous excerpts by prominent personalities who praised Giurjian's literary merits, but we will simply mention the fact that Yervant Odian, the greatest satirist of his time, was very close to Giurjian. Flipping through Odian's memoirs convinces one of the truth of his statement. Odian often used words of sympathy and praise for Giurjian and his work, beginning with expressions of admiration for the novel, *Mardig Agha*, and ending with the wit he points at in Giurjian's editorials and chronicles.

As early as 1898, Giurjian longed to know Odian personally. Arpiar Arpiarian, who was in Alexandria, Egypt, before leaving for London, introduced them. The two writers met for the first time at a candy store called Zola. "We sat and began to talk. From the first moment, we felt a mutual empathy; an empathy that eventually turned into a steady and pure, friendly affection,"[9] wrote Odian in his memoir, *Twelve Years Outside Constantinople* [Dasnergu dari Bolsen turs]. This mutual empathy and affection stemmed from similarities in their personalities, ideas, and literary styles.

Therefore, it is not surprising that only a few years after their acquaintance, the two writers co-authored chronicles they signed as Y. M. Giurod—a combination of their initials and the first syllables of their last names. Co-authoring is rare enough in literature in general, and unique in the Armenian literature of the early twentieth century.

Odian, who published the periodical *Azad Pem* [Free Podium] from 1903 to 1905, remarked: "Mikayel Giurjian was a permanent contributor to the newspaper; he flooded the pages of *Azad Pem* with his boundless wit."[10] Odian continued: "*Azad Pem* did not cause me much trouble. I went to the press only a few hours a week to write articles or proofread. The rest of my time I spent in the pleasant companionship of Mikayel Giurjian."[11]

The collaboration between Giurjian and Odian continued in later years when they co-authored and published the comedy, *The Franco-Turkish War* [Franko-trkagan baderazmê], which continues to be staged in Armenia and the Diaspora. Yervant Odian would only co-author with Mikayel Giurjian, and this collaboration also resulted in the comedy, *Heroic Play.* Audiences followed *Heroic Play* with interest, and it continues to be performed today.

On February 16, 1904, when Odian traveled from Alexandria to Bombay upon the invitation of his brother who traded in diamonds, Giurjian took over the editorship of *Azad Pem* until Odian's return. Later, as *Azad Pem* became a purely partisan newspaper, Giurjian, Tekeyan, and Odian departed one after the other. Odian went on to publish a small daily called *Tertig* [Newsletter] for a month, and then, in 1908, he founded the newspaper *Arev* [Sun] in Alexandria. Mikayel Giurjian took part in the publishing association of *Arev* as a founding member.

In Odian's final memoir, *After Sixteen Years* [Dasnvets dari yedkê], which he wrote after his return to Egypt, he spoke of Giurjian anew in positive words. After a sixteen-year absence, Alexandria was no longer familiar to Odian. In the harbor, embellished with new streets instead of the old cafés; in the city where "the prelacy had become a kindergarten, and the kindergarten had turned into a prelacy"; in a city where "everything was different," Odian sought out his friend and wrote about him: "Then I saw my beloved Mikayel Giurjian and together we spent long hours digging into old memories. What a change! Where is that thin, pale, Turianistic, idealistic Mikayel, for whom Arpiar and I often thought in distress: Will the poor man live? Now I have a bourgeois, bulky mass of flesh before me. But when he begins to talk, the old Mikayel appears with his witty, sparkling, unequalled energy."[12]

More recently, Yervant Azadian, a Western Armenian journalist, critic, and cultural and social activist, gathered his articles previously published in Diasporan Armenian newspapers in a volume entitled, *Fixations in Literature and Fine Arts* [Kragan kegharvesdagan severumner][13]. The articles are titled: "Who Will Plant a Flamboyant" [Ov bidi dngé vareni mê?], "Mikayel Giurjian the Writer" [Mikayel Giurjian kroghê], "The Vast Contents of a Small Book" [Pokrig kirki mê layn povantagutiunê], and "Mikayel Giurjian in Intimacy" [Mikayel Giurjianê mdermutean mech].

Azadian considers Giurjian "the last Mohican of our artistic generation," "the living witness of the past amongst us," who "has registered in him the life of all past national and literary figures" and "who carried in him a greatness throughout his life."

During the years Azadian acted as the editor-in-chief of *Arev*, he had the opportunity to know Giurjian intimately, enjoy his presence, and take pleasure in his friendship, since Giurjian spent five to six months a year in Cairo during which he visited the editorial office of *Arev* daily. Sensing Azadian's literary curiosity, Giurjian entrusted his archives and their fate to him—testament that Azadian was a trustworthy companion, close friend, and affiliated writer.

Azadian extensively analyzed Giurjian's play, *Twenty Years Later*, and more than ten of his realistic, thoughtful, and emotional works and Oriental sketches. He presented a vivid portrait of the author in an essay he wrote, "The Vast Contents of a Small Book," on the occasion of the publication of a collection of some of Giurjian's works in a volume called *Twenty Years Later*,[14] which was published by Simon Simonian, a notable Diasporan Armenian writer, journalist, editor, and owner of Sevan publishing house. In that work, Azadian praised the mastery, success, delicate expressions, multifaceted talent, exceptional literary qualities, and sharp satire of Giurjian, commenting, in particular, on his beautiful language and style. Azadian wrote: "With his beautifully colored style and infallible and flexible language he was a master of the study of manners."

It was thanks to Azadian's suggestion that Giurjian wrote his many memoirs about the writers he knew: Arpiar Arpiarian, Diran Chrakian, Yervant Odian, Vahan Tekeyan, and others. As their contemporary, and as someone who had close and long-lasting relationships with them, Giurjian stored many valuable and interesting episodes in his bright memory, and was able to recall them in full detail, the same way he recalled poems he had learned by heart by Musset, Verlaine, Hugo, and Lamartine.

A Constantinoplean Armenian by birth, Giurjian remained a well-liked, praised, and respected writer to the end, even during his old age. When he died, many intellectuals, including Vahé-Vahian and Hmayag Kranian of Beirut, Lebanon; Daria Gamsaragan and Hovhannes Boghosian of Paris, France; and Aleksandr Sarukhan of Cairo, Egypt, praised him in articles published throughout the Diasporan Armenian media.

THE PATH OF GIURJIAN'S LIFE

Mikayel Giurjian, son of Sahag, was born in 1879, in suburban Scütari [Üsküdar, a neighborhood of Constantinople] located on the beautiful Constantinoplean shore, into a family of intellectuals. His parents had migrated from Kayseri [Caesarea]. His father, Sahag Effendi, was a clerk. Despite his luxurious past, his father was a simple and polite person, a good father, and a caring husband who sustained his family. Diran Chrakian portrayed old Sahag Effendi, son of Armenag, as follows: "In the evenings he would pass through the streets alone, carrying, in the semi-savage self-containment of asocial isolation, an astonishingly pensive gaze and slowness—so mysterious was his silhouette in the shadow of dusk."

In a letter that Diran Chrakian wrote to Giurjian on September 22, 1901, from Scütari, he commented on Sahag Effendi's intellectuality and his modest contribution to the Armenian media of Constantinople, saying: "I have not found your father's *Dziadzan* [Rainbow] yet. The *Dziadzan*s I found are in Turkish, and the names of the editor, the owner, manager, etc., are not Armenian. As for the content (at least of those that I have seen) there is nothing interesting in it; in a word, they are not what you are looking for. Later, I might find more important issues and, particularly, the one your father published."

Diran Kelegian, a famous Constantinoplean Armenian journalist, in a letter dated November 14, 1904, and mailed from Cairo to Giurjian, talked about Sahag Effendi's involvement in publishing activities during the 1880s, saying: "Your father, Sahag Effendi, has been a favored visitor of our house for years. Personally, I enjoyed a very good relationship with him as a novice writer in the Constantinoplean media, almost a quarter century ago. Also, I continue to hold a very profound memory of your uncle with whom I feel like a brother since the time we shared together as exiles in Athens some fourteen years ago."

Doctor Hrutiun Tireakian also knew Giurjian's uncle, Serop [Serovpé] Giurjian, well. At the end of a letter he wrote from New York on September 2, 1915, he asked: "Any news from Serovpé? I think he and I are the only survivors of our generation, if he is alive." Serop was born in Talas, Turkey. After graduating from College of Bodwin, Maine, he returned to Istanbul to become a merchant. Later, he moved to Athens as a photographer.

Giurjian's mother, Miurig (née Altunian), was a smart, kind, sharp-minded Armenian woman. She attended to her children, and her innate wit, metaphoric descriptions, and ingenious expressions left profound impressions on the people she came in contact with, including, of course, her children. Giurjian often recorded his mother's metaphors, epithets, and her artistic definitions of various phenomena: "My mother has ingenious moments where one finds the personalized stamp of a uniquely gifted disposition, rather than the folksy occasional inspirations of a natural person."[15]

There are many instances when Giurjian used his mother's wonderful words, the witty expressions of a Constantinoplean Armenian woman, as proverbs or puns. In 1909, in contemplations he entitled *My Mother's Famous Words* [Mors nshanavor khoskerê], we read: "Once again she rose to Goethe's level without effort, without literature, but with an excellent rationality." Giurjian stated that the divine intuition of life could suddenly turn an illiterate woman into "the equal of a great poet-thinker." Giurjian admired his mother's beautiful words, metaphors, and analogies. He wrote: "My mother spoke wonderful poetry to describe a marvelous woman ... she used the expression 'crystal glass' ... I do not know any other such admirable, illustrative word ... indeed, a glass, a clean, thin, authentic glass reflects water like a transparent soul." Analogous to the popular folk maxim, "The sound of a gun cannot be heard when the cannon shoots," his mother was fond of saying, "It slips like the stick of a cotton ginner"; that is, the sound released cannot be distinguished amongst the buzzing noises of the stick. Another favorite example of an expression she used was her description of a very skinny person: "If a crow pecked the person, it would not find flesh on him."

Giurjian believed that he inherited his skill for puns from his mother. He wrote the following dialogue, which he thought had the merit of a proverb:

"Mother! Why do you whine and worry, repeating that we do not have money? Why?"

"Indeed I whimper much," she said, "but you know not how much I ponder."

Indeed a wonderful pun.

Giurjian's maternal uncle, Arshag Effendi Altunian, was the author of a novel called *The Poor Man's Honor* [Aghkadin badivê] and a well-known personality in Western and Eastern Armenian circles.

The following excerpt from Diran Chrakian's letter of October 16, 1902, pertains to Giurjian's uncle: "I was told that someone wearing glasses had come to see me. I went down and saw your uncle, Altunian, sitting face to face with Nshan Effendi in the courtyard. It's impossible not to recognize his strange countenance at once. O, is that you, Altunian Effendi; where have you been, etc.? We conversed for quite a while. The government had ... hosted him for four months; he had been ill and his arthritis had become worse, he said. I told him that the pains he described were something else, and that the *iodure* he referred to as useless was not what he needed. He suffers from neuralgia; the body of the poor man is full of neuralgia; he feels pain with every movement he makes. He told me that he had been moved to the prisoners' hospital and released eight days later. Then he was transferred to a less unbearable location, namely the Armenian National Hospital, where, of course, he took sulfuric baths, that were useless, naturally. After spending twenty-eight days there, seven or eight days ago he secured his release by bribing one person or another with a little money (six or seven pounds), otherwise he would have had to surrender himself to the government had he recovered. Now, he is being hosted at someone's house in Silihdar Garden (Scütari). He spoke, also, about his most recent activities: he took his new novel to Russia with him and it sold wonderfully, thereby generating some good income for him. He spoke, too, of many more things from his past."

In 1903, while visiting the Giurjians at their former house in Ramleh, Alexandria, the same uncle, whose hearing was somewhat impaired, stepped in mud without realizing it. But Giurjian immediately noticed and teasingly asked his uncle: "Uncle, are your feet also deaf?"

In a letter dated March 4, 1904, Chrakian asked Giurjian about Arshag Altunian: "Have you received any news from your uncle who visited Istanbul recently?"

Giurjian recorded his uncle's significant and witty expressions in his diary, such as: "Our desires surpass eternity – A. Altunian."

During the years 1919 through 1932, Hayganush Mark directed and edited *Hay Gin* [Armenian Woman]. It was a magazine published in Istanbul in support of the moral, intellectual, physical, and aesthetic progress of Armenian women. By publishing the works of Taniel Varuzhan, Vahan Tekeyan, Yervant Odian, Yeghishé Turian, Shushanig Gurghinian, and others, the magazine also helped popularize Armenian literature. In the 1920–1923 issues of the magazine, articles and letters signed by Giurjian's sister, Alice, often appeared. These discussed the pressing issues of her time, and were published under titles such as *Feminism among Us* [Feminizmê mer mech], *Our Orphans* [Mer vorperê], and *Should the Letters be Opened?* [Namagnerê bedk é patsvin?]. In addition to writing articles in support of Armenian interests, Alis actively participated in the Committee of the Armenian Women of Alexandria and in functions organized to support the Armenian homeland.

It was to such an exemplary and intellectual family that Mikayel was born and raised. Then his achievements increased his family's fame by adding the name Mikayel Sahag Giurjian to the history of Armenian literature, and by gaining respect and recognition as "a unique talent" (Yetvart Kolanjian) and as "a most capable writer," "a promising literary talent," and "an ever-shining star on the intellectual horizon" (Reteos Berberian).

Beautiful Scütari and Istanbul—the cradles of poetry—were the world of Giurjian's childhood and adolescence, and he was destined to relive the first impressions he gathered there throughout his life. Indeed, the magical sky of Istanbul, with its hills looking at the sea, and the beautifully vivid shores of Marmara not only inspired Giurjian but many other gifted writers and artists, including Bedros Turian, Zabel Yesayan, Diran Chrakian, and Levon Pashalian.

* * *

Giurjian received his primary education, first, at Nersesian School located in the Ijadiyé quarter, and then at Berberian School where he began his studies in 1891, graduating in 1895. Reteos Berberian, the laborious principal and famous pedagogue of that school, greatly affected the intellectual progress of Constantinoplean Armenians. The generation that came of age under Berberian's supervision demonstrated significant intellectual abilities. On April 24, 1911, standing by Berberian's tomb surrounded by Armenian teachers, doctors, scientists, clergymen, artists, statesmen, and businessmen—whom belonged to the generation empowered by Berberian's spirit—and in observation of the fourth anniversary of Berberian's death, Teotig announced: "Here I see men of letters: Pashalian, Shaklian, Sh. Shavarsh, Bartevian, B. Akatan [Giurjian's pseudonym], Tekeyan, Indra [Diran Chrakian's pseudonym], Sinanian, Kechian, Nazariants, Cheogiurian, Kolanjian, R. Sevag [R. Chilingirian's pseudonym]."[16]

Reflecting upon his student years at Berberian School, Giurjian described himself in the following words: "I was literally a tiny person at the time, both physically and morally: a humble student, with the timidity that is characteristic of quiet students who are striving for learning having reached an extreme in me."[17]

Later, as Giurjian entered high school, he listened with admiration to the rich, meaningful, and influential lectures Berberian delivered. The great educator taught, amongst other subjects, psychology, logic, philosophy, Greek and Latin literature, the history of civilization, and ethics. "Driven by the splendid enthusiasm of his exuberant rhetoric and cascading thoughts," wrote Giurjian about his teacher, "he continued to speak, like Crysostom and with a silvery voice, when interpreting a philosopher's doctrine or energetically analyzing a poet's work."[18]

Giurjian, the studious and bibliophilic adolescent, sensed in himself the embryo of the future writer manifesting itself through compositions. Ten years after Giurjian's graduation, Berberian recalled comments he made in regard to his former student's comprehension, emphasizing in a letter: "I could never forget you as one of our best students, but you yourself have reminded yourself with your beautiful achievements. ... Long live! One should honor his alma mater in this way, and one should reward the efforts of his educators in this way. Long live!"[19]

Recalling his adolescence, Giurjian confessed: "The devil of literature caught and apprehended me, too." Thus, in 1893, the thirteen-year-old teenager wrote his first work, *Roland* [Rolan], for the handwritten school magazine, *Arshaluys* [Dawn]. About twenty years later, when speaking of this novella which he wrote at the request of the publishers of the newfound magazine, Giurjian wrote: "Its one and only merit or justification is that it was written in one breath, in one pen from A to Z, with an ease of inspiration and splendor, and with the abundance of an enthusiasm that later I never found, having lost forever the literary inexperience, the illiteracy, and self-confidence that—together with my adolescent imagination nourished and ignited by novels and feuilletons—deservedly presided over my first literary product."

What was the subject of this first literary attempt? Here is how the author presented it: "The theme was a love drama, as gloomy and tragic as a stormy dusk or the skies of Delacroix. What else did you expect a thirteen-year-old would write about, if not the thing that he thinks about most and knows nothing about—Love? As if I had had numerous love affairs and been deceived and abandoned by at least ten women, I wrote about an episode of humiliated and revengeful love, with tattling, which covered many long pages.

"A rich lover collapsed one day. His lover, or 'mistress,' as the French say, dismissed him and found another wealthy lover, as you predicted. The young man, wounded deeply and furious, vowed revenge from the traitorous woman. So he disguised himself and one day presented himself at the home of his former lover to apply for the vacant position of coachman. He was hired. O heavens, or O hell! Here he was; a poor lover now employed to drive the couple on trips in their cart. Patience! The righteous hour of revenge is close. Then, one evening, the fake coachman took the cart to a desolate place, jumped down from the seat, and showing his real face while holding a pistol, he stood before the horrified woman who, I think, was pursuing a kiss. Tableau! I do not recall the rest well, but you can imagine. Bang, bang! Death and destruction! Revenge! Somewhere in my novella, while describing a love scene, I wrote: 'Rolan stamped a clangorous kiss on Rosali's hand.'

"A psychologist perhaps would see in this expression the spiritual state of a boy who knows nothing about the world, who has never heard the sweet melody of romantic embraces, and in his insatiably hungry imagination turns it into a noise and a clang—much like an extremely thirsty person might swallow a glass of water offered to him in a few big gulps accompanied by loud engulfing sounds. People took the magazine to Shaklian, seeing him as the only skilled critic whose opinion mattered, and then they broke the news that Shaklian had found the 'clangorous kiss' phrasing very rude, very tasteless, and very vulgar. What a shame to me!

"I remember that I listened to the verdict with humiliation and a broken spirit; it was a verdict I could not possibly appeal. Shaklian was the undisputable authority in my student world. This was the first wounding of my writer's ego. Fortunately ... I did not continue to author, and published nothing for years, until 1898, when my first printed work, *Mardig Agha* appeared in *Nor Geank* [New Life]—*de scandaleuse mémoire,* wasn't it, my good residents of Alexandria?"[20]

Giurjian continued to enrich the education he received at school through independent study. He loved to read. While mastering the French and English languages, he acquainted himself with the works of the greatest figures of Western European literature. In particular, he loved to read the works of romantic poets and, later, of realist authors. Victor Hugo, Alphonse de Lamartine, Alfred de Musset, Pierre de Ronsard, Charles Baudelaire, Alphonse Daudet, Paul Verlaine, Honoré de Balzac, Arthur Rimbaud, Stéphane Mallarmé, François Villon, Jean Moréas, and prominent British authors, especially Charles Dickens, were Giurjian's favorite writers.

Giurjian possessed rich libraries both in Constantinople and Alexandria. Diran Chrakian wrote: "After I returned from Alexandria, The Soanjians (now in Pera), who were neighbors of mine at the time, asked me to look through the piles of books they had in their attic that belonged either to your father or you." Chrakian chose the books he considered useful to Giurjian to be shipped to him in Alexandria. He selected several books such as "a small minéralogie, an Armenian *Empiric Physics* published in Vienna, Flammarion's *Lumen,* and a section of a book or a magazine in which I found Bourget's study on Baudelaire." These selections prove that his library contained books of diverse nature. Those who knew Giurjian in Alexandria testified that the walls of his residence were lined with books, often containing various editions of the same book.

As a book lover, Giurjian always carried books with him when he traveled, and he wrote often in his memoirs that when he visited France, he frequented old bookstores in order to purchase books for reading. Gathered across the years, these books formed a rich private library, a portion of which is now housed in his personal archive at the Museum of Literature and Art of Armenia.[21]

* * *

Giurjian began to work at the age of seventeen, starting as a clerk for master Hetum Setian in Istanbul. His employment, though, did not last long in Istanbul because of the bloody events of 1894–1896 when the Anglophile government of Kiamil Pasha began its monstrous plan to annihilate Armenians in Western Armenia. Even Istanbul, that city of wonderful geographical location and beauty, witnessed massacres and became a hellish city, defiled by the calamities.

On August 14, 1896, as a consequence of the incident known as the "Demonstration of the Ottoman Bank in Istanbul," the Sultan's government organized new massacres against the Armenians. Within two days, from August 14 to August 16, more than 10,000 Armenians fell victim to the massacres. As a result of the massacres of the 1890s, which preceded the massacres and deportations of 1915, almost 300,000 Armenians were killed, 100,000 Armenians were forced to convert to Islam, and more than 100,000 Armenians were compelled to emigrate from Western Armenia.

Giurjian, a man of sensitive character, could not remain indifferent toward his people's calamity and misery. The massacres organized by the Turkish authorities deeply shook the young patriot's spirit and found expression in many of his future works: *The Tribute* [Durkê], *The Ineffaceable Tome, The Magic Carpet* [Mokagan korkê], *What the Angel Saw* [Inch vor hreshdagê desav], etc.

In 1896, Giurjian left Constantinople with his sister and mother, and moved to Alexandria, Egypt. Thanks to this relocation, he survived the claws of the executioner and was saved from martyrdom, unlike most of the Armenian intellectuals of Constantinople and the more than 1.5 million hardworking, peaceful, and creative Armenian people who were brutally killed in 1915 regardless of their position, gender, or age.

Giurjian left Constantinople, but he never forgot his birthplace. It was impossible to forget the charming sky and beautiful hills of Constantinople where he and his close friend Diran Chrakian had talked and dreamed the daring dreams of adolescence in their homes or under the trees or while silently enjoying nature's beauty by the sea. They especially took pleasure in watching the Black Sea. They both felt the breath of simplicity and kindness before its unlimited space.

Giurjian's father, Sahag Effendi, remained in Constantinople. He planned to join his family later. But the comfortable life of the Giurjians was interrupted, and Sahag Effendi never had the opportunity to join his wife and children in Alexandria.

In May 1897, a year after Giurjian family's departure, Diran Chrakian wrote to Mikayel: "When exiting Beyler's garden, I approached your closed gate for the first time in so long a time, and I entered the empty and abandoned garden. The trees were green with a living, strong greenness after the rains had washed them during recent days… It was as if nobody had entered after you left. There was abandonment and destruction everywhere... The trees and shrubs extended their shadow over the round iron table that no longer had my rocking chair around it... A damp cushion lay naked and crooked under one of the trees. I do not know why it was left there, unfit to be sitting on, but it was ready for the infrequent visits of cats and to get soaked by the rains... The house was more abandoned and sad than the garden. At least the garden had its trees and Miss Simmer's bushes in the background. Your room was full of disorderly fallen chairs, crookedly moved cushions, uselessly crowded furniture all intertwined one piece on top of another, and the dim looking glasses left the impression that a thick dust had come down to cover the lifeless, sad pile. Birds were singing... but not even a single cat was there. The fruits of the medlar tree (I do not know its Armenian, French, or family name) were beginning to bud under the tree's broad leaves, and the mulberry tree was covered with green, unripe mulberries that would be eaten by the birds mostly."

This was the state of the sad, desolate, and uninviting house, and its sweet-scented garden, a garden that had once been synonymous with happiness and dreamy moods, a garden that had bloomed rich with the beauty of the spring and the charm of autumn dusks, and was alive with the soft sweetness of so many evenings.

On Tuesday, June 26, 1897, the day Sahag Effendi decided to obtain a passport in order to prepare for his travel to Egypt to join his loved ones, he died. Giurjian's auntie asked Diran Chrakian to break the news to the family in Alexandria, whereupon Chrakian wrote in his letter of July 12, 1897, from Scütari: "Levon Tashjian, Sdepan, and I followed his coffin with a fine, sad pleasure, because in your absence, we replaced you. I am sure that my friends also felt you in themselves as I did... Perhaps this was the reason escorting your father's coffin was beautiful and poignant. The group that followed the deceased was composed of neighbors, one or two acquaintances and ... several brainless Scütarians who carry loads, do easy errands, and accompany every dead person with profound and incomprehensible drive—everyone certainly comprehended very well the sadness of your father's dying alone and as a stranger."

The newly resettled family faced spiritual, moral, and financial difficulties. Contrary to the soft, delicate, and pure spring air he experienced in Constantinople, Giurjian burned in the Egyptian sun, whose scorching beams are eternally endured by the Sphinx only. The environment aggravated Giurjian and provoked "desperate feelings" in his young mind.

In a thick notebook he had made out of blue papers and used as a diary to sometimes pen accounts, or write out Turkish poems in the Armenian alphabet, Sahag Effendi wrote, referring to his son: "He does not have even five paras in his pocket." Indeed, Giurjian's moral, spiritual, and financial state was burdensome.

In order to make a change in his sad life, he began working at the court as a clerk. But the court also pressured him. It was during this time that he received the news of his father's death, which added grief to his anguish. The separation from birthplace and friends, the sadness of loneliness, the absence of Scütari's nature, and the Egyptian climate combined to effect Giurjian's health negatively. His mother also became very ill.

Here is how Diran Chrakian described Giurjian upon receiving his photo in May 1897: "Your photo presents you loyally. Loyally?... But your smile is missing... Your ever present smile that particularly (not to say exclusively) cheered your face—which would have been destined to sadness and grief—when you were with your friends. A smile in your photo, however, would not seem appropriate after your letters. This is the loyal image of *current* Mikayel, better to say current Mikayel Giurjian, who looks at matters with calm and convinced disparagement. With your crushed, fatigued, and desperate appearance, and with the bloodlessness of your cheeks that are framed by an ill-looking and vague beard, your image reveals both your boredom and your anguish, which through the physiological interpretation of your thick eyebrows, sculptured lips, and daring (but sad) expression still indicates your capricious, fantasist, and independent spirit. It is as if your image, with the proud stature of your head that sticks out and upon your depressed body, and with the wild, neighing expressions of flared nostrils sprouting from between weak cheeks, states: 'The detestable abundance that surrounds and presses me, and the irresistible force of fate does not deserve my loftiness.' The image seems to wait, wait, again, for the fate of new agitations and storms through its seemingly calm and simple, yet angry and aggravated appearance, an image ready to contract its brows. The image shows your talent and suffering through the apparent gushes of a forehead with shuddered circumference, through the thoughtful, sad, and mesmerized perforation of deep eyes, through the ill shadows of the cheeks, through the delicate edges of a moustache that hangs down sadly—rather than twirl and twist—and through retreat of the thorax."

The years 1896 and 1897 were the most desperate in Giurjian's life. On the one hand, he thought of teaching at Makriköy's school whose principal, upon Diran Chrakian's intercession, had agreed to accept Giurjian as a teacher. On the other hand, he wanted to go to Paris for a better life.

Disillusionment from the "moldy atmosphere of the court" led Giurjian to leave the following entry in his diary in December 1900: "I sincerely regret that I left Constantinople and my master Hetum Setian. That was a very interesting life, rich with multifaceted tunes. I would have become a good person, a businessman, a man of life; I would have benefited financially and romantically. Now I comprehend the essential truth of my master's words of wisdom. If I ever visit Constantinople, I'll go to him; yes, I miss the store, the faces, Krikor, Yorgi, Diran, Vahan, and Setian. I miss my desk, the dim atmosphere, and the appearance of the merchandise."

Giurjian longed for his birthplace to the end of his life. He never had the opportunity to return.

From 1898 forward, thanks to his strong will, Giurjian attentively cared for his health. He began to eat and sleep regularly, strengthen and improve his body through physical exercise and baths, and he made two to three hours of daily walk a habit. And this fanatically sad man, who was addicted to sadness and loved sadness, in October 1900 recorded this entry in his diary: "It has been almost two years or a year and a half that I have not been sad. I dismissed sadness, erased it, and killed its presence within me. I killed death. Instead of death killing me, I killed death. I did well, didn't I? I do not want anything related to death in me; rather, only life and its offshoots."[22]

In 1902, the Giurjians moved from central Alexandria to a lush suburb called Ramleh. There, his mother's health improved. Along with his daily work, Giurjian began to teach. He loved the young, gentle souls and became a compassionate teacher. Teaching, however, did not hinder his involvement in literature, an involvement that was an intellectual pleasure for a well-read person like him.

It might be more illustrative to use his words to describe the tremendous difficulties he faced and the sad life he lived in those years. "The centrifugal movement or stream of migration," he wrote on February 20, 1908, to Doctor Harutiun Tireakian, "has thrown us here into wreckage. After several months of joblessness, I entered the mixed courts of Alexandria as a humble employee... I spent eight years earning a salary only large enough to cover daily expenses, until two years ago, when I became an employee of the Ottoman Bank with a salary higher than what I received at the court. Today, praise God, as people say, without needing anybody's support, without much distress, we have all that is necessary to live. I hope to have rank advancement gradually and to reach what is called *Ezance*. I am temperate by nature; I mean to say I am free from devastating addictions and alien and indifferent to luxury, sumptuousness, and vainglorious things."[23]

In the publication of excerpts from five letters Giurjian addressed to his father, Mihrtad Tireakian wrote: "In the 1880s, my father was a close friend of Mikayel Giurjian's father, uncle, and entire family in Constantinople."[24]

Giurjian viewed this relationship as a source of satisfaction and comfort: "I feel myself very proud and happy that my father, my poor, deceased father had a friend like you, and that I have inherited, too, a friend like you: it is a moral inheritance more precious than those thousands of pounds he could have left me, but did not."[25]

Giurjian served at the mixed courts of Alexandria as a clerk until 1915. Thereafter, he assumed many different and high positions in various branches of the Ottoman Bank until his retirement in 1935 (in 1917–1919 he was the manager of the Minieh branch of the Ottoman Bank in Upper Egypt).

In 1919, Giurjian returned with his mother and sister from Upper Egypt to Alexandria and betrothed Miss Lucy (Lusntak Tahdajian), a divorced woman from Aintab, Turkey. Later, on February 19, 1920, he married her, with Levon Mgrdichian acting as godfather.

In those days, his mother's liver pains intensified, torturing her frequently and for long hours. Miurig died in the summer of 1921. The family was then composed of only Giurjian, his wife Lucy, and his sister Alis. Then, Lucy's illness began to trouble Giurjian, and the family traveled to Europe several times seeking treatment.

In Europe, Giurjian was particularly and profoundly impressed by the snow-covered Alps, the magnificent scenery of Mont Blanc, the wonderful panorama of Annecy, the heavenly peace of the lakes of Savoie, the industrial appearance of Dijon, the multi-styled art of the statues of Paris, the beauty of Bois de Boulogne, the paintings and statues of Versailles, and the rare and internationally acclaimed art in the Louvre.

Giurjian's third and fourth journeys (in 1927 and 1933, respectively) were of particular interest. Making optimal use of his time, he met with famous Armenian and non-Armenian writers and artists. He had literary conversations with Dikran Gamsaragan, Arshag Chobanian, Vahan Malezian, Vahan Tekeyan, Aram Andonian, Daria Gamsaragan, Mikayel Alemshah, Krikor Tellalian, and others. He also met with famous French writers and critics. In the offices of *Les Nouvelles Littéraires* he met with Frédéric Lefèvre, a fan of Giurjian's French pieces.

The visit Giurjian made on October 1, 1927, to the graves of Alfred de Musset and Rossini in Père-Lachaise cemetery left an indelible impression on him. On October 23, 1927, Arshag Chobanian and Giurjian participated in a commemorative ceremony that took place near the grave of Charles Baudelaire—Giurjian's beloved poet—where Paul Bourget, a member of the French Academy, delivered a lecture, and the poems of the poet were recited. Giurjian also considered the Saturday of October 15, 1927, an eternally memorable day, because he visited the museum of Victor Hugo, a writer he loved so much.

He left the following words of admiration in his diary: "V. Hugo's sketches and paintings are absolutely unparalleled and striking works. Perhaps I have never been so shocked..."

In Egypt, the Giurjian family entertained a circle of close friends composed of intellectuals and cultural activists. Included were Levon Mgrdichian, Arpiar Arpiarian, Mgrdich Antranigian, Yervant Odian, Vahan Tekeyan, Mihran Damadian, Yervant Gamsaragan, Dikran Gamsaragan, Hagop Papazian, Hrant Nasibian, and Fermanian.

It is noteworthy that during the eighty-six years of Giurjian's life, he abstained from active roles in political parties. It is true that Giurjian was a member of the Armenian Democratic Liberal Party from early on and remained faithful to it to the last day of his life, but literary support marked the only facet of his active participation during his years of membership. Not only did he try to keep a distance from political agitations and crises, but also he advised Arpiarian, Tekeyan, Bartevian, and others to stay away from political fights and revolutionaries. It is known that in 1905, when Arpiar could no longer live in Italy and moved to Egypt, Giurjian tried to keep him away from political circles. Odian wrote: "Uselessly, Giurjian and I tried to keep him away and isolate him."

It is a well-established fact that Arpiarian was deceitfully killed in 1908 as a result of political fights after the second assassination attempt against him. Giurjian and Odian also opposed Tekeyan's involvement in political activities. Odian wrote in his memoirs: "Tekeyan made a mistake after arriving in Alexandria, which Mikayel Giurjian and I often felt sorry for: Tekeyan became a revolutionary when he joined the Reformed Hnchags."[26]

Giurjian blamed also Suren Bartevian for joining the Tashnag Party, and Bartevian replied in a letter he wrote from Cairo on September 5, 1913: "Quit this ugly and despicable rumor that I have become a Tashnag. Neither am I Tashnag, nor Ramgavar. I am an individual journalist who belongs only to the party of his conscience. I know the Tashnags and the Ramgavars, and I have no disposition whatsoever to discredit or praise one's store for the other's sake. I do not believe that these parties, by spending the vigor of our active elements against each other, will bring any benefit to our nation."

* * *

Like his contemporaries, from the day he published his first work, Giurjian used many pseudonyms. Sarkis Sahagian, an Egyptian Armenian poet, in his essay, "Egyptian Armenian Prose Writers" [Yekibdahay artsagakirner], published in the eleventh volume of the album-book, *Life and Letter* [Geank yev kir], wrote: "Giurjian used the pseudonyms Baruyr, Bond, and Bedros Akatan. If I am not mistaken, he was also one of the Hamshirags (Hamshirag A., Hamshirag B.) of the *Shirag* magazines." The brief nature of the article indicates that Sahagian did not try to mention all the pseudonyms Giurjian used, and that he was unaware that Hamshirag A. was Giurjian's pseudonym, whereas Hamshirag B. belonged to Tekeyan.

Philologist Karekin Levonian mentioned in his book, *Dictionary of Armenian Literary Pseudonyms* [Pararan hay kragan dzadzganunneru],[27] that Giurjian signed using the following pseudonyms: Hamshirag A., Zarmayr, Y. M. Giurod, Arsen Molar, Bedros Akatan, Hrand, Men Gen, Mkhitar Bondatsi, Baruyr, Bond, and Srjep A.

Levonian was wrong to relate the pseudonym Y. M. Giurod only to Giurjian, and in crediting only two pseudonyms to Yervant Odian: Yerod and Zhirayr.[28] As mentioned earlier, the signature Y. M. Giurod belonged to the two writers and was composed from the initials of their first names and the first syllables of their last names. In Levonian's alphabetical list of pseudonyms there is another mistake. He related the pseudonym Mkhitar Bondatsi to Melkon Giurjian who portrayed the lives of Armenian refugees.[29] But Mkhitar Bondatsi, as we know, was a pseudonym used by Mikayel Giurjian. Later, we find this same pseudonym used also by Prof. H. Kayayan.[30]

In his extensive and laborious work, *Armenian Bibliography and Encyclopedia of Armenian Life* [Haygagan madenakidutiun yev hanrakidaran hay geanki], Father Arsen Ghazigian said while discussing Giurjian's life and works: "His pseudonyms are Zarmayr Sahagian, Arsen Molar, Bedros Akatan ([in] Constantinople), Baruyr, Bond, Men Gen, Hamshirag A., and

Y. M. Giurod (a pseudonym he selected for the satirical essays he co-authored with Yervant Odian in *Azad Pem*) [abroad], etc."[31]

It is evident that this list also stopped short of including all the pseudonyms Giurjian used, although when Ghazigian reached the letter G of his work, he wrote a letter on September 9, 1910, from Venice to Giurjian asking him to send "the list of his articles related to Armenian life," to list the titles in detail, and to mention the pseudonyms he used, etc. A month later, on October 10, 1910, Ghazigian, who was one of the members of the Mekhitarist Congregation of St. Lazar, sent a letter of gratitude to Giurjian for his response-letter, saying he hoped to benefit from it soon. It can be concluded that Father Arsen Ghazigian certainly benefited from the information Giurjian furnished him, but, unfortunately, the information was not complete, ending with an etcetera.

In 1963, Giurjian's three short stories—*The Name Day Night*, *New Dress*, and *A Family* [Êndanik mê]—were published in one volume.[32] In the introductory note, Giurjian mentioned that *The Name Day Night* was published in 1901 in *Arshaluys* daily of Cairo under the pseudonym Tidag, whereas *A Family* appeared in 1902 in *Nor Or* [New Day] newspaper of Cairo under the pseudonym Zarmayr Sahagian.

Although the number of pseudonyms Giurjian used numbered thirteen, based on the above Hagop Oshagan listed only nine.

Perhaps the most comprehensive list of Giurjian's pseudonyms was the one published in the special edition of *Spiurk* [Diaspora] weekly on December 31, 1965 (No. 49–52, p. 11) in an article entitled "Mikayel Giurjian (Memoires and Notes)" [Mikayel Giurjian (Husher yev noter)]. The list was compiled by Giurjian and Azad, when the latter visited him in Alexandria in 1964. Here is the list: Tidag, Zarmayr Sahagian, Hamshirag A., Zarmayr, Y. M. Giurod, Arsen Molar, Bedros Akatan, Hrand, Men Gen, Mkhitar Bondatsi, Baruyr, Srjep A., Kandag, and Bond.[33]

So, we discover that Giurjian used fourteen pseudonyms. Consequently, Giurjian's example also proves that the Armenian authors of the 1890s continued the tradition common among authors of the 1880s in the liberal use of pseudonyms. The reason for this phenomenon seems to lie in the struggle these authors bore against the ideologies and actions of Armenian and non-Armenian authorities.

It appears that it was Piuzant Kechian who credited the pseudonym Bedros Akatan for the short story *The Name Day Night*, because had Giurjian himself sent the story with a pseudonym, he would have naturally used the pseudonym Tidag, which he used in 1901 when he contributed to *Arshaluys*. Besides, before publishing the story in *Piuzantion* [Byazntium],

Kechian advertised it in his newspaper without mentioning the author's name. We know that initially Giurjian established contact with Kechian through his close friend, Diran Chrakian. This is evidenced through the letters in Giurjian's archive, where, acting as an intermediary between the famous reporter and Giurjian, at times Chrakian asked whether Giurjian wanted to be published under his real name or a pseudonym.

In his letter of May 25, 1902, after offering some information about his book *Inner World* [Nerashkharh], Chrakian wrote in response to Giurjian's inquiry: "But let us discuss Bedros Akatan a little, my dear Mikayel. It appears that Kechian changed your name because of your outrageous family name, and placed the folksy name Bedros Akatan under your story." It is possible that Kechian considered the name Giurjian outrageous, because Giurji means Georgian. It is a fact, though, that the reference in this letter belonged to a changed name. Giurjian would have not asked Chrakian for an explanation, had it been known to him, and Chrakian would have not tried to bring up the theory of an "outrageous family name."

It is worthwhile to mention that Giurjian himself was the creator of a pseudonym for another person, namely Vahan Tekeyan and his pseudonym, Asub [Comet].

* * *

Having mastered the French language, loving French literature, and being captivated by the works of 19th century French authors, Giurjian made his literary debut in French, contributed to French newspapers, wrote poems in French, and wrote, for a time, about the Armenian literary movement in *La Revue* magazine of Paris. His famous work, *The Scribe's Dream*, was first published in French. Later also we find his French verse published in Teotig's *Amenun Daretsuytsê* [Everybody's Almanac] in 1915, 1925, and 1926.

Giurjian entered Armenian literature with his masterpiece, *Mardig Agha*, which caused quite a stir after it was published in the 1898–1899 issues of London's *Nor Geank* [New Life] Armenian literary and political magazine.

From that date on, and until the article, "How I Made Vahan Tekeyan's Acquaintance" [Inchbes dzanotatsa Vahan Tekeyani hed],[34] which he wrote on June 30, 1965, a few days before his death, Giurjian's works appeared in close to forty different newspapers, magazines, and yearbooks. His death on July 3, 1965, in a tram accident, prevented Giurjian from fulfilling his plan to gather all of his works written and published in the Armenian periodicals of Alexandria, Cairo, Constantinople, Smyrna, London, Paris, Saint Petersburg, and the United States.

The collection and study of Giurjian's works, especially in the initial stage, was difficult, because his archive was not dispatched to the Museum of Literature and Art of Yeghishé Charents of the Ministry of Culture of the Republic of Armenia in one batch. In order to study the works not included in that batch, I had to examine the ill-gathered Diasporan Armenian periodicals located at the National Public Library, the Scientific Fundamental Library of the National Academy of Sciences, and the Library of the Institute of Scientific Research of Manuscripts of Mesrob Mashdots (Madenataran) in Yerevan. In the course of this collection process, I found that other authors' signatures corresponded with the pseudonyms Giurjian had used. For example, I discovered that an Armenian from Baku had most likely used the initials M. G. in *Ararad* monthly and that the signature Baruyr in *Zhamanag* [Time] newspaper of Constantinople belonged to a writer from Paghesh (Bitlis). Unfortunately, during the eighty-six years he lived, Giurjian never had the opportunity to write his memoirs, which would have been a valuable resource, because of the interesting and important details about him and his contemporaries they might have contained. His archive does contain handwritten diaries and notebooks covering the years 1900 through 1933 but there are long lapses within these documents. They rather prove that he did not keep a regular diary. Found in these documents are thoughts, proverbs, aphorisms, descriptions of people he met, outlines for literary projects, travel impressions, incidental notes, and incomplete or inappropriate remarks, more than important biographical data or valuable literary observations.

Also problematic, Giurjian himself could not recall the complete list of newspapers and periodicals to which he had contributed. For example, even the list published that he and Azad prepared on page 11 of the joint issue 49–52 of *Spiurk* weekly in 1965, comparatively the most extensive listing of his works, was incomplete. The list did not mention Mihran Askanazian's *Bardez* [Garden] weekly where Giurjian published a free poem, *The Song of the Sword* [Surin yerkê]; two short stories, *A Liberal Girl* [Azadamid aghchig mê] and *Post Mortem* [Hed mahu]; a fable, *Balance and Mind* [Gshirk u khelk]; and two translations: *Favors of the Moon* of Charles Baudelaire, and the epic novel of Alphonse Daudet, *The Prodigious Adventures of Tartarin de Tarascon*. The list also omitted the *Hay Kraganutiun* literary, scientific, and art monthly of Smyrna where in 1911–1913 Giurjian published short stories and poems, such as *Drtad and Dajad*, *The Power of a Word* [Pari mê uzhê], *Mister Politician* [Baron kaghakakedê], *The Story of a Miracle* [Hrashki mê badmutiunê]. Also forgotten was *Miutiun* [Unity] monthly—the official organ of the Armenian General Benevolent Union, which contains in more than twenty issues, dating from the second decade of the twentieth century, Giurjian's chronicles; Aram Andonian's *Kharazan* [Whip] illustrated satirical weekly; *Ani* magazine and *Nayiri* weekly of Beirut, Lebanon; *Baykar* periodical of Boston, Massachusetts; and many others. Finally, located in the United States, as I reviewed the materials I had gathered over the past two decades in order to finalize this study, and converted the orthography to Western Armenian standards, then prepared for publication, I had no access to the libraries in Yerevan so I was unable to make necessary changes or additions.

Regretfully, until 1960, only the following works had been published in the form of individual publications: *The Franco-Turkish War* that Giurjian co-authored with Yervant Odian (1909 and 1923), *A Heroic Play* (1928), and *The Salvation* (1910). If gathered and published as a complete collection, Giurjian's best works alone would require huge volumes.

It is hard to make peace with the fact that even though Cairo was once the "third city in the world," after Constantinople and Smyrna, well-known for the quantity of Armenian books published, in essence, Giurjian's works remain scattered in periodicals and have not yet been published in book form.

Perhaps Giurjian also was responsible for the fact that today we have, in addition to those previously mentioned, only the following works published as separate books: *To the Adored, from the Bottom of My Heart* (Beirut, Donigian Press, 1960, 53 pages), a collection of free verse; *Twenty Years Later* (Beirut, Sevan Press, 1961, 100 pages), an anthology of fifteen short stories and sketches published in addition to the play that shares the same title; and a third anthology, *The Name Day Night and Other Stories from Constantinoplean Manners* [Anunin kisherê yev ayl badmvadzkner bolsahay parkeré] (Cairo, Vosgedar Press, 1963, 55 pages).

In the 1890s, because of partisan pressure and his deteriorating health, and then in the early 1900s, because of economic and family hardships and the intensifying persecutions and massacres in Turkey, Giurjian's contributions to the Armenian media were sometimes separated by great intervals of time. Regardless, he always remained attached to his people and expressed his patriotic sentiments and progressive thoughts regarding the pressing issues of the day. For example, on April 18, 1909, he wrote to Doctor Harutiun Tireakian: "The new regime has forced me to do a little more literature," even though "official and family anxieties have brought forth a distressed situation."[35]

Despite these factors, the years 1898–1915 were the most productive period of Giurjian's life. His realistic novellas and short stories shone, especially in his portrayal of the life of Armenians in Western Armenia and Constantinople, as did his Oriental literary sketches, satirical works, witty chronicles, and literary-critical essays.

Giurjian made noteworthy contributions to the Armenian press. He diligently edited and stylized literary and journalistic writings, essays, and reports. Most important, in addition to temporarily editing *Azad Pem*, Giurjian published *Shirag* literary magazine (1905–1907), and acted as the editor-in-chief of *Arev* daily (1920–1923).

He was also known as a civic activist dedicated to his nation and its culture. During the first two decades of the twentieth century, amidst dissensions that had surfaced between Armenian revolutionary parties in Alexandria, a handful of young Armenians founded three new entities: the Armenian Reading Hall, which was established in a modest store in support of the Armenian language, literature, and culture; the Dikran Yergat Armenian Cultural Association; and the Culture-Loving Armenian Women's Association [Kegharvesdaser Hayuhyats]. Giurjian became an active and dedicated member of Dikran Yergat through which he supported a variety of cultural functions.

The founders of Dikran Yergat wanted to benefit from the close literary relationship Giurjian had with Odian, so they asked the two authors to write a play, the proceeds of which would be used to enrich the association's treasury. Pleased with the idea, Giurjian and Odian wrote *The Franco-Turkish War* comedy in a month by allocating two- to three-hour writing sessions per week to its authoring. Like other translators, such as Mihran Damadian, Levon Mgrdichian, Sisag Shaljian, Khachig Sandaljian, and Baydzar Yergat, who Armenianized plays and operettas for the association, Giurjian also volunteered to translate works. He employed his graceful style to those translations for the benefit of the association.

In the spring of 1911, Gomidas Vartabed visited the Armenian community in Egypt for the purpose of introducing Armenian folk songs. He organized a choir and gave concerts in Cairo and Alexandria. Giurjian, as the chairperson of the educational board of the Boghosian Armenian School, played an instrumental role in the success of Gomidas's visit. To him, "the unforgettable and immortal Gomidas" was "one of the greatest persons born to the creative race of Mashdots [the inventor of the Armenian alphabet in A.D. 405]."

Giurjian also participated in the literary-cultural functions of the Armenians of Egypt. He was an actor in *The Franco-Turkish War* (September 1903). He translated a comedy (February 1912) for a festival[36] organized by the Armenian Constitutional Democratic Party and he adapted Arpiar

Arpiarian's work, *My Nation's Benefactors* [Azkis parerarnerê] into a satirical theatrical production (staged in February 1912). As a member, he also participated in a committee that organized a jubilee honoring the forty years of literary and educational services of Hovhannes Setian, a talented poet and meritorious teacher (January 1913).

Moreover, Giurjian paid homage to Eastern Armenian intellectuals. He contributed a literary-critical essay, "The Novella Writer" [Noravebakirê],[37] to the anthology *Shirvanzaté and His Work* [Shirvanzaté yev ir kordzê] that Dikran Gamsaragan compiled. In addition, he acknowledged the fortieth anniversary of *Mshag* [Cultivator], the political, social, and literary newspaper of Tbilisi,[38] in June 1912 with a telegram greeting.

In 1920, when General Antranig Ozanian, the national hero of the Armenians visited Egypt with his two aides, Jim Chankalian and Doctor Bonapartian, the directors of *Arev* daily initiated a fund-raising effort to raise money to donate a precious sword that the Armenian goldsmiths of Egypt had prepared for the General. The General received the sword during a ceremony of unprecedented pomp and circumstance held in Dikran Yergat Association's hall. Giurjian participated in the ceremony, along with the Primate, Archbishop Torkom Kushagian, and he was among a group of ten people who were treated to a photo opportunity with the national hero.

Giurjian was a drama lover. He had the opportunity to know such masterful actors of the Armenian theater as Levon Shishmanian, Hovhannes Apelian, Hovhannes Zarifian, and Siranush and he enjoyed their performances in Alexandria.

Left to right, Mikayel Giurjian, Vahan Tekeyan, and Yervant Odian, c. 1908.

GIURJIAN'S TUMULTUOUS DEBUT WITH A MASTERPIECE

THE SATIRICAL NOVEL, *MARDIG AGHA*

The situation of Armenians living in Western Armenia became increasingly dangerous as the nineteenth century came to an end. Day after day, Sultan Abdülhamid II intensified his persecution of Armenians. The massacre that took place in Sasun in 1894 and the wider spread Armenian massacres of 1895–1896 shook the civilized world. In Turkey, the Armenians were terrorized. Many were unable to endure the endless and violent brutality of the Turks. With broken hearts, they abandoned their homes and birthplaces and left for foreign countries.

Eventually, the Armenian communities in Bulgaria, Rumania, Greece, Egypt, France, the Unites States, and other hospitable countries swelled with the influx of refugees. This eleventh-hour escape and the harsh conditions suffered by refugees were recorded in the Armenian media, memoirs, and literary works of the time. The misery of the constantly increasing number of refugees was grievous. Even in the United States, an attractive destination for people from various nations, life was not easy for the Armenian refugees who found work mainly as laborers. To sustain themselves and their families, they labored under demanding physical conditions. It was only after overcoming harsh initial hurdles that Armenian storekeepers, businessmen, and artisans began to earn incomes commensurate with the middle classes.

The final five years of the nineteenth century were extraordinary for the Armenian community of Egypt, too. The Armenians of Alexandria lived through heartrending days. After the 1896 calamities in Constantinople, many Armenian families panicked, abandoned their houses, and, in order to escape death, took refuge under the blue, star-studded, hospitable, yet unfamiliar Egyptian sky. Many arrived in almost half-dead condition.

Eozhen Papazian, a Diaspora-Armenian musician, wrote in his memoirs that his family, unwilling to live any longer under Turkish oppression, moved from Smyrna to Alexandria in August 1885, where they found barely sixty Armenian families. But when "the sad news of the Armenian massacres of 1895–96 reached us," recalled Papazian, referring to his childhood, "thousands of Armenians fled Turkey, stampeding to Alexandria. Refugees filled Boghosian School's classrooms, gardens, and so on, and instead of desks, we were placed on seats lined up against the inner walls of the church."[39]

Levon Mgrdichian also discussed the refugee movement of 1896 in an article entitled, "Recollections from Alexandria's Community Life" [Verhishumner Agheksantrio hamaynkayin geanken].[40] Mgrdichian mentioned that each boat that arrived in Alexandria after the incident of the Ottoman Bank in 1896 carried hundreds of refugees. "Within several weeks," wrote he, "at least three thousand refugees were housed in the church compound. The school, a portion of the diocese, and the large church garden all served as temporary residence. It was a Babylonian confusion made up of a mixed crowd from the provinces of Armenia and the quarters of Constantinople. Three thousand people needed to be fed, cared for, and...managed."

Mgrdichian was the head of the chancery of the Armenian diocese of Alexandria at the time. In this capacity, he was directly involved in refugee affairs. He related that the Parish Council had created a seventeen-member Committee for Refugees that convened every evening from 5:00 to 9:00 p.m. to raise funds for the refugees and find jobs for them. "When the refugees felt that they could not continue to dwell in the diocesan and school buildings, and they moved to a large area in the church garden, within less than a month, the garden turned into a very interesting and unique quarter filled with small houses, streets, tea and coffee shops, and a market," Mgrdichian wrote.

Teacher and writer Hovhannes Setian, in his turn, briefly described the misery of the refugees, most of whom were deprived of means, confused, and depressed. Here is an excerpt from his article, "The Great Migration" [Medz kaghtumê]: "The courtyard and garden of the church of Alexandria rendered the most doleful scene of haphazardly piled-up old furniture, hastily installed small tents, wooden huts, dinner tables ... under which you would see an old woman or a breastfeeding mother, pale, hair falling loose, grievously indifferent to themselves, and with a gaze reflective of the confusion of unheard disasters and horrors. Or you would see young girls, dressed carelessly, hiding their embarrassment and despair in a poor tent or wooden cell. All seemed stamped with the seal of hopelessness and doubt about the future." Setian continued: "Later, when I moved to Cairo, I witnessed similar scenes there."[41]

The distress and horror of the survivors of the brutal massacre was so heartrending that even youngsters lost their sanity. In his short story, *A Wreck* [Khleag mê],[42] Setian described the story of the fate of Ardashes who had barely survived events in the calamitous city. On an August morning in 1896, while crossing the wharf of Galata, the main character of the story, thirty-five-year-old Ardashes, saw horrified-looking people running away from other people armed with cudgels and clubs. He understood. Noticing a steamboat by the shore, and knowing how to swim, he jumped into the sea. He boarded the boat where he found other Armenians. The boat took the young Armenian to Alexandria. Ardashes could not find a job there so he moved to Cairo, where he found work as a mechanic. The smart, dexterous, silent young man always seemed absent-minded. Day after day, his intellectual faculties deteriorated irrecoverably—fear, wrath, and "the fury over his inability to do something were causing him harm," wrote Setian about the young man, who was able to save himself but not his kin from the massacre, nor was he able to avenge his losses from the barbaric and monstrous Turks. One night, the residents of Bein-el-Suren heard a noise and recognized the voice of Ardashes, who had lost his sanity. "He was shouting and cursing against the Sultan, the author of the Armenian massacres" with the hatred of an unstoppable rebel. Nobody saw the patriotic Ardashes after that night.

Armenian newspapers provide much information on the misery of Armenian refugees, whether in Europe or the United States. In *Nor Geank* weekly, Levon Pashalian, signing as L. Zartumian, wrote about the hardships Armenian refugees faced in London and the United States. In his memoir, *Twelve Years Outside Constantinople*, Yervant Odian reported on the destitute Armenian refugees from various provinces of Western Armenia, who found refuge in the Greek harbor of Piraeus.

In 1898, *Sharzhum* [Movement], a newspaper printed in Varna, Bulgaria, published a short novel entitled, *The Price of Bread* [Hatsin kinê], about a refugee Armenian woman and her children. *Balkanian Mamul* [Balkan Media] later reprinted the work as a feuilleton.

The work portrayed the destruction of a modest and honest Armenian family. The couple, Diran and Asdghig, had two children, Vahé and Anush, who brought them happiness in their initial years of marriage. Then the horrors of 1896 engulfed Asdghig's village with the bloody flames of fire. The mob launched its first attack on Asdghig's house, because many coveted this beautiful woman. After facilitating the escape of his wife and children out the back door, Diran bravely fought and killed many of the attackers until he was killed when the furious mob fired ten or twenty gunshots.

As the swords and fire spread from house to house, Asdghig and her children left her paternal home, which had been reduced to ashes, and ran across the hill along with other half-naked, confused, miserable people of all ages, most of whom had jumped out of windows and off of roofs in the dark.

While enduring with strength all the physical afflictions and hardships she encountered, the horrors multiplied. Asdghig anxiously wandered through villages and towns, until she left the damned country she loved to settle in Varna on the European shores of the Black Sea, where a sizeable Armenian community was established.

Thanks to help provided by the Bulgarian government and the Armenian community, the refugees gradually settled. Asdghig's family, however, was destined to fall victim to Margos Agha—who was close to forty-five-years old, a prominent personality in the town, and the owner of a large business. He had been in Varna for quite a while. This dissembling agha, who presented himself as a skilled community activist or a person concerned about political issues, changed his attitude toward the political parties daily. One day he was a fanatic Hnchag, applauding their achievements; the next day he was praising the Tashnags.

The reader eventually discovers the nets that this cunning leader lay to entrap the provincial woman, whose beauty had captivated him from the first day, even at a time when her children had begun to lose weight and color from malnutrition and from the unsanitary dark and damp room in which they had to live. Disguised under the "reputation of a good man," Margos Agha shamelessly defiled Asdghig in return for the bread he offered her children, who were wearing away like melting candles. Because of her inner turbulence and anguish, Asdghig lost her sanity and was sent to the asylum that was part of the Armenian Hospital of Constantinople. Her daughter, Anush, grew sicker and died without a father and mother. Her son, Vahé, ended up in a remote orphanage.

While one could continue to write numerous pages highlighting the literary works of contemporaries who portrayed the heartbreaking conditions the Armenian refugees faced after the tragedies of 1894–1896, it is pertinent to examine instead how Giurjian, who himself escaped the massacres of Constantinople and lived the miserable refugee life, reflected on both old and new settlers of the Armenian community of Egypt in his first satirical novel, published in serial form in *Nor Geank* of London under the title, *Mardig Agha.*

Giurjian began his novel thus: "After the massacres of 1896, the great wind of migration, that uprooted the Armenian people from their birthplace and scattered them throughout the world, drove a great number to Egypt." He went on to describe the miseries of the unfortunate self-exiles and refugees, as well as the encouraging and vivifying atmosphere of the free and safe life they found in Egypt. In describing the deplorable conditions and state of the refugee laborers, artisans, merchant clerks, market apprentices, and families, who had somewhat managed to make a living in Constantinople but were deprived of all means in Alexandria, Giurjian commented on their financial and economic hardships, and their most common feelings, including the panic attacks, confusion, and feverish anxieties many of them suffered. He found their situation so pitiful and disturbing that he wrote: "You would think a funeral procession was passing, with the people singing the same heartrending introduction of looting, massacre, and complete immiseration, the same entreating, tearful refrain that concluded with the plea, 'Give us work, give us money, give us food'; a plea directed at the members of the Relief Committee who had gathered to deal with refugee issues." Two members out of the committee of eight were absent. One sat lazily in a green armchair, reading a French newspaper. "He threw an indifferent glance at the pleaders during moments he felt the urge to smoke."[43] Two other committee members argued political or economic issues intensely. The remainder of those on the committee, in turn, and often all three together, dealt with the refugees, "sending the parade of refugees away with indifference and empty promises. 'Very well,' they said. 'Your name has been written… we will look for… wait… God willing…'"[44]

There were also people who revolted against the duplicity of polite refusals, such as the brave, daring, and sincere "Adanatsi Hagop, who after openly insulting and embarrassing the parish council member that reproached him in the garden, dared to enter the meeting room and repeat the scene there, throwing into the faces of offended and tremulous council members words of rage and wrathful contempt as harsh as fist strikes, perhaps to the joy of the refugees whose feelings he expressed."[45]

At that moment, Mardig Agha arrived and tried to enter.

He was told, "There is someone else inside; it can't be, wait!" Then harshly and with unstoppable haughtiness he said: "Let me in, brother, I tell you! I am not like others you know. They call me Mardig Srmakeshian. I have served as a council member in Constantinople ... I have not come to ask for money, rather I have come to give money, do you get it?"[46]

Then forcefully he opened the door, entered the room, and donated ten British pounds for the purpose of "remedying, as much as possible, the huge damages caused by insolent revolutionaries to our poor nation." The council members barely managed to interrupt Mardig Agha's anti-revolutionary speech and shoo him away once they gave him a receipt.

In the fourth chapter, Giurjian described the life in an Egyptian Armenian salon located in the oddly hospitable and ostentatious house of Dikran Agha Beylerian's family, who had settled in Alexandria less than three months before. The luminous hall was full of invitees on Sunday evening. The visitors followed each other: Sarkis Effendi Khabarajian, a rich Constantinoplean merchant and his snobbish and boastful wife; Sdepan Margosian, a clerk from Constantinople who was now jobless in Alexandria;

Kavafian, "a mixture of a bear and a pig" and his wife, Zaruhi; Mr. and Mrs. Krikorian, a young merchant from Pera, Mrs. and Miss Semerjian, Mr. Aram Seghposian, the deaf but talkative Miss Sarafian, and, finally, the main characters of the novel: merchant Mardig Agha and "hero" and "revolutionary" Levon Surian.

Giurjian was particularly inspired by the indecisive and mercurial character of Mardig Agha (Mardig Srmakeshian), who grew wealthy in Scütari thanks to the riches gathered by his merchant father who was originally from Kayseri. Mardig Agha then moved to Alexandria with his mother and daughter. There, influenced by Levon Surian, a member of the Armenian Revolutionary Federation, Mardig Agha, who was fond of only himself and had never liked the revolutionaries, changed his views and became a "revolutionary" himself, announcing that he was no longer against all revolutionaries, but just against the Hnchags. So, the person who had previously used every opportunity to speak against the revolutionaries, after reading a set of *Troshag* newspapers [the official publication of the Armenian Revolutionary Federation], and upon Surian's advice, became a stout promoter of revolutionary views and a person who did not spare his wealth in support of them.

After cunningly and deceitfully getting Mardig Agha into his claws, Surian captured the heart of his daughter. Together they left for Paris so that Surian could realize his venal plans with regard to Mardig Agha's wealth and daughter.

Levon Surian, who pretended to be the ideologist of a revolutionary organization and who the author severely ridiculed, was as real a character as were all others in the novel. Upon first reading, it was evident that the anti-partisan nature of the novel would be met with bayonets and animosity. The Hnchag leaders launched an offensive against it and tried to stop its publication, because Surian, although presented as a member of the Tashnag Party, was a well-known Hnchag activist in Alexandria.

After publishing the first part of the novel in seven large installments, the editor of *Nor Geank* curtailed its publication. He announced in the March 1, 1899, issue: "The rest in the upcoming issue." Indeed, in the issue of March 15, the "second and final part" of the satirical novel appeared in an extremely abridged form (pages 91–96).

According to the abridged manuscript, the author ended the novel with a dialogue between two people sitting in the corner of a café in Alexandria.

In a long letter one of them had received from his friend in Paris, the friend wrote that Mardig Agha was disappointed with Surian who, after traveling with Mardig Agha's daughter from Paris to Italy on a wedding trip, decided to confess the truth to his father-in-law, saying that he had associated himself with the revolutionaries simply to deceive Mardig Agha because he had been in love with his daughter. The man listening to this revealing letter understood nothing; wherefore, the reader of the letter summed up the matter in his own words: "Didn't you get it? Surian wrote a letter to Mardig Agha, saying give up your dreams, stay away from revolution, and return to your former opinions. Everything I said was a lie; I was compelled to deceive and take advantage of you in order to establish a position and gain my fortune. Now I have come to ask for your forgiveness. Forget these things of the past and let's live together happily."[47]

Mardig Agha, after receiving the unexpected letter from his son-in-law, "stayed home for a whole week, filling the rooms and deafening the ears of his servants and mother with extremely agitated wrathful screams, like a wounded wild beast roaring and pacing in his cage."[48]

It is true that Giurjian basically concluded the funny tragedy of Mardig Agha. But by leaving out whole chapters from the manuscript, *Nor Geank* affected the gradual progression of the novel, and limited its aesthetic merits. Those omissions led to unfounded speculations.

In *Mardig Agha,* Giurjian mocked the vainglory of Armenian nationalist parties and the meanness of the leaders of the Armenian community of Alexandria. He realistically described the customs and habits of the Armenians of Egypt at the end of the nineteenth century, and stripped naked the snobs—the nouveau riche—and those who pompously preached revolution. By doing so, his satire gained social resonance and was no longer innocent entertainment.

Mardig Agha first appeared in *Nor Geank* from October 1898 to March 1899. Prudently, Giurjian concealed his identity by writing under the pseudonym Baruyr, which saved him many unpleasant incidents, according to the testimony of contemporary authors.

The novel, despite initially qualifying as pleasant reading material, soon caused great upset within the Armenian community of Alexandria, where there was much speculation about the true identity of the author and many rumors circulated. "It must be Dikran Gamsaragan ..., no, Arpiar is the author definitely ... perhaps it's Odian," wrote Odian.[49] "H. Alpiar narrowly escaped a beating, because he had unwisely announced somewhere, 'Only I can write such a novel,' which amounted to exaggerated self-praise," wrote Odian in his memoirs.[50]

According to Suren Bartevian, when at the offices of *Nor Geank* he and Levon Pashalian read the first episodes of *Mardig Agha,* they were "shocked by the unexpected and masterful discovery of a new talent who, in the person of Mikayel Giurjian, rose up in such a way as to suddenly impose himself upon our judgment, enthuse us, and simultaneously bewilder us."[51]

Bartevian wrote also that *Mardig Agha* caused such a storm that it could have potentially hit Giurjian on the head, "had he not protected himself under the pseudonym *Baruyr.*"

Giurjian, indeed, showed great audacity with his "untamed novel of derision" (in Bartevian's words). It is debatable whether to characterize this satirical novel as derision, because Giurjian was not a man of crude mockery; rather, he was a delicate satirist who caused a tempest.

Why did the novel generate so much commotion, and what was the primary reason behind this excitement? The answer can best be attributed to the primary subject of the novel. *Mardig Agha* opened with the description of the deplorable situation many self-exiles faced immediately after the 1896 massacres. The events of 1894–1896 resulted in much panic, commotion, and fear, which in turn led to the migration of Armenians to Egypt. In the novel, Giurjian described the life of both old and new migrants to Alexandria in the late nineteenth century. Alexandria was the kind of city where they could breathe freely and enjoy the liberty of speech and action, exempt from the constant threat of the police, arrests, imprisonments, and tortures that were prevalent at the time in the Armenian provinces of Turkey, and especially pronounced in the capital, Constantinople.

Giurjian described the garden and the courtyard of the Alexandrian church with its turbulent crowd. Amongst the multitude gathered in the courtyard were representatives of various provinces from many walks of life: the laborer and the fisherman; the provincial porter and the elegant young man sporting the appearance of an educated person; the newly graduated from school, and the *esnaf,* or craftsman; the young businessman and the fez-wearing merchant. Mardig Agha Srmakeshian, the main character of the novel, appeared suddenly in front of a backdrop of tents that housed poor refugees, other types of improvised shelters, and shops built with two logs. The scene was reminiscent of a miniature village. At different times in the novel, the author used his versatility as a writer to portray his main character in the business world, at home, or mingling with the wealthy.

In his memoir *Twelve Years Outside Constantinople,* Yervant Odian discussed the "unprecedented crisis" the author Baruyr (this was the pseudonym Giurjian used) generated with *Mardig Agha.* Odian felt Baruyr was "certainly not a neophyte writer" and noted: "After a few installments, the [serialized] novel presented an Armenian salon in Alexandria, in which many well-known individuals were portrayed in most accurate and yet superbly caricatured lines. Nobody, male or female, was spared. They appeared in the novel with all their ridiculous features unmasked. Their faces, bodies, ways of sitting, clothes—in short, everything was exposed with insolent naughtiness."[52]

As examples, Odian cited the descriptions of many figures in the novel who were known to all. These included a wealthy Constantinoplean merchant, Sarkis Effendi Khabarajian and his wife, as well as Kavafian and his wife—whom the author blamed and mocked mercilessly.

As a consequence of the novel, Odian remarked: "A terrible storm erupted in the city. At home, in the cafés, and in the parks, everybody was preoccupied with *Mardig Agha*. Those who had not yet appeared in the novel, waited with heart pounding anxiety for their turn; those who had already been mocked, consoled themselves, saying: 'Our turn has passed.' But no one forgave Baruyr, whose true identity was unknown."[53]

Referring to those turbulent days, Odian testified that Arpiarian suffered greatly because of *Mardig Agha*, and that the novel stirred up angry confrontations within political party circles. "Levon Pashalian confidentially revealed Baruyr's real name to Arpiar, asking him to reveal his true identity to no one except me," wrote Odian. "On the other hand, Levon Mgrdichian, as one of the [Reformed] Hnchagian Party leaders, wrote to colleagues in London in an effort to discover the name of the author, but Pashalian refused to disclose the satirist's identity. Mgrdichian demanded that the newspaper stop the publication of the novel, but Arpiar and Pashalian opposed him. Mgrdichian then ordered, by telegram, the termination of the novel, but publication continued. Consequently, Mgrdichian threatened to resign and retire from the party."[54]

One of the funniest elements in the novel is Surian being a member of the Armenian Revolutionary Federation. In real life he was a well-known Hnchagian Party activist. This, too, was a stumbling block for party members aware of the issues.

Giurjian described himself also in *Mardig Agha*; therefore, readers who were provoked by "Baruyr" sympathized with Mikayel Giurjian, who portrayed himself as the character Kurchian, "a nineteen- to twenty-year-old pallid, thin, distressed young man with the complexion of a cadaver, an unsteady glance, a stumbling walk, and extinguished eyes."

Odian asserted: "Even years later, the aggravation against Baruyr had not faded within the Armenian community of Alexandria, and finally, when the real name of the author was revealed, a true persecution began against Mikayel Giurjian, to the point that, in order to live undisturbed in the city, the poor man was compelled to announce that his intention in writing *Mardig Agha* was the shaping of a literary fancy for which he was regretful."[55]

Yet in truth, by breaking past the thematic limitations of a number of contemporary Western Armenian writers, through the use of satirical language and the comedy of manners, Giurjian produced a sophisticated, aesthetic, and witty criticism of the inner essence and external peculiarities of people well-known to his contemporaries.

Giurjian portrayed his characters, and particularly the main heroes, with great mastery:

"Rich Constantinoplean merchant Sarkis Effendi Khabarajian and his wife. A most appropriately yoked couple. The man is short, fat, has a big mountain-like head, a forehead as stubborn as a rock, a thick falling moustache, and a curved hanging nose. There is something similar to the thick-headedness, coarseness, and slowness of ruminating animals in the undulation of his hoarse, rich voice and his body language. His head, stuck in the middle of broad, edgy shoulders, reminds one of the head of an ox slowly proceeding before the yoke, shaping its outline with its shoulders.

"His similarly fat wife is squeezed next to him with cheeks blowing, a double chin, her obese breasts resting like inflated packages on her bloated belly, and her arms crossed on her chest. Her movements and intonation possessed a kind of haughtiness and egotism. Contemptuous folds surrounded her lips when she spoke. She was the kind of woman who continuously brags about herself, her house, pleasures, luxury, and spending, with the snobbish boasting of a girl born from the poor class who married a rich person. Whereas her husband—a man who accumulated wealth with his own hard work—talks everywhere and to everybody about money, thanks to deprivations, humiliations, patience, and stinginess, preaching saving, decrying the badness of the times, dissuading from 'unwise expenditure,' asking people he just met about their business, honoring only businessmen, and turning his back on the unemployed, the clerks, and those who 'could read and write.'"[56]

Giurjian described the attendees of the large hall of the Beylerian family, one at a time, with the same mercilessness.

"Sdepan Margosian, a thirty year old man was a clerk in Constantinople, but jobless in Alexandria. He was said to be educated, which amongst us meant one who knew French. Once upon a time, he had published a book, *18 Novellas Translated from French*, which only he recalls. It was amusing to see how obesity flattened and softened his scabrous body, like the snow does to the ground, had almost ironed away his perimeters, broadening his legs to the extent that they reached the protrusion of the belly. His neck, too, was hidden in the folds of his flesh, making his head an uninterrupted part of the rest of his body, which he had successfully turned into a round and heavy, barrel-like and cylindrical pile of flesh and fat, like a short Egyptian cucumber or zucchini.

"Despite his physical state, Margosian chose to wear gold-threaded eyeglasses, as if attempting to correct his body's roughness and density with the lightness and noble delicacy of his eyeglasses, like an ox that vaingloriously wants to wear the elegant eye-flaps of a horse."[57]

A few lines later, Giurjian went on to ruthlessly describe Mr. and Mrs. Kavafian.

"This is another fat man; the mixture of a bear and a pig. The most striking thing about him is his head; a huge, multivolume head shaped like a large watermelon that was attached almost without a neck to a short-legged impressive body, burdened with a belly that protruded forward like a barrel. His eyebrows were made of tow. A bushy moustache, a large, broad nose, big blotted eyes with salient eyeballs, a face dug deep with cavernous wrinkles, and a voice corresponding to these. In contrast, his wife shared with him only his last name. That pile of heavy, rough, and obese elements was married to a thin bundle of nerves, the coquette body of a woman whose beauty had faded a little; a restless, dynamic woman who seemed like a flute and a goat next to the big drum and buffalo that was her husband."[58]

In the same issue of *Nor Geank*, Giurjian continued to describe the skinny guests of the salon, using a similar palette and comparable wit.

"A young merchant from Pera who has established a new business here; is as dry as a wringed and pressed piece of cloth, as contracted as the residum of melted tallow, a man whose flesh is stuck to his bones, seemingly with a skulled face and a neck that is reminiscent of the friend of Daumier's immortal Robert Macaire. Dark black holed eyes that look like the piercing of twigs. His wife thin and sweet."

Miss Beylerian is the living link between the people of different genders, personalities, and ideologies gathered together in the salon: "Seemingly as prating as a magpie, as restless as a fish, constantly talking, unwisely saying whatever crosses her mind, unable to hide or conceal anything, jumping from one idea to another and from one word to another like a sparrow jumping from one perch to another, spouting incoherent, absurd, unrelated words like an ever-flowing wave and laughing loud and obnoxiously, interrupted with unexpected, sudden pauses—as if to take a breath—only to once again resume, jump, and fly into the whirling and turning vortex of words and movements, like the dusty flight of pieces of paper, cloth, and feather that frantically, disorderly, and haphazardly dance in a street."[59]

The novel goes on to portray the main characters, Mardig Agha Srmakeshian and Levon Surian, with more interesting and uncompromising criticism. The central character, Mardig Agha, is described as: "Looking forty or forty-five years old, but brisk, stout, and tall, with a big belly shaped like a capital S. A pretentious man with a fat, round body, ash-colored hair, a forehead that is bloated like a bourgeois belly, a face colored with the redness of adobe, eyebrows as thick as moustaches, big and commanding eyes burning through their bushes in swollen eyeballs, a majestic Armenian nose, Arabic lips that are completely covered with a handle bar moustache twisted like a rope, a haughty chin reaching down three-stories to victoriously rest on his vested chest, a big belly circling his girth like the drum of a drummer, his tall fez slanted backward, an umbrella in one hand, the other hand in his pocket. He entered the church walking between two adults who were thin, serious-looking men, also wearing fezes—most certainly they were merchants who seemed to be listening to the fat man who walked using big, authoritative steps, who was threateningly swinging his umbrella, and whose strong head movements made the fringe of his fez swing like the malfunctioning pendulum of a watch."[60]

Levon Surian, a cold, calm, and serious man, was the opposite of Mardig Agha Srmakeshian—a man with a fiery nature, he was a naive believer. Unlike the other characters, Giurjian portrayed Surian as an elegant person. He refrained from ridiculing his external look, but in reality reserved the harshest criticism for him by clearly reprehending his inner world and essence, his knavish act. Giurjian successfully unmasked Surian, exposing the crafty and cunning man inside. By doing so, Giurjian underlined the disgusting ingenuity of Surian who initially presented himself as a revolutionary and only after reaching his goal lowered himself to write a letter asking Mardig Agha's forgiveness for his action.

Before he met Surian, Mardig Agha was prone to loud complaints about political parties and revolutionaries, holding them responsible for the poor and deplorable state of the refugees.

Mardig Agha's meeting with Surian at the Beylerians is noteworthy. Levon spoke of his "revolutionary life," whereas Mardig Agha related incidents from his "patriotic activity." Two weeks later, Surian managed to blackmail and collect a ten pound fine from Mardig Agha "as punishment for the mean insults" he was expressing openly against revolution—in particular, against the Tashnag Party.

Surian successfully subverted the naive Mardig Agha who, driven by terror and the vainglory of wanting to leave a mark in history as a national benefactor, became a member of the Tashnag Party. Thus "the man who could not spell even the alphabet of politics," became an ideologist, analyzing events and making political predictions.

Through dialogues taking place between Mardig Agha and his audience, Giurjian successfully portrayed the faith of a new convert that grew stronger daily. In this regard, of particular interest is Mardig Agha's encounter with a refugee dressed and looking like a provincial man. Having heard that the Effendi was kind, benevolent, and generous toward the nation, he appealed to him.

"'Effendi,'" said the man entreatingly ... then, speaking of his misery he said: He was doing quite well in Constantinople, then he suffered much loss, and now he finds himself in a desperate situation here.

"Mardig Agha bloated like a turkey and smoked one cigarette after another in rapid succession. The provincial man begged Mardig Agha to kindly help him, to reach out to him and his family 'for God's sake, for his pretty daughter's sake.'

"'Eh,' said Mardig Agha, 'are you a revolutionary?'

"The man—who was indeed a revolutionary affiliated with the Tashnags—had had the opportunity to acquaint himself with Mardig Agha's beliefs at the church and elsewhere, outlined a movement of strong protest upon that question.

"'What did you say, Effendi, I a revolutionary? God forbid ... These disgraceful...'

"'Who are you alluding to,' interrupted Mardig Agha, 'the Hnchags or Tashnags?'

"'May all be damned, Hnchag or Tashnag alike ... especially the Tashnags who...'

"Barely had this sinister remark slipped from the man's mouth, when he, stunned and horrified, ceased speaking before Mardig Agha who partially stood up on his cushion and showed him the door, gesturing with threatening, angry, and commanding movements:

"'Shut up, get out, get lost, you worthless man ... how dare you insult the Tashnags?'

"Caught by surprise, confused, as if suddenly realizing that he has fallen down the moon, the man took on the appearance of a person who had swallowed the burning fire of a rooster thinking that he would drink water, or one who hit the floor, having been assured that he would sit on a chair."[61]

Giurjian used secondary characters to criticize Mardig Agha's conversion, vainglory, and other character flaws, after he becomes a Tashnag propagandist.

Reverend Yervant Karageozian is one of those secondary characters. Contrary to Mardig Agha, who believed Russia was behind every incident, repeating, "Look for the Russian, look for the Russian," and motivated by the love of arguments, Karageozian said with quarrelsome intentions: "If you ask me, Effendi, England is behind everything."

Noteworthy also is the Russian Armenian socialist, who argued: "The Tashnag leaders profess the socialist doctrines of Marx and Lassalle," and "they will seize the wealth and distribute it to others after liberation."

Terrorized by these words, Mardig Agha replied: "What are you talking about? You are wrong ... They do not say such things." Ignorant in the sciences, he continued and concluded: "What does this mean? ... Why would my wealth be distributed to others? ... What kind of a statement is this? ... Let everybody work and become rich ... How did I get rich with my own efforts? ... If that is socialism, it's void then...." Earlier, Surian had assured him that after successfully resolving the Armenian Question and achieving liberty, in the very near future, the National Bank would return all voluntary donations with added interest.

Sarkis Effendi, a Constantinoplean merchant, also seeks an audience with Mardig Agha. He lived off the remnants of his wealth and claimed sizeable demands on the Ottoman Government. Mardig Agha had convinced him that the Russians would destroy the Turks within the next several years. Russia, he had assured, "would occupy Turkey and you would be able to collect all your money back."

There is also another noteworthy secondary character, a talkative Constantinoplean physician addicted to politics, who matched Mardig Agha in analyzing and predicting.

The work concludes: "People like Mardig Agha need people like Surian."

Although Giurjian completed the novel, it was published in an extremely abridged version with an abrupt ending. The original was surely longer, since its publication was halted due to partisan pressures and threats. This assumption is based on Odian's account in his memoir, *Twelve Years Outside Constantinople*, which covered the years 1896 through 1908: "When I was in London, whenever we felt upset, Levon Pashalian and I would take out the unpublished manuscripts of *Mardig Agha* and spend a pleasant time reading them at night."[62]

Odian referred to unpublished manuscripts. This means that the unpublished portion was more than a handful of written pages, because Odian mentioned reading them on many nights, not just one. Otherwise, he and Pashalian could have read and finished the manuscript in one night and there would have been no need to mention multiple nights.

Aside from *Nor Geank, Mardig Agha* was published in *Hayrenik* [Fatherland] of Constantinople, *Azk* [Nation] of Boston, and *Arev* of

Cairo—twice in the latter—but always in its incomplete form. It was finally published complete in 1999, after I obtained copies of the manuscripts of the unpublished chapters, deciphered and edited them, and presented the satirical novel to readers, on the 120th anniversary of the author's birth, thanks to the financial support of book- and- literature–lover Harutiun Simonian.

Although *Mardig Agha* was written more than a century ago, people read the satirical novel with great interest today, too. The novel was not appreciated fairly during its time because of a number of factors: its publication was interrupted, it was published incomplete because of threatening partisan pressures, and its abridged version appeared only in the media and not in the form of a book.

Some scholars never paid attention to the novel, while others did not examine it with adequate depth and interest. Therefore, certain writers and critics have concluded that it lacked "a masterful action" or "structure and design," "its second part is weak," "the author most likely did not complete it before submitting it for publication," or "the initial youthful passion of the novel gradually weakens at the end."

The *Mardig Agha*'s manuscripts reveal that Giurjian wrote on ledger-size papers and noted in the margins the date and time the section was written, the number of hours he wrote, and the reason he stopped writing: the visit of an acquaintance, for example. Interestingly, he omitted Sundays and holidays as regular writing sessions. Often, he authored the section he had planned early in the morning, before he left for work, or after he returned from work. He seemed to work steadily, composing for two, three, or even five or more hours a day during a given week. This is an indication of his strong passion to write, his powerful desire to create, and his mighty ability to compose a literary work.

The manuscripts show that Giurjian completed *Mardig Agha* before sending it for publication. He wrote chapters ten through twenty of the second part of the novel between July 31 and October 14, 1898; that is, by the time the second and third chapters of part one were published on October 15 and November 1, 1898, respectively.

Odian wrote: "Several issues later, the novel presented an Armenian salon in Alexandria where many well known figures of the refugees appeared with most precise and yet excellently ridiculed sketches," and "a terrible storm belched in the city." Then, definitely, the Armenians of Alexandria became upset once the successive chapters were published on November 1 and November 15, and arrived in Egypt—after the novel was completed on October 14, 1898.

Even the seasoned critic Hagop Oshagan—who after reading the incomplete version of *Mardig Agha* in *Nor Geank,* stated: "Giurjian's talent is unquestionable" and "his work has a powerful charm," and further admitted that it has "splendid merits"—pronounced it "incomplete, if not insufficient capacity." The critic regretfully mentioned that the work was "structured and designed carelessly" then continued: "It does not lack life, truth, authenticity, rather it lacks a masterful action, the benefit of structure, and the character of progression, which are the requirements of a novel." Nevertheless, Oshagan praised Giurjian's "sharp, sarcastic style, illustrative delicacy."

Had Oshagan had the opportunity to read the entire novel, he probably would not have hesitated to place it next to Arpiarian's *Red Offering* [Garmir zhamuts] novella and *Golden Bracelet* [Vosgi abaranchan] short story.

It is noteworthy that Giurjian, by virtue of reading the works of world-renowned writers and particularly French authors, was influenced by Alphonse Daudet, whose work *Tartarin of Tarascon* he translated into Armenian. These literary influences helped awaken his own talent and lead him to find his unique literary path, exempt from mechanical duplications and full of creativity.

Mardig Agha is positioned to be considered, more than the internationally acclaimed *The Prodigious Adventures of Tartarin de Tarascon,* a masterpiece of world literature. Whereas Tartarain victoriously returned to his Tarascon town in southern France after killing a blind lion in the African desert, Mardig Agha pursued national and patriotic dreams, rejoiced at the revival of his homeland, and only became a victim of his boastful vainglory when he was deceived by the fake promise that he would become the financial minister of a future Armenia. He returned with broken wings to his initial convictions and innate principles after he was disillusioned.

Mardig Agha analytically portrayed the large picture—the lives of individuals and their participation in society. It showed the progress of characters within the broader environment and lifestyles, and the relationships between social classes. The events, acts, human bonds, and the characters were presented most successfully. The author consistently and skillfully exposed the inner essence of his characters: the vainglory of frivolous Mardig Srmakeshian and the fraudulence of cunning and deceitful Levon Surian.

Giurjian described his main characters and the Armenian refugees in the courtyard of the church in Alexandria, in the room of the Relief Committee, at the Armenian café Masis, in the garden of the Louvre, and in many different settings. Parallel to describing the external look of his characters,

Giurjian exposed their inner worlds. The sharp contrast between the characters and their descriptions in the novel enabled the author to express his ideas more profoundly.

The satirical novel also consistently developed themes, because the natural succession of events in the second part, similar to that of the first part, is set within the parameters of a given historic period.

Giurjian wrote *Mardig Agha* when he was nineteen or twenty years old. With it he proved that he was a talented writer who knew how to make fun of life's negative aspects, criticize the blemishes of social life and human imperfections, condemn peoples' ignoble behavior, strip venality, defame vanity, ridicule deceitfulness, mock vainglory; in a word, expose the shortcomings of life and human blunders. Giurjian expressed his irreconcilable hatred through sharp, deliberate sarcasm and unique literary style. He constructed a coherent fabric of characters and descriptions, woven with meticulous language and masterful metaphors.

The novel abounds with significant epithets, witty comparisons, and the skillful use of parallelism. Indeed, as a master of the art of sarcastically portraying the imperfections of life, and thanks to his well-crafted language, Giurjian successfully observed the funny situations of people and events, transformed them into literary themes, and illustrated them with striking ability.

Giurjian lacked the bitter, hateful, mortally stinging satire of Bernard Shaw, because he did not intend to destroy. Giurjian's satire was constructive, instructive, and educating.

Mardig Agha opened a unique world to Giurjian's readers; a world spiced with a Constantinoplean and Egyptian spontaneity. Having appropriated the love of literature from his school days, he made his literary debut with the skill of an experienced writer. He demonstrated dexterity in his satire. His smooth and attractive style, together with his undeniable giftedness in sarcasm, revealed itself in his very first novel. He used Eastern Armenian, French, Turkish, and Egyptian words and sentences that helped create a vivid atmosphere and individualize his characters.

Mardig Agha can rightfully be considered a successful satirical novel with its structure, picturesque language, and wit. It is one of the best works of Armenian realistic literature of the late nineteenth century.

GIURJIAN AS PROMOTER OF THE REALISTIC LITERARY "NEW SCHOOL"

New School is Giurjian's second satirical novel. The manuscript can be found at the Museum of Literature and Art of Armenia. Giurjian wrote the following words as its proto-title: *Human Comedy – Armenian Part.* On the title page, he mentioned that the novel was written in Alexandria between July 9 and July 31, 1899, in nine sessions.

I have at my disposal copies of 113 large format pages. I have deciphered the novel, compiled a glossary of Armenian and foreign words, and indexed the proper names along with annotations. I was inclined to publish this work as a separate book, like Giurjian's other works, in order to make it available to a larger readership, but later changed my mind because it was not a complete work. Giurjian never went back to it after his initial writing to polish the initial imperfections and errors, or publish it. I am convinced that the manuscript remained incomplete, neglected by both the author and other men of letters. And I am positive that I am the first reader of the work, because had the author read it, he would have noticed and corrected its faults.

Publishing the work requires omitting repetitions, completing sporadic sentences that were left incomplete, finding the Armenian equivalents of foreign terms—in other words, fundamentally editing the work. However, I do not have the right to do so, because that would make me co-author. If I mentioned in brackets or through annotations the portions not belonging to Giurjian, there would be scores of insertion on each page. Besides, its publication without intervention would be inappropriate, because Giurjian was a meticulous author, both linguistically and stylistically.

When Shirvanzaté wrote a preface for the three-volume collection of his own works published in Tbilisi in 1903, he stated: "In reviewing the products of the initial phase of my literary activity, I found essential faults in terms of content and, particularly, language. At first, I thought to postpone the publication of my general anthology by a year or two, in order to correct the faults, refine the style and language of my first works, and then publish them. Later, I decided that I do not have the right to do so."

Shirvanzaté went on: "I would have sinned against the tradition adopted and sanctified by authors, had I corrected and straightened the mistakes of my inexperienced pen in accordance with my current experience." Therefore, he chose to republish his initial works intact, "as they were published the first time." In conclusion, I felt I did not have the right to capriciously complete, correct, and prepare for publication Giurjian's *New School.*

Despite its imperfections and incompleteness, the content of *New School* is interesting. Giurjian described a poorly furnished room, lit by a lantern, located on the second floor of a building on one of the streets of Pera, a suburb of Constantinople. There were three young men there: painter Aram, the owner of the room; prose writer Sarkis, and clerk Levon, a Baudelaire-style ambitious poet who spends the entire day behind the desk counting, writing, and playing with sums. Their dialogues were intense. They loved melancholy, tranquility, and the darkness of night. Armaghanian, Vahan, and a young man referred to as "Stupid" visited them. Influenced by Rodenbach's *L'Amour et la Mort* [The Love and Death], impressed by the mysterious association of love and death, and fond of the positive effects of the trinity of Verlaine's mystique death—night, darkness, and sleep—Levon intoned a poem.

Levon shared the experiences of miserable people drained of exhaustion, loved the ill magic and dark charm of evening, and always worked under the gloomy and vulgar master's watch as "he was compelled to endure that hellish condition like the endurance of a convict to the chains," wrote Giurjian.

To change atmosphere, the characters went to a modest Greek winery to drink uzo, and then gathered in the Crystal Palace where the waitresses, girls, and women "were under the disposal of all men as obedient as tools and as marketable as products, and stretched their divine bodies and exposed them to the dominating, almost raping looks of men."

Levon, who recalled lines and sentences from Verlaine, Baudelaire, Musset, and Rimbaud, watched the public performances of the dancing girls and women of the shiny Crystal Palace with disgust and found them "abominable."

Giurjian wrote: "The music began and the dancer entered. She was fat, heavy, and possessed the broad movements of the marquise of a melodrama; a barely moving marvelous mass of flesh and fat, she stuck her huge chest out and when she did, it rose and fell like the bellows of a blacksmith."

In the second part of the novel, Giurjian described the same room where Levon read Rodenbach and Armaghanian a newspaper. Laughingly, Armaghanian made a pun with Rodenbach's name: "His name already tells you to look closely—*moden bak*."[63] Levon envied Armaghanian who loved to laugh and generate laughter; whereas he, Levon, professing sadness as the main Muse of true poetry, cited aphorisms from Goethe, Lamartine, and other famous writers, and advised Armaghanian to think about mankind's vanity, despicability, and bitterness. Right then, Vahan, Sarkis, and Askanaz—an artist, painter, and a little bit of poet—entered the room. Aram came in with Hovhannes Mesrobian, a short provincial young man wearing a fez. He had come from one of the villages of Van to earn his living as a clerk at a Constantinoplean merchant's establishment.

The dark room, filled with melancholy the previous Sunday night, turned into a place accommodating the exchange of opinions of fine literary minds. Sarkis read a reverie, *Autumn Eve*, where he declared all to be vanity. Vahan read a poem, *The Violin*, which lacked harmony. Hovhannes began to read his prose, *The Corner of the Hearth*, with a trembling, shy voice, despite the laughter and exchanged sarcastic signs that threatened to interrupt him. The article sketched the provincial life—the lonely life of a dreaming soul on a winter day. Hovhannes had to interpret the provincial idioms and words for the laughing audience. The metaphors and comparisons he used "sounded strange to Armenian ears accustomed to listening to French music. The article was the product of the paternal land after all."

Levon was the only one to say "not bad" to the provincial man, "who collapsed on a chair like an offender waiting for a verdict." To the astonishment of Aram, Sarkis, and Armaghanian, Levon admired Yervant's piece too, because he was familiar with some of Yervant's other poems.

Giurjian's novel portrayed the clash of two literary schools—romanticism and realism.

In the second part of *New School*, Giurjian made Yervant a spokesman. Sitting in a bar alone with Levon, Yervant told him that he did not like the inappropriate laughter and sarcastic remarks of some of the audience, and only in Levon's works did he find jewels of thoughts. He added that the products of the Armenian writers writing at the close of the nineteenth century, "their half realistic, half poetic, half nihilistic, and half hard to say what-ism literature is the reflection, copying, parroting, caricature of the French literature of the end of the century that Shaljian, the head of the new school introduced to us."

Levon related how he snatched one of Hovhannes's articles and took it to the editor of *Arshaluys* newspaper. The editor and his colleagues considered it a masterpiece. "The author of this piece is a great writer" and "this is a great treasure that we have found for our newspaper," said the editor who asked Levon to promise to bring all of Hovhannes's written and to-be-written pieces to their newspaper. Then, publishing them under the general heading of folk literature, Yervant himself praised Hovhannes: "These silly ones were mocking such a unique, gifted, and self-made talent that day. They were telling a man born writer to learn French... But this young man is a splendid observer and poet, sincere, simple, yet with an unusual breath of life palpitating in his language that seemed so rough and un-literary to you. There is emotion, there is conveyance, and there is nerve in his writings. His metaphors, comparisons, and descriptions are authentic, expressive, beautiful, and new. This young man has harmonious theme and style. He is not a pedant, nor is he a monkey. He has not read books; he is not writing by plagiarism or memory; he has banished all of these from his life and soul; he has seen, felt, and thought."

Levon, who after meeting Yervant has found in him the real artist and compared and contrasted him to his friends, felt that something was changing in him because of Yervant's statement: "Balzac is the greatest man of knowledge and thought, and the greatest artist of this and coming years, because he has analyzed, examined, tested, decomposed, and composed life and humanity."

Yervant encouraged Levon, saying: "See how you will heal slowly, how you will find yourself and will always be great in literature, a sincere and authentic writer who will bring his theme and frame, fished freshly from the depth of his soul." Yervant added that he studied the *Human Comedy* from A to Z—the only book that he read with great pleasure and fascination—and created ten portraits of Balzac's characters.

Unfortunately, Giurjian's last session of composition of this novel began at 2:30 p.m. on Monday, July 31, 1899, and ended at 4:00 p.m., after covering eleven large papers. He interrupted his work to go with a visitor, Ardashes Unjian, to Roset harbor. Giurjian wrote: "Now I will tell you a memoir, etc., etc." but never again did he touch the novel, according to the 113 pages I have in my possession. It is clear the author planned to say more, but left his work incomplete.

Portraying the clash of literary schools, the novel is interesting in its simple thematic structure, the literary ideas and psychology of the characters, and the sharp contrast between the opinions of poets and artists. It proceeded from Giurjian's belief in realism and populism, and from his zeal to raise Armenian literature to a new level. Indeed, at the end of the nineteenth century, Armenian literature prospered as never before thanks to a group of realist writers who, in Western Armenian literature, followed Hagop Baronian and Madteos Mamurian. Noteworthy among them were Dikran Gamsaragan with his first Western Armenian realistic novel, *The Teacher's Daughter* [Varzhabedin aghchigê]; Arpiar Arpiarian with his public support for the aesthetic principles of the realist school and his short novel *Red Offering*; Levon Pashalian with *The Disillusioned* [Hmayatapê] novella; Krikor Zohrab with his novellas that portrayed reality as authentically as possible, *The Storm* [Potorigê], *Ayinga, Tefarig, Posdal, The Obligation* [Jidin bartkê]; Srpuhi Diusap with her *Mayda, Siranush,* and *Araxia* novels;

Melkon Giurjian, Arshag Chobanian, Zabel Yesayan, Hrant Asadur, Yervant Odian, Rupen Zartarian, and other contributors to the literary movement of the 1880s.

Giurjian himself defended the principles of realism in art and through his writings established this literary belief, which he publicized through the precise expression of truth and popular literature.

Mikayel S. Giurjian, by Arakel Badrig, c. 1943.

Mikayel Giurjian's Plays

Plays are the least developed genre in Armenian literature in general, and for Western Armenian writers in particular. Turkish persecution is the main reason for the weakness of Armenian dramatic literature. Mikayel Giurjian, however, made an important contribution in this field. His realistic and sarcastic plays deserve separate study and publication. The following is a complete list of his dramatic works:

The Franco-Turkish War or Charshêlê Artin Agha, a comedy in three acts written in 1903 with Yervant Odian;

"The National Activist," or the Greatness and Fall of Mr. Iknadios Rupinian, a comedy in three acts written during the years 1903–1933;

The Tribute, a drama in one act, 1905;

The Salvation, a drama in three acts, authored in 1910 with Dikran Gamsaragan;

Heroic Play, a comedy in one act, co-authored with Yervant Odian;

The Franco-Turkish War Continues or Mrs. Yevpimé's Victory, a comedy in one act, 1934.

As in his other literary works, Giurjian discussed in these plays themes, chose heroes, and expressed ideas that reflected real life and its demands. As these are not fortuitous, it is necessary, in order to accurately assess Giurjian's literary heritage, to consider the historical, economical, political, and social conditions of Western Armenians during the time he wrote.

A writer cannot produce a worthy literary work without experiencing life, assimilating his topic, and expending much labor, for literature is not a trade; it is creation. One characteristic of Giurjian's work is that he drew his themes from the life of the people; consequently, his dramatic creations closely mirrored the mentality, conceptions, and emotions of the Armenian people. Giurjian has yet another essential characteristic: his dramatic works abound with the exposition of the inner selves of his heroes, and their progressive actions influence the audience to the end. The author tried to present the spiritual world of his characters through their actions and relationships. The following is a summary of Giurjian's plays.

* * *

Giurjian's most famous play is the one he authored with Yervant Odian, *The Franco Turkish-War.* It is a witty and captivating comedy, known to the public as *Charshêlê Artin Agha.* The theme of the work stems from the manners of the Constantinople Armenians, and reflects the conflict between Europeanism and Turkism—a very important issue at the time.

Hagop Baronian was the first to touch on this subject, but Odian and Giurjian enriched drama, that barren field in Armenian literature, thanks to their profound knowledge of Constantinoplean life and their satiric talents and skilled penmanship. The clash of eastern and western manners, Yevpimé's extreme and fanatic love for everything western, and Artin Agha's caricaturistic and funny nature provided audiences with pure enjoyment when the play was performed in numerous cities of Egypt, Turkey, Syria, Lebanon, Iran, Iraq, France, Greece, Romania, Bulgaria, Australia, and the United States.

The comedy was first performed on September 13, 1903 in a theater made of wood called Pyramid by the seaside in Alexandria. The play created a small scandal, because most of the audience knew the prototypes for the rough and vulgar à la Turkish husband and his à la French wife who was endowed with the pretensions of an educated person. The day after the performance, rumors spread in the community and the caricatured couple severed their relationship with the author. The Russian Armenian character in the play was a well-known Egyptian Armenian in life. He was a general manager employed by the oil magnet Mantashef, and he, too, was not pleased about being ridiculed publicly.

In his article, "The Story of *The Franco-Turkish War*" Giurjian wrote: "The first performance was a complete success; the theater roared with continuous laughter and applause. Even now, though successive generations have departed from the environment so familiar to their predecessors—the manners and language of Constantinople Armenians—the play has kept its ability to cause laughter and entertain."[64]

In the play's first performance, actor Levon Shishmanian played Artin Agha's role, and the talented actress Mari Beylerian played the important role of Mrs. Yevpimé. The other actors were amateurs, including Giurjian himself, who performed the role of the editor.

After debuting in Egypt, the first performance in Constantinople was staged in 1909, at the winter theater of Petit Chain of Pera. There, too, Levon Shishmanian played the role of the main character. Thereafter, the presentations were repeated at the winter theater of Kadiköy, the Mnagian Theater of Shahzadé Pash, and the Variété Theater of Pera.[65]

In his *Kharazan* weekly, Aram Andonian wrote: "The Constantinoplean Armenians practically proved that they have become truly peaceful people after July 11.[66] The theater fans who have applauded so many stupid plays [in the past] did not show even the slightest reaction to the truly captivating comedy of Odian and Giurjian, because... they were afraid of war. How true is the designation 'banality.'[67] The result of the four plays, presented or to be presented, or half-presented, was that Mr. Levon Shishmanian, the main character of the play, arrived fat from Egypt and is going back slim. Had he performed a few more times, he would have returned skinny."[68]

The play was also staged in 1923 before a huge crowd in Korfu, Greece, where Armenian refugees landed from Samson after escaping the massacres of 1923 and from the Kemalists. "The intellectuals and amateurs formed a theatrical group and presented the well-known comedy, *Charshêlê Artin Agha* in a local hall," wrote Shahnazar Keotahian.[69] Kevork Garvarents, a composer, played Artin Agha's role, while Nshan Beshigtashlian, a writer, personified Dr. Shavarsh in the play.

The audience watched and enjoyed the comedy in Armenia, too. The first staging there took place on April 28, 1962, at the Theater of Musical Comedy in Yerevan, followed by a performance in Giumri on December 25, 1962. In Yerevan, Henri Aslanian and Gegham Vosgian, two repatriates well versed in the Constantinoplean Armenian dialect, played Artin Agha. Another repatriate, Meliné Hamamjian, played Yevpimé. In Giumri, Garo Ardzrunian, a meritorious actor, and Garo Sarksian personified Artin Agha, while Yevpimé's role was performed by the meritorious actress Arus Aznavurian and Mania Garabedian. Presentations of the play in Armenia were frequent. Two years after the first performance, Mania Aslanian wrote to Giurjian: "*Charsêlê Artin Agha* has been played in Yerevan 110 times to date. Artist Krateon Keorkian designed the set and composer Vagharshag Godoyan composed the music."[70]

We have seen a frequently repeated mistake in the works of scholars and the Armenian media pertaining to the date the comedy was written. It is claimed that the play was written in 1906, but 1903 is the accurate date.

In his article, "Sketches from Yervant Odian's Life" [Kidzer Yervant Odiani geanken], H. J. Siruni wrote: "He did not have time to write plays worthy of his talent. And the ones he did write numbered not more than four. The most successful was *Charshêlê Artin Agha*, co-authored with Mikayel Giurjian in 1906."[71]

Anushavan Magarian, who specialized in the study of Odian's life and work, placed the wrong year, 1906, at the end of the play *The Franco-Turkish War or Charsêlê Artin Agha.*[72] Later, in the section of annotations, the scholar confirmed: "Odian wrote this comedy with the famous Western Armenian satirist Mikayel Giurjian in 1906."[73]

In his article, "The Story of *The Franco-Turkish War,*" Giurjian wrote: "Recently, I was flipping through the pages of *Azad Pem* weekly... After several pages, I reached, finally, the issue of September 12, 1903 and... I stopped to read the following lines of the editorial: 'Next Tuesday evening, on September 15, a theatrical presentation will take place in Pyramid Theater to support the library of Dikran Yergat Union.'" Three lines down, the author asserted: "Sixty years later... Yes, 1963 is Yervant Odian's and my sixtieth anniversary." Thereafter, he confirmed: "*The Franco-Turkish War* is sixty years old and, despite its advanced age, remains energetic and young."[74]

* * *

Eighteen years after Odian's death, in 1934, Giurjian continued to treat the confrontation of à la French with à la Turkish alone by writing a new comedy in one act and one image: *The Franco-Turkish War Continues or Mrs. Yevpimé's Victory.*

In this later composition, Artin Agha and Yevpimé were influenced by the new conditions in Turkey, in general, and Atatürk's reform mandating wearing hats instead of fezes, in particular. In the play, Artin Agha insisted upon wearing the fez, whereas Yevpimé, relying on Atatürk's decree, at times struggled against and at times tried to convince Artin Agha to give up his fez and use a hat. Aside from the implacable war she declared against Artin's fez, Yevpimé also struggled against regressive rich trustees with provincial mentality, triumphing at the end.

In the last scene of the comedy Artin Agha entered the house wearing a cylinder hat and shouted in rage: "Take this 'furnace pipe' and put it next to the others." In response, Yevpimé remarked to her offspring: "Not only the cylinder, but even if you piled all the hats of the world on him like a pyramid, your father's head will not change." Artin Agha's stubbornness reached the point where he announced that he had decided to move to Europe in order to wear his fez.

* * *

Giurjian's drama, *The Tribute* was published in 1905, in *Shirag* monthly,[75] which Giurjian and Vahan Tekeyan founded and published jointly in Alexandria.

In this one-act play, the author described the horrific nights the Armenians of Constantinople lived through after the massacres of 1895 due to persecutions, apprehensions, and imprisonments ordered by Sultan Abdülhamid. Giurjian described those frightening days when the youngsters, in particular, lived with the nightmare of apprehension. The same alarming situation was prevalent for the Armenians living in Western Armenia and Cilicia at the time.

Through Aram, his mother Surpig, and his childhood girlfriend Makruhi, Giurjian portrayed the overall situation during the terrorizing era of Abdülhamid's rule.

Aram was a person who would return home from the market in a good mood, eat his food in uplifting spirit, speak about the events that took place in the store, and generate laughter by his jokes. But he was no longer the same. The deplorable state of the Armenians began to take a toll on him and he became sad and pensive. At the end of the drama, when the police knocked on the door, Aram asked for the door to be opened after a delay of five or ten minutes. Then he ran to the next room to collect the papers he wrote and the newspapers he read with his revolutionary comrades.

This was the state of affairs at the time, and this was the fate of young men who thought about and worked for their nation—prosecution, searches, apprehension, and imprisonment.

This was what prompted Armenians to leave their homeland during the massacres of 1894–1896 and find refuge in foreign countries.

I have not found any information that the play was ever staged, but it is apparent that the author was eager to see it reprinted in another periodical or presented on the stage, because he, too, like many other writers and intellectuals, had fled from Constantinople in 1896 in search of a safer life in Alexandria.

In the postscript of a letter addressed to Giurjian, Tekeyan wrote: "I have no hopes that *The Tribute* will be staged, but I will try once."[76]

* * *

The Salvation is a remarkable drama in three acts that Giurjian co-authored with Dikran Gamsaragan in 1910 in Alexandria.

The events took place in Constantinople. Kapriel Totvanian, a retired man of more than sixty decades, lived on the savings he made throughout his career. His daughter, Arsiné, was engaged to Suren Srabian, an employee. Certain of Arsiné's love, Srabian demanded a dowry of 2000 pounds from Totvanian. Arsiné's brother, Adom, did not like Suren from the beginning, because Suren brought nightclub songs and taught them to his sister under their family's sacred roof. Adom tried to dissuade his sister from marrying Suren, but Arsiné's love prevailed. To fulfill his promise with regard to the dowry, Totvanian desperately played the stock market, but he lost the entire fortune of his life and suffered a stroke. The thought that after losing everything he would end up owing money to others terrified him. Suren, a venal person, when he did not receive the dowry, abandoned Arsiné, thus destroying the Totvanian family.

The play portrayed the clash between people of opposing principles and morals—Suren and Adom. Although the reason for Arsiné's separation from Suren seemed to be a matter of customs—the dowry—in reality it was a social issue that exposed Suren's covetousness and inhumane conduct.

The Salvation is Arsiné's salvation from a venal and manipulative person like Suren for whom love was a means to improve his social status through the dowry he demanded and expected. Suren, who once declared: "I would not replace you, my priceless Arsiné, with all the treasures of the world," and stated that the dowry was "a casual matter," "an insignificant financial detail," or "a meaningless financial matter," was unmasked at the end. Arsiné, who thought that her dream to love and to be loved had come true, was transformed into a grief-stricken and humiliated victim of deceit.

When Dikran Gamsaragan read the play to Siranush in Constantinople, the actress called it "a noble play." In July 1910, Shirvanzaté wrote about his impressions of the play in a number of letters to Gamsaragan he sent from Le Vaud, Switzerland. He found it to be "fine, interesting, and literary," After congratulating the authors, he suggested they submit *The Salvation* for consideration for the Magarian Award of the Armenian Dramatic Association of Tbilisi. "You do not need to be afraid of the competition, because you will not have a strong competitor, since I know well the worth of the 'idiosyncratic' Russian Armenian plays. Finally, as a work portraying Turkish Armenian life, yours will be more interesting to the jury. Good luck, then!"

The Salvation was first staged on November 18, 1912, in Alexandria. Thereafter, it was performed in Baku, Constantinople, and Paris in 1923, and in other cities, later.

* * *

Odian and Giurjian, the two realist authors, illustrated a contemporary social issue—addiction to heroism—in the one-act comedy, *Heroic Play*, that they authored together. In the drama, the authors unmasked the fake heroes who in their addiction to heroism during the first quarter of the twentieth century were the mockery of revolution. At times in the play, more than one fake hero arrived from Constantinople in Alexandria or Cairo, all using the name of the one and same true hero at the same time.

This witty play was published in book form in 1928, two years after Odian's death, in Pera, as a publication of *Tidag* series. It blasted the revolutionaries addicted to heroism and criticized the adventures of pretentiously "brave heroes." The action took place in a bar in Samatia, a suburb of Constantinople, in the aftermath of the fake Constitution of

1908. After wandering in Bulgaria, Rumania, Athens, Alexandria, and Cairo, Tumig, a jobless man referred to as the Unbaptized, returned to Constantinople. Sercho the barman gave him the clothes a hero had left behind, and advised him to act as a hero and to assume the name Vartan Khorkhoruni.

Teacher Suren, choirmaster Saghatel, and goldsmith Mihrtad, among other attendees of the bar, believed in Tumig and listened to the fabricated feats of imposter Vartan Khorkhoruni. Blacksmith Husep, however, knew the fake heroes, Tumig and Janig, who were pretending to have been imprisoned and starved for the sake of the sacred causes of the nation.

Growing impatient, Husep slapped Tumig and said: "This is called Mischievous Janig and this is called Unbaptized Tumig. Aren't the shameful deeds you did in Bulgaria, Rumania, and Egypt enough? Wasn't it enough that you rotted in the prisons? Shame on you, you shameless people, now that you have come to present yourselves as revolutionaries! Apparently you learned nothing from the strikes you received at the café in Varna and are now looking for trouble here, too..."

Tumig's last words to Sercho were significant: "Is this the good job you found for me? The stupid person is I for I have listened to you and pretended to be a revolutionary."

This comedy has been staged and appreciated by many lovers of the theatrical arts. In a letter dated March 13, 1913, Vahan Tekeyan wrote to Giurjian: "I have to say I have received and read the precious play with pleasure not only for myself, but also for several others, including Papelian and his sister."[77]

* * *

Aside from being a witness of his own times, Giurjian vivified the period he lived through his realistic works. Analyzing the psychology of certain people and classes was the author's main ideological objective, and he successfully attained his goal in the comedy, *"The National Activist," or the Greatness and Fall of Mr. Iknadios Rupinian*, as he did with his short stories and sketches.

Giurjian's criticism of national activism and the oppression of the wealthy was not imaginary or abstract, but rather rooted in real life. Iknadios Rupinian, his wife Zaruhi, and Setrag Effendi Eliasian, Janfesian Effendi, Nigoghos Agha, and Sahag Agha who illegally ran the parish council for three years were the personification of real life characters.

It was the late nineteenth century. Upset with the wealthy people in positions of leadership and convinced that the parish council was illegitimate, a group of people (Shirinian, Sirkejian, Elmasian, Sisag Jshmardakhosian, his wife Armenuhi, and others) gathered around Iknadios Rupinian to put an end to the oppressive and unjust operations of the parish council of their village.

At the time, family being a pressing issue, the main theme of the play was Anahid's love for Parunag; a love that could fail because of Iknadios's extreme adherence to the Constitution and struggle against community leaders. Rupinian's activism also was discussed in this play, including an analysis that revealed the main and secondary characteristics of his approaches.

The comedy started with a conflict risen from Rupinian's "vengeful" and "liberating" article as a champion of civil rights and as a responsible citizen who loved the Constitution. The conflict then expanded into arguments between Rupinian and his wife Zaruhi.

Parunag Eliasian, the son of the wealthy Eliasian Effendi, had confessed to Anahid that he loved her, and that his parents had agreed to their marriage. This happy news coincided with the publication of Rupinian's unusual article. Rupinian was surprised to hear from Zaruhi that Parunag Effendi wanted to marry their daughter, because he was certain that the son of "a wealthy and boastful great Agha" would not ask to be wed with "the daughter of a proletarian like himself, especially one known for his democratic principles." The situation was Hamletesque—to be a good father, or not; to be a good citizen, or not? He, who struggled for the sake of people, law, and constitution, faced a delicate situation, thinking: "I will lose either my daughter, or my honor and reputation."

Zaruhi, too, was portrayed with a realistic palette in the play. As a conscientious mother, she skillfully and prudently pulled Iknadios out of the battlefield to save the sacred love of Anahid and Parunag, which she had been trying to bring to fruition for years.

Giurjian masterfully depicted the inner confusion of Iknadios Rupinian, the main character of the comedy. Iknadios was nourished by the Armenian Constitution from the day he was born, and had led the life of a loyal national activist for thirty years. But now people blamed him for abandoning the struggle and violating their trust, and he lived a tragedy.

Zaruhi's last words to Iknadios are significant: "Now that you have become closer to the leaders of the village and are their in-law, you have more opportunities and means to help your people. Before you relied only on your regular adherents."

Meanwhile, the secondary characters in the play created a natural environment for the main characters' actions and helped explain the work's essential idea by presenting the embellished aspects of conservatism and oppression. Of these secondary characters noteworthy are barber Onnig, a hypocrite; the trio Shirinian, Sirkejian, and Elmasian, all addicts of principles; the tyrannical quartet comprised of Eliasian, Janfesian, Nigoghos Agha, and Sahag Agha; and Mihrtad, a quarrelsome man.

The actions, which unfold through monologues and dialogues, revealed the relationship among the characters and the events.

The play is a fine work in general, thanks to the author's mastery, and to the natural succession of events and crafty solutions of the conflicts.

Giurjian's sarcasm is constructive in all the plays he authored individually or jointly, because he ridicules life's imperfections and the characters in order to expose their faults and educate them, rather than to negate those who personified the imperfections. His sarcasm is friendly.

The characters successfully portray the various episodes of real life. The progressive tendencies of the era are effectively expressed through positive and negative characters and their engagement in essential conflicts.

The plays are interesting in their argumentative nature and come to a peaceful end.

The exposition of the inner worlds of Giurjian's characters is excellent and expressive in many ways.

In works full of daring and general criticism of the reality, Giurjian reflects phenomena pertinent to social customs and family ties. He is not merely an indifferent describer, but rather a man of specific disposition, who makes his views and socio-political stands clear. His style is clear, flexible, mordant, and kind.

There is no wonder that when referring to the drama, Oshagan stated: "After Hagop Baronian, we had A. Arpiarian, Y. Odian, and M. Giurjian, if mentioning only the true talents in that genre."[78]

Mikayel S. Giurjian with his pipe, c. 1950.

THE CHARM OF BEWITCHING NOVELLAS, SHORT STORIES, AND LITERARY IMAGES

The nineteenth century represented a unique period in the centuries-old history of the Armenian people. Historic and political events, economic and social changes, and tendencies of national and patriotic self-recognition created conditions for the progress of Armenian social thought, media, literature, and arts. Armenian intellectual and spiritual life were rejuvenated, new art and literary schools and trends emerged.

The second half of the nineteenth century, in particular, was an unprecedented period in Armenian literature. Classic poetry, previously a dominant literary genre (Hovhan Vanantetsi, Father Arsen Pakraduni, Father Ghevont Alishan), gradually lost ground even though certain lyric traditions continued to develop. Of the writers writing during the 1850 to 1860 decade, noteworthy were Mikayel Nalbantian, Rapayel Badganian, Mgrdich Beshigtashlian, the author of the best lyric and military songs of Zeitun, and Bedros Turian, the short-lived master of lyricism.

The following decade, which in history is usually referred to as the literature of 1870–1880, was significant for the parallel existence of the realistic and romantic schools. Realism reached its peak in that decade, whereas the years between 1875 through 1885 witnessed the rise of classic romanticism, when the generation of Kapriel Suntugian, Berj Broshian, Ghazaros Aghayan, Raffi, Hagop Baronian, Dzerents, and Srpuhi Diusap passed the baton of Armenian literature to the next generation—Muratsan, Shirvanzaté, Nar-Tos, Hovhannes Tumanian, Vrtanes Papazian, Arpiar Arpiarian, Dikran Gamsaragan, Krikor Zohrab, Levon Pashalian, and other contemporaries.

Indeed, Armenian literature transitioned from romanticism to realism during the last two decades of the nineteenth century.

It was during this period of fast-paced transformations that Giurjian made his literary debut with his novel, *Mardig Agha,* in 1898.

Before writing in Armenian, Giurjian wrote in French. He contributed to the French media of Cairo and Alexandria as of 1896. His famous work, *The Scribe's Dream,* was first published in the French media. Judging from the poems uncovered during my research, Giurjian was a master of the French language. Like his Armenian works, his French poems and prose were written with a smooth style and meticulous language. He dedicated his

French poem, *The Harmonies of Night*, published in Teotig's almanac, to Lucy, whose colorful face, as gorgeous as a summer night, made his soul dream like a sea that rested quietly, and whose sweetness and softness resembled the disappearing tides of the sea, and whose countenance brought to his soul the divine peace of quieting nights. And in all of these, Giurjian emphasized the frailty of life.

The poem, which consisted of three quatrains, ended with these lines:

Ta douceur fait rêver les flots évanouis
De mon âme mirant ta face blanche et rose...
Dans le calme divin des soirs épanouis
Ah! que la vie, ma chère, est une faible chose...

Giurjian wrote another French poem, *Tears in the Night*, published again in Teotig's almanac of 1907. Giurjian dedicated this poem to Herminé Askanaz, the daughter of the educator and Armenologist Mihran Askanazian, as a way to mourn her death at a very young age. Giurjian emphasized the powerlessness and absence of life, and the boundless, deadly, and profound resting silence. No, the silence was not disturbed; it listened to the whisper of the remote, clear fountain that dripped into the old pool. It seemed to the poet that he heard the lonely silence of the mysterious hour, crying drop after drop like an inconsolable soul in the nostalgic night:

Car il me semble entendre,- illusions magique,-
Le Silence esseulé
Qui pleure goutte à goutte en la nuit nostalgique
Comme un inconsolé.

The magazine *Hay Gin* [Armenian Woman] published Giurjian's French poem, *The Queen*,[79] which was dedicated to his lover. Giurjian wanted to make his lover a queen and to place his young, incense-scented soul like a luminous palace at her disposal. He expected to see her dressed in royal dresses made of diamonds, pearls, and jewels in bright heavenly and marine colors, and seated round the clock on the victorious throne, reigning over the poet's entire being. He offered his thoughts and contemplations to her as an entourage, and his poems as royal bodyguards and protecting soldiers. He hoped she would see his dreadful wishes—sometimes daring and mad, and sometimes thoughtful and affable—accompanying her everywhere.

The poem, *The Queen,* started and ended with the following lines:

Dans mon âme qui vit sans passions ni loi
Dans mon coeur libre ainsi qu'une foule sans roi,
Je voudrais t'installer en Reine, ô Bien-Aimée!

In his French poem, *The Mysterious Death*, Giurjian's poetic flight and zeal to attain his goal dominate the work from beginning to end. In this four-verse poem, the author expressed himself in a very impressive and influential fashion. He contemplated and emphasized the mysteriousness of horrible death by describing the night's progression with heavy steps, the domination of darkness, the everlastingness of peace, and the eternal existence of soul. The lines carried Baudelaire's and Verlaine's scent of sadness, sorrow, and melancholy, and Giurjian reached conclusions he had gathered from the burdensome experiences of life. Here is the poem.

La Mort Mystique

S'évanouit du jour l'espoir d'azur et d'or...
Le Soir s'aggrave, hélas! comme un mal incurable
Et très mystérieux... En lente et douce Mort,
L'universelle Nuit monte, incommensurable...

O mon âme, voici venir sans bruit
L'heure de lentement mourir avec les choses
Exhalant en secret dans l'unanime Nuit,
Leur âme de lumière et de métamorphoses...

En toi s'apaise enfin le rythme frémissant
Des diurnes émois de la Vie et du Songe.
Pendent qu'occulte et grave, au fond de toi descend
La paix de cette mort qui dure et se prolonge...

Le Temps s'immobilise en une heure infinie,
Plane la solitude immense du néant...
Tu ne vis plus, mon âme, et tu goûtes, ravie,
L'universel bonheur d'être éternellement.

At different times and in different years, found in his intermittently kept diaries and notes, Giurjian penned impressions from his European travels and notes in French. Included are valuable literary idioms, descriptions, and sensual reflections, such as:

La nuit marche à pas d'ombre et de silence
(The night walks with the steps of shadow and silence)
or
Le soleil m'enforce dans l'oeil ses doigts d'or
(The sun inserts her golden fingers in my eye)
or
La douceur du ciel fondue dans le lac
(The sweetness of the sky melted in the lake)
or
L'abus fait le moins
(The abuse escapes less)

Seemingly, Giurjian liked this idea so much that he initialed it.

Another sample:

Les anciens Grecs étaient épiques,
les modernes épiciers
(The ancient Greeks were epics
The modern grocers)

Here, Giurjian demonstrated his ability to create puns in French, using the words epic and grocer with wit.

Here is another sample:

Les littérateurs font de peinture
Et les peintres font de la littérature
(The writers paint
And the painters write)

Notice how Giurjian compared the painters with writers, and how he used the rhyme—*peinture, litterature.*

As mentioned earlier, Giurjian visited Europe four times. During his second visit, he penned his impressions of Victor Hugo's museum, which he toured on Saturday, October 15, 1927:

> Les dessins et tableaux de V. Hugo sont choses absolument uniques foudroyantes! Jamais je n'ai été peut être autant secoué...
>
> Mon impression en sortant est celle-ci:
>
> Si Hugo n'avait pas voulu être le plus grand poète lyrique de son siècle et de tous les tempe, il eut été le plus grand peintre-dessinateur des temps modernes, comme Rembrandt moderne! Jamais paintres n'a dessiné et peint comme lui, car jamais peintre n'a été grand poète comme lui.
>
> Je suis sorti de ce musée, titulant, ivre... tout tremblant. La décharge de beauté, de mystère et de sublime avait été trop forte!

> (The drawings and paintings of Victor Hugo are absolutely unique and devastating. Never have I been so shocked.
>
> As I leave, this is my impression:
>
> Had Hugo not wanted to be the greatest lyric poet of his century and of all times, he would have been the greatest painter-drawer of modern times, just as Rembrandt. Never have painters drawn and painted like him, because never has a painter been a great poet as he was. I exited this renowned museum drunk, intoxicated... in total shock. The sense of comfort offered by the beauty, mystery, and sublimity was overpowering.)

During this trip, Giurjian also toured the museum of Luxembourg in Paris on October 13, and wrote: "The impressionists impressed me very much."

According to his diary entries, Giurjian's fourth trip to Europe was not as happy as the previous ones. "I am in Paris for the fourth time... but I do not feel myself the same; great diminution of joy and living." He was not sure of the cause: his age, improper health, or the events of the last two years? Perhaps the reason was his wife's absence? He was more energetic and happier when in 1927 they traveled together. He had a strong and compassionate love for her, and he felt more secure in her presence.

Noteworthy was Giurjian's hour-long meeting with Frédéric Lefèvre, the editor of *Nouvelles Littératures.* After acquainting himself with Giurjian's French works (*Le Rêve de Kiatib, Le Café, Le Vin de l'Hivrer, Harem,* etc.), Lefèvre particularly liked *The Scribe's Dream,* saying: "This is very beautiful, very good."

A diary entry dated October 25, 1907, presents the high praise for Giurjian's work, *Le Café,* which an employee of the Anglo-Egyptian Bank of Cairo wrote in a letter: "I cannot resist the pleasure of shaking your hand and expressing my most profound greetings of compliment for the excellent article, *The Café,* that I read in *L'Orient* this morning." The employee went on: "I think that many well educated French authors would have wanted to sign those lines. With a pure and clear French that leaves no room to strive for elegance, simplicity, and modernity, this article alone would have sufficed to place you in the company of the elite of famous writers." He also stated: "I consider you a rare Armenian who knows how to best use the language of Baudelaire and Guy de Maupassant."

I do not have at my disposal other works by Giurjian in French, but these few creations seem sufficient to justify the high praise he received about the style and language of his French works. Presumably he exercised the same meticulous and cautious approach toward every word, sentence, and punctuation mark.

Giurjian was a central figure within intellectual circles at the beginning of the twentieth century, and he enjoyed authority within non-Armenian literary circles.

* * *

In his short novels and stories, Giurjian also reflected upon real characters and events. Memories of his birthplace had a profound influence on him and his works.

Giurjian created close to twenty Constantinoplean Armenian characters under the general subheading, *Constantinoplean Armenian Manners.*

In 1901, *Arshaluys* daily of Cairo published his short story, *The Name Day Night* under the pseudonym Tidag.

The work presented vivid descriptions of the manners of the bigwigs of the small village. Grocer Sarkis of Scütari was the main character of this short story. This bigwig celebrated his name day "with a ceremony commensurate to the great idea he had of himself," surrounding himself with Krikor, a vegetable seller, Hagop, a seller of fabrics, Khachig, a carpenter, Aleksan, a barber, Hampar, a baker, Nshan, a shoemaker, Mihran, a diamond setter, Boghos, a blacksmith, Levon, a café owner, and other representatives of the lower class, while he put up the appearance of hosting his guests with an open heart and happy face. By honoring others, he simply pursued the vainglory of honoring himself.

In his review of Viken Khechumian's anthology, *Book of Migration* [Kirk bantkhdutean], Baruyr Sevag stated: "It is impossible to be a writer without the ability to observe. At the same time, one can possess a very sharp eye, but still not be a writer. One needs to make what he has observed observable and what he has seen visible. To do so, the writer has one tool only—the word."[80]

The main character, grocer Sarkis of *The Name Day Night,* was significant in this regard. He contrasted the nouveau riche—the users of frock coats and "bonjour." He was a pure Armenian follower of the old ways in his patriarchal traditional clothes.

Loyal to his picturesque style, Giurjian painted Sarkis with original colors: "One cannot imagine a true grocer without a belly. The belly of a grocer is the most significant and symbolic part of his store; one could say it constitutes one body with some of his products; it is a close relative of the leather containers, barrels, and bags, and is often confused with them. The belly of a grocer sings the glory of all the fatty, buttery, round, tasty, scented, and colorful things that he sells, and therefore it is his best advertisement, the breathing announcement, and wandering crier of his store."

Next to the sarcastic character of Sarkis Agha, Giurjian presented the simple people of the artisan class with positive inclination: "Happy people, who, instead of wealth, possess abundant health, and who work much but earn little." Their manners are significant: "Their speeches and movements are broad, free, and unhindered, without the leash that is called limit or taste. You feel that when they move or speak, they do not feel any reverence for the preacher called 'civility,' or the police called 'it's a shame.'"

Sarkis Agha's vanity and ostentatiousness were criticized throughout the story, including the way he dressed, played the deck, arranged the table with food and drinks, served the guests, and bid them farewell.

Giurjian presented what he saw and experienced in Scütari with daring and a smooth pen, He used elements of satire artistically. He was a true artist in his best short stories. He knew how to begin, continue, and end at the right time. His ability to observe, his deep knowledge, penetrating sharp mind, and delicate style were samples of perfection, deserving appreciation and praise.

This particular short story is a testimony to the fact that at the turn of the twentieth century Giurjian was a serious, mature, original personality. His standards and principles were firmly established in his idiosyncratic literary world.

With his novel, *Mardig Agha*, and with his marvelous short stories, short novels, chronicles, and free or metric verse Giurjian debuted like a mature and experienced writer, without making the straying steps of a beginner needing to publish in experimental publications or preparatory wanderings. This lack of apprenticeship was the foundation for Yervant Azadian to state in his article, "Who Will Plant a Flamboyant?,"[81] which he wrote on the first anniversary of Giurjian's death in *Arev* (issue of July 11, 1966): "Mikayel Giurjian was a great literary PROMISE at the age of nineteen."

Giurjian's short story, *A Family*, was published in 1902 in *Nor Or* newspaper of Cairo under the pseudonym Zarmayr Sahagian. It portrayed the boringly silent house of Sarkis Effendi Hampartsumian, a merchant from Kayseri, whose bourgeois taste was reflected in how he furnished his house.

Unlike the room full of guests, with their loud conversations, exclamations of upset card players, the troubled expressions of the losers, the children's fights and cries, the interference of beating parents, reproaches, arguments, and sometimes shouted insults that shaped the atmosphere of the story *The Name Day Night*, the story *A Family* described a winter night and its perfect, depressing silence. During the long periods of waiting in the story, only the following short conversations took place between the mother-in-law and the bride:

"What time is it, Mari?"

"Seven thirty."

...

"Will you give me threads from there?"

"Very well."

...

"What day is today, Mari?"

"Wednesday."

...

"My son will come any moment now."

"Yes."

Sarkis Agha, too, was reticent.

"It's very cold, isn't it?"

...

"What's up; what did you do today?"

"What else; like every day."

...

"OK; let's have lunch; tell Margos; I am hungry."

...

After dining silently like penitent monks, away from each other, Sarkis sat at the desk, pulled a pile of papers out of his pocket to flip through them, read and jot down some figures; then, putting an end to the monotonous and uninteresting daily life of the family, he said: "It's late; let's go to bed."

Sarkis Effendi and his mother were portrayed as still as the lifeless objects of the richly furnished house, maybe more so since they were deprived of the glamour of the objects. The after midnight arrival of the merchant made no difference to the boring atmosphere in the room or in the cold and silent environment of the family where the swish of a robe touching the ground, the murmur of an opening or closing drawer, and the sound the servant made when straightening something were enough to disturb the mortal silence. Giurjian wrote of a home where the strikes of the clock's pendulum roared as if in ridicule of the dominant, numbing hush.

In 1902, *Piuzantion* daily published the short stories *March* [Mard] and *Mister Sisag* [Miusiu Sisag] in the form of a series entitled, *Constantinoplean Armenian Manners. March* depicted Kevork Agha and Takug Dudu, both over eighty, who have been fighting death daily for more than twenty years. Year after year the desire to live as long as possible and the need to postpone the last deadly hour grew stronger in them. They were always afraid of the dangerous winter season and, in particular, the month of March. "Easterners use the adjective 'crazy,' placed on March's head like a madhouse hat," wrote Giurjian.

The couple owned a large terrace on the upper floor of their house that overlooked a deep gorge. Every year, a week before March, they would retreat to their room to spend the entire month of March there, refusing to go out to breath the clean air and "see the sun's face" on the terrace until March's departure. They would constantly ask their children and grandchildren: "How many more days are there? How many days are left before the 'crazy' leaves?"

They would wait until March was over, and then one nice day they would hang on each other for support and walk out on the terrace. Once outside, they would badmouth March, jump, shake and move their hands, legs, heads, and tongues, thus bidding the month farewell.

Finally, however, their last March arrived. Two days after their retreat into their room, their health deteriorated. A strong flu knocked them both down. The wife died first, thinking, "Kevork will go to the terrace alone." Three days later, her husband passed away. His last thought was of the terrace: "Takug will go alone."

In *Mister Sisag,* Giurjian criticized the deceitful and impudent Sisag who went from house to house, saying: "If you give me this girl without a dowry, I'll marry her." He "ingeniously" played the game of groom-to-be in order to enjoy the good days of his youth. Families grabbed him, with the hope of owning him. Sisag, however, found imperfections in their daughters and moved on to find others "without dowries." Sisag had his own philosophy: "Do not become a groom without staying a groom-to-be for long." After pretending for three to four years that he was willing but had not found a suitable spouse, Sisag was finally compelled to marry laundress Nunig's daughter. The groom-to-be did not intend to marry Horop "without a dowry," but rather flirt with her. "But he fell a fall that he could not recover from," wrote Giurjian about Sisag, the insolent.

These two short stories are interesting with regard to the themes they present. Like many other stories by Giurjian, these can be read with ease and fascination, because they are written in a simple language, without expatiation or obscurity. They are concise and unembellished compositions, written with the pertinent meticulousness that Giurjian exercised with regard to each word, sentence, and punctuation mark.

In 1903, Giurjian published the short story, *A Liberal Girl,* in *Bardez* literary-pedagogical weekly of Alexandria. The story depicted Verzhini's vanity. Driven by free speech, and convinced of his liberalism, Verzhini tried to make others believe that she was liberal, using means pertinent to liberals. To seem educated, she mixed such phrases as *on the contrary, undoubtedly, indeed, particularly, possibly, extremely, nevertheless, in my opinion, generally, truly,* etc. She also used scores of French words: *comme il faut,* a *tour,* a *promenade,* we are *d'accord,* I do not have any *disposition,* what a *scandale,* etc. Throughout the story, Miss Verzhini Sinemian fell in love several times, consistently acted like a spoiled person, confused her insolent daringness with liberalism, did not approve of her "ignorant" parents, ignored the residents of the quarter, and looked down upon other girls, only to find herself alone upon her parents' death, seeking shelter in a relative's house where "they used her as... honorary maiden." Giurjian concluded: "This is the mildest of fates liberal girls like her are subjected to."

Giurjian was familiar with feminine liberalism: portrayed by the character, Zaruhi, the novel, *Mardig Agha,* presented an elaborate description of female revolutionary and liberal behavior through various events.

The short stories *Post Mortem* [Hed mahu] and *The Power of a Word* also belonged to the series *Constantinoplean Armenian Manners. Post Mortem* was an impressive story written on the occasion of the funeral of Janig Effendi Krikorian, a poor barber. The more Petrag Effendi, Janig's brother-in-law, prospered in business, the more Petrag was elevated in the society, adopting the relationships and manners of the "upper class." His wife, too, although Janig Effendi's sister and of the same origin, began to look down upon his brother. Petrag Effendi's disgust for Janig turned into hatred. Unable to endure their treatment and hateful expressions, Janig left his sister's house and moved from Scütari to Balat, while Petrag Effendi, "the honorable merchant," grew wealthier and moved from Scütari to Kadiköy.

Twenty years later, before his death, Janig Effendi revealed that he was Akabi Markarian's brother and, therefore, the brother-in-law of Petrag Effendi Markarian, one of the bigwigs of Kadiköy, "a rich and respectful merchant," the chairman of his town's council, and a well-known member of several councils of the Armenian Patriarchate. Consequently, the priests of Balat refused to bury the deceased free of charge. Akabi found a cunning solution to this complex situation. She threw her arms around her husband's neck and suggested moving his brother's body to Kadiköy, saying, "Let us put up a great funeral ... we did nothing when he was alive, at least we can do something after his death; I do not want my brother to be buried like a stranger with one priest." Realizing the opportunity to add more shine to their reputation, the couple organized a solemn funeral with ten priests, three vartabeds, and a bishop for Janig whom they despised in life and whose death they had learned about in the media and through news from Balat's church. Giurjian wrote, "Let those who die not be deceived. Often funerals tell the glory of the living instead of the dead."

The theme of *The Power of a Word* is taken from the life of the Armenians of Scütari. Giurjian described the visit of some businessmen and their families to the home of the goldsmith, Kapriel Agha. While gathered around a magnificent fire on a winter evening, after being served sour cherry jam, a glass of cognac, and chestnuts, and relaxing in the enjoyable atmosphere, Giurjian, as someone who "reads and writes," or "as a reader of newspapers and novels," was asked to enliven the waning conversations of the party by coming up with a new subject of discussion.

"Okay. Go ahead, tell us something so that we can listen." After some feigned refusals, Giurjian accepted, saying, "I read what I am about to relate in a newspaper." He barely had pronounced the word "newspaper" when the entire room erupted in turbulence. To end the incident, Giurjian was compelled to continue his story. He then turned to Arshag, Surpig Hanum's son, and asked: "Of course you are going to wear the alb, aren't you?" A renewed and even more intense commotion followed, this time together with Surpig Hanum's tears. In response to Giurjian's inquiry about the reason for Surpig Hanum's tears, the latter burst out agitatedly: "The hell with the gazette and the gazetteers, and with gazette readers…" She explained that her only happiness and ideal was to see her son, Arshag, become a priest.

When Giurjian commented that he did not understand the connection between gazetteers and Surpig Hanum's happiness, Kapriel Agha explained that a reporter, in an article, had used the word "priest" in the sense of lizard-like, inexperienced and childish, three or four times. Arshag read the article and decided to not to wear the alb thereafter.

Suddenly Surpig Hanum again began to curse the gazetteers. Comprehending the damage caused, Giurjian kissed Surpig Hanum's hand, to the astonishment of the audience, and exclaimed: "Look at me, mother! I promise you that your son will wear the alb this Christmas…" Hearing that, Surpig gushed a flood of blessings.

True to his word, Giurjian published an article in the same newspaper criticizing the previous article and chastising its author, emphasizing, in particular, that priests are beings worthy of respect and admiration. As a result, at Christmas, Arshag joined the acolytes, consequently "reviving" his mother and bringing joy to the entire quarter. The author then concluded his story: "The evil that came from a pen had been removed by a pen. Therefore, blessed be the pen…"

Giurjian addressed the same issue he broached in *The Power of a Word* in the humorous story entitled, *The Determinative Role of Various Words in Human Life* [Inch inch khoskeru jagadakragan terê martgayin gentsaghi mech], published in the Armenian weekly of Constantinople *Dzaghig* on February 7, 1904, under the pseudonym Bedros Akatan. The author cited three incidents, all related to words that unavoidably played decisive negative roles in the lives of human beings.

The first incident concerned a beautiful girl. People were cautioned against the use of praises: "Don't say much, she will encounter the *nazar* [evil eye, in Turkish]." Sure enough, she was forced to marry a rich and extremely rough and ugly outsider called Nazar.

In the second case, a man accustomed to comment about everything, "It's a misunderstanding, brother, and nothing more!" was struck on the back instead of another man and killed because of a misunderstanding.

The third incident related to an Armenian endowed with a luxurious moustache. This man was in the habit of using the expression, "If this is not so… I will shave my moustache." In the story, he is compelled to shave his moustache in order to get a good job as a cart driver for a rich British man, thus depriving himself of the grounds to repeat his usual words in reference to his moustache. Nevertheless, during heated arguments he often forgot and said, "I will shave my moustache," which made the audience laugh.

The short story *New Dress* was published in *Shirag* magazine, which Giurjian and Tekeyan founded and published in 1905 in Alexandria. The author described Merger, a blacksmith, who had not worn new clothes since adolescence. During the turbulent period of local elections in his village, opposite political parties competed in trying to gain Merger to their side because of the popularity he enjoyed. Merger went to the leader of a party and offered his support in return to "a new dress." Then, working with an unusual energy, he secured his party's victory. The following day, the party leader fulfilled his promise and sent a man to take Merger to a shoemaker, shirt-maker, and a dress barn to dress him in new clothes from head to toe.

After staying away from the cafés and bars that evening, the day after Merger entered the café with the look of a man who was being tortured in his new clothes. In view of his transformation, his friends mocked him and laughed at him, saying: "Enjoy it"; "How can you forget your old friends because of a new dress?"; "May God give us many local councils and ... you new dresses." The following day, Merger went to the bar at the same time in his former look and old clothes. When asked, "What happened to the new clothes?" he threw a handful of coins on the table and said: "Here! I sold my new clothes, guys. I am rich tonight. Eat and drink as much as you want."

He returned to his old clothes, friends, and habits for the sake of his comfort and freedom. Thereafter, Merger lived comfortably with his old clothes.

The merit of Giurjian's works is in their true and colorful reproduction of real life. He demonstrates not only the peculiarities of a writer who possesses an amazingly sharp ability to observe, but also the grace to illustratively and authentically present what he observes. He is a crafty storyteller who charms the reader with his pure Western Armenian language, spiced with the idioms of the Constantinoplean Armenian dialect.

Diran Chrakian, Giurjian's childhood peer, who maintained correspondence with the "true writer" for years, often sincerely reflected upon his works, expressing his admiration. In a letter dated November 29, 1912, he wrote from Scütari: "You never demonstrated the apprenticeship and rawness of a beginner as I did in the arena, and it was on the occasion of your first writing (signed Zarmayr Sahagian) that Yeghia Demirjibashian told me in Geneva that you were already an accomplished master. I had the opportunity to read *Mardig Agha* in the issues of *Nor Geank*, and I testify that it is barely worth less than any of the recent works that carry your signature, and I cannot think of a truly able person, except you, whose literary life has been free of the weakness of revealing the story of his *progress.* It was a sublime pleasure when in Yervant Odian's serial, *Twelve Years Outside Constantinople*, published in the local newspaper *Zhamanag,* I found him mentioning you with praise—something Yervant Odian rarely does—while relating the commotion your *Mardig Agha* brought forth, and in another instance, on the occasion of publishing your articles in *Azad Pem* newspaper in the columns of which you poured *floods of wit* (these are almost verbatimely Odian's words). I will borrow the collection of the newspaper from Vahan, who has it, sometime soon, to read what you have written."[82]

Didn't I Tell You? [Yes tsezi chêsi?] is another short story depicting the life of Constantinoplean Armenians and ridiculing, in particular, women's vaunt. Giurjian presented many braggers of whom the most significant was a widow, Parantsem, a more than sixty-year-old woman who lived in a small village on the Asian shore of Constantinople and whom the superstitious villagers declared a "fortuneteller" because of her predictions and craftiness. Some women, though, headed by Koharig, the wife of a rich merchant, ridiculed her prophetic ambitions. Every time Parantsem said: "Didn't I tell you... Haven't I told you... Don't you recall?," she aggravated Koharig. One day, a woman talked about a Simonian who had divorced his wife and Parantsem immediately shouted: "Didn't I tell you?" Unable to take it any more, Koharig categorically refuted Parantsem's claim and pulled out of her pocket a notebook in order to read the list of her unrealized predictions by date. The latter, also the host, stood up and shouted: "Didn't I tell you this woman is a bad woman, evil, jealous... Tell me! Haven't I said?" Giurjian concluded that from that day on, the idol began to come down off her platform.

The short story about goldsmith Krikor Agha and his son Vahram, a schoolboy, is touching. During the days of sudden apprehensions, imprisonment, and exile, when the books of patriotic writers such as Raffi, Khrimian, and Khoren Nar-Bey, and even songbooks were considered "dangerous," Krikor Agha wanted to burn, along with some of his library books, his son's concise textbook of Armenian history. He was utterly surprised, though, when his son, a day after begging to extend the fifteen-day-long deadline by a night, with a happy and victorious appearance gave his book to his father, saying: "Here Pa, take it! Now you can burn it." In response to his surprised father, Vahram revealed the mystery. "'I learned the entire book by heart,' Vahram said stressing every syllable separately. 'I stayed awake all night long and read.'"

Giurjian titled this story *The Ineffaceable Tome*, not only because of the fact that despite burning a textbook that contained "so many nice things, so many wonderful stories," the contents of which remained ineffaceable in the young boy's brain, but also because the author wanted to emphasize that the history of the Armenian people is as ineffaceable and eternal as the Armenian people who made it. The patriotism of the young hero attains pan-Armenian resonance; therefore, it would be appropriate to be included in Armenian textbooks designed to strengthen national sentiments and patriotism in young Armenians.

Vahan Tekeyan, too, addressed the "danger" Armenian books posed in Armenian homes during the years of barbaric and tyrannical persecution and oppression in Ottoman Turkey. In a short story entitled *The Fire* [Kharuygê][83] and published in Chobanian's *Anahid* Magazine of Paris (Vol. II, issues 9, 10, and 11, 1900), Tekeyan related that having Armenian books at home was a source for daily anxieties after the events of 1894 and 1895 in Constantinople. The young man of the family, upon his mother's request, first put the books in a tin can and hid them behind the beams of the ceiling. Then, for added security, he buried them near the bed of violets in the garden. Later, when he heard that the Turkish police had searched the neighbor's house the night before and had taken even the smallest piece of paper away together with the young man of the house, he burned the books one after another in the kitchen's chimney.

One of Giurjian's most successful works is the short novel *The Lie True, the Insane Sane,* published in Smyrnia's *Arevelian Mamul* [Eastern Media] on

March 22 and 29, 1903, under the pseudonym Bedros Akatan. In this masterpiece portraying Armenian life, Giurjian described a village on the European shore of the Bosporus that Armenian families frequented in summer. Nasib, a twenty- or twenty-five-year-old insane but kind and hardworking young man, was born in this village and orphaned when he was twelve. He helped everybody cut wood, wash floors, get water from the wells, and so on, in return for food, money, and clothes he needed for his sustenance, and cash he saved. He was also a jester who entertained the residents of the village and the vacationers with his funny plays, jokes, mimics, and "strange" and ambiguous responses. His clothes were as comic as the destitute way he dressed. The most striking part of his outfit was his belt—a belt as famous as a historic person in and around the village.

In the second part of the short novel, the author revealed that Nasib had been in love for years. He, too, had a heart, knew how to love, and was in love with fisherman Bedros's daughter Horopig, a girl from the village he had known since childhood. The love between these two humble and poor creatures met with the fisherman's rejection, to Nasib's surprise who never second guessed his success.

In the third part of the story, Giurjian related that the following summer the village was again filled with vacationers who did not believe that Nasib would drown himself or that Horopig would set herself on fire with matches if their love was denied. Nasib's pleas to several aghas and ladies for them to mediate before the fisherman were futile. Consequently, the unbelievable and seemingly impossible event took place: Nasib jumped into the sea to end his life. Fortunately, fishermen passing by saved him. The deed of a jester like Nasib was a surprise epilogue for the vacationers who could not see the profound spiritual sensitivity and seriousness under his comic appearance. Those who used to laugh at him were stunned when confronted with such a magnanimous act. Some even cried and felt uncomfortable about the indifferent and uncompassionate treatment they had shown him.

Two months later, the bells of the village church tolled and declared Nasib's marriage with Hripsimé Bedrosian, because the local villagers and vacationers had persuaded the fisherman to allow the union with promises to combine efforts to prepare his daughter's dowry, pay the wedding expenses, and to open a drapery store for Nasib with a small investment of capital.

This work on Nasib's odyssey is a marvelous literary product that was produced with a tight frame, polished style, and simple, neat language spiced with the dialect of Constantinoplean Armenians. Giurjian focused his attention on the honest and humble people of the village and made their customs and manners, thoughts and aspirations live with authentic sketches.

This short novel, too, like Giurjian's other works, captures readers, rewarding them with spiritual enjoyment and intellectual satisfaction. The simple people become lofty with their virtues, positive characteristics, and benevolence.

In his chronic report on the literary events of the passing year, *The Turkish Armenian Literature in 1903* [Trkahay kraganutyunê 1903in], critic Hovhannes Kazanjian (1870–1915) wrote at the threshold of 1904: "Moving from novellas to short novels and novels, we find Kasim's *Complicated Knot* [Gnjrod hankuyts] and Bedros Akatan's *The Lie True, the Insane Sane* short novel worthy of consideration."[84]

After reading the story of Nasib's adventurous life, Diran Chrakian wrote to Giurjian from Malgara on April 26, 1908: "You are telling me that we have not had a work like the *Inner World* [Chrakian's work]. Well, then, it is as true that we have not had works like *The Name Day Night* and *Nasib*; this genre did not previously exist; our stupid songs did not have that much love for the nation, nor did our 'realists' possess so much attentive observation, or our 'populists' feel the poetry, depth, and, one could say, 'scientificity' of the most trivial realities."

Chrakian was so deeply moved by the story that he wrote: "O how beautiful it was! I was reading it (I mean the epilogue) in the classroom. Almost in a rush, I read Nasib's wedding, jumping over the minutes because of the emotions I had. I am certain my eyes would have moistened at a different, more opportune moment."

In a different letter, Chrakian wrote: "I read Nasib... Most men would have generated their best works, masterful works, had they known, each individually, what they were capable of, had they simply known themselves. Few are the writers who know themselves amongst us: among them, Berberian, Agheksantr Panosian, Alpiar, and you. This supreme property is enough for a talented writer to call a masterful work. Fortunately, the mindless people who do not know themselves are many and they limit the number of the masters and glorify them. The 'Know Yourself' should be an ordinance for writers, as it is for everyone else. From the incoherent works of 'writers' who do not know themselves, one realizes that their self-knowledge—or, if you prefer, their self-ignorance—results from incomplete cultivation combined with a lack of observation and *sense* of reality. Now, you are not one of them; you have not done things above and beyond you in the most part of what you have published to date."

He continued: "From *The Name Day Night* to *The Lie True, the Insane Sane* there is so much reality in your stories and literature that you have the right to be one of those who are as masterful as firmly cognizant of the nature of their ego; that is, who are simply masters of their genres. It is so apparent that to know what we can do is the requisite of our work's perfection. Now, Nasib's story was as marvelous as *The Name Day Night* (although the latter is a superb work in that it contains a richer study, more literature, and more life), and it had the following advantage (which is not an insignificant advantage, rather a property one can announce like a tiding in general): it reconciled and amalgamated the novel and the *reality*, the creation and the *story*, simply the fiction and truth, as if dictating the rule that *the word novel should remain the name of a form only*, and not the object of art, and that *reality should be created*. Of course *The Name Day Night* also had the same characteristic of your last work, but it did not have the appearance of a novel, whereas Nasib has and explores the boundary of the novelness of the story that is being told; in other words, how the novel should constitute an artsy *frime*[85] of reality."

Giurjian gathered the theme of the short story *Drtad and Dajad* from Constantinoplean Armenian life. It is a popular story about the animosity between Drtad the fisherman and Dajad the vegetable seller. The antagonism between the two stemmed from the fact that they both loved Noyemzar and she gave the assurance of her love to each. Their animosity was portrayed in a kind of daily bragging and boasting, mixed with threats, insults, and challenges, even though the adversaries never left their quarters or had a decisive confrontation.

Their fight was, in reality, a quarrel of words relayed through others. Realizing that there was no end to their fighting, Noyemzar married a third person. Nevertheless, Drtad and Dajad continued feuding for thirty years.

"Well, did you tell him what I told you last night?"

"Well, let's see what he said."

"Go tell him that..."

The day after Dajad's death, Drtad put on a black suit and for the first time in thirty years left Selamsiz to go to Yenimahallé in order to participate in the funeral. He went to the cemetery like a mourning relative, opened the coffin before it was lowered into the ditch, kissed the corpse, and whispered in his dead foe's ears, to the astonishment of the audience who later expressed their condolences to him.

Giurjian turned the story told him by the aged people of Scütari into a marvelous psychological literary piece, adding new content and charm.

Giurjian liked the genre of the short story so much that he wrote numerous stories where he exercised a realistic approach and remained loyal to the principle that a writer should be a trustworthy witness of his times in his writings. Giurjian's ability to observe was an important factor in his success. He noticed minute details others often missed.

It is unquestionable that Giurjian was a talented individual who knew how to portray people of diverse characters, natures, and psyches in various environments and situations. In addition to these, he had the gift of effortless composition.

In the short story *Mirijan*,[86] for example, Giurjian described a man who frequented a café. He was one of those characters who "take you away from your thoughts, reading, or an interesting conversation with a close friend," cause you to get a headache from their light and colorless words, one who gradually consumes your patience and turns those present victims of civility by wasting their time.

In the funny short story *A Story from the Other World* [Antrashkharean batmutiun],[87] Giurjian sharply ridiculed Nigoghos Agha, a man who, after spending his whole life in councils that dealt with local, educational, and religious matters, found the gates of heaven open upon his death so he walked in. Noticing the presence of a stranger, the Apostle Peter employed tricks to send him away, but nothing worked: neither threats, nor convincing, nor entreating words. Suddenly, an ingenious idea came to the Apostle. He went to the Archangel and suggested that he gather several hundred angels outside heaven to talk and laugh loudly. Then he returned to Nigoghos Agha. The two suddenly sensed a commotion outside. Curious, Nigoghos Agha asked what was happening. The Apostle said: "A local council must be arguing either about the beadle, or the archpriest."

When Nigoghos Agha learned that meetings and arguments were forbidden in heaven, in order to continue arguing, even postmortem and even if it meant he could not remain, he opened the gate and exited, saying: "I don't want your Kingdom... enjoy it... I do not envy you. If one cannot be a council member, why would I pay a dime for your Kingdom; why didn't you tell me this beforehand?"

Another short story Giurjian wrote is entitled, *The Story of a Miracle* [Hrashki mê badmutiunê], in which Kapriel Agha Der Sarkisian denied what he owed to a man. In the absence of documents or witnesses, the matter was to be settled through oaths. The arguing parties went to the church, placed their hands on the Bible before a priest, and successively said: "Grant me a sudden death within the next fifteen days if I took the money and am denying it," "Grant me a sudden death within the next fifteen days if I did not lend the money and am demanding its return unjustly." Fifteen days later, Kapriel Agha's adversary died of a stroke and Kapriel Agha was viewed in the community as a saint. Years later, Kapriel Agha summoned a priest "to confess." Confusion caught the priest when he learned that Kapriel Agha's adversary, who had died of a stroke forty years ago, had told the truth, and that Kapriel had made the daring false oath, because at the time he faced bankruptcy. To remedy his deed, later, he had become a benefactor, "giving to the poor hundred-folds of what he had unjustly usurped from the deceased."

The story is shocking and impressive, and the characters are presented through their emotions.

Another successful short story is *Mister Politician.* Soghomon, the main character, frequented the café daily to discuss complex issues, immerse himself in newspapers, or surround himself with an audience to discuss politics. With his noble sarcasm, Giurjian criticized this character who read the European tabloids from A to Z, memorized them, discussed politics, found subjects he could spin into two-hours-long discussions in a four- or five-line-long telegram, and pretended to be a skilled politician. Soghomon, who never relinquished his duty of running analytical and informative conversations on politics during peaceful times, literally had no time to even scrub his head during war—instead of him trying to find or hunt down audiences, audiences begged him to analyze for them the news, and praise or criticize the policies of the great powers, especially from the viewpoint of seeing the British behind every issue. Soghomon was a firm believer that the British were "the universal axis around which world politics rotated, from Asia to Europe and from Africa to America."

Giurjian wrote his significant short story *New Year's Gift* [Gaghantchek] in 1909. This three-page-long, compact story is a moving and heartrending work, describing psychological situations. The author presented two opposite conditions: poverty and wealth, misery and luxury, sadness and joy. Mariam, an orphan, as thin as a skeleton, wrapped in old and torn clothes, on the eve of the New Year, knocked on the door of a family she knew. The house was full of joyful smiles, loud laughter, and happiness. The painfully suffering creature was shocked when she realized the contrast between the cold welcome and the toys and presents scattered all around, and the festive dresses of the participants. As she hurried to wrap her head with her ragged shawl and leave, the lady of the house pulled out a used shawl from the drawer and said: "Take, Mariam! Let this be my New Year's gift to you." Mariam declined and left, saying: "Thank you. I don't want it. Keep it for yourself." The lady and her husband started philosophizing about the pride of the poor, with hearts hardened by happiness. From their point of view, the poor were not allowed to turn down a present. They neglected the possibility that offering an old shawl was inappropriate.

This story is touching and pitiful at the same time, because the reader anticipates finding something else under the title *New Year's Gift,* not the merciless, indifferent, and inhumane attitude of the wealthy toward a poor, orphan Armenian girl, who after witnessing the gorgeous, shiny, and expensive toys, naturally refused to accept a used shawl as a gift.

* * *

Giurjian also produced literary sketches, such as *The Fountain* [Aghpiurê], *The Runaway Horses* [Pakhadz tsierê], and *The Café,* which are some of the best impressionist works in Armenian literature. Often Giurjian turned insignificant things that inspired him into universal themes with philosophical and psychological depth, thanks to his poetic soul and alert sensitivity. Ultimately, these works reached the apex of world literature.

The Fountain stemmed from an inspiration Giurjian experienced when viewing a painting his friend Diran Chrakian presented to him in 1898. The painting portrayed a magnificent fountain with tall pine trees as a distant background. A young girl was offering a cup of water to a thirsty, tired old man. Giurjian immortalized the painting with words, emphasizing the contrast between lively youth and the hunched old man who slowly approached the woods that would someday extend their eternal shadow upon his exhausted body. Chrakian's painting must have been as moving and beautiful as this image for it to have inspired Giurjian and move his mind and soul.

The Scribe's Dream and *The Café* are fascinating works, and as such have been anthologized in Armenian textbooks for their exemplary language and style. Both fall under the general title *Eastern Sketches,* because both are creations pertinent to typically Middle Eastern countries.

The Scribe's Dream was first published in *Shirag* magazine in 1909. A talented scribe had inherited his profession from his father and was going on with it. His life had been spent writing letters for others. The scribe who "had darkened mountains of papers, poured out seas of ink, and consumed forests of pens" was old and fatigued. Then one night, this kind, patient, and conscientious scribe had a dream: He was on top of the mosque's dome, holding the minaret as a pen, using the blue sky as paper, and writing an entreaty to God, this time begging a little comfort for himself. God received the scribe's appeal, accepted his entreaty, and transitioned him from life to death, granting him eternal rest.

Giurjian treated this humanitarian theme that relates to all diligent, hardworking people masterfully. It reflected the Middle Eastern life, psyche, emotions, and aspirations, which are all so different from Western civilization and traditions.

Many are the writers and critics who expressed their admiration for *The Scribe's Dream.* Diran Chrakian opined: "*The Scribe's Dream* made me cry. You will not believe me. It was a jewel, perfection itself. Here is what I thought on this occasion: a pure intellectual also (such as you have been) who can move the heart, achieve the results of emotionalism, thanks to (à force de ...) accuracy, *mastery.* You are the only person to claim *mastery* in its European sense amongst us, and I have had the honor to find, see, and enthusiastically present you to those who cannot see on their own."[88]

The Café, an impressionist sketch, portrayed an ordinary place that many would consider unimportant. Giurjian, however, brought a unique meaning, spirit, and substance to it, emphasizing particularly the vivacious atmosphere as well as the Middle Eastern spirit and manners. The Café corner provided the author with the opportunity to ponder, contemplate, and philosophize on the indisputable intimacy of the café.

The *Runaway Horses* is an impressionist work also. Giurjian described the mad galloping of the unleashed horses, their freedom, exempt from controls and restricting bonds. The author compared their independence with the freedom of nations. He admired the uncontrolled freedom of the naked, galloping, runaway horses whose manes flew with the wind.

Giurjian wrote another noteworthy impressionist piece, *The Pine Trees* [Shojinerê], which he dedicated to his friend, Simon Simonian. On a beautiful morning, at dawn, Giurjian admired Lebanon's natural elegance and the pine trees, in particular, for their silent existence as he admired the cicadas for their endless singing. As he contemplated Mother Nature, it seemed to him that he heard nature's voice telling him that people fatigued by civilized, noisy cities and congested with thoughts, feelings, and passions rarely feel the happiness of living. The author materialized his beliefs with regard to life in an unparalleled manner and suggested that people should be satisfied by the mere fact of being alive.

Giurjian wrote his sketch, *The Happy Ones* [Yerchanignerê], while under the impressions he gathered from newly married lovers whom he met in a Lebanese hotel. The work is reminiscent of the following two lines of La Fontaine's fable, *Two Doves:*

Be a new world to one another,
Always diverse, always nice.

Giurjian's works, whether short stories, novellas, or images, are the result of impressions gathered from real life. They are not mere duplications because the author is present in them with his unbridled imagination, deep thoughts, and creative art. They are remarkable philosophically, especially in terms of their penetrating, sharp observations and analytical approach to human feelings. As a contemplative and humanitarian writer, he examined world issues with kindness and candid vigilance. For this reason, one could place him next to the greatest writers of world literature: Goethe, Schiller, Hugo, Zola, Tolstoy, and Dostoyevsky.

The genocide and deportation of the Armenian people deeply affected Giurjian's fragile and sensitive soul. The inhumane, barbaric oppression by the Ottoman Turks shook his being. In his late twenties, Giurjian could not stay silent in view of the suffering of wretched mothers, the inconsolable conditions of orphans, the martyrdom of Armenians at the hand of horrible torturers, and the agony of an entire nation. So he described the catastrophe in not only journalistic articles, but also literary works.

What the Angel Saw is an unparalleled work. An angel illuminating the morning of Armenian Christmas with the first rays of the day found the Armenian land unidentifiable. He saw endless desolation and vast silence where villages and towns, peasant houses, and humble huts once abounded. Witnessing ruins instead of buildings and scorched lands instead of fields, and feeling that he would not be able to stand this hell until eve, he hurried back to the Lord and tearfully reported of his findings: corpses, lakes of blood, piles of ashes, and wild half-naked people heading toward unknown calamities, howling from hunger and fright, and persecuted by hideous people. With eyes full of unusual glitter, the angel related to Jesus that the entire country seemed like a boundless earthen cross, an entire Christian nation crucified on it. The scene reminded Christ of the cruel peak of Golgotha. After a long silence and mute cry, Christ said: "It will resurrect."

In this way, Giurjian turned the national grief and anguish of the genocide into a humanitarian theme. He described the wreckage the horrendous crime had left, and, as in his other works, concluded with optimism and certainty that the nation would resurrect.

The Magic Carpet, a fantasy, also drew upon impressions of the genocide. Giurjian called this work a tale of hallucination. Even a summarized description of this work affects people of all kinds. As a token of gratitude and appreciation, Turkish delegates presented a magnificent oriental rug to Pièrre Loti—a Frenchman fond of the Orient and the Turks. Influenced by a mixture of tobacco and opium, and under the heavy pressure of numbness, Loti took fright when he thought he saw the carpet replaced by a group of girls, seated on the floor, and saying: "It is we who made the rug that you admire as a wonder of art and talent... and we are Armenian Christians, not Moslems." Momentarily, a new voice filled the room. Loti saw moving skeletons—the ghosts of the rug owners. They told him that the Turks, transformed into devils, invaded their village, massacred the inhabitants, appropriated their belongings, and burned their ancestral homes. This rug was one of the most beautiful of the stolen artifacts. The skeletons pointed to a bloodstain of a family member the Turks had killed on the rug. Suddenly, the bloodstain grew, expanding fast, until it covered the rug, and Loti felt the cool, disgusting caress of the bubbling pool on his skin. Releasing a horrible scream, Loti fell on the cushion, and the blood of the victims—having grown into a sea—threatened to drown him, for he had been a protector and a friend of the executioners.

With this work, too, Giurjian turned a national theme into a humanitarian issue, inviting attention to the Armenian suffering and reminding the readers and, in particular, the French Turcophil writer. The marching ghosts of martyred Armenians sought justice from the world to overcome the psychological state they were subjected to because of the genocide.

Giurjian's many other noteworthy works depict the lives and manners of the humble Constantinoplean Armenian people and working classes, and touch upon community leaders and social life in the Diaspora. Giurjian's prose is characterized by depth, compact style, firm structure, and clear and carefully crafted language. He is a master describer and reproducer of nature, society, and human emotions in vivid artistic molds. One finds in his descriptions of scenery, circumstances, and intense psychological situations unique inspiration, delicate thoughts, and sensitivity. Giurjian did not report factually, nor did he limit his objective to simple notations on events, and characters. Rather, he added artistic meaning to reality through the production of excellent works of art. Consequently, he became one of those talented writers who shaped the pride of Armenian literature.

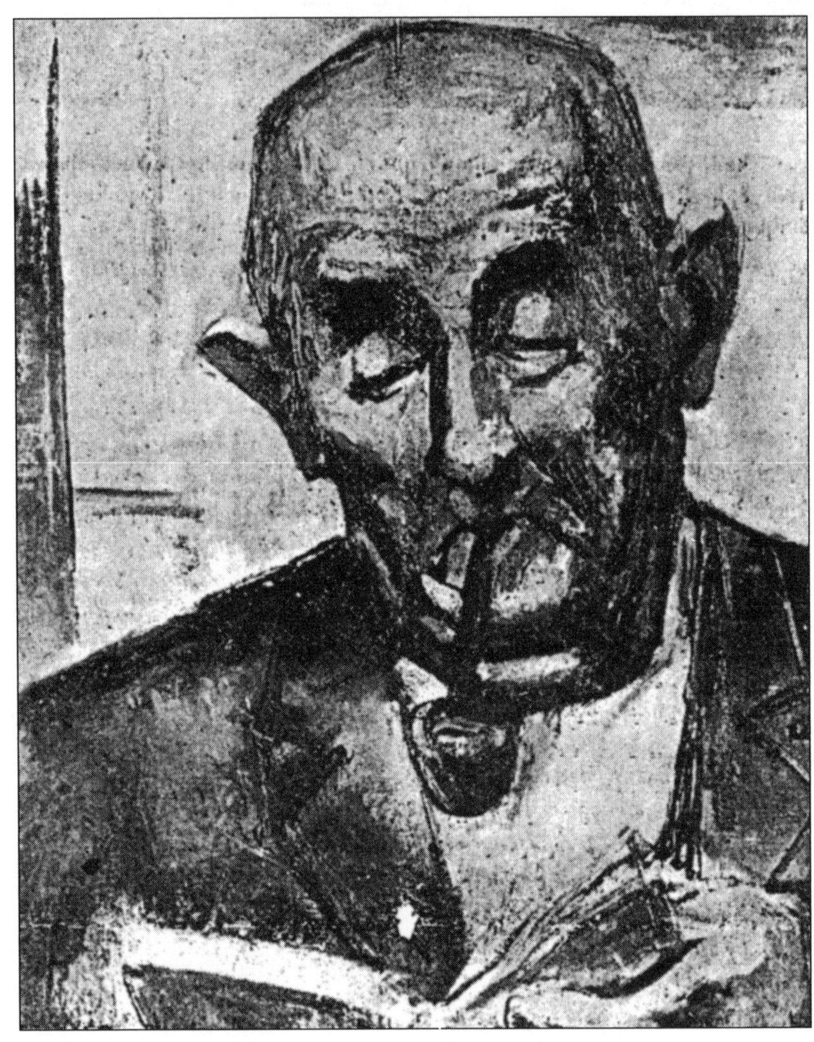

Mikayel S. Giurjian, by Ashod Zorian.

GIURJIAN AS A POET OF METRIC AND FREE VERSE

Mikayel Giurjian was well known as a poet. His poetry possesses a certain social, lyric, and romantic resonance. He wrote metric and free verse from a young age into his elder years.

Panper Kraganutean Yev Arvesdi [Herald of Literature and Art] of Saint Petersburg, Russia, one of the most valued literary periodicals of the early twentieth century, published the works of the most renowned and best writers of the time, such as Tumanian and Tekeyan. It hosted Mikayel Giurjian's lyric poems under the general title, *Minutes and Syllables* [Vayrgeanner yev vanger] (1903, pp. 138–142), with the following individual titles: "Pale Woman" [Talguhi], "Evening" [Irigun], "My Soul in the Sea" [Hokis i dzov], "Song of Memories" [Husherk], "Night" [Kisher], and "The Poem of the Window" [Baduhanin kertvadzê]. The same periodical published in its second volume in 1904 Giurjian's "The Twins" [Yergvoreagnerê], together with poems from Avedik Isahagian, Vahan Tekeyan, Adom Yarjanian, and Hovhannes Hovhannesian.

Influenced by romantic French poets, and driven by the somber realities of the time in which he lived, Giurjian expressed, in his early poems, thoughts and feelings reminiscent of Charles Baudelaire. Giurjian wrote of the dull shadow and musical silence, describing how "Here, the sorcerer night descends wrapped in darkness, silence..." at the twilight.

> With the dense steps of darkness, and sounds of silence
> Infinite Anthem of the Dead, mourning the death of the light
> Do you hear the progression and lament of the great night...
>
> (*Night*)

Giurjian broke the sad news of the death of the light only after describing the miraculous colors of twilight. He used Baudelaire's following line to summarize the main idea of his poem:

> *Entends, ma chère, entend la douce Nuit qui marche*
> (Hear, my dear, hear the sweet Night that marches.)

The poet's dreaming spirit was wrapped in a terrible premonition, as he felt the fading and shuddering of the evening ("Evening"). An evening dying of consumption, an evening in whose womb of immortality "my fatigued soul dreams like a resting sea," he wrote in his poem, "Pale Woman."

There was a sublime lyricism in Giurjian's poem, "The Twins." The poet sang of shadows without luminescence and of musical silence. He considered both reflective of his estranged soul.

He composed the poem in three stanzas with alternating rhyme:

> The lusterless shadow is the somber color of Silence,
> And the silence is the music of the Shadow...
> They are so fit to each other and similar
> As if they were poor twin orphans...
>
> They are the adopted family of the dreamer
> These discreet twins, one of which
> Listens to his singing soul,
> While the other smiles to him with his dark face.
>
> What a pleasure, when, perturbed and resigned
> Of this life, he goes to rest next to them...
> The estranged soul finds sweet comfort there
> With the overflowing intimacy of families.
>
> ("The Twins")

In the poem, "My Soul in the Sea," which he dedicated to Diran Chrakian, Giurjian described his profound thoughts upon hearing the breathing life of the sea by night, and his fright upon hearing the cries and moans of the waves:

> Because I feel, alas, that before this gloomy sea
> My entire soul shivers as if prey,
> Like a poor, weak, lonely thing would shiver
> Before a strange monster, or a frightful giant

The poet found resemblance between an open window and a heavenly eye. Both, he said, poured sensations through an opening framed with reality that brought forth vibrant, luminous feelings ("The Poem of the Window").

"The Fire" (1903) and "A Cry at Night" (1905) were two poems Giurjian wrote in his youth. "The fire" was written in memory of a girl who died prematurely. Giurjian likened her essence to a fire that the girl needed to nourish with all her feelings, hopes, and dreams in order to keep it alive:

To the day when your lungs lost their power,
And nothing was left in you to serve as fuel...
The fire collapsed; turned ashy and forgotten
And death contained it in its limitless womb.

"A Cry at Night," also, was a sad poem. The poet drew parallels between the sound of water dripping into a pool and the endless crying out of a lonely soul in the silence of night, indicating the absence of life in the advanced night.

Three other poems, "Ode to Armenian Letters," "Entreaty," and "He Will Go," are additional evidence of Giurjian's poetic accomplishments.

In "Ode to Armenian Letters," the author addressed Mesrob Mashdots and Sahag Bartev, the inventors of the Armenian alphabet, wondering if they would be regretful if they knew of the degeneration and disfiguration of the mother tongue, and the ugly articles in the Armenian media, so numerous that if stacked they would form piles as high as the pyramids.

In "Entreaty," Giurjian begged the dainty ladies not to be kind in disseminating coquetry, "look and smile—light, flame, and alcohol" to the old man "who was turned down as a lover."

But he owns a heart; and don't you know that
While his body ages day by day,
His heart always remains twenty
And he always hopes, O, foolishly?

The poem, "He Will Go," was a hymn written with optimism and enthusiasm. A choir made up of young Armenian women of Scütari performed this uplifting hymn in 1909 in Constantinople, during a concert organized to raise funds for the starved inhabitants of Armenia. Even during the bitter days of the Ottoman "freedom," Giurjian predicted a bright future for Armenians—for a people heading from the land of widespread prisons and graves toward happiness. The poem concluded:

His eyes mesmerized to the luminous distances to come,
He dashes forward and forward from ages to ages,
He dashes forward and forward from ages to ages.[89]

Giurjian was always optimistic about the future of the Armenian people. He consistently hoped and predicted bright days to come. In the free verse "The Song of the Sword," Giurjian praised General Antranig's sword, calling it a magical weapon that made the truth shine. This poem was an ode dedicated to the sharpness of the national hero's sword whose death-spreading motions "beautify death with art." Giurjian wrote: "The wound you open should be a terrible delight for someone who likes forms," because the sword "is lightening transformed into metal by a miracle," or "a thunderbolt suddenly frozen."

The poet wrote this work in 1903, seventeen years before the editorial office of *Arev* daily initiated a fundraising effort to donate a sword in honor of the national hero General Antranig in the name of the Armenians of Egypt. The national hero, so popular in those and following years amongst Western Armenians, later, gifted the sword to the Museum of History of Armenia.

Earlier, in 1903, Siamanto, while visiting Paris, wrote a poem, "Antranig," in which he also extolled the bravery and invincibility of the national hero.

In a series of articles entitled *Love* [Ser],[90] Giurjian elaborately and penetratingly analyzed the meaning and essence of love. Studying the definitions given by Musset, Baudelaire, Lamartine, and other European authors, Giurjian stated: "Love is a kind of divinity. We see, enjoy, and carry the good and evil, the pleasures and suffering, and the bounties and punishments it brings, generates, or disseminates, but it always remains invisible, untouchable, and veiled with mysteries for us, like all the divinities people have worshipped." Then he defined the word himself, saying: "Love is the lyric of craving."

Giurjian's love was worldly and exempt from mysticism and sentimental elements. In his lyric poems, love and hatred, joy and sorrow, and present and future were always intertwined, because his artistic ideal aimed at raising up the society and the individual.

Nature represented the uppermost essence for him. He portrayed the profound feeling of suffering in love through a unique integration of realistic and romantic images:

> Your gorgeously pure naked body, O virgin,
> Is a pitcher with colorful lights,
> Is a masterpiece of a secret art,
> Shaped by Nature the artist.

These are the lines he penned in his poem, "The Pitcher."[91] The vessel, filled with a drink tasting like heaven, will remain closed and sealed, "Until the rising of the predetermined day when the privileged man comes."

Giurjian's poetry was woven with fine spiritual threads. It possessed a resonant breath, and the artistic images defined his beliefs and the depth of his thoughts and feelings through multiple themes and motifs. He enjoyed broad recognition for his lyric poetry.

Giurjian's free verse was of particular value. The Russian Ivan Turgenev, the French Charles Baudelaire, the Hindi Rabindranath Tagore, and the Belgian Émile Verhaeren are some of the most renowned authors of free verse. In Armenian literature, only a few writers attempted free verse, starting at the beginning of the twentieth century. Their names include Avedik Isahagian, Indra, Misak Medzarents, Vrtanes Papazian, Rupen Vorperian, Movses Arazi, among others.

In the Armenian version of the 1931 edition of Turgenev's *Free Poems* (Yerevan, 1968), the critic Tomashevski stated: "My good reader, do not read these poems all at once in succession; you will become sad and drop the book. Rather, read them one by one: one today, another tomorrow, and then perhaps one of them will leave a mark on your soul."

The same applies to those who read Giurjian's book, *To the Adored, from the Bottom of My Heart.* Thirty-one free poems are found in this volume, all written separately, during a time stretching from the early twentieth century to the 1960s. In them, Giurjian's feelings were interwoven with deep sadness, and his lyric heroes were shaped with emotions, not actions. His free poems stimulated the mind and soul of the reader with their warmth, sincerity, and directness.

This tiny book is evidence of the Giurjian's limitless poetic gush. It was as if the author experienced a flow from the heart that resulted in a volume of poetry that can be compared to a bouquet of beautiful flowers, each petal captivating on its own.

The thirty-one poems are connected to one another as a whole. The volume is a wonderful anthology of intellectual-philosophical pieces. Giurjian discussed life and philosophy with emotional and intellectual flights, with love being the core issue. He treated love with impressive sincerity and original expression. Giurjian's love songs charmed and attracted the reader, because their author came out of his isolated self and gushed like a fountain that vibrated the palpitating heart of the reader. Love is an almighty humanistic force, after all.

Oddly enough, the poet, ailed by love, loved his ailment and was reluctant to exchange it for all the health of the world (*I Refuse to Be Treated* [Chem uzer puzhvil]). He accepted and admitted: "My day was desolate until eve: a perfect desert, for your grace was absent" (*Oasis* [Ovasis]). Before he met his lover, his soul wandered in desolation until she suddenly appeared like an oasis, providing shadow and coolness to his burning soul, rejuvenating him with a drink made from light and honey. Giurjian admitted wanting to "never heal" to avoid the monotonous and careless way he had lived before loving her. With conviction, he declared: "Not only do I not want to heal, but also I will try to do my best to deepen and eternalize my ailment." Finally, he blessed the day he was caught by the sublime illness of love that overflows with life's sensations.

In the poem "Let Me Give You a Rose" [Vart mê dam kezi], Giurjian compared the rose—the queen of flowers—with his lover, because the two look alike in their royal gorgeousness. They both open only their external petals, hiding their breathtaking scent deep inside the internal leaves, "in the deepest folds of the soul."

Giurjian began his poem "Thrice Great Drunkard" [Yeramedz kinov] with an epithet by his favorite poet, Charles Baudelaire: "Get intoxicated, drunk, with wine, virtue, or poetry." Giurjian considered love the tastiest of wines, the greatest of virtues, the poetry of poetries; in other words, the never-ending source of all inspiration, excitement, and fascination. He wrote: "I am intoxicated, intoxicated, my adored one, but neither with wine, nor with virtue or poetry; rather, with your love, your love only." By doing so, he drew a parallel between the trinity of virtue, poetry, and love and the divine trinity of faith, hope, and love.

Giurjian's romantic poems are warm and passionate, because his richly harmonious poetic inner world was deep and saturated with anxieties and anguish.

In the aforementioned series of articles, *Love*, Giurjian wrote: "This monosyllabic word is so similar to the word Lord. True love is the lord of life and soul: A capricious Lord, stringent and tyrant, who demands absolute obedience, submission, and sacrifice, and who inspires us with the most sublime, noble, and epic, as well as the most foolish and tragic thoughts and deeds."

There is no doubt that love reached lofty heights in Giurjian's poetry. It is noteworthy that Giurjian did not reduce himself to vulgarity when describing the external and internal virtues of his lover; rather, he expressed his troubled soul and talked about the fine shades of his love and emotions with civilized modesty and purity.

In the poem "You Come Close, You Leave" [Gê modenas, gê heranas], Giurjian seemed to have felt that at times his lover's soul had touched his poetic spirit, and at other times, escaped to an inapproachable summit. The poem concluded: "You are a heavenly lamp that at times kindly illuminates my estranged loneliness, and at times you are a remote star that glitters above my soul ... When you talk and smile at me, you give me the illusion that you are a mortal creature like myself, but then suddenly, the moment I stretch my hands to test your realness, you ascend and disappear, wrapped in a cloud, like a goddess who, inspired by heavenly caprice, appears for a moment to mortal eyes, blinds them, then returns to the realm of the immortals."

Kissing the hair of his lover and breathing her sweet scent, the lyrist assumed he was sniffing the inexpressible mystery of her miraculously grown body, since "all the scents of Arabia and elsewhere were seemingly gathered, intermingled, and concentrated in her hair," scents which "were light and soft, and yet so strong that a net of metal knots would not have entrapped my soul so tightly" ("The Imperishable Scent" [Angorncheli puyrê]).

By establishing similarities between phenomena, and considering the properties of an object, Giurjian made beautiful comparisons: "The presence of the adored one is the sun of my nature, light and warmth in its entirety, and her memory is a pale moon that sprinkles a mystic radiance on me" ("Sun and Moon" [Arev ev lusin]).

These illustrative comparisons, resulting from Giurjian's impressions of life, render his work particularly striking. They are expressions of his artistic style.

"Today, we did not meet. Today, I was deprived of the happiness of your sight, O marvelous image. No museum can offer me your parallel. I was deprived of the happiness of hearing you, O magnificent music. I can enjoy your equal in no concert," wrote Giurjian in the poem, "Sun and Moon." Thinking of his lover and writing free verse were the only means with which he was able to dismiss his sadness as a lonely man, because his loneliness then was expelled "by an invisible presence" and "an unexplainable happiness" filled his soul.

The loving poet compares himself with an arrow heading for its target—the bird that flies home and the river that heads for the sea—as he hastens to find his adored one ("The Happy Going" [Yerchanig knatskê]).

Giurjian developed his philosophical and pensive inclusions through the use of metaphors. He did not limit himself to epithets or the use of adjectives to describe his emotions and impressions. Rather, he portrayed phenomena through metaphors and original comparisons, which serve to stimulate the inner world of readers and affect the delicate strings of their conscience.

Love is the pseudonym of happiness, according to Giurjian. A happiness that is a mixture of tears and moans, which shakes him by tormenting his poor heart, and excites him with the most moving countenance, expressive eyes, soft and sweet smile, breathtaking voice, and passionate soul of his lover ("I praise You and Myself" [Gê kovem kez yev inkzinks]). Even the autocrat of a most populous country or the mightiest emperor of the world is not loved and adored as much as the empress of the uninhabited island—his adored queen ("The Empress and Her Subject" [Vehabeduhin yev ir hbadagê]).

The lyrist believed that his lover was almighty. He promised: "I will bless you when you grant me happiness. I will not damn you if you give me unhappiness." He says he is ready to accept anything from his lover regardless of whether it could equally make him happy or unhappy,[92] confessing: "My love is total bravery and selflessness. It is a hero who strives for the laurels of glory, and, simultaneously, a mystic believer who is ready to accept the thorny crown of martyrdom any moment for the love of the deity he worships" ("Confession" [Khosdovanank]).

It seemed that even if the poet—that humble child of nature chained with the chains of the Aether—possessed the power of Sampson, he would not be able to break the chains. He admitted: "I am a captive, I know; but I do not exchange my captivity with all the freedoms of the world," adding with confidence: "I lost a treasure—my freedom. I gained a greater treasure—my happiness of love" ("Loss and Gain" [Gorusd yev shah]).

The magical presence of the lover energized Giurjian's soul, her radiant face illuminated his day, her vivifying breath animated his lifeless hours, and her glances brought light to his soul. "Without you, the world is a limitless void and death to me," stated the melancholic weaver of words who had been wounded by his lover.

Giurjian longed to be like Endymion, the fair shepherd of Latmos, who had been sentenced to eternal sleep. He wanted to receive a similar punishment—to sleep eternally and to dream of his lover—the goddess living on earth ("Endymion" [Antimion]). In another poem, he compared the four elements of the universe—earth, air, water, and fire—with the love of his small mono-elemental universe, which he concluded, is as powerful as the four elements combined ("Beyond the Pain and Joy" [Tsaven yev urakhutenen antin]).

In the poem, "Do You Remember?" [Gê hishes?], Giurjian reminisced about the summer night when the lover and he reached the shore "sharing their words and silence": his lover "like an unapproachable goddess," the infinite song of the waves singing, the magical whiteness of the moon lighting their way, while he outcried his infinite love. After some comparisons and analogies, the poet concluded: "And it seemed to me suddenly—O passing illusion—when I was uttering, with ever-growing excitement and fascination, that my love was the sea lifting the endless cry of a limitless passion unto the moon, and you, my adored, were that moon, that sublimely peaceful moon dispatching her lofty beams to the sea like mysterious smiles." It is with such radiant colors that the poet recalled the memorable past, the days of fortune and happiness that would never return.

At night, for a poet hypnotized before the window of the creature he loves, there is no brighter, more mysterious, or more gravitating point in the universe than the luminous canvas—the window—which seems to be the gate of a palace saturated with mysteries, or the entrance of a cave of the *A Thousand Nights and a Night*, opening onto shiny treasures and wonders ("Light and Mystery" [Luys ev khorhurt]).

Giurjian's soul tossed between two equally strong poles: the flamboyance of his lover's presence and the bliss of her absence, because she was always with him whether in person or in memory, each provoking different, distinct feelings within the author ("Between Two Poles" [Yergu peverneru michev]).

Giurjian's style, artful images, ingenious comparisons, and rich metaphors are living witness of the author's profound knowledge of life, deep understanding of reality, and sensitivity in comprehending phenomena and relationships.

Women and nature were the poet's primary sources of inspiration. As his adored one excited and intoxicated him, so did nature stir and provoke his soul. The wind agitated the tideless, calm lake so much that he favored his perturbed state more than the entire tranquility of heaven and earth. "The wind is the lake's life, love is the soul's wind," wrote Giurjian in "The Lake and the Wind" [Lijê yev hovê]. His meaning was that the lake's only wish was that wind to never cease blowing, so that its happy waves might sing the wind's glory.

Giurjian was at odds with boring sagacity. He praised wine, because just as the drunkard views the world in vibrant colors, so does a quiet person feel happier under the influence of love ("I Say the Same in a Different Way" [Nuyn pane gêsem darper tsevov]).

Thinking of dreams as the continuation of the thoughts and events of the day, the author resolved the puzzle by saying: "The dream, the real, true dream, is my life during the day; it is my daily life, when I am granted the opportunity to see you, talk to you, constantly think of you, be captivated by your presence and surrounded by your memory." Whereas sleep is reminiscent of a pale reality—the place where passionless people live ("The Real Life" [Jshmarid gyankê]).

The deep harmony that prevailed in three perfect images—the sky, desert, and sea —horrified the poet who pondered whether he would feel immense pressure from the indifference, carelessness, and insensitivity of a slice of the unaltered blue, a grain from the sands of the desert's desolation, or a drop from the monotonous sea onto his lover's soul ("Nature and Woman" [Pnutiun yev gin]).

The author drew parallels between the clouds progressing across the heavenly fields and a flock of sheep shepherded by the wind. Then, when the wind suddenly gusts, the sheep scatter as if they are deserters. Likewise, for the poet, love begins like a calm, light breeze only to strengthen and drive its flock to unfamiliar territory. What a beautiful metaphor: the shepherd, the flock, and the deserters compared with the wind, the clouds, and the cooled atmospheric steam headed in an indefinite direction ("The Wind" [Hovê]).

In the poem "Victory March" [Haghtanagi yerk], Giurjian described how he avoided the immediate return to his home after departing from his lover, in order not to feel secluded, nor to think of or write about her. Rather, he described how light and joyful he felt; so light and joyful that he wanted to jump, dance, and fly. He walked for hours, wishing to walk endlessly toward immortality "carrying the immense load of the happiness of love for days, months, and years."

Giurjian's poems are pleasant because they are simple, harmonious, and musical. They generate the delight and inner turbulence that only true art can offer.

For Giurjian, to love and to live in romantic dreams and fantasies was what mattered. When we penetrate into the psyche of the poet, we feel his profound optimism, unshakable faith, and philosophy of life. Like the romantic, fantastic, delicate dreams of Vahan Derian, Giurjian's philosophy of life in this tiny book was the source of his never-ending suffering, the root of his optimistic and bright generalizations, and the condensation of his love.

The publication of *To the Adored, from the Bottom of My Heart* shook the Armenian literary world. Father Zaven Chinchinian (later, Archbishop and Primate of the Armenians in Egypt) said in the introduction he wrote for this book: "These pages, written some thirty years ago, are in the form of free verse—a favorite of the aesthetic writers of the early 1900s, and revered, at the time. Rarely has free verse been a successful literary genre, and then only under the pen of the most talented." Emphasizing Giurjian's multifaceted talent and pleasing language, Chinchinian praised the literary and artistic merits of the book: "These are poems written in succession on the theme of love. They possess a beautiful style, rich language, and conductibility, as is the case of all works of true art written with emotions."

The collection of poems in this booklet caught the family of Victoria Arsharuni, a talented writer, by surprise. Although neighbors of the

Giurjians for a long time in Alexandria, they never realized that "their sharp, sarcastic friend, who was always ready to forge a pun and who spread much joy, was, at the same time, such a sensitive poet. Who would have thought?"

The surprised writer expressed her fascination and admiration by praising the romantic poems she found so beautiful and touching in their substance and so perfect in their shape: "These poems are noteworthy for their sincerity, their deep and intense feelings, and the juvenile warmth that animates them. Authenticity being their greatest attribute."[93]

In a long article published in the section of *Books, Profiles* [Kirker, temker] in his periodical, Hrant Paluyan praised Giurjian's book.[94] After mentioning that Giurjian's extensive works remain buried in old and scattered periodicals, he went on: "More than sarcasm, he was one of the forefront representatives of our beautiful literature." He added that the new book "offers impressive images, confessions, and the soft murmur of music that engulfs your soul." The critic recommended the book to the readers, because "the captivating ode, written several decades ago, is the deification of love, given through a rich explosion."

In 1962, Hmayag Kranian dedicated a review to the book in Beirut, Lebanon, in which he wrote: "Rarely has the Armenian language worn the richness of its lyric beauty and princedom so elegantly as under Giurjian's aesthetical pen."

Hovhannes Boghosian, the editor-in-chief of *Arev* daily, said in an article entitled "Mikayel S. Giurjian"[95] that he felt himself lucky for having enjoyed Giurjian's intimacy. Briefly reflecting upon Giurjian's literary activities, Boghosian mentioned: "He was an attentive observer of the phenomena and expressions of human society, looking down upon events and people, with his pipe squeezed in the corner of his mouth, from the peaceful atmosphere of his office, where one could hardly hear an external noise over the bluster of the tides of the nearby sea." Thereafter, referring to Giurjian's analytical and rich expressions, linguistic skills, and the spirit and style of olden times, he wrote: "It was very pleasant to hear his heart pound with youthful energy mix with the prudent thoughts of an aged man when he spoke to his 'adored one' from the bottom of his heart."

Yervant Azadian described Giurjian's stirring romantic free verse as the book "where Giurjian surfaced as a true poet."

Indeed, this book is saturated with the fascinating and moving expressions of the colorful and beautiful creations of non-metric poetry. His free verse was written with limitless poetic flight, with volcanic explosion of emotions, and, particularly, with romantic heat and literary charm.

Mikayel S. Giurjian with Yervant Odian, by Krikor Keusseyan, c. 1961.

Mikayel Giurjian the Essayist

Giurjian lived and created in a period of complex, confusing, and contradictory national and international events. The Armenians in Eastern and Western Armenia lived under harsh conditions. The European Powers despite moving the Armenian Question from one conference to another, were unable to solve it and, the situation in Western Armenia became graver. After the bloody demonstration of Kum Kapu in 1890, the lives of Christians and, in particular, Armenians became more insecure. Sultan Abdülhamid II intensified his policy of persecution against Armenians. The prisons of Turkey were filled with thousands of Armenian intellectuals and national activists, all accused as revolutionaries. The massacres of Sasun in 1894 and of all Armenian provinces in 1895–1896 shook the civilized world. On July 11, 1908, telegrams broke news to the world of the "tiding" of the declaration of the Ottoman Constitution.

The Constitution announced that all Ottoman subjects, including the Christians of the Ottoman Empire, would have equal rights. Less than a year later, on March 31, 1909, the Ittihadists toppled Sultan Abdülhamid with a coup d'état. My father, Hagop Mekeryan, a Constantinoplean at the time, used to tell me that he witnessed the dethronement of the Sultan—the Red Executioner—and that he felt unbounded joy in watching the Sultan be pulled from the palace and forced to walk the streets in humiliation. However, ensuing massacres, plunders, lootings, exiles, and persecutions revealed that the "educated" Young Turks were as thirsty for Armenian blood and as covetous of the belongings and wealth of Armenians as their fanatic, jealous, and ruthless predecessors.

Taniel Varuzhan, Adom Yarjanian (Siamanto), Arpiar Arpiarian, Yervant Odian, Vahan Tekeyan, Levon Pashalian, Dikran Gamsaragan, Mikayel Giurjian, Arshag Chobanian, Yervant Srmakeshkhanlian, Suren Bartevian, Levon Shant, Rupen Zartarian, Krikor Zohrab, Zabel Yesayan, and other writers moved abroad under these politically confusing and deceiving conditions.

In his book *History of the 19th Century Turkish Armenian Literature* [Badmutiun ZhT taru Turkio hayots kraganutean] (Cairo, 1944), Arpiarian wrote: "Before 1880, censorship was decreed for neither books, nor newspapers. Once in a while, an author or a publisher were apprehended and imprisoned without any explicit violation of law… In 1888, censorship included the Armenian media, too." In this way, although losing its freedom, the Armenian media continued to enjoy some privileges, which Armenian books were deprived of, since they were subjected to more scrutiny. Under these circumstances, writers and essayists were drawn more and more to the benefits of publishing in newspapers.

At the time, there were many publications, mostly partisan and revolutionary, in the comparatively well-organized Armenian communities of the United States, Egypt, Bulgaria, and Rumania. Both refugee and resident Armenians read the editorials and articles of political, social, and national nature with great interest. The media played an important role in guiding the Armenian people and inspiring hope and optimism. Meritorious authors and young writers of talent focused on many issues pertinent to mankind and the Armenian people.

Political, economic, social, and cultural issues related to Armenians and their homeland remained in consistent focus for Mikayel Giurjian. Often sounding like a daily toll, Girujian wrote about many international and national problems from the days of his youth until old age.

The Armenian people entered the twentieth century under historical-political conditions that opened the doors wide for internal dissensions and arguments, threats and commotions, agitation and terror, and the struggle between conservatives and liberals or constitutionalists, with the political parties actively engaged in all matters. The Armenian media and intellectuals were unable to remain indifferent toward these developments. Across the Diaspora, many newly formed publications began to preach prudence to their Armenian readership through alerting articles.

In Egypt, the constitutionalists launched a struggle against a national council elected by fraud. They did not trust the ability of the Central National Administration of Constantinople to reestablish order.

Odian mentions that after publishing three issues of *Azad Khosk* [Free Speech] in France, when he continued the publication of his periodical in Alexandria, Dikran Gamsaragan and Mikayel Giurjian began to contribute to it.

At the time, Giurjian was already contributing to *Paros* [Lighthouse] of Dikran Arpiarian, the former editor-in-chief of *Masis*, and satirist Harutiun Alpiar in Cairo; to Yeghishé Torosian's fifteen-year-old *Arshaluys* of Cairo; and to the semiweekly *Piunig* [Phoenix] of Alexandria, which became a daily in July 1903.

Many of the Armenian intellectuals who had escaped the Turkish persecutions were engaged in teaching and publishing new periodicals. Mihran Askanazian, for example, aside from teaching, published a literary and pedagogical weekly, *Bardez*. Mari Beylerian, a renowned revolutionary, taught at the Kalusdian National School of Cairo and published, in 1902–1903, a literary, family monthly, *Ardemis* [Artemis]. In 1903, Avedis Balian launched *Zhoghovurt* [People], as monthly in Cairo, which then became a weekly in Alexandria. Diran Kelegian became editor-in-chief of two French publications: *Le Journal du Caire* and *La Bourse Egyptienne.* In addition, he found time to establish a Turkish language monthly, *Yeni Fikir* [New thought]. Levon Pashalian edited *Nor Geank,* the official publication of the Reformed Hnchag Party in London. Odian published a daily, *Tertig* [Newsletter], from July 11 through August 17, 1906, twenty-eight issues altogether.

One can list many more periodicals published in Egypt at the turn of the twentieth century, such as Smpad Piurad's *Nor Or* (1900–1901), Diran Papazian's *Hayeli* [Mirror] (1903–1904), Vahan Kiurkjian's *Lusaper* [Lucifer] (1904–1908), Smpad Piurad's *Sisuan* (1905) with Yervant Srmakeshkhanlian as co-editor, and Sisag Muradian's *Bidzag* [Wasp] (1906).

Of the newly founded periodicals in Egypt, most noteworthy were Odian's publications, *Azad Khosk, Azad Pem, Tertig, Arev,* and *Grag* [Fire], along with two others: *Shirag,* a joint publication of Tekeyan and Giurjian, and *Nor Zhamanagner* [New Times], which Tekeyan published alone.

Giurjian frequently contributed literary works and essays to all these publications.

In his memoirs, *Twelve Years Outside Constantinople,* Odian praised Giurjian's contributions, writing: "The collection of the year-long issues of *Azad Pem,* which I do not have with me, alas, is quite rich, I can say, and they occupy an honorable place in the collections of Armenian newspapers. Mikayel Giurjian was a regular contributor to the newspaper. He flooded the pages of *Azad Pem* with his endless wit." Odian went on: "*Azad Pem* did not cause me much fatigue. I visited the press only several hours a week to write an article or correct a proof. I spent the rest of my time with Mikayel Giurjian, in pleasant companionship. Often, we sat together in a café on the shore writing chronicles, which we signed Y. M. Giurod, intertwining our names with one another." It was for this reason that when Odian's brother invited him to Bombay, Odian immediately agreed, because he had easily found a way for his newspaper to continue. The Reformed Hnchags of Alexandria had been planning on establishing an official organ, and *Azad Pem* was laboring under heavy debts. So Odian transferred the newspaper to the Reformed Hnchags, on the condition that Giurjian would edit it during his absence, and that Odian would resume the editing when he returned from India. This was evidence of the great trust Odian had for Giurjian's literary and editorial abilities, as well as testimony to their close relationship.

As the new editor of *Azad Pem* in 1904, Giurjian wrote a fantasy under the title, *The Subscriber* [Pazhanortê]. His main character, Senekerim Ghugasian, was a uniquely odd character: he never turned down an Armenian newspaper and he paid his dues regularly, although his Armenian was mixed with Turkish, and all he could do was sign his name and write a two-liner. However, he was portrayed as a new Armenian role model who had found an easy way to demonstrate his love for his nation—"to accept all the newspapers delivered to him, paying each of them with a piece of his love for the nation" in order to help his nation to the extent his financial means allowed him, even if the unopened packages piled up on the shelves of a closet, as if the papers were sacred objects and not things people should open and read.

In December 1904, when Odian returned to Alexandria, Giurjian turned the newspaper back over to him and kept contributing to it. Odian testified: "*Azad Pem* was regularly published during my absence, under the editorship of Giurjian and with the assistance of Vahan Tekeyan, who arrived several months ago from Marseilles to settle in Alexandria."[96]

Later, when Levon Larents also arrived in Alexandria, *Azad Pem* became an official organ of the Reformed Hnchag Party, and Odian, Giurjian, and Tekeyan retired from it.

Odian's *Azad Khosk* was published at irregular intervals. To help improve the situation, Krikor Nazaretian, a press owner and a photoengraver, offered his help in turning the periodical into an illustrated satirical weekly. *Azad Khosk* continued to focus on local issues every week from 1906 to 1907 in Alexandria. Arpiarian, Tekeyan, Giurjian, and Parsegh Shahbaz were regular contributors.

Giurjian's most important editorial contribution was the publication of *Shirag* literary monthly in 1905 with Tekeyan's collaboration. The first editorial outlined the objectives of the magazine: "To try to revive Armenian literature in the Diaspora with the assistance of a group of chosen writers. Since it will be impossible for an Armenian writer not to reflect upon the ongoing pains of the homeland and absorb the blood of his sensations and the juice of his thoughts from these pains, *Shirag* will present a national literature exempt from the entanglements of partisan considerations. It will open the gates wide for all true and authentic writers by presenting them with the means to fulfill their obligation toward Armenian literature and, through literature, toward a national renaissance."[97]

It is clear in hindsight that a magazine with those literary and social objectives could have helped the nation rise during those harsh days. Indeed, the editors and contributors often described the chaotic situation of Western

Armenians in successive issues, and the best Western Armenian writers (Arpiarian, Odian, Vrtanes Papazian, Adom Yarjanian, Diran Chrakian, Hovhannes Setian, etc.) contributed both prose and poems.

During the first year of its publication, from January to November 1905, Tekeyan and Giurjian published eleven issues. After a brief interruption, the editing was entrusted to Arpiar Arpiarian who had moved to Cairo, and Arpiarian published nine issues from 1906 to 1907. This second period of the magazine came to a halt when Arpiarian accepted the editor-in-chief position at *Lusaper.*

Shirag began its third phase as a literary and political weekly in Constantinople, under the lone editorship of Tekeyan, who published twenty-six issues from February through August 1909, when the magazine's life ended.

This interesting magazine ranked foremost amongst all the Armenian periodicals of Egypt, with regard to content.

Profoundly aware of the important role journalism played in lifting the spirit of Armenians and strengthening their morale, Giurjian supported his people with encouraging words and humanitarian ideals during those distressful days. He offered his insight on the most pressing issues and events of his times.

Unfortunately, Giurjian's numerous editorials and articles, so pleasant to read, remain scattered in many Western Armenian newspapers and magazines.

Referring to Odian, Siruni says: "Odian's daily humor is scattered in his chronicles, because thousands of witty pages lay in the collections of dailies. They await a caring hand to collect them into a bouquet." Similarly, there are many masterpieces of sarcasm and wit, useful tips, wise thoughts, prudent advice, and helpful opinions in the persuasive essays Giurjian wrote almost daily for the Armenian media.

In his chronicles and essays, Giurjian discussed social and political matters with metaphoric emotions, scientific-philosophical inquiry, and noteworthy artistic breath.

As he made his literary debut in 1898 with his novel, *Mardig Agha,* likewise he entered the field of journalism as an ingenious journalist with the article "Though We Cry, We Leave" [Hem lank, hem yertank] that appeared in Alpiar's *Paros* in 1900. The title was a perfect reflection of the content and spirit of the article. At the same time, it also embodied the invincible will of the Armenian people and their hopes for a bright future.

The article was a philosophical analysis of the Armenian proverb, "Though we cry, we leave." Giurjian explained that despite suffering for centuries, Armenians have shown the faith and endurance required to stay attached to life. Crying at times and bleeding at times, they have always been energetic, struggling and persistent, their character unflappable.

Indeed, despite all the disastrous events, Armenians have persisted throughout the centuries, and continued to walk even while crying. Giurjian was convinced that disasters could destroy the weak, but that they strengthened the strong, even instilling resilience. Therefore, the proverb was not only a lament, but also a marching tune for the Armenians who have suffered for so long. The always-optimistic writer was confident that "the day will come for sure, when Armenians will receive the reward and crown in honor of their wonderful ability to live and survive, and for their unparalleled ingenuity, attaining *a kind of a happy life*. That day will finally eliminate the *lament* and preserve only the sacred march," because suffering has been the preserving force for Armenians since ancient days.

In 1909, in the aftermath of the Ottoman Turkish revolution, when people naively believed that the new regime would erase the memory of past calamities and bring to the Ottoman subjects the bounties of a happy life, this article was reprinted in *Piuzantion* daily with a minor change in the epilogue.

History proved that the Armenians were deceived in their optimism and hopes. With the eruption of World War I, the Armenian people cried as never before.

Giurjian published the same article again sixty-five years later in *Arev* daily with an introductory explanation that emphasized: "Although the majority of Western Armenians were annihilated with unprecedented barbarism, and the 'remnants' of those who survived the flood of blood comprise today, more or less, prosperous communities in many different countries and they have lost their gloomy features for quite a while, Armenians no longer cry; rather, they walk triumphantly, and will walk to attain their goal." He added that the hope for a better future he had formulated at the end of the article when it was first published had come true thanks to the existence and wonderful growth of Armenia.[98]

In his letter of September 27, 1909, Diran Chrakian wrote to Giurjian: "Your *Though We Cry, We Leave*—that article, which unfortunately has remained only in a newspaper (even if it were the newspaper of Kechian the Great)—was a masterpiece."

In 1906, Cairo witnessed the foundation of the Armenian General Benevolent Union, which later became the most vital charitable organization in the Armenian Diaspora. Guided by the slogan "Unity is strength," the AGBU established an official monthly publication in Cairo in 1912.

Giurjian became one of its most active contributors. Sharing his rich literary and sociological knowledge with readers, he published witty and instructional articles that sought to shape characters and refine manners.

In an article entitled "The Role of Great People" [Medz martots terê], Giurjian refuted the common belief that "great historical moments give birth to critically historical personalities." Instead he asserted that a nation should consider itself fortunate if it had a providential famous person or persons capable of defending its existence against imminent dangers. To support his opinion, Giurjian referred to the history of the Greek people. After an unsuccessful battle in 1896, and after a period of military weakness, unpreparedness, and internal dissensions and disagreements, Venizelos came from Crete to successfully change Greece's image within several years. "The civil administration, army, and navy were put into order, reformed, and strengthened, and Greek diplomacy transformed itself into an alert, clever, and active presence," he wrote.

Giurjian showed how the former lawyer from Crete unified all the rival factions and, like a great conductor, he conducted "a great, national, harmonious Halleluiah," subjecting all of the players to the masterful waves of his stick.

Concluding his article, Giurjian advised: "It would be better if we, Armenians, pay attention to these realities, because no other nation is in more need of prominent personalities at this critical moment, and no other nation has as many obligations as we do, to recognize and appreciate the persons or person whom fortune has given us."

In the article "Prudence and Heroism" [Voghcmdutiun yev tiutsaznutiun] Giurjian mentioned that these two attributes complement each other in human beings. Prudence serves during peace, heroism when danger looms. He then stated: "We are a nation that has the right to live" and that "will live free and happy" by its heroic will and profound rectitude.

The education of the younger generation was an essential issue during the first decade of the twentieth century. Giurjian discussed the issue in a series of articles in *Miutiun* as of 1912 in which he advocated the improvement of Armenian schools. He emphasized the importance of a well-rounded education, the shaping of students both morally and physically, and the theoretical and practical roles of schools ("Total Education" [Ampoghchagan tasdiaragutiun]).

"School should not be an artificial environment where students are in touch with life through the books alone. Rather, it should be a small world—a real and positive one—that places the student as close to nature and reality as possible. The student should not learn only the theoretical, but also the practical, and these two elements should be tightly joined in the school curriculum, as they are around us, so that when a young person enters life, he will not enter a world he was not prepared for and where he will be confused and directionless."

Giurjian acquainted the readers of *Miutiun* with the views of Edmond Demolins, the best apprentice of the famous economist and sociologist Le Play, on education. Demolins referred the British school system to French parents, saying that it was better adapted for the newest demands of life and that it more successfully prepared capable, daring, and self-sufficient individuals "who are able to find their way through all kinds of difficulties and situations in life" (*Total Education*).

As both a searcher and reader, Giurjian was well acquainted with the theories of famous economists and sociologists, such as Hyppolyte Taine, Gustave Le Bon, Joseph Renan, Voltaire, Gabriel Tarde, and others. As a lover of education, he particularly reflected upon Demolins' work, *Anglo-Saxon Superiority: to what it is due* [A quoi tient la supériorité des Anglo-Saxons], emphasizing that Demolins' ideas were useful for Armenians. According to the author, Anglo-Saxon parents did not treat their children as their property. On the contrary, they viewed them as beings destined to gradual independence from their parents. Anglo-Saxon parents dealt with their children as adults and independent individuals. French parents, like Armenians, were more inclined to see their children as immature people even when they attained maturity. Anglo-Saxon parents focused on meeting the demands of the future life and not the past.

In another article, Giurjian suggested that parents should care for not only their children's health, but also, and in particular, for the normal and complete development of their physical strength. Again referring to Anglo-Saxon parents who trained their children from early on in handwork and familiarized them with objects, he said that training should constitute the method of parental education and not pressure or enforcement. A parent's role was mostly to advise, convince, and suggest, rather than dictate or threaten. Giurjian underlined: "Unless we rise again and are renewed physically, our nation will not be renewed morally" ("Physical Education" [Fizikagan grtutiun]). He thought we needed to hold tight to the branch of physical training, on the physical education of school children, because the shoots of our intellectual and moral renaissance would rise from it. For Giurjian, the intellectual development and character shaping of young students were essential components of the educational program. "By moral education, one should primarily understand the kind of direct, living, positive, and, therefore, influential education that the teacher can and should offer to the students through his or her manners within and outside the school, by the impressive and expressive example of his or her movements and actions" ("Moral Education" [Paroyagan grtutiun]).

Giurjian provided similar correct and useful tips on national education in many other educational and pedagogical articles, such as the one entitled, "How Should We Educate Our Children?" [Inchbes grtelu enk mer zavagnerê?] According to him: "The boys that graduate—and often half-graduate—from our schools demonstrate an excessive inclination toward two things: *literature* and *politics*—the two most 'unpositive' things that exist on earth *when they are Armenian.*" Considering that "we have too many literature lovers and *national activists*, it is time to realize that the situation is grave and that it is necessary to develop the means for healthy positivism, because education, media, and politics are in the hands of these people—these ill-prepared activists." Giurjian stated: "No other race produces 'literature lovers' and 'writers-to-be' as abundantly as we do" ("A Little Positivism" [Kich mê traganutiun]).

In a long article entitled, "The Armenian's Mind" [Hayun midkê], Giurjian asserted that "we are unquestionably a smart and intellectual race, but as the French say, 'Il y a fagots et fagots' [All fagots are not alike]; likewise, there are brains and brains." Citing the theory of Gustave Tard, the famous sociologist, that "creation and imitation" are the driving forces of social life, Giurjian concluded that the Armenian civilization is a more or less successful imitation of foreign civilizations. We have borrowed myths, religion, literature, arts, and political and social manners from civilized nations that have surrounded or ruled us. The Armenian mind, in its general and essential lines, is more imitating than creating, more receptive than productive, more analytical than synthetic. The primary characteristic of the Armenian mind is appropriation. Due to the unfavorable conditions our nation has been destined to from the beginning, the Armenian mind has not been able to freely develop or the seeds of creative forces to flourish.

Giurjian signed the articles he wrote in *Miutiun* with his real name and not with pseudonyms. His editorials and essays, scattered in the Diaspora Armenian media, remain instructive and educative today, even though he wrote them many decades ago.

In the article "What We Have and What We Lack" [Inch vor unink yev inch vor gê bagsi mezi][99] Giurjian wrote: "We could say, without the fear of being wrong, that an Armenian with average ability, intellectually speaking—possessing a thinking, comprehending, and benefiting mind—has more than an average French, British, or German. Even the most illiterate Armenian has a unique 'traditional' and experiential wisdom." He cited the words of Nubar Pasha, the world-renowned diplomat: "One Armenian is worth three Europeans." Then went on: "Yes, but *intellectually*; that is, by mind, cunningness, and reason. However, often ten Armenians are not worth one European morally; that is, measuring by character and will power. This is the main problem." He then emphasized: "Our giftedness is predominantly intellectual, mental," concluding: "Our boys learn too many things in school; perhaps an Armenian graduate of a school knows more language than an Anglo-Saxon student, but they do not learn the one great thing that the latter does learn and that is so crucial in succeeding—the knowledge of how to act and govern himself in life."

In another article, "The Ego" [Yesê], Giurjian wrote: "One of the reasons, and perhaps the main reason amongst us for the disruption or destruction of social affairs, or, otherwise speaking, for the almost impossibility of creating a productive and permanent public activity is nothing but the personal *I,* or partisan *we*, which is the aggrandizement of the previous one." In the end, the human ego turns to vanity, vainglory, and egoism. Therefore, Giurjian suggested to all those who undertake national duties to replace their personal egos with the *public ego* and learn how to show devotion.

Discussing the disunion of Armenians and their inability to unite, Giurjian argued for solidarity, because "evil has never been as great as it is in these times; therefore the need for unity has never been as great as it is in these days" ("For the Sake of Unity" [Vasn miutean]).

In an article titled, "The Insufficiency of the Mind as Means for Success" [Midkin anpavaganutiunê iprev hachoghutean michots], Giurjian found that one should know how to act, and also possess the will and character to succeed in life. "The mind can conceive and think many things… but it is the will, the character, and the physiology of man that executes." He referred to the attributes of Napoleon, Rockefeller, and the Romans, and then, after citing Pascal—"Man is a thinking reed"—he commented that the aphorism was incomplete. Man is not only a thinking reed, but also an acting one. "The reed" could have done nothing, created nothing, had he been only a thinker. "We know how to *think*; let's learn a little how to *act*," Giurjian concluded.

Borrowing the title of Racine's tragedy, Giurjian named one of his articles "Enemy Brothers" [Tshnami yeghpayrner]. There, he discussed the realm of organizations and individualism. "The Armenian nation has always suffered from the lack of a conductor," because each one of us thinks as a leader. "We all want to command; *obedience is beyond our ability*, or *below our dignity*. … We cannot tolerate an Armenian, a national activist, commanding us, giving us the word of order, showing us a common path to follow. It is as if we are constantly and inexorably competing with each other as individuals, organizations, or political parties." Referring to the Anglo-Saxons, Germans, Latins, and French, Giurjian suggested that we should adopt the spirit of order and obedience in pursuit of national objectives, whether significant or not, so that we might concentrate our efforts, avoid wasting our vigor, and be rewarded by productive, regular, and permanent activity.

Giurjian demonstrated political savvy, skill in describing events and figures, and rich knowledge about the international media and historic personalities or statesmen. He cited an article by Maurice Barrès and a speech by Nubar Pasha, as well as Napoleon, General Joffre, Lorris Melikof, Aivazovski, Edgar Shahin, Dikran Yergat, Eprem Khan, and others who, thanks to their exceptional talent and entrepreneurship, attained brilliant positions and international fame in the arts, politics, trade, military, and other fields.

In an article he entitled, "Our Individualism" [Mer anhadabashdutiunê], Giurjian invited the Armenians to be collectivists and not individualists in social life, and to work in solidarity.[100] He appealed to the Armenians to stop partisan fights and hatred, and to be alert, honest, and calm in order to lift the minds and reconcile the hearts of the nation ("Silence, Gentlemen, People Are Dying There!" [Lrutiun, baronner, hon gê mernin]). He preached the love of nation. He commemorated the brave brethren who died regiment after regiment to reestablish the honor of Armenians before the world, and he reminded that "there, on the cursed land of Turkey, which has been nourished with crimes and renewed bloodshed, our unfortunate compatriots are being martyred in hellish torments, suffering of starvation." He reminded people of the Spanish-American war that was taking place during those days in which the American armada destroyed the Spanish and battleships sank accompanied by the loud blasts of fire and smoke.

Inviting attention to the criticism of some French parliamentarians against the Ministry of War, Giurjian reflected upon the emotional speech Millerand, the Minister of War during World War I, delivered to his supporters and to the opposition in the parliament: "For the sake of the homeland, let's stay united and in solidarity until victory day." By doing so, Millerand wanted to stop political agitations and social conflicts, because the enemy had entered French borders and the danger had not departed their country.

Giurjian was concerned about the small Armenian nation. The disaster looming over Armenians and the dangers threatening their existence were by far graver; therefore, in order to survive, "we have to be collectivist more than ever, pan-national as never before, give up our individualism, belong to the race, be driven by its infallible instinct, and palpitate with its boundless heart," for the sake of the sacred interests of the homeland. He appealed patriotically: "O Armenians, let's unite; O Armenians, let's stay united *at least until the fatal danger is over*" ("At Least until the Victory Day" [Koné minchev haghtutean orê]).

Giurjian's article "Our Character" [Mer ngarakirê] is noteworthy, for its plea for being independent in life, learning from the achievements of other nations, not depending on others more than depending on ourselves, staying away from vainglory and loving everything foreign, and becoming a developed and perfect nation.

In 1911, Suren Bartevian settled in the country of the pyramids, where a significant number of Armenian intellectuals had already gathered. When Bartevian began to publish *Hosank* [Current] weekly in 1912, Giurjian contributed to the periodical along with others, including Vahan Malezian, Dikran Gamsaragan, Levon Mgrdichian, Hovhannes Setian, Hovhannes Kayayan, Ardavazt Hanêmian, Agheksantr Shaklian, Karnig Fndklian, Bishop Mushegh Seropian, Diran Kelegian, Vahan Tekeyan, Diran Chrakian, Yervant Odian, Ardashes Harutiunian, Onnig Chifté-Saraf, Tlgadintsi, Rupen Vorperian, and Aram Andonian.

In the first, third, eighth, twelfth, and eighteenth issues of the first year of *Hosank*, and under a general header, "Thunder... Notes" [Tnta... Noter],[101] Giurjian discussed the National Assembly of Constantinople, Krikor Zohrab's speeches, the delegates of the Ottoman Parliamentary Council, the deliberations about a constitutional article, the need to terminate the struggle against the Tsarist government, and other national and international issues, always defending the interests of the Armenian people.

Speaking of newly established political streams, doctrines, organizations, and parties, Giurjian pointed to a new French political party that referred to itself as Political Futurism. The party's main principle—futurism—was derived from a school of art and literature that distinguished itself with the same *-ism* ending and denied the past and focused only on the future. The founder of the party, Lefèvre, had presented his candidacy for the municipal elections of Paris in order to bring the "Golden Age" back to the planet Earth or establish a "worldly paradise."

One of Giurjian's important journalistic contributions was his role as the editor of *Arev* daily. The editorship of *Arev* was entrusted to him in the years 1920–1923. The articles and editorials he wrote during this period were the best expressions of his progressive political views and testimonies for the faith and optimism he held for the Armenian homeland.

Many Diasporan Armenian newspapers reprinted several of Giurjian's articles and editorials for the weight they carried. One of them was an editorial entitled, "Why Did Boghos Pasha Nubar Not Sign the Peace Treaty?" [Inchu Boghos pasha Nubar chsdorakrets hashdutean tashnakirê], which *Gochnag Hayasdani* [Bell of Armenia] of New York reprinted on October 16, 1919 (pp. 1346–1347). Giurjian invited attention to the dialogue he had with Aleksandr Khadisian, the Prime Minister of the Republic of Armenia, during a dinner at Hotel Savoy in Paris. Khadisian mentioned that at the last minute, as Boghos Nubar Pasha was about to sign the Peace Treaty, the Turks argued that he did not have the authority to sign it. Khadisian and Avedis Aharonian, the president of the delegation of the Republic of Armenia to the Peace Treaty, asked the Pasha to insist on his right to sign. However, since the Allied Powers had accepted that the Turkish objection was based on "legal" ground, they found that the absence of Boghos Nubar's signature would serve the Armenian interests better. They did not want to give the Turks any pretext on which to protest the treaty as a tool executed with irregularities.

"His Highness [Boghos Nubar], after thoroughly studying the matter and discussing it with authoritative Armenophils and men of law, voluntarily sacrificed the personal satisfaction that would have been the rightful reward of his selfless and relentless patriotic efforts, had he placed his signature under an international treaty sanctifying the nation's independence..." He decided not to sign for another consideration. Had he signed the treaty, he would have consented to the unsatisfactory boundaries delimited for Armenia. By not signing, he maintained "the freedom to protest and act in favor of the realization of the unfulfilled aspirations of the Armenian nation."

Indeed, later, with an official letter dated August 14, 1920, Boghos Nubar expressed his gratitude to the Allied Powers for the portion of Armenian provinces they liberated and turned into an independent state. Simultaneously, he protested that the greater part of Cilicia and the province of Kharpert which should have been detached from the Ottoman Empire and joined to the French zone had been left under Turkish rule; whereas Adana, the capital of Cilicia, Sis, the religious capital of Armenians, and Zeitun, which half a century ago the French had recognized as a semi-autonomous territory even under Ottoman regime, remained under Turkish rule.

It is impossible to list, analyze, and comment here on all of Guirjian's editorials and articles. They would fill many volumes. The best of them should be gathered and published in the form of volumes, because they abound with Giurjian's mature thoughts, clear and simple style, prudent love for his nation, and radiant patriotism. Each of these writings reflects the noble intellectual who suffered with the nation's anguish.

Mikayel S. Giurjian as seen by Aleksandr Sarukhan, c. 1962.

GIURJIAN AS MASTER OF AUTHENTIC TRANSLATIONS

Giurjian contributed to the enrichment of Armenian literature by translating many works from foreign literature.

The art of translation began amongst Armenians immediately after the invention of the Armenian alphabet in the fifth century. Armenians first translated the Holy Bible from Greek and Syriac, and then the works of ancient philosophers and scientists, such as Plato, Aristotle, Euclid, Eusebius of Caesarea, Athanasius of Alexandria, Epiphanius, Ephraem Syrus, and Dionysus of Thrace.

In the nineteenth century, when many of the Armenian intellectuals of Constantinople and Smyrna studied European languages—French in particular—they undertook translating the masterpieces of world literature into Armenian. According to Arpiar Arpiarian, "Translations from French, particularly novels, began to train people's minds, realign them, and gradually Europeanize their taste."[102]

Armenian authors felt that translating the works of foreign writers enlightened and educated society, and promoted cultural communication between various peoples. Thus, they enriched Armenian literature with the additions of numerous and valuable translations.

While searching for and studying Giurjian's translations in more than fifty periodicals, I realized that there were numerous translated works awaiting serious research. For example, novels such as *The Wandering Jew, The Wretched* [Les Miserables], *Raphael, The Secrets of Paris, The Three Musketeers, The Mysterious Island, Faust, Ivanhoe, Twenty Years Later, Around the World in Eighty Days*, etc., are scattered throughout the Armenian media.

Armenian translators favored works by Victor Hugo, Eugène Sue, Alexandre Dumas, Jules Verne, Anatole France, Alphonse Daudet, Gustave Flaubert, Alphonse de Lamartine, Jean-Jaques Rousseau, Molière, Voltaire, Musset, Shakespeare, Byron, Shelley, Walter Scott, Daniel Defoe, Charles Dickens, Goethe, Schiller, Heine, Tasso, Edgar Allan Poe, Émile Verhaeren, Tolstoy, Pushkin, Lermontov, Nekrasov, Krylov, Gogol, et al.

A master of his mother tongue, Giurjian used a purified Armenian language in his metric and free translations. Giurjian's translations abound with emotion and creativity. He was not a casual translator; rather more a creator who considered mastery of the original and target languages, with their idioms and allegories, a prerequisite for successful translation.

If Giurjian's metric and free translations were collected, they would fill two large volumes. The list of his translations was not as impressive and long as that of Fr. Arsen Pakraduni, Yetvart Hiurmiuz, or Fr. Arsen Ghazigian, nor as systematically planned as that of Arshag Chobanian. However, in quality, Giurjian surpassed many of the authors who surpassed him in quantity.

The following is a translation of Baudelaire's poem, *Exotic Perfume:*

When, closing my eyes on a tepid autumn evening,
I delightfully breathe the scent of your naked breast,
I see the path of brave shores
Burned by the dazzling fires of a steady sun.

And I see an island where nature is birthing
Fantastic plants, trees and delicious fruits,
Men with slim and vigorous bodies,
Daring women looking at you with sharp glances.

Led by your scent toward calm climes,
I see a harbor, sails, and masts
Battered by tides, resting here immovably.

While the trees release incensed perfumes
That fill the warm air and caress the nostrils
Blend in my soul with the sailors' chorus.

(Parfum exotique

Quand, les deux yeux fermés, en un soir chaud d'automne,
Je respire l'odeur de ton sein chaleureux,
Je vois se dérouler des rivages heureux,
Qu'éblouissent les feux d'un soleil monotone:

Une île paresseuse où la nature donne
Des arbres singuliers et des fruits savoureux;
Des hommes dont le corps est mince et vigoureux,
Et des femmes dont l'oeil par sa franchise étonne.

Guidé par ton odeur vers de charmants climats,
Je vois un port rempli de voiles et de mâts
Encore tout fatigués par la vague marine,

Pendant que le parfum des verts tamariniers,
Qui circule dans l'air et m'enfle la narine,
Se mêle dans mon âme au chant des mariniers.)

Without altering the meaning of Baudelaire's text and while artfully maintaining the poet's spirit, Giurjian's reproduction leaves one with the impression the poem was originally written in Armenian.

One of the most important requirements for a successful translation is the love and admiration a translator harbors for an author or a work. Indeed, Giurjian's creative spirit and style were very much in sync with Baudelaire's spirit and the way the French poet expressed his thoughts or impressions.

Giurjian successfully translated *The Rose* by Pierre de Ronsard, *The Dawn* by Alfred Droin, and *The Cracked Bell* by Charles Baudelaire.

In the seventeenth and eighteenth centuries, people placed fairly rigid requirements on poetry in Europe. Nowhere were these as effective, rigid, and scrutinized as in France.

For example, the poems of Jean Racine, the seventeenth century French playwright, were always rhymed. The lines were arranged according to complex and inflexible rules that reflected the grammatical structure. The same phenomenon occurred with Milton and Shakespeare. Looking for perfect harmony of metric works and maintaining the clarity of mind until his death, Baudelaire developed the poetic sensation to a great extent.

Originally, French poetry was not based on the numbers of metric strokes, as was the case with British poetry, nor did it rely on the number of vowels, as was the case with Latin poems. It was established around the number of syllables in a given line. The French silent "e" is considered as syllable if it occurs between consonants, and at times it is neglected or not pronounced before a vowel. Despite the presence of an audible "e," sometimes the "-es" and "-ent" endings are silent. There is also the case of combined vowels. For example, when combined with other vowels, "i" and the vowel it is annexed to are sometimes considered one syllable and sometimes two.

Having all these nuances in mind, Giurjian rendered an authentic translation of Baudelaire's poem, *The Cracked Bell*. When the original and reproduced poems are compared, it is obvious that Giurjian accurately reproduced the style and spirit of the piece.

The Cracked Bell

It is bitter and sweet at the same time, on a long winter night,
To listen to, by the fire that sputters and smokes,
Distant memories that slowly rise
Through the nearby bells that sing in the fog.

Lucky the bell whose throat is strong,
Always healthy and alert, despite its age,
Like an old soldier, always watchful in the tent,
Lifting its pious cry up all day long.

My soul is cracked, alas, and when it wants, in its despair,
To spirit with its songs the cold air of night,
It often happens that its poor and weak sound

Resembles the snore of a wounded soldier
Forgotten under corpses by the edge of a bloody pool
Dying slowly with a horrible torment.

(La Cloche Fêlée

Il est amer et doux, pendant les nuits d'hiver,
D'écouter, près du feu qui palpite et qui fume,
Les souvenirs lointains lentement s'élever
Au bruit des carillons qui chantent dans la brume.

Bienheureuse la cloche au gosier vigoureux
Qui, malgré sa vieillesse, alerte et bien portante,
Jette fidèlement son cri religieux,
Ainsi qu'un vieux soldat qui veille sous la tente!

Moi, mon âme est fêlée, et lorsqu'en ses ennuis
Elle veut de ces chants peupler l'air froid des nuits,
Il arrive souvent que sa voix affaiblie

Semble le râle épais d'un blessé qu'on oublie
Au bord d'un lac de sang, sous un grand tas de morts,
Et qui meurt, sans bouger, dans d'immenses efforts.)

Giurjian relied on the inner meaning of the words and not their appearance, thus expressing the spirit of the poem more truthfully. The comparison shows that Giurjian took the liberties such as replacing a verb with an adjective or changing a plural into a singular. His rendition gives the reader the impression that it is an original rhymed and metric Armenian composition. In the last line, for example, the literal translation is, "And he dies, motionless, in horrible efforts." But grouping the syllables as 4+3+4+3 poetic measure, Giurjian wrote "Dying slowly with a horrible torment."

After comparing the Armenian version with the following English translation, one can conclude that Giurjian was more faithful to the original.

The Cracked Bell

How bittersweet it is on winter nights
To hear old recollections raise themselves
Around the flickering fire's wisps of light
And through the mist, in voices of the bells.

Blessed is the bell of clear and virile throat
Alert and dignified despite his rust,
Who faithfully repeats religion's notes
As a soldier keeps a watchman's trust.

My spirit, though, is cracked; when as she can
She chants to fill the cool night's emptiness,
Too often can her weakening voice be said

To sound the rattle of a wounded man
Beside a bloody pool, stacked with the dead,
Who cannot budge, and dies in fierce distress![103]

The English translator limited his work to a literal rendition, whereas Giurjian produced a work as valuable as the original, with the charm of a unique creation.

The great poet Tumanian said that even a well-done translation is like a rose placed in a glass container. He emphasized that one can see the shape, but cannot smell the scent. He felt that a translator "should possess the grace to reflect the authentic shape and to transfer the original scent."[104]

French Romanticism came to life in 1820, when Alphonse de Lamartine published his volume, *Poetic Meditations,* and followed it, in 1823, with the

New Poetic Meditations. Romanticism formulated literature based on the senses. This literary revolution was not the result of the bravery of critics; rather, it was born from the creation of poets whom playwrights and novelists followed.

In 1827, in the preface of his tragedy, *Cromwell*, Victor Hugo supported these revolutionary ideas and criticized the classical theory of the unity of action, time, and place used by playwrights of earlier centuries (with the exception of Shakespeare). Hugo announced that he intended to replace tragedy with a new kind of play and a broader historic reflection. He suggested that the most relevant characteristics of Romanticism were to be found in poetry, not plays. The Romantic poet expressed his personal emotions in the name of the society, in effect: "Foolish you who believes I am not you!"

Hugo stirred motions, Lamartine awakened music, whereas Vigny dissected philosophical ideas. Musset sang about romantic encounters, Sainte-Beuve portrayed city scenes, and Nerval struggled in the hell of symbols. For these reasons the young generation of Romantic poetry greeted Lamartine as their master, although this first voice of the Romantic chorus later died, somewhat forgotten and impoverished.

Lamartine's works have been translated into many languages. Western and Eastern Armenian writers and translators also translated many poems by Lamartine. In 1859, Khoren Kalfayan (Nar-Bey, 1832–1892) translated and published a collection of poems by Lamartine under the title, *Lamartine's Songs* [Tashnagk Lamartina]. Krikor Odian (1834–1887), a journalist and political-national activist, and Minas Cheraz (1852–1929), a poet and cultural-educational activist, also translated a selection of Lamartine's poems. Later, Krikor Chilingirian (1839–1923), Arshag Chobanian, Archbishop Yeghishé Turian, Archbishop Torkom Kushagian, Father Arsen Ghazigian, Vahan Tekeyan, Mikayel Giurjian, Mari Atmajian, Kuidon Lusinian (Amprosios Kalfayan), and others translated Lamartine's works.

In 1811, the Mediterranean brightened Lamartine's world while he was traveling in Italy, and awakened his first romantic emotions. Later, in 1816, while spending time at the spa Aix-les-Bains, the poet met Mrs. Charles, the wife of a physicist. Their meeting stirred his inner world and he praised her, referring to her as Elvir. In one of his most peculiar poems, "*Le Lac*" [The Lake], Lamartine expressed of his intense love for her, with strong eruptions of poetic genius and romantic imagery.

In "The Lake," the poet concentrated on the artistic reflection of reality in order to reconstruct life in accordance with his aesthetical ideal. The poem describes the lake where, a year before, he spent time with his lover, "She."

Recalling the sweet memories of beautiful and graceful past days, the author asked the time and the hours not to hasten by and escape, because he wanted to savor the joys of a short-lived, pleasant life.

Not only Giurjian, but also Yeghishé Turian, Mari Atmajian, and others translated this poem into Armenian. I have two translated versions of the poem at my disposal, both apparently "translated by Mikayel Giurjian." The first version, however, which was published in the second signature of the fourth volume of the periodical *Geank yev kir* [Life and Letter] (pp. 25–26), is not Giurjian's. His translation was published in *Arev* daily, first in 1942, and later, revised, on June 8, 1963. This translation is far superior to the plagiarized one.

When Giurjian's translation first appeared in *Arev*, Vahan Tekeyan, then the editor-in-chief, wrote an editorial note, saying: "Lamartine's poem has been translated at least twice amongst us. This is incomparably the best, and it is beautiful per se, as we have come to expect from Giurjian the delicate artist."

The first version is an example of the worst violation of literary ethics. In an article entitled "A Literary Mystery and a Personal Matter" [Kragan areghdzvadz mê yev antsnagan khntir mê],[105] Giurjian condemned the attempt to steal his name, calling it an immoral act. But he did not disclose the name of the plagiarizer.

Here is Giurjian's revised translation that follows Lamartine's original poem:

Le Lac

Ainsi, toujours poussés vers de nouveaux rivages,
Dans la nuit éternelle emportés sans retour,
Ne pourrons-nous jamais sur l'océan des âges
Jeter l'ancre un seul jour?

O lac! l'année à peine a fini sa carrière,
Et près des flots chéris qu'elle devait revoir,
Regarde! je viens seul m'asseoir sur cette pierre
Où tu la vis s'asseoir!

Tu mugissais ainsi sous ces roches profondes,
Ainsi tu te brisais sur leurs flancs déchirés,
Ainsi le vent jetait l'écume de tes ondes
Sur ses pieds adorés.

Un soir, t'en souvient-il? nous voguions en silence;
On n'entendait au loin, sur l'onde et sous les cieux,
Que le bruit des rameurs qui frappaient en cadence
Tes flots harmonieux.

Tout à coup des accents inconnus à la terre
Du rivage charmé frappèrent les échos
Le flot fut attentif, et la voix qui m'est chère
Laissa tomber ces mots:

"O temps! suspends ton vol, et vous, heures propices!
Suspendez votre cours:
Laissez-nous savourer les rapides délices
Des plus beaux de nos jours!

"Assez de malheureux ici-bas vous implorent,
Coulez, coulez pour eux;
Prenez avec leurs jours les soins qui les dévorent,
Oubliez les heureux.

"Mais je demande en vain quelques moments encore,
Le temps m'échappe et fuit;
Je dis à cette nuit: Sois plus lente; et l'aurore
Va dissiper la nuit.

"Aimons donc, aimons donc! de l'heure fugitive,
Hâtons-nous, jouissons!
L'homme n'a point de port, le temps n'a point de rive;
Il coule, et nous passons!"

Temps jaloux, se peut-il que ces moments d'ivresse,
Où l'amour à longs flots nous verse le bonheur,
S'envolent loin de nous de la même vitesse
Que les jours de malheur?

Eh quoi! n'en pourrons-nous fixer au moins la trace?
Quoi! passés pour jamais! quoi! tout entiers perdus!
Ce temps qui les donna, ce temps qui les efface,
Ne nous les rendra plus!

Éternité, néant, passé, sombres abîmes,
Que faites-vous des jours que vous engloutissez?
Parlez: nous rendrez-vous ces extases sublimes
Que vous nous ravissez?

O lac! rochers muets! grottes! forêt obscure!
Vous, que le temps épargne ou qu'il peut rajeunir,
Gardez de cette nuit, gardez, belle nature,
Au moins le souvenir!

Qu'il soit dans ton repos, qu'il soit dans tes orages,
Beau lac, et dans l'aspect de tes riants coteaux,
Et dans ces noirs sapins, et dans ces rocs sauvages
Qui pendent sur tes eaux.

Qu'il soit dans le zéphyr qui frémit et qui passe,
Dans les bruits de tes bords par tes bords répétés,
Dans l'astre au front d'argent qui blanchit ta surface
De ses molles clartés.

Que le vent qui gémit, le roseau qui soupire,
Que les parfums légers de ton air embaumé,
Que tout ce qu'on entend, l'on voit ou l'on respire,
Tout dise: Ils ont aimé!

(The Lake

Driven toward new shores, thus, uninterruptedly,
Carried away in the night without return or trace
On the ocean of ages will we never be able
To drop anchor at least a day?

Beloved lake! Hardly a year has passed by and here
Near your waves where we promised to meet again
Look! Alone and sad I come to sit on the stone
Where she sat last year.

You were roaring thus below these profound rocks,
Breaking against their ragged sides furiously,

And the wind was throwing thus the light foam of the waves
To her adored feet.

One eve, remember? we were rowing silently and speechless,
Over your waters and under the sky, not a single sound but
The splash of oars harmoniously stroking in cadence
Your floating waves.

Suddenly, odd sounds, unknown to this world,
Aroused the echoes of the enchanted bank;
The wave became attentive, and the voice, dear to me,
Cried out sadly:

"O time! stop your flight, and you, happy moments,
Stop your mad getaway;
Let us enjoy the temporal delights
Of our most beautiful days!

"Too many are the unhappy ones here that always implore you
Pass by swiftly for them;
Take away all of their pains with their lives,
Forget the happy ones!

"But in vain I ask still a few more moments;
Time evades.
I say to the night: 'Slow down!' and the dawn
Here comes to disperse the night.

"Let's love, then; O, let's love! These slippery moments
Let's hasten to enjoy.
Man has no harbor and time has no shores;
It flows; we pass by."

O time, shattered by jealousy, why do these unforgettable hours
In which love intoxicates us with unbound happiness,
Like days of misfortune and mourning, rapidly
Fly far away?

Can we not keep to the least their trace?
What! gone forever! are they totally lost?

Time that gave us, then ravished them,
Will not ever give us back?

Eternity, past life, nothingness, dark abyss,
Say! what do you do with the days that you relentlessly engulf?
Will you not give us back the sublime ecstasies
That you always ravish from us?

O lake, rocks, cave, obscured forest!
You who time treats with so much mercy,
Keep, at least, Nature, do not erase the memory
Of this brave night!

Let it be in your calm, in your storms,
And in the appearance of, O beautiful lake, your lavish hills,
And in the gloomy firs, and also in the giant rocks
That hang over you.

Let it be in the breeze that flies shiveringly,
In the whisper of your shores echoed from your shores,
In the silver-shining moon that floods you entirely
With a pleasant brightness.

Let the wind that moans, and the reed that sighs,
Let the scents spread in your balmy air,
Let all that we saw, heard, and breathed, say:
"Here they loved!")

Why did many Armenian writers translate Lamartine's works and, in particular, "The Lake"? The answer is clear. Because with his book, *Poetic Meditations*, Lamartine introduced a new breath into lyric poetry. The meditations carried the resonance of the author's personal voice; they brought a new daring and intimate nuance to the flat prose characteristic of his time. "The society," as Lamartine phrased once, "rather than a book, saw a human being." The mountain, the river, the sun, the moon, and the lake were not presented for their own sake—as Roucher or Saint-Lambert of the preceding generation had presented them—but rather for the impressions they left upon the author.

The French author Alfonse Daudet was another favorite of Armenian writers. T. Zakarian, a physician, translated *Tartarin de Tarascon* [Tartarin of

Tarascon] into Armenian in a volume he published in Tbilisi in 1891. Giurjian translated the same work in 1903. It appeared in the Armenian media three times: In Mihran Askanazian's *Bardez* weekly, in 1903–1904; in Suren Bartevian's *Tashink* [Alliance] daily of Smyrna, in 1912; and in *Arev* daily of Cairo, in 1965.

Dikran Gamsaragan not only was fond of Daudet, but also, perhaps, influenced by him. In 1893, he wrote in *Masis* weekly: "Daudet was the great sharpener of my senses and gradually became an inseparable friend. Moreover, he was, in particular, an adviser to whom I said nothing, but he told me everything."

Alfonse Daudet was the main representative of provincial literature. His first literary works were poems that he published in 1858 under the title, *Les Amoureuses* [Women in Love]. His masterpiece, *Lettres de mon moulin* [Letters from My Mill], was followed by a few plays in 1866. These made him famous and led to the publication of his epic work, *Tartarin de Tarascon.* Daudet wrote in a simple and natural manner. Zola, the French writer, in his eulogy at Daudet's funeral, stated: "Alfonse Daudet was an exception—sweet and lofty in French literature. He was unique—sweet but powerful—and he was born with vigor. That is, he felt and produced with an art in which every page will always express his emotions so long as our language lives."

The literature of adventure is a type of narrative literature. In adventures, the actions are developed using fast, successive events, combined often with improbable, accidental developments. Daudet intertwined his vibrant imagination, the action-filled theme, and characters with substance when he wrote *Tartarin de Tarascon.* He presented a detailed account of Tartarin's features, body language, and clothes, to such an extent that these components reflected Tartarin's inner self.

A summary of the work may lead one to believe that everybody who lived in Tarascon, near Avignon city in Bouches du Rhone province, was a hunter. Tartarin, a brave and cautious man of epic nature with well developed muscles, spent his Sunday mornings hunting caps. The rest of his time he divided between the club, the market square, and the shop of Costecalde the gunsmith, delivering justice to arguing hunters. Tartarin, who had not left his hometown until the age of forty-five, decided to quench his thirst for hunting and travel to Algeria to hunt lions. He had read stories of African travelers and he had trained himself to endure hunger, thirst, and other hardships. After filling his chests with guns and provision, he put on Algerian clothes and left Tarascon.

In the three episodes of the epic work, Daudet related Tartarin's adventures and failures. In one instance, Tartarin charged with a bear sword at porters whom he confused with pirates; in another instance, at night, from his hideout, he fired into a vegetable garden at every moving object, assuming they were Saharan lions, to only discover the following morning that he had killed a donkey. After a series of unfortunate events, while tearfully contemplating the consequences of a lost wallet and other matters, Tartarin suddenly saw a lion and within seconds shot it dead. Consequently, he was compelled to give everything he possessed to the owners of the blind and domesticated lion in order to save his skin. Nevertheless, the Tarasconians ceremoniously welcomed home their townsman upon his return.

In making this novel available to Armenian readers, Giurjian maintained the charm and power of the original work by reproducing it with its imagery intact. Only twenty-three or twenty-four years old at the time, he easily found the Armenian equivalents of rarely used words. This, prompted Mihran Askanazian[106] to write in his *Bardez* weekly: "The publication of Alfonse Daudet's famous satirical novel will appear in this weekly as a serial, in increments. The immortal author of this admirable jewel of French literature would have felt fortunate, no doubt, had he learned of its translation into Armenian by a translator who equally masters the two languages. The Benjamin of the Egyptian Armenian writers, indeed, translated it with great success, not so much because of his linguistic erudition, but rather because the work was commensurate with his sarcastic talent and nature. The editor expresses his pleasure and gratitude to Mr. Mikayel Giurjian, his kind friend and selfless contributor, for the worthwhile translation of this precious work."

In translating prose, Giurjian demonstrated the same linguistic precision, and employed the same skill of coining new words as he did in poetry. To render his translation more accessible to readers of all walks of life, Giurjian also explained French proper names or idioms in annotations or footnotes.

* * *

Aside from *Tartarin of Tarascon*, Giurjian translated Leopold Lalué's one-act comedy, *In the Spring*, in 1912, as well as twenty-year-old Daria Gamsaragan's short novel, *Blood Destiny* [Ariuni jagadakraganutiunê]. *In the Spring* was staged as a musical for the Armenian Constitutional Democrat Party, whereas *Blood Destiny* appeared in *Arev* daily.

GIURJIAN'S VIEWS AS LITERARY CRITIC

In addition to his literary works and translations, Giurjian authored many critical articles, book reviews, introductions to other writers' works, biographies of writers and artists, studies on literary works and authors, portraits, and much more.

Because he was a systematic reader and thus exposed to the principles of literary criticism and the richness of the international literary treasure, Giurjian continued the critical tradition of famous nineteenth century Eastern and Western Armenian literary activists: Krikor Odian, Sdepan Vosganian, Harutiun Svajian, Hagop Baronian, Arpiar Arpiarian, Leo, Manug Apeghian, Aleksandr Shirvanzaté, and others. He helped develop the artistic content and moral substance of literature through solid analysis, emphasizing, in particular, that literature should strive to educate the public and play an important role in the multifaceted intellectual progress of the people.

The Importance of Criticism and Its Lack amongst Us [Knnatadutean garevorutiunê yev anor bagasê mer mech] was one of Giurjian's noteworthy studies. He published this almost one-signature-long essay in *Shirag* magazine (June 1905, No. 5, pp. 439-453), using the following epigram: "Criticism is the science of art."

In the study, Giurjian extensively discussed the views of many critics, such as Nicolas Boileau, a member of the French Academy, a famous writer and critic, and author of *The Poetic Art*; or Charles Augustin Sainte-Beuve, another writer and critic and member of the French Academy. After praising good critics and pointing out the inevitable damage that faulty critics cause, Giurjian reflected upon Armenian criticism. He emphasized the lack of systematic criticism in Armenian literature despite the presence of a handful of noteworthy Western Armenian critics who had produced fine critical works. By admitting that he was a "very hard-to-please person in literature," he underlined the point that his favor could not be sought with regard to mediocre, a low quality literary works.

Giurjian dedicated another significant study, *The Novella Writer,* to Aleksandr Shirvanzaté, praising his merits. After opening with a proverb—"He who can do more, can do less also"—Giurjian referred to Balzac, Flaubert, Daudet, Maupassant, and Dickens. He stated: "Shirvanzaté, our great playwright and novelist, appears an equally skilled and perfect story teller in his short writings." Having read some of the "smaller works" of Shirvanzaté, as well as from his long works, Giurjian concluded that they represented "the style and craft of the artist."

He extensively analyzed Shirvanzaté's psychological sketch, *One of the New Ones* [Norerits megê], a psychological novella, *The Exiled from the Region* [Shrchanits ardaksvadzê], and the short story, *Precious Bond* [Tangakin gabank]. Giurjian included a wide range of citations in his study. In addition, he found that Kamalian, the main character of *One of the New Ones,* was the embodiment of the catastrophic effects of an undisciplined education, targeting only the mind while neglecting the body. Giurjian found this analogous to the foundation of the building, the character being its *culmination.*

While discussing *The Exiled from the Region,* Giurjian portrayed Shirvanzaté as a great observer of social manners and prejudices.

The Precious Bond was a moving presentation of the mutual love of a mother and son. The son, Smpad, was the only consolation Hripsimé had after losing her husband and another son. Smpad, feeling extremely pressured under his mother's constant watch, wanted to move to Europe. The poor mother—who repeatedly said, "I cannot live without you"—begged, wept, and retreated to her room sickened, convinced that no medicine could heal her. Giurjian was deeply touched and fascinated by the way Shirvanzaté expressed his ideas. He was also impressed by Shirvanzaté's use of description. Giurjian wrote: "There is a most beautiful scene here, and I cannot resist the temptation to reproduce it in its entirety." Consequently, he cited a fifty-line-long segment of the novella.

Shirvanzaté's work ends with the mother fainting as her Smpad departs. Frightened, he shouts: "Mother, mother!" The mother begs: "Don't leave; don't go!" And Smpad says: "Breaking this precious chain is impossible."

Giurjian phrased his praise: "A beautiful expression from the author that summarizes the subject and reveals the aesthetic moral of the story. It does not sound as false 'literature,' because the sentiments expressed rise from the well of a heartbreaking theme, completely immersed in its reality, and moist. 'The expression of sonly love to be kissed for.'"

In an essay, *The Novella Writer,* Giurjian testified: "Shirvanzaté presents himself in his 'short stories' with the double and intertwined properties of a novelist and a playwright. If his skills as a novelist are abridged in any way because of the mandatory reduction and abridgement of psychological, analytical, and descriptive parts—which can be extended only in the broad boundaries of a novel in accordance with the author's caprice and the demands of the theme—his powerful giftedness as dramaturge (as our

Russian Armenian brethren say) helps him, on the other hand, to a great extent. Because the novella is the expansion of an often short but impressive and emotional action where the quick and skillfully woven sequence of scenes and situations should result in 'a fatalistic' outcome (dénouement), an end that shocks the feelings or shakes the mind from its root. This end then is suddenly explained and often illuminated through the author's word, as dictated in theatrical lexicon."[107]

Although the book *Shirvanzaté and His Work* was a "literary banquet" that the Armenian writers of Turkey organized on the occasion of his jubilee, Simon Vratsian criticized it in *Azadamard* [Freedom Battle], calling the volume "a tombstone placed on sixteen of the seventeen authors of the volume, as well as on the subject, Shirvanzaté."

Responding to Vratsian in an article called *"Shirvanzaté and His Work* and His Critic,"[108] Vahan Tekeyan justified the anthology as an expression of reverence for the jubilee. He emphasized that considering it a tombstone was wrong, saying: "Three months ago, we met with Shirvanzaté in Tbilisi and he invited Chifté-Saraf and me to a club one night. Since his words were intended for all the writers who contributed to the volume dedicated to his honor, I have to mention here the joy and thankfulness the author of *For Honor* [Badvi hamar] expressed toward his Turkish Armenian brethren for the way they honored him, which, he said, was the most precious of all presents he had been offered on the occasion of his jubilee." Shirvanzaté added: "For me you have done something that never before has been done for any writer amongst us. You did hundred-fold more than what my Russian Armenian brethren have done, and I am thankful to you from the bottom of my heart."

It would be worthwhile to cite an excerpt from a letter that Shirvanzaté wrote to Dikran Gamsaragan: "The unwillingness of the Russian Armenian media was placed, from the beginning, on one wing of balance deciding my literary fate. On the other wing daringly rose the sincere affection of Turkish Armenians, which was particularly precious to me because Constantinople is closer than Tbilisi to Europe."

* * *

From his school days, Giurjian read and enjoyed Yervant Odian's writings, and Odian read Giurjian's *Mardig Agha* in the successive issues of *Nor Geank* without knowledge of the real identity of its author, Baruyr. In 1898 the two writers met for the first time, face to face, in Alexandria and became close friends. Their collaboration lasted almost twenty-eight years, being, as Giurjian phrased it, a friendship that turned "gradually closer, warmer, and more intimate, strengthened and sanctified by literary collaboration."

On the occasion of Odian's death, Giurjian expressed his distress in the article, "To His Memory" [Ir hishadagin], saying: "Today, an infinite void has opened in our literature."

Recalling his last meeting with the renowned satirist, Giurjian wrote: "My poor beloved friend had already received the last blow of the merciless ailment, which he was unable to defeat. Where had his inconsumable cheerfulness gone? His wonderful ability to smile and generate smiles? His comic enthusiasm so known to be able to revive even the most morbid joy, or his supply of tasty stories that never seemed to end?"

Deploring the loss of his vivacious, sincere, witty and joyful, close ideological associate, Giurjian testified: "The pain of the loss of my unforgettable friend very powerfully twitches inside me and I cannot talk about the writer without my blood turning cold. But there is no need to do so. Is there, amongst us, an author who has been more known, liked, and popular than Odian in the best sense of the word? His countless fans indiscriminately belong to all the classes of our people. From the ill-educated reader to the most delicate lover of fine literature and including the most hard-to-please writer, everybody feels today the irreplaceable loss our literature has suffered because of Odian's passing. Of course Odian's glory is secure as is his immortality—so long as the Armenian nation and language live—through the numerous works and several masterpieces he has left as lordly inheritance to our poor literature." Giurjian concluded: "He should have been allowed to continue to produce for many more years, bringing us greatest pleasure and for the sake and glory of Armenian literature."

* * *

Panchuni is an important work in Armenian literature. In it, Odian mocked and condemned the activities of the Socialists in Western Armenia.

Caricaturist Aleksandr Sarukhan, a close friend of both Odian and Giurjian, was deeply impressed by *Panchuni*. In 1931, he planned on republishing the work in a separate volume. After reading it again and poring over his impressions, he completed the caricatures in 1934. The illustrated masterpiece was published in 1938.[109]

Giurjian wrote the introduction for the volume upon Sarukhan's request. In it, he thoroughly analyzed the works of two masters: Odian for his satirical talent and international literary merit, and Sarukhan for his giftedness and caricaturistic grace. "The immortal Panchuni is the stereotype of an Armenian with stagnant mind. Despite its authentically Armenian characteristics, it belongs, in many aspects, to the greater human family, thus allowing him access to the universal gallery of famous characters. He takes his place next to the Spanish Don Quixote, the British Pickwick, and the French Tartarin."

Assessing Sarukhan's work, Giurjian stated: "The illustrations he drew are more expressive than any comment" and "they are wonderfully truthful, fraternal, and, at the same time, reflect the powerful personal seal Sarukhan stamped on Odian's masterpiece."

The work was the result of a combination of two artistic talents unprecedented in the history of Armenian printed books. Giurjian highlighted this event in a brief statement: "*Dzablvar* is the satirical masterpiece of Yervant Odian, and its illustration is the caricaturistic masterpiece of Al. Sarukhan."

In an article entitled "Sarukhan … As Seen by the Reader" [Sarukhan … êntertsoghin agnotsov],[110] Giurjian analyzed the gift and art of Sarukhan with regard to his ability to generate laughter, drawing parallels between him and Molière: "Sarukhan does not always exercise his sarcasm and caricatures without sadness, without bitterness." Giurjian also compared Sarukhan with Balzac, who "was never satisfied by noticing funny, despicable, and horrible characters exclusively; rather, next to them, he placed human beings who deserve to be loved, pitied, and admired."

When referring to Sarukhan's three books and journalistic essays that are full of thoughtful viewpoints, Giurjian asserted: "Today, Sarukhan deservedly continues the satiric work of his predecessors, Baronian and Odian, with the significant addition of caricature."

Giurjian wrote another article, "Sarukhan,"[111] in which he called Sarukhan a "multifaceted talent" as well as a "great talent" that was "fully defined." The author considered Sarukhan "an Armenian Daumier; that is, the prince of Armenian caricaturists, as Daumier was for the French." He added: "Sarukhan, of course, does not bring to mind the French giant with the style of his caricatures; but more so with regard to his creative power, inconsumable and stunning productivity, and in the flawless technique of his drawings." Indeed, Sarukhan ranked as one of the greatest caricaturists of the world, with his bright artistic gift, exceptionally sharp eye, and extraordinary wit—a meritorious and brave artistic creator who always carried his pencil and pen with him, to write down his thoughts and, particularly, to caricature.

* * *

The series of articles entitled *Honoré de Balzac* is the most extensive biographical and critical piece Giurjian ever wrote on writers and artists. It was published in increments in *Arev* daily from July 2 to September 3, 1949.

Honoré de Balzac was a thorough analysis of this renowned author's works, including biographical data and an evaluation of the significance of these works in the advancement and enrichment of world literature. Giurjian admitted that getting to know Balzac was "the greatest discovery of his intellectual-literary life, the others [great discoveries] being his acquaintance with [the works of] Shakespeare, Baudelaire, and our genius, the unmatched Indra (Diran Chrakian)."

When Giurjian read about the novel *Human Comedy*, his interest in Balzac was sparked. Consequently, he purchased and read Balzac's *Béatrix* in Alexandria when he was nineteen or twenty years old. A day later he acquired all the other novels by Balzac he could find and placed orders for those missing. Then he read the books more than once, "always finding new things, and always adding new reasons for contemplation and admiration."

Giurjian stated: "With his unique genius, Balzac lifted the novel from its abject position, renewed it, recreated it, drew its frames and boundaries, and established its rules, just as Corneille and Racine had done in the 17th century for the tragedy and Molière for the comedy."

Giurjian briefly discussed the state of the French novel before Balzac: the masterpiece of Marie de la Fayette, *La Princesse de Clèves*, which paved the road for the psychological novel (1678); Abbé Prévost's novel, *Manon Lescaut* (1731), which was a profound study of romantic passion; Benjamin Constant de Rebecque's famous psychological short novel, *Adolphe* (1806); "the poetic or epic novels and short novels of Chateaubriand, Hugo, Vigny, and Lamartine, and the so popular feuilleton-novels of Alexandre Dumas and Eugène Sue that entertained imaginations and horrified readers with unreal stories."

Regretfully, Giurjian mentioned that until 1830, Balzac wrote numerous novels and illusory, gloomy, or melodramatic stories under different pseudonyms that were unfit for his vocation and genius, because they were written "with bad style" and "unleashed imagination." Evidently, Balzac hastily produced volumes "full of unnatural characters and unreal events," neglecting all kinds of considerations with regard to taste, style, theme, and the "academic" matters of truth, simply because he needed the income with which to pay his debts.

Finally, in 1830, Balzac's true literary talents came to the front with the novel, *Les Chouans*.[112] The realist author was a knowledgeable and pensive artist with an analytical mind and creative brain. Armed with the rich knowledge of his century's sciences and trades, he played the role of historian and painter of human manners, willing to preach and lead the society. Giurjian wrote: "I would like to designate him as the greatest contemporary *master of the sciences of life*," because "Balzac's novels generate thoughts, make one contemplate life and all the major and minor issues concerning man and human society, without causing harm to the essential properties of a novel. The reader's attention is kept agitated and strained, the imagination captured, the senses impressed, and the emotions deeply moved. Had he not, the product would have become a didactic writing or a long sermon, deprived of body and soul and the warmth and beat of life."

Giurjian further stated: "One cannot read Balzac's novels without becoming rich and productive." He added: "As far as I know, there is no other example of a great writer in the literary history of all nations who has had so unsuccessful and so tragic a start. But also there is no other author who has miraculously matured, found his way, and stayed at the pinnacle of his vocation for such a short time—barely twenty years—and produced such a voluminous work and so many marvels."

Referring to the novelty of Balzac's themes, Giurjian said: "It was the first time ever that a novelist undertook to present, portray, and tell, with all their apparent and hidden facets, life among all the classes of a society, including the commoners, the peasants, the lower and middle bourgeoisies, and the wealthy and aristocrat classes."

Before, in the novels written from the 15th century on, the main characters belonged to the ruling class and, therefore, they lacked the elements needed to attract readers. Giurjian emphasized: "Balzac's work reflected contemporary society with all of its strata and classes. All characters were represented and their history, psyche, manners, traditions, and stages of life were the subject of his examination. They stirred hearts and charmed imaginations"—factors that are most important for a narrative work.

Giurjian regretfully wrote that Balzac did not enjoy the glory he deserved, and that he was not placed on the front line of French literature, next to the most glorious great ones at a time when, too often, almost unknown authors would suddenly attain fame with one sonorous article and find the road to glory stretching before them. In this regard, Giurjian blamed Sainte-Beuve, the prince of French critics, who, despite his great skill, delicate taste, and penetrating mind, did not reprimand his contemporary writers and acclaimed critics who thought ill of Balzac.

In Giurjian's view, the role of criticism, in addition to pointing out the merits and faults of a work, should be an enlightening guide for readers, acquainting them with new literary values. Giurjian also touched upon the opinions of many French critics, such as Hippolyte Taine and Edmond Jaloux. With a bold conviction Giurjian stated: "I dare to say that Balzac is for French literature what Shakespeare was for the English. He belongs to the group of geniuses who are unique not only in their, but rather in all nations' literature; geniuses such as the Italian Dante, the Spanish Cervantes, the English Shakespeare, and the German Goethe."

Giurjian cited the words of sorrow offered by the greatest and most glorious writer of the nineteenth century, Victor Hugo, before Balzac's coffin: "Alas! This powerful and diligent researcher, this philosopher, this thinker, this poet, this genius lived amongst us and experienced the storms, battles, and struggles common to the great personalities of all ages."

Giurjian went on: "The realistic and naturalistic schools have come forth directly from Balzac's works, irrefutably born of his influence." Flaubert, the Goncourts, Daudet, Maupassant, Zola, and others' works are considerably tiresome and boring, because they are written with suppressed imagination and moderated vigor. They are not created with Balzac's powerful brush and bright colors. They lack the aesthetical genius of a thinker and creator comparable with Balzac.

Giurjian demonstrated in this series of articles his prudence as a critic, his skill as a successful artist, and his deep knowledge of French literature.

* * *

Giurjian's friendship with Tekeyan began in 1903, when Parsegh Ohanian, Tekeyan's cousin, invited Tekeyan from Marseilles to Alexandria. The two writers most likely met in Constantinople, because they were both born and raised in Scutari and had read each other's work in the media.

They shared similar values, thoughts, ideas, literary preferences, and, in particular, a worship of meticulously crafted art created from original inspirations. These paved the ground for the close relationship between the two writers.

Giurjian often wrote about Tekeyan and his delicate literature, including the articles "Vahan Tekeyan's Life" [Vahan Tekeyani geankê], "Recollections" [Verhishumner], "Complaint" [Drdunchk]. Unfortunately, when Tekeyan published his first collection of poems in 1901 under the title *Solicitudes* [Hoker], Giurjian responded with a negative article entitled "A Poet Caught by Flu" [Harpkhod panasdeghdz mê]. Despite admitting that "Tekeyan was one of the most authoritative representatives of modern Armenian literature in Europe," and that he possessed "the evident signs of an authentic poet" and "the promise of future better works," Giurjian criticized Tekeyan's sentimentality and melancholy, attributing them to Baudelaire, Verlaine, Leconte de Lisle, Rodenbach, Rimbaud, Mallarmé, and Mirbeau. He found Tekeyan too influenced by romantic and symbolist writers. Giurjian himself had loved to read the works of these writers, which led him to despair when he was twenty and suffering a physical crisis. But that was before he changed his lifestyle and replaced these works with more uplifting literature. It is possible that Giurjian wrote his harsh, sarcastic article during this inner transformation. In a letter dated November 2, 1901, Tekeyan wrote a very curbed, polite letter that implied there was no need for such violent criticism: "The merciless article is the result of a haphazardly reading ... you will realize your mistake later, although you will admit it neither to your readers nor to me."

Indeed, two decades after Tekeyan's death, on June 30, 1965, Giurjian wrote of his regret in, "How I Made Vahan Tekeyan's Acquaintance" [Inchbes dzanotatsa Vahan Tekeyani hed]. This article appeared in *Arev* daily on July 15, 1965, twelve days after Giurjian's death. There, Giurjian expiated a sin he had committed as a young man by invoking mercilessly harsh criticism. Tekeyan's death was an occasion for Giurjian to mourn the disappearance of his "most beloved and precious friend." "A poet and journalist who was endowed with rare moral characteristics," whose death was "a great and irremediable loss for the Armenian nation and literature."

Giurjian praised the clear vision, righteousness, and bravery of the noble journalist. He commended the selfless work of the civic activist whom for more than forty years he befriended, shared ideas and penmanship with, and whom he regarded "a precious, irreplaceable friend of the mind and the heart."

In an article entitled "Complaint," which Giurjian published on the occasion of the fortieth day after Tekeyan's death, he commemorated "the prince of Armenian literature and journalism." He wrote: "It is the eternal Tekeyan that will live hereafter; shall live so long as the Armenian race and language are alive."

On May 10, 1963, on the eighteenth anniversary of Tekeyan's death, Giurjian emphasized in *Arev* daily: "Tekeyan had great influence on poetry, which is the favorite genre of Armenian literature for our young writers." He added: "Today, all the poets of the Armenian Diaspora are influenced more or less efficiently or profoundly by this poet, whose work was perfect in content and form."

Referring to Tekeyan's devoutness and patriotism, Giurjian considered "this unparalleled Armenian, this hero, who dedicated his entire life to beauty, which is the art and poetry, to the good, which is the love of nation and humanity, and to truth, which is the crowning of these two" a model, a guideline, and a source of inspiration. He suggested that all those serving or willing to serve the nation verbally, in writing, or by their works follow Tekeyan's example, because he loved his nation and the truth, he possessed civic valor. In particular, Tekeyan possessed a readiness to sacrifice, and a complaint-free dedication toward the service of his nation.

In his article, "Vahan Tekeyan's Life,"[113] Giurjian related that the talented poet, who lived much of his life deprived of the care and attendance of a mother, a sister, a wife, or a lover, felt proud and lucky to the end of his life, happy with the knowledge that he was a creative artist and a benevolent patriot who served the nation.

* * *

The evaluative report Giurjian submitted to the Patriarch of the Armenians in Jerusalem—the head of the Holy Translators' Turian Committee—with regard to Hagop Oshagan's study, *The Western Armenian Literature and Vahan Tekeyan* [Arevmdahay kraganutiunê yev Vahan Tekeyan], bears a unique weight of its own in terms of literary criticism. In it, after recognizing that criticism has never been a well-cultivated and developed genre in Armenian literature, he valued Oshagan's study as unique, valuable, and unprecedented. Never before had "a Western Armenian writer been subjected to such a complete, multifaceted, skilled, and detailed study," performed neither through the application of Hippolyte Taine's[114] 'purely objective plan and inclinations' nor Ferdinand Brunetière's[115] 'dogmatic objectives.' Rather, Oshagan's study was based on an initial sympathy toward Tekeyan as the best match to his ideal of a poet who had not been recognized as occupying the first class place his poetic talent and work made him worthy of."

Giurjian stated that Oshagan, the writer, critic, and man in possession of the sensitivity and expressions of an artist, was well versed in the works of the major representatives of Armenian and non-Armenian literature and the ideological trends of various literary schools. He "irrefutably had the necessary literary taste, skill, and baggage of readings" and chose Vahan Tekeyan the poet with affection and empathy. He "truthfully reflected his charms and mysteries" with numerous citations, comparisons, and contrasts to other works."

Sharing Oshagan's view that Tekeyan was a symbolist, Giurjian concluded: "Vahan Tekeyan is our most noble, sensitive, personal, and *perfect* poet," because he was endowed "with all the authentic properties and graces that are pertinent to and necessary for poets."

Referring to the theory of Edmond Jaloux, a French critic, that "every true poet is romantic, is born romantic," Giurjian pointed out that Tekeyan was the most classic amongst Armenian romantics with his exigency, taste, and instinctive balance and modesty. Tekeyan stayed away from corruption, rhetoric, harangue, and bragging, and had a deep, shuddering sensitivity, without excess lavishness and ostentation. According to Giurjian: "Indeed, Tekeyan is perhaps the only poet amongst us, who, except for some of his patriotic poems—where rhetoric is justifiable to a certain extent—has been exempt from the original sin of rhetoric. For this very reason one can compare him with 'artist' poets, such as Baudelaire, Mallarmé, Régnier, Moréas, Rodenbach, and even Verlaine who was less 'artist,' but the first to announce the new creed in his *Art Poetic,* 'Take eloquence and wring its neck!'"

Giurjian admitted that Oshagan was a talented, original writer with a great ability to express himself. Nevertheless, he concluded his report with some negative remarks about the complexity of Oshagan's language, his extreme use of parentheses and intermediary sentences, and the abundance of footnotes. He found Oshagan's contempt for Tovmas Terzian exaggerated and his evaluation of Reteos Berberian's valuable work, *Thoughts and Memoirs* [Khohk yev hushk] unfair.

* * *

Giurjian left behind numerous aphorisms on many writers, artists, and their creations: Hagop Baronian, Yeghia Demirjibashian, Yervant Odian, Shirvanzaté, Diran Chrakian, Reteos Berberian, Aleksandr Sarukhan, Vahan Malezian, Daria Gamsaragan, Hrant Antranigian, et al.

According to Giurjian, Baronian's life was a constant struggle against ill health and poverty. He lived poor and died of tuberculosis. Nevertheless, like Molière, he adhered to his vocation and gifted the people with his comedies and farces. Thanks to his humor and his ability to laugh and generate laughter, "Thalia, the Muse of comedy, inspired him throughout his life."[116]

In an article entitled, "The Spring Under the Pens of R. Berberian and Indra" [Karunê R. Berberiani yev Indrayi krchin dag], Giurjian evaluated Berberian's style of expression. After using in his initial works a language mixed with the elements of Ancient Armenian, Berberian eventually purified his language and came to use words so elegant, harmonious, rich, and precise that "they could serve as example and guide to many modern writers inclined to disfigure and distort the beautiful modern Armenian language that many generations of talented writers, from 1880 and on, began and continued to build, shape, and develop to almost perfection."

Giurjian also praised the best of the free verse and spiritual poetry of Yeghia Demirjibashian. He commented that Demirjibashian wrote with emotions and sighs drawn from the bottom of his heart "with an intense dash... inspiration, enthusiasm, and self-gushing abundance."[117]

Giurjian had nothing but admiration for Diran Chrakian, whom he considered the greatest Armenian artist-poet-thinker, and whose *Inner World* "reached an unparalleled summit in Armenian literature, shining with eternal glory."

He stated that Diran Chrakian "was the greatest Armenian genius, our most 'universal' genius in a European sense, and our greatest artist-poet-thinker." Like Goethe did in *Faust*, Chrakian "mixed philosophy and art in *Inner World*," underlined Giurjian, who regretfully added that we would have had "a new Chrysostom, a second Naregatsi" had Chrakian continued to walk in the same path. But: "Alas, we had a common *Sabbatarian* who became the victim of the religion he preached. He died after killing in himself Indra, the genius poet. I do not know what was Jehovah's gain in this sacrifice, but I do know that Armenian literature suffered a huge, irremediable loss."[118]

* * *

"Withdrawing from Literature" [Hrazharumn i kraganutené] is an interesting article Giurjian published first in the *Hayasdani Gochnag* weekly and then in *Arev* daily. The article stemmed from a report Giurjian read in a French magazine on George Moore, who had decided to bid literature farewell after his last publication. Giurjian was skeptical. He doubted Moore could stay firm in his decision, and he wrote: "Those who have begun to write obeying a powerful inner drive will continue to write, more or less regularly, so long as they live. Often, they will write even before the ghost of death, if not with the futile hope of pushing it back, at least to increase their chance for literary immortality."

To support his opinion, Giurjian offered as evidence Bedros Turian, who wrote "his most *inspirational* poem, that alone was enough to eternalize his name in Armenian literature" when as a young man he had reached the gate of death and, naturally, the "foams" of the "bottom" of his soul gushed out with a sublime gush. "George Moore, however, is aged, has produced many works, has said whatever he had to say. In a word, he is consumed by writing."

Giurjian thought that if the British writer indeed retreated from the arena, broke his pen, and stopped writing forever, his actions "would indicate the extreme diminution of vitality in him; a sort of physiological inability, because, in reality, for a person born to be a writer, writing is a way of life, an expression of life—a way and an expression appropriate and favorable to his disposition and nature more than anything else."

In literature, Giurjian referred to two rare phenomena of people who did retire from writing: Arthur Rimbaud in French literature and Diran Chrakian in Armenian. Both were promising writers, even geniuses; nevertheless, they abandoned literature when the devil of art and literature left their souls. Rimbaud was driven by the frenzy of wealth accumulation when he was twenty. Chrakian, after presenting marvelous poetic masterpieces such as the *Inner World* and *Cypress Grove* [Nojasdan], dedicated himself to preaching God's Word.

Giurjian emphasized that writers and artists create because they feel a powerful inner vocation: "Once the sacred fire burns inside a man, only death extinguishes it." As evidence, he related the case of the French painter, August Renoir. Reputedly, Renoir arranged, right before dying, to have a palette fixed on his paralyzed hand so he could try to paint.

In a critique of Daria Gamsaragan's *Voyage avec une ombre* [Travel with a shadow], a psychoanalytical novel written in French, Giurjian reaffirmed the truth of the inner vocation. He testified that Daria, the famous artist and original sculptor who had tried a multitude of genres at a young age—poetry, music, painting, and sculpture—"never severed her ties with literature, which was her first love from the beginning. She loved to write and never ceased to do so. Her first and second novels to which she is getting ready to add a successor are proof of this."

Daria[119] was the cousin of writer Dikran Gamsaragan and daughter of Armenag Gamsaragan. She was a talented sculptor who won the gold prize at the international exhibit of Paris in 1937. She was acclaimed for her sculptures *The Nude Man, The Cry, The Christ, Eve, The Pretender, The Woman with the Pitcher, Lotus, Don Quixote,* and *Salute to Peace.* She was only twenty when she wrote an emotional novel, *Blood Destiny,* in which the main character was a sculptor. Giurjian translated and published this novel in *Arev* daily, while Arshag Chobanian highly praised it in his magazine, *Anahid.*

* * *

In his article on contemplations and spiritual reflections selected from Hrant Antranigian's book,[120] Giurjian presented a thorough analysis of the thoughts that have troubled this diarist. Hrant was one of the three sons of Mgrdich Antranigian, a founder of the Armenian General Benevolent Union. Though Hrant suffered from a physical misfortune, his diary was free of references to his physical condition. "The analyses carry the stamp of a developed erudite and bright-sighted mind," wrote Giurjian.

The small book, rich with interesting daily thoughts that are adorned with virtues, expressed determination rather than depression, optimism as opposed to pessimism, and a sense of satisfaction rather than complaint. It revealed Antranigian's erudition and the prudence of a sensitive analyzer who observed the soul with thoughtful examination and logical interpretation. Giurjian asserted that the author had alert thoughts about life, happiness, joy, sadness, love, and, in particular, misfortune, because Giurjian's inner world itself suggested to him that to love was essential, whereas to be loved was secondary. To be loved depended on another person. The unfortunate person is not one who is not loved, but rather one who does not know loving, because human love brings happiness.

* * *

Giurjian's article, "Thoughts on Mr. Vahan Malezian's 'Album'" [Khorhrtadzutiunner B. Vahan Maleziani "Hushamadean"i aritov], which was published in *Hayasdani Gochnag,* is interesting in terms of literary criticism. Giurjian reflected upon the memoirs of the famous French writer Marcel Proust, *À la Recherche du Temps Perdu* [Remembrance of Things Past], analyzing his own and other peoples' emotions. He then moved on to examine the memoirs of historian and chronicler Philippe de Comines about King Charles VIII and Louis XI, then Jean Jacques Rousseau's *Confessions,* poet Alfred Vigny's *Diary,* Joseph Renan's *Memoirs,* and the memoirs or autobiographies of François Chateaubriand and other statesmen, activists, clergymen, actors, and writers of historic and literary merit.

Giurjian regretfully stated: "Our literature has had a great lack and deficiency from the beginning: it is a field left almost completely barren. In the likeness of foreign literatures, certain literary genres have been more or less successfully developed amongst us—poetry, comedy, novel, novella, and even drama—however, and painfully, the genre of the memoir has been neglected, even while it flourished in European and particularly in French literature since the 13th and 14th centuries." Searching for the reason behind this absence, Giurjian wrote: "The life of Armenians from the 18th century on—in Turkey alone—has been full of most important events: intellectual renaissance, revolutionary activities, disasters engulfing the entire nation." He went on to refer to Arpiarain as "a great writer as having the dough of a true memorialist." Arpiarian's chronicles and articles, published over the course of years under the titles "The Day's Life," "Obituary," and "Pages of Contemporary History" [Zhamanagagits badmutean echer], are documentaries and memoirs about his times and Armenian life that provide substance for future historians.

To Giurjian, Yervant Odian's *Twelve Years Outside Constantinople* also was a valuable memoir, thanks to the author's sharp memory and tasteful narration. Unfortunately, Giurjian himself did not leave memoirs or works of a more autobiographical nature, which would have also contained valuable facts about his contemporaries.

With regard to Malezian's other book, *Past Days: An Album of the Literary Matinees of Kadi-Köy* [Antsadz orer—Hushamadean Kadi-Köyi kragan yereguytneru], Giurjian designated it as an interesting work, because most of it "is dedicated to reproducing haphazardly composed pages read today with much pleasure and interest." In reality, the book is an anthology of questions and answers and puns, in the form of rhymed free verse that representatives of Constantinoplean Armenian literature and media spent time producing during their literary matinees.

Giurjian, the writer and philologist, left us with a rich heritage of critical articles, literary portraits of writers and artists, book reviews, aesthetical writings, and literary studies, with the evidence of a skilled critic and erudite artist in every one of them. He was well versed in international literature, and he possessed the temperament of an impartial critic. As a researcher of vanguard concepts, Giurjian tried to develop the Armenian culture and, in particular, literature, thereby contributing to the intellectual progress of his people.

GIURJIAN AS SKILLFUL NEOLOGIST

Study of Giurjian's manuscripts reveals that he was meticulous about the purity of the Armenian language and the precision of words in a given context.

Not only was he an erudite lexicologist, but also a dexterous creator of phrases and new words, whether derivative or complex. From the Golden Age of Armenian culture in the fifth century to the present, Armenian literature counts numerous writers and philologists who created new, complex words by joining two root words and suffixes or prefixes to one another. However, none of Giurjian's contemporaries used as many new words as Giurjian did.

Although not a lexicologist by profession, nor a linguist who made the study of word roots and semantics his profession, Giurjian was a conscientious chooser and user of words.

In an article entitled "Flipping Through Dictionaries" [Pararan tghtadelov],[121] he stated through a rhetorical question: "Flipping through dictionaries has been a long favorite hobby of mine. The writer should be a lover of words before being … a lover of glory, shouldn't he?"[122] He mentioned that dictionaries contain, along with many very popular words, a handful of very useful words generally limited to high-level conversations or literature, and as such are destined to remain at the bottom of dictionaries, away from attention or utilization. An example of such a word is *khapegha*, which etymologically means a fake or cheating monk. He added: "This is a wonderful pun that reflects our ancestors' wit, especially since the word can be used as a synonym to *khapepa* [cheater]."

In the same article, Giurjian listed the word *gardzekhos* for a person who thinks he is talking, but in reality he is babbling. In its likeness, Giurjian created a new word, *gardzekir* [one who thinks he is writing]; that is, those who add the sin of writing to their sin of talking. "Let this word be from me," he wrote.

The Armenian language has the great advantage of easily creating new words by adding suffixes or prefixes to a root word. This advantage has helped writers and philologists create and use new words. The coinage of new words continues to contribute to the progress of the Armenian language, whether in Armenia or across the Diaspora.

Giurjian was a neologist who loved to use new, unusual words. In Armenian, for example, there are many complex words made from the root *nor* [new], such as *norakiud* [newly discovered], *noradzak* [newly risen], *norabsag* [newly wed], etc. Similarly, Giurjian created the word *norasdats* [newly received], which cannot be found in the works of other writers.

Hrasheg [as red as fire] is a popular word in Armenian. Giurjian, however, preferred to use the word *adrasheg,* the root of which (*adr* = fire) is no longer used in colloquial or written Armenian.

The verb *ayoyel* [to say yes, to accept] is another word Giurjian created and often used in his works. It is neither found in dictionaries, nor has it become popular in colloquial or literary language.

In his article entitled, "Let's Protect and Enrich Our Mother Language" [Bahbanenk yev harsdatsnenk mayrenin], Baruyr Sevag stated: "The Armenian language has prospered throughout centuries not by its own means alone; it has also been enriched through necessary loans."[123] Sevag proved through his works that "the Armenian language, for example, has an advantage that a few other languages of the world have: the ease and flexibility of coining words. And if any language, even a language richer and more flexible than Armenian, ought to borrow words because of the scarcity of the possibilities for coinage, then a language like the Armenian ought to Armenianize such a word, because, as a general rule, the foreign word says much less to Armenians than the successful coinage of a word in their mother tongue."[124]

Giurjian opposed the use of foreign words and avoided foreign borrowings. Instead, when writing or translating, he searched for the equivalents of foreign words or created their Armenian counterparts, often placing the foreign word next to them in parentheses.

After meeting with Giurjian at the offices of *Arev* daily and discussing matters of word coinage, Sarukhan wrote an article entitled, "Mikayel Giurjian as Talented Word Coiner" [Mikayel Giurjian daghantavor paragerd], mentioning that in response to his question, Giurjian recalled about twenty new words he has authored.

The two intellectuals had agreed to expand upon the subject in future discussions, but their intention remained unfulfilled because of Giurjian's death.

In addition to creating new words, Giurjian enjoyed reviving rarely used words, or making a noun from a verb or an adjective, or changing a simple word into a complex one.

EPILOGUE

Mikayel Giurjian the writer, during the eighty-six years of his life, adored his people, walked the road of popularity, adhered to new literary principles, and supported all that was progressive in arts and literature. He followed in the footsteps of the worthy representatives of the realistic writers of the 1880s, and defended the aesthetic fundamentals of the realistic school, enriching Armenian literature with valuable and high-quality works of art. He amalgamated the national with the universal without weakening national individuality, and yet remained loyal to the principles of truthful and holistic mirroring of reality.

Giurjian selflessly served the Armenian people and culture. He masterfully and aesthetically portrayed real people and environments, without covering their ugly and unpleasant facets, always striving to portray the full aspects of an object or a person.

Although some of Giurjian's works have been included in textbooks as exemplary samples,[125] not a single monograph has been dedicated to his life and work.

In 1914–1915, in his two-volume textbook, *History of Armenian Literature,*[126] teacher, philologist, linguist, and writer Hovhannes Kazanjian presented Giurjian as one of the meritorious figures of Armenian culture, deeming the study and teaching of his life and works in Armenian schools appropriate.

Kurken Mkhitarian, on the other hand, in his work *A Quarter Century of Literature* [Karort tar kraganutiun] (Cairo, 1946), and Garo Sasuni in his book, *History of Modern Western Armenian Literature* [Badmutiun arevmdahay arti kraganutean] (Beirut, 1951), ignored Giurjian's name, whereas Father Mesrob Janashian in his textbook, *Concise History of Modern Era Armenian Literature* [Hay kraganutean nor shrchani hamarod badmutiun] (Venice, 1973), mentioned Giurjian simply as the co-author of Odian's play, *Heroic Game,* and co-editor of *Shirag* magazine with Tekeyan.

There is no doubt that the critics in Armenia will remedy this negligence and that Giurjian will eventually assume the place he deserves next to his colleagues of the pen.

Being well versed in international literature, and particularly familiar with the works of French classical, romantic, naturalist, and symbolist authors (Corneille, Molière, Bossuet, Racine, La Fontaine, Boileau, La Bruyère, Voltaire, Chateaubriand, Stendhal, Lamartine, Hugo, Vigny,

Musset, Sainte-Beuve, George Sand, Balzac, Mérimée, Zola, Baudelaire, Verlaine, Rimbaud, and Mallarmé), Giurjian enriched Armenian literature with his original works. He adhered to the fundamentals of realism. He kept his distance from surrealism, cubism, existentialism, unanimism, fantasism, Dadaism, modernism, and all other -isms.

Thanks to his realistic beliefs, Giurjian created such unforgettable characters as Mardig Srmakeshian and Levon Surian in *Mardig Agha*; the couple Iknadios and Zaruhi Rupinian, Anahid and Parunag Bey, Setrag Eliasian and barber Onnig in *"The National Activist," or the Greatness and Fall of Mr. Iknadios Rupinian*; Kapriel Totvanian and Suren Srabian in *The Salvation*; Unbaptized Tumig, Unlucky Janig, Barman Sercho, and Uncle Hovsep in *Heroic Game*; Artin and Yevpimé in *Franco-Turkish War, or Charshêlê Artin Agha*; Aram, Surpig, and Makruhi in *The Tribute*, and many more.

Most of Giurjian's characters are simple people rooted in the womb of the society and struggling to live under harsh circumstances.

Endowed with a great ability to observe and examine, and knowing well the driving forces behind life and human relations, Giurjian successfully revealed the connection between individuals and societies and between dispositions and actions. Not only did he truthfully portray life, but he also created characters that carried in them the power of popularity. The most striking and essential characteristic of Giurjian's literary heritage is the authentic projection of real life, people, objects, and events. True, Giurjian did not bring us the riches of Balzac's three thousand characters, nor the diversity of the more than twelve hundred characters Émile Zola portrayed in his series of twenty naturalistic novels under the collective title, *Les Rougon-Macquart*. However, Giurjian graced the altar of Armenian literature with many hundreds of characters, each with unique properties and original characteristics.

Remaining loyal to ancient Armenian customs and traditions, Giurjian pictured in his works the life that he examined thoroughly. For this reason, his works generated active interest amongst readers and gained him popularity within the broadest layers of Armenian society.

People read Giurjian with pleasure, because he meticulously reflected reality, described people and events with profound emotion, expressed sorrows and joys skillfully, while conjoining sadness with laughter and suffering with cheerfulness.

Giurjian's literary legacy is charming, educative, and original. He kept pace with international and national innovations and the new and progressive literary tendencies of his day.

Giurjian's works are characterized by their keenness and ideological content, authentic descriptions and genuine manners, metaphoric thoughts and artistic merits, good-natured sarcasm and original wit, simple style and polished language.

Giurjian's inner world is all-inclusive. At the core of his writings are the pressing issues and the real lives of the people of his time. His works are instructive and noteworthy. They carry the emphasis of a delicate style and meticulously purified language.

Giurjian's numerous translations, scattered throughout various magazines and newspapers, present him as a skilled translator who possessed a fine aesthetic giftedness.

Cognizant of the sublime social value of satire, Giurjian played an instrumental role in popularizing literature and establishing the realistic school, thus immortalizing his name and works.

With his works addressing the most burning issues of his time, Giurjian deserves place amongst those who continued the tradition established by the great Baronian. Armenian literature and criticism are obliged to keep Giurjian's torch burning, because he was endowed with unarguable creative talent, literary mastery, a fine and natural sarcastic gift, and superb aesthetic taste.

Annotations

1 *Bardi* in Armenian means "owes." One of Giurjian's successful puns.

2 *Arev*, July 9, 1965.

3 *The Salvation*, the realistic drama that Gamsaragan and Giurjian authored together.

4 Teotig, *Amenun Daretsuytsê* [Everybody's Almanac], Constantinople, 1910, fourth year, p. 120.

5 Teotig, *Amenun Daretsuytsê*, Paris, 1928, p. 468.

6 Vahan Malezian, *The End of My Path* [Jampus dzayrê], Vol. II, *Olden Letters and Literary Relics* [Hnatroshm namagner yev kragan nshkharner], Paris, 1955, p. 59.

7 Speaking of Oshagan's high demands, Kurken Mkhitarian says: "His eyes capture the disfigurations first, before looking for beautiful things. In general, he has no admiration—the sickness of our century. He has no friendship—the exchange of our days. For these reasons, he first sees the deformed, and only establishes the solid portion later, if he finds it." *A Quarter Century of Literature* [Karort tar kraganutiun], Cairo, Husaper Publishing, 1946, p. 178.

8 Hagop Oshagan, *Armenian Literature* [Hay kraganutiun], Jerusalem, 1942, p. 565.

9 Yervant Odian, *Collected Works* [Yergeri zhoghovadzu], Vol. IV, Yerevan, 1962, p. 134.

10 Ibid., p. 134.

11 Ibid., p. 301.

12 Ibid., p. 533.

13 Yervant Azadian, *Fixations in Literature and Fine Arts* [Kragan kegharvesdagan severumner], La Vern, California, a publication of the Armenian International College, 1988, 333 pages.

14 Mikayel Giurjian, *Twenty Years Later; The Franco-Turkish War Continues or the Victory of Mrs. Yevpimé; Stories and Images* [Ksan dari yedk; Franko-trkagan baderazmê gê sharunagvi gam digin Yevpiméi haghtanagê; badmvadzkner yev badgerner], Beirut, Sevan Press, 1961, 100 pages.

15 *Diary and Notes* [Orakrutiun yev nshumner], M. S. Giurjian's archive, Museum of Literature and Arts of Armenia.

16 *Zhamanag* [Time] daily, Istanbul, May 8, 1911.

17 Bartevian Suren, *Yekibdahay Daretsuytsê*, 1914, p. 198.

18 Ibid.

19 Reteos Berberian's letter of November 16, 1904 to M. Giurjian.

20 Bartevian Suren, *Yekibdahay Daretsuytsê*, 1914.

21 Yervant Azadian inherited these books from Giurjian. He shipped some to Armenia and donated the rest to the library of Dikran Yergat Club in Alexandria.

22 Yervant Azadian wrote: "On the occasion of Giurjian's death I had published a special issue of *Arev* that included Giurjian's apology to Tekeyan for the harsh critique he wrote in *Paros* [Lighthouse] in 1901, on the occasion of the publication of Tekeyan's first work, *Solicitudes* [Hoker]. There, Giurjian described how he wanted to be like the poets Turian and Medzarents by depriving himself of light and sun, and opening himself to tuberculosis. One day, when he found blood in his saliva, he went to the doctor who advised him to take long walks in the open air. By doing so, he returned to life and in his intense emotions as a new convert, he found something sick, 'flu-like' in Tekeyan's first book. The entire issue of *Arev* is included in the book *Tekeyan's Letters* [Tekeyani namagani] that Avedis Sanjian published."

23 *From Mikayel S. Giurjian's Letters to Doctor Harutiun Tireakian,* published in *Baykar* [Struggle], Watertown, MA, July 25, 1965.

24 Ibid.

25 An excerpt from a letter Giurjian wrote to Doctor Harutiun Tireakian in November 1908 and the copy of which his son Mihrtad Tireakian sent to me from New York.

26 Yervant Odian, *Collected Works*, Vol. IV, Yerevan, 1962, p. 378.

27 Levonian compiled his work based on memory, oral information, and written notes. It was published postmortem, in *Works* [Yerger], Yerevan, 1963.

28 Karekin Levonian, *Works*, Yerevan, 1963, p. 471.

29 Ibid., p. 478.

30 Ibid., p. 458.

31 Arsen Ghazigian, *Armenian Bibliography and Encyclopedia of Armenian Life* [Haygagan madenakidutiun yev hanrakidaran hay geanki], Vol. II, Venice, St. Lazar, 1912, column 1319.

32 Yervant Msrlian, the editor of *Savarnag* [Airplane] satirical weekly, wrote to me in his letter of April 18, 1967, that these short stories were published by using the same galleys prepared for *Arev* daily, and that only the book's cover was printed by Vosgedar Press.

33 The name Srjep A. was misspelled in *Spiurk* as Arjep A.

34 *Arev* daily, July 15, 1965. Published postmortem.

35 I received a copy of this letter from the doctor's son, Mihrtad Tireakian of New York.

36 Giurjian translated for the festival Leopold Lalué's *In the Spring* comedy, which, adapted as a musical fantasy, was staged in Alexandria on March 1912.

37 *Shirvanzaté and His Work*, Constantinople, 1911, pages 91–110.
38 *Mshag* was published from 1872 to 1921. The founder and the editor of the first twenty years was Krikor Ardzruni, a reporter, critic, and social activist.
39 Eozhen Papazian, *Autobiography and Memoirs* [Inknagensakrutyun yev husher], p. 5.
40 Suren Bartevian, *Yekibdahay Daretsuytsê*, 1914, pp. 88–95.
41 Ibid, pp. 29–32.
42 Suren Bartevian, *Yekibdahay Daretsuytsê*, Cairo, 2nd year, 1915, pp. 64–72.
43 *Nor Geank*, London, Vol. I, No. 20, October 15, 1898, p. 308.
44 Ibid., p. 308
45 Ibid., p. 309.
46 Ibid.
47 Ibid., Vol. II, March 15, 1899, p. 95.
48 Ibid., p. 94.
49 Yervant Odian, *Collected Works*, Vol. IV, Yerevan, 1962, p. 132.
50 Ibid., p. 134.
51 Suren Bartevian, *Yekibdahay Daretsuytsê*, 1914, first year, Cairo, p. 211.
52 Yervant Odian, *Collected Works*, Vol. IV, Yerevan, 1962, p. 132.
53 Ibid., p. 133.
54 Ibid., pp. 133–134.
55 Ibid, pp. 135.
56 *Nor Geank*, Vol. I, No. 22, November 15, 1898, p. 345.
57 Ibid., p. 346.
58 Ibid.
59 Ibid., No. 23, December 1, 1898, p. 361.
60 Ibid., No. 20, October 15, 1898, p. 307.
61 Ibid., Vol. II, No. 5, March 1, 1899, p. 79.
62 Yervant Odian, *Collected Works*, Vol. IV, Yerevan, 1962, p. 135.
63 *Modén bak* is half Armenian and half Turkish phrase, meaning "watch from close."
64 *Arev* daily, Cairo, December 27, 1963.
65 *Shirag*, Constantinople, 1909, No. 2, p. 72.
66 Reference to the fake Constitution the Ottoman government declared on July 11, 1908.
67 Andonian resorted here to a pun. In Armenian, the word *hasaragutiun* means both "public" and "banality."
68 *Kharazan* weekly, Vol. I, No. 4, February 28, 1909, p. 59.
69 Shahnazar Keotahian, *Memoirs and Notes* [Husher u nisher], Los Angeles, 1990, p. 165.
70 *Arev* daily, May 22, 1964. The letter was dated April 7, 1964.

71 *Hayrenik* [Fatherland] monthly, 1927, Vol. V, No. 8(56), p. 50.
72 Yervant Odian, *Collected Works*, Vol. I, Yerevan, 1960, p. 687.
73 Ibid., p. 714.
74 *Arev* daily, December 27, 1963.
75 *Shirag* literary and social monthly, Alexandria, 1905, Vol. I, No. 2, pp. 101–112.
76 Avedis Sanjian, *Vahan Tekeyan's Letters*, Los Angeles, 1983, p. 174.
77 Ibid., p. 189.
78 Hagop Oshagan, *Armenian Literature* [Hay kraganutiun], Jerusalem, 1942, p. 404.
79 *Hay Gin*, semimonthly magazine, Vol. III, No. 6, January 16, 1922, p. 867.
80 Baruyr Sevag, *Collected Works*, Vol. V, Yerevan, 1974, p. 52.
81 Yervant Azadian, *Fixations in Literature and Fine Arts*, La Vern, California, 1988, pp. 65–76.
82 *Arev* daily, Cairo, July 9, 1965.
83 Vahan Tekeyan, *Collected Works*, Cairo, Vol. IX, pp. 66–71.
84 *Masis* periodical, Constantinople, Vol. XCIV, fifth cycle, No. 2, January 10, 1904, p. 19.
85 This French word means "demonstration" or "show."
86 *Kharazan* [Whip] satirical daily, Constantinople, Vol. I, No. 9, March 25, 1909, pp. 68–69.
87 *Dzaghig* [Flower] weekly, Constantionple, February 21, 1904, Vol. XVII, No. 8 (592), pp. 105–106.
88 Chrakian wrote this letter to Giurjian from Scütari on November 27, 1909.
89 Teotig, *Amenun Daretsuytsê*, Constantinople, 1909, Vol. 3, pp. 278–279.
90 *Arev* daily, Cairo, May 14, 21, 28, and June 4, 1949.
91 This poem, dedicated to Vahan Tekeyan, is published in the AGBU's *Husharar-Miutiun* [Reminder-Unity] periodical in 1925, in *Amenun Daretsuytsê*, and other Armenian periodicals.
92 Yervant Azadian testifies: "This assertion is authentic and true literally, because during the period Giurjian authored these lines, his lover had found another love, taking Giurjian in the web of a tripod. With a strange altruism, Giurjian was happy that his lover was happy ... though with someone else. It is difficult to penetrate into the depths of this romantic-sexual triangle, lest we ignore the circulating rumors and gossips."
93 *Arev* daily, Cairo, November 4, 1960.
94 *Zvartnots* monthly of literature and arts, Paris, new period, Vol. 5, No. 5–6, p. 14.
95 *Arev* daily, Cairo, August 21, 1965.
96 Yervant Odian, *Collected Works*, Vol. IV, Yerevan, 1962, p. 362.

97 *Shirag* literary, political, and social magazine, Alexandria, 1905, No. 1, p. 2.

98 *Arev* daily, Cairo, June 23, 1965.

99 *Miutiun* monthly official publication of the AGBU, Vol. I, No. 7, July 1912, p. 102.

100 *Miutiun* monthly, Vol. I, No. 6, June 1912.

101 The header presents a pun. It dissects the Armenian word for cannon, to leave the impression that the notes are as resonant as the cannons.

102 Arpiar Arpiarian, *History of the Nineteenth Century Turkish Armenian Literature*, Cairo, 1944, p. 83.

103 *Six French Poets of the Nineteenth Century*, edited by E. H. and A. M. Blackmore. Oxford University Press, 2000, pp. 165–166.

104 Hovhannes Tumanian, *Collected Works*, Vol. VI, Yerevan, p. 152.

105 *Arev* daily, Cairo, June 15, 1963.

106 Mihran Askanazian, a scholar of Ancient Armenian and a pedagogue, published the weekly *Dzaghig Mangants* [Children's Flower] in Constantinople. Before he was compelled to leave Constantinople in 1896 and move to Alexandria to teach at Boghosian School, he buried his manuscripts and papers in the garden of the Turkish Fuad Bey in the Jevizlik quarter of Kadiköy.

107 *Shirvanzaté and His Work* [Shirvanzaté yev ir kordzê], an anthology, Constantinople, 1911, pp. 93–94.

108 *Shant* [Thunderbolt] illustrated literary and art semimonthly magazine, Vol. I, No. 19, May 1912, pp. 311–312.

109 Yervant Odian, *Comrade P. Panchuni in Dzablvar and Vasburagan* [Ênger Panchuni Dzablvari yev Vasburagani mech], caricatures by Al. Sarukhan, Cairo, Sahag-Mesrob Press, 1938, 248 pages.

110 *Arev* daily, Cairo, April 11, 1962.

111 Ibid., April 4, 1964.

112 The Chouans were French rebels Jean Chouan led against the Bourbon kings.

113 *Arev* daily, Cairo, April 6, 1949.

114 Hippolyte Taine (1828–1893) based his critical theories on the unity of race, milieu, and moment.

115 Ferdinand Brunetière (1849–1906) implemented the theory of the evolution of literary genres in his studies.

116 Thalia is one of the three countenances (Agalé, Thalie, and Euphrosyne) of the sculpture *Three Goddesses* by the French sculptor Philon (1573–1590). They personify the most charming elements of beauty.

117 "On the Occasion of a Handwritten Poem by Yeghia Demirjibashian" [Yeghia Demirjibashiani még tserakir kertvadzin aritov], *Armenian Literature*, Smyrna, Vol. 1, June 14, 1912, No. 12, pp. 11–15, or *Armenian Rattle*, Vol. 29, No. 1, January 1929, pp. 12–14.

118 "The Spring Under the Pens of R. Berberian and Indra," *Arev* daily, Cairo, May 2, 1964.

119 Daria Gamsaragan was born in Alexandria in 1907. In 1924, she moved to Paris. She engaged herself in sculpture with the Russian sculptor Gonsdan who lived in Egypt. In Paris, Daria apprenticed to Émile Antoine Bourdelle (1861–1929), a famous French sculptor who created the statue *Hercules* that stands on General Alvear's mausoleum.

120 *Arev* daily, Cairo, 10–11 April, 1964.

121 Ibid., March 19, 1963.

122 Giurjian uses a pun here. In Armenian, "lover of word" is *paraser* and "lover of glory" is *paraser.*

123 Baruyr Sevag, *Collected Works*, Vol. V, Yerevan, 1974, p. 152.

124 Ibid.

125 Giurjian's *The Scribe's Dream* and *The Café* are published in the first volume of the fourth revised edition of A. Biberjian's *A Taste of Modern Armenian Literature* [Jashag arti hay madenakrutean] (Constantinople, 1910, pp. 313–319 and 336–340). The *New Dress* and *The Scribe's Dream* are included in Oshagan's textbook, *Armenian Literature* (Jerusalem, 1942), the first in the first volume with minor abridgements (pp. 217–218), and the second in the second volume (pp. 563–565).

126 Hovhannes Kazanjian, *History of Armenian Literature,* Vol. II (From mid 19th century to our days), Yevtogia, 1915, Antelias [Lebanon], 1970, p. 124.

Index of Proper Names, Periodicals, and Giurjian's Works

Յարութիւն Մէքէրեան

ՄԻՔԱՅԷԼ Ս. ԿԻՒՐՃԵԱՆ

(Կեանքը Եւ Գործը)

Խմբագրեց

Վաչէ Ղազարեան

Լոս Անճելըս
2005

Այս հատորին հրատարակութիւնը կարելի դարձաւ շնորհիւ
ՏՈԼՈՐԷՍ ԶՕՀՐԱՊ ԼԻՊՄԱՆ ՀԻՄՆԱԴՐԱՄԻՆ
առատաձեռն օժանդակութեան:

ՁՕՆ

Այս գիրքը կը ձօնեմ իմ գաղթական ծնողներուս՝
ՅԱԿՈԲ ՅԱՐՈՒԹԻՒՆԻ ՄԷՔԷՐԵԱՆԻ (1887-1959) եւ
ՄԱՐԻԱՄ ՅԱԿՈԲԻ ՄԷՔԷՐԵԱՆԻ, ծնեալ՝ ԴԱՒԻԹԵԱՆ (1895-1979)
խնկելի եւ օրհնելի յիշատակին:

ՇՆՈՐՀԱԿԱԼԻՔ

Հեղինակը, երախտագիտութեամբ, իր խորին շնորհակալութիւնը կը յայտնէ Dolores Zohrab Liebmann Fund-ի վարչութեան, որ յանձն առաւ այս մենագրութեան հրատարակութեան մեկենասութիւնը՝ մոռացումէ փրկելով Միքայէլ Կիւրճեանը եւ ընթերցասէր հասարակութեան ու գրականագէտներուն հանգամանօրէն ծանօթացնելով Յակոբ Պարոնեանի, Արփիար Արփիարեանի, Երուանդ Օտեանի եւ այլ անմահ հայ գրողներու գործը շարունակող Կիւրճեանի արուեստն ու գրական վաստակը:

Հեղինակը շնորհակալութիւն կը յայտնէ նաեւ իր մտերիմ բարեկամ, Կիւրճեանի արխիւի պատասխանատու Երուանդ Ազատեանին, որ սիրայօժար այս մենագրութեան մասին իր գնահատական տողերը արձանագրեց «Վերականգնելով Կիւրճեանի գրական ժառանգութիւնը» յառաջաբանին մէջ:

Շնորհակալութեան խօսք նաեւ Դոկտ. Վաչէ Ղազարեանին, թարգմանիչի իր ուշադիր եւ բարեխիղճ մօտեցումին համար:

ԲՈՎԱՆԴԱԿՈՒԹԻՒՆ

ՎԵՐԱԿԱՆԳՆԵԼՈՎ ԿԻՐՃԵԱՆԻ ԳՐԱԿԱՆ ԺԱՌԱՆԳՈՒԹԻՒՆԸ

Այստեղ արդէն տեղին է անկեղծ խոստովանութիւն մը - երբ մամուլի մէջ առաջին անգամ սկսայ կարդալ Միքայէլ Ս. Կիրճեանի գրական ժառանգութեան մասին ընդարձակ ուսումնասիրութիւն մը՝ նախանձի, կողոպտուած ըլլալու եւ զարմանքի զգացում մըն էր որ պատեց զիս. չէ՞ որ ե՛ս էի հանդիսացած գրագէտի վերջին տարիներուն մտերիմն ու գործակիցը, որուն իսք ժառանգած էր բոլոր արխիւներն ու գրադարանը՝ այն յանձնարարութեամբ որ պահպանէի եւ ըստ կարելւոյն արժեւորէի իր գրական ժառանգութիւնը: Եւ ահա անծանօթ մը կը միջամտէր մեր մտերմութեան ու կը համարձակէր այդ արժեւորումի փորձը կատարել, կարծէք ինձմէ խլելով անկողոպտելի իրաւունք մը:

Սակայն, քանի ծանօթացայ այդ անծանօթին՝ Յարութիւն Մէքէրեանի բարեխիղճ ու բոլորանուէր աշխատանքին՝ նախ ամօթի զգացում մը սկսաւ պատել զիս որ ուշացած էի գործադրելու ինծի առաջադրուած առաքելութիւնը՝ Կիրճեանի գործին ու յիշատակին հանդէպ եւ ապա այդ զգացումը հետզհետէ սկսաւ վերածուիլ հիացման, ոչ անպայման անոր համար որ Մէքէրեանի անձին մէջ սրտակից հիացող մը կը գտնէի Կիրճեանի գրականութեան հանդէպ, այլ մանաւանդ անոր համար որ լիիրաւ բանասէր մը ձեռք կ'առնէր Կիրճեանի ժառանգութիւնը՝ ամբողջական ու գիտական վերլուծումի, վերծանման ու գնահատման ենթարկելու, այնպէս ինչպէս հայրենական բանասիրութեան լաւագոյն մեկնաբանները գիտեն ընել եւ ըրած են անցեալ տասնամեակներուն մեր դասական գրողներուն նկատմամբ:

Զգացումներու սահմանէն անցնելով՝ գործակցութեան առիթ մը ստեղծեց նաեւ Կիրճեանի «Մարտիկ Աղա» վէպին վերականգնումն ու հրատարակութիւնը Մէքէրեանի աշխատասիրութեամբ: Կիրճեան կիսատ թողած էր այդ վէպին ամբողջական հրատարակութիւնը, երբ ան թերթօնային շարքով սկսած էր լոյս տեսնել Արփիարեանի խմբագրած «Նոր Կեանք» թերթին մէջ (Լոնտոն) վէպին յարուցած աննախադէպ փոթորիկին պատճառաւ:

Վէպին մասնակի հրատարակութիւնը բնականաբար դուռ բացած էր թիւր մեկնաբանութեանց եւ մինչեւ անգամ թերգնահատումի. Օշականի նման գրականագէտ մը որ այլապէս միայն հիացում ունէր Կիրճեանի գեղագիտական ճաշակին ու գրական լայն ըմբռնումներուն նկատմամբ՝ անկատար նկատած էր վէպը՝ Բ. մասի կառոյցի կաղացման պատճառաւ: Մէքէրեանի բծախնդիր եւ անձանձիր աշխատանքով վէպին ցանուցիր մասերը, անկատար հրատարակութիւնները եւ անընթեռնելի ձեռագիրները ի մի գալով բացայայտած էին վէպին ամբողջական դիմագիծը՝ գրասէրներու եւ գրականագէտներու դատումին յանձնելով զայն:

Կիւրճեանի ողջութեան՝ ամէն անգամ որ խնդրած էի վէպին ամբողջական ձեռագիրը պատրաստել հրատարակութեան՝ միշտ կէս կատակ ու կէս իրաւ ան ոգեկոչած էր վէպին հրատարակութեան առիթով յարուցուած ազգային ու կուսակցական փոթորիկը որ ատենին մինչեւ անգամ ֆիզիքական սպառնալիք մը դարձած էր հեղինակին: Այդ վախը տարիներու ընթացքին աւելի եւս ամրապնդուած էր 1908ին իր մտերիմ գրչակիցին, Արփիար Արփիարեանի սպանութեամբ եւ ուրիշ մէկ մտերիմին՝ Վահան Թէքէեանի խոշտանգումով 1916-ին, որ որբ ձգած էր անոր մէկ աչքը: Անհաբեկման այդ արարքները աւելի եւս ամրապնդած էին Կիւրճեանի երկիւղը թէ խօսքի ուժին դիմաց բիրտ ուժն էր որ հաշուեյարդար կը կատարէր հայ իրականութեան մէջ: Մինչեւ Կիւրճեանի արկածահար մահը՝ 66 տարիներ ամբողջ անկատար մնացած էր վէպը, զլանալով առիթը անոր ամբողջական վայելքին ու արժեւորման: Միայն վէպին յօրինման հարիւրամեակին առիթով է որ շնորհիւ Մէքէրեանի աշխատասիրութեան «Մարտիկ Աղա» արժանացաւ ամբողջական հրատարակութեան մը՝ իրաւացիօրէն հաստատելով այն իրողութիւնը թէ վէպը ոչ միայն գլուխ-գործոցն էր Միքայէլ Կիւրճեանի գրականութեան, այլ նոյնինքն գլուխ-գործոց մը մեր երգիծական գրականութեան մէջ, ամուր կանգնած համաշխարհային գրականութեան տուեալներուն վրայ: Այդ կերպով Կիւրճեանի գրական դիմագիծը յայտնուեցաւ նոր լոյսի մը տակ:

«Մարտիկ Աղա» վէպին ճակատագիրը դժբախտաբար տարածուած է Կիւրճեանի ամբողջ գրականութեան վրայ. հակառակ անոր բեղուն գրիչին, գրական բազմակողմանի դիմագիծին եւ անվերջ գրական-թատերական-ազգային բեմին վրայ գտնուելու իրողութեան՝ մեծաւ մասամբ անտէր մնացած էր անոր գրականութիւնը:

Ճակատագրի հեգնանքով մը՝ Կիւրճեան մինչեւ անգամ «զրկուեցաւ» նահատակ գրագէտներու «բախտ»էն. արդարեւ, եղեռնի վաղորդայնին, «Նահատակ Գրագէտներու Բարեկամները» փորձեցին արդարութիւն ընել նահատակ գրագէտներուն՝ շարք մը հրատարակելով նահատակ գրագէտներու գործերէն, ու Կիւրճեան, անգամ մը եւս տուժեց՝ նահատակ գրագէտ մը չըլլալուն պատճառաւ, ու ճակատագրի հեգնանքը կայացաւ հոն ուր այդ գրագէտները ֆիզիքապէս նահատակուեցան, բայց մասամբ փրկուեցաւ իրենց գրականութիւնը, մինչ Կիւրճեան ֆիզիքապէս փրկուած ըլլալով՝ նահատակութեան ճամբան բռնեց իր աժէքաւոր գրականութիւնը: Յարութիւն Մէքէրեանի ձեռնարկած աշխատանքը կը միտի այդ նահատակութեան ճիրաններէն ազատագրել Կիւրճեանի գրականութիւնը եւ զայն զետեղել այն բարձունքին վրայ, որուն արժանի է ան՝ թէ՛ հայ գրականութեան պատմութեան եւ թէ՛ համաշխարհային գրականութեան մէջ:

«Միքայէլ Ս. Կիւրճեան (Կեանքը Եւ Գործը)» աշխատասիրութեամբ մենագրութիւն մը իրականացուցած է հեղինակը, ոչ այն քնոյթով որ Հանրի Թրուայա կատարած էր՝ փաստագրական-վիպական սահմանումներով ուրուագծելով Թոլսթոյի, Թուրկենեւի եւ այլ ռուս դասական գրողներու դիմագիծը, ոչ ալ Զօպանեանի թրթռուն զգայնութեամբ անմահացուցած մեռնող քերթողին՝ Դուրեանի շիջման օրերը: Մէքէրեան կը ցուցաբերէ աւելի գործնապաշտ մօտեցում մը, հաւատալով ու թելադրելով որ Կիւր-ճեանի ժառանգութեան ամբողջական վերականգնումով հայ գրականու-թիւնը եւ գրականագէտները պիտի օժտուին ամբողջական տուեալներով արդար վերագնահատում մը կատարելով անոր ժառանգութեան եւ անխուսափելի վերադասաւորում մը տալով անիրաւուած գրագէտին:

Կիւրճեան ինք եւս, իր կեանքի վերջին տասնամեակին, ընդվզելով իր կոթողային վաստակին հանդէպ ցուցաբերուած անտարբերութեան դէմ, շօգեկառքէն ուշացած ճամբորդի մը փութկոտութեամբ ջանաց կորուստէ փրկել իր ստեղծագործութեանց մէկ մասը, ու երբ ան յանկարծամահ եղաւ իր այդ անկատար ճիգին մէջ՝ իր գրական ժառանգորդը կարգելով զիս, պարտք սեպեցի անոր արխիւները փոխադրել հայրենիք՝ կորուստէ փրկելու համար Գրականութեան Եւ Արուեստի Թանգարանին մէջ, անյուսօրէն յուսալով որ խնամատար ձեռք մը, օր մը կրնայ ըստ արժանւոյն կեանքի կոչել գրական այդ ժառանգութիւնը:

Այն կառոյցը որով հանդէս կու գայ Մէքէրեան այս հատորին մէջ դուրս կը մնար իմ երեւակայութենէս, ու մինչեւ անգամ Կիւրճեան գրագէտին յիշողութենէն, որ վերջին տարիներուն սկսած էր աղօտիլ: Մեր գրական զրոյցներուն ընթացքին, տալով հանդերձ ճշմարիտ ճաշակը իր գրական հոգեխառնութեան, երբեք չէր կարողացած ան տպաւորել իր շուրջինները իր ստեղծագործութեանց բազմաբնոյթ ծաւալով ու ահեղ քանակութեամբ: Այստեղ կարծէք կը սահմանագծուին դիմագիծերն ու իրաւասութիւնները գրագէտին, գրական քննադատին ու գրականութեան պատմութեան մասնագէտին:

Այս գործին մէջ Մէքէրեան, ծաւալելով մեր ծանօթութիւնը Կիւրճեանի գրական վաստակին շուրջ՝ սահմանած կ'ըլլայ նաեւ տպաւորիչ զանգուածը գրական այն բերքին որ արգասիքն է Կիւրճեանի բազմալար գրիչին: Մէկ խօսքով՝ այս գիրքը կիզակէտի տակ առնելու փորձ մըն է Կիւրճեանի վաստակը, առաջին անգամ ամբողջական դասաւորումի հսկայ ճիգ մըն է, ու միանգամայն մարտահրաւէր մը՝ խորաչափելու անոր գրական տաղանդը:

Յուզիչ է հեղինակին անխառն հիացումը Կիւրճեանի վաստակին հան-դէպ. անսակարկ է անոր սէրը գրագէտին հանդէպ ու մանաւանդ՝ անաղարտ է անոր յանձնառութիւնը եւ հայ գրականութեան պատմութիւնը անզան-ցառելի բացով մը լրացնելու խիզախութիւնը: Կ'արժէ նաեւ ընդգծել թէ Մէքէրեան իր անխառն հիացումին մէջ չէ փթացուցած գրական քննադատի իր զգայարանքը՝ տեղին կատարելով նշումներ Կիրճեանի կարգ մը գործերու թերութեանց:

Ուրուագծելէ առաջ հատորին տարբեր գլուխները, պէտք է կանխաւ յայտնեմ թէ մինչեւ այս գործին ընթերցումը միշտ ունեցած էի այն յաւակնութիւնը թէ ամբողջապէս ծանօթ էի Կիրճեան գրողի անձին ու գրականութեան ու զանոնք սիրած էի անվերապահ հիացումով մը. Մէքէրեանի գործին ընթերցումը աւելի եւս ծանօթացուց Կիրճեանը ինծի, եւ աւելի սիրցուց զայն, եթէ ի հարկէ, տեղ կար այդ անմնացորդ սիրոյ սահմանին մէջ:

Քաղաքակիրթ երկիրներու մէջ գրողներու արխիւները աւելի բախտաւոր ճակատագրի մը կ'արժանանան՝ ամփոփուելով ազգային գրադարաններու, թանգարաններու կամ սեփական հաւաքածոներու մէջ, քիչ բաժին թողելով բախտին ու հետախուզական ու հետազօտական աշխատանքին: Մասնագէտները պարզապէս կը դիմեն այդ կեդրոնները կատարելու համար իրենց ուսումնասիրութիւնները. մեր պարագային՝ գրողներուն հետ կը նահատակուին նաեւ անոնց ստեղծագործութիւնները՝ սահմանափակելով ուսումնասիրութեան ծիրը, կամ այդ ժառանգութիւնը կը ցրուի աշխարհի տարածքին՝ գրողին աստանդական կեանքին բերումով, եւ անկարելի պատնէշներ կը հիւսուին ուսումնասիրողին դիմաց: Կիրճեանի գրական ժառանգութիւնը տարածուած է իրեն ժամանակակից գրական ու հասարակական մամուլին մէջ՝ Պոլիսէն Թիֆլիս ու Գահիրէէն Եւրոպա, միշտ հաւանականութիւն մը ստեղծելով որ հետազօտողը գտնուի բացթողումներու դիմաց: Մէքէրեան չէ յուսալքուած այդ ահաւոր փորձութեան դիմաց եւ համբերատարութեամբ հաւաքած է իր նիւթերը՝ ուսումնասիրելէ առաջ զանոնք. եւ երբ ան ձեռնարկած է գործի՝ ի ձեռին ունեցած է պատկառելի պաշար մը գրողին ստեղծագործութիւններէն, ու խղճամիտ բանասէրի իր համբերութեամբ իր նիւթերը բաժնած է առանձին գլուխներու՝ ամբողջական մոզայիքի մը մտային նախագծումով:

Իր հակիրճ նախաբանէն ետք հեղինակը առանձին գլուխով մը անդրադարձած է այն գնահատումներուն, զորս իր ժամանակակիցներն ու գրական քննադատները կատարած են անոր գրականութեան նկատմամբ. ապա կու գայ Կիրճեանի կենսագրութիւնը՝ անտիպ ու շահեկան տուեալներով: Գլուխ մը յատկացուած է գրողին երկու երգիծավէպերուն՝ «Մարտիկ Աղա»ին եւ «Նոր Դպրոցը»ին. առաջինը՝ անկատար հրատարակութեամբ եւ երկրորդը՝ անտիպ: Կիրճեանի գրականութեան ուրիշ մէկ երեսը անոր թատերական վաստակն է: Նորավէպերու, պատմուածքներու եւ գրական պատկերներու բաժինը իւրայատուկ տեղ մը կը գրաւէ անոր գրական ասպարէզին մէջ: Կիրճեան բանաստեղծը ուրիշ յայտնութիւն մըն է, իսկ հրապարակագիրը՝ ամենէն շահեկան երեսն է գրողին: Երախտաշատ գործ մըն է անոր թարգմանական վաստակը: Մէքէրեան առանձնացուցած է

Կիւրճեանի գրականագիտական դիմագիծը, եւ ապա՝ բաժին մը յատկացուած է անոր բառակերտումի շնորհին՝ երեւոյթ մը որ բացառիկ է գրականութեան պատմութեան մէջ: Հատորը իր վախճանին կը հասնի պատշաճ «Վերջաբան»ով մը:

Վերեւ նշուած իւրաքանչիւր գլուխը արժանի է առանձին անդրադարձումի. այնքան հում նիւթ կուտակուած է այնտեղ, այնքան հարուստ պաշար, որ կարելի չէ առանց վայելքի անդրադառնալ այդ բոլոր բաժիններուն:

Հակառակ իր անխառն հիացումին՝ Յարութիւն Մէքէրեան անհաշիւ վճիռներ չ'արձակեր Կիւրճեանի գրականութեան մասին. աւելի իր դերը կը տեսնէ գրողի ստեղծագործութեան յայտնաբերումին ու ծանօթացման մէջ, հաւատալով թէ այդ յայտնաբերումը, այդ հրապարակումը պիտի երաշխաւորէ արդար արժեւորում մը Կիւրճեանի տաղանդին՝ այսօրուան ու վաղուան գրականագէտներուն կողմէ: Այդ ճիգին մաս կը կազմէ համադրումը արդէն առկայ գնահատումներուն, որոնց արժանացած է Կիւրճեան իր ժամանակակից մեծերուն կողմէ:

Մէքէրեան իր արժեւորումները կը կատարէ հիմնուած սկզբնաղբիւրներուն վրայ եւ ոչ անպայման արդէն հրատարակուած գրութեանց ու վերլուծումներու վրայ: Ան նախ արխիւներէն, նամականիներէն, փոշիի տակ ինկած մամուլի էջերէն կը հաւաքէ սկզբնաղբիւրները՝ ետքէն համադրելու եւ համայնապատկերի մէջ զետեղելու իր կատարած գիւտերը: Այս աշխատանքին մէջ կը նմանի Մանուկ Աբեղեանին, երբ ան կը շարադրէր «Հայոց Հին Գրականութեան Պատմութիւնը» երբ մէկ կողմէ սկզբնաղբիւրները կը պեղէր ու միւս կողմէ զանոնք կ'ենթարկէր գրական արժեւորումի:

Մէքէրեանի այս աշխատութիւնը Կիւրճեանի գործին նուիրուած առաջին մենագրութիւնն է. ան չունի իր նախընթացը: Նոյնիսկ առանձին յօդուածներ եւ ուսումնասիրութիւններ ցանցառ են հայ մամուլին մէջ: Այս հատորով լուրջ հիմքերը կը դրուին *կիւրճեանագիտութեան*:

Չարենց՝ Թումանեանի մասին պատկերալից գնահատում մը կատարած է ըսելով թէ ան Հոմերոսի, Կէօթէի եւ այլ մեծերու հետ թաս խփած է. նոյն պատկերը կը պատշաճի նաեւ Կիւրճեանին, որ ոչ միայն թաս խփած է համաշխարհային գրականութեան մեծերուն հետ, ինչպէս Քորնէյ, Ռասին, Պալզաք, Տոտէ եւայլն, այլ անձնապէս մտերիմը եղած է իր ժամանակին մեծերուն — Թէքէեանի, Ինտրայի, Արփիարեանի, Օտեանի, Եղիա Տէմիրճիպաշեանի, Օշականի, Բաշալեանի, Կամսարականի եւ այլոց հետ: Եթէ պահ մը խորհինք թէ անոնցմէ իւրաքանչիւրը ինչպիսի տաղանդի եւ իւրայատուկ բնաւորութեան տէր մարդ էր որ չէր կրնար ներդաշնակուիլ վերոյիշեալ հոյլին այլ տաղանդներուն հետ. օրինակ, Օտեան, իր կենսասիրութեամբ եւ անսանձ գինարբեցութեամբ ճիշդ հակապատկերն էր ներամփոփ եւ խստամբեր Թէքէեանի մը կամ Եղիա մը, իր բնազանցական զառանցանքներու կատաղութեան մէջ հազիւ թէ համադրուէր «Օրուան

Կեանք»ի բազկերակին վրայ իր մատը դրած Արփիարեանի մը հետ. սակայն Կիւրճեան լեզու կը գտնէր բոլորին հետ՝ Օտեանին հետ կը հինովնար, Թէքէեանին հետ կը զգաստանար ու դեռ՝ Ինտրային հետ կը սգար ոռճիներուն խորհուրդը: Կենցաղով պոհէմ՝ միտքով ազնուական, անկեղծօրէն կը սիրուէր բոլորէն ու մանաւանդ կը գնահատուէր բոլորէն՝ իր տաղանդին բազմակողմանի այլազանութեան համար:

Այսպէս, հայ գրականութեան մութ հանճարը՝ Ինտրա նամակի մը մէջ կը գրէր Կիւրճեանին «ոչ ոք աւելի վարպետ է քան դուն», Տիգրան Կամսարական «իրական տաղանդ մը» կը հռչակէր զինք: Իսկ հայ երգիծանքի վարպետը՝ Երուանդ Օտեան, հետեւեալ բնորոշումը կու տար անոր երգիծելու ձիրքին մասին. ««Ազատ Բեմ»ի մշտական աշխատակիցն էր Միքայէլ Կիւրճեան որ իր անսպառ սրամտութեամբ, սրամիտ, կայծկլտուն եւ աննման աւիւնով կ'ողողէր «Ազատ Բեմ»ի էջերը»: Իսկ խստապահանջ Օշական, որ աւելի հակամէտ էր «հարթել»ու քան գնահատելու, իր ժլատ գրիչով հետեւեալ գնահատականը կ'ընծայէ Կիւրճեանին. «իր սերունդին մէջ Միքայէլ Կիւրճեան կը ներկայանայ այդ սերունդին ամբողջ կենդանութեամբը, անոր հետաքրքրութիւններովը, խոր ցանկութիւններովը: Ու նման անոնց ամէնէն տաղանդաւորներուն՝ գրեթէ միշտ մնալով իր մտադրութեանց եզրին»: Եթէ Օշական գիտնար Կիւրճեանի մասին այն ինչ Մէքէրեան գիտէ, կամ կրցած է մակաբերել, վստահաբար այդ եզրէն հեռացնելով աւելի կեդրոնական տեղ մը պիտի յատկացնէր Կիւրճեանին, իր ժամանակի գրականութեան մէջ:

Մէքէրեան տակաւին հաստատումներ ունի Թէոդիկէն, Բաշալեանէն, Թէքէեանէն, Սարուխանէն եւ ուրիշներէ, նոյնիսկ օտար գրագէտներէ, որոնք կարդացած էին Կիւրճեանի ֆրանսերէնով գրած ստեղծագործութիւնները: Եւ այս կերպով համապատկերը կը կազմէ Կիւրճեանի վաստակին եւ այդ վաստակէն յառաջացած արժեւորումներուն: Հեղինակը չէ բաւարարուած հաւաքելով այն արժեւորումները եւ գնահատական արտայայտութիւնները որոնք ուղղուած են Կիւրճեանի հասցէին, այլ քննադատութեան առած է նաեւ գրականութեան պատմութեան նուիրուած այն հատորները, որոնց հեղինակները կա՛մ թերագնահատած են Կիւրճեանի գրականութիւնը եւ կամ՝ ամբողջութեամբ անտեսած են զայն — Մերուժան Պարսամեան, Գուրգէն Մխիթարեան, եւայլն:

ԿԵԱՆՔԻ ՈՒՐՈՒԱԳԻԾ

Մէքէրեան կը հաւատայ թէ գրողի մը կամ արուեստագէտի մը յայտնաբերումը հանրագումարն է անոր ծիներուն (gene) մէջ սերունդէ սերունդ մթերուած եւ յաճախ ալ շրջապատի ազդեցութեամբ խմորուած արժանիքներուն: Օրինակ, Լէոփոլտ Մոցարթ չափուած ձեւուած երաժիշտը ծնունդ տուած է Ուլֆկանկ Ամատէուս Մոցարթի հանճարեղ պոռթկումին, կամ Պախի քսան զաւակներուն բոլորն ալ երաժշտական տաղանդի փշրանք մը կրած են իրենց տիեզերահռչակ հօր փայլատակումներէն: Մեր մէջ ալ, Ծահնուր շատ բան կը պարտի իր բանահիւսաք մօրեղբօր՝ Թէոդիկին:

Մէքէրեան այս եզրերով մօտեցած է նաեւ Կիւրճեանի կեանքին, մի առ մի մանրելով անոր ընտանեկան ժառանգութեան երեսակները — հօրը՝ Սահակ էֆէնտիի խմբագրական գործունէութիւնը, մօրեղբօր՝ Արշ. Ալթունեանի վիպագրական փորձերը («Աղքատին Պատիւը») եւ ի վերջոյ մօրը անսպառ սրամտութիւնն ու պատկերալից արտայայտութիւնները: Այս բոլորը ի մի գալով կերտած են Կիւրճեանի գրականութեան ենթահողը:

Մէքէրեան մասնաւորաբար շեշտը կը դնէ Կիւրճեանի յանկարծական ու ամբողջական յայտնութեան վրայ: Արդարեւ, 19-20 տարեկանին «Մարտիկ Աղա»ի նման կատարեալ երգիծավէպ մը յօրինելը կանխահաս տաղանդի մը վկայութիւնն է: Հեղինակը մէջբերումներ կը կատարէ այս ուղղութեամբ իր ժամանակակիցներէն, որոնք զարմանք կը յայտնէին թէ ականատեսը չէին հանդիսացած Կիւրճեանի տաղանդին հասունացման գործընթացին, որովհետեւ ան անակնկալօրէն յայտնուած էր մեծերու վայել յղկուած միտքով եւ գրական տաղանդով: Երեւոյթ մը որ ընդհանրապէս յատուկ է բանաստեղծութեան, ինչպէս օրինակ մեր մօտ Մեծարենցի եւ Դուրեանի պարագային, կամ՝ անգլիական գրականութեան մէջ Շելլիի, Քիցի եւ Լորտ Պայրընի պարագաները: Վէպի մէջ, օրինակ, կ'ըսուի թէ Պալզաքի գրական հանճարը իր հասուն լիութեան հանգրուանը թեւակոխած է անոր քառասուն տարեկանէն վերջ:

Կիւրճեանի կենսագրութեան մաս կը կազմեն նաեւ իր բարեկամութիւնները Թէքէեանի, Արփիարեանի, Եղիայի, Ինտրայի, Շիրվանզադէի, Կամսարականի, Բաշալեանի, Ռէթէոս Պէրպէրեանի (որուն աշակերտած էր) եւ այլոց հետ:

Կիւրճեանի գրականութեան կրակը, անկասկած անզուսպ կենսասիրութիւնն էր: Իր երիտասարդ տարիքին օր մը ան իր օրագրութեան մէջ կ'արձանագրէ. «Մահը մեռցուցի: Մահը հեռացուցի: Ան ինծի մեռցնելուն ես ան մեռցուցի: Մահուան ցեղակից բան չեմ ուզեր մէջս»:

Մահուան դէմ այս անհաշտ պայքարը միշտ զուգահեռ ընթացած է Կիւրճեանի անձին ու գրական ստեղծագործութեան մէջ: Օրինակ, «Մարտ» վերնագրեալ պատմուածքին մէջ ծերունի ամոլ մը Մարտ ամիսը մահաբեր կը նկատէ ու ամէն տարի Մարտ ամիսը վանելով կը կարծէ տարի մըն ալ կեանք շահած ըլլալ: Ականատես վկան եղած եմ այդ պատմուածքի վերախմբագրումին երբ Կիւրճեան ծերունի ամոլին զառամած դիմագիծերը կը վերագրէր անոնց 80-ը անցուցած ըլլալու փաստին. այդ վերախմբագրումի պահուն Կիւրճեան ինք եւս արդէն անցած էր 85 տարիքը. զգալով որ այդ տարիքին կրնար մահը իրեն ալ մօտեցած ըլլալ, յանկարծ, գրիչի միամիտ խաղով մը ծերունիներուն տարիքը բարձրացուց 90-ի՝ հաւատալով որ մահը քանի մը տարի եւս անդին հրած եղաւ…: Կիւրճեանի հետ մեր վերջին գիշերուան խօսակցութիւնը եւս կը դառնար մահուան շուրջ: Ան կ'ըսէր թէ ինք անցուցած է բոլոր հիւանդութիւնները եւ փորձանքները եւ շատ հետաքրքիր է գիտնալու թէ ի՞նչ բանը կրնար իր մահուան պատճառ դառնալ: Յաջորդ առաւօտ հանրակառքի արկածի մը զոհ գնաց ան: Կ'երեւի թէ այդ պարագան հաշիւի չէր առած…:

Կիւրճեան իր կեանքը գրականութեան վերածած էր եւ գրականութիւնը՝ կեանքի. կը հաւատար երկուքին ալ յաւիտենականութեան:

Մէքէրեան իրայատուկ մօտեցում մը ցուցաբերած է երբ փորձած է վերականգնել անոր կենսագրութիւնը: Ան գրողին կեանքը միահիւսած է ժամանակի գլխաւոր անցքերուն հետ, որոնք իրենց անդրադարձը ունեցած են գրողին միտքին, հոգիին ու գրականութեան վրայ: Յուշերով, նամակներէ մէջբերումներ ընելով, մամուլի հատուածներ պրպտելով՝ կենդանի կերպով վերականգնած է այն ժամանակաշրջանը որուն մէջ ապրած եւ ստեղծագործած է Միքայէլ Կիւրճեան: Կիւրճեան կուսակցական պայքարներու լուսանցքին վրայ ապրող քրոնիկագիրը եղած է իր դարուն:

Աննշան իրագործում մը չէ նաեւ Կիւրճեանի բոլոր ծածկանուններուն յայտնաբերումը: Բանասէր Գարեգին Լեւոնեանի «Բառարան Հայ Գրական Ծածկանուններու» եւ հայր Արսէն Ղազիկեանի «Հայկական Մատենագիտութիւն Եւ Հանրագիտարան Հայ Կեանքի» հատորները ուսումնասիրելով անբաւարար գտած է Կիւրճեանի ծածկանուններուն յատկացեալ բաժինները եւ իր կարգին առաջնային աղբիւրներու վրայ հիմնուելով ան լրացուցած է Կիւրճեանի հաւանական ծածկանուններու գրեթէ լրիւ ցուցակը — Համշիրակ Ա., Զարմայր, Պարոյր, Արսէն Մոլար, Պետրոս Ագաթան, Պոնտ, Սրճեփ եւ այլն:

Կիւրճեան ոչ միայն կը սիրէր ինքզինք պաճուճել ծածկանուններով, այլեւ կը զուարճանար նաեւ այլոց ծածկանուններով: Կը պատմէր թէ Վահրամ Փափազեան օր մը կ'այցելէ Եգիպտոս՝ տեղական ուժերով թատերախաղ մը սարքելու, ինք ստանձնելով գլխաւոր դերը: Անգամ մը բեմի վրայ խաղընկեր կ'ունենայ բարձր դասակարգէն մեծահարուստ տիկին մը որուն թանկարժէք մատանին կ'անհետանայ Փափազեան, գաղութին մէջ գայթակղութիւն մը յառաջացնելով: Տարիներ վերջ Փափազեան դարձեալ կ'այցելէ Եգիպտոս, այս անգամ իտալական խումբի մը հետ եւ այս անգամ ծպտուած Վահրամ Պարտի ծածկանունով: Կիւրճեան այդ ծածկանունին հրապոյրով հմայուած թատերախօսական յօդուած մը կը գրէ մամուլին մէջ, իբրեւ եզրակացութիւն աւելցնելով. «Այո՛, Վահրամ Պարտի … մատանի մը եգիպտահայ գաղութին»:

«ՄԱՐՏԻԿ ԱՂԱ» ԵՐԳԻԾԱՎԷՊԻՆ ՏԵՂԸ ԳՐԱԿԱՆՈՒԹԵԱՆ ՄԷՋ

«Մարտիկ Աղա» երգիծավէպին անկատար երեւումը մամուլի մէջ եւ

առանձին հատորով հրատարակութեան մը չարժանանալը՝ բացասական եւ ողբերգական հետեւանքներ ունեցած են Կիրճեանի գրականութեան եւ տաղանդին վրայ, եւ միշտ սեպ մը խրած են անոր կարողութեան ու կարողականութեան միջեւ: Երգիծավէպը չէ արժեւորուած ըստ բաւականին կարենալ ճշդելու համար Կիրճեանի հարազատ դիմագիծը մեր գրականութեան մէջ, հետեւաբար նաեւ անոր տեղը հայ գրականութեան պատմութեան մէջ:

Այդ ճակատագիրը Կիրճեանին չափ, եւ հաւանաբար՝ անկէ ալ աւելի տոչորած է գրականութեան պատմութեան հմուտ մասնագէտը՝ Յարութիւն Մէքէրեանը, որ անհրաւութեան զգացումէն մեկնելով ջանացած է դարմանել այդ անարդարութիւնը. եւ այդ դարմանումի գործը կարելի չէր իրականացնել ներբողելով Կիրճեանի տաղանդը կամ պարսաւելով գրական քննադատներու վերաբերումը անոր ստեղծագործութեանց նկատմամբ. այդ դարմանումը կարելի էր իրականացնել միայն վէպին ամբողջականութիւնը յանձնելով պատմութեան դատողութեան. ուրեմն գիրքին յօրինումէն հարիւր տարի վերջ Մէքէրեան գոհունակութեամբ կ'արձանագրէ. «Ուրախ ենք որ երկար տարիներու մեր երազը իրականցաւ եւ վերջապէս յաջողեցանք ունենալ «Մարտիկ Աղա» վէպին շարունակութիւնը, անտիպ գլուխներու ձեռագիրներուն պատճէնները հաւաքելով կարողացանք վերծանել, մշակել եւ երգիծավէպը 1999ին ամբողջական ձեւով մատուցանել ընթերցողներուն»:

Այս իրագործումը այնքան համեստ նուաճում մը չէ, ինչպէս պարզօրէն կը խոստովանի Մէքէրեան. իրականութեան մէջ Կիրճեանի գրականութեան նոր կեանք մը երաշխաւորելու պատասխանատու եւ ողջունելի կենսագործում մըն է որ առիթ կու տայ ընթերցողներուն ու գրականագէտներուն նոր լոյսի տակ դիտելու անիրաւուած գրողին հարազատ դիմագիծը եւ կայացնելու նոր ու աւելի բարենպաստ դատում մը անոր հարուստ վաստակին նկատմամբ:

Կիրճեանի գրականութիւնը ունի բազմաթիւ երեսներ. ան իր օգտագործած բոլոր սեռերուն մէջ ալ յաջողած է փայլուն էջեր արձանագրել շնորհիւ իր գեղագիտական խորունկ զգայարանքին. սակայն պարզ է թէ անոր գլուխ գործոցը կը հանդիսանայ «Մարտիկ Աղա» երգիծավէպը:

Մէքէրեան մեծ հիացում մը տածելով հանդերձ Կիրճեանի գրականութեան եւ ժառանգութեան նկատմամբ՝ չի կորսնցներ նաեւ իր դատողութեան կշիռը անոր անվաւեր գործերուն նկատմամբ:

Օրինակ Կիրճեանի բոլոր կենսագրութիւններուն մէջ կը յիշուի ուրիշ վէպի մը անունը՝ «Նոր Դպրոցը», որ միշտ անտիպ մնացած է հեղինակին կենդանութեան, զանազան ենթադրութեանց առաջնորդելով գրականութեան պատմութեամբ զբաղողները եւ յառաջացնելով նաեւ *միթիք* մը — թէ՝ ինչպիսի յաւելում մը պիտի ըլլար անոր հրատարակութիւնը Կիրճեանի վաստակին արժեւորման մէջ: Սակայն, փաստը այն է որ Կիրճեան երբեք չէ վերանայած այդ գործը, որ միշտ մնացած է իր անկատար վիճակին մէջ: Պէտք է խոստովանիմ որ իբրեւ Կիրճեանի ձեռագիրներուն ժառանգորդ իմ կարգիս, առիթը չեմ ունեցած ամբողջապէս աչքէ անցընելու վէպը՝ այդ ձեռագիրները Հայաստան փութացնելու արտորանքիս մէջ:

Մէքէրեան հաւանաբար առաջին անձն էր, հեղինակէն ետք, որ աչք մը նետած էր այդ ձեռագրին վրայ, զոր լուրջ քննութենէ մը անցընելէ ետք կը վճռէր ««Նոր Դպրոցը» Մարտիկ Աղա մը չէ», ու գրագէտը բարեխղճու-թեամբ կը խուսափի զայն վերամշակելու փորձութենէն:

Հատորը կը բնութագրէ վիպապաշտ եւ իրապաշտ դպրոցներու հակա-մարտութիւնը, առանց, անպայման ստեղծագործական հրայրք մը կամ գրական մշակման խնամք մը դրսեւորելու:

Միւս կողմէ «Մարտիկ Աղա»ն կը ծանուցանէ Կիրճեանի շնդալից մուտքը հայ գրականութեան անդաստանէն ներս, տակաւին հազիւ թեւակոխած 20 տարիքը:

Պատմութեան ճակատագրական պահերուն, ջրբաժան հանգրուան-ներուն, գրողները - երգիծող, վիպասան թէ բանաստեղծ — անստգիւտ յայտնաբերումներ կ'ընեն ազգերու նկարագրէն: Օրինակ, կ'ըսուի թէ երբ 1453-ին Ֆաթիհ Սուլթան կը պաշարէր Պոլիսը բիւզանդացի պալատա-կանները վէճի մէջ կը գտնուէին՝ ստուգելու համար թէ քանի՞ հրեշտակ կարելի էր կանգնեցնել գնդասեղի մը ծայրը: Կամ, հայոց պարագային՝ Մեծն Տիգրան, ի տես մօտեցող հռոմէական բանակին կը գոչէ. «Եթէ եկողները պատգամաւոր են՝ շատ են, իսկ եթէ զինուորականներ են՝ քիչ են». սակայն հռոմայեցիք կը հասնին ու կը տապալեն հայոց պատմութեան առաջին ու վերջին կայսրութիւնը:

Կրնան այս փաստերը չհամապատասխանել պատմական իրողութեան, սակայն այնքան ճշմարտանման են ու դիպուկ որ հարազատ կերպով կը բնութագրեն ժամանակն ու կացութիւնները. մանաւանդ կարելի է նկարագրի ուղիղ գիծ մը տեսնել Մեծ Տիգրանի փքուռոյց եւ յանձնապաստան յայտա-րարութենէն մինչեւ «Փանջունի» եւ «Մարտիկ Աղա»: Սերվանդէսի «Տոն Քիշոթ»ն անգամ, իր անսահման երգիծանքին մէջ, ասպետական ժամա-նակներու անկման տխուր շրջանը կը բնորոշէ:

Վերադառնալով «Մարտիկ Աղա»ին, անիկա ալ իր կարգին, երգի-ծական ժամանակագրութիւնն է ազգային նոր իրադարձութեանց: Արդարեւ, 1894-96-ի համիտեան ջարդերը մարդկային հեղեղ մը թափած էին Եգիպտոս եւ այլուր: Մարդկային այդ զանգուածները, իրենց բնօրրաններէն արմատախիլ՝ կը ջանային յուսահատօրէն պատշաճիլ նոր եւ անօրինակ պայմաններու՝ դրսեւորելով տագնապալի ժամանակներու յատուկ մարդկա-յին ու ազգային նկարագրի գիծ մը, որ անսովոր տաղանդով մը կը սեւեռուէր Կիրճեանի այս վէպին մէջ:

Այս վէպը իր ուժականութեամբ երկու կարեւոր հաստատում կ'ընէր – նախ կը ցնցէր օրուան հասարակական կեանքը՝ մեծ գայթակղութիւն մը յառաջացնելով եւ ապա՝ կը ծանուցանէր յայտնաբերումը կազմուած վիպագիրի մը:

Վէպին մասին բազմաթիւ վկայութիւններ կան Օտեանէն, Բաշալեանէն, Պարթեւեանէն եւ ուրիշներէ. սակայն, ամենէն բնորոշը կարծէք Ինտրայի նամակներէն մէջ բերուած հատուած մըն է որ լաւագոյնս կը բնութագրէր Կիւրճեանի հասուն տաղանդին յայտնութիւնը – այսպէս, Ինտրա կը գրէ. «Դուն ինծի պէս *տէպի*ի մը համբակութիւններն ու խակութիւնները ցուցադրած չես երբեք հրապարակի վրայ, եւ առաջին գրութեանդ (Զարմայր Սահակեան ստորագրութեամբ) առթիւ էր որ Եղիա Տէմիրճիպաշեանը Ժընեւի մէջ ըսաւ ինծի թէ իբրեւ վարպետ կը ներկայանայիր: Բախտ ունեցայ *Նոր Կեանք*երուն մէջ *Մարտիկ Աղադ* կարդալու, եւ կը վկայեմ թէ հազիւ քիչ մը նուազ կ'արժէ քան ստորագրութիւնդ կրող մէկ վերջին ռեւէ երկդ, եւ կարծեմ թէ չկայ մեր մէջ ճշմարիտ կարողութեան տէր մէկը որուն գրական կեանքը զերծ ըլլայ, քուկինիդ պէս, իր զարգացման պատմութիւնը պարզած ըլլալու տկարութենէն»:

ԿԻՒՐՃԵԱՆԻ ՏԱՂԱՆԴԻՆ ՈՒ ՎԱՍՏԱԿԻՆ ԲԱՂԱԴՐԻՉ ԱՅԼ ՏԱՐՐԵՐԸ

Կիւրճեան իր օրերուն մեծ մասը անցուցած է համաշխարհային տիտաններու մտերմութեան մէջ՝ արգասաւորելով իր տաղանդը անոնց գործերով եւ անգիտակցօրէն նաեւ մատչելով անոնց բարձունքին. պարբերաբար աչքէ անցուցած ըլլալով Կիւրճեանէն ինծի ժառանգ մնացած գիրքերը – մեծ մասամբ՝ ֆրանսերէն, գիրքերու լուսանցքներուն վրայ տեսած եմ Կիւրճեանի գրիչով արձանագրուած հիացական տողեր, մեկնաբանութիւններ ու գիրքերէն թելադրուած թեւաւոր խօսքեր, որոնք կարծէք նախածրագրուած ըլլային իբրեւ հում նիւթ օգտագործուելու իր արձակ թէ չափածոյ գործերուն մէջ:

Այդ բոլոր միտքերը, փայլատակումներն ու ներշնչումները Կիւրճեանի տաղանդին պրիսմակէն անցնելով ցոլացած են իր պատմուածքներուն, պատումներուն ու քերթուածներուն մէջ:

Այս հատորին մէջ առանձին գլուխ մը յատկացուած է Կիւրճեանի այս սեռի ստեղծագործութեանց, որոնց շարքին գնահատման ու վերլուծման ենթարկուած են «Քեաթիպին Երազը», «Սրճարանը», «Ինչ Որ Հրեշտակը Տեսաւ», «Նոր Լաթ», «Մարտ», «Փախած Ձիեր», եւ այլ գործերը: «Քեաթիպին Երազը» նախ լոյս տեսած է ֆրանսերէնով եւ արժանացած ջերմ գնահատանքի: Անոր հայերէն տարբերակին հրատարակութեան առիթով Ինտրա կը գրէ Կիւրճեանին. ««Քեաթիպին Երազը» զիս լացուց. գոհար մըն է ան». արդարեւ արեւելեան շռայլ գոյներով, համեմունքներու բուրմունքներով եւ անօրինակ դիտողականութեամբ օժտուած կտորներ են անոնք:

Այդ բոլորը դասաւորելէ եւ վերլուծելէ ետք Մէքէրեան արդարօրէն կ'ըսէ Կիւրճեանի մասին. «ահա թէ ինչո՞ւ կարելի է զայն դասել Կէօթէի, Շիլլէրի, Հիւկոյի, Թոլսթոյի եւ Տոսթոեւսքիի շարքը»:

ԿԻՒՐՃԵԱՆ ԲԱՆԱՍՏԵՂԾԸ

Կիւրճեանի միտքերը միշտ բանաստեղծական պատկերներով կը յառաջանան: Նոյնիսկ իր արձակ գործերուն մէջ ներկայ է պատկերաւոր մտածողութեամբ յօրինելու անոր բնազդական գիծը: «Մարտիկ Աղա»ն որ վէպ մըն է եւ սեռի պատկանելիութեամբ արձակ, այնտեղ անգամ Կիւրճեան տեղ տեղ դադար կ'առնէ իր պատումին մէջ նկարագրելու համար բնութեան քնարական տեսարանները:

Իսկ իր քերթողութիւնը կերպով մը մեր գրականութեան մէջ կը ցոլացնէ Պոտլէրի, Վերլէնի, Ռեմպոյի վիպապաշտ դպրոցին մթնոլորտը:

Բացի իր տաղաչափեալ բանաստեղծութիւններէն, որոնց հանգամանօրէն կ'անդրադառնայ Մէքէրեան — Կիւրճեան ընթերցող հասարակութիւնը անակնկալի առջեւ դրաւ հասուն տարիքին հրատարակելով իր «Ի Խորոց Սրտի Խօսք Ընդ Պաշտելւոյն» արձակ բանաստեղծութիւններու հատորը՝ պատանեկան սիրոյ թարմ թրթռացումներով:

ԿԻՒՐՃԵԱՆ ՀՐԱՊԱՐԱԿԱԳԻՐԸ

Անհաւատալիօրէն ընդարձակ է թիւը այն հրատարակութեանց, որոնց աշխատակցած է Կիւրճեան՝ Պոլիսէն Եգիպտոս, Պուլկարիա, Ֆրանսա, Ամերիկա, Լիբանան եւ այլուր: Մէքէրեան անխոնջ պրպտումներով գտած եւ իր մենագրութեան մէջ նշած է բոլոր այդ թերթերուն անունները, յաճախ անդրադառնալով կարեւոր յօդուածներուն ու տեղին մէջբերումներ ընելով անոնցմէ:

Կիւրճեանի գրիչը շատ սուր նշտրակի մը նման խրուած է մեր ազգային եսին: Ան իր վերլուծման առարկայ դարձուցած է մեր ազգային կեանքի շատ մը երեսները, եւ իբրեւ պատասխանատու եւ գիտակ մտածող՝ ան միշտ խիզախութեամբ անդրադարձած է հարցերուն ու երեւոյթներուն, երբեմն ցուցնելով մեր զգայնութիւններն ու ազգային սնափառութիւնը:

Այսպէս, Ծահնուրէն շատ առաջ, ան խիզախութիւնն ունեցած է հակադրուելու մեր սնափառութեանց եւ բնութագրելու մեր ցեղին միտքը, այնպէս ինչպէս որ է:

Օրինակ, ան «Հայուն Միտքը» վերնագրեալ յօդուածի մը մէջ կը գրէ. «Հայ միտքը իր ընդհանուր եւ էական գիծերուն մէջ, կը ներկայանայ իբրեւ աւելի նմանող քան ստեղծագործող միտք մը, աւելի ընկալուչ քան արտադրող միտք մը, աւելի հասկցող եւ ըմբռնող քան ստեղծող, աւելի տպաւորական քան ներգործող, աւելի վերլուծող քան համադրող: Հայ միտքի գլխաւոր յատկանիշը իւրացումն է: Մեր ցեղին ի սկզբանէ անտի ճակատագրուած գոյութեան անձպաստ պայմաններուն պատճառաւ հայ միտքը չէ կրցած ազատօրէն զարգացնել ու փթթեցնել ստեղծագործ ուժի սերմերը»:

Ամէն առիթով Կիրճեան նման համարձակ հաստատումներ կը կատարէ եւ հայուն թերութիւնները մատնանշելով կը ցանկայ անոր մէջ զօրացած տեսնել ազգային հաւաքական կամքը. ուրիշ տեղ մը ան յանկարծ կը պոռթկայ. «պէտք է հաւաքապաշտ ըլլանք, պէտք է համազգային ըլլանք, հրաժարինք մեր անհատականութիւններէն եւ պատկանինք ցեղին, անոր անսխալական բնազդէն վարուինք, անոր անհուն սիրովը բաբախենք»:

Ինչպէս կը տեսնուի քնարական ներանձնական ապրումներու զգայուն երգիչը գիտէ նաեւ հաւաքական ուժին արժէքն ու տարողութիւնը՝ երբ ձեռք կ'առնէ ան իր հրապարակագիրի գրիչը:

ԹԱՐԳՄԱՆԱԿԱՆ ԳՐԱԿԱՆՈՒԹԻՒՆ

Արդի հայ գրականութեան բեղմնաւորման կազմաւորման մէջ կարեւոր ներգործութիւն մը ունեցած է թարգմանական գրականութեան հսկայ պաշարը որ իրագործուեցաւ յատկապէս 19րդ դարուն, հայ ընթերցողին մատչելի դարձնելու եւրոպական գրականութեան եւ մասնաւորապէս՝ ֆրանսական գրականութեան ամէնէն ժողովրդական վէպերը: Մէքէրեան այս հատորին մէջ կը ներկայացնէ ցանկը թարգմանուած այդ երկերուն, որոնք առաւելաբար ժողովրդական ճաշակի պատշաճող վէպեր են. դարավերջին, սակայն, թարգմանական գրականութիւնը աւելի նրբանալով ընդգրկեց բանաստեղծութիւնը եւ աւելի որակեալ գրական ճաշակի գործերը: Այնպէս ինչպէս ոսկեդարը հին աշխարհի գրականութիւնը բերած էր մեր ժողովուրդին, 19րդ դարն ալ նոյն դերը կատարեց ժամանակակից գրականութեան պարագային:

Մէքէրեան մասնայատուկ տեղ մը կը վերապահէ Կիրճեանին թարգմանական գրականութեան կալուածէն ներս:

Կիրճեան լեզուական երկակենցաղութեան վկայութիւնը տուած էր արդէն քերթողական իր առաջին գործերը ֆրանսերէնով հրատարակելով եւ կամ՝ իր ամենէն նշանաւոր արեւելապատումները երկու լեզուով ալ հրատարակած ըլլալով: Հետեւաբար, անոր համար մէկ լեզուէն միւսին անցումը եւ կամ մէկ լեզուէն միւսին գրական վերածումներ կատարելը դարձած էին երկրորդ բնութիւն: Իր այս մենագրութեան մէջ Մէքէրեան ընտրած է ընտիր թարգմանութիւններ Պոտլէրէն, Վերլէնէն, Լամարթինէն, Ռոնսարէն եւ այլ ֆրանսացի գրողներէ եւ զանոնք բաղդատութեան դրած է ուրիշ հայ գրողներու կատարած թարգմանութիւններուն հետ, ցոյց տալու համար Կիրճեանի հմտութիւնն ու վարպետութիւնը այդ մարզէն ներս: Այստեղ կը դրսեւորուի նաեւ Մէքէրեանի լեզուական եւ գրական հմտութիւնը, երբ ան Կիրճեանի կատարած թարգմանութիւնները, ֆրանսերէնէ, բաղդատութեան կը դնէ միեւնոյն գործերու անգլերէն թարգմանութեան հետ — օրինակ՝ Վերլէնի «Ծածուկ Ջանգակը» եւ Լամարթինի «Լիճը». ան նոյն ատեն վեր կ'առնէ իւրայատկութիւնները ու տաղաչափական օրէնքները իւրաքանչիւր լեզուի մէջ:

Գիրքին ամենէն շահեկան գլուխներէն մէկն է Կիւրճեանի թարգմանական արուեստին նուիրուած բաժինը: Սակայն, այստեղ անհրաժեշտ է նկատողութիւն մը ընել արձակ ու տաղաչափեալ թարգմանութեանց նուիրուած բաժիններուն մասին, որոնք հաւասարակշռուած չեն. օրինակ Ալֆոնս Տոտէի «Թարասքոնցի Թարթարէն» երգիծավէպին տրամադրուած բաժինը կարելի էր շատ աւելի ընդարձակել ի հաշիւ տաղաչափեալ գործերուն: Արդարեւ, Տոտէի վէպին թարգմանութիւնը ինքնին գլուխ-գործոց մըն է՝ վէպին հոգեբանական թափանցումներով, համապատասխան բառերու կերտումով եւ նուրբ զուարթախոհութեան հարազատ փոխադրումով:

Տոտէ հեռացած էր Փարիզէն եւ իր գաւառական օճախէն դիպուկ դատումներ կ'ընէր Փարիզի եւ ընդհանրապէս մեծ քաղաքներու կենցաղին ու մտայնութեանց մասին, իր այլաբանական գործերով եւ թէ մանաւանդ՝ «Նամակներ Իմ Ջաղացքէն» գործով: «Թարթարէն»ը անոր հսկայական ներդրումն էր աշխարհի երգիծական գրականութեան: Ալ. Սարուխանի նկարազարդած Օտեանի «Փանջունի»ին նախաբանին մէջ Կիւրճեան Տոտէի երգիծավէպը կը դասէ Տիքընզի «Փիքուիք Փէյփըրզ»ին, Սերվանդէսի «Տոն Քիշոթ»ի կարգին: Կիւրճեան միեւնոյն հրայրքով (verve) թարգմանած է «Թարթարէն»ը, պահպանելով ոչ միայն անոր ոգին, այլեւ՝ համն ու բոյրը:

«Մարտիկ Աղա» վէպին ամբողջական հրատարակութեան կցուած իմ վերջաբանին մէջ (որ ենթադրուած էր նախաբանը ըլլալ), այս գործին անդրադառնալով գրած էի որ եթէ Տոտէ հայերէն գիտնար եւ ծանօթացած ըլլար Կիւրճեանի այդ թարգմանութեան, առաջին հերթին ինք պիտի ուզէր հայերէն գրած ըլլալ վէպը, որովհետեւ, շնորհիւ Կիւրճեանի տաղանդին՝ այնքան հարազատ արտայայտութիւն մը գտած էր Տոտէի տաղանդը:

ԳՐԱԳԷՏԸ՝ ԿԻՒՐՃԵԱՆԻ ՄԷՋ

Բոլոր անոնք որոնք հպանցիկ կերպով ծանօթ են Կիւրճեանի գրաքննադատական գործերուն՝ հաւանաբար փորձուին լուսանցքային նշանակութիւն մը ընծայել անոնց. դժբախտաբար այս վիճակը կրնայ պարտադրուիլ շատերու, որովհետեւ Կիւրճեանի գրաքննադատական գործերը, որոնք խորունկ տարողութիւն մը ունին, չեն համախմբուած հատորի մը ծածկին տակ:

Այստեղ եւս Մէքէրեան շնորհակալ աշխատանք կատարած է պրպտելով մամուլը, հաւաքելով գրաքննադատական գործերու ստուար պաշար մը՝ հաստատելու համար որ այս մարզէն ներս եւս Կիւրճեան կը մնայ հեղինակութիւն մը: Ան վերլուծած եւ արժեւորած է կարգ մը ժամանակակից գրողներ. իսկ միւս կողմէ վէճի բռնուած է հեղինակաւոր քննադատներու հետ՝ պաշտպանելու համար իրական արժէքները. օրինակ, ան Եղիա Տէմիրճիպաշեանի լաւագոյն էջերն ու ոգեկանութիւնը կը բնորոշէ հետեւեալ սահմանումով. ըստ Կիրճեանի, այդ գործերը յօրինուած են՝ «խելայեղ խոյանքով ... ներշնչումով, միացայտ աւիւնով եւ ինքնաբուխ յորդումով»: Միւս կողմէ ան կը դիմադարձէ Օշականին՝ Ինտրայի մասին արձակած անոր մէկ վճիռին առիթով, գրելով. «ապշեցուցիչ եւ ընդվզեցուցիչ կերպով անարդար կը գտնեմ զինքը Տիրան Չրաքեանի մասին, որ իմ համոզումովս, եւ ինծի պէս մէկ քանիներու համոզումովը՝ որ ապագայ սերունդներունը պիտի ըլլայ ապահով, մեր մեծագոյն հանճարն է, եւրոպական իմաստով մեր ամենէն «տիեզերական» հանճարը, մեր մեծագոյն արուեստագէտ-բանաստեղծ-խորհողը»:

Հայ գրականութեան մասին ընդհանրացումներ կատարելով Կիրճեան կ'ողբայ հայ գրականութեան մէջ պակասը յուշագրութեան — մեմուարային գրականութեան — որ այսօր եւս, յատկապէս ամերիկեան գրականութեան մէջ նոր զարթօնք մը կ'ապրի: Այս մարզէն ներս յաջող օրինակներ կը նկատէ Արփիարեանի «Հողվրտիք»ն ու «Օրուան Կեանքը», ինչպէս նաեւ Օտեանի «Տասներկու Տարի Պոլսէն Դուրս» գործը:

ԲԱՌԱԿԵՐՏՈՒՄԻ ՀՐԱՑՔԸ

Միքայէլ Կիրճեան մեր գրականութեան մէջ ամենէն գեղագէտ գրողներէն մէկն է՝ եթէ ոչ ամենէն գեղագէտը, ոչ միայն խորքային իմաստով, այլ նաեւ ու մանաւանդ, իր մշակելու արուեստագէտ հնարաւորութիւններով, լեզուի ճկունութեամբ ու բառերու ոգին արտահանելու իր բացառիկ շնորհներով:

Կիրճեանի լեզուն հիւթեղ է եւ պատկերալից. ան մանաւանդ կ'ախորժի բառախաղերէ եւ բառակերտումներէ: Գրողներն են որ լեզուական չափանիշներ պիտի հաստատեն գրականութեան, մամուլի, բեմի եւ մինչեւ անգամ՝ առօրեայ խօսակցութեան համար. անոնք է որ քաղաքացիութեան իրաւունք կ'երաշխաւորեն նորակերտ բառերուն ու կեանք կը պարգեւեն անոնց:

Մէքէրեանի այս մենագրութիւնը ամբողջական պիտի չըլլար՝ եթէ այս մարզէն ներս Կիրճեանի բերած ուսանելի նպաստը չընդգրկէր այստեղ:

Լեզուական այդ մակարդակի նուաճումը, ընթացիկ բառերուն նոր տրամագիծ ընծայելու շնորհը, արտայայտիչ բառակերտումներու ստեղծումը կ'նեթադրեն խորունկ հմտութիւնը մեր լեզուին, մանաւանդ՝ ընտանութիւնը գրաբարին, որ մեզի թոյլ կու տայ կատարելու ճիշդ ստուգաբանութիւններ եւ յօրինելու նոր եւ արտայայտիչ բառեր:

Լեզուական այս հնարաւորութենէն զրկուած են խորհրդային շրջանի գրողները, որովհետեւ նոր ուղղագրութեան որդեգրումը անհնար դարձուցած է բառերու դիմագիծին եւ արմատներուն ճանաչումը եւ հետեւաբար ածանցումներով եւ բարդացումներով նոր բառեր կերտելու հնարաւորութիւնը:

Հասկնալի կը դառնայ ուրեմն, որ այդ շրջանի ամենէն շնորհալի գրողներն անգամ — որոնք ծանօթ չեն եղած գրաբարին կամ դասական ուղղագրութեան — կալանաւորը մնացած ըլլան մակերեսային եւ յաճախ՝ անդիմագիծ լեզուային պաշարի մը:

Նոր բառակերտումներու պակասը, միւս կողմէ, դուռ կը բանայ օտար բառերու որդեգրումին, աւելի եւս աղքատացնելով մեր լեզուն: Կիւրճեանի գրականութիւնը կրնայ իքնին ուղեցոյց մը դառնալ բոլոր այն գրողներուն որոնք կը փափաքին լեզուական ճաշակով հանդէս գալ կամ գեղարուեստական շնորհ մը աւելցնել իրենց լեզուին ու ոճին: Մէքէրեան բազմաթիւ օրինակներ կը ներկայացնէ Կիւրճեանի լեզուական գիւտերէն:

Պարոյր Սեւակ այն հազուագիւտ խորհրդային գրողներէն է որոնք բանաստեղծութեան մէջ լեզուի գեղարուեստական արժէքը գիտեն եւ կը գործածեն — Մահարի տեղ մը ըսած է թէ Պարոյր Սեւակ իր իւրայատուկ լեզուն ստեղծեց իր «Անլռելի Զանգակատունը» պոէմին համար, որ անկրկնելի մնաց իր գրականութեան մէջ անգամ:

Մէքէրեան յաջողած է Սեւակի այդ յաջողութեան ետին կեցող սկզբունքը գտնել ու մէջբերել նոյնինքն Սեւակի խօսքերը, որ, աւելորդ չ՚ըլլար կրկնել այստեղ: Ուրեմն «Պահպանենք Եւ Հարստացնենք Մայրենին» յօդուածին մէջ Սեւակ մասնաւորաբար կը գրէ. «Հայերէնը, օրինակ, ունի մի առաւելութիւն, որ աշխարհի քիչ լեզուներ ունեն. բառակազմութեան հեշտութիւնն ու շահաւէտութիւնը: Ու եթէ որեւէ լեզու, հայերէնից նոյնիսկ աւելի հարուստ ու ճկուն մի լեզու, ստիպուած է օտար բառն ընդունել, որովհետեւ բառակազմութեան իր հնարաւորութիւնները սուղ են, ապա հայերէնի պէս մի լեզու պարտաւոր է հայացնել այդ բառը, որովհետեւ օտար բառը, իբրեւ ընդհանուր օրէնք, շատ աւելի քիչ բան է ասում հային, քան մայրենի լեզուի յաջող բառակազմութիւնը»:

Այսօր մեծ է պաշտամունքը Հայաստանի մէջ Սեւակի վաստակին, անուան ու յիշատակին նկատմամբ. սակայն այդ պաշտամունքը ունեցող շատ մը մտաւորականներ կը յամառին մեր լեզուն պահել զայն աղքատացնող բռնաշապիկի մէջ:

* * *

Յարութիւն Մէքէրեան այս հատորին երկնումով արձանագրած կ՚ըլլայ միանգամայն քանի մը իրագործում. ա) ան նշանակալից ներդրում մը կատարած է հայ գրականութեան պատմութեան, լրացնելով հսկայ բաց մը. բ) վերականգնած է Կիւրճեան գրագէտի հարուստ ժառանգութեան դիմագիծը. գ) ուղեցոյց մը պատրաստած է կիւրճեանագիտութեան, մեր գրականութիւնը հարստացնելով այս շատ շնորհալի գրողի տաղանդին ամբողջական ուժով. դ) անարդարութեան եւ անտեսուած ըլլալու տագնապը,

որով բաժնուեցաւ Կիրճեան այս աշխարհէն, մասամբ դարմանուած կ'ըլլայ.
ե) այս հատորով Մէքէրեան նախագիծ մը հրամցուցած կ'ըլլայ Կիրճեանի գործերու գիտական եւ ակադեմական հրատարակութեան, միանգամընդմիշտ անոր տեղը ամրագրելով մեր դասական գրականութեան պատմութեան մէջ:

* * *

Իր կեանքի օրերուն Կիրճեան միշտ հմայուած էր Եգիպտոսի մէջ ամառնամուտին ծաղկող վառ կարմիր ծառերով, որոնք այդ շրջանին առատ ծաղիկներ կու տային բնկեցնելով պուրակներն ու ճամբեզրները. Կիրճեան անոնց հմայքով արբշիռ կը քալէր փողոցներէն, իր խոշոր կօշիկներով, իբրեւ յաւիտենական ճամբորդը այդ ուղիներուն: Այդ ծառերը ֆրանսերէնով կը կոչուին flamboyant (ֆլամպուայան). Կիրճեան յաջող թարգմանութեամբ մը այդ ծառերը կոչած էր *վառենի.* այնքան կը սիրէր այդ ծառերը որ կը ցանկար իր հողակոյտին վրայ վառենիի մը տնկումը: Անոր մահէն տարիներ վերջ երբ այցելեցի Եգիպտոսի մէջ Հելիոպոլսոյ հայոց գերեզմանատունը, շքեղ դամբարաններու կողքին, մեր գրականութեան ոստանին նման անոր անշուք հողակոյտը տեսնելով գրած էի տեղ մը թէ «Ո՞վ պիտի տնկէ վառենի մը» Կիրճեանի հողակոյտին վերեւ:

Յարութիւն Մէքէրեան իր այս շնորհակալ երկով խորհրդանշականօրէն տնկած է այդ վառենին:

Երուանդ Ազատեան

ՆԱԽԱԲԱՆ

Հայ մտաւորականութեան քաջ ծանօթ Միքայէլ Կիրճեանի անունը ցաւօք սրտի տակաւին անյայտ է հասարակութեան լայն խաւերուն, հակառակ անոր որ իր արձակ եւ թատերական ստեղծագործութիւններով ան իր պատշաճ եւ ուրոյն տեղը գրաւելու արդար իրաւունքն ունի հայ նոր գրականութեան պատմութեան մէջ: Արդարեւ, արեւմտահայ գրողներու փայլուն համաստեղութեան մէջ Կիրճեան իր գրական վաստակով իւրայատուկ ստեղծագործող մը եղած է հայ լուսափայլ գրողներու շարքին, մշակութային, հասարակական եւ անարատ հայրենասիրական գործունէութեամբ՝ միշտ հաւատարիմ մնացած է իր դաւանանքին եւ 19րդ դարու վերջին տասնամեակի տարիներէն մինչեւ 20րդ դարու 60ական թուականները ստեղծագործած է որպէս արձակագիր ու բանաստեղծ, թատերագիր ու նորավիպագիր, խմբագիր ու թարգմանիչ, անցնելով մի քանի սերունդներու մէջէն եւ միշտ հարազատ մնալով իր գրական իրապաշտ սկզբունքին ու երգիծական տաղանդին՝ յաւէտ մնալով բարձր, առաջաւոր ու պատուաւոր պատնէշի վրայ: Անոր բեղուն ու բազմալար գրիչին կը պատկանին «Մարտիկ Աղա» երգիծավէպը, «Չարշըլը Արթին Աղա» կատակերգութիւնը (գրուած Երուանդ Օտեանի հետ), «Փրկանքը» տրամը (գրուած Տիգրան Կամսարականի հետ), «Հերոսախաղ» ազգային երգիծական թատրերգութիւնը (գրուած Երուանդ Օտեանի հետ), «Քսան Տարի Ետք...» կատակերգութիւնը, «Անունին Գիշերը», «Նոր Լաթ», «Սուտը Իրաւ՝ Խենթը Խելօք», «Տրդատ Եւ Տաճատ», «Անջնջելի Մատեանը» հայկական եւ տոհմային կեանքը պատկերող բազում պատմուածքներն ու նորավէպերը, «Քեաթիպին Երազը», «Սրճարանը» արեւելեան պատկերները, «Ի Խորոց Սրտի Խօսք Ընդ Պաշտելւոյն» արձակ քերթուածներու ժողովածուն, բազմաթիւ քրոնիկներ, խմբագրականներ, գրախօսականներ, յօդուածներ, արձակ ու չափածոյ թարգմանութիւններ, եւայլն:

Հանճոյքով ընթերցուող գրող մը եղած է Կիրճեան, որ գիտէ գեղարուեստօրէն պատմել ու նկարագրել: Հանդէս գալով մեր գրականութեան իրապաշտ շրջանին՝ ան նկարած է կեանքը պահանջկոտ բծախնդրութեամբ, նկարագրած է դէպքերն ու դէմքերը խորունկ զգացումով, վիշտն ու ծիծաղը խառն, սուր *հիւմըր*ով, յուզումներով, ապրումներով: Օժտուած ըլլալով դիտելու ու զննելու մեծ վարպետութեամբ եւ քաջ գիտակցելով երգիծանքի հասարակական վեհ նշանակութիւնը, ան վճռական դեր կատարած է գրականութեան ժողովրդականացման, իրապաշտ գրականութեան հաստատման ու զարգացման գործին մէջ, որով պայմանաւորուած է գրողի անուան անմահութիւնը: Իր գրուածքներուն նիւթը եւ խորքը եղած են ազգային դաստիարակութեան եւ ժամանակի հրատապ խնդիրները, որոնք մշակած եւ հրատարակութեան տուած է իր օրերու տարբեր երկիրներու հայ մամուլին մէջ: Կիրճեանի գործերը ուշագրաւ են ու թելադրական, շեշտուած են նուրբ ոճով եւ մշակուած են խստապահանջօրէն՝ մաքուր եւ սահուն լեզուով:

Այս մենագրութեան նպատակն է փորձ կատարել ներկայացնելու Միքայէլ Կիրճեանի գրական ժառանգութիւնը՝ արձակը, բանաստեղծութիւնը, թատրերգութիւնը, հրապարակախօսութիւնը, տեսական-գեղագիտական յօդուածները, գրախօսականները, թարգմանութիւնները, ինչպէս նաեւ կենսագրութիւնը, հասարակական գործունէութիւնը եւ գրական կապերը՝ ծանօթացնելու համար հայ գրականութեան գրեթէ չգնահատուած տաղանդաւոր ներկայացուցիչը ընթերցասէր հասարակութեան ու գրականագէտներուն, որոշելու համար անոր արժանի տեղը հայ նոր գրականութեան մէջ:

Այս աշխատութիւնը Միքայէլ Կիրճեանի նուիրուած առաջին ծաւալուն ուսումնասիրութիւնն է, ուստի, հասկնալի է, որ հեղինակը երբեք յաւակնութիւն չունի այս երկը անթերի ու սպառիչ համարելու՝ յանիրաւի անուշադրութեան եւ մոռացութեան մատնուած տաղանդաւոր հայ գրողին վերաբերեալ: Մենագրութեան հեղինակը երկար տարիներու ընթացքին պրպտած, փնտռած, հաւաքած է տարբեր երկիրներու մէջ լոյս տեսած եւ Հայաստանի ու Լոս Անճելըսի գրադարաններուն մէջ գտնուող հայ պարբերականներու մէջ ցիր ու ցան տպագրուած Միքայէլ Կիրճեանի ստեղծագործութիւնները, զորս ուսումնասիրած եւ անոնցմէ խնամքով ընտրուած «Հատընտիր» ժողովածու մը պատրաստած է տպագրութեան: Ուսումնասիրած է նաեւ Հայաստանի Գրականութեան եւ Արուեստի Թանգարանի Միքայէլ Ս. Կիրճեանի արխիւը, նամակները, ձեռագրերը եւ յուշատետրերը, որոնց մէջ գրողը արձանագրած է սեփական ապրումները, ճանապարհորդական տպաւորութիւնները, անձնական նօթագրութիւնները եւ գրական մտորումները:

Միքայէլ Կիրճեանի կեանքը եւ գրական ժառանգութիւնը ուսումնասիրող գրականագէտը վերջին տարիներուն վերծանած, խմբագրած ու հրատարակութեան պատրաստած է Կիրճեանի ««Ազգայինճին» Կամ Մեծութիւն Եւ Անկում Իգնատիոս Ռուբինեանի» երեք արար կատակերգութիւնը եւ հռչակաւոր «Մարտիկ Աղա» երգիծավէպը՝ ձեռագիրներէն, որոնք սփիւռքահայ գրականասէր Յարութիւն Սիմոնեանի մեկենասութեամբ լոյս տեսած են 1999ին՝ երգիծաբանին ծննդեան 120ամեակին առթիւ, Հայաստանի Գրականութեան եւ Արուեստի Թանգարանի հրատարակութեամբ: Վերծանած եւ ծանօթագրած է նաեւ Կիրճեանի «Նոր Դպրոցը» ձեռագիր անտիպ երգիծավէպը:

Կիրճեանի տաղանդը բարձր գնահատած են Արփիար Արփիարեանը, Եղիա Տէմիրճիպաշեանը, Գրիգոր Զօհրապը, Տիգրան Կամսարականը,

Լեւոն Բաշալեանը, Երուանդ Օտեանը, Երուանդ Սրմաքէշխանլեանը, Արշակ Չօպանեանը, Վահան Թէքէեանը, Թէոդիկը, Յակոբ Օշականը, Սուրէն Պարթեւեանը, Սիմոն Սիմոնեանը, Երուանդ Ազատեանը, Ալեքսանտր Սարուխանը, Հմայեակ Գրանեանը եւ ուրիշ հայ գրողներ ու արուեստագէտներ:

Կիւրճեանի մասին առաջին գիրքն է այս, ուր գլխաւորաբար տրուած է ամփոփ վերլուծութիւնը գրողին գեղարուեստական ստեղծագործութիւններուն՝ իրենց յատկանշական կողմերով: Արդարեւ, ընթանալով Յակոբ Պարոնեանի եւ 19րդ դարու ութսունականներու բացած ճանապարհով, Կիւրճեան, որպէս վիպասան-արձակագիր, զարգացուցած է հայ գրականութիւնը, մասնաւորաբար երգիծաբանութիւնը, իրապաշտ խորութեամբ եւ ընդհանրացման ուժով կերտուած տիպական կերպարներով:

ՄԻՔԱՅԷԼ ԿԻՒՐՃԵԱՆ ՀԱՅ ԳՐԱԿԱՆ ՄԻՏՔԻՆ ԳՆԱՀԱՏՄԱՄԲ

Միքայէլ Կիւրճեան գրչակիցն է եղած Արփիար Արփիարեանի, Գրիգոր Զոհրապի, Եղիա Տէմիրճիպաշեանի, Տիգրան Կամսարականի, Լեւոն Բաշալեանի, Երուանդ Օտեանի, Երուանդ Սրմաքէշխանլեանի, Օննիկ Չիֆթէ-Սարաֆի, Տիրան Չրաքեանի, Արշակ Չօպանեանի, Վահան Թէքէեանի, Վահան Մալէզեանի, Թէոդիկի եւ հայ նոր գրականութեան ուրիշ երախտաւորներու, որոնք դրուատանքով արտայայտուած են անոր մասին, գովաբանած են գրագէտի իր իրապաշտ ստեղծագործութիւններուն արժանիքները, բարձր գնահատած են գրաքննադատական հարցերու շուրջ իր խորաթափանցութիւնը, հիացումով արտայայտուած են նաեւ իր երգիծական տաղանդին ու խնամուած ոճին մասին:

Արեւմտահայ բանաստեղծ Տիրան Չրաքեան, գրական ծածկանունով՝ Ինտրա, Կիւրճեանին ուղղուած 16/29 Նոյեմբեր 1912 թուակիր նամակին մէջ[1] կը գրէ. «Ես որ Իզմիրի *Հայ Գրականութիւնը* առնելուս պէս քու անունդ կը փնտռեմ նախ եւ առաջ, *Լուսաբեր-Արեւը* տեսած ատենս ալ կը նայիմ թէ հո՞ն ես թէ ոչ. ես ոչ մէկ գրագէտի համար ունիմ երբեք այս փոյթն ու անձկութիւնն, այս կարօտը, այս պէտքը, ինչ որ արդիւնքն է ոչ միայն այն մասնաւոր կապին որով կապուած եմ քեզի հետ, այլ մանաւանդ իրողութեան թէ ստուգիւ ոչ ոք աւելի վարպետ է քան դուն: Կան քանի մը հոգիներ, որոնց գրածներն անպատճառ կը կարդամ. ինչպէս Օտեանը, Քէչեանը, Լեւոն Մկրտիչեանը, նաեւ Յովհաննէս Սէթեանը, որովհետեւ անոնք ալ իրենց տեսակին մէջ անմրցելի են, մանաւանդ Օտեանն ու Քէչեանը,- երբ այս վերջինը գրէ իր մեծ խմբագրականներէն մին,- բայց ուրիշ է կարօտը որով զքեզ կը կարդամ. կամ լաւ եւս՝ կարօտ մըն է այն զգացումը որով կը փնտռեմ մէկ յօդուածդ, եւ միայն գոհացման ապահովութիւն մը այն զգացումը, որով անոնց գրութիւններով կը հետաքրքրուիմ: ... Կ'ուզէի ըսել որ, սիրելի Միքայէլս, ամենէն առաջ զքեզ կը կարդամ. ինչ որ կը նշանակէ թէ *մանաւանդ* զքեզ, երբեմն *միայն* կ'ուզեմ կարդալ»:

Տիգրան Կամսարական իր ինքնակենսագրութեան մէջ կը գրէ. «... Ձեռքիս տակ ունիմ pièce (թատրերգութիւն – Յ.Մ.) մը[2] զոր կը յուսամ «ոտքի վրայ դնել» յառաջիկայ տարի Պոլսահայ բեմին վրայ՝ աշխատակցութեամբ Կիւրճեան Միքայէլի, որուն *իրական տաղանդը ծանօթ է ձեզ*»:[3]

Երուանդ Օտեանի մահուան կապակցութեամբ Թէոդիկ կը գրէ. «... Քանէ առաջ՝ անդարձ մեկներ էին հին մտերիմներդ՝ Արփիար, Քէլէկեան, Զոհրապ ու Պարթեւեան: *Լուսաւոր փաղանգէդ կը մնան միայն Ծանհնազար,*

Բաշալեան, Կամսարական, Թէքէեան ու Կիւրճեան, որոնց ճիտի պարտքն է անշուշտ վերապրեցնել զքեզ՝ կեանքիդ պէս ցրիւ այլ լրիւ քու գործերովդ»:[4]

Արեւմտահայ բանաստեղծ եւ խմբագիր Մերուժան Պարսամեան Պոլիսէն Վահան Մալէզեանին ուղղուած 11/24 Փետրուար 1909 թուակիր նամակին մէջ խօսելով քաղաքական պայքարի պատճառով գրականութեան մեռելային վիճակին մասին, միաժամանակ կ'անդրադառնայ «Փրկանքը» թատերգութեան հեղինակներուն ազնուական գրագէտներ ըլլալու հանգամանքին եւ կը գրէ. «... Ո՜ւֆ, սա քաղաքական կեանքը, սա քաղաքական պայքարը: Ո՞ր գեղեցկագէտի ականջ արդեօք կը յամառի դեռ լսել ուզելու: Գրական ուսումնասիրութիւն մը պատրաստած եմ «Քաղաքական Կեանքին Ազդեցութիւնը՝ Մեր Գրագէտներուն Վրայ», զոր հրատարակել կ'ուզեմ, եւ որուն երեւումը թերեւս մեծ պաղութիւն մը առաջ բերէ իմ եւ կարգ մը բարեկամ գրագէտներու միջեւ: Պէտք է ըսեմ, որ ես պաղարիւնութիւնով չեմ կրնար նայիլ այս իրադարձութիւններուն վրայ: Մեռած ենք գրականապէս: Ցաւալի է ասիկա, չէ՞: *Ո՞ւր մնաց Կամսարականին եւ Կիւրճեանին թատերգութիւնը: Կ'երեւակայեմ որ աղուոր բան մը ըլլալու է ան: Երկուքն ալ, ազնուական գրագէտներ, ոչ մէկ ձիրք կը պակսի իրենց գրականութեան սալոնին ամենէն բարձր աթոռները գրաւելու համար*»:[5]

Գրաքննադատութեան հարցերու մէջ խստապահանջ Յակոբ Օշական[6] բարձր կը գնահատէ Կիւրճեանի «սուր տաղանդը», որ «դուրս է կասկածէ»: «Իր սերունդին բոլոր ջոջերուն նման,- կը գրէ Օշական,- անիկա ստորագրած է քերթուածներ՝ արձակ եւ ոտանաւոր, որոնց մէջ զգացումէն եւ ստեղծումէն աւելի, խնամքն ու ձեւը կը մնան տիրական: Բազմաթիւ են օրուան հարցերուն շուրջ զուտ լրագրական գրուածքներ իրմէն: *Իր սերունդին մէջ Միքայէլ Կիւրճեան կը ներկայանայ այդ սերունդին ամբողջ կենդանութեամբը, սուր հետաքրքրութիւններովը, խոր ցանկութիւններովը: Ու նման անոնց ամենէն տաղանդաւորներուն՝ գրեթէ միշտ մնալով իր մտադրութեանց եզրին*»:[7]

Կիւրճեանի գրական արժանիքները փառաբանող ու բարձր գնահատող անուանի մարդոց խօսքերէն շատ քաղուածքներ կարելի է կատարել, սակայն մենք պիտի բաւականանանք նշելով միայն այն փաստը, որ իր ժամանակի ամենամեծ երգիծաբան Երուանդ Օտեան չափազանց հարազատ ու մտերիմ կապերու մէջ եղած է անոր հետ: Համոզուելու համար կը բաւէ գէթ մէկ անգամ թղթատել Օտեանի յուշագրական գործերը, որոնց մէջ հեղինակը յաճախ կ'արձանագրէ Կիւրճեանի մասին համակրանքի խօսքեր եւ անոր ստեղծագործութեան վերաբերեալ վաւերական գնահատականներ՝ սկսած «Մարտիկ Աղա» վէպի մասին հիացումի արտայայտութիւններէն մինչեւ իր խմբագրական յօդուածներու եւ քրոնիկներու սրամտութիւնը մատնանշող վկայութիւններ:

Հետաքրքրական է նշել, որ տակաւին 1898ին Միքայէլ Կիւրճեան ուզած է մտնէն ծանօթանալ Օտեանի հետ: Ծանօթացնողը եղած է Արփիար Արփիարեանը, որ այդ ժամանակ Աղեքսանդրիա կը գտնուէր՝ նախքան Լոնտոն մեկնիլը: Առաջին անգամ Կիւրճեան եւ Օտեան իրարու կը հանդիպին «Զոլա» կոչուած շաքարավաճառին խանութը: «Նստեցանք եւ սկսանք իրարու հետ խօսակցիլ: Առաջին վայրկեանէն ջերմ համակրութիւն մը զգացինք փոխադարձաբար իրարու հանդէպ, համակրութիւն մը որ յետոյ, կամաց-կամաց, հաստատուն ու բարեկամական անխառն սիրոյ մը փոխուեցաւ»,[8] կը գրէ Օտեան «Տասներկու Տարի Պոլսէն Դուրս» իր յուշագրական լաւագոյն երկին մէջ: Իրարու նկատմամբ փոխադարձ համակրանքն ու սէրը կու գար իրենց թէ՛ անհատական խառնուածքի, թէ՛ գաղափարներու, թէ՛ գրելաոճի նմանութենէն: Ուստի բնաւ զարմանալի չէ որ իրարու հետ անձնապէս ծանօթանալէ հազիւ քանի մը տարի ետք, երկու գրագէտները միասին կը գրեն քրոնիկներ, որոնց տակ կը ստորագրեն Ե. Մ. Կիւրօտ ծածկանունով, որ կը հանդիսանայ իրենց անուններու սկզբնատառերուն եւ ազգանուններու առաջին վանկերուն միախառնումը: Հարկ է նշել, որ գրականութեան մէջ այս բացառիկ երեւոյթը վառ ապացոյց մըն է որ երկու գրողներուն միջեւ փոխադարձ սէրն ու համակրանքը չէր բխեր միայն բարեկամութենէ եւ մտերմութենէ, այլ պայմանաւորուած էր Օտեանի եւ Կիւրճեանի աշխարհահայեացքի, բնաւորութեան եւ գրելաձեւի համապատասխանութեամբ:

Խօսելով 1903-1905 թուականներուն իր հրատարակած «Ազատ Բեմ»ի մասին, Օտեան կը նշէ որ «թերթին մշտական աշխատակիցն էր Միքայէլ Կիւրճեան, որ իր *անսպառ սրամտութեամբ կ'ողողէր «Ազատ Բեմ»ի էջերը*»:[9] ««Ազատ Բեմ» մեծ յոգնութիւն մը չէր տար ինծի,- կը շարունակէ Օտեան,- շաբաթը հազիւ քանի մը ժամ կ'երթայի տպարան յօդուած գրելու կամ փորձ սրբագրելու համար: *Մնացած ժամանակս կ'անցընէի Միքայէլ Կիւրճեանի հաճելի ընկերակցութեամբը*»:[10]

Կիւրճեան-Օտեան գրական համագործակցութիւնը շարունակուած է նաեւ հետագայ տարիներուն եւ անոնք որպէս հեղինակակից լոյս ընծայած են «Ֆրանքօ-Թրքական Պատերազմը» կատակերգութիւնը, որ մինչեւ այսօր կը ներկայացուի սփիւռքահայ եւ հայրենի բեմերէն: Հետաքրքրական է նշել, որ բեղմնաւոր գրող Երուանդ Օտեան հեղինակակցած է միայն Կիւրճեանի հետ եւ այդ համագործակցութեան արդիւնքն է նաեւ «Հերոսախաղ» կատակերգութիւնը, որ նոյնպէս հետաքրքրութեամբ դիտուած է հասարակութեան կողմէ:

Աղամանդի առեւտուրով զբաղող եղբօր հրաւէրով երբ 16 Փետրուար 1904ին Օտեան Աղեքսանդրիայէն կը մեկնի Պոմպէյ, իր բացակայութեան ժամանակ «Ազատ Բեմ»ի խմբագրապետ կը դառնայ Կիւրճեան, որ կանոնաւորաբար կը շարունակէ լոյս ընծայել թերթը՝ մինչեւ Օտեանի վերադարձը Հնդկաստանէն Եգիպտոս: Հետագային, երբ «Ազատ Բեմ»ը կամաց-կամաց կը սկսի դառնալ զուտ կուսակցական թերթ, իրարու ետեւէ թերթէն կը հեռանան Կիւրճեան, Վահան Թէքէեան եւ Օտեան: Աւելի ուշ, մէկ ամսուան կեանք ունեցած «Թերթիկ» փոքրածաւալ օրաթերթէն ետք, երբ Օտեան 1908ին կը հիմնէ «Արեւ»ը Աղեքսանդրիոյ մէջ, հրատարակչական ընկերութեան կազմին անդամ կ'ըլլայ նաեւ Կիւրճեան՝ որպէս հիմնադիրներէն մէկը:

«Տասնվեց Տարի Ետքը» խորագրով յուշագրական իր վերջին գործին մէջ, զոր գրած է 1925ին Եգիպտոս վերադառնալէ ետք, Օտեան դարձեալ դրական խօսքերով կ'արտայայտուի Կիւրճեանի մասին: Տասնվեց տարուան բացակայութենէ ետք անոր համար Աղեքսանդրիան անճանաչելի դարձած կ'ըլլայ: Հին սրճարաններու փոխարէն նորաշէն փողոցներով գեղեցկացած նաւահանգիստին մէջ, «առաջնորդարանը վարժարանի վերածուած, ման-կապարտէզը առաջնորդարան եղած» քաղաքին մէջ, «ամէն բան փոխուած» Աղեքսանդրիոյ մէջ Օտեան փոխուած կը գտնէ նաեւ իր բարեկամը, որուն մասին կը գրէ. «Յետոյ կը տեսնեմ իմ սիրականս, Միքայէլ Կիւրճեանը, որուն հետ երկար ժամեր կ'անցընենք հին յիշատակներ պրպտելով: Ի՜նչ փոփոխութիւն: Ուր է այն նիհար, տժգոյն, դուրեկանական, իդէալական Մի-քայէլը, որուն համար յաճախ Արփիարին հետ անձկութեամբ կը խորհէինք.

«- Արդեօք պիտի ապրի՞ խեղճը:

«Հիմա քաղքենիացած, զանգուածային մսակոյտ մը ունիմ դէմս: Բայց *երբ կը սկսի խօսիլ, երեւան կու գայ հին Միքայէլը իր սրամիտ, կայծկլտուն անմահ ոգիովը*»:[11]

* * *

Կիւրճեանագիտութեան մէջ իր ուրոյն տեղն ունի արեւմտահայ հրապարակագիր, գրաքննադատ, մշակութային եւ հասարակական գործիչ Երուանդ Ազատեան, որ գրողին կեանքին ու ստեղծագործութիւններուն մասին սփիւռքահայ մամուլին մէջ լոյս տեսած իր յօդուածները զետեղած է նաեւ «Գրական գեղարուեստական սեւեռումներ» խորագրով հատորին մէջ՝ «Ո՞վ Պիտի Տնկէ Վառենի Մը», «Միքայէլ Կիւրճեան Գրողը», «Փոքրիկ Գիրքի Մը Լայն Բովանդակութիւնը», «Միքայէլ Կիւրճեանը Մտերմութեան Մէջ» վերնագրերով:[12]

Ազատեան Կիւրճեանը կը համարէ «մեր արուեստագէտ սերունդի վեր-ջին մոհիկանը», «անցեալին ապրող վկայութիւնը մեր մէջ», որ «ազգային ու գրական բոլոր դէմքերուն կեանքը արձանագրած է իր մէջ» եւ «ամբողջ կեանքին ընթացքին մեծութիւն մը պտտցուցած է իր հետ»:

Ազատեան «Արեւ»ի իր խմբագրապետութեան տարիներուն անձնապէս մօտէն ծանօթանալու, գրագէտին հաճոյալի ընկերակցութիւնը ըմբոշխնելու եւ անկեղծ մտերմութիւնը վայելելու բախտաւոր առիթն է ունեցած, որովհետեւ Կիրճեան վերջին տարիներուն տարեկան շուրջ 5-6 ամիս կ'այցելէր Գահիրէ եւ գրեթէ ամէն ցերեկ կը յաճախէր «Արեւ»ի խմբագրատուն: Զգալով վերջինիս գրական հետաքրքրասիրութիւնը, հայկական արժէքները արժեւորելու եւ պահպանելու հոգատարութիւնը, Կիրճեան յարմար դատած է անոր վստահիլ իր խունացած արխիւներուն ժառանգութիւնը եւ անոնց ճակատագիրը տնօրինելու որոշումը. կտակը՝ որպէս հաւատարիմ մտերիմի, սրտակից բարեկամի եւ համակիր գրական մշակի:

Սփիւռքահայ անուանի գրող, հրապարակագիր եւ խմբագիր Սիմոն Սիմոնեանի նախաձեռնութեամբ ու «Սեւան» հրատարակչատան տպագրութեամբ Կիրճեանի անհամար գործերէն դոյզն մաս մը ընդգրկող «Քսան Տարի Ետք. Պատմուածքներ Եւ Պատկերներ» հատորին[13] լոյս ընծայման առթիւ Ազատեան «Փոքրիկ Գիրքի Մը Լայն Բովանդակութիւնը» յօդուածին մէջ հանգամանօրէն կը վերլուծէ գրողին «Քսան Տարի Ետք» թատերախաղը, մէկ տասնեակէ աւելի իրապաշտական, խոհական, զգացական ստեղծագործութիւնները եւ արեւելապատումները՝ ներկայացնելով հեղինակին վառ դիմագիծը: Ազատեան յատկապէս կ'ընդգծէ որքան գրագէտին վարպետութիւնը, յաջողականութիւնը, արտայայտուելու նրբութիւնը, նոյնքան ալ՝ տաղանդի բազմակողմանիութիւնը, գրչի բացառիկ յատկութիւնը եւ սուր երգիծանքը: Գրաքննադատը մասնաւորապէս կը դրուատէ նաեւ Կիրճեանի գեղապաշտ լեզուն եւ գրելաոճը, գրելով. «ան բարքերու ուսումնասիրութեան վարպետ մըն էր, իր գունագեղ ոճով, անվրիպելի եւ ճկուն լեզուով»:

Հարկ է արձանագրել որ Ազատեանի առաջարկով է որ Կիրճեան գրած է իր անսպառ, հետաքրքրաշարժ բազում յուշերը ճանչցած գրողներու՝ Արփիար Արփիարեանի, Տիրան Չրաքեանի, Երուանդ Օտեանի, Վահան Թէքէեանի եւ այլ գրչեղբայրներու մասին, որոնց ժամանակակիցը ըլլալով եւ անոնց հետ սերտ եւ երկարատեւ կապ ունենալով, շահեկան, ուշագրաւ ու հետաքրքրական դրուագներ ամբարած է իր պայծառ յիշողութեան մէջ՝ զանոնք յիշելով ամենայն մանրամասնութեամբ, ինչպէս Միսսէն, Վերլէնէն, Հիւկոյէն, Լամարթինէն անգիր սորված բանաստեղծութիւնները:

Ծնունդով պոլսահայ Միքայէլ Կիրճեան մինչեւ վերջ մնաց սիրուած գրող մը, որ գնահատուած եւ յարգուած էր իր ծերունազարդ տարիքին ալ: Ականաւոր գրագէտին մահուան կապակցութեամբ՝ ի շարս այլ մտաւորականներու՝ Վահէ-Վահեանն ու Հմայեակ Գրանեանը Պէյրութէն, Տարիա Կամսարականն ու Յովհաննէս Պօղոսեանը Փարիզէն, Ալեքսանտր Սարուխանը Գահիրէէն եւ ուրիշներ գովասանքի խօսքերով արտայայտուած են սփիւռքահայ մամուլին մէջ:

ԿԵԱՆՔԻ ՇԱՒԻՂԸ

Միքայէլ Սահակի Կիրճեան ծնած է 1879ին Կ. Պոլսոյ կապուտագեղ ծովափի Սկիւտարի արուարձանը, կեսարացի պանդուխտ մտաւորական ծնողներու ընտանիքին մէջ: Հայրը՝ Սահակ էֆէնտի, գրագիր էր, եւ հակառակ իր չքեղ անցեալին՝ եղած է պարզ ու բարեկիրթ մարդ, իր ընտանիքին ապրուստը ապահովող հոգատար ամուսին եւ բարի հայր: Տիրան Չրաքեան հետեւեալ խօսքերով կը նկարագրէ ծերունի Սահակ Արմենակի Կիրճեան էֆէնտիին կերպարանքը. «իրիկունները կ'անցնէր մեռաւոր փողոցներէն, իր տարօրինակ կերպով խոհուն նայուածքն ու դանդաղութիւնը տանելով՝ մարդամերժ կղզիացումի մը կիսավայրի ինքնամփոփումով՝ վերջալոյսին ստուերին մէջ այնքան խորհրդաւոր էր այդ կերպարանքը...»:

Ապացուցելու համար Սահակ էֆէնտիի մտաւորական ըլլալն ու պոլսահայ մամուլին իր բերած համեստ մասնակցութիւնը, այստեղ կը մէջբերենք Տիրան Չրաքեանի Սկիւտարէն Աղեքսանդրիա՝ Միքայէլ Կիրճեանին գրած 9/22 Սեպտեմբեր 1901 թուակիր նամակէն հետեւեալ հատուածը. «Հօրդ Ծիածանը չգտայ դեռ. գտած Ծիածաններուս լեզուն տաճկերէն է, եւ խմբագրին, արտօնատիրոջ, տնօրէնին եւլն. անունները օտար են: Իսկ պարունակութիւնը (գէթ իմ տեսածներուս) ոչինչ կը ներկայացնէ հետաքրքրական. վերջապէս փնտռածդ չէ: Յառաջիկային թերեւս աւելի կարեւոր թիւեր եւ մանաւանդ քու հօ'րդ հրատարակածը գտնեմ»:

Պոլսահայ նշանաւոր հրապարակագիր Տիրան Քէլէկեան Գաhիրէէն Կիրճեանին գրած 14 Նոյեմբեր 1904 թուակիր նամակին մէջ նոյնպէս կը հաստատէ գրողին հօր՝ Սահակի հրատարակչական գործունէութիւնը տակաւին 1880ական տարիներուն:

Ան կը գրէ. «Ձեր հայրը՝ Սահակ էֆէնտին տարիներով մեր տանը սիրուած այցելուներէն մէկը եղած էր, անձնապէս շատ աղէկ յարաբերութիւններ ունեցայ իրեն հետ, երբ Պոլսոյ մամուլին մէջ սկսնակ գրող մըն էի, քառորդ դար կայ արդէն: Շատ խորունկ յիշատակ մը պահած եմ նաեւ ձեր հօրեղբայրէն, որուն հետ Աթէնքի մէջ վտարանդիի կեանքի եղբայրակցութիւնը ունեցանք շուրջ 14 տարի առաջ»:

Միքայէլի հօրեղբօրը՝ Սերոբ Կիրճեանին քաջ ծանօթ եղած է նաեւ բժիշկ Յարութիւն Թիրեաքեանը, որ 2 Սեպտեմբեր 1915ին Նիւ Եորքէն գրած նամակին վերջաւորութեան կը հարցնէ. «Սերովբէէն ի'նչ լուր, կարծեմ ան ու եւ մնացինք մեր սերունդէն, եթէ ողջ է...»: Թալասցի Սերոբ սառնաշունչ Մէյնի Պոտոնին Գոլէճէն վկայական ստանալէ ետք Պոլիս կը մեկնի վաճառականութեամբ զբաղելու համար, բայց յետոյ կը հաստատուի Աթէնք իբրեւ լուսանկարիչ:

Միքայէլի մայրը՝ Միրիկ հանըմ (ծնեալ՝ Ալթունեան), եղած է խելացի, ազնիւ եւ սրամիտ հայուհի մը: Ան զբաղած է իր երախաներուն դաստիարակութեամբ եւ իր բնածին սրամտութեամբ, պատկերաւոր նկարագրութիւններով ու հաճճարեղ արտայայտութիւններով լեցուն խօսակցութիւններով միշտ ալ ազդեցիկ տպաւորութիւն է ձգած իր շրջապատի մարդոց եւ անշուշտ, առաջին հերթին, իր զաւակներուն վրայ: Կիրճեանի օրագրին մէջ յաճախ կը հանդիպին իր մօր պատկերաւոր խօսքերը, մակդիրներն ու երեւոյթներու գեղարուեստական բնորոշումները: «Հաճճարեղ վայրկեաններ ունի մայրս, ուր բնական մարդուն, ժողովրդական դիպուածականներշնչումներէն աւելի, կամ զատ, կայ մասնաւոր կերպով օժտուած խառնուածքի մը անհատական կնիքը»:[14]

Կիրճեան յաճախ որպէս բառախաղ կամ ասացուածք գրի առած է իր մօր սքանչելի խօսքերը, պոլսահայ կնոջ բնածին սրամիտ արտայայտութիւնները: 1909ի իր խորհրդածութիւններուն մէջ «Մօրս Նշանաւոր Խօսքերը» վերնագրով կը կարդանք. «Անգամ մըն ալ մինչեւ Կէօթէ բարձրացաւ sans effort, sans litterature (առանց ճիգի, առանց գրականութեան – Յ.Մ.), հոյակապ բանականութեամբ մը...»: Այնուհետեւ կ'եզրակացնէ, որ կեանքի աստուածային բնազդը կրնայ անգրագէտ կին մը յանկարծ դարձնել «մեծ բանաստեղծ-խորհողի մը հաւասար»:

Կիրճեան հիացումով կ'արտայայտուի ոչ միայն մօր գեղեցիկ խօսքերուն մասին, այլեւ՝ անոր պատկերաւոր համեմատութիւններուն, նմանութիւններուն, գրելով. «Մայրս ի՞նչ բանաստեղծութիւն ըրաւ սքանչելի աղուոր կին մը նկարագրելու համար ... գործածեց *պիլլօր* բառը ... ասանկ հիանալի, ասչափ նկարիչ բառ չեմ գիտեր ... եւ իրաւ, գաւաթ մը, մաքուր, բարակ, տոհմիկ գաւաթ մը ջուրը կը ցոլայ թափանցիկ հոգիի մը պէս:» «Թնդանօթ արձակուած ատեն, հրացանին ձայնը չի լսուիր» յայտնի ժողովրդական առածի պէս, մայրը կ'ըսէ. «հալաճի տէղի պէս կը փախի», այսինքն՝ հալաճին փայտին թաքաթաքա, դըղդըղի ձայներուն մէջէն չի լսուիր արձակուած ձայնը:

Ուրիշ օրինակ մը զոր Կիրճեան սիրած է շատ նիհար անձի մը համար ըսուած արտայայտութիւնն է. «խառղան կոցելու ըլլայ նէ վրան միս չի գտնար»: Կիրճեան իր բառախաղի ունակութիւնն ալ մօրմէն ժառանգած կը համարէ՝ մօր նշանաւոր խօսքերէն առակի արժանի հետեւեալ հարց ու պատասխանը նօթագրելով.

«– Մայրիկ, վիրա կը մոմռաս, ... տէրտ կ'ընես, բարա չունինք, բարա չունինք, կ'ըսես. ինչո՞ւ համար...

«– Ասչափ կը մոմռամ նէ, ըսաւ, գիտէ՞ք որչափ կը մտմտամ»:

Իսկապէս հոյակապ բառախաղ:

Արեւմտահայ եւ արեւելահայ շրջանակներուն մէջ յայտնի անձնաւորութիւն եղած է նաեւ Միքայէլի մօրեղբայրը՝ Արշ. Էֆէնտի Ալթունեանը, որ գրած է «Աղքատին Պատիւը» վէպը:

Անհա անոր մօրեղբօր մասին տեղեկութիւններ պարունակող Տիրան Չրաքեանի 3/16 Հոկտեմբեր 1902ին գրած նամակէն հետեւեալ հատուածը. «Ակնոցաւոր մէկը եկեր է, քեզ տեսնել կ'ուզէ, ըսին: Վար իջայ, նայեցայ որ բակը Նշան էֆէնտիին հետ դէմառդէմ նստեր է մօրեղբայրդ, Ալթունեանը, որուն տարօրինակ դէմքը անկարելի է չճանչնալ խսկոյն: Օ ... դո՞ւք էք, Ալթունեան էֆէնտի, աս ուրկէ կու գաք, եւայլն,- բաւական տեսնուեցանք: Չորս ամիս հիւր եղեր է ... կառավարութեան. տախտակներուն վրայ հիւանդացեր է. յօդացաւը սաստկացեր է, ըսածին նայելով. թէեւ հասկցուցի իրեն թէ իր նկարագրած ցաւերը ուրիշ բան են, եւ թէ իր ըսած իօդիւրը (iodure) որմէ իրօք օգուտ չէ քաղեր՝ անյարմար է իրեն. névralgie է ունեցածը, խեղճ մարմինը լեցուն է névralgie-ով, բոլոր շարժումները կը ցաւին կոր: Ջինքը փոխադրեր են բանտարկեալց հիւանդանոցը, ուրկէ 8 օրէն ելեր է, կրցեր է հանուիլ, այսինքն, փոխադրուելու համար նուազ անտանելի տեղ մը, այսինքն ազգային հիւանդանոցը. ծծումբի լոգանքներ ըրեր է, բնականաբար անօգուտ, 28 օր ալ հոն մնացեր է, եւ 7-8 օրէ ի վեր հոնկէ ալ ելեր է եղեր, քիչ մը դրամ (6-7 ոսկի) կերցնելով հոս հոն, վասնզի աղէկնալու պարագային պէտք է եղեր որ կառավարութեան յանձնուի դարձեալ: Հիմա Զիլիֆտար Պաճչէսիի մէջ (Սկիւտար) մէկուն տունը հիւր է եղեր: Պատմեց իր վերջին գործերը. այսինքն Ռուսիա երթալը՝ տանելով իր նոր վէպը, որ սքանչելապէս սպառեր է հոն, շատ շահ բերելով իրեն: Եւ դեռ այլեւայլ բաներ ալ իր անցեալէն»:

1903ին, մօրեղբայրը, որ ականջը քիչ մը ծանր կը լսէր, Աղեքսանդրիա՝ Կիւրճեաններուն Ռամլէի նախկին տան մէջ գտնուած ժամանակ պարտէզը մէկ ոտքը ցեխաջուրի մէջ կը մտնէ եւ չ'իմանար...: Միքայէլ իսկոյն կը նկատէ եւ կատակով կը հարցնէ. «Մօրեղբայր, ոտքե՞րդ ալ խուլ են»:

Չրաքեան Սկիւտարէն 4 Մարտ 1904 թուակիր նամակին մէջ կը հետաքրքրուի Արշ. Ալթունեանով եւ կը հարցնէ. «Տեղեկութիւն ունի՞ս մօրեղբօրմէդ, որ Պոլիս եկած էր վերջերս»:

Կիւրճեան իր մօրեղբօր յիշարժան եւ սրամիտ խօսքերն ալ նօթագրած է իր օրագրութեան մէջ:

Անհաւասիկ օրինակ մը. «Մեր տենչերը յաւիտենականութիւնը կ'անցնին ... (dépassent) Ա. Ալթունեան»:

1919-1932 թուականներուն Հայկանուշ Մառքի տնօրէնութեամբ եւ խմբագրութեամբ Կ. Պոլիս լոյս տեսած է «Հայ Կին» հանդէսը, որ նպատակ ունէր նպաստել հայ կնոջ բարոյական, մտաւոր, ֆիզիքական եւ գեղագիտական զարգացման: Հանդէսը օգտակար եղած է նաեւ գրականութեան ժողովրդականացման գործին՝ իր էջերուն մէջ տպագրելով Դանիէլ Վարուժանի, Վահան Թէքէեանի, Երուանդ Օտեանի, Եղիշէ Դուրեանի, Ծուշանիկ Կուրղինեանի եւ ուրիշ հայ գրողներու ստեղծագործութիւնները: Հանդէսին 1920-1923 տարիներու թիւերուն մէջ յաճախ տպագրուած են նաեւ Միքայէլ Կիւրճեանի քրոջ՝ Ալիս Ս. Կիւրճեանի ստորագրութեամբ յօւուածներ ու նամակներ՝ այդ օրերու հրատապ հարցերուն արծարծմամբ: Սիպիլի, Արշակուհի Թէոդիկի, Մարի Պէյլէրեանի, Զ. Պէրպէրեանի, Ա. Գույումճեանի եւ ուրիշներու գրութիւններու շարքին, Ալիս Կիւրճեանի գրչին կը պատկանին «Ֆէմինիզմը Մեր Մէջ», «Մեր Որբերը», «Նամակները Պէ՞տք Է Բացուին» եւ այլ խորագրերով հետաքրքրական ու հայանպաստ գրութիւններ: Ալիս գործօն մասնակցութիւն ունեցած է նաեւ Աղեքսանդրիոյ Հայուհեաց յանձնախումբի կազմին մէջ՝ ի նպաստ հայրենիքի կազմակերպուած օգնութիւններու ձեռնարկներուն:

Ահա այսպիսի յայտնի, տիպար եւ մտաւորական հայ ընտանիքի մէջ ծնած ու դաստիարակուած է Միքայէլ, որ առաւել հանրայայտ դարձուցած է իր գերդաստանին անունը՝ հայ նոր գրականութեան պատմութեան մէջ մտցնելով «Միքայէլ Սահակի Կիւրճեան» սիրուած գրողի անունը, խորապէս յարգել տալով իր «ինքնատիպ տաղանդը» (Եդուարդ Գոլանճեան), եւ իր ժամանակի պարբերականներուն մէջ հանդէս գալով իբրեւ «կարողագոյն գրիչ մը», «գրական խոստմնալից տաղանդ մը», «մտաւոր հորիզոնի վրայ մշտափայլ աստղ մը» (Ռէթէոս Պէրպէրեան):

Կիւրճեանի մանկութեան եւ պատանեկութեան մեծ աշխարհը եղած է բանաստեղծութեան օրրան՝ նուիրական Պոլիսը, գեղատեսիլ Սկիւտարը, ուր ստացած առաջին տպաւորութիւնները վերապրած է ամբողջ կեանքի ընթացքին: Արդարեւ, Պոլսոյ մոգական երկինքը, ծովահայեաց բարձունքները, Մարմարայի գեղածիծաղ ափերը գրական ներշնչումներով օժտած են նաեւ մեր անմահ Պետրոս Դուրեանի, Զապէլ Եսայեանի, Տիրան Չրաքեանի, Լեւոն Բաշալեանի ու շատ ուրիշ գրողներու եւ արուեստագէտներու քնարական զգացումներն ու շնորհալի հոգիները:

* * *

Կիւրճեան իր կրթութիւնն ստացած է Պոլիս, նախ յաճախելով Իճատիէի Ներսէսեան թաղային դպրոցը, իսկ 1891էն՝ Պէրպէրեան վարժարանը, զոր աւարտած է 1895ին: Վաստակաւոր ուսուցչապետ եւ մեծանուն մանկավարժ Ռէթէոս Պէրպէրեան մեծապէս նպաստած է պոլսահայ հաւաքականութեան մտաւոր կեանքին: Ռ. Պէրպէրեանի շունչին տակ հասակ առնող երիտասարդութիւնը զարգացաւ իմացական ճիգերու ընդունակութեամբ: Այստեղ կը մէջբերենք Թէոդիկի վկայութիւնը, խօսուած Սկիւտարի գերեզմանատունը 24 Ապրիլ 1911ին, Ռ. Պէրպէրեանի հողակոյտին առջեւ՝ թաղման չորրորդ տարեդարձին առթիւ: Պէրպէրեանականութեամբ հզօրացած պատուաբեր սերունդի մը՝ հայ ուսուցիչներու, բժիշկներու, գիտնականներու, եկեղեցականներու, արուեստագէտներու, պետական եւ այլ պաշտօնեաներու, առեւտրականներու շարքին ան կը նշէ. «Անհա գրչի մարդիկ.- Բաշալեան, Ծաքլեան, Ճ. Ճաւարշ, Պարթեւեան, Պ. Ագաթան (Մ. Կիւրճեան _ Յ.Մ.), Թէքէեան, Ինտրա (Տիրան Չրաքեան _ Յ.Մ.), Սիմանեան, Քէչեան, Նազարեանց, Չէօկիւրեան, Գոլանճեան, Ռ. Սեւակ (Չիլինկիրեան _ Յ.Մ.)»:[15]

Անդրադառնալով Պէրպէրեան դպրոցին մէջ իր աշակերտական տարիներուն, Կիւրճեան այսպէս կը նկարագրէ ինքզինք. «Ես խլէզ մըն էի այն ատեն, բառին ֆիզիքական եւ բարոյական առումներովը,- խոնարհ աշակերտ մը, «ուսումնատենչ» հանդարտաբարոյ պատանիներուն յատուկ երկչոտութեամբը, իմ մէջս ծայրայեղութեան հասած»:[16]

Հետագային, երբ Կիւրճեան կը դառնայ բարձր դասարանի սան, հիացումով կ'ունկնդրէ Ռ. Պէրպէրեանի կարդացած փարթամ, բովանդակալից եւ ազդեցիկ դասախօսութիւնները: Կրթական մեծ մշակը, ի թիւս բազմաթիւ առարկաներու, կը դասաւանդէ հոգեբանութիւն, տրամաբանութիւն, իմաստասիրութիւն, յոյն եւ լատին դպրութիւն, քաղաքակրթութեան պատմութիւն, բարոյախօսութիւն եւ այլ գիտութիւններ: «Իր մտածումներուն ջրվէժումէն ու յորդաբուղխ պերճախօսութեան շքեղ աւիւնէն տարուած,- կը գրէ Կիւրճեան իր ուսուցչին մասին,- կը շարունակէր բարբառիլ, ոսկեբերան եւ արծաթաձայն, մեկնաբանելով այսինչ փիլիսոփային վարդապետութիւնը կամ այնինչ բանաստեղծին երկը վերլուծելով խանդավառօրէն...»:[17]

Ուսումնասէր եւ գրասէր Կիւրճեան պատանի հասակին կը զգայ սաղմնային վիճակի մէջ ապագայ գրող դառնալու զգացումը, որ կը դրսեւորուի տակաւին դպրոցական շարադրութիւններ գրելու ժամանակ: Ծրջանաւարտ ըլլալէն շուրջ տասը տարի ետք, Պէրպէրեան կը յիշէ իր աշակերտին շարադրութիւններէն մէկուն առթիւ ըրած դիտողութիւնները, միաժամանակ նոյն նամակին մէջ շեշտելով. «իբրեւ մեր լաւագոյն աշակերտներէն մին չէի կրնար զքեզ մոռնալ երբեք, բայց դու իսկ փոյթը ունեցար քու գեղեցիկ արդիւնքներովդ զքեզ յիշել տալու: ... Ապրի՜ս, ասա՛նկ պատիւը ըլլալու է դպրոցի մ'ուր մարդ ուսած է, ասա՛նկ մարդ իր դաստիարակին փոխարինելու է անոր ջանքն իր վրայ: Ծա՜տ ապրիս»:[18]

Յիշելով իր պատանեկութեան օրերը, Կիւրճեան կը խոստովանի. «գրականութեան դեւը զիս ալ ըմբռնած կալանած էր»: Եւահա դպրոցական ձեռատիպ «Արշալոյս» գրական հանդէսին մէջ 1893ին լոյս կը տեսնէ հազիւ 13 տարեկան պատանի Միքայէլի երախայրիքը «Ոոլան» խորագրով: Նորաստեղծ թերթին հրատարակիչներուն կողմէ իր աշխատակցութիւնը խնդրող դիմումին ընդառաջելով գրած բաւական երկար այս նորավէպին «միակ արժանիքը կամ մեղմացուցիչ պարագան մէկ շունչով, գրչի մէկ ցայտով ծայրէ ի ծայր գրուած ըլլալն է,- կը գրէ Կիւրճեան շուրջ երկու տասնեակ տարի անց,- ներշնչումի դիւրութեամբ մը, աւիւնի ճոխութեամբ մը, առատութեամբ մը, զոր մէյ մըն ալ չգտայ վերջէն, կորսնցուցած ըլլալով անդարձ, գրական անփորձութիւնը, տգիտութիւնը եւ ինքնավստահութիւնը, որոնք արժանաւորապէս նախագահեցին, թերթօններով, վէպերով սնած եւ բորբոքած պատանիի երեւակայութեանս հետ աթոռակից, գրական այս անդրանիկ արտադրութեանս...»:

Ի՞նչ է այս անդրանիկ գրական փորձին նիւթը: Բերենք հեղինակին խօսքերը. «Նիւթը սիրային դրամա մըն էր մռայլ ու եղերական, փոթորկոտ վերջալոյսի մը կամ Տըլակռուայի երկինքներուն պէս...: Ի՞նչ բանի վրայ կ'ուզէիք որ գրէր 13 տարեկան պատանի մը, եթէ ոչ այն բանին որու վրայ ամենէն շատ կը մտմտայ եւ զոր բնաւ չի ճանչնար. Սէրը...: Եւ իբր թէ սիրային աճագին արկածներ ունեցած եւ առնուազն տասը կիներէ խաբուած եւ լքուած ըլլայի, նախատեալ եւ վրէժխնդիր սիրոյ դրուագ մը կը պատմէի, բազմէջեան շաղփաղփութեամբ:

«Հարուստ տարփածու մը օրին մէկը կը կործանի. իր սիրուհին կամ «տիրուհին» -ֆրանսացւոց պէս խօսելու համար- կը վռնտէ զինքը, եւ ուրիշ ընչեղ հոմանի մը կը ճարէ, ինչպէս որ գուշակեցիք: Երիտասարդը, կարեվէր խոցուած, կատղած, կ'ուխտէ ահռելի վրէժ մը լուծել դրուժան կնոջմէն: Կը ծպտուի, աննանաչ կ'ըլլայ եւ օրին մէկը կը ներկայանայ իր նախկինին եւ թեկնածութիւնը կը դնէ կառապանի բաց մնացած պաշտօնի մը համար: Կ'ընդունուի՞, ո՛վ երկինք, կամ ո՛վ դժոխք: Ահա՛ խեղճ սիրահարը որ ստիպուած է ամոլը պտոյտի տանիլ, կառքով: Բայց համբերութի՜ւն, մօ՛տ է վրէժին իրաւարար ժամը: Իրիկուն մը ուրեմն՝ կեղծ կառապանը ամայի վայր մը կը տանի կառքը, եւ նստարանէն վար ցատկելով, կը ցցուի յանկարծ, իր ճշմարիտ դէմքով, ատրճանակ ի ձեռին, զահանդած կնոջ դիմաց, որ զբաղած էր կարծեմ ինքզինքը համբուրել տալու: Tableau! Մնացածը լաւ չեմ յիշեր. բայց կրնաք երեւակայել: Բա՛ն, բա՛ն: Մա՜հ եւ աւե՜ր: Վրէ՜ժ:

Նորավէպիս մէջ տեղ մը, նկարագրելով սիրոյ տեսարան մը, ըսած էի. Ոռլան *մեծաշառաչ* համբոյր մը դրոշմեց Ռոզալիի ձեռքին վրայ...:

«Հոգեբան մը թերեւս տեսնայ այս միամիտ բացատրութեան մէջ հոգեկան վիճակը աշխարհքէն անգէտ տղու մը, որ սիրային զգուանքներ աղու միւզիքէն ոչինչ լսած է, եւ իր անկուշտ անօթի երեւակայութեան մէջ՝ ժխոր մը, շառաչիւն մը կ'ընէ զայն,- քիչ մը ճիշդ ինչպէս որ խիստ ծարաւած մէկը իրեն երկնցուած գաւաթ մը ջուրը կուլ պիտի տար խոշոր ումպերով, մեծաձայն ընկլուզմամբ: Այդ հանդէսը կը տանին ձեռքը կը դնեն Ծաքլեանին, իբր միակ ձեռնհաս քննադատին, որուն կարծիքը առնել անհրաժեշտ էր: Եւ ինծի լուր կը բերեն որ Ծաքլեան այդ «մեծաշառաչ համբոյր» բացատրութիւնը շատ կոշտ, շատ աննաշակ, շատ գռեհիկ գտեր է: Ո՜վ մեծի ամօթապարտութեանս...:

«Կը յիշեմ որ այդ դատավճիռը մտիկ ըրի կորագլուխ, ջախջախուած,- դատավճիռ, որուն դէմ անկարելի էր վերակոչման դիմել: Ծաքլեան գրական գերագոյն, անվիճելի հեղինակութիւն էր ուսանողական աշխարհին մէջ...: Ասիկա եղաւ գրողի անձնասիրութեանս առաջին վէրքը...: Բարեբախտաբար ... չշարունակեցի արտադրել եւ տարիներով ոչինչ հրատարակեցի, մինչեւ 1898 թուականը, ուր «Նոր Կեանք»ի մէջ երեւցաւ առաջին տպուած գործս, «Մարտիկ Աղա» վէպը,- de scandaleuse mémoire (գայթակղեցուցիչ յիշողութիւն - Յ.Մ.),- այնպէս չէ՞, ո՞վ բարի Աղեքսանդրիացիք»:[19]

Դպրոցական տարիներուն իր ստացած գիտութեան պաշարը Կիրճեան շարունակած է հարստացնել ինքնազարգացումով: Ան եղած է չափազանց ընթերցասէր: Լաւ տիրապետելով ֆրանսերէն եւ անգլերէն լեզուներուն, ան հնարաւորութիւն ունեցեր է ծանօթանալու արեւմտաեւրոպական գրականութեան խոշորագոյն դէմքերու գործերուն:

Ան յատկապէս սիրած է կարդալ ռոմանթիք բանաստեղծներու, իսկ հետագային նաեւ իրապաշտ հեղինակներու գործերը:

Կիրճեանի սիրած հեղինակներն են եղած Վիքթոր Հիւկօն, Ալֆոնս տը Լամարթինը, Ալֆրէտ Միւսէն, Փիէռ տը Ռոնսարը, Շարլ Պոտլէրը, Ալֆոնս Տոտէն, Փոլ Վերլէնը, Օնորէ տը Պալզաքը, Արթիւր Ռէմպօն, Սթեֆան Մալարմէն, Ֆրանսուա Վիյոնը, Ժան Մոռէասը եւ ուրիշ ֆրանսացի գրողներ, ինչպէս նաեւ անգլիական գրականութեան ականաւոր հեղինակները, յատկապէս՝ Չարլզ Տիքընզ:

Կիրճեան թէ՛ Պոլսոյ, թէ՛ Աղեքսանդրիոյ մէջ ունեցած է ճոխ գրադարան: Տիրան Չրաքեան կը գրէ. «Աղեքսանդրիայէն դառնալէս վերջը մեր այն ատենուան դրացի Սօանճեաններր (հիմա Բերա) զիս կանչեցին, որ իրենց վերնայարկը գտնուած քու կամ հօրդ գիրքերու եւայլն մէկ դէզը աչքէ անցունեմ»: Տիրան ըստ իր հայեցողութեան կ'ընտրէ այդ գիրքերու դէզէն այն ինչ որ կարող էր օգտակար ըլլալ Կիրճեանին, որպէսզի Սօանճեաններր ատոնք ուղարկեն Միքայէլին՝ Աղեքսանդրիա: Չրաքեան միաժամանակ այդ գիրքերէն կ'առանձնացնէ իրեն օգտակար մի քանի հատորներ՝ «պզտիկ minéralogie (հանքաբանութիւն _ Յ.Մ.) մը, վիէննական «փորձառական բնագիտութիւն» մը հայերէն, Ֆլամմարիոնի Lumen-ը, մէյ մըն ալ գիրքի մը կամ թերթի մը հատուկտորը, ուր Պուրժէի մէկ ուսումնասիրութիւնը կար Պոտլէրի վրայ», որոնք ապացոյց են գրադարանին բազմաբնոյթ բովանդակութեան: Աղեքսանդրիոյ մէջ Կիրճեանը ճանչցողները նոյնպէս կը վկայեն, որ իր բնակարանին պատերը ծածկուած էին գիրքերով, որոնց մէջ գտնուած են գիրքի մը զանազան հրատարակութիւնները: Միքայէլ շատ սիրած է գիրքը, ճամբորդելու ժամանակ չէ մոռցած առաջին հերթին իր հետ վերցնել որեւէ գիրք, իսկ իր յուշերուն մէջ բազում տեղեր նշումներ կան այն մասին թէ Ֆրանսա գտնուած շրջանին յաճախած է հին գրատուներ եւ գնած է մի քանի հատոր գիրք՝ ընթերցանութեան համար: Այդ գիրքերը ժամանակի ընթացքին հաւաքուելով դարձած են անձնական ճոխ գրադարան մը: Այդ գիրքերուն մէկ մասը այժմ կը գտնուի իր անձնական արխիւին մէջ՝ Հայաստանի Գրականութեան եւ Արուեստի Թանգարանը:[20]

* * *

17 տարեկանին, Միքայէլ կը մտնէ կեանքի ասպարէզ: Պոլսոյ մէջ կը սկսի աշխատիլ որպէս գրագիր վարպետ Հէթում Սէթեանի մօտ: Սակայն շատ շուտ կ'ընդհատուի անոր աշխատանքային գործունէութիւնը Պոլսոյ մէջ: Պատանի հասակին կը զուգադիպին 1894-1896 թուականներու արիւնալի դէպքերը, երբ անգլիասէր Քեամիլ փաշայի կառավարութեան մշակած հայ ժողովուրդի ֆիզիքական բնաջնջման հրէշային ծրագիրը կը սկսի կիրարկուիլ Արեւմտեան Հայաստանի մէջ եւ բացայայտ ջարդերէն զերծ չի մնար նաեւ Պոլիսը՝ իր աշխարհագրական դիրքով եւ գեղեցկութեամբ հրաշալի, սակայն այդ օրերուն արհաւիրքներով պղծուած եւ դժոխային դարձած քաղաքը:

14 Օգոստոս 1896ին, Օսմանեան Դրամատան դէպքին կը յաջորդէ Պոլսոյ մէջ սուլթանական կառավարութեան թելադրանքով կազմակերպուած հայերու նոր կոտորածը, որու ժամանակ երկու օրուայ ընթացքին (Օգոստոս 14-16) կը կոտորուի աւելի քան տաս հազար հայ:

1915ի բռնագաղթէն, կոտորածներէն, ջարդէն առաջ, հինգունական թուականներու հայկական կոտորածներու հետեւանքով Թուրքիոյ մէջ սպաննուած հայերու թիւը կը հասնի մօտ երեք հարիւր հազարի, բռնի մահմետականացածներու թիւը՝ հարիւր հազարի, Արեւմտեան Հայաստանէն հարկադրաբար գաղթածներու թիւը՝ աւելի քան հարիւր հազարի:

Բնականաբար, զգայուն խառնուածքի տէր Միքայէլը չէր կրնար անտարբեր գտնուիլ տեսնելով իր ժողովուրդի աղէտն ու դժբախտութիւնը: Բարբարոս թուրքերու կողմէ կազմակերպուած ջարդերը խորապէս կը ցնցեն ներբազգաց, ազգասէր ու հայրենասէր երիտասարդին հոգին եւ իրենց արտայայտութիւնը կը գտնեն անոր հետագայ կարգ մը ստեղծագործութիւններուն մէջ՝ «Տուրքը», «Անջնջելի Մատեանը», «Մոգական Գորգը», «Ինչ Որ Հրեշտակը Տեսաւ», եւայլն: 1896ին, Միքայէլ, իր մօր եւ քրոջ հետ, կը հեռանայ Պոլիսէն, կը տեղափոխուի Եգիպտոս եւ մշտական բնակութիւն կը հաստատէ Աղեքսանդրիոյ մէջ: Ծնորհիւ ճակատագրական այս բարեբախտ տեղափոխութեան, ան կ'ազատի դահիճի ճիրաններէն եւ կը փրկուի 1915ի մեր զոհուած, խողխողուած մտաւորականներու հոյլին հետ նահատակուելու աղէտէն, որ սրախողխող ըրաւ պոլսահայ մտաւորականութիւնն ու աւելի քան մէկ ու կէս միլիոն աշխատասէր ու շինարար, խաղաղ ու գործունեայ հայ բնակչութիւն՝ առանց դիրքի, սեռի ու տարիքի խտրութեան:

Կիւրճեան հեռացաւ Պոլիսէն, բայց երբեք չմոռցաւ իր ծննդավայրը: Անհնար էր մոռնալ Պոլսոյ հմայիչ երկինքը եւ անոր գեղանի բարձունքները, ուր իր մտերիմ ընկերոջ՝ Տիրան Չրաքեանի հետ գրեթէ ամէն օր Սկիւտարի տան մէջ կամ պարտէզի ծառերուն տակ կ'առանձնանար, կը խօսակցէր, կամ լուռ կ'ըմբոշխնէր գեղատեսիլ բնութիւնը՝ պատանեկութեան եւ վաղ երիտասարդութեան սխրալի երազներով, Սեւ Ծովը՝ պարզութեան եւ բարութեան շունչը զգալու համար անծայրածիր տարածութեան առջեւ:

Միքայէլի հայրը՝ Սահակ էֆէնտի, կը մնայ Պոլիս՝ հետագային ինք եւս միանալու համար իր գաղթական ընտանիքին: Այսպիսով կ'ընդմիջուի իրենց բարեկեցիկ կեանքը եւ Սահակ էֆէնտին բախտը չ'ունենար միանալու իր կնոջ եւ զաւակներուն: Ընտանիքին մեկնումէն տարի մը ետք, 1897ի Մայիսին, Տիրան Չրաքեան Միքայէլին ուղղուած նամակին մէջ հետեւեալ ձեւով կը նկարագրէ. «Երբ դուրս ելլելու համար Պէյլէրին պարտէզէն, ձեր փակ դրան մօտեցեր էի այսքան ժամանակ ետքը առաջին անգամ ըլլալով մտայ թափուր ու լքուած պարտէզը»: Ան կը նկատէ որ «ծառերը կանանչցեր էին, եւ՝ առջի օրերուն անձրեւներէն լուացուած ըլլալով՝ կենդանի, ուժգին կանաչութիւն մը ունէին...»: Այնուհետեւ կը շարունակէ. «Կարծես թէ ձեր մեկնելէն ետքը ոչ ոք մտած էր հոն: Ամէն կողմ լքում ու աւեր էր...: Ծառերը, թուփերը հովանի կ'ընէին երկաթէ բոլորշի սեղանին որուն շուրջը իմ ճօճաթոռս չկար...: Ծառի մը տակ, խոնաւ բազմոց մը, մերկ, ծուռ, երկնցած էր, չեմ գիտեր ինչ բանի համար հոն թողուած,- վրան նստելու խիստ անյարմար՝ բայց կատուներու ցանցառ այցերու համար ու անձրեւներէն թրջելու շատ պատրաստ դիրքի մը մէջ...: Տունը, պարտէզէն աւելի լքուն ու տխուր էր: Գէթ պարտէզը ծառեր կային, ու fond-ը (խորքը – Յ.Մ.)՝ Միս Սիմմէրին հոծ թաւուտները: Սենեակդ տակնուվրայ էր ինկած աթոռներով, ծուռ տեղափոխուած բազմոցներով, կարասիներու անպէտ խճողումով մը իրարու վրայ, իրարու խառնուած, եւ պղտոր ապակիները կարծել կու տային թէ թանձր փոշի մը իջած էր ծածկելու այդ տխուր անկենդան դէզը: Թռչուններու ճռուողիւններ կային...: Կատու մը անգամ չկար: Ֆրէնկ մուշմուլասին (որուն ոչ հայերէնը գիտեմ ոչ գաղղիերէնը, ոչ ալ ընտանիքին անունը) պտուղները սկսեր էին տեսնուիլ լայն թուփ տերեւներուն տակէն, եւ թթենին ծածկուեր էր կանաչ, խակ թութերով, որոնք թռչուններուն կեր պիտի ըլլային մեծ մասամբ»:

Ահա այս էր երբեմնի անոյշ խոովքներու եւ երազելու տրամադրութիւն ստեղծող, գարնանային գեղեցկութեամբ ու աշնանային վերջալոյսի չքնաղութեամբ հարուստ, ցերեկուան ստուերներուն բարի գաղջութեամբ եւ երեկոներու մեղմ քաղցրութեամբ լեցուն անուշաբոյր պարտէզին ու տան տխուր, ամայի ու անհրապոյր վիճակը:

Ճիշդ այն օրը երբ Միքայէլի հայրը՝ Սահակ էֆէնտի, որոշած կ'ըլլայ անցագիր հանել, որպէսզի պատրաստուի Եգիպտոս երթալ իր հարազատներուն միանալու համար, 1897 թուկանի Յունիս 26ին, Երեքշաբթի օր կը մահանայ: Միքայէլի մօրաքրոջ խնդրանքով այս մահագոյժը Աղեքսանդրիա կը յայտնէ Տիրան Չրաքեան, որ Սկիւտարէն գրած իր 30 Յունիս/12 Յուլիս 1897ի նամակին մէջ կը գրէ. «Հետեւեցանք իր դագաղին, Թաշճեան Լեւոնը, Ստեփանը ու ես, աղուոր տրտմագին հանդյքով մը, որովհետեւ ձեր բացակայութիւնը կը փոխարինէինք ինչպէս ես՝ անշուշտ ընկերներս ալ իրենց մէջ զձեզ կը զգային...: Ասո՞ր համար էր արդեօք որ մեր յուղարկաւոր գնացքը հօրդ դագաղին ետեւէն՝ գեղեցիկ էր ու յուզիչ: Այն խմբակին մէջ որ կը հետեւէր ննջեցեալին,- կազմուած դրացիներէ, մէկ երկու ծանօթներէ ու ... Սկիւտարի այն մէկ երկու ապուշներէն որոնք բեռ կը կրեն, դիւրին յանձնարարութիւններ կը կատարեն եւ, խորին, անհասկնալի ձգտումով մը ամէն մեռելի կ'ընկերանան ... եւ որ շատ լաւ զգալու էր անշուշտ հօրդ պանդուխտ ու միակ մեռնելուն թախիծը...»:

Շատ ծանր կ'ըլլայ նոր գաղթած Կիւրճեաններու կացութիւնը՝ հոգեկան, բարոյական եւ նիւթական վիճակը: Գարնանային փափուկ, դիւրաբեկ, բիւրեղեայ պոլսական օդի փոխարէն եգիպտական արեւի տակ կ'այրի Միքայէլ, այն արեւին՝ որուն կիզիչ ճառագայթներուն տակ միայն Սֆինքսը կրնայ տոկալ յաւիտեան: Միջավայրը կը ջղագրգռէ Միքայէլը, «վհատութեան զգացումներ» կը յառաջանան անոր դեռատի մտքին մէջ: Պէտք է նշել, որ կապոյտ թուղթերով պատրաստուած, բաւական հաստ այն տետրակին մէջ,- զոր իբրեւ օրագիր օգտագործած է հայրը երբեմն հաշիւներ, երբեմն ալ հայատառ եւ թուրքերէն երկար տողերով ոտանաւորներ գրելու համար,- Սահակ էֆէնտին իր ընտանիքի հարկադրական գաղթին մասին նշած է «... ճէպտէ պէշ բարա եօգ» (գրպանին մէջ հինգ փարա չկայ - Յ.Մ.) խօսքը: Արդարեւ, շատ ծանր կ'ըլլայ Միքայէլի թէ՛ բարոյական, թէ՛ հոգեկան, թէ՛ ալ տնտեսական վիճակը: Վշտագին կեանքին մէջ փոփոխութիւն մտցնելու նպատակով Միքայէլ կը սկսի աշխատիլ դատարանին մէջ որպէս գրագիր: Դատարանը եւս կ'ազդէ անոր վրայ: Եւ ահա վրայ կը հասնի հօր մահուան լուրը, որ աւելի եւս կը խռովէ երիտասարդին կիսով խաղաղած տառապանքը նոր վիշտով: Ծննդավայրէն ու բարեկամներէն բաժանումը, մենութեան տրտմութիւնը, Սկիւտարի բնութեան բացակայութիւնը, Եգիպտոսի կլիմայական պայմանները խիստ բացասաբար կ'անդրադառնան իր առողջութեան վրայ: Ծանր կերպով կը հիւանդանայ նաեւ մայրը:

Ահա թէ ինչպէս Տիրան Չրաքեան կը նկարագրէ Միքայէլը, 1897 Մայիսին ստանալով անոր Պոլիս ուղարկած մէկ լուսանկարը. «Քու պատկերդ քեզի կը ներկայացնէ հաւատարմօրէն: Հաւատարմօրէ՞ն...: Բայց ժպիտդ կը պակսի...: Այն ժպիտը որով ներկայացած էր շարունակ կերպարանքդ ինծի, եւ որ մանաւանդ (չըսելու համար մի միայն) բարեկամներուդ քով եղած ատենդ կը զուարթացնէր տխրութեան ու վշտի դատապարտուած դէմքդ: Սակայն պատկերիդ վրայ ժպիտդ շատ աղուոր չպիտի հնչէր՝ նամակներէդ ետքը: *Ներկայ* Միքայէլին կամ լաւ եւս ներկայ Միքայէլ Կիւրճեանին հաւատարիմ պատկերն է այս, որ հանդարտ, համոզուած արհամարհանքով կը նայի իրերուն, որ քիչ մը ընկճուած, յոգնած ու վհատ երեւոյթով ու այտերուն անարիւնութեամբ զոր հիւանդագին ու անորոշ մօրուք մը կը շրջանակէ, կը թերայայտէ ձանձրոյթը ու տառապանքը,- որ թաւ յօնքերուն, որոշ քանդակով շրթունքին, եւ համարձակ (բայց տխուր) նայուածքին բնախօսական նշանակութեամբ կը ցուցնէ քմահաճ, fantaisiste (երեւակայող - Յ.Մ.) ու անկախ հոգին,- որ, ընկճուած մարմինէն վեր ցցուող գլխուն խրոխտ կեցուածքով, եւ վառոյժ այտերուն միջեւ ուռեցող ռունգերուն *անընտել*, խրխնջող արտայայտութեամբ կարծես կը հարցնէ. «Ձեր գարշելի առատութիւնը, որով զիս կը շրջապատէք ու կը սեղմէք, եւ ճակատագրին անդիմադրելի ոյժը կ'արժե՞ն իմ բարձրութեանս...»- որ իր զայրացկոտ, ջղագրգիռ, յօնքերը պռստելու պատրաստ, առերեւոյթս հանդարտ ու պարզ երեւոյթով կը սպասէ դեռ, կը սպասէ դարձեալ նոր խռովքներու, մրրիկի, ճակատագրին,- եւ որ իր քստմնած շրջագիծով ճակտին նշանակելի ցայտերով, իր խորունկ աչքերուն խոհուն, տխուր ու սեւեռած փորուածքովը, այտերուն հիւանդագին ստուերներովը, տրտմօրէն վար կախուող նուրբ ծայրերովը պեխին,- որ գալարուելով չ'ոլորուիր թեթեւօրէն,- ու լանջքին ընկրկումով կը ցուցնէ տաղանդ ու տառապանքը»:

1896-1897 տարիները ամենայուսահատականները կ'ըլլան Միքայէլի կեանքին մէջ: Մէկ կողմէ կը մտածէ ուսուցչութեամբ զբաղիլ Մագրիգիւղի դպրոցին մէջ, որու տնօրէնին հետ խօսած կ'ըլլայ Տիրան Չրաքեան եւ այս վերջինիս խնդրանքով դպրոցի տնօրէնը պատրաստակամութիւն կը յայտնէ Միքայէլը ընդունիլ որպէս ուսուցիչ: Միւս կողմէ, կը խորհի երթալ Փարիզ, աւելի ուրախ եւ յաջող կեանք մը ապրելու համար: Ան շատ շուտ կը հիասթափուի նաեւ «դատարանի մգլոտ մթնոլորտէն» եւ իր օրագրին մէջ 1900 թուականի Դեկտեմբեր ամսուն կը գրէ. «Արդէն անկեղծօրէն կը ցաւիմ կոր Պոլսէն ելլելուս, Սէթեան Հէթում վարպետիս քովէն ելլելուս. ի՜նչ շահեկան, այլազան նօթերով ճոխ կեանք էր ան. ինչպէս մարդ պիտի ըլլայի հոն, գործի մարդ, կեանքի մարդ. որքան նիւթապէս եւ վիպասանօրէն պիտի օգտուէի. ինչպէս հիմա կ'ըմբռնեմ վարպետիս տուած խրատներուն կենսական ճշմարտութիւնը. Պոլիս երթամ նէ քովը պիտի մտնամ. այո՛, կարօտցայ խանութը, դէմքերը, Գրիգորը, Եօնկին, Տիրանը, Վահանը, Սէթեանը, կարօտցայ գրասեղանս, կիսալոյս մթնոլորտը, ապրանքներուն տեսքը»: Միքայէլ երկար ժամանակ կը տառապի իր ծննդավայրին՝ Պոլսոյ կարօտով ու տենչանքով, որ մինչեւ իր կեանքին վերջը կը մնայ չիրականացուած երազ:

1898էն սկսեալ, շնորհիւ իր կամքի ոյժին, լրջօրէն կը զբաղի իր առողջութեամբ. կը սկսի կանոնաւոր ուտել ու քնանալ, շնորհիւ մարմնամարզութեան ու լոգանքներու ֆիզիքապէս կը կազդուրուի եւ կ'ամրապնդուի, իսկ օրական 2-3 ժամ քալելը իրեն համար սովորական բան կը դառնայ: Եւ այդ մոլի, մոլեռանդ տխուրը, տխրութեան սիրահարը Հոկտեմբեր 1900ին իր օրագրին մէջ կը գրէ. «2 կամ 1 1/2 տարի կայ գրեթէ որ տխուր եղած չեմ: ...Տխրութիւնը վանեցի մէջէս, ջնջեցի, մեռցուցի: Մահը մեռցուցի: Ան ինծի մեռցնելուն, ես ան մեռցուցի: Աղէկ չըրի՞: Մահուան ցեղակից բան չեմ ուզեր մէջս. կեանք միայն եւ իր ծնունդները»:[21]

1902ին Աղեքսանդրիոյ կեդրոնը թողելով՝ ընտանիքը կը փոխադրուի Ռամլէ կոչուած դալարագեղ արուարձանը, ուր մօր առողջական վիճակը քիչ մը կը բարելաւուի:

Այդ տարիներուն իր առօրեայ աշխատանքին զուգահեռ կը զբաղի նաեւ ուսուցչութեամբ: Շատ կը սիրէ գողտրիկ ու քնքուշ հոգիները, կ'ըլլայ գուրգուրացող դաստիարակ: Սակայն ուսուցչական ասպարէզն ալ չի խանգարեր զինք որ զբաղի գրականութեամբ, որ մտաւորական հաճոյք մըն էր բուռն ընթերցասէր Միքայէլին համար:

Գաղթականութեան բազմատանջ դժուարութիւնները եւ իր վշտալի կեանքին դրութիւնը պատկերացնելու համար աւելի լաւ է որ մէջբերենք իր իսկ խօսքերը. «Գաղթումի կեդրոնախոյս շարժումը կամ հոսանքը,- կը գրէ 20 Փետրուար 1908ին Աղեքսանդրիայէն բժիշկ Յարութիւն Թիրեաքեանին ուղղած նամակին[22] մէջ,- զմեզ հոս նետեց իբրեւ խլեակ մը: Մի քանի ամիս անգործ, Աղեքսանդրիոյ խառն դատարաններն մտայ իբր խոնարհ պաշտօնեայ մը... Ութ տարի հոն մնացի օրը օրին ապրելու համար բաւող ամսականով մը, եւ երկու տարի առաջ պանք Օթոմանը պաշտօնեայ եմ դատարանը առած ամսականէս աւելի բարձր ամսականով մը: Այսօրուան օրս, փա՜ռք Աստուծոյ, ինչպէս կ'ըսեն, առանց մէկու մը պէտք ունենալու, առանց շատ նեղուելու, կ'ապրինք, ունենալով կարեւորը (le nécessaire) ապրելու համար: Կը յուսամ պաշտօնիս մէջ յառաջանալ կամաց կամաց եւ օր մը հասնիլ *էզան* ըսուածին...: Ես ի բնէ ըլլալով ժուժկալ, ըսել կ'ուզեմ սպառիչ եւ կործանարար մոլութիւններէ զերծ, *լիկփ, ճախայի*, ընկերական եւ սնափառութեանց բոլորովին օտար եւ անտարբեր»:

Միհրդատ Թիրեաքեան հատուածաբար հրատարակելով իր հօր ուղղուած Կիւրճեանի նամակներէն հինգ հատը կը գրէ. «Հայրս 1880ական թուականներուն, Պոլիս մտերիմ բարեկամը եղած էր Միքայէլ Կիւրճեանի հօրը, հօրեղբօրը եւ բոլոր ընտանիքին»:[23] Այդ պարագան մեծ գոհունակութիւն եւ սփոփանք պատճառած է նաեւ Միքայէլին, որ կը գրէ. «Ի՜նչ հպարտ եւ երջանիկ կը զգամ ինքզինքս հայրիկիս, հեգ յաւէտ ողբացեալ հայրիկիս Ձեզի պէս բարեկամ մը ունեցած, Ձեզի պէս բարեկամ մը ինծի ժառանգութիւն ձգած ըլլալուն, բարոյական ժառանգութիւն մը աւելի թանկագին քան այն հազարաւոր ոսկիները, զորս կրնար ձգել ինծի, բայց չձգեց»:[24]

Կիւրճեան Աղեքսանդրիոյ խառն դատարաններուն մէջ պաշտօնավարած է որպէս քարտուղար մինչեւ 1915 թուականը, որմէ յետոյ աշխատած է Օսմանեան Դրամատան զանազան մասնաճիւղերուն մէջ եւ վարած է բարձր պաշտօններ՝ մինչեւ իր հանգստեան կոչուիլը՝ 1935 թուականին (1917-1919 տարիներուն եղած է Օսմանեան Դրամատան Մինիէի՝ վերին Եգիպտոսի մասնաճիւղի տնօրէն):

1919ի գարնան Միքայէլ իր մօր եւ քրոջ հետ վերին Եգիպտոսէն կը վերադառնայ Աղեքսանդրիա, կը նշանուի օրիորդ Լիւսիի՝ այնթապցի ապահարզան եղած Լուսնթագ Թահտաճեանի հետ, ապա կ'ամուսնանայ անոր հետ 19 Փետրուար 1920ին՝ կնքահայրութեամբ Լեւոն Մկրտիչեանի: Այդ օրերուն աւելի կը սաստկանան մօր լեարդի ցաւերը, որոնք յաճախակիօրէն եւ երկարատեւ կը տառապեցնեն զինքը: 1921ի ամրան կը մահանայ մայրը՝ Միւրիկ հանըմ, եւ ընտանիքին մէջ կը մնան Միքայէլը, կինը՝ Լիւսի, եւ քոյրը՝ Ալիս: Այս անգամ Լիւսիի հիւանդութիւնը կը սկսի անհանգստացնել Միքայէլը եւ բուժման համար մի քանի անգամ կը ճանապարհորդեն Եւրոպա: Կիւրճեանի վրայ առանձնապէս խոր ներգործութիւն կ'ունենան Ալպեան ձիւնածածկ լեռները, Մօն Պլանի մեծաշուք տեսարանը, Աննէսիի[25] հրաշալի համայնապատկերը, Սաւուայի[26] լիճերուն դրախտային խաղաղութիւնը, Տիժօնի[27] արդիւնաբերական տեսքը, Փարիզի պատմական յուշարձաններու բազմառնճ ճարտարապետութիւնը, Պուլոնեան անտառներու գեղեցկութիւնը, Վէրսայի պալատի նկարներուն եւ քանդակներուն արուեստը, Լուվրի թանգարանի համաշխարհային արուեստի եզակի ու հազուագիւտ ցուցանմուշները:

Յատկապէս շահեկան են Կիւրճեանի երրորդ եւ չորրորդ ճանապարհորդութիւնները Փարիզ (1927 եւ 1933 թուականներուն), երբ ան լաւագոյնս կ'օգտագործէ այդ առիթները հանդիպումներ ունենալով իր ժամանակի հայ եւ օտար անուանի գրողներուն եւ արուեստագէտներուն հետ: Գրական գրոյցներ կ'ունենայ Տիգրան Կամսարականի, Արշակ Չօպանեանի, Վահան Մալէզեանի, Վահան Թէքէեանի, Արամ Անտոնեանի, Տարիա Կամսարականի, Միքայէլ Ալէմշահի, Գրիգոր Թելլալեանի եւ ուրիշներու հետ: Ան հանդիպումներ կ'ունենայ նաեւ ֆրանսացի անուանի գրողներու եւ քննադատներու հետ: Les Nouvelles Littéraires-ի գրասենեակին մէջ հանդիպում կ'ունենայ Ֆրետերիք Լըֆեւրի[28] հետ, որ շատ կը հաւնէր Կիւրճեանի ֆրանսերէն ստեղծագործութիւնները: Կիւրճեանի յիշողութեան մէջ անջնջելի տպաւորութիւն կը գործեն իր այցելութիւնները Ալֆրէտ տը Միւսէի եւ Ռոսսինիի գերեզմանները՝ Փարիզի Փէր Լաշէզ գերեզմանատան մէջ՝ 1 Հոկտեմբեր 1927ին: Իսկ 23 Հոկտեմբեր 1927ին Արշակ Չօպանեանի հետ կը մասնակցի իր շատ սիրած բանաստեղծ Ծարլ-Փիէռ Պոտլէրի շիրիմին մօտ կազմակերպուած յիշատակման արարողութեան, ուր Ֆրանսայի Ակադեմիայի անդամ Փօլ Պուրժէ[29] կը կարդայ ճառ մը եւ կ'ըսթերցուին բանաստեղծութիւններ: Կիւրճեան յաւէտ յիշարժան օր մը կը համարէ Ծաբաթ, 15 Հոկտեմբեր 1927 թուականը, երբ կ'այցելէ նոյնպէս իր շատ սիրելի Վիքթոր Հիւկոյի թանգարանը: Կիւրճեանի օրագրին մէջ կայ հետեւեալ հիացական գրութիւնը. «Վ. Հիւկոյի գծագրութիւնները եւ նկարածները բացարձակապէս անզուգական եւ շանթահարիչ գործեր են: Գուցէ երբեք ես այնքան ցնցուած չեմ եղեր...»:

Կիւրճեան ընտանիքը Եգիպտոսի մէջ ալ ունեցած է մտաւորական եւ մշակութային ներկայացուցիչներէ բաղկացած ծանօթներու մտերմական ու ընտանեկան շրջապատ (Լեւոն Մկրտիչեան, Արփիար Արփիարեան, Մկրտիչ Անդրանիկեան, Երուանդ Օտեան, Վահան Թէքէեան, Միհրան Տամատեան, Երուանդ Կամսարական, Տիգրան Կամսարական, Յակոբ Փափազեան, Հրանդ Նաժիպեան, Ֆէրմանեան եւ ուրիշներ):

Կարեւոր է նշել, որ իր 86ամեայ կեանքի ընթացքին Միքայէլ հեռու մնացած է մեր քաղաքական հոսանքներէն որեւէ մէկուն մէջ գործօն դեր ստանձնելէ: Ճիշդ է թէ Կիւրճեան Ռամկավար Ազատական Կուսակցութեան շարքերը ընդգրկուած է շատ շուտ, որուն հաւատարիմ մնացած է մինչեւ իր կեանքին վերջը, սակայն իր անդամակցութեան ընթացքին ան ունեցած է միայն գրական աջակցութիւն: Ան ոչ միայն աշխատած է հեռու մնալ մեր քաղաքական յուզումներու ստեղծած տագնապներէն, այլեւ իր ժամանակին խորհուրդ տուած է Արփիարեանին, Թէքէեանին, Պարթեւեանին եւ ուրիշներու, որ անոնք եւս հեռու մնան կուսակցական պայքարներէ եւ յեղափոխականներէ: Օրինակ, մեզի յայտնի է որ 1905ին երբ Արփիարեանի կեանքը անտանելի կը դառնայ Իտալիոյ մէջ եւ կ'երթայ Եգիպտոս, Կիւրճեան շատ կը փորձէ զայն հեռու պահել կուսակցական շրջանակէն:

«Ի զուր,- կը գրէ Օտեան,- ես ու Կիւրճեան կը ջանայինք զինքը առնել տանիլ առանձնացնել»:[30]

Ինչպէս գիտենք, նոյնինքն Արփիարեան կուսակցական պայքարի հետեւանքով նենգօրէն սպաննուեցաւ 1908ին՝ իր վրայ կատարուած երրորդ մահափորձէն ետք:

Կիւրճեան եւ Օտեան դէմ կ'ըլլան նաեւ Թէքէեանի կուսակցական գործունէութեան: Օտեան իր յուշերուն մէջ կը գրէ. «... Միայն թէ Վահան Թէքէեան Աղեքսանդրիա գալով՝ ապուր մը կերեր էր, որուն ես ու Միքայէլ Կիւրճեան յաճախ կ'ափսոսայինք: Վահան Թէքէեան յեղափոխական եղեր էր եւ վերակազմեալ հնչակեան»:[31]

Միքայէլ կը պարսաւէ նաեւ Սուրէն Պարթեւեանը՝ իր դաշնակցականութեան համար եւ Պարթեւեան Գահիրէէն Աղեքսանդրիա՝ Կիւրճեանին ուղղուած 5 Սեպտեմբեր 1913 թուակիր նամակին մէջ կը պատասխանէ. «Վա՛զ անցէք սա՛ *դաշնակցականացումիս* տգեղ ու *միսքին* սպրդուքը ուղղելու ինծի: Ես ո՛չ Դաշնակցական կ'ըլլամ եւ ո՛չ ալ Ռամկավար եմ: Ես անհատ հրապարակագիր մըն եմ, որ իմ խղճմտանքիս կուսակցութեանս միայն կը պատկանիմ: Դաշնակցութի՛ւնն ալ կը ճանչնամ, Ռամկավարութի՛ւնն ալ, եւ մէկուն խանութին համար միւսինը վարկաբեկելու կամ պանծացնելու բնա՛ւ տրամադրութիւն չունիմ: Ես *չե՛մ հաւատար* որ այս կուսակցութիւնները՝ մեր կենսունակ տարրերուն կորովը իրարու դէմ վատնել տալով՝ ոեւէ օգուտ կրնան հասցնել Ազգին»:

* * *

Արեւմտահայ իր ժամանակակիցներուն պէս, Կիւրճեան առաջին ստեղծագործութիւններէն սկսեալ օգտագործած է ծածկանուններ: Եգիպտահայ բանաստեղծ Սարգիս Սահակեան «Կեանք Եւ Գիր» գիրք-յիշատակարանի ԺԱ. պրակին մէջ տպագրուած «Եգիպտահայ Հայ Արձա-կագիրներ» վերնագիրը կրող յօդուածին մէջ կը գրէ. «Կիւրճեան գործածած է Պարոյր, Պոնտ, Պետրոս Ագաթան ծածկանունները: «Շիրակ»ներու Համշիրակներէն (Համշիրակ Ա., Համշիրակ Բ.) մին ալ ինքն է, եթէ չեմ սխալիր» գրած է: Յօդուածին համառօտ բնոյթէն կ'երեւայ թէ Սահակեան չէ փորձած թուարկել Կիւրճեանի բոլոր ծածկանունները եւ անգիտացած է թէ Համշիրակ Ա. Կիւրճեանի ծածկանունն էր, իսկ Համշիրակ Բ.՝ Թէքէեանի:

Արուեստասէր եւ բանասէր Գարեգին Լեւոնեան «Բառարան Հայ Գրա-կան Ծածկանուններու»[32] խորագրով աշխատութեան մէջ կը յիշատակէ, որ Կիւրճեան գործածած է Համշիրակ Ա., Զարմայր, Ե. Մ. Կիւրօտ, Արսէն Մոլար, Պետրոս Ագաթան, Հրանտ, Մէն Կէն, Մխիթար Պոնտացի, Պարոյր, Պոնտ, Սրճեփ Ա. ծածկանունները:[33]

Լեւոնեան կը սխալի երբ Ե. Մ. Կիւրօտ ծածկանունը կը վերագրէ միայն Միքայէլ Կիւրճեանի, իսկ Երուանդ Օտեանի անուան դիմաց որպէս ծածկանուն կը թուարկէ միայն երկու կեղծանուններ՝ Երօտ եւ Ժիրայր:[34] Ինչպէս արդէն ըսինք, Ե. Մ. Կիւրօտ ստորագրութիւնը կը պատկանի երկու գրողներուն եւ ան կազմուած է անոնց անուններու սկզբնատառերէն եւ ազգանուններու առաջին վանկերէն: Լեւոնեանի ծածկանուններու այբբենա-կան ցանկին մէջ սխալ է նաեւ Մխիթար Պոնտացի ծածկանունը մեր պանդուխտ կեանքի երգիչ Մելքոն Կիւրճեանին վերագրելը:[35] Մեզի յայտնի է որ Մխիթար Պոնտացի ծածկանունը գործածած է Միքայէլ Կիւրճեան: Հետագային, այս ծածկանունը կը տեսնենք նաեւ փրոֆէսէօր Յ. Գայաեանի անուան մօտ:[36]

Հայր Արսէն Ղազիկեան իր «Հայկական Մատենագիտութիւն Եւ Հանրագիտարան Հայ Կեանքի» վերնագրուած ծաւալուն գործին մէջ, Մ. Կիւրճեանի կեանքին եւ ստեղծագործութեան մասին խօսելով, կը նշէ. «ծածկանուններն են Զարմայր Սահակեան, Արսէն Մոլար, Պետրոս Ագաթան (Պոլիս), Պարոյր, Պոնտ, Մէն Կէն, Համշիրակ Ա., Ե. Մ. Կիւրօտ (*Ազատ Բեմ*ի մէջ՝ Երուանդ Օտեանի աշխատակցութեամբ գրած երգի-ծական յօդուածներուն ընտրած ծածկանուն), Արտասահման, եւայլն»:[37]

Ինչպէս կը տեսնենք այս ցուցակին մէջ ալ լրիւ չեն թուարկուած Կիւրճեանի ծածկանուններըը, հակառակ անոր որ երբ Ղազիկեան իր աշխատութեան Կ. տառին հասած է, նամակագրական կապի մէջ եղած է Միքայէլի հետ եւ Վենետիկէն գրած 9 Սեպտեմբեր 1910 թուակիր նամակին մէջ անկէ խնդրած է ուղարկել «հայ կեանքով գրաղող յօդուածներուն ցանկը», մանրամասն գրել խորագրերը, լրագրի անունը եւ թիւը, յիշատակել գործածած ծածկանունները, եւայլն: Մէկ ամիս ետք Ս. Ղազարի Մխիթարեան Միաբանութեան բազմաբեղուն անդամներէն Ղազիկեան 10 Հոկտեմբեր 1910 թուակիր նամակով շնորհակալութիւն կը յայտնէ Կիւրճեանին՝ իր պատասխան-նամակին համար, եւ յոյս կը յայտնէ շուտով օգտուիլ անկէ: Անկէ կարելի է եզրակացնել որ Հայր Արսէն Ղազիկեան Կիւրճեանի մասին գրելու ժամանակ անպայման օգտուած է անոր տուած տեղեկութիւններէն. սակայն ցաւօք սրտի կը տեսնենք որ ան ամբողջական չէ եւ կը վերջանայ եւայլնով:

1963ին առանձին գրքոյկով լոյս տեսան կիւրճեանի «Անունին Գիշերը», «Նոր Լաթ», «Ընտանիք Մը» պատմուածքները:[38] Այդ գիրքին «Ծանօթութիւն» բաժնին մէջ Կիւրճեան կը նշէ որ «Անունին Գիշերը» պատմուածքը 1901ին հրատարակուած է Գաբիրէի «Արշալոյս» օրաթերթին մէջ Դիտակ ծածկանունով, իսկ «Ընտանիք մը» պատմուածքը 1902ին՝ Գաբիրէի «Նոր Օր» լրագրին մէջ Զարմայր Սահակեան ծածկանունով: Հակառակ անոր որ Կիւրճեանի օգտագործած ծածկանուններուն թիւը այսպիսով կը հասնի 13ի, Յակոբ Օշական կը թուարկէ միայն 9 ծածկանուն:

Հաւանաբար Կիւրճեանի ծածկանուններուն լրիւ ցանկը պէտք է նկատել «Սփիւռք» շաբաթաթերթին 1965 թուականի Դեկտեմբեր 31ի բացառիկին մէջ, թիւ 49-52, էջ 11ի վրայ՝ «Միքայէլ Կիւրճեան (Յուշեր Եւ Նօթեր)» յօդուածին մէջ հրատարակուած ցանկը, որ կազմած են Կիւրճեան եւ Ազատ 1964ին, վերջինիս Աղեքսանդրիա գտնուած պահուն: Ահա եւ այդ ցանկը.- Դիտակ, Զարմայր Սահակեան, Համշիրակ Ա., Զարմայր, Ե. Մ. Կիւրօտ, Արսէն Մոլար, Պետրոս Ագաթան, Հրանտ, Մէն Կէն, Մխիթար Պոնտացի, Պարոյր, Սրճեփ Ա., Քանտակ, Պոնտ:[39]

Այսպիսով Կիւրճեանի գործածած ծածկանուններուն թիւը կը հասնի 14ի: Հետեւաբար, անոր օրինակով եւս կ'ապացուցուի որ 90ական թուականներու հայ գրողները ստիպուած էին շարունակել նախորդ սերունդի՝ ութսունականներու՝ հայ հեղինակներու կողմէ զանգուածային բնոյթ ստացած ծածկանուններու օգտագործման սովորութիւնը, որուն պատճառները պէտք է փնտռել հայ թէ օտար իշխող խաւերու գաղափարախօսութեան եւ գործունէութեան դէմ մղած պայքարին մէջ:

Հետաքրքրական է նշել, որ Պետրոս Ագաթան ծածկանունը, ըստ երեւոյթին, Բիւզանդ Քէչեանն է դրած «Անունին Գիշերը» պատմուածքին տակ, որովհետեւ եթէ Միքայէլ ինք պատմուածքը ծածկանունով ուղարկած ըլլար, բնականաբար գրած պիտի ըլլար Դիտակ, ինչպէս որ այդ ծածկանունով աշխատակցած էր 1901ին «Արշալոյս»ին: Բացի այդ, պատմուածքը հրատարակելէ առաջ, Քէչեան անոր ծանուցումը տպած է «Բիւզանդիոն»ի մէջ՝ առանց գրելու հեղինակին անունը: Մեզի ծանօթ է թէ սկզբնական շրջանին Կիւրճեան Քէչեանի հետ կապեր հաստատած է իր մտերիմ ընկերոջ՝ Տիրան Չրաքեանի միջոցով. այդ բանը կը վկայեն նաեւ Կիւրճեանի արխիւին մէջ գտնուող նամակները, որոնց մէջ Չրաքեան որպէս միջնորդ հանդէս գալով անուանի լրագրողին եւ Միքայէլի միջեւ երբեմն հարց կու տայ թէ արդեօք կ'ուզէ իսկակա՞ն ազգանունով լոյս տեսնել, թէ՞ հրատարակուիլ ծածկանունով:

Տիրան Չրաքեան 12/25 Մայիս 1902 թուակիր նամակով իր «Ներաշխարհ»ին մասին տեղեկութիւններ տալէ ետք, պատասխանելով Կիւրճեանի հարցին, կը գրէ. «բայց քիչ մըն ալ Պետրոս Ագաթանին գանք, սիրելի Միքայէլս: Հաւանօրէն Քէչեանն է որ փոխած է անունդ, գայթակղական մականունիդ համար, եւ Պետրոս Ագաթան ժողովրդաբոյր ծածկանունը դրած է՝ գրութեանդ ներքեւ»: Շատ հաւանական է, որ Չրաքեան Կիւրճեան ազգանունը «գայթակղական» համարած է անոր համար որ կիւրճի կը նշանակէ վրացի: Բայց փաստը կը մնայ փաստ, որ հոս խօսքը կը վերաբերի փոխուած անունին, որ եթէ յայտնի ըլլար Միքայէլին, բնականաբար հարցուցած պիտի չըլլար Տիրանին, որ իր կարգին կը փորձէ բաղդատութեան միջոցով բացատրել «գայթակղական մականունը» ժողովրդական ծածկանունով փոխելու հարցը: Օգտուելով այս առիթէն կ'ուզենք մէջբերել իրողութիւն մը այս մասին, որ Կիւրճեան ինքն ալ եղած է ուրիշ անձի ծածկանուն ստեղծող՝ յղանալով Վահան Թէքէեանի «Ասուպ» ծածկանունը:

* * *

Քաջ տիրապետած ըլլալով ֆրանսերէն լեզուին, սիրելով ֆրանսական գրականութիւնը, հրապուրանքով ընթերցելով 19րդ դարու ֆրանսացի գրողներու երկերը, Մ. Կիւրճեան իր գրական նախափորձերը կատարած է ֆրանսերէն լեզուով, աշխատակցած է ֆրանսական թերթերու, ոտանաւորներ սկսած է գրել ֆրանսերէնով, որոշ ժամանակ ներկայացուցած է հայ գրական շարժումը Փարիզի La Revue հանդէսին մէջ. անոր «Քեաթիպին Երազը» հուչակաւոր գործը առաջին անգամ լոյս տեսած է ֆրանսերէն լեզուով: Հետագայ տարիներուն եւս իր ստորագրութեամբ ֆրանսերէն չափածոյ գործերու կը հանդիպինք Թէոդիկի «Ամէնուն Տարեցոյցը» հրատարակութեան 1915, 1925 եւ 1926 տարեթիւերու հատորներուն մէջ եւ այլուր:

Միքայէլ մեր գրականութեան մէջ մտաւ աղմկայարոյց գլուխ գործոցով՝ «Մարտիկ Աղա» վէպով, որ լոյս տեսաւ Լոնտոնի «Նոր Կեանք» ազգային, գրական, քաղաքական հանդէսին մէջ 1898-1899 թուականներուն: Ահա այս թուականէն մինչեւ 30 Յունիս 1965ին իր մահուընէ քանի մը օր առաջ գրած «Ինչպէս Ծանօթացայ Վահան Թէքէեանի Հետ» յօդուածը,[40] Կիւրճեանի գրութիւններուն կը հանդիպինք սփիւռքահայ շուրջ 40 անուն թերթերու, հանդէսներու, տարեգիրքերու մէջ: Աղեքսանդրիոյ, Գահիրէի, Պոլսոյ, Զմիւռնիոյ, Լոնտոնի, Փարիզի, Ս. Փեթերսպուրկի եւ մինչեւ իսկ Ամերիկայի հայատառ պարբերականներուն մէջ տպուած են անոր գրչի արգասիքը ներկայացնող բազմատեսակ ու բազմաթիւ գործեր, որոնք ջանասիրաբար ի մի հաւաքելու համար վերջին տարիներուն իր թափած ջանքերը չաւարտած՝ վերջնականապէս հրաժեշտ տուաւ կեանքին 3 Յուլիս 1965ին, հանրականքի արկածի մը հետեւանքով:

Պատկերացում մը տալու համար անոր ստեղծագործութիւններուն հաւաքման եւ ուսումնասիրութեան հետ կապուած աշխատանքներու դժուարութեան մասին, նշենք գէթ հետեւեալ իրողութիւնները: Առաջին, Հայաստանի Հանրապետութեան Մշակոյթի Նախարարութեան Չարենցի անուան Գրականութեան եւ Արուեստի Թանգարան ուղարկուած «Մ. Կիւրճեանի Արխիւը» միանուագ չուղարկուելուն պատճառով, ամբողջական չէր իմ ուսումնասիրութեան սկիզբի տարիներուն, իսկ հնարաւորութեան սահմաններուն մէջ զայն համալրելու համար անհրաժեշտ էր պրպտումներ կատարել նաեւ Երեւանի մի քանի գլխաւոր գրադարաններու (Հանրային Ազգային Գրադարան, Գիտութիւններու Ազգային Ակադեմիայի Գիտական Հիմնակազմ Գրադարան, Մ. Մաշտոցի անուան հին ձեռագիրներու գիտահետազօտական հիմնարկութեան գրադարան՝ Մատենադարան) պարբերական մամուլի հաւաքածոներուն մէջ, որոնք ցաւօք սրտի թերի են համալրուած արեւմտահայ մամուլով: Երկրորդ, Կիւրճեանի ստեղծագործութեան ուսումնասիրման նպատակով արեւմտահայ եւ արեւելահայ մամուլին էջերէն անոր գրութիւններու հաւաքման ժամանակ մենք հանդիպեցանք ուրիշ հեղինակներու ստորագրութիւններու, որոնք կը համընկնէին Միքայէլի ծածկանուններուն, օրինակ՝ Մ. Կ.՝ հաւանաբար պաքուցի հայու մը ստորագրութիւնը «Արարատ» ամսագրին մէջ, իսկ Պոլսոյ «Ժամանակ»ին մէջ Պարոյր ստորագրութիւնը, որ նոյնպէս Կիւրճեանինը չէր, այլ՝ Բաղէշէն թղթակիցի մը, ինչպէս նաեւ ուրիշներ: Երրորդ, 86ամեայ իր կեանքին ընթացքին գրողը չէր հասցուցած գրել իր յուշերը, որոնք արժէքաւոր պիտի ըլլային թէ՛ իր, թէ՛ իր ժամանակաշրջանի գրական գործիչներուն մասին հետաքրքրական եւ կարեւոր մանրամասնութիւններով: Ճիշդ է, անոր արխիւին մէջ կան օրագրի մը ձեռագիր տետրակներն ու նօթատետրեր, որոնք կ'ընդգրկեն 1900-1933 տարիները միայն, այն ալ ժամանակագրական երկար ընդհատումներով: Ատոնք աւելի շատ կը վկայեն անոր անհետեւողական վերաբերումը դէպի կանոնաւոր օրագրութիւնը: Այդ նմոյշներուն մէջ կը հանդիպինք խորհրդածութիւններու, առածներու, ասացուածքներու, կեանքի ընթացքին հանդիպած զանազան տիպերու նկարագրութիւններու, իր ստեղծագործութիւններուն համար կերպարներու բնութագրումներու, գրական ուրուագծային ծրագիրներու, ճանապարհորդական տպաւորութիւններու, դիպուածական գրառումներու, կիսատ կամ անտեղի նշումներու, քան՝ կենսագրական կարեւոր տեղեկութիւններու կամ գրական արժէքաւոր դիտողութիւններու: Չորրորդ, կարելի է արձանագրել նաեւ այն իրողութիւնը, որ ինքն իսկ չէ յիշած իր աշխատակցած թերթերուն եւ պարբերականներուն լրիւ ցանկը:

Օրինակ, նոյնիսկ «Սփիւռք» շաբաթաթերթի 1965ի 49-52 թիւի 11-րդ էջին վրայ տպագրուած ցանկը, որ համեմատաբար ամենաընդարձակն է, չի պարփակեր այն բոլոր պարբերականներուն անունները, որոնց մէջ լոյս տեսած են իր գրութիւններն ու թարգմանութիւնները: Այդ ցանկը, զոր կազմած են ինք ու Ազատը, թերի է. հոն չէ յիշատակուած Միհրան Ասքանազեանի «Պարտէզ» շաբաթաթերթը, ուր լոյս տեսած են «Սուրին Երգը» արձակ բանաստեղծութիւնը, «Ազատամիտ Աղջիկ Մը», «Յետ Մահու» պատմուածքները, «Կշիռք Ու Խելք» առակը եւ Շարլ Պոտլէրի «Լուսնին Բարիքները» արձակ բանաստեղծութեան ու Ալֆոնս Տոտէի «Թարասքոնցի Թարթարէնը» դիւցազնավէպին թարգմանութիւնները: Այդ ցանկին մէջ չէ նշուած նաեւ Զմիւռնիոյ «Հայ Գրականութիւն» գրական, գիտական եւ գեղարուեստական ամսօրեայ հանդէսը, որուն 1911-1913 թուականներու թիւերուն մէջ տպագրուած են «Տրդատ Եւ Տանատ» ժողովրդական պատմութիւնը, «Բանի Մը Ոյժը» պատմուածքը, «Պարոն Քաղաքագէտը», «Հրաշքի Մը Պատմութիւնը», ինչպէս նաեւ այլ պատմուածքներ եւ արձակ քերթուածներ: Նոյնպէս մոռացութեան ենթարկուած է Հ.Բ.Ը. Միութեան ամսօրեայ «Միութիւն» պաշտօնաթերթը, որուն անցեալ դարասկիզբի տասական թուականներու քսանէ աւելի թիւերուն մէջ տպագրուած են իր քրոնիկները: Այդ ցանկին վրայ նշուած չեն նաեւ Արամ Անտոնեանի «Խարազան» երգիծական պատկերազարդ շաբաթաթերթը, Պէյրութի «Անի» հանդէսն ու «Նայիրի» շաբաթաթերթը, Ամերիկայի «Պայքար» պարբերականը եւ ուրիշներ, որոնց էջերուն մէջ եւս լոյս են տեսած Կիւրճեանի տարբեր ժամանակներու ստեղծագործութիւնները: Հինգերորդ, երկու տասնամեակներու ընթացքին մեր հաւաքած նիւթերը Ամերիկայի Միացեալ Նահանգներուն մէջ վերջնականապէս շարադրելու, խմբագրելու, արեւմտահայերէնի վերափոխելով՝ դասական ուղղագրութեան վերածելու եւ հրատարակութեան պատրաստելու համար վերջերս կատարած մեր աշխատանքին ընթացքին կտրուած ենք Երեւանի գրադարաններէն եւ Կիւրճեանի արխիւին միջոցով անհրաժեշտ ճշդումներ եւ լրացումներ կատարելու հնարաւորութենէն:

Ցաւով կը նշենք նաեւ այն տխուր վիճակը, որ մինչեւ 1960 թուական իր երկերէն առանձին հրատարակուած են միայն Երուանդ Օտեանի հետ Կիւրճեանի գրած «Ֆրանքօ-Թրքական Պատերազմը» (1909ին եւ 1923ին),

«Հերոսախաղ»ը (1928ին) եւ «Փրկանքը» (1910ին): Կիւրճեանի միայն լաւագոյն ստեղծագործութիւնները ի մի հաւաքելու պարագային, հազիւ թէ հնարաւոր ըլլայ հաստափոր քանի մը հատորներու մէջ ամփոփել անոր մտքի ու գրչի արգասիքը հանդիսացող գոհարները: Եւ ինչպէ՞ս հաշտուիլ այն իրականութեան հետ, որ եղած է ժամանակաշրջան մը, երբ Գահիրէն հանդիսացած է աշխարհի մէջ երրորդ քաղաքը, ուր ամենէն շատ տպագրուած են հայատառ գիրքեր Պոլիսէն եւ Զմիւռնիայէն յետոյ: Իր աշխատութիւնները հիմնականին մէջ մամուլի մէջ ցրուած եւ ոչ թէ առանձին հատորներով հրատարակուած ըլլալու մէջ գուցէ մասամբ մեղաւոր է ինքը՝ Կիւրճեան, որմէ այսօր հրապարակի վրայ կան միայն «Ի Խորոց Սրտի Խօսք Ընդ Պաշտելւոյն» (Պէյրութ, տպ. Տօնիկեան, 1960, 53 էջ) արձակ քերթուածներու ժողովածուն, «Քսան Տարի Ետք» (Պէյրութ, տպ. Սեւան, 1961, 100 էջ) ժողովածուն, ուր նոյնանուն կատակերգութենէն բացի տպագրուած են տասնհինգ պատմուածքներ ու պատկերներ, եւ վերջապէս «Անուշին Գիշերը Եւ Այլ Պատմուածքներ Պոլսահայ Բարքերէ» գիրքը (Գահիրէ, տպ. Ոսկետառ, 1963, 55 էջ):

Տասնիններորդ դարու իննսունական թուականներուն, կուսակցական ճնշումներու եւ իր առողջական վիճակին վատթարացման պատճառով, իսկ ինն հարիւրական թուականներու սկիզբին՝ տնտեսական ու ընտանեկան նեղ կացութեան, ինչպէս նաեւ Թուրքիոյ մէջ սաստկացող հալածանքներու եւ կոտորածներու հետեւանքով ան որոշ ընդմիջումներով հանդէս կու գայ մամուլին մէջ, սակայն չի կտրուիր իր ժողովուրդէն ու գրիչով կ'արտայայտէ իր ներքին հոգեկան ու մտային խռովքը, պոռթկումը՝ աւուր պատշաճի հարցերու շուրջ գրելով եւ ոգեւորեալ հայրենասիրութեամբ եւ ազգային-քաղաքական առաջադիմական գաղափարներով: Այնուամենայնիւ, «նոր րեժիմը ստիպեց զիս քիչ մը աւելի գրականութիւն ընելու», կը գրէ Կիւրճեան բժիշկ Յարութիւն Թիրեաքեանին իր 18 Ապրիլ 1909 թուակիր նամակով,[41] հակառակ անոր որ «պաշտօնական եւ ընտանեկան հոգեր յառաջ կը բերեն անտրամադիր վիճակ»:

Վերոյիշեալ բոլոր հանգամանքները նկատի ունենալով հանդերձ պէտք է նշել թէ Կիւրճեանի կեանքին ամենաբեղմնաւոր շրջանը կազմած են 1898-1915 տարիները, երբ ան փայլեցաւ իրապաշտ նորավէպերով, պոլսահայ եւ արեւմտահայ կեանքը արտայայտող պատմուածքներով, արեւելեան պատկերներով, երգիծական երկերով, սրամիտ քրոնիկներով, գրական-քննադատական յօդուածներով:

Կիւրճեան անուանի է նաեւ խմբագրական գործունէութեամբ: Բացի «Ազատ Բեմ»ի ժամանակաւոր խմբագիր ըլլալէ, անոր խմբագրական գործունէութեան կարեւորագոյն շրջանները եղած են «Շիրակ» գրական հանդէսի հրատարակութեան (1905, 1907, 1909) եւ «Արեւ» օրաթերթի խմբագրապետութեան (1920-1925) տարիները, երբ ժրաջանօրէն կ'աշխատէր խմբագրել ու ոճաւորել գրական եւ հրապարակախօսական գրութիւններ, յօդուածներ, թղթակցութիւններ:

Կիրճեան յայտնի է նաեւ որպէս հասարակական գործիչ, որ միշտ ցուցաբերած է նուիրուածութիւն հայութեան եւ հայ մշակոյթին: Յատկապէս քսաներորդ դարու առաջին տասնամեակներուն ան եռանդուն մասնակցութիւն ունեցած է եգիպտահայ մշակութային կեանքի մէջ: 1900ական թուականներուն, երբ յեղափոխական կուսակցութիւններուն միջեւ տարակարծութիւններ սկսած էին ծայր տալ Աղեքսանդրիոյ մէջ, հեռնուածեալ մասէն քանի մը զարգացած երիտասարդներ կը հիմնեն Հայկական Ընթերցասրահը անշուք կրպակի մը մէջ՝ նպաստելու համար հայ գիրին, գրականութեան, ընթերցասիրութեան եւ մշակոյթին:

Տիգրան Երկաթ հայ մշակութային միութեան կողքին, իբր աջակից քոյր միութիւն, կը ստեղծուի Գեղարուեստասէր Հայուհեացը, որ բեղուն գործունէութեամբ կը սկսի աչքառու դիրք գրաւել: Կիրճեան կը դառնայ Տիգրան Երկաթ միութեան գործօն ու նուիրեալ անդամներէն մէկը, օգնելով գեղարուեստական զանազան ձեռնարկներու: Միութեան հիմնադիրները կ'ուզեն օգտագործել Օտեանի եւ Կիրճեանի սերտ գրչեղբայրակցութիւնը եւ կը խնդրեն գրել թատերախաղ մը, որուն ներկայացման հասոյթը պիտի պարարտացնէր միութեան դրամարկղը: Առաջարկը հաճելի ըլլալով իրենց, մէկ ամսուան ընթացքին շաբաթական երկուքէն երեք ժամ տեւող նիստերով, յիշեալները կը գրեն «Ֆրանքօ-Թրքական Պատերազմը» կատակերգութիւնը, սատարելու համար հայկական հանրօգուտ ձեռնարկի յաջողութեան: Միութեան թատերական եւ օփերէթային ներկայացումներու թարգմանիչներ Միհրան Տամատեանի, Լեւոն Մկրտիչեանի, Սիսակ Ծալճեանի, Խաչիկ Սանտալճեանի, Պայծառ Երկաթի եւ ուրիշներու շարքին, Միքայէլ ալ սիրայօժար թարգմանութիւններ կը կատարէ շնորհալի ոճով:

1911ի գարնան Կոմիտաս Վարդապետ Պոլսէն կ'այցելէ Եգիպտոս՝ սփիւռքի այդ հայ գաղութին մէջ եւս հնչեցնելու հայկական ազգայինժողովրդական երգը եւ հայ հոգիին մէջ դնելու երգերու թրթիռը: Կոմիտաս Եգիպտոսի մէջ կը կազմակերպէ երգչախումբ եւ համերգներով հանդէս կու գայ Գահիրէ ու Աղեքսանդրիա: Կիրճեան, որպէս Պօղոսեան ազգային վարժարանի հոգաբարձութեան ատենապետ, մեծապէս կ'օժանդակէ այդ ձեռնարկին յաջողութեան, քանի որ «անմոռանալի եւ յաւիտենական Կոմիտասը» ան կը համարէ «մին այն ամենէն մեծ մարդերէն, որոնց ծնունդ տուած ըլլայ մաշտոցներու գիտարար ցեղը»:

Կիրճեան իր երիտասարդութեան ճիգ չէ խնայած նաեւ եգիպտահայ գրական-գեղարուեստական ասպարէզին մէջ ալ, եւ մենք իր մասնակցութիւնը կը տեսնենք որպէս «Ֆրանքօ-Թրքական Պատերազմը»ի դերակատար (1903ի Սեպտեմբերին), որպէս կատակերգութեան թարգմանիչ (1912ի Փետրուարին) Ռամկավարներու փառատօնին համար,[42] որպէս Արփիար

Արփիարեանի «Ազգիս Բարերարները» երկը երգիծական աւիւնով բեմական պատկերի վերածողի (բեմադրուած 1912 թուականի Փետրուարին), եւ որպէս տաղանդաւոր բանաստեղծ ու բազմերախտ ուսուցիչ Յովհաննէս Սէթեանի գրական-դաստիարակչական քառասնամեայ յոբելեանը կազմակերպող յանձնախումբի անդամի (1913ի Յունուարին): Միաժամանակ, ան իր պարտքը կը կատարէ արեւելահայ մտաւորականներու հանդէպ՝ գրական-քննադատական ուսումնասիրութեամբ մասնակցութիւն բերելով Տիգրան Կամսարականի կազմած «Ծիրվանզադէ Եւ Իր Գործը» ժողովածուին «Նորավէպագիրը» ընդարձակ յօդուածով[43] եւ այլ եգիպտահայ մտաւորականներու շարքին, ողջոյն ուղարկելով Թիֆլիս՝ «Մշակ» քաղաքական, հասարակական, գրական օրաթերթի քառասնամեայ յոբելեանին առթիւ (1912ի Յունիսին):[44]

Զօրավար Անդրանիկ երբ իր փառքի օրերուն, 1920ին կ'այցելէ Եգիպտոս, ընկերակցութեամբը իր զոյգ տեղակալներուն՝ Ճիմ Ջանգալեանի եւ Տոքթոր Պօնաբարդեանի, Աղեքսանդրիոյ մէջ «Արեւ» թերթի վարչութեան նախաձեռնութեամբ տեղի կ'ունենայ հանգանակութիւնը Զօրավարին նուիրուած թանկարժէք թուրին, զոր կը պատրաստեն եգիպտահայ ոսկերիչները: Թուրը Զօրավարին կ'ընծայուի Տիգրան Երկաթ հանդիսասրահին մէջ, արտակարգ հանդիսականութեամբ: Կիւրճեան ոչ միայն կը մասնակցի հանդիսութեան, այլեւ կ'երեւի այդ օրը լուսանկարուած տասը հոգինոց խմբանկարին մէջ, Անդրանիկի, իր տեղակալներուն, Թորգոմ Արք. Գուշակեանի եւ այլոց կողքին:

Կիւրճեան արուեստասէրը առիթ ունեցած է ճանօթանալու հայ բեմի վաստակաշատ արուեստագէտ դերասաններ Լեւոն Ծիշմանեանի, Յովհաննէս Աբէլեանի, Յովհաննէս Զարիֆեանի, Սիրանոյշի հետ եւ ըմբոշխնելու անոնց ներկայացումները անոնց Աղեքսանդրիա այցելութեան առիթով:

Կիւրճեանի երկերն արժանացած են արեւմտահայ ընթերցողներու լայն շրջաններու ջերմ ընդունելութեան. իսկ եթէ հաշուի առնենք նաեւ զինք ճանչցող եւ գնահատող արեւելահայ մտաւորականութեան շատ ներկայացուցիչներ, ապա կարելի կ'ըլլայ ըսել որ ան սիրուած գրող մը եղած է եւ կը շարունակէ այդպիսին մնալ ընթերցասէր հայ հասարակութեան համար, երբ առանձին հատորներով կը հրատարակուին անոր գրական հարուստ ժառանգութիւնն ու կեանքին ու գործին մասին ուսումնասիրութիւններ:

ՄՈՒՏՔ՝ ՓՈԹՈՐԿԱՅԱՐՈՅՑ ԳԼՈՒԽ ԳՈՐԾՈՑ ԵՐԱԽԱՅՐԻՔՈՎ

Ա. «ՄԱՐՏԻԿ ԱՂԱ» ԵՐԳԻԾԱՎԷՊԸ

19րդ դարու աւարտին Արեւմտեան Հայաստանի հայերուն վիճակը նոր եւ աւելի վտանգաւոր հանգամանք մը կը ստանայ: Սուլթան Համիտ օր օրի կը սաստկացնէ հայահալած քաղաքականութիւնը: 1894ին Սասունի եւ 1895-1896ին հայկական ընդհանուր կոտորածները կը յուզեն եւ կը ցնցեն քաղաքակիրթ աշխարհը: Ամբողջ հայ ժողովուրդը վախի ու սարսափի արհաւիրքով կ'ապրի Թուրքիոյ իշխանութեան տակ, որ կատարեալ դժոխքի կերպարանք կը ստանայ: Շատեր չկարողանալով հանդուրժել թրքական տեւական, անվերջ ու վայրագ բարբարոսութիւններուն, սրտաբեկ ու յուսահատ, կը թողուն իրենց տուները, կը հեռանան իրենց ծննդավայրէն ու կը գաղթեն օտար երկիրներ:

Գաղութահայութեան թիւը աստիճանաբար կ'անի Պուլկարիոյ, Ռումանիոյ, Յունաստանի, Եգիպտոսի, Ֆրանսայի, Ամերիկայի եւ այլ հիւրընկալ, ապաստանական երկիրներու մէջ: Այս մազապուրծ փախուստը եւ գաղթականներու տաժանելի կացութիւնը արտացոլուած են այդ ժամանակներու հայ պարբերական մամուլին, յուշագրական յօդուածներուն եւ գեղարուեստական ստեղծագործութիւններուն մէջ:

Բնականաբար շատ ծանր, տխուր եւ թախծալից կ'ըլլայ հայ նոր գաղթականներու թշուառութիւնը՝ շարունակ անոր գաղթականութեան հուանքին պատճառով: Աշխարհի բոլոր կողմերէն տարբեր ազգերու ներկայացուցիչներ հրապուրող եւ տնտեսական մարզի մէջ յաղթանակներու հասնելու պայմաններ ընծայող Ամերիկայի մէջ անգամ դժուար կ'ըլլայ Թուրքիոյ հայաբնակ վայրերէն պարտադրաբար գաղթած հայոց վիճակը, քանի որ հայ գաղթականութիւնը ստուար մեծամասնութեամբ իր ապրուստը հոգալու համար կը զբաղէր բանուորութիւն ընելով, ինչ որ կը պահանջէր անսպառ ֆիզիքական ուժ, մեքենական արագութեամբ սպասարկութիւն եւ չարքաշ աշխատանք: Բոլոր գաղութներուն մէջ ալ սկզբնական դժուարութիւնները յաղթահարելէ ետք է որ ժամանակի ընթացքին տարբեր երկիրներու մէջ կը սկսի հանդէս գալ հայ փոքր խանութպաններու, մանր վաճառականներու եւ արհեստաւորներու դասակարգ մը՝ հազիւ միջին մակարդակով ապրելակերպ ապահովող վաստակով:

Տասնիններորդ դարու վերջին հնգամեակը արտասովոր կ'ըլլայ նաեւ եգիպտահայ գաղութին համար: Սրտաճմլիկ օրեր կ'ապրին աղեքսանդրիաբնակ հայերը: 1896ի Պոլսոյ աղէտէն յետոյ, սարսափէն կիսամեռ վիճակի մէջ, մահուան առջեւէն մազապուրծ ազատած, իրենց տուներէն խուճապահար փախած, խելակորոյս հայ ընտանիքներ կը գաղթեն եւ ապաստան կը գտնեն ասպնջական սակայն օտար Եգիպտոսի կապոյտ, աստղափայլ երկինքին տակ:

Սփիւռքահայ երաժշտասէր Էօժէն Բաքազեան կը գրէ թէ երբ իրենց ընտանիքը չուզելով ապրիլ թրքական ճնշիչ, տագնապալի մթնոլորտի մէջ, 1885ի Օգոստոս ամսուն Իզմիրէն կը փոխադրուի Աղեքսանդրիա, հոն կը գտնէ հազիւ վաթսուն հայ ընտանիք: Իսկ երբ «յանկարծ վրայ եկան 1895-96ի հայկական ջարդերու տխուր գոյժերը,- կը նշէ Բաքազեան՝ վերյիշելով մանկութեան օրերը,- հազարաւոր հայեր Թուրքիայէն փախստական, եկան թափեցան Աղեքսանդրիա: Պօղոսեան վարժարանին դասարանները, պարտէզները, եւայլն, լեցուեցան գաղթականներով. փոխանակ գրասեղաններու, մեզի տեղաւորեցին եկեղեցիին ներքին պատերուն երկայնքը շարուած նստարաններու վրայ»:[45]

Հրապարակագիր Լեւոն Մկրտիչեան նոյնպէս անդրադարձած է 1896ին ծաւալած գաղթականական շարժումին: «Վերյիշումներ Աղեքսանդրիոյ Գաղթային Կեանքէն» յօդուածին մէջ[46] ան յուշագրած է թէ «դէպք»էն՝ Օսմանեան Դրամատան ցոյցին յաջորդող Պոլսոյ ջարդէն յետոյ, իւրաքանչիւր շոգենաւ հարիւրներով գաղթական կը փոխադրէր Աղեքսանդրիա: «Քանի մը շաբթուան մէջ,- կը գրէ Մկրտիչեան,- առնուազն երեք հազար գաղթական ունեցանք եկեղեցւոյ շրջափակին մէջ: Վարժարան, առաջնորդարանի մէկ մասը, եկեղեցւոյ ընդարձակ պարտէզը առնց առժամեայ բնակութեան յատկացուեցան: Բաբելոնեան խառնակութիւն մըն էր: Հայաստանի բոլոր գաւառներէն եւ Պոլսոյ զանազան թաղերէն խառնախուռն ամբոխ մը գրաւած էր տեղւոյս ազգային հաստատութիւնը: Հարկ էր այս երեք հազար հոգին կերակրել, խնամել եւ... կառավարել»:

Մկրտիչեան, որ այդ ժամանակ Աղեքսանդրիոյ ազգային առաջնորդարանի դիւանապետի պաշտօնը վարելով անմիջականօրէն կը զբաղէր գաղթականներու հարցերով, կը նկարագրէ թէ ինչպէս թաղական խորհուրդը ստեղծած է տասնեօթ հոգիներէ բաղկացած «գաղթականաց յանձնաժողով» մը, որ ամէն օր երեկոյեան ժամը հինգէն ինը նիստ կը գումարէր՝ մէկ կողմէն հանգանակութեան ձեռնարկելով ի նպաստ գաղթականներուն, իսկ միւս կողմէն գաղթականներուն համար հեւզհեւոէ աշխատանք գտնելով:

«Երբ գաղթականները զգացին թէ չէին կրնար յաւիտենապէս առաջնորդարանի եւ դպրոցի շէնքին մէջ բնակիլ, ու երբ եկեղեցւոյ պարտէզին ընդարձակ մէկ մասը փոխադրուեցան, ամիս մը չանցած, այդ պարտէզը վերածուեցաւ յոյժ շահեկան եւ ինքնատիպ թաղի մը, իր տնակներով, փողոցներով, թէյարաններով, սրճարաններով եւ շուկայով...»:

Բազմավաստակ ուսուցիչ եւ գրող Յովհաննէս Սէթեան նոյնպէս համառօտակի կը նկարագրէ ապրուստի միջոցներէն բոլորովին զուրկ, շուարած ու ջլատուած խեղճ գաղթականներուն թշուառութիւնը: Ահա հատուած մը անոր «Մեծ Գաղթումը» յօդուածէն. «Աղեքսանդրիոյ եկեղեցիին բակն ու պարտէզը ամենէն աղիողորմ տեսարանը կ'ընծայէր խառնիխուռն շեղջաշեղջ կարկատակոյտ հնոտի կահ կարասիներու, ափ յափոյ կանգնուած վրանիկներու, տախտակակերտ տնիկներու, ճաշի սեղաններու, թերաքամ վրաններու ... որոնց տակ պառաւ մը, կամ դիեցիկ մանուկ մը սնուցանող մայր մը աչքիդ կը զարնէր, գունատ, հերարձակ, վիշտէն անձնամոռաց, նայուածքնին անլուր աղէտքներու եւ սոսկումներու տեսարանէն դեռեւս մոլոր ու ճերմակ. կամ դեռատի աղջիկներ, անխնամ կերպով հագուած, իրենց ամօթը եւ յուսահատութիւնը պարտկելով վրանի մը կամ փայտաշէն խցիկի մը խեղճութեանը մէջ, ամէնքն ալ կրելով իրենց կերպարանքին վրայ վհատութեան, վաղուան կասկածի մութ կնիքը...»: Այնուհետեւ, Սէթեան կը շարունակէ. «Վերջէն, երբ Գահիրէ եկայ, նոյնօրինակ տեսարաններ պարզուեցան աչքերուս...»:[47]

Վայրագ ջարդէն փրկուածներու արհաւիրքն ու սարսափը այնքան սրտաճմլիկ եղած է, որ նոյնիսկ երիտասարդներու հոգեկան վիճակը խախտած է: Սէթեան «Խլեակ Մը» պատմուածքին մէջ[48] գեղարուեստական վարպետութեամբ կը նկարագրէ արհաւիրալից քաղաքէն մազապուրծ ազատած Արտաշէսի ողբերգական ճակատագրին պատմութիւնը: Ստեղծագործութեան հերոսը՝ 35 տարեկան Արտաշէսը, 1896ի օգոստոսեան առաւօտ մը երբ Ղալաթիոյ քարափէն կ'անցնէր, կը տեսնէ մարդիկ, որ լեղապատառ կը վազէին, հալածուած բիրերով, մահակներով զինուած մարդոց կողմէ: Կը հասկնայ: Ծովեզերքին շատ մօտ շոգենաւ մը նկատելով եւ լողալ գիտնալով կը նետուի ծովը: Ջիւք կ'առնեն նաւը, ուր ուրիշ հայեր ալ կ'ըլլան: Երիտասարդ հայորդին այդ պատահական նաւով կը հասնի Աղեքսանդրիա, ուր աշխատանք չգտնելով կը փոխադրուի Գահիրէ եւ կը սկսի աշխատիլ որպէս մեքենագործ: Խելացի, ճարպիկ, լռակեաց երիտասարդը միշտ մտազբաղ հայեցք կ'ունենայ: Օր օրի անվերականգնելիօրէն կը փոխուի անոր իմացականութիւնը, որովհետեւ սոսկումը, զայրոյթը եւ «բան մը ընելու անկարող ըլլալու կատաղութիւնը իրեն մէջ աւերում գործած էին», կը գրէ Սէթեան, միայն իր ֆիզիքական գոյութիւնը փրկած երիտասարդին մասին, որ ոչինչով կրցած էր օգնել փրկելու իր ազգակիցները ահաւոր ու գազանային ջարդէն եւ կամ իր վրէժը լուծել բարբարոս ու հրէշային թուրքերէն: Եւ ահա, գիշեր մը Պէյն-էլ-Սուրէնի բնակիչները փողոցին մէջ աղմուկ կը լսեն եւ կը ճանչնան հաւասարակշռութիւնը կորսնցուցած Արտաշէսի ձայնը, որ անզուսպ ապստամբի ատելութեամբ «կը պոռար ու կը հայհոյէր հայերու ջարդերու հեղինակ սուլթանի դէմ»: Այդ գիշերէն վերջ այլեւս ոչ ոք կը տեսնէ մոլեգին հայրենասէր Արտաշէսը:

Այդ օրերու պարբերական մամուլին մէջ շատ տեղեկութիւններ կան հայ ինքնաքսորեալ գաղթականներու թշուառութեան մասին, ըլլա՛յ Եւրոպայի, ըլլա՛յ Ամերիկայի մէջ: Լեւոն Բաշալեան «Նոր Կեանք»ի մէջ Լ. Զարթումեան ստորագրութեամբ տխուր տեղեկութիւններ կը հաղորդէ Լոնտոնի եւ Միացեալ Նահանգներու հայ գաղթականներու կեանքի դժուարութիւններուն վերաբերեալ: Երուանդ Օտեան «Տասներկու Տարի Պոլսէն Դուրս» յուշագրութեան մէջ կը նշէ Յունաստանի Բիրէա նաւահանգիստը ժամանած շոգենաւէն իջնող եւ Արեւմտեան Հայաստանի զանազան նահանգներէն այնտեղ ապաստան գտնող հազարաւոր հայերու ընչազուրկ եւ չքաւոր վիճակը:

1898ին Պուլկարիոյ Վառնա քաղաքին մէջ հրատարակուող «Ծարժում» թերթը հրատարակած է գաղթական հայուհիի մը եւ իր զաւակներուն կեանքը պատկերող «Հացի Գինը» վիպակը, որ հետագային արտատպած է «Պալքանեան Մամուլ»ը որպէս թերթօն:

«Հացի Գինը» կը նկարագրէ թրքահայ համեստ ու պատուախնդիր հայ ընտանիքի մը կործանումը: Տիրան եւ Աստղիկ ամոլը կը բախտաւորուի երկու զաւակով՝ Վահէ եւ Անուշ, որոնք առաւել եւս կ'երջանկացնեն անոնց կեանքի ամուսնական առաջին տարիները: Սակայն 1896ի սարսափները արիւնոտ կրակի բոցերով կը պաշարեն Աստղիկենց գիւղն ալ: Առաջին խուժումը կ'ըլլայ իրենց տան վրայ, քանի որ շատեր աչք ունէին այդ գեղանի կնոջ վրայ: Աստղիկն ու երախաները տան ետեւի դռնէն փախցնելէ ետք, Տիրան արիաբար կը կռուի եւ յարձակողներէն շատեր գետին փռելէ ետք, անշունչ վար կ'իյնայ՝ գազազած ամբոխի տասը քսան զէնքերու պայթիւնէն յետոյ:

Մինչ գիւղին մէջ սուրն ու կրակը տունէ տուն կը փոխադրուին, անդին, խաւարին մէջ, պատուհաններէն ու տանիքներէն վար ցատկած՝ ամէն տարիքէ ու սեռէ կիսամերկ եւ ուշացիր այլ թշուառներու հետ բլուրէն այն կողմ կը փախչին Աստղիկ եւ իր երկու անչափահաս զաւակները՝ ետին թողլով մոխրացող հայրական երդիքը: Դիմադրելով ուղեւորութեան առթած ֆիզիքական տուայտանքներուն եւ դժուարութիւններուն, սարսափէն կրկնապատկուած ուժով եւ հոգեկան բուռն տագնապներով գիւղէ գիւղ եւ քաղաքէ քաղաք թափառելէ վերջ, Աստղիկ կը հեռանայ իր սիրած բայց անիծեալ երկրէն, կը հաստատուի Սեւ Ծովի եւրոպական եզերքին վրայ գտնուող Պուլկարիոյ Վառնա քաղաքը, ուր վաղօրօք հաստատուած նկատառելի թիւով հայ գաղութ մը գոյութիւն ունէր:

Պուլկարական կառավարութեան եւ տեղական հայ գաղութին օգնութեան շնորհիւ օր ըստ օրէ իրենք զիրենք կը վերագտնեն այս զրկուածները: Սակայն բոլորովին այլ բախտ կը վիճակուի Աստղիկի ընտանիքին, որ զոհ կ'երթայ շատոնց այնտեղ հաստատուած, 45 տարեկանի մօտ, առեւտրական ընդարձակ տան մը տէր, քաղաքի աչքառու դէմքերէն Մարկոս աղային: Այս վերջինը իբրեւ ատենապետ աղքատախնամ վարչութեան կը զբաղէր գաղթականներու գործերով: Ինքզինք ազգային գործերու մէջ հմուտ եւ քաղաքական հարցերով հետաքրքրուող ներկայացնող, սակայն իրականութեան մէջ առեւտուրէն ու իր շահէն անդին չտեսնող այս կեղծաւոր աղան ազգային յեղափոխական շարժումներուն հանդէպ օրը օրին կը փոխէր իր դիրքը. օր մը թունդ Հնչակեան կ'ըլլար եւ անոնց յաջողութիւնները կը ծափահարէր, ուրիշ օր մը կը սկսէր Դաշնակցութիւնը փառաբանել:

«Հացի Գինը»ին մէջ ընթերցողը հետզհետէ կը ծանօթանայ «ի բնէ խորամանկ» ջոջին վարպետօրէն փռած ցանցերուն՝ թակարդը ձգելու համար այդ գաւառացի կինը, որուն գեղեցկութիւնը առաջին օրէն իսկ հրապուրած էր զինք եւ այդ ալ ա՛յն ժամանակ, երբ սնունդի նուազութենէն, ինչպէս նաեւ իրենց բնակած մութ ու խոնաւ սենեակին հակառողջապահական մթնոլորտին պատճառով երախաներն սկսած էին նիհարնալ ու տժգունիլ:

Աստիճանաբար մոմի պէս հալող ու մաշող երախաներուն կտոր մը հացի փոխարէն «բարի մարդու համբաւ»ի տէր Մարկոս աղա խայտառակօրէն կը կորզէ Աստղիկի թանկագին պատիւը: Ներքին ալեկոծութենէն եւ տանջանքէն կը խելագարի Աստղիկ եւ զինք կ'ուղարկեն Պոլսոյ Ազգային Հիւանդանոցի խենթերու արգելարանը: Անուշի հիւանդութիւնը սաստկանալով՝ կը մեռնի առանց հօր ու մօր, իսկ Վահէին կը վիճակուի հեռաւոր որբանոց մը:

Կարելի է բազում էջերով շարունակել գրել 1894-1896 թուականներու ողբերգական արհաւիրքներէն յետոյ հայ գաղթականներու սրտայոյզ ու վշտալի վիճակները պատկերող գրուածքներու մասին, սակայն բաւականանանք այսքանով եւ տեսնենք թէ կոտորածներու պատճառով Պոլիսէն փախած եւ գաղթականներու թշուառ կացութեան ականատես Միքայէլ Կիւրճեան ինչպէս արտացոլացուցած է իր օրերու եգիպտահայ գաղութի հին ու նոր գաղթականներու կեանքն ընդհանրապէս «Մարտիկ Աղա» խորագրով իր անդրանիկ երգիծավէպին մէջ:

Վէպը կը սկսի այսպէս. «96ի ջարդերէն վերջը, գաղթականութեան մեծ հովը, որ սարսափահար հայ ժողովուրդը՝ իր ծննդավայրէն արմատախիլ ընելով՝ աշխարհի չորս կողմը կը ցրուէր, անոր մէկ մասն ալ քշած էր Եգիպտոս»: Այնուհետեւ կը նկարագրէ սարսափին առջեւէն փախչողներու, ինքնաքսորեալներու թշուառ խումբերու, արիւնոտ արհաւիրքներէ ճողոպրած գաղթականներու դժբախտ վիճակը, անոնց հոգեկան ապրումներն ու մութ ապագայի անձկալից մտատանջութիւնը, ինչպէս նաեւ Պոլսոյ հաւատքննական մթնոլորտէն ոստիկաններու, ձերբակալումներու, բանտի, տանջանքի մշտական սպառնալիքի զարհուրելի մղձաւանջէն զերծ՝ Եգիպտոսի ազատ ու ապահով կեանքի պայմաններու քաջալերական ոգեւորութեան տրամադրութիւնը:

Նկարագրելով գաղթական բանուորներու, արհեստաւորներու, վաճառականի գրագիրներու, շուկայի աշկերտներու, Պոլսոյ մէջ գէշ աղէկ ապրիլ կրցող, բայց Աղեքսանդրիոյ մէջ ամէն միջոցէ զուրկ ընտանիքներու խեղճուկրակ պայմանները ու կացութիւնը, Կիւրճեան կը պատկերէ նաեւ անոնց նիւթական եւ տնտեսական ծանր վիճակը, հոգեկան յուզումները ու խումապայինն տագնապները, շուարած խռովքները ու տենդային մտատան-ջութիւնները:

Անոնց վիճակը այնքան խղճալի եւ յուզիչ է, որ ան կը գրէ. «Յուղարկաւոր թափօր մը կարծես, որ կ'անցնի՝ շարականելով միեւնոյն աղիողորմ յառաջաբանը կողոպուտի, ջարդի, ամբողջական թշուառացումի, միեւնոյն աղաչական, արտասուալից յանկերգը, «գործ տուէ՛ք, դրամ տուէ՛ք, ուտելիք տուէ՛ք...»»: Անոնք նման աղերսանքով կը վերջացնեն իրենց խօսքը, ուղղուած Նպաստամատոյց Յանձնաժողովի անդամներուն, որոնք գաղթականներու վերաբերեալ գործերով զբաղելու համար են հաւաքուած: Ութ հոգիներէ կազմուած յանձնաժողովի անդամներէն երկուքը կը բացակային, մէկը կանանչ թիկնաթոռին մէջ ընկղմած յուլօրէն ֆրանսերէն թերթ մը կը կարդայ՝ «ծխելու ստիպուած վայրկեաններուն՝ անտարբեր նայուածք մը ձգելով խնդրարկուներուն վրայ»:[49] Ուրիշ երկու անդամներ քաղաքական կամ առեւտրական հարցերու շուրջ տաք կը վիճաբանին: Յանձնաժողովի անդամներէն մնացածները փոխն ի փոխ, յաճախ երեքը մէկանց, կը զբաղին գաղթականներով, անուշադրութեամբ եւ խոստում-ներով կը ճամբեն տողանցող գաղթականները «- Շատ աղէկ... անունին գրուեցաւ... կը փնտռենք... սպասեցէք... ինշալլահ...» ըսելով:[50]

Թախանձողներու մէջ կան նաեւ քաղաքավար մերժումներու կեղծաւո-րութեան դէմ ընդվզողներ, ինչպէս, օրինակ, քաջ, յանդուգն, անկեղծ «Ատանացի Յակոբը, որ զինքը յանդիմանող թաղականը պարտէզը ամէնուն առջեւ նախատելէն, խայտառակելէն ետքը, կը համարձակի նոյն իսկ ժողո-վասենեակ մտնել ու հոն կրկնել տեսարանը, զայրոյթի ցասկոտ արհամար-հանքի ջախջախող, բռունցքի հարուածներու պէս բիրտ խօսքեր նետել՝ գայթակղած ու վախկոտ շուարումի մը մէջ դողահար լռող թաղականներու երեսին, ի մեծ ուրախութիւն թերեւս գաղթականներու, որոնց սրտէն կը խօսէր»:[51]

Այդ միջոցին Մարտիկ աղա կու գայ եւ ներս մտնել կը փորձէ:

«- Ներսը ուրիշ մա՛րդ կայ ճանըմ, չըլլար, սպասեցէ՛ք» խօսքին վրայ կոպտօրէն ու անզուսպ գոռոզութեամբ կ'ըսէ.

«- Թող տուր կ'ըսեմ կոր, աղբա՛ր, ես քու ճանչցածներէդ չեմ, ինծի Մարտիկ Սրմաքէշեան կ'ըսեն, ես թաղականութիւն ըրած եմ Պոլիս... ես ստակ ուզելու չեմ երթար կոր, այլ ստակ տալու, կը հասկնա՞ս»:[52]

Դուռը ուժգնօրէն բանալով ներս կը նետուի եւ 10 անգլիական ոսկի կը նուիրէ որպէսզի «կարելի եղածին չափ դարմանենք սա անամօթ յեղափոխականներուն մեր խեղճ ազգին հասցուցած անհագին վնասները»: Ժողովականները հազիւ կը յաջողին ընդհատել Մարտիկ աղայի հակայեղափոխական ճառը եւ ընկալագիր մը տալով ազատիլ անկէ:

Չորրորդ գլուխին մէջ Կիւրճեան կը նկարագրէ եգիպտահայ սալոնական կեանքը, տարօրինակապէս հիւրասէր ու ցուցամոլ, հազիւ երեք ամիսէ ի վեր Աղեքսանդրիա հաստատուած Տիգրան աղա Պէյլերեան ընտանիքին տունը, որուն լուսաշող սրահը կ'այցելեն հիւրընկալները կիրակնօրեայ երեկոյին: Ահա իրարու ետեւէ կու գան պոլսեցի հարուստ վաճառական Սարգիս էֆէնտի Խապպազաճեան եւ իր չտես ու պարծենկոտ կինը, Պոլսոյ մէջ որպէս գրագիր աշխատող, սակայն Աղեքսանդրիոյ մէջ տակաւին անգործ Ստեփան Մարկոսեանը, «արջի ու խոզի խառնուրդ» Գավաֆեանն ու իր կինը՝ Զարուհին, բերացի երիտասարդ վաճառական պարոն եւ տիկին Գրիգորեանները, տիկին եւ օրիորդ Սէմէրճեանները, պարոն Արամ Սեղբոսեանը, խուլ բայց շատախօս օրիորդ Սարաֆեանը եւ վերջապէս վէպին գլխաւոր դէմքերը՝ վաճառական Մարտիկ աղան ու «հերոս» և «յեղափոխական» Լեւոն Սուրեանը:

Կիւրճեան ոգեւորուած է յատկապէս անհաստատամիտ ու վերափոխուող, անկայուն ու դիւրափոփոխ Մարտիկ աղայի կերպարով, որ իր կեսարացի վաճառական հօր դրամով կը հարստանայ Սկիւտարի մէջ, ապա իր մօր եւ աղջկան հետ կը տեղափոխուի Աղեքսանդրիա: Այստեղ, Դաշնակցական Լեւոն Սուրեանի ազդեցութեամբ, միայն ինքզինքը հաւնող եւ յեղափոխականները չսիրող Մարտիկ Սրամաքէշեանը իր հայեացքները կը փոխէ եւ կը դառնայ «յեղափոխական», յայտարարելով թէ ինք ոչ թէ բոլոր յեղափոխականներուն դէմ է, այլ՝ Հնչակեաններուն: Ահա ամէն առիթով յեղափոխականներուն դէմ արտայայտուողը Սուրեանի խորհուրդով «Դրօշակ»ներու հաւաքածոն կարդալէ ետք կը դառնայ յեղափոխական սկզբունքներու բուռն ջատագով, յեղափոխութեան գործին համար նոյնիսկ հարստութիւնը չխնայող մարդ:

Խորամանկութեամբ եւ խաբէութեամբ Մարտիկ աղան իր ճիրաններուն մէջ առնելէ ետք, «Դաշնակցական» Սուրեան կը յաջողի գրաւել նաեւ Սրմաքէշեանի աղջկան սիրտը: Մարտիկ աղայի հարստութեան եւ աղջկան նկատմամբ իր շահամոլ նկատումները իրագործելու համար աղան եւ ինք կը մեկնին Փարիզ:

Վէպին մէջ հանդէս եկող բոլոր կերպարներուն պէս իրական է նաեւ յեղափոխական կուսակցութեան գաղափարախօս ձեւացող Լեւոն Սուրեանի կերպարը, որուն մենամոլութիւնը խստօրէն ծաղրած է հեղինակը: Պարզ է թէ վէպին հակակուսակցական բնոյթը սուիններով եւ թշնամութեամբ պիտի դիմաւորուէր. հետեւաբար, բնական է այն պայքարը, որ Հնչակեան պետերը կը մղեն վէպին հրատարակութիւնն անմիջապէս դադրեցնելու համար, քանի որ որպէս Դաշնակցական ներկայացուած Լեւոն Սուրեանը այդ ժամանակ

Աղեքսանդրիոյ հայ հասարակութեան քաջ ծանօթ Հնչակեան գործիչ մըն էր:

Վէպին առաջին մասը եօթ ծաւալուն գլուխներով հրատարակելէ յետոյ, «Նոր Կեանք»ի խմբագրութիւնը ստիպուած կը կրճատէ վէպը, եւ 1899ի Մարտ 1ի թիւին մէջ կը յայտարարէ «մնացեալը յաջորդով», իսկ Մարտ 15ի թիւին մէջ լոյս կը տեսնէ երգիծավէպին «Բ. եւ վերջին մասը»՝ խիստ յապաւուած (էջ 91-96): Ըստ խմբագրութեան կրճատած հրատարակեալ մասին, հեղինակը վէպը կը վերջացնէ Աղեքսանդրիոյ սրճարաններէն մէկուն անկիւնը նստած երկու հոգիի միջեւ ընթացող խօսակցութեամբ: Անոնցմէ մէկուն Փարիզի իր բարեկամներէն ստացած բազմաթերթ նամակին մէջ շարադրուած է Մարտիկ աղային յուսախաբութիւնը Սուրեանէն, որ անոր աղջկան հետ Փարիզէն կը մեկնի Իտալիա ամուսնական ճանապարհորդութեան եւ այնտեղէն ինքզինքը արդարացնելու համար կ'որոշէ ճշմարտութիւնը խոստովանիլ իր աներոջ, թէ ինք յեղափոխութեան մէջ մտած է խաբելու համար Մարտիկ աղան, որովհետեւ սիրած է եղեր անոր աղջիկը: Այս տարօրինակ գաղտնիքը պարզող նամակին ընթերցումին հետեւողը բան մը չհասկնալով, իր երիտասարդ խօսակիցը իր իսկ բառերով կ'ամփոփէ.

«- Զհասկցա՞ր: Սուրեանը Մարտիկ աղային նամակ մըն է գրեր, ըսելով որ ա'լ *վազ անցիր* այդ քու երազներէդ, յեղափոխութեան պոչը ձգէ, նորէն քու առջի կարծիքներուդ դարձիր, բոլոր ըսածներս սուտ էին, դիրք մը ստեղծելու, իմ բախտս շինելու համար ստիպուեցայ քեզի խաբել ու շահագործել, հիմակ կու գամ քենէ ներում խնդրել, մոռցիր ատ բաները, եւ եկուր միասին ապրինք երջանիկ»:[53]

«Հերոս» Սուրեանին զոհ գացած, վախի եւ փառասիրութեան նահատակ դարձած, ոտքէն մինչեւ գլուխը Դաշնակցական դարբնուած Մարտիկ աղան փեսայէն ստացած անսպասելի նամակէն յետոյ «Ծաքաթ մը ամբողջ, առանց տունէն դուրս ելլելու, տան սենեակները, սպասաւորին եւ մօր ականջները լեցուցեր, խլցուցեր է գերագրգռուած զայրոյթի մը պոռչտուքներովը, վիրաւորեալ վայրի գազան մը դարձած, որ վանդակին մէջ մռնչելով՝ կը դառնար ու դառնար»:[54]

Ճիշդ է, Կիրճեան հիմնականին մէջ իր աւարտին կը հասցնէ Մարտիկ աղայի ծիծաղաշարժ ողբերգութիւնը, սակայն ձեռագիրէն ամբողջ գլուխներ դուրս ձգելը խիստ կ'ազդէ վէպին աստիճանական բնական շարունակութեան եւ գեղարուեստական արժանիքներուն վրայ, եւ սխալ ենթադրութիւններու պատճառ կը հանդիսանայ:

«Մարտիկ Աղա» երգիծավէպին մէջ Կիրճեան ծաղր ու ծանակի նիւթ կը դարձնէ ազգայնական կուսակցութիւններու սնափառութիւնը եւ Աղեքսանդրիոյ հայ գաղութի ջոջերուն փոքրոգութիւնը: Ան իրապաշտօրէն կը նկարագրէ 19րդ դարավերջի եգիպտահայ բարքերն ու սովորութիւնները, կը մերկացնէ նոր հարուստ կոչուող չտեսները, յեղափոխութիւն քարոզող մեծխօսիկները: Այս առումով ալ անոր ծաղրը կը ստանայ հասարակական քաղաքական նշանակութիւն եւ հեռու կը մնայ անմեղ զուարճաբանութիւն ըլլալէ:

«Մարտիկ Աղա»ն առաջին անգամ լոյս տեսած է Լոնտոնի «Նոր Կեանք» պարբերականին մէջ 1898ի Հոկտեմբերէն 1899ի Մարտ ամիսներու ընթացքին: Կիրճեան խոհեմութիւն ունեցած է երկին հեղինակը ըլլալու իրողութիւնը ծածկելու «Պարոյր» ծածկանուան տակ, ինչ որ զինք փրկած է շատ անհաճոյ միջադէպերէ, ինչպէս կը վկայեն իր ժամանակի գրողներ: Բաւական է նշել որ հրատարակութեան սկիզբը իբրեւ գեղեցիկ երկ հանոյքով կարդացուելով հանդերձ, շուտով վէպը յառաջ կը բերէ խսկական փոթորիկ մը, որ կ'ալեկոծէ Աղեքսանդրիոյ ամբողջ հայ գաղութը, ուր կարծիքներ կը շրջին թէ հեղինակը «Տիգրան Կամսարականը ըլլալու է ... չէ, անպատճառ Արփիարն է գրողը ... թերեւս Օտեանն է ...», կը գրէ Օտեան:[55] «Մազ մնացեր էր որ Յ. Ալփիար ծեծ ուտէր, որովհետեւ տեղ մը անխոհեմութեամբ յայտարարած էր թէ «Ասանկ վէպ մը ե՛ս միայն կրնամ գրել», ինչ որ չափազանց ինքնագովութիւն էր իրեն համար», կը գրէ դարձեալ Երուանդ Օտեան իր յուշագրութեան մէջ:[56]

Սուրէն Պարթեւեան կը վկայէ որ եգիպտահայ բարքերէն վերցուած «Մարտիկ Աղա» վէպին առաջին դրուագները Լեւոն Բաշալեանի հետ կարդալու ժամանակ Լոնտոնի մէջ «Նոր Կեանք»ի խմբագրատունը, «միասին ապշահար մնացած ենք անակնկալ ու տիրական յայտնագործումին հանդէպ նոր տաղանդի մը, որ յանձին Միքայէլ Կիրճեանի կու գար մէկէն ի մէկ հարկադրուիլ մեր գնահատումին, մեզ խանդավառել ու սահմռկեցնել միանգամայն»:[57]

Պարթեւեան կը գրէ նաեւ որ «Մարտիկ Աղա»ն այնպիսի փոթորիկ մը յառաջ բերաւ իր շուրջը, որ կրնար այդ փոթորիկը իր գլխին պայթիլ, «եթէ Կիրճեան ինքզինքը պատսպարած չըլլար «Պարոյր» ծածկանունին տակ»:

Իսկապէս, Կիրճեան գրական մեծ յանդգնութիւն ցուցաբերած է «սանձակոտոր ծաղրավէպ»ով (ըստ Պարթեւեանի): Բայց մենք գիտենք որ ճիշդ չէ երգիծավէպը ծաղրավէպ համարել, որովհետեւ Կիրճեան ոչ թէ կոպիտ ծաղրող է, այլ՝ նրբազգաց երգիծող:

Բայց ինչո՞ւ վէպը այդքան աղմուկ բարձրացուց եւ ի՞նչ էր այդ յուզումներու պատճառը:

Այդ պէտք է բացատրել վէպին գլխաւոր սիւժէթային գիծով, որուն գործողութիւնները կը զարգանան հեղինակին անվերապահ քննադատութեամբ:

«Մարտիկ Աղա» վէպը կը սկսի 1896ի ջարդերէն յետոյ ինքնաքսորեալներու թշուառ խումբերու ողբալի վիճակին նկարագրութեամբ: Միքայէլ կը նկարագրէ եկեղեցիի պարտէզն ու բակը իր ալեկոծ ամբոխով. այդ խառնիճաղանճ բազմութեան մէջ մենք կը տեսնենք զանազան տարազներով տարբեր գաւառներու ներկայացուցիչներ՝ բանուորն ու ձկնորսը, գաւառացի բեռնակիրն ու զարգացածի երեւոյթով վայելուչ երիտասարդը, նոր շրջանաւարտն ու *էսնաֆը*, շուկայի երիտասարդն ու փէսաւոր նախկին վաճառականը: Տեսակ մը գիւղի մանրանկար յիշեցնող աղքատ գաղթականներու բազմաթիւ վրաններու, յանկարծակերտ բնակարաններու, երկու տախտակով շինուած խանութներու ֆօնին վրայ կը յայտնուի վէպին գլխաւոր հերոսը՝ Մարտիկ աղա Սրմաքէշեան: Հեղինակը բազմակողմանիօրէն կը պատկերէ այս կերպարը թէ՛ շուկայական ասպարէզի մէջ, թէ՛ տունը, թէ՛ մեծահարուստներու շրջապատին մէջ:

Օտեան իր «Տասներկու Տարի Պոլսէն Դուրս» յուշագրութեան մէջ մանրամասնօրէն կը գրէ «ապահովաբար ոչ սկսնակ գրող» Պարոյրի «Մարտիկ Աղա» վէպին եւ անոր յառաջ բերած «անօրինակ տագնապ»ին մասին: Օտեան կը նշէ. «քանի մը թիւ ետքը՝ վէպը կը ներկայացնէ Աղեքսանդրիոյ մէջ հայկական սալօն մը, ուր կ'երեւային գաղթականութեան շատ մը ծանօթ դէմքերը ամենաճշգրիտ եւ սակայն գերազանցօրէն ծաղրանկարուած գիծերով. կին, էրիկմարդ եւ ոչ մէկուն խնայուած էր, ամէնքը հոն, իրենց ծիծաղելի կողմերուն բովանդակ մերկութեամբը կ'երեւային: Իրենց դէմքը, մարմինը, խօսուածքը, հագուստը, ամէն ինչ մէջտեղ հանուած էր անպատկառ չարաճճիութեամբ մը»:[58]

Օտեան վէպէն ընդարձակ մէջբերումներ կը կատարէ բոլորին ծանօթ ջոջերու նկարագրութիւններէն՝ պոլսեցի հարուստ վաճառական Սարգիս էֆէնտի Խապառաճեան եւ իր կինը, Գավաֆեան եւ իր կինը, ինչպէս նաեւ Աղեքսանդրիոյ մէջ ծանօթ ուրիշ անհատներ, զորս անողոք կերպով կ'այպանէ, կը հեգնէ երգիծավէպին հեղինակը:

Այնուհետեւ Օտեան կը շարունակէ. «Անհելի փոթորիկ մըն էր բրդաւ քաղաքին մէջ: Տուները, սրճարանները, զբօսավայրերը, ամէն մարդ Մարտիկ աղայով կը զբաղէր: Անոնք որ տակաւին վէպին մէջ չէին երեւցած՝ սրտատրոփ անձկութեամբ կը սպասէին իրենց կարգին, արդէն իսկ ծաղրուածները կը ջանային իրենք զիրենք մխիթարել՝ ըսելով.

- Մենք մեր կարգը անցուցինք:

Եւ սակայն եւ ոչ մէկը կը ներէր Պարոյրին, որուն ով ըլլալը չէին գիտեր»:[59]

Օտեան կը վկայէ որ «Մարտիկ Աղա»ի պատճառով Արփիարեան փորձանքի հանդիպած էր. իսկ կուսակցական շրջանակներու մէջ ան վերածուած էր ներկուսակցական զայրալի պայքարի:

«Լեւոն Բաշալեան գաղտնաբար Արփիարին իմացուցած էր Պարոյրին ո՛վ ըլլալը, սակայն պատուիրելով, որ ինէ զատ ոչ մէկուն յայտնէ,- կը գրէ Օտեան: Միւս կողմէ՝ Լեւոն Մկրտիչեան, իբրեւ Հնչակեան պետերէն մին, դիմած էր Լոնտոն՝ հեղինակին իսկական անունը իմանալու համար, սակայն Բաշալեան մերժած էր յայտնել: Մկրտիչեան պահանջած էր, որ վէպին հրատարակութիւնը դադրեցնեն. Արփիար եւ Բաշալեան ընդդիմացած էին ասոր: Մկրտիչեան հեռագրով հրահանգ տուած էր դարձեալ վէպը դադրեցնելու, սակայն շարունակուած էր: Ասոր վրայ Մկրտիչեան սպառնացեր էր հրաժարելու եւ կուսակցութենէն քաշուելու:

Ամենէն զուարճալին այն էր, որ վէպին հերոսներէն Սուրեան՝ որ իբրեւ Դաշնակցական ներկայացուած էր՝ Հնչակեան ծանօթ գործիչ մըն էր: Ա՛յս ալ ոչ նուազ գայթակղութիւն կը պատճառէր խնդրին տեղեակ կուսակցականներուն մէջ»:[60]

Կիւրճեան ինքզինքն ալ նկարագրած է «Մարտիկ Աղա»ի մէջ: Այդ իսկ պատճառով Պարոյրի դէմ կատղած ընթերցողներն իսկ կը խղճահարին Կիւրճեանին, որ վէպին մէջ պատկերուած է Քուրջեան անունին տակ, որպէս 19-20 տարեկան տժգոյն, նիհար, սմքած, սատկած երեւոյթով երիտասարդ մը, տարտամ ակնարկով, փլփլող քալուածքով, մարմրած աչքերով, եւայլն: Օտեան կը հաստատէ. «Տարիներ անցնելէ ետքն ալ Պարոյրի դէմ գրգռումը չանցաւ Աղեքսանդրիոյ հայ գաղութին մէջ, եւ ի վերջոյ, երբ իմացուեցաւ անոր իսկական անունը, ճշմարիտ հալածանք մը սկսաւ Միքայէլ Կիւրճեանի դէմ, այն աստիճան որ խեղճը, քաղաքին մէջ հանգիստ ապրելու համար, ստիպուեցաւ հրապարակաւ յայտարարել, թէ «Մարտիկ Աղան» գրելով՝ գրական *ճախա* մը ընել ուզած էր, որուն համար կը զղջար»:[61]

Արդարեւ, դուրս գալով արեւմտահայ շարք մը գրողներու թեմաթիք սահմանափակումներէն, Կիւրճեան գաղափարական ու գեղարուեստական բարձր մակարդակով երգիծական խօսքի միջոցով ու բնաւորութիւններու քոմիզմով սրամտօրէն կը քննադատէ իրեն ժամանակակից սերունդին շատ ծանօթ մարդոց ներքին էութիւնն ու արտաքին յատկանիշները:

Կիւրճեան մեծ վարպետութեամբ կը պատկերէ բոլոր կերպարները, մասնաւորաբար՝ գլխաւոր հերոսները, եւ դժուար է զանոնք նոյն պատկերաւորութեամբ վերարտադրել: Ուստի, խօսքը տանք տակաւին երկու տասնամեակները չբոլորած հեղինակին:

«Ողլսեցի հարուստ վաճառական Սարգիս էֆէնտի Խապառաճեան, եւ իր կինը: Շատ յարմար լծուած զոյգ մը: Մարդը, կարճահասակ, գիրուկ, խոշոր լեռնոտ գլուխ մը, ժայռի պէս յաման ճակատ, հաստ իլնող պեխեր, կախուող կոր քիթ: Խոպոտ, պարարտ ձայնի ելեւէջներուն, մարմնին շարժումներուն, ձեւերուն մէջ՝ որոնացող կենդանիներու դանդաղութենէն, կոշտութենէն, պինդ գլխութենէն բան մը: Արդէն գլուխը միխրճած իր լայն ու ծայրալից ուսերուն մէջտեղ, յիշեցնելով եզի մը գլուխը՝ յամրերեր իր լուծին առաջ, որուն՝ ցիր ուսերը շրջագիծը կը ձեւացնեն:

«Իր քովը տոտոզուած է կինը, նմանապէս գէր, պայթող այտերով, կրկնակ ծնօտով, յոյր ծիծերը մաէ ծրարներու պէս նստած ուռած փորին վրայ, ու թեւերը կուրծքին վրայ ծալլուած: Իր ձեւերը, շեշտը տեսակ մը գոոզութիւն, եսեմութիւն ունին, ու շրթունքներուն քովերը՝ արհամարհոտ ծալքեր երբ խօսի: Միշտ իր վրայ, տանը վրայ, պերճանքի, ճոխութեան, ծախքի վրայ, հարուստ մէկու մը հետ ամուսնացած աղքատ դասակարգի աղջկան մը չտես պարծենկոտութիւնովը, մեծքիթութիւնովը մեծաբանող կին մը, մինչ իր ամուսինը, ճակտին քրտինքովը,- զրկանքներու, նուաստացումներու շնորհիւ, ժամանակով համբերութեամբ ու կծծիութեամբ հարստացած մէկը, ամէն տեղ, ամէնուն, գործի, դրամի վրայ խօսող, խնայողութիւն քարոզող, «ժամանակներուն» գէշութեան վրայ ողբացող, «յիմար ծախքեր» ընելէ տարհամոզող, նոր տեսած մէկու մը իր գործը հարցնող,- միայն առեւտուրի մարդոց պատիւ ընող, անգործներուն, գրագիրներուն, «գրող կարդացողներուն» կռնակ դարձնող...»:[62]

Կիւրճեան հերթով կը նկարագրէ նաեւ Պէյլէրեան ընտանիքի ընդարձակ հիւրասրահի ներկաները՝ նոյն անգթութեամբ:

«Ստեփան Մարկոսեան, երեսուն տարեկան երիտասարդ մը, Պոլիս գրագիր, հոս անգործ: Զարգացած կ'ըսեն զինքը, ինչ որ կը նշանակէ մեր մէջ ֆրանսերէն գիտցող: Գիրք մըն ալ հրատարակած է ատենով, «18 Նորավէպք, Թարգմանեալք Գաղղիերէնէ», զոր ինք կը յիշէ միայն: Զուարճալի է տեսնել թէ ինչպէս գիրութիւնը --ինչպէս ձիւնը հողինները-հարթած, կակուղցուցած է այդ մարդուն քով մարմնին խորտուբորտութիւնները, գրեթէ արդուկած է անոր շրջագիծը, սրունքները անչափօրէն լայնցուցած, մինչեւ զանոնք հասցնելու աստիճան փորին ցցուածքին, մսի ծալքերուն մէջ անհետացնելով վիզը, գլուխը՝ առանց փոխանցումի՝ շարունակութիւնը ընելով մարմնին մնացորդ մասին, զոր յաջողած է այսպէս վերածել մսի, ճարպի կոյտի մը կլոր ու ծանր, տիկ ու գլան, եգիպտական կարճ վարունգի կամ դդմակի ձեւով:

«Հակառակ ասոնց, Մարկոսեան ոսկեթել ակնոց դրած է, կարծես փափաքելով իր մարմնին կոշտութիւնը, թանձրութիւնը սրբագրել ակնոցին թեթեւ, ազնուապետական նրբութիւնովը, եզի մը պէս որ ուզած ըլլար, սնափառօրէն, ձիու մը վայելուչ աչապահները հագնիլ»:[63]

Մի քանի տող յետոյ, Կիւրճեան անողոքաբար կը նկարագրէ նաեւ պարոն եւ տիկին Գավաֆեանները:

«Գէր մըն ալ աս: Արջի ու խոզի խառնուրդ մը: Էն ցայտող բանը իր մէջ իր գլուխն է, ահագին բազմահատոր գլուխ մը, խոշոր ձմերուկի մը ձեւով, գրեթէ առանց վզի փակցուած կարճոտն պատկառելի մարմնի մը, տակառաձեւ ցցուած փորով մը բեռնաւորուած: Խծուծէ յօնքեր, մացառուտ պեխեր, լայնշի, մեծափոր քիթ մը, խոշոր աչքեր ուռած, ցցուած ակնագուններով, ահագին խորշոմներով խորխորատուած դէմք մը. ձայնը ասոնց համեմատ: Կինը իրմէ միայն անունը ունի: Ծանր, կոշտ, լայնփոր բաներու այդ դէզը, ամուսնացած՝ ջիղերու նիհար ծրարիկի մը, կնկան պչրող մարմնի մը հետ, քիչ մը անցած գեղեցկութիւնով — անհանդարտ, աշխոյժ, որ կը սրնգէ ու կ'այծուըղտէ այդ խոշոր թմբուկին, այդ գոմէշին քով»:[64]

Պէյլէրեանները սալօնը ներկայացնող «Նոր Կեանք»ի այդ նոյն թիւին մէջ Կիւրճեան նոյնպիսի գունագեղութեամբ կը պատկերէ նաեւ այդ սրահին նիհար հիւրերը՝ նոյնանման սրամտութեամբ.

«Բերացի երիտասարդ վաճառական մը որ այս տեղ նոր գործ մը բացած էր. քամուած անռուած լաթի պէս չոփ չոր, խարխնծիի պէս կռնծած, մսերը ոսկորներուն փակած մարդ մը, կարծես գանկէ դէմքով, Տոմիէի անմահ Րօպէր Մաքէրին ընկերինը յիշեցնող ճիտով մը: Սեփ սեւ փոսացած աչքեր, որոնք կը նային ինչպէս գզիրները կը ծակեն: Իր կինը նիհար ու անուշ»:

Սակայն այդ սրահին մէջ հաւաքուած տարբեր սեռի, տարբեր բնաւորութեան, տարբեր գաղափարներու տէր մարդոց կեդրոնն ու կապը օրիորդ Պէյլէրեանն է՝ «կարծես, կաչաղակի պէս չանչան, ձուկի պէս անհանդարտ, անդադար խօսող, մտքէն անցածը անխորհրդաբար դուրս թափող, բան մը պահելու, ծածկելու անկարող, գաղափարէ գաղափար, խօսքէ խօսք ցատքտելով ինչպէս ճնճղուկ մը թառէ թառ, մշտահոս ալիքի մը մէջ անկապակից, անհեթեթ, իրարու հետ չկարուած խօսքերու, ծայրայեղ, խօլ շարժումներու, լիակոկորդ անպատկառ քրքիջներու, յեղակարծ անշարժաորիթ կայքերով - շունչ առնելու համար կարծես — նորէն սկսելու, նետուելու, թռելու համար բառերու, շարժումներու բուռն յորձանքի մը մէջ, որ կը պտուտքի, կը դառնայ՝ թղթի, կտաւի, փետուրի կտորներու փոշեխառն թռիչքի մը պէս՝ փողոցի մէջ հովէն խօլաբար պարող, շփոթ ու տակնուվրայ»:[65]

Ինչպէս ըսինք, վէպին մէջ նկարագրուած են աղեքսանդրիաբնակ հայ շատ ծանօթ դէմքեր, որոնք իրենք իրենց վերոյիշեալ պատկերաւոր եւ անողոք ձեւով նկարագրուած ըլլալը կարդալով չէին կրնար չընդվզիլ:

Երգիծավէպին մէջ աւելի հետաքրքրական ու անզիջող քննադատութեամբ բնութագրուած են գլխաւոր հերոսները՝ Մարտիկ աղա Սրմաքէշեան եւ Լեւոն Սուրեան:

Ահա՛ վէպի կեդրոնական հերոս Մարտիկ աղան: «40-45 տարեկան երեւցող, կայտառ ու յաղթանդամ սակայն, երկայնահասակ, գլխագիր Տ-ի պէս մեծ-փոր, յաւակնոտ, կուռ ու կլոր մարմինով մարդ մը,- մոխրոտած մազեր, քաղքենի փորի պէս լայն ու ուռած ճակատ, աղիւսի կարմրութեամբ դէմք,- պեխերու պէս հաստ յօնքեր որոնց խիտ մացառուտին մէջէն խոշոր ու հրամայական աչքեր կը վառէին, ուռած ակնագունտերով, հայկական վեհաշուք քիթ մը, արաբ շրթունքներ զոր առատ պեխերը չուանի պէս ոլորուած կը ծածկէին ամբողջովին, եռայարկ ծնօտ մը գոռոզ՝ յաղթականօրէն հանգչող լանջաշապիկին վրայ, խոշոր փոր մը առջեւը ձգած ինչպէս թմբկահար մը իր թմբուկը, բարձրահասակ ֆէսը տիրաբար ետեւ նետուած, մէկ ձեռքը հովանոց ու միւս ձեռքը լայն տաբատին գրպանը՝ այդ վայրկեանին եկեղեցիին դռնէն ներս կը մտնէր, երկու չափահաս, նիհար, լրջերեւոյթ մարդերու մէջտեղէն, նմանապէս ֆէսով,- վաճառականներ ապահովաբար, որոնք կը թուէին միայն մտիկ ընել գէր մարդը, որ կը յառաջանար խոշոր ու հեղինակաւոր քայլերով, բարձրաձայն կը խօսէր, ձեռքի հովանոցը երերցնելով սպառնագին, գլխի բուռն շարժումներով որոնց համեմատ փէսին ծոպը կ'երերար խանգարուած ժամացոյցի մը ճօճանակին պէս»:[66]

Մարտիկ աղա Սրմաքէշեանի կրակ խառնուածքի տէր եւ միամիտ հաւատացող մարդու հակապատկերն է պաղ, հանդարտ, լուրջ Լեւոն Սուրեանը: Ի տարբերութիւն միւս կերպարներուն, Կիրճեան շատ վայելուչ կը ներկայացնէ Սուրեանը, չի ծաղրեր անոր արտաքինը, սակայն իրականին մէջ ամենասուր քննադատութիւնը կը վերապահէ անոր՝ քննադատելով անոր ներքինը, անոր էութիւնը, անոր խաբեբայ արարքը: Կիրճեան յաջողած է դիմակազերծել Լեւոն Սուրեանը եւ ցոյց տալ այդ արտաքինին ներքեւ թաքնուած խարդախ եւ վարպետորդի անձնաւորութիւնը: Այսպիսով, Կիրճեան աւելի շեշտուած կերպով մատնացոյց կ'ընէ Սուրեանի զազրելի հնարամտութիւնը՝ որ սկիզբը որպէս յեղափոխական կը ներկայանայ, իսկ իր նպատակին հասնելէ վերջ, նամակ կը գրէ եւ կը խնդրէ, որ Մարտիկ աղա ներողամիտ գտնուի իր արարքին համար:

Մինչեւ Սուրեանին հետ հանդիպումը Մարտիկ աղա գաղթականներու խեղճութիւնն ու թշուառութիւնը տեսնելով բարձրաձայն դժգոհանք կը յայտնէր կուսակցութիւններու եւ յեղափոխականներու դէմ, տրտնջալով որ «խեղճ ազգը այս վիճակին հասցուցին»:

Ուշագրաւ է Սրմաքէշեանի եւ Սուրեանի հանդիպումը Պէյլէրեաններու տան մէջ, ուր Լեւոն իր «յեղափոխական կեանքէն» կը ճառէ, իսկ Մարտիկ աղա իր «հայրենասիրական գործունէութենէն» միջադէպեր կը պատմէ: Առաջին հանդիպումէն երկու շաբաթ ետք, Սուրեան կը կարողանայ ահաբեկութեան սպառնալիքով 10 ոսկի տուգանք վերցնել Մարտիկ աղայէն «ի պատիժ այն ցած նախատինքներուն» որ ամէնուրեք, հրապարակաւ կ'արտայայտէ ան յեղափոխութեան եւ մասնաւորապէս Դաշնակցութեան դէմ: Սուրեան կը յաջողի հեշտութեամբ յեղաշրջել միամիտ Սրմաքէշեանը, որ իբրեւ ազգային բարերար իր անունը պատմութեան մէջ արձանագրուած տեսնելու սնափառութենէն ու տեռորի վախէն մղուած դաշնակցական կը դառնայ, եւ ահա «քաղաքականութեան այբուբենը հեգել չգիտցողը» տեսաբան կը դառնայ, կը սկսի մեկնաբանել դէպքերը եւ քաղաքական գուշակութիւններ ընել:

Կիրճեան վարպետօրէն կրցած է Մարտիկ աղայի եւ անոր ունկնդիրներուն միջեւ տեղի ունեցող խօսակցութիւններուն միջոցով ցոյց տալ օրաւուր ամրացող անոր նորադարձի հաւատքը: Հետաքրքրաշարժ է յատկապէս Մարտիկ աղայի հանդիպումը գաւառացիի տարազով ու դէմքով թշուառ գաղթականի մը հետ, որ իմացած ըլլալով որ էֆէնտին բարեսիրտ ու բարեգործ մէկն է, ազգին շատ բարիքներ ըրած է, կը դիմէ անոր.

«- Էֆէնտի, ըսաւ մարդը, աղաչական ... ու սկսաւ պատմել իր թշուառութիւնը — Պոլսոյ վիճակը բաւական գոհացուցիչ, ունեցած անագին վնասները, հոստեղի յուսահատ կացութիւնը:

Մարտիկ աղա հնդկահաւի պէս կ'ուռենար, ու իրարու ետեւէ կը ծխէր, արագ արագ:

Գաւառացին կու գար աղաչել, որ Մարտիկ աղա հաճի օգնել իրեն, ձեռք կարկառել, «Աստծու սիրուն, աղուորիկ աղջկանը սիրուն», իր եւ իր թշուառ ընտանիքին:

- Հը', ըրաւ Մարտիկ աղա, դուն յեղափոխակա՞ն ես:

Մարդը — իրօք յեղափոխական, նոյն իսկ Դաշնակցական ատենօք — որ առիթ ունեցած էր, եկեղեցին կամ այլուր, Մարտիկ աղան տեսնալու իր նախորդ հաւատքին զանազան արտայայտութիւններուն մէջ,ատ հարցումին՝ բողոքի բուռն շարժում մը ուրուագծեց:

- Ի՞նչ կ'ըսես, էֆէնտի, ե՞ս յեղափոխական ըլլամ, քա'ւ լիցի ... ան խայտառակները ...

- Որո՞նց համար կ'ըսես կոր, ընդմիջեց Մարտիկ աղա, Հնչակեան-նեռու՞ն թէ Դրօշակեաններուն:

- Հնչակեան Դրօշակեան ամենքն ալ գետնին տակը անցնին ... մանաւանդ Դրօշակեանները որ ...

Հազիւ այս ձախող խօսքը բերնէն փախած էր որ լռեց մէկէն, ապշած ու անհաբեկ՝ Մարտիկ աղային առջեւ որ բազմոցին վրայ կէս մը ոտքի ելած՝ սպառնագին ու խոժոռ՝ հրամայող շարժումով մը դուռը կը ցուցնէր իրեն:

- Լռէ', դուրս ելիր այստեղէն, կորսուէ' անպիտան ... դուն ո՞վ Դրօշակեանները նախատողը ո՞վ ...

Մարդը շուարած յանկարծակիի եկած, լուսնէն ինկած երեւոյթը ունէր մէկու մը, որ ջուր խմել հաւատալով՝ աքլորին այրող կրակը կը կլլէ, կամ, աթոռին վրայ նստելու ապահովութեամբ տախտակամածին անակնկալին կը բաղխի»:[67]

Ընթերցողը չի կրնար իր հեգնական ժպիտը զսպել կարդալով ժամանակ մը զայրոյթով ու նախատինքով յեղափոխականները խարազանող, ամէն առիթով կուսակցականներու դէմ կատաղի յարձակումներ գործող, անընդհատ «անոնց խերը պիտի անիծեմ» նախադասութիւնը կրկնող, իսկ այս անգամ թնդացող ձայնով ճիշդ հակառակ դիրքէն արտայայտուող, գունափոխ եղած Մարտիկ աղայի խօսքերը, որ այժմ կուսակցականներուն ու յեղափոխականներուն օգնելու իր նոր սկզբունքով շարժելով տունէն դուրս կը վռնտէ «հակադրօշակեան» գաւառացին:

Վէպին մէջ կան նաեւ ուրիշ երկրորդական դէմքեր, որոնց միջոցով եւս կը քննադատուի Դաշնակցութեան բրոբականտիսդ դարձած Մարտիկ աղայի հաւատափոխութիւնը, փառասիրութիւնը եւ բացասական այլ թերութիւններ: Հետաքրքրական կերպար է պատուելի Երուանդ Գարակէօզեանը, որ քաղաքական ամէն դէպքի տակ Ռուսիոյ մատը փնտռող ու գտնող Մարտիկ աղային «Ծէոշէ լը Ռիւս, շէոշէ լը Ռիւս» յանկերգին հետեւանքով վիճամոլութենէ դրդուած «ինծի հարցնես նէ, էֆէնտի, Անգլիան է ամէն բանի պատճառը» ըսելով կը վիճաբանի կոուազան յաւակնութիւններով: Ուշագրաւ է նաեւ ռուսահայ ընկերվարականը, որ կը հակաճառէ թէ «Դաշնակցական պետերը ամբողջ Մարքսի, Լասալի ընկերվարական վարդապետութիւններն դաւանում են» եւ թէ «ազատութիւն ստացուելէն ետքը՝ հարստութիւնը գրաւելով ուրիշներուն պիտի բաշխեն»: Այս խօսքէն սարսափած, Մարտիկ աղա կը պատասխանէ. «Չէ՛ ճանըմ, դուն սխալ կ'ըսես կոր ... անոնք անանկ բաներ չեն ըսեր»: Գիտական բացատրութիւններէն բան չհասկնալով, ան կը շարունակէ. «Ատ ինչ ըսել է ... ինչո՞ւ իմ հարստութիւնս ուրիշներու բաժնուի ... ի՞նչ ըսել է ... թող ամէն մարդ աշխատի հարստանայ ... ես ի՞նչպէս եմ հարստացեր իմ ջանքերովս ... ատ է նէ ընկերվարականութիւնը պարապ բան է եղեր ...», կ'եզրակացնէ ան, հակառակ անոր որ Սուրեան զինք ապահովցուցած էր թէ շատ մօտ ապագային հայկական հարցի յաջող լուծումէն ու ազատութենէն վերջ յեղափոխութեան շրջանին մէջ եղած բոլոր կամաւոր նուիրատուութիւնները Նորակազմ Ազգային Դրամատան կողմէ ամբողջովին պիտի վերադարձուին, իրենց տոկոսներովը: Մարտիկ աղայի ունկնդիրներուն մէջ էր նաեւ պոլսեցի վաճառական Սարգիս էֆէնտին, որ իր հարստութեան թափթփուքներով կ'ապրէր եւ դրամական կարեւոր պահանջներ ունէր օսմանեան կառավարութենէն: Իսկ Մարտիկ աղա համոզած էր զինքը՝ թէ ռուսը քանի մը տարիէն տաճիկին խերը պիտի անիծէ եւ վստահեցուցած՝ թէ «Թուրքիան պիտի գրաւէ, դուն ալ քու ստակներդ ամբողջովին կրնաս գանձել»: Երկրորդական դէմքերէն կարելի է յիշատակել նաեւ քաղաքականութեան մենամոլ, Մարտիկ աղային չափ մեկնաբանող, գուշակող ու շատախօս պոլսեցի բժիշկը եւ ուրիշներ:

Հետաքրքրական եւ ծիծաղաշարժ է վէպին վերջաւորութիւնը, ուր զարգացուած է այն միտքը թէ «Մարտիկ աղաներուն Սուրեաններ են հարկաւոր»:

Կարեւոր է նշել թէ երգիծավէպը կիսատ չէ մնացած. ան աւարտած է, սակայն հրատարակուած է չափազանց յապաւուած, խիստ կրճատումներով եւ կտրուկ վերջաւորութեամբ: Մենք կ'ենթադրէինք եւ հաւատացած էինք որ անոր բնագիրը եղած է աւելի ընդարձակ, քանի որ փաստ է թէ անոր հրատարակութիւնը դադրեցուած էր կուսակցական ճնշումներով եւ սպառնալիքներով: Մեր ենթադրութեան գլխաւոր ապացոյցն այն էր, որ Օտեան 1896-1908 թուականները ընդգրկող իր «Տասներկու Տարի Պոլսէն Դուրս» յուշագրութեան մէջ կը գրէր. «Լոնտոն գտնուած միջոցիս, երբ սրտերնիս նեղանար *գիշերները*, Լեւոն Բաշալեանի հետ *կը հանէինք Մարտիկ աղայի անտիպ մնացած ձեռագիրները* եւ զանոնք կարդալով՝

հաճելի ժամանց մը կ'ընծայէինք մենք մեզի»:[68] Ինչպէս կը տեսնենք, Օտեան կը վկայէ անտիպ մնացած ձեռագիրներու գոյութիւնը, որ կը հաստատէ թէ չտպագրուած մասը շատ էր եւ ոչ թէ մէկ քանի ձեռագիր թերթ, մանաւանդ որ Օտեան կ'ակնարկէ ոչ թէ մէկ գիշերուան, այլ՝ գիշերներու: Եթէ անտիպ մնացած ձեռագիրները քիչ ըլլային, Օտեան եւ Բաշալեան մէկ գիշերուան մէջ կարդացած ու վերջացուցած պիտի ըլլային եւ ակնարկութիւն պիտի չըլլար գիշերներու:

Բացի Լոնտոնի «Հայ Կեանք» հանդէսէն, «Մարտի Աղա»ն լոյս տեսած է նաեւ Պոլսոյ «Հայրենիք»ի ու Ամերիկայի «Ազգ»ի մէջ՝ մէկական անգամ, եւ «Արեւ» օրաթերթին մէջ երկու անգամ, այդ պակասաւոր վիճակով: Ուրախ ենք որ մեր երկար տարիներու երազը իրականացաւ եւ վերջապէս յաջողեցանք ունենալ «Մարտիկ Աղա» վէպին շարունակութիւնը, անտիպ գլուխներու ձեռագիրներուն պատճէնները, եւ կարողացանք վերծանել, մշակել ու երգիծավէպը 1999ին ամբողջական ձեւով մատուցանել ընթերցողներուն՝ հեղինակին ծննդեան 120ամեակին առիթով, շնորհիւ գրասէր ու գրականասէր Յարութիւն Սիմոնեանի մեկենասութեան:

Երգիծավէպը մեծ հետաքրքրութեամբ կ'ընթերցուի մեր օրերուն ալ, եւ թէեւ ան գրուած է աւելի քան դար մը առաջ, կը հրապուրէ ժամանակակից ընթերցողը՝ շնորհիւ իր շահեկան եւ հետաքրքրական բովանդակութեան եւ գեղարուեստական-գեղագիտական արժանիքներուն:

Դժբախտաբար, «Մարտիկ Աղա»ի հրատարակութեան աննախադէպ ընդհատումը, կուսակցական սպառնալից հրահանգներու պատճառով կիսատ հրապարակումը, որոշ գլուխներու անտիպութիւնը, որպէս վէպի Բ. մաս միայն վերջաբանին տպագրութիւնը, ինչպէս նաեւ լոկ մամուլի մէջ յապաւեալ վիճակով լոյս ընծայուած ըլլալը պատճառ դարձած են որ վէպը ըստ արժանւոյն չգնահատուի գրականագէտներու կողմէ: Ոմանք բնաւ չեն անդրադարձած երգիծավէպին, ուրիշներ չեն քննած զայն գիտական անհրաժեշտ հետաքրքրութեամբ: Ուստի, որոշ գրողներ ու գրաքննադատներ հետեւցուցած են թէ ան չունի «տիրական գործողութիւն», «կառուցում ու մշակում», թէ՝ «վէպին երկրորդ մասը թոյլ է», թէ՝ «շատ հաւանաբար հեղինակը չէր ամբողջացուցած զայն՝ հրատարակութեան տալէ առաջ», թէ՝ «վէպին սկզբնական երիտասարդական հրայրքը կը սկսի հետզհետէ թուլնալ վերջաւորութեան», եւայլն:

«Մարտիկ Աղա»ի ձեռագիրներուն վերծանման ընթացքին նկատեցինք որ Կիւրճեան սովորութիւն ունեցած է սովորական չափէ մեծ՝ հաշուապահական թուղթերու վրայ գրելու ժամանակ բարեբախտաբար լուսանցքներուն նշելու թէ ո'ր օրը, ո'ր ժամերուն գրուած է հատուածը, քանի՛ ժամ նստած է գրելու, ինչու՛ ստիպուեր է ընդհատել գրելը ծանօթի մը ժամանմանն պատճառով, եւայլն: Ուշագրաւ է որ ան միշտ չէ որ գրելու նստած է Կիրակի կամ ազատ օրերուն: Ան յաճախ իր ծրագրած նիւթը հեղինակած է առաւօտ կանուխ, մինչեւ աշխատանքի երթալը, կամ աշխատանքէն վերադառնալէ ետք, եւ շատ անգամ շաբթուան մէջ մի քանի օր շարունակ շարադրած է օրական երկու, երեք, նոյնիսկ հինգ եւ աւելի ժամ, որ ապացոյցն է իր հեղինակելու բուռն կիրքին, ստեղծագործելու զօրաւոր տենչին, գեղարուեստական գործ մը յօրինելու հզօր կորովին ու կարողութեան:

Ճշմարտութիւնը պարզելու նպատակով կ'ուզենք յատկապէս նշել այն իրողութիւնը, որ Կիւրճեան «Մարտիկ Աղա»ն գրած եւ աւարտած է ամբողջութեամբ նախ քան տպագրութեան ուղարկելը: Ստուգիւ, երգիծավէպին Բ. մասը՝ Ժ.էն Ի. գլուխները յօրինուած են 31 Յուլիսէն 14 Հոկտեմբեր 1898ին, այսինքն՝ մինչեւ Ա. մասի Բ. գլուխի (15 Հոկտեմբեր 1898) եւ Գ. գլուխի (1 Նոյեմբեր 1898) լոյս ընծայումը:

Օտեան կը գրէ. «*Քանի մը թիւ ետքը* վէպը կը ներկայացնէր Աղեքսանդրիոյ մէջ հայկական սալոն մը, ուր կ'երեւային գաղթականութեան շատ մը ծանօթ դէմքերը ամենանճշգրիտ եւ սակայն գերազանցօրէն ծաղրանկարուած գիծերով» եւ «*Ահռելի փոթորիկ մըն էր փրթաւ քաղաքին մէջ*» (Ծեղագրումներն իմն են - Յ.Մ.): Ուրեմն, հաստատապէս, աղեքսանդրիահայերու իրարանցումը սկսած է յաջորդող գլուխներէն ետք, որոնք լոյս տեսած են Նոյեմբեր 1ին ու 15ին, եւ Լոնտոնէն Եգիպտոս հասած՝ այդ թուականներէն ետք. հետեւաբար՝ վէպը 14 Հոկտեմբեր 1898ին աւարտելէն շատ վերջ:

Նոյնիսկ հմուտ գրականագէտ Յակոբ Օշական,- որ կը հաստատէ թէ «Կիւրճեանի տաղանդը դուրս է կասկածէ» եւ «անոր ստեղծագործութիւնը ունի հզօր հրապոյր»,- «Նոր Կեանք»ի մէջ կարդալով «Մարտիկ Աղա»ի կիսատ տպագրութիւնը եւ ընդունելով հանդերձ վէպին «շքեղ արժանիքները», զայն կ'որակէ «անաւարտ, չըսելու համար անբաւարար տարողութիւն»: Գրաքննադատը ցաւով կ'արտայայտուի «կառուցման ու մշակման անփութութեան» մասին եւ կը շարունակէ. «անոր կը պակսին ոչ թէ կեանքը, ճշմարտութիւնը, հարազատութիւնը, այլ վէպ մը պայմանող տիրական գործողութիւնը, կառուցման բարիքը եւ յառաջատու նկարագիրը»: Այնուամենայնիւ, Օշական կը գովէ Կիւրճեանի «սուր, հեգնող ոճը, նկարուն նրբահիւսութիւնը»:

Վստահ ենք որ եթէ Օշական հնարաւորութիւն ունեցած ըլլար վէպը ամբողջութեամբ կարդալու, պիտի չզլանար զայն դասելու Արփիարեանի «Կարմիր Ժամուց» վիպակին եւ «Ոսկի Ապարանջան» պատմուածքին շարքին:

Ուշագրաւ է նաեւ որ Կիւրճեան յափշտակութեամբ ու հրապուրանքով ընթերցելով համաշխարհային հռչակաւոր գրողներու եւ առաւելաբար ֆրանսացի գրագէտներու երկերը, յատկապէս ներշնչուած է Ալֆոնս Տոտէի գործերէն, որոնցմէ հայերէնի թարգմանած է «Թարասքոնցի Թարթարէն» դիւցազնավէպը, կրած է անոր բարերար ներգործութիւնն ու գրական ազդեցութիւնը, որոնք օգնած են արթնցնելու իր մէջ սեփական տաղանդը եւ Կիրճեան գտած է իր մասնայատուկ, ինքնուրոյն ուղին գրականութեան մէջ, զերծ մեքենական ընդօրինակութենէ, այլ՝ ինքնատիպ ստեղծագործական մօտեցմամբ:

«Թարասքոնցի Թարթարէն»ը թերագնահատել եւ «Մարտիկ Աղա»ն գերադրել չէ մեր նպատակը. սակայն չափազանցութիւն չենք համարեր, այլ՝ իրականութիւնը մատնանշելու դիտաւորութեամբ եւ մեր դաւանածը հրապարակաւ յայտնելու մտադրութեամբ եւ առաջադրութեամբ կ'ուզենք հաղորդել որ Կիրճեանի ստեղծագործած կերպարը՝ Մարտիկ աղա, Թարթարէնի պէս փառամոլ ու սնափառ, եւ անոր պէս չարադէպօրէն ընկճուած է, սակայն եւ այնպէս ունի աւելի ազնիւ ու ազգային փառատենչութիւն քան Տոտէի արկածասէր «հերոսը», որ անիմաստ, անխոհեմ, լոկ անձնասիրական փառքի մը կ'ուզէր արժանանալ՝ որսորդական ճանապարհորդութեամբ: Ուստի, «Մարտիկ Աղա» վէպը ֆրանսական ու համաշխարհային փառքի ու հռչակի արժանացած «Թարասքոնցի Թարթարէն»էն աւելի իրաւունք ունի համաշխարհային գրականութեան գլուխ գործոցներէն համարուելու, որովհետեւ երբ Թարթարէն Ափրիկէի անապատները թափառելով իր սպաննած կոյր առիւծով յաղթականօրէն կը վերադառնայ Ֆրանսայի հարաւը գտնուող Թարասքոն գիւղաքաղաքը, ապա Մարտիկ աղա ունենալով ազգային ու հայրենասիրական վառ հեռանկարներ՝ կ'ուրախանայ հայրենի երկրի հետագայ վերականգնումով եւ իբրեւ պարծենկոտ փառամոլ կը խաբուի մայր հայրենիքի ապագայ ելեւմտական նախարար ըլլալու սուտ խոստումէն, կը հիասթափուի՝ յուսացածը, երազածը չգտնելուն պատճառով եւ ի վերջոյ թեւաբեկ կը կառչի իր սկզբնական համոզումին եւ նախկին տարերային սկզբունքին:

«Մարտիկ Աղա» վէպը վերլուծաբար կը ներկայացնէ հասարակական եւ անհատական կեանքի ընդարձակ պատկերը, բնաւորութիւններու զարգացումը, միջավայրն ու կենցաղը, հասարակական տարբեր խաւերու կեանքն ու յարաբերութիւնները: Դէպքերը, գործողութիւնները, մարդկային կապերը, կերպարներու զարգացումը մատուցուած են շատ յաջող: Մինչեւ վերջ ճարտարօրէն բացայայտուած է գլխաւոր հերոսներուն՝ սնոտի ու նանիր Մարտիկ Սոմաքէշեանի սին փառամոլութիւնը եւ խորամանկ ու ենեգ Լեւոն Սուրեանի խաբեբայութիւնը՝ դրսեւորելով անոնց բնաւորութիւններուն ներքին էութիւնը: Կիրճեան իր գլխաւոր հերոսներն ու գաղթականները կը նկարագրէ ինչպէս Աղեքսանդրիոյ եկեղեցիի բակին մէջ, այնպէս ալ Նպաստամատոյց Յանձնաժողովի սենեակին, «Մասիս» հայոց սրճարանին, Լուվրի պարտէզին մէջ եւ այլուր: Հերոսներուն արտաքին նկարագրութիւններուն զուգահեռ, Կիրճեան կը բացայայտէ անոնց ներաշխարհը: Երգիծավէպին մէջ նկատելի է կերպարներու եւ նկարագրութիւններու սուր հակադրութիւն, որուն միջոցաւ աւելի ցայտուն կերպով կ'արտայայտէ ան իր գաղափարը:

Երգիծավէպը բարեյաջող է նաեւ սիւժէթային հետեւողական զարգացմամբ, որովհետեւ, ինչպէս առաջին մասին, այնպէս ալ երգիծավէպին Բ. մասին մէջ կենսական դէպքերու բնական յաջորդականութիւնը՝ որպէս երկին բովանդակութիւնը մարմնաւորող հիմնական միջոց, կ'արտացոլացնէ տուեալ պատմական ժամանակաշրջանը:

Յատուկ ուշադրութեան արժանի է այն հանգամանքը որ Կիւրճեան, 19-20 տարեկան հասակին գրած «Մարտիկ Աղա» վէպով կ'ապացուցէ թէ ինք երգիծաբանի տաղանդով օժտուած գրող մըն է, որ գիտէ ծաղրել կեանքի բացասական երեւոյթները, այպանել հասարակական կեանքի արատներն ու մարդոց թերութիւնները, դատապարտել մարդկային հոգեբանութեան անազնիւ վարմունքը, մերկացնել շահամոլութիւնը, խայտառակել փառամոլութիւնը, նշաւակել խաբեբայութիւնը, ծանակել սնափառութիւնը, մէկ խօսքով՝ բացայայտել կեանքի անկատարութիւններն ու մարդոց սայթաքումները: Կիւրճեան իր անհաշտ վերաբերումն ու ատելութիւնը կ'արտայայտէ սուր եւ միտումնաւոր ծաղրով՝ իր ուրոյն գրական ոճով եւ անձնական տաղանդին յատկանշական դրոշմով: Ան կը կերտէ կերպարներու եւ նկարագրութիւններու կուռ կառուցուածք մը մշակուած՝ լեզուի խստապահանջ առանձնայատկութեամբ եւ լեզուական պատկերաւորութեան վարպետութեամբ: Վէպը գրուած է սեղմ եւ խնամուած ոճով, լեզուական անաղարտութեամբ, սուր երգիծանքով:

Վէպին մէջ նկատելի է յատկանշական մակդիրներու, սրամիտ համեմատութիւններու եւ բնորոշ զուգահեռականութիւններու օգտագործման վարպետութիւնը: Ան հարուստ է նաեւ պատշաճ դարձուածքներու լայն կիրարկումով, որոնք հանդէս կու գան կայուն եւ ճշգրիտ մակդիրներու գործածութեամբ: Արդարեւ, Կիւրճեան քաջ տիրապետելով կեանքի թերութիւնները երգիծական ձեւով պատկերելու արուեստին եւ շնորհիւ իր երգիծական գրչի ճարտարութեան, յաջողապէս կը նկատէ դէմքերու եւ դէպքերու ծիծաղելի երեւոյթները, զանոնք գրականութեան նիւթ կը դարձնէ, արտայայտիչ ձեւով կը պատկերէ՝ գեղարուեստական ցայտուն կարողութեամբ: Ահա թէ ինչու Կիւրճեան կարողացած է կեանքի եւ մարդու մասին իր ունեցած բարձր դիրքերէն պատկերել ու մերկացնել այլանդակ երեւոյթները: Այստեղ է որ ի յայտ կու գայ Կիւրճեան երգիծաբանին անզիջող բայց բարի ծիծաղը: Ան չունի Ճորճ Պեռնար Շոյի կծու, ատելութեամբ լեցուած, խայթիչ երգիծանքով սպաննիչ բնոյթը, որովհետեւ ան չի ծաղրեր քանդելու, ոչնչացնելու նպատակով, այլ անոր ծաղրը շինիչ է ու բարեհոգի, հրահանգիչ է ու կրթիչ:

Կիւրճեան իր այս վէպով ինքնատիպ աշխարհ մը կը բանայ ընթերցողին առջեւ՝ իրեն իւրայատուկ պոլսական եւ եգիպտական բնական անմիջականութեամբ համեմուած: Գրիչը բռնելու սէրն ու ընդունակութիւնը դպրոցէն իւրացուցած՝ ան ի յայտ կու գայ գրելու արուեստին տիրացած փորձառու գրողի հմտութեամբ, երգիծաբանի ճարտարութեամբ եւ իքնուրոյն ոճով: Իր այս առաջին գործին մէջ իսկ նկատելի է անոր սահուն ու հմայիչ գրիչը, երգիծելու աներկբայելի ձիրքը եւ հրապուրիչ մայրենի լեզուն՝ հայերէնը: Լեզուի մասին խօսելով, պէտք է նշել տեղ-տեղ ճիշդ գործածութիւնը արեւելահայերէն, թուրքերէն, ֆրանսերէն եւ արաբերէն բառերու եւ նախադասութիւններու, որոնք կենցաղային գունաւորում ստեղծելու, կերպարները անհատականացնելու եւ տիպականացնելու նպատակով գործածուած են:

«Մարտիկ Աղա» վէպը իրաւացիօրէն կարելի է բնութագրել բարեյաջող երգիծավէպ մը, իր կառուցուածքային զարգացմամբ ու պատկերաւոր մտածողութեամբ, եւ մանաւանդ ծիծաղաշարժ սրամտութեամբ հեղինակուած գործ մը, զոր կրնանք դասել 19րդ դարավերջի հայ իրապաշտ գրականութեան լաւագոյն գրական ստեղծագործութիւններու շարքին:

Բ. ԳՐԱԿԱՆ ԽԱՐԱՊԱՇՏ «ՆՈՐ ԴՊՐՈՑ»Ի ՋԱՏԱԳՈՎԸ

Առաջին երգիծավէպէն ետք Կիրճեան գրած է «Նոր Դպրոցը» երգիծական պատկերներով վէպը, որ ձեռագիր վիճակով կը գտնուի Հայաստանի Գրականութեան եւ Արուեստի Թանգարանը, իր իսկ արխիւին մէջ: Հեղինակը որպէս նախավերնագիր գրած է՝ Մարդկային Կատակերգութիւն — Հայկական Մաս: Ձեռագրին տիտղոսաթերթին վրայ Կիրճեան նշած է թէ երգիծավէպը գրուած է Աղեքսանդրիա 9-31 Յուլիս 1899ի ժամանակաշրջանին եւ ան արդիւնք է ինը նիստով աշխատանքի:

Ձեռքի տակ ունինք 113 մեծադիր էջերու պատճէնները: Վերծանած ենք վէպը, կազմած՝ անոր բառարանը (հայերէն եւ օտար լեզուներով) եւ պատրաստած՝ յատուկ անուններու ցանկը ծանօթագրութիւններով հանդերձ: Կիրճեանի միւս գործերուն նման մտադիր էինք առանձին գիրքով հրատարակել եւ ընթերցող հասարակութեան մատչելի դարձնել այդ գրական գործն ալ, սակայն մեր պատրաստածը մնաց ձեռագիր վիճակով, առանց մաքրագրութեան եւ մեքենագրութեան, որովհետեւ անիկա աւարտուն գործ մը չէ: Կիրճեան չէ փորձած զայն գէթ անգամ մը կարդալ, նախնական թերութիւններն ու վրիպակները վերացնել, մաքրագրել եւ հրատարակել: Համոզուած եմ որ 1899-1965 տարիներուն՝ նոյն անկատար վիճակին մէջ մնացած է ձեռագիրը, առանց արժանանալու հեղինակին կամ ոեւէ գրական մշակի հոգատար ուշադրութեան՝ աւարտուն վիճակի հասցնելու համար: Իմ տպաւորութիւնն ու հաստատ համոզումն այն է, որ առաջին ընթերցողը մենք եղանք, որովհետեւ գրելէ ետք եթէ հեղինակը անգամ մը կարդացած ըլլար զայն, անպայման նկատած պիտի ըլլար անկատարութիւններն ու վերացուցած՝ թերութիւնները: Երկը հրատարակելու համար հարկ է կրկնութիւնները ջնջել, հոս ու հոն կիսատ նախադասութիւնները շարունակել ու բաց ձգուած տեղերը լրացնել, օտար բառերու համապատասխան հայերէն արտայայտութիւնները գտնել. մէկ խօսքով՝ ձեռագիրը հիմնովին խմբագրել: Այդ ընելու իրաւունքը չունինք, որովհետեւ այդ պարագային հեղինակակից կը դառնանք: Իսկ եթէ ուղիղ փակագիծներով եւ էջատակի ծանօթագրութիւններով նշենք Կիրճեանին չպատկանող հատուածները, իւրաքանչիւր էջի վրայ տասնեակներու պիտի հասնին անոնք: Անոր առանց հպումի հրատարակութիւնը անվայելուչ եւ անպատշաճ է Կիրճեանի նման լեզուական եւ ոճական պահանջկոտութեան ու ճշդապահանջութեան տէր հեղինակի մը համար:

Տեղին է յիշել Շիրվանզադէի հետեւեալ կարծիքը իր «Ժողովածու Երկերի» եռահատոր հրատարակութեան (Թիֆլիս, 1903) առաջին հատորին սկիզբը, «Ներկայ Հրատարակութեան Առիթով» գրութեան մէջ. «Աչքի անցկացնելով իմ գրական գործունէութեան առաջին շրջանի արդիւնքները, ես նրանց մէջ գտայ էական թերութիւններ թէ՛ բովանդակութեան եւ թէ մանաւանդ լեզուի կողմից: Այս պատճառով սկզբում մտածեցի ընդհանուր ժողովածուիս հրատարակութիւնը մի կամ երկու տարով յետաձգել, ուղղել այդ թերութիւնները, մշակել սկզբնական երկերիս ոճն ու լեզուն, ապա լոյս ընծայել: Բայց յետոյ որոշեցի, թէ իրաւունք չունիմ այս անելու»:

Երբ Ծիրվանզադէ կը հաստատէ. «Ես մեղանչած կը լինէի հեղինակների կողմից ընդունուած եւ գրեթէ սրբագործուած աւանդութեան դէմ, եթէ անփորձ գրչիս սխալները ուղղէի եւ շիտկէի ներկայիս համեմատական փորձառութեամբ» եւ, հետեւաբար, անփոփոխ տպագրութեան կը յանձնէ իր սկզբնական շրջանի երկերը, «ինչպէս նրանք տպագրուել են առաջին անգամ», մենք առաւել եւս իրաւունք չունինք Կիւրճեանի «Նոր Դպրոցը» երգիծավէպը քմահաճօրէն համալրելու, սրբագրելու եւ հրատարակութեան պատրաստ վիճակի հասցնելու:

Հակառակ իր անկատար, թերի, անաւարտ վիճակին, «Նոր Դպրոցը» ունի հետաքրքրական բովանդակութիւն: Կիւրճեան կը նկարագրէ Պոլսոյ թաղամաս Բերայի փողոցներէն մէկուն մէջ շէնքի մը երկրորդ յարկի կանթեղով լուսաւորուած, վատ կահաւորուած սենեակը: Հոն են երեք երիտասարդներ՝ սենեակի տէր նկարիչ արուեստագէտ Արամ, արձակագիր Սարգիս եւ առտուընէ իրիկուն գրասեղանին գամուած, հաշուելով, գրելով ու ամբողջ օրը գումարներու հետ խաղացող, գրական յաւակնութիւններով, պոտլէրեան ոճով բանաստեղծ՝ գրագիր Լեւոնը: Կը խօսակցին անոնք բուռն ոգեւորութեամբ, սիրելով մելամաղձոտութիւնը, անդորրը, գիշերուան մթութիւնը: Հոն կը ժամանեն Արմաղանեանը, Վահանը եւ ապուշ ծանուցուած երիտասարդը: Ռոտենպաքի L'Amour et la Mort (Սէրը եւ Մահը - Յ.Մ.) գործէն ազդուած, սիրոյ եւ մահուան խորհրդաւոր աննշակցութեամբ տպաւորուած եւ այդ զգացումով տոգորուած, Վէրլէնի մահուան միսթիք երրորդութեան՝ գիշերուան, մթութեան եւ քունի բարերար ազդեցութեան սիրահար Լեւոն կը մոմռայ.

Լոյսէն յոգնած երերուն, ինչ անուշ է գիշերուան
Գգուանքը մութ, խաղաղութիւն ու մոռացումն անսահման.
....
Կեանքէն յոգնած հոգիին, կեանքէն մաշած մարմինին
Ի՞նչ անուշ պիտ' թուի, վսեմ գիշերը յիշել
- Քունն ունենալ զոր չպիտի արշալուսէ զարթումը վատ.
Անաստղ երկինքը ամբաւ ու չի ծաղկիր այգն իսպառ:

Այս է հոգեվիճակը ամբողջ օրը թիւերու, անուններու, գումարներու հետ գործ ունեցող, առտուընէ իրիկուն թուանշաններու հետ կեանքը մաշեցնող, իրիկուան հիւանդագին մոգութիւնը, իրիկուան մութ հմայքը սիրող Լեւոնի, որ աշխատանքի ժամանակ միշտ քովը՝ գլխուն վրայ տնկուած ունեցած է խոժոռ ու գռեհիկ իր վարպետը, մինչ հիք «ստիպուած է եղած դիմանալ այդ դժոխային վիճակին՝ ինչպէս թիապարտը իր շղթային», կը գրէ Կիւրճեան:

Իրենց տրամադրութիւնը փոխելու նպատակով անոնք կ'երթան յունական անշուք գինետուն մը օղի խմելու եւ ճաշէն վերջ պոլսածանօթ Բալէ Քրիսթալ կը հասաքուին, ուր կարսօնուհիներ, աղջիկներ եւ կանայք «ամէն մարդերու տրամադրութեան տակ գտնուող, գործիքի մը պէս հլու ու ապրանքի մը պէս ծախու այդ կիները, որոնք այդպէս կու գան իրենց աստուածային մարմինը կոշտ ու բիրտ մարդերու տիրացող, բռնաբարող գրեթէ նայուածքին կը ծաւալեն ու կը պարզեն»:

Վէրլէնէն, Պոտլէրէն, Միւսէէն, Ռեմպոյէն տողեր, նախադասութիւններ յիշող ու երազող Լեւոն զգուանքով կը դիտէ ու «գարշելի» կը գտնէ լոյսերով ողողուած Բալէ Քրիսթալի (Բիւրեղեայ Պալատ - Յ.Մ.) պարուհի աղջիկներու եւ կիներու հրապարակային ելոյթները:

Նկարագրելու, պատկերելու եւ համեմատութիւններու վարպետ Կիրճեան կը գրէ. «Նուագը սկսաւ եւ պարուհին ներս մտաւ: Ասիկա գէր, ծանր, մելոտրամի մարքիզուհիի լայն ու վեհ շարժումներով. մսի ու ճարպի հոյակապ զանգուած մը հագիւ երերուն, վիթխարի կուրծք մը առաջ կարկառած, եւ որ կ'ելեւէջէր դարբնոցի փքոցի մը պէս»:

Վէպին երկրորդ մասին մէջ Կիրճեան կը նկարագրէ միեւնոյն սենեակը, ուր Լեւոն Ռոտենպաք կը կարդայ, իսկ Արմաղանեան թերթ կ'ընթերցէ: Երկրորդը, խնդալով, պելճիքացի բանաստեղծին անունը բառախաղի կ'ենթարկէ. «արդէն անունը կ'ըսէ կոր մօտէն նայէ— մօտէն պաք...»: Լեւոն երան կու տայ Արմաղանեանին, որ միշտ խնդալ եւ խնդացնել կը սիրէ, իսկ ինք որ տրտմութիւնը ճշմարիտ բանաստեղծութեան ներշնչարանը եւ աղբիւրը կը համարէ, Կէօթէի, Լամարթինի եւ ուրիշ անուանի գրողներու խօսքերէն յատկանշական բնորոշումներ եւ ասոյթներ թուելով՝ խորհուրդ կու տայ մտածել կեանքի ունայնութեան, մարդկային խեղճութեան եւ դառնութիւններուն վրայ:

Այդ միջոցին կը ժամանեն Վահանը, Սարգիսն ու արուեստագէտ, նկարիչ, քիչ մըն ալ բանաստեղծ Ասքանազը: Արամ ներս կը մտնէ կարճահասակ ու ֆէսաւոր Յովհաննէս Մեսրոպեանի հետ, որ Վանայ մէկ գիւղէն եկած եւ Պոլսոյ վաճառականի մը քով գրագրութեամբ իր ապրուստը ապահովող գաւառացի երիտասարդ մըն է:

Նախորդ Կիրակի գիշերուան եւ իրիկուան տխուր ու մութ, մելամաղձոտութեամբ պարուրուած խուցը կը վերածուի գրական մթնոլորտով ընտրեալ միտքերու խմբակի մտորումներու փոխանակման սենեակի մը: Սարգիս կը կարդայ կեանքը մահերգող, ամէն բան ունայնութիւն հռչակող «աշնան իրիկունով» երազանքը: Վահան կը կարդայ «Ջութակը» բանաստեղծութիւնը, որուն կը պակսի ներդաշնակութիւնը: Օհաննէս կը սկսի ընթերցել դողդողացող, շիկնող ձայնով մը իր արձակ գործը՝ «Թոնիրին Անկիւնը», հակառակ քրքջոտ ընդմիջումներուն, փոխանակուած հեգնական նշաններուն:

Յօդուածը գաւառական կեանքէն պատկեր մըն էր, ձմեռ օրով մենակեաց երազող հոգիի մը պատմութիւնը գաւառական դարձուածքներով, բառերով, զոր կը ստիպուէր թարգմանել իր ունկնդիրներուն քրքիջներուն տակ, պատկերներով, նմանութիւններով, որոնք «օտար եւ խորթ կը հնչէին գաղղիական ճաշակի երաժշտութեան վարժուած հայ ականջներուն, հայրենի հողի ծնունդ յօդուած մը»: Ներկաներէն միայն Լեւոն հաւնելով «գէշ չէ» կ'ըսէ գաւառացիին, «որ դատապարտուելու սպասող յանցաւորի տեսքովը ընկճած էր աթոռին վրայ»: Ի զարմանս Արամի, Սարգիսի եւ Արմաղանեանի, Լեւոն իր հիացմունքը կը յայտնէ նաեւ Երուանդի ընթերցածին մասին, որովհետեւ կարդացած էր նաեւ անոր գրած մէկ քանի քերթուածները:

Փաստօրէն երկու գրականութիւններու կռիւն է պատկերուած այստեղ՝ վիպապաշտութեան եւ իրապաշտութեան պայքարը:

«Նոր Դպրոցը» վէպին երրորդ մասին մէջ Կիրճեան իր գրական հայեցակէտը եւ գրականագիտական տեսակէտը կ'արտայայտէ Երուանդի բերանով, որ չախորժելով սենեակին մէջ գտնուողներէն ոմանց անտեղի բարձրաձայն քրքջոցներէն եւ այպանելի ծաղրական նշմարներէն, այդ գլուխներուն մէջ լոկ Լեւոնի յաւերժութիւնը անկեղծ գտնելով ու Լեւոնի գրածներուն մէջ մտածումի գոհարներ գտնելով, եւ գարեջրատան մը մէջ Լեւոնի հետ առանձնացած կը պարզէ իր միտքը, թէ մեր այս վերջին գրականութիւնը՝ տասնիններորդ դարավերջի հայ գրողներու արտադրութիւնները «կէս իրապաշտ, կէս բանաստեղծական, կէս սնանկապաշտ, չեմ գիտեր դեռ ինչապաշտ գրականութիւնը, ցուք, կապկում, թութակում, ծաղրանկար է վերջին գաղղիական վերջաւորութեան գրականութեան ... զոր մեր մէջ մտցուց նոր դպրոցին պետը՝ Ծալճեանը», կը գրէ Կիրճեան:

Լեւոն օրինակ բերելով կը պատմէ թէ ինչպէս ինք Յովհաննէսի մէկ յօդուածը բռնի կ'առնէ եւ «Արշալոյս»ի խմբագրատունը կը տանի. կը հիանան, գլուխ գործոց կը համարեն: «Բայց այս մեծ գրագէտ մըն է գրողը», «աս ինչ գանձ գտանք մեր թերթին համար», կ'ըսէ խմբագրապետը եւ խոստում կ'առնեն որ այնուհետեւ իր բոլոր գրածները եւ գրելիքները հոն բերէ: Ապա *գուսանական գրականութիւն* ընդհանուր տիտղոսով կը սկսին հրատարակել այդ յօդուածները: Խօսակիցը ինք ալ կը գովէ Յովհաննէսը: Անհաւասիկ Երուանդի կարծիքը Յովհաննէսի մասին. «Եւ սասանկ խիկատիպ, սասանկ օժտուած, ինքնածին տաղանդի մը այդ տխմարները կը խծբծէին կոր այն օրը, մատենագէտ ծնած մէկու մը գաղղիերէն սորվէ կ'ըսէին կոր... բայց այդ տղան սքանչելի դիտող մը ու բանաստեղծ մըն է, անկեղծ, պարզ, բայց իր անտաշ, ոչ-գրական ձեր կարծիքով լեզուին մէջ կեանքի անօրինակ շունչ մը կը բաբախէ, յոյզ կայ, աւիւն կայ, ջիղ կայ, բայց անոր պատկերները, նմանութիւնները, բացատրութիւնները խիկատիպ են, արտայայտիչ, գեղեցիկ, նո՛ր, այս տղան նիւթը եւ ոճը ունի երկուքն ալ ներդաշնակ. անիկա իմաստակ չէ՛, կապիկ չէ՛, գիրք կարդացած չէ՛, բանագողութեամբ, յիշողութեամբ չգրեր կոր ան. իր կեանքէն ու իր հոգիէն հանած է բոլոր ատոնք, տեսած է, զգացած է, խորհած է»:

Լեւոն, որ այս նկարիչ արուեստագէտը՝ Երուանդը տեսնելէն ի վեր ճշմարիտ artist-ին յայտնութիւնը ունեցած էր ու բաղդատութիւն մը ըրած անոր ու իր ընկերներուն միջեւ, կը զգայ որ բան մը կը փոխուի իր մէջ, որովհետեւ Երուանդ կը յայտնէ թէ իրեն համար «ներկայ եւ ուրիշ տարիներուն ամենէն մեծ գիտունը, ու ամենէն մեծ խորհողը, ամենէն հսկայ, ինչպէս նաեւ ամենէն մեծ արուեստագէտը Պալզաքն է, որ կեանքն ու մարդկութիւնը վերլուծած, զննած, փորձարկած, տարբաղադրած ու համադրած է...»:

Երուանդ քաջալերելու նպատակով կը յուսադրէ ու կը խրախուսէ Լեւոնը. «Տես դուն ինչպէս պիտի բուժուիս կամաց, ինչպէս պիտի գտնաս ինքզինքդ ու միշտ պիտի ըլլաս մեծ՝ գրականութեան մէջ, անկեղծ ու իսկատիպ մատենագիր մը, որ իր նիւթը պիտի քերէ ու իր տարազը, կեանքի ու իր հոգիին խորերէն տաք տաք դուրս հանած»: Երուանդ կը յայտնէ նաեւ որ ինք ծայրէ ծայր ուսումնասիրած է «Մարդկային Կատակերգութիւնը», միակ գործը զոր հաճոյքով ու հիացումով կարդացած է եւ 10 հատ ալ դիմանկար յօրինած է Պալզաքի ստեղծած կերպարներէն:

Դժբախտաբար, վերջին անգամ ըլլալով Երկուշաբթի 31 Յուլիս 1899ին, ժամը երկուքուկէսին, իններորդ նիստով շարունակած է շարադրել մինչեւ ժամը չորս եւ տասնմէկ մեծադիր էջերու վրայ գրելէ ետք ընդհատած է գրելը՝ Արտաշէս Ունճեանի ժամանման պատճառով՝ երթալու Ռօզէթ նուահանգիստը: Կիրճեան «Հիմա քեզի պատմեմ յիշատակ մը ... եւայլն ... եւայլն» արձանագրելով այլեւս չէ շարունակած վէպը՝ ըստ իմ ստացած 113 ձեռագիր էջերու պատճէններուն: Պարզ է թէ գրողը մտքին մէջ ունէր պատմելիք մը, որ չէ շարունակած եւ կիսատ մնացած է աշխատութիւնը:

Գրական դպրոցներու պայքարը պատկերող այս վէպը հետաքրքրական է սիւժէթային պարզ կառուցուածքով, հերոսներու գրականագիտական գիտելիքներու եւ անոնց հոգեբանութեան իւրօրինակ լուսաբանութեամբ, բանաստեղծներու եւ արուեստագէտներու հայեացքներու եւ գաղափարներու սուր հակադրութեամբ: Ստուգիւ, Կիրճեան իր ստեղծագործական կեանքի ընթացքին եռանդուն ոգեւորութիւն ցուցաբերած է գրական-գեղարուեստական հարցերու նկատմամբ: Այդ հետաքրքրութիւնը պատահական ու դիպուածական չէ. ան բխած է իր իրապաշտութենէն ու ժողովրդայնութենէն, հայ դպրութիւնը նոր մակարդակի բարձրացնելու նպատակէն, ձգտումէն ու տենչէն: Արդարեւ, 19րդ դարավերջին, հայ գրականութիւնը բուռն վերելք ապրեցաւ շնորհիւ հոյլ մը իրապաշտ գրողներու, որոնք արեւմտահայ հատուածի մէջ հետեւորդներն էին Յակոբ Պարոնեանի ու

Մատթէոս Մամուրեանի: Ցիշատակութեան արժանի են Տիգրան Կամսարականը իր «Վարժապետին Աղջիկը» առաջին արեւմտահայ իրապաշտ վէպով, Արփիար Արփիարեանը գրականութեան իրապաշտ դպրոցի գեղագիտական սկզբունքներու հրապարակային պաշտպանութեամբ եւ «Կարմիր Ժամուց» վիպակով, Լեւոն Բաշալեանը իր «Հմայաթափը» նորավէպով, Գրիգոր Զոհրապը իրականութիւնը կարելի հարազատութեամբ ներկայացնող իր «Փոթորիկը», «Այինկա», «Թէֆարիկ», «Փոստալ», «Ճիտին Պարտքը» նորավէպերով, Սրբուհի Տիւսաբը իր «Մայտա», «Սիրանուշ» եւ «Արաքսիա» գործերով, Մելքոն Կիւրճեանը, Արշակ Չօպանեանը, Զապէլ Եսայեանը, Հրանդ Ասատուրը, Երուանդ Օտեանը, Ռուբէն Զարդարեանը եւ 1880-ականներու գրական շարժման միւս անուանի մասնակիցները:

Կիւրճեան ինք եւս հանդէս եկաւ իրապաշտական արուեստի տեսական դրոյթներու պաշտպանութեամբ եւ իր ստեղծագործութիւններով հաստատեց իր գրական դաւանանքը՝ գրականութեան ժողովրդայնութեան եւ ճշմարտութեան ճշգրիտ արտայայտութեամբ յատկանշուած:

ՄԻՔԱՅԷԼ ԿԻՒՐՃԵԱՆԻ ԹԱՏԵՐԳՈՒԹԻՒՆՆԵՐԸ

Ընդհանրապէս հայ գրականութեան մէջ եւ յատկապէս արեւմտահայ գրողներու մօտ թատրերգութիւնը քիչ մշակուած գրական սեռն է: Թատերական գրականութեան ամենէն տկար ճիւղն ըլլալու գլխաւոր պատճառը թրքական հալածանքն է:

Կիւրճեան յայտնի է նաեւ որպէս թատերագիր: Ան ստեղծած է երգիծական արձակի եւ թատերագրական սեռի այնպիսի արժէքաւոր իրապաշտ գործեր, որոնք արժանի են առանձին ուսումնասիրութեան եւ հրատարակութեան: Ահաւասիկ անոր թատրերգութիւններուն ամբողջական ցանկը՝

«Ֆրանքօ-Թրքական Պատերազմը Կամ Չարշըլը Արթին Աղա», կատակերգութիւն, 3 արար, գրուած 1903 թուականին, Երուանդ Օտեանի հետ միասին.

««Ազգայինճին» Կամ Մեծութիւն Եւ Անկում Պարոն Իգնատիոս Ռուբինեանի», կատակերգութիւն, 3 արար, գրուած 1903-1933 թուականներուն.

«Տուրքը», տրամ, 1 արար, 1905.

«Փրկանքը», տրամ, 3 արար, գրուած 1910 թուականին, Տիգրան Կամսարականի հետ.

«Հերոսախաղ», կատակերգութիւն, 1 արար, գրուած Երուանդ Օտեանի հետ.

«Ֆրանքօ-Թրքական Պատերազմը Կը Ծարունակուի Կամ Տիկին Եւփիմէի Յաղթանակը», կատակերգութիւն, 1 արար, 1934:

Ինչպէս իր գրական միւս ստեղծագործութիւններուն, այնպէս ալ իր թատրերգութիւններուն մէջ Կիւրճեանը յուզող թեմաները, անոր ընտրած հերոսները եւ արտայայտած գաղափարները պատահականութեան արդիւնք չեն, այլ կը բխին իրական կեանքէն եւ անոր թելադրած պահանջներէն: Ուստի Կիւրճեանի գրական ժառանգութիւնը ճիշդ գնահատելու համար պէտք է նկատի ունենալ այն պատմական, տնտեսական, քաղաքական եւ հասարակական պայմանները, որոնց մէջ կը գտնուէր արեւմտահայութիւնը այդ ժամանակ:

Էական է նկատի ունենալ որ ոեւէ գրող առանց ապրումի, առանց նիւթը մարսելու, առանց երկունքի՝ անկարելի է որ ստեղծէ գրական արժէք ներկայացնող որեւէ գործ, քանի որ գրականութիւնը ստեղծագործութիւն է եւ ոչ թէ արհեստ: Կիւրճեան շարժած է այդպէս:

Կիւրճեանի միւս առանձնայատկութիւնն այն է, որ ան ընտրած է ժողովուրդի կեանքէն առնուած նիւթեր, հետեւաբար իր ստեղծագործութիւնները ժողովուրդի միտքին, հասկացողութեան եւ զգացումներուն համապատասխանող թատրերգութիւններ են, որոնք կը պատկերեն ժողովուրդի կեանքին բուն հանգամանքները եւ կ՚արտացոլեն անոր հոգեբանական բարդութիւնները:

Ուրիշ յատկանիշ մը այն է, որ Կիւրճեան իր թատրերգութիւններուն մէջ կը դիմէ հերոսներու ներքին էութեան յայտնաբերումին եւ գործողութեան զարգացման, որոնք ընթերցողը կամ հանդիսատեսը կը յուզեն մինչեւ վերջ, քանի որ հեղինակը կը ջանայ կերպարներուն հոգեվիճակը տալ հերոսներու գործողութեամբ եւ յարաբերութեամբ:

* * *

Կիւրճեանի թատրերգութիւններէն ամենէն հանրայայտը Երուանդ Օտեանի հետ հեղինակած «Ֆրանքօ-Թրքական Պատերազմը» սրամիտ եւ հրապուրիչ կատակերգութիւնն է, որ հանրութեան ծանօթ է «Չարշըլը Արթին Աղա» խորագրով: Նշելէ ետք թէ Տիգրան Երկաթ միութեան գրադարան-ընթերցարան մը կազմակերպելու ծրագրին թատերախաղի մը միջոցով աջակցելու առաջարկը անհանոյ չէր Օտեանին եւ իրեն եւ զիրենք ի վիճակի կ՚ընէր սատարելու հանրօգուտ ձեռնարկի մը յաջողութեան, Կիւրճեան կ՚աւելցնէ. «Ես տուի նիւթը, զոր յղացած էի արդէն եւ կը խորհէի աւելի վիպակի ձեւով գրի առնել»:

Թատերախաղին նիւթը քաղուած է պոլսահայ բարքերէ եւ կը ներկայացնէ իր ատենին խիստ կարեւոր ալաֆրանկայի եւ ալաթուրքայի պայքարը. նիւթ մը, որ առաջին անգամ մշակած է Յակոբ Պարոնեանը, եւ որ շնորհիւ Օտեանի եւ Կիւրճեանի երգիծական տաղանդին եւ ճարտար գրիչներուն՝ եկած է հարստացնելու հայ գրականութեան համեմատաբար ամուլ մարզը՝ թատրերգութիւնը:

Արեւելեան եւ արեւմտեան բարքերու եւ սովորութիւններու ճակատումը, Եւփիմէի ծայրայեղ ու մոլեռանդ արեւմտասիրութիւնը, Արթին աղայի ծաղրանկարչային ու ծիծաղաշարժ տիպարը, իրենց բնաւորութեան եւ վարքագիծի որոշակի յատկանիշներով, հոգեկան անխառն վայելքի լաւագոյն առիթներ են պարգեւած բազմահազար հանդիսատեսներու՝ Եգիպտոսի եւ Թուրքիոյ, Սուրիոյ եւ Լիբանանի, Իրանի եւ Իրաքի, Ֆրանսայի եւ Յունաստանի, Ռումանիոյ եւ Պուլկարիոյ, Աւստրալիոյ եւ Ամերիկայի բազմաթիւ քաղաքներու մէջ:

Կատակերգութիւնը առաջին անգամ ներկայացուած է 1903 թուականի Սեպտեմբերի 13ին Աղեքսանդրիոյ Փիրամիտ ծովեզերեայ փայտաշէն թատրոնին մէջ, տեղի տալով փոքր գայթակղութեան մը, քանի որ թատրերգութեան կոշտ ու գռեհիկ երեւոյթով ալաթուրքա ամուսինին ու անոր զարգացածի յաւակնութիւններով ալաֆրանկա կնոջ նախատիպ ծառայող ամոլը ծանօթ էր հանդիսատեսներէն շատերու: Ներկայացման հետեւեալ օրն իսկ շշուկներ կը տարածուին գաղութին մէջ եւ հեղինակին յարաբերութիւնները կը խզուին ծաղրանկարուած ամոլին հետ: Թատերախաղին մէջ պատկերուած ռուսահայու կերպարը եւս եգիպտաբնակ յայտնի անձ մըն էր՝ Մանթաշէֆի ընդհանուր գործակալը, որուն եւս ապահովաբար հաճելի չէր հրապարակաւ ծաղրուիլը:

Իր ««Ֆրանքօ-Թրքական Պատերազմ»ին Պատմութիւնը» յօդուածաշարքին մէջ Կիւրճեան կը գրէ. «Առաջին ներկայացումը եղաւ կատարեալ յաջողութիւն մը, թատրոնը չդադրեցաւ թնդալէ քրքիջներով եւ ծափահարութիւններով եւ մինչեւ այսօր ալ, հակառակ որ իրարու յաջորդող սերունդները հետզհետէ կը հեռանան իրենց նախորդներէն այնքան ընտանի միջավայրէ մը —պոլսահայ բարքերէն եւ լեզուէն- ան կը պահէ միշտ իր խնդացնելու եւ զուարճացնելու կարողութիւնը»:[69]

Արթին աղայի դերը կատարած է դերասան Լեւոն Շիշմանեան, իսկ Տիկին Եափիմէի կարեւոր դերը ստանձնած է տաղանդաւոր դերասանուհի Մարի Պէյլէրեան: Միւս բոլոր դերակատարները եղած են սիրողներ, ներառեալ Կիւրճեանը ինք՝ խմբագրի դերով:

Եգիպտոսէն ետք, Պոլսոյ մէջ առաջին ներկայացումը տեղի ունեցած է 1909 թուականին, Բերայի Բըթի-Շանի ձմեռնային թատրոնին մէջ, Լեւոն Շիշմանեանի դերակատարութեամբ, եւ ապա Գատըգիւղի ձմեռնային թատրոնը, Շահզատէ Բաշի Մնակեան թատրոնը եւ վերստին Բերա՝ Վարիէթէ թատրոնը:[70]

Արամ Անտոնեան իր խմբագրած «Խարազան» շաբաթաթերթին մէջ կը գրէ. «Պոլսահայերը գործնականապէս ապացուցեցին, թէ Յուլիս 11էն ասդին ճշմարտապէս խաղաղասէր ժողովուրդ մը դարձած են: Այնքան եւ այնքան ապուշ թատերախաղեր ծափահարող թատերասէր հասարակութիւնը ոչ իսկ տեղէն շարժեցաւ Օտեանի եւ Միքայէլ Կիւրճեանի ճշմարտապէս հրապուրիչ կատակերգութեան համար, որովհետեւ... պատերազմէն կը վախնար: Որչա՜փ ճիշդ է «հասարակ»ութիւն բառը: Տրուած կամ տրուելիք եւ կամ կիսովին տրուած չորս ներկայացումներուն արդիւնքը սա եղաւ, որ Տիար Լեւոն Շիշմանեան, խաղին գլխաւոր դերակատարը, «շիշման» եկաւ Եգիպտոսէն եւ «զայիֆ» կը վերադառնայ: Եթէ քանի մը ներկայացում ալ տար՝ բոլորովին «սըսխա» պիտի դառնար»:[71]

1922 թուականի եղեռնէն ազատած, քէմալականներէն հազիւ ճողոպրած, Սամսոնէն Յունաստան խուճապահար փախած հայ գաղթականները, անորոշ ապագայով եւ դժուարին պայմաններու մատնուած այդ հայորդիները 1923 թուականին Գորֆուի մէջ խուռներամ բազմութեան մը ներկայութեան կը բեմադրեն այս կատակերգութիւնը: «Մտաւորականներէն եւ սիրողներէն թատերախումբ մը կը կազմուի եւ տեղւոյն սրահներէն միոյն մէջ կը ներկայացուի «Չարշըլը Արթին Աղա» ծանօթ կատակերգութիւնը», կը գրէ Ծաղկազար Քէօթահեան:[72] Գէորգ Կաուլարենց կը խաղայ Արթին աղայի, իսկ Նշան Պէշիկթաշլեան՝ Տոքթոր Ծաւարշի դերը:

«Ֆրանքօ-Թրքական Պատերազմը» դիտած ու վայելած են նաեւ հայրենի հանդիսատեսները եւ թատրոնի սիրահարները: Հայաստանի մէջ առաջին ներկայացումը տեղի ունեցած է Երեւանի Երաժշտական Կոմէտի-այի Թատրոնին մէջ, 28 Ապրիլ 1962ին, իսկ Գիւմրիի մէջ՝ 25 Դեկտեմբեր 1962ին: Երեւանի մէջ Արթին աղայի դերը կատարած են Հէնրի Ասլանեանը եւ Գեղամ Ոսկեանը, երկուքն ալ պոլսահայ լեզուին լաւ տիրապետող հայրենադարձներ: Եւփիմէի դերը խաղացած է հայրենադարձ դերասանուհի Մելինէ Համամճեանը: Գիւմրիի մէջ Արթին աղան մարմնաւորած են վաստակաւոր դերասան Կարօ Արծրունեանը եւ Կարօ Սարգսեանը, իսկ Եւփիմէն՝ վաստակաւոր արթիսթուհի Արուս Ազնաւուրեանը եւ Մանիա Կարապետեանը: Հայրենի բեմադրութիւնները այնքան յաճախակի կ'ըլլան, որ երկու տարի վերջ Մանիա Ասլանեան Կիւրճեանին կը գրէ. ««Չարշըլը Արթին Աղան» Երեւանում առ այսօր խաղացուել է 110 անգամ: Բեմադրութիւնը ձեւաւորեց նկարիչ Գրադէոն Գէորգեանը, երաժշտութիւնը յօրինեց կոմպոզիտոր Վաղարշակ Կոտոյեանը»:[73]

«Ֆրանքօ-Թրքական Պատերազմը» թատերախաղին գրութեան թուա-կանին շուրջ հանդիպած ենք գրականագէտներու աշխատութիւններուն եւ հայ մամուլին մէջ տարիներէ ի վեր շարունակուող սխալի մը, որ որպէս կա-տակերգութեան թուականը կը նշէ 1906ը, մինչդեռ ան գրուած է 1903ին:

Յ. Ճ. Սիրունի «Գիծեր Երուանդ Օտեանի Կեանքէն» յօդուածին մէջ կը գրէ. «Ատեն չունեցաւ իր տաղանդին արժանի թատերախաղեր գրելու: Ու գրածներուն թիւը չորսը չանցաւ: Ամենէն յաջողը «Չարշըլը Արթին Աղա»ն է՝ 1906ին գրուած Միքայէլ Կիւրճեանի աշխատակցութեամբ»:[74]

Օտեանագէտ Անուշաւան Մակարեան նոյնպէս 1906 սխալ թուականը գրած է «Ֆրանքօ-Թրքական Պատերազմը Կամ Չարշըլը Արթին Աղա» կատակերգութեան վերջաւորութեան:[75] Այնուհետեւ, ծանօթութիւններ, բառարան բաժնին մէջ հաստատապէս կը գրէ. «Այս կոմեդիան Օտեանը գրել է արեւմտահայ ականաւոր երգիծաբան Միքայէլ Կիւրճեանի հետ միասին, 1906 թուականին»:[76]

Կիւրճեան իր ««Ֆրանքօ-Թրքական Պատերազմ»ին Պատմութիւնը» յօդուածաշարքին մէջ կը գրէ. «Վերջերս կը թղթատէի «Ազատ Բեմ» շաբաթաթերթը... բաւական էջեր յետոյ հասայ վերջապէս 1903 Սեպտեմբեր 12ի թիւին եւ... կանգ առի, կարդալու համար խմբագրականին հետեւեալ տողերը.- Թատերական ներկայացում մը տեղի պիտի ունենայ յառաջիկայ Երեքշաբթի գիշեր, Սեպտեմբեր 15ին, «Փիրամիտ» թատրոնին մէջ, ի նպաստ «Տիգրան Երկաթ» Միութեան գրադարանին»: Երեք պարբերութիւն ետք կը վկայէ. «Վաթսուն տարի ետք... Այո, 1963ը իմ եւ Օտեանի կատա-կերգութեան վաթսուներորդ տարեդարձն է...»: Այնուհետեւ վստահօրէն կը հաստատէ թէ ««Ֆրանքօ-Թրքական Պատերազմը» վաթսուն տարեկան է եւ հակառակ իր յառաջացած տարիքին, տակաւին առոյգ է եւ երիտասարդ»:[77]

* * *

Օտեանի մահէն տասնութ տարի ետք, Կիրճեան մինակը կը շարունակէ ալաֆրանկայի եւ ալաթուրքայի պայքարը եւ 1934 թուականին կը գրէ «Քսան Տարի Ետք. Ֆրանքօ-Թրքական Պատերազմը Կը Շարունակուի Կամ Տիկին Եփիմէի Յաղթանակը» մէկ արարով եւ մէկ պատկերով կատակերգութիւնը, որ շարունակութիւնն է «Ֆրանքօ-Թրքական Պատերազմը» երգիծական գոհարին:

Թուրքիոյ նոր պայմանները, Աթաթիւրքի բարենորոգութիւնները եւ ֆէսի փոխարէն գլխարկ կրելու որոշումը կ'ունենան իրենց հակազդեցութիւնը Արթին աղայի եւ Եփիմէի մօտ: Արթին աղա կը յամառի ֆէս կրելու իր որոշումին մէջ, իսկ Եփիմէ, ապաւինելով Աթաթիւրքի հրովարտակին, մերթ կը պայքարի եւ մերթ կը փորձէ համոզել Արթին աղան, որ հրաժարի ֆէսէն եւ գլխարկ գործածէ:

«Քսան Տարի Ետք» զաւեշտախաղին մէջ Եփիմէ կը պայքարի նաեւ գաւառական մտայնութեամբ յետադէմ հոգաբարձու աղաներու դէմ ու անողոք պատերազմ կը յայտարարէ Արթին աղայի ֆէսին դէմ, յաղթական բայց նուաղած դուրս գալով անկէ: Կատակերգութեան վերջին տեսարանին մէջ Արթին աղա սիլինտր գլխարկ մը հագած տուն մտնելէ ետք կատաղութեամբ կը պոռայ. «Ա'ռ այս «զոպայի պօռու»ն տէ մէկալներուն քովը դիր»: Յատկանշական է նաեւ Եփիմէի պատասխանը. «Սիլինտր չէ, աշխարհի բոլոր գլխարկներն ալ եթէ բուրգի պէս վրան բեռցնենք, հորդ գլուխը փոխուելիք չունի»: Արթին աղայի յամառութիւնը կը հասնի հոն, ուր կը յայտարարէ թէ որոշած է Եւրոպա երթալ, որպէսզի ֆէս կարենայ գործածել:

* * *

Վահան Թէքէեանի եւ Միքայէլ Կիրճեանի հիմնադրութեամբ եւ տնօրէնութեամբ Աղեքսանդրիա լոյս տեսնող «Շիրակ» ամսաթերթի 1905 թուականի երկրորդ թիւին մէջ հրատարակուած է Կիրճեանի «Տուրքը» տրամը:[78] Այս մէկ արարուածով թատրերգութեան մէջ հեղինակը կը նկարագրէ պոլսահայերու այն ժամանակի արհաւրալի գիշերները, համիտեան հետապնդումներն ու հալածանքները, ձերբակալութիւններն ու բանտարկութիւնները, այն սոսկալի օրերը, երբ ամբողջ հայութիւնը եւ յատկապէս երիտասարդները ահ ու դող կ'ապրէին ամէն վայրկեան ձերբակալուելու եւ բանտարկուելու մղձաւանջով:

Ազգային կեանքէ առնուած այս մէկ արար տրամին գործողութիւնը կը ներկայացնէ 1895ի բռնութիւններու եւ ջարդերու դէպքերէն յետոյ Պոլսոյ մէջ հայերու ապրած սարսափահար օրերը: Նոյն արհաւիրքին մէջ էր նաեւ Թուրքիոյ տիրապետութեան տակ գտնուող Արեւմտեան Հայաստանի եւ Կիլիկիոյ ամբողջ հայութիւնը:

Գործող երեք անձերու՝ Արամի, անոր մօր՝ Սուրբիկ հանըմի, եւ առաջինին մանկութեան ընկերուհի Մաքրուհիի միջոցով Կիւրճեան կը նկարագրէ ընդհանրապէս հայերու եւ մասնաւորապէս պոլսահայերու կացութիւնը համիտեան չարաշուք ժամանակներուն: Սկիզբը շուկայէն ուրախ զուարթ տուն եկող, քէֆով, խնդալով հաց ուտող, խանութին մէջ անցած-դարձածները պատմող, խնդալէն մարեցնող, կատակներ ընող Արամը հայ ազգին այդ ժամանակուան ահռելի վիճակով մտահոգ՝ տխուր եւ մտածկոտ դարձած ու փոխուած է: Տրամին վերջաւորութեան, թուրք ոստիկաններու կողմէ իրենց դուռը զարնուելուն պէս, Արամ կը խնդրէ հինգ-տասը վայրկեան վերջ դուռը բանալ, իսկ ինք կը վազէ միւս սենեակը՝ յեղափոխական ընկերներուն հետ իր գրած թուղթերը եւ կարդացած լրագիրները հաւաքելու համար:

Ա՛յս էր հայութեան վիճակը. ա՛յս էր իրենց ազգին մասին մտածող եւ գործող երիտասարդներուն ճակատագիրը՝ հետապնդում, խուզարկութիւն, ձերբակալութիւն, բանտարկութիւն: Ա՛յս էր պատճառը, որ 1894-1896 թուականներու ջարդերէն ետք բազմահազար հայեր ամէն ինչ լքելով փախուստ տուին իրենց պապենական տուներէն՝ ապաստանելու եւ ազատ ապրելու համար օտար երկիրներու մէջ:

Թատերգութեան բեմադրութեան մասին որեւէ տեղեկութեան չենք հանդիպած, սակայն յայտնի է, թէ գրողը կը փափաքէր ուրիշ պարբերականի մը մէջ եւս տեսնել տրամին տպագրութիւնը կամ բեմի վրայ ներկայացումը, քանի որ ինք ալ պոլսահայ շատ գրողներու եւ մտաւորականներու նման իր մօր եւ քրոջ հետ Պոլսէն փախած էր Աղեքսանդրիա 1896ին՝ ապահով ապրելու համար:

Վահան Թէքէեան Պոլսէն Կիւրճեանին գրած բազմաթիւ նամակներէն մէկուն յետ գրութեան մէջ կ'ըսէ. ««Տուրք»դ չեմ յուսար, որ խաղան, բայց կը փորձեմ մէյ մը»:[79]

* * *

Կիւրճեանի թատերգութիւններէն առանձին ուշադրութեան արժանի է «Փրկանքը» երեք արարով տրամը, գրուած Տիգրան Կամսարականի հեղինակակցութեամբ 1910ին, Աղեքսանդրիա:

Տրամին գործողութիւնները տեղի կ'ունենան Պոլսոյ մէջ: Վաթսունը անցնող Գաբրիէլ Թոփվանեանը ծերութեան պատճառով այլեւս չ'աշխատիր եւ իր ամբողջ կեանքի ընթացքին հաւաքած խնայողութիւններով կ'ապրի: Աղջիկը՝ Արսինէն, նշանուած է պաշտօնեայ Սուրէն Սրապեանի հետ: Այս վերջինը համոզուելով որ Արսինէ վճռականօրէն սիրահարած է իրեն, Թոթվանեանէն կը պահանջէ 2000 ոսկի օժիտ: Արսինէի եղբայրը՝ Ատոմ, սկիզբէն եւէթ չէր համակրած Սուրէնի, քանի որ ան café chantant-ի երգեր կը բերէ եւ կը սորվեցնէ իր սիրեցեալին, իրենց ընտանեկան սուրբ յարկին տակ: Ատոմ կը փորձէ համոզել որ քոյրը ետ կենայ այդ ամուսնութենէն: Բայց Սուրէնի հանդէպ սէրը կը յաղթէ Ատոմի ցանկութեան: Գաբրիէլ, իր սիրելի աղջկան օժիտը տալու խոստումը կատարելու համար, յուսակտուր՝ սակարանին մէջ կը խաղայ շահելու ակնկալութեամբ, սակայն ամբողջ կեանքին վաստակը կորսնցնելով՝ կաթուածահար կ'ըլլայ: Ծահամոլ Սուրէն օժիտը չստանալով՝ անհոգաբար երեսի վրայ կը ձգէ Արսինէն եւ պատճառ կը դառնայ ամբողջ Թոթվանեան ընտանիքի կործանման:

Այս թատրերգութեան մէջ կը բախին երկու տարբեր, ներհակ սկզբունքներու եւ բարոյախօսութիւններու տէր Սուրէնը եւ Ատոմը, եւ հակառակ որ Արսինէի եւ Սուրէնի բաժանման պատճառը շատ որոշ կենցաղային օժիտի հարցն է, խորքին մէջ ատիկա հասարակագիտական հարց մըն է, որ կը բացայայտէ եւ կը մերկացնէ Սուրէնի ընչասէր արծաթասիրութիւնը եւ անմարդկային վարմունքը:

«Փրկանքը» Արսինէի փրկութիւնն է Սուրէնի պէս շահամոլ, դրամօժիտով իր դիրքը շտկել ուզող եւ սէրը գործիք դարձուցած անձէ մը: «Աշխարհիս բոլոր գանձերուն հետ չեմ փոխանակեր քեզ... իմ անգին Արսինէս» ըսող Սրապեանը, որ դրամօժիտը կը յայտարարէր «սովորական խնդիր», «նիւթական չնչին մանրամասնութիւն» կամ «նիւթական ճղճիմ հարց», ի վերջոյ կը դիմակազերծուի: Արսինէն, որ սիրելու եւ սիրուած ըլլալու երազը իրականութիւն դարձած կարծելով՝ ինքզինք երջանիկ կը համարէր, խաբէութեան զոհ երթալով, մեծ վիշտ կ'ապրի եւ նուաստացած կը զգայ: Կաթուածահար հայրը՝ Գաբրիէլ Թոթվանեան, գուցէ եւ մեռնի՝ մտածելով «ունեցածս չունեցածս երթալէն ետքը պարտական ալ պիտի մնամ այս տարիքիս մէջ, աս ճերմակ մազերովս»:

Երբ Տիգրան Կամսարական Պոլսոյ մէջ թատերախաղը կը կարդայ Սիրանոյշին, դերասանուհին «պատուաւոր պիէս» կը կոչէ զայն. իսկ Ծիրվանզադէ 1910 Յուլիսին Լը Վոյէն, Զուիցերիա, Կամսարականին գրած քանի մը նամակներու մէջ իր տպաւորութիւնները յայտնելով եւ քննադատական դիտողութիւններ ընելով հանդերձ, զայն կը գտնէ «յաջող, հետաքրքրական ու գրական», կը շնորհաւորէ հեղինակները եւ կ'առաջարկէ «Փրկանքը» անպայման ղրկել Թիֆլիսի Հայ Դրամատիկական Ընկերութեան՝ Մակարեան մրցանակին համար: «Մրցումից վախենալու տեղիք չունիք, վասնզի զօրեղ մրցակից չէք ունենալու, քանի որ ես լաւ եմ ճանաչում ռուսահայ «ինքնուրոյն» պիէսների արժէքը: Վերջապէս, իբրեւ տաճկահայ կեանքից մի երկ, ձերն աւելի հետաքրքրական պիտի լինի ժիւրիի համար: Ուրեմն յաջողութիւն»:

«Փրկանքը» առաջին անգամ ներկայացուած է 1912 թուականի Նոյեմբեր 18ին Աղեքսանդրիոյ մէջ: Այնուհետեւ բեմադրուած է Պաքու եւ Պոլիս, ապա՝ Փարիզ 1923ին, իսկ հետագային նաեւ ուրիշ քաղաքներ:

* * *

Իրապաշտ գրողներ Երուանդ Օտեան եւ Միքայէլ Կիրճեան իրենց ժամանակակից ընկերային խնդիրներէն հերոսամոլութեան իրական պատկերներ կը ներկայացնեն միասնաբար հեղինակուած «Հերոսախաղ» ստեղծագործութեան մէջ: Այս մէկ արարով կատակերգութեան մէջ դիմակազերծուած են յեղափոխութեան ծաղրը հանդիսացող հերոսամոլ կեղծ հերոսները, որոնք շատ տարածուած էին քսաներորդ դարու առաջին քառորդին: Նոյն հերոսին անունով երբեմն կը յայտնուէին մէկէ աւելի կեղծ «հերոսներ», որոնք իրարու ետեւէ Պոլիսէն եւ գաւառներէն կը ժամանէին Աղեքսանդրիա եւ Գահիրէ:

Երկու տաղանդաւոր երգիծաբաններուն հեղինակած այս սրամիտ թատրերգութիւնը, որ առանձին հրատարակուած է Օտեանի մահուընէ երկու տարի ետք՝ 1928ին, Բերայի մէջ, «Դիտակ» մատենաշարով, կը խայտառակէ «հերոսամոլ յեղափոխականներու» տիպարները եւ կը քննադատէ «սխրագործ հերոսներու» շահատակութիւնն ու բախտախնդրութիւնը:

Կատակերգութեան գործողութիւնը տեղի կ'ունենայ Սամաթիոյ (Պոլիս) գինետան մը մէջ, Սահմանադրութենէն ետք: Մէռօնօղլու Թումիկ Պուլկարիա, Ռումանիա, Աթէնք, Աղեքսանդրիա, Գահիրէ թափառելէ ետք կը վերադառնայ Պոլիս: Գինեպան Սէրչօ իր գինետան մէջ ուրիշ հերոսի մը թողած հագուստները անգործ Թումիկին տալով, կ'առաջարկէ որ ան ինքզինք յեղափոխական ծախէ՝ իբր քաջ ընկեր Վարդան Խոռխոռունի:

Ուրիշ յաճախորդներու շարքին գինետուն կը յաճախեն նաեւ վարժապետ Սուրէն, դպրապետ Սաղաթէլ, ոսկերիչ Միհրդատ, որոնք հաւատալով Թումիկի՝ պահ մը ունկնդիր կը դառնան կեղծ Վարդան Խոռխոռունիի յերիւրածոյ քաջագործութիւններուն: Երկաթագործ Տայի Յուսէփ, սակայն, կը ճանչնայ կեղծ հերոսներ Թումիկը եւ Ճանիկը, որոնք իբր թէ ազգին սուրբ գործը գլուխ հանելու համար բանտ նստած եւ անօթի ալ մնացած են: Համբերութիւնը հատած, Տայի Յուսէփ կ'ապտակէ Թումիկը եւ կը բացագանչէ. «Ասոր Ուղուրօղլու Ճանիկ կ'ըսեն, ասոր ալ Մէռօնօղլու Թումիկ... Պուլկարիա, Ռումանիա, Մըսըր ըրած խաղքութիւննիդ, ըրած *քէֆազէնութիւննիդ* չօգտեց, բանտերը *չիրիւմիշ* եղաք... Թո՛ւ ձեզի, անամօթնե՛ր, մէյ մըն ալ եկեր էք հոս ինքզինքնիդ յեղափոխական կը ծախէք կոր հէ՞... Վառնայի *խահվէն* կերած ծեծերնիդ չօգտե՞ց, հո՞ս ալ *պէլանիդ* կը փնտռէք կոր...»:

Յատկանշական է Սէրչոյին ուղղուած Թումիկի վերջին խօսքը. «Ա՞ս է ինծի գտած *խըլեախ* գործդ... ապուշը եւ եմ *քի* խօսքդ մտիկ ըրի *տէ*, յեղափոխական եղայ...»:

«Հերոսախաղ» ազգային երգիծական կատակերգութիւնը բեմադրուած եւ արժանացած է հայ թատերասէրներու գնահատանքին:

Վահան Թէքէեան Կիւրճեանին ուղղուած իր 28/13 Մարտ 1913 թուակիր նամակին մէջ կը գրէ. «Թանկագին pièce-ի (թատերախաղի) մասին պէտք է ըսել, որ ստացած եմ եւ քէյֆով կարդացած՝ ո՛չ միայն ինծի, այլ ուրիշ մէկ քանիներու համար ալ, որոնց մէջ Բաբէլեանը եւ իր քոյրը»:[80]

* * *

Միքայէլ Կիւրճեան լոկ ականատես վկան չէ եղած իր ժամանակին, այլեւ իր ժամանակաշրջանը ապրեցուցած է իրապաշտական գործերով: Գրողին գաղափարական հիմնական խնդիրը եղած է մերկացնել որոշ խաւերու եւ մարդոց հոգեբանութիւնը: Այդ խնդիրը յաջողութեամբ լուծուած է ինչպէս իր շատ պատմուածքներու եւ պատկերներու, այնպէս ալ ««Ազգայինճին» Կամ Մեծութիւն Եւ Անկում Պարոն Իգնատիոս Ռուբինեանի» կատակերգութեան մէջ: Ազգայինճիութեան եւ Մեծն-աղայական բնատիրութեան հասցէին եղած քննադատութիւնը երեւակայական կամ վերացական չէ, այլ հեղինակը նկատի ունեցած է իրական կեանքը, իրական տիպարներով՝ Իգնատիոս Ռուբինեանի, անոր կնոջ՝ Զարուհիի, երեք տարիներէ ի վեր ապօրինի կերպով պաշտօնի անցած թաղական խորհուրդի անդամներ Սեդրակ էֆէնտի Էլիասեանի, Ծանֆէսեան էֆէնտիի, Նիկողոս աղայի, Սահակ աղայի եւ ուրիշ կերպարներու միջոցով:

Գործողութիւնը կը ծաւալի 19րդ դարու վերջին: Կատակերգութեան գլխաւոր հերոսին՝ Իգնատիոս Ռուբինեանի շուրջը կը հաւաքուին տիրապետող Մեծն-աղաներէն դժգոհ խումբ մը մարդիկ (Ծիրինեան, Սիրքէճեան, Էլմասեան, Սիսակ Ճշմարտախօսեան, վերջինիս կինը՝ Արմենուհի, եւ ուրիշներ), որոնք անզիջում համոզում ունին թէ թաղական խորհուրդը անօրինական է: Անոնք նոյնպէս չեն հանդուրժեր իրենց գիւղի թաղական խորհուրդի գործունէութիւնը, բռնութիւնն ու անիրաւութիւնը:

Ընտանիքի խնդիրը 19րդ դարու վերջաւորութեան գլխաւոր հարցերէն մէկն էր. ուստի սիւժէին հիմքը Անահիտի եւ Բարունակի նուիրական սէրն է, որ կրնայ յաջող վախճան չունենալ Իգնատիոսի մոլի սահմանադրապաշտութեան, ազգայինճիութեան եւ թաղականներու դէմ կռիւներուն պատճառաւ: Այնպէս որ Ռուբինեանի ազգայինճիութիւնը նոյնպէս սկիզբէն մինչեւ վերջ նիւթ դարձած է այս ստեղծագործութեան, որ ունի գլխաւոր եւ երկրորդական ենթակայական գիծեր՝ միասնաբար բացայայտող անոր բովանդակութիւնը:

Կատակերգութեան նիւթը առանց նախադրութեան կը սկսի սահմանադրասէր քաղաքացիի պարտականութեան գիտակցութեամբ օժտուած եւ ժողովրդային իրաւունքներու պաշտպանութեան անվեհեր ախոյեան Ռուբինեանի գրած «վրիժառու» եւ «ազատարար» յօդուածին հանգոյցով, որ հետագայ զարգացում կ'ունենայ Իգնատիոսի եւ իր կնոջ՝ Զարուհիի բանավէճերով: Ճակատագրի բախտաւոր բերումով, մեծահարուստ Սեդրակ էֆէնտիի որդին՝ Բարունակ Էլիասեան, Ռուբինեանի դստեր՝ Անահիտին կը բանայ իր սիրտը՝ անկեղծօրէն յայտնելով իր ծնողներուն հաւանութիւնը անոր հետ ամուսնանալու: Դժբախտաբար համաձայնութեան այդ ուրախալի լուրը կը զուգադիպի Ռուբինեանի խիստ արտասովոր յօդուածին հրապարակման: Ռուբինեան կը զարմանայ երբ Զարուհի իրեն կը յայտնէ թէ Բարունակ էֆէնտի իր աղջկան ձեռքը կը խնդրէ, քանի որ Իգնատիոս հաստատապէս համոզուած է որ «հարուստ եւ գոռոզ Մեծ-աղայի մը զաւակը» չի կրնար կնութեան խնդրել «ընչազուրկ եւ իր ռամկավարական սկզբունքներովը ծանօթ մէկու մը աղջիկը»: Ահա եւ կը ստեղծուի համլէթեան կացութիւն մը... լինե՞լ, թէ՞ չլինել բարի հայր, լինե՞լ, թէ՞ չլինել բարի քաղաքացի: Ինքը, որ ի փառս Օրէնքի ու Սահմանադրութեան կը պայքարի յօգուտ հանրութեան, այժմ դժուար կացութեան կը մատնուի՝ մտածելով. «կա՛մ աղջիկս վրայ պիտի տամ, կա՛մ՝ պատիւս ու համբաւս»:

Թատրերգութեան մէջ իրապաշտական խտացուած գոյներով ներկայացուած է նաեւ Զարուհին, որ մայրական պարտականութեան գիտակցութեամբ, զգօն խելացութեամբ եւ լրջախոհութեամբ պայքարի դաշտէն դուրս կը մղէ Իգնատիոսը՝ տարիներէ ի վեր իր թափած համբերատար ջանքերուն արդիւնքը հանդիսացող Անահիտի ու Բարունակի նուիրական սէրը չվթարելու համար: Զարուհիի բացայայտ եւ թաքուն պայքարը յաջողութեամբ կը պսակուի, եւ իր աղջկան երջանիկ ապագան չի զոհուիր ճամբուած վարժապետ մը կամ տնտես աղբար մը իրենց պաշտօնին մէջ վերահաստատուած տեսնելու Իգնատիոսի եւ իր համախոհներուն համար:

Կիւրճեան վարպետօրէն դրսեւորած է կատակերգութեան գլխաւոր հերոսին՝ Իգնատիոս Ռուբինեանի խառն հոգեվիճակը: Իր ծնած օրէն Ազգային Սահմանադրութեան կաթը ծծած, անոր օդը շնչած եւ անոր մթնոլորտին մէջ ապրած ու մեծցած Իգնատիոսի՝ երեսուն տարուան անբասիր եւ հաւատարիմ գործիչի կեանքը կը խայտառակուի դասալքութեան եւ ուխտազանցութեան պատճառաւ եւ ան ողբերգութիւն կ'ապրի: Այնուամենայնիւ, յատկանշական է Զարուհիի վերջին խօսքը Իգնատիոսին. «Հիմա, որ գիւղին մեծերուն ես մօտեցած եւ անոնց գլխաւոր խնամի եղար, շատ աւելի հնարաւորութիւն եւ միջոց ունիս ժողովուրդին ծառայելու, քան երբ կը կոթնէիր քու սովորական կուսակիցներուդ վրայ»:

Կատակերգութեան մէջ անշուշտ կան նաեւ երկրորդական տիպարներ, որոնք բնական միջավայր կը ստեղծեն գլխաւոր հերոսներուն գործունէութեան համար, կ'օգնեն աւելի կատարեալ կերպով բացայայտելու երկին էական գաղափարը, կը նպաստեն աւելի լրիւ ներկայացնելու պահպանողականութեան, բռնապետութեան եւ Մեծ-աղայութեան արատաւոր կողմերը: Երկրորդական կերպարներէն նշանաւոր են սափրիչ Օննիկը՝ իր կեղծաւորութեամբ ու երկերեսանի բնաւորութեամբ, Ծիրինեան, Սիրքէճեան, Էլմասեան եռեակը՝ սկզբունքի մոլի սիրահարութեամբ, Էլիասեան, Ծանփէսեան, Նիկողոս աղա, Սահակ աղա քառեակը՝ իր բռնապետական իշխանութեամբ, Միհրդատ՝ իր կռուասիրութեամբ եւ ուրիշներ:

Ուշագրաւ է որ հեղինակը մենախօսութիւններու եւ երկխօսութիւններու միջոցով կը զարգացնէ գործողութիւնը՝ դրսեւորելով հերոսներուն փոխյարաբերութիւնները եւ դէպքերուն վերարտադրող պատկերները:

Պէտք է ըսել թէ թատերախաղը ընդհանրապէս յաջող գործ մըն է, կենսական դէպքերու բնական յաջորդականութեամբ եւ հանգոյցի հնարագէտ լուծումով՝ շնորհիւ գրողին վարպետութեան:

Միքայէլ Կիւրճեանի երգիծանքը շինիչ է, որովհետեւ կեանքի թերութիւններուն եւ զանոնք կրող հերոսներուն նկատմամբ գրողը ծաղր կը կիրարկէ ոչ թէ այդ թերութիւնները կրողները բացասելու, այլ անոնց պակասութիւնները վերացնելու, զանոնք որոշ ուղղութեամբ դաստիարակելու նպատակով: Անոր ծաղրը բարեկամական է:

Կիւրճեան թէ՛ առանձին եւ թէ հեղինակակցաբար գրած թատրերգութիւններուն մէջ կատարելապէս յաջողած է ստեղծել իրական կեանքի զանազան դրուագներ ընդգրկող եւ մանաւանդ առօրեայ կեանքի մէջ գոյութիւն ունեցող իրապաշտ կերպարներ: Դրական ու բացասական կերպարներու, բնաւորութեան եւ վարքագիծի որոշակի յատկանիշներ ունեցող գործող անձերու միջոցով եւ կենսական հակասութիւններու պատկերումով ան յաջողութեամբ կրցած է արտայայտել իր ժամանակի առաջաւոր հասարակական ձգտումները:

Թատերախաղերը հետաքրքրական են իրենց բանավէճային բնոյթով եւ կ'աւարտին հաշտ ու խաղաղ: Պէտք է մատնանշել նաեւ, որ Կիւրճեանի ստեղծագործութիւններուն հերոսներու հոգեբանութեան բացայայտումը շատ կողմերով անթերի եւ արտայայտիչ է:

Ժամանակի իրականութեան համարձակ եւ ընդհանրացնող քննադատութիւն պարունակող իր ստեղծագործութիւններուն մէջ ան ցայտուն գիծերով կ'արտացոլէ հասարակական բարքերն ու կենցաղային եւ ընտանեկան յարաբերութիւններու բնորոշ երեւոյթները: Անհրաժեշտ է նկատի ունենալ նաեւ, որ գրողը լոկ անտարբեր նկարագրող մը չէ, այլ որոշակի վերաբերում կ'արտայայտէ, եւ պարզ կ'երեւայ հեղինակի հայեացքն ու վերաբերումը դէպի գրականութիւնը, անոր հասարակական-քաղաքական դիրքորոշումը: Եղած են տարիներ, որոնց մէջ անիկա ամէնօրեայ պահանջն էր ընթերցող հասարակութեան: Կիւրճեանի ոճը յստակ, ճկուն, խայթող ու բարի է:

Պատահական չէ որ Օշական կը հաստատէ. «Յակոբ Պարոնեանէն վերջ ունեցանք Ա. Արփիարեանը, Ե. Օտեանը, Մ. Կիւրճեանը, յիշելու համար միայն վաւերական տաղանդները այդ սեռէն»:[81]

ԴԻԻԹԻՉ ՆՈՐԱՎԷՊԵՐՈՒ, ՊԱՏՄՈՒԱԾՔՆԵՐՈՒ ԵՒ ԳՐԱԿԱՆ ՊԱՏԿԵՐՆԵՐՈՒ ՀՐԱՊՈՅՐԸ

Հայ ժողովուրդի բազմադարեան պատմութեան մէջ իւրայատուկ ժամանակաշրջան մըն է 19րդ դարը: Պատմական ու քաղաքական իրադարձութիւնները, տնտեսական ու ընկերային փոփոխութիւնները, ազգային ինքնաճանաչման ու հայրենասիրական ինքնագիտակցութեան միտումները պայմաններ ստեղծեցին հայ հասարակական միտքի, պարբերական մամուլի, գրականութեան եւ արուեստներու զարգացման: Մտաւոր ու հոգեկան կեանքի աշխուժացման հետ յառաջացան նաեւ արուեստի եւ գրականութեան նորանոր ուղղութիւններ: Հայ գրականութեան պատմութեան մէջ իւրայատուկ շրջան է յատկապէս 19րդ դարու երկրորդ կէսը, երբ իշխող գրական սեռը դասական բանաստեղծութիւնն էր (Յովհան Վանանդեցի, Հայր Արսէն Բագրատունի, Հայր Ղեւոնդ Ալիշան): 1850-1860ական թուականներուն նկատելիօրէն կը նուազի հետաքրքրութիւնը բանաստեղծութեան նկատմամբ: Բնականաբար, սակայն, քնարերգութեան որոշ աւանդութիւններ կը շարունակեն գոյատեւել ու զարգանալ նաեւ այդ եւ հետագայ տարիներուն:

1850-1860ական թուականներու գրողներէն յիշատակութեան արժանի են Միքայէլ Նալբանդեանը, Ռափայէլ Պատկանեանը, զէյթունեան ռազմական երգերու եւ քնարական լաւագոյն երկերու հեղինակ Մկրտիչ Պէշիկթաշլեանը, քնարերգական խօսքի վարպետ սակաւակեաց Պետրոս Դուրեանը:

Յաջորդ տասնամեակը, որ գրականութեան մէջ սովորաբար կ'անուանուի 1870-1880ական թուականներու գրականութիւն, յատկանշական է երկու հիմնական ուղղութիւններու՝ իրապաշտական եւ վիպապաշտական մեթոտներու համատեղ ընթացքով, որոնցմէ իրապաշտականը կը հասնի իր զարգացման բարձունքին, իսկ 1875-1885 տարիներն ընդգրկող տասնամեակը դասական վիպապաշտութեան վերելքի շրջանը կը դառնայ, երբ Գաբրիէլ Սունդուկեանի, Պերճ Պռոշեանի, Ղազարոս Աղայեանի, Րաֆֆիի, Յակոբ Պարոնեանի, Ծերենցի, Սրբուհի Տիւսաբի սերունդը հայ գրականութեան ղեկը կը յանձնէ յաջորդ սերունդին՝ Մուրացան, Շիրվանզադէ, Նար-Դոս, Յովհաննէս Թումանեան, Վրթանէս Փափազեան, Արփիար Արփիարեան, Տիգրան Կամսարական, Գրիգոր Զօհրապ, Լեւոն Բաշալեան եւ ուրիշ ժամանակակիցներ:

19րդ դարու գրականութեան պատմութեան մէջ իր ուրոյն տեղն ու դերն ունի «ութսունականներ»ու գրական-հասարակական գործունէութիւնը: Արդարեւ, զարգացման նոր շրջան մը կը թեւակոխէ հայ գրական շարժումը՝ անցում կատարելով վիպապաշտական ոճէն դէպի իրապաշտական:

Այս գրական արագ փոփոխութիւններու այս շրջանին է որ Միքայէլ Կիւրճեան 1898ին իր «Մարտիկ Աղա» վէպով մուտք կը գործէ գրական ասպարէզ, հարստացնելով Պէրպէրեան վարժարանէն իր ստացած գիտելիքները ընթերցանութեամբ ու ինքնազարգացմամբ, եւ կատարելագործելով իր բնածին գրական ձիրքերը:

Հետաքրքրական է նշել թէ Կիւրճեան հայերէն գրելէ առաջ սկսած է գրել ֆրանսերէն լեզուով 1895էն սկսեալ եւ 1896էն աշխատակցած է Գահիրէ եւ Աղեքսանդրիա հրատարակուող ֆրանսերէն թերթերու: Ուշագրաւ է որ իր «Քեաթիպին Երազը» նշանաւոր գործը գրած է ֆրանսերէն եւ առաջին անգամ լոյս տեսած է ֆրանսական մամուլի մէջ: Մեր պրպտումներու ընթացքին հանդիպած ոտանաւորներէն դատելով, Կիւրճեան գերազանցօրէն կը տիրապետէր ֆրանսերէն լեզուին եւ ինչպէս իր մայրենի լեզուով ստեղծագործութիւնները, այնպէս ալ իր ֆրանսերէն ոտանաւորներն ու արձակ գործերը գրուած են սահուն ոճով եւ խնամուած լեզուով, որ ապացոյց է ֆրանսերէնի լաւ իմացութեան: Թէոդիկի տարեցոյցին մէջ լոյս տեսած «Harmonies du Soir»ը («Գիշերուան Ներդաշնակութիւններ» - Յ.Մ.) ձօնուած է Լիւսիին, որուն գունագեղ դէմքը ամառնային շքեղ գիշերուան պէս իր հոգիին երազել կու տայ, ինչպէս ծով մը, որ անխռով կը հանդարտի ու կը հանգչի, որուն քաղցրութիւնն ու մեղմութիւնը կը նմանի ծովուն անհետացող ալիքներուն ու ծփանքներուն եւ որուն դէմքը իր հոգիին կը պարգեւէ հանդարտող գիշերներու աստուածային խաղաղութիւնը՝ եւ այս բոլորէն Կիւրճեան յատկապէս կը շեշտէ կեանքի տկարութիւնը:

Երեք քառեակներէն բաղկացած բանաստեղծութիւնը կը վերջանայ հետեւեալ տողերով.

Ta douceur fait rêver les flots évanouis
De mon âme mirant ta face blanche et rose...
Dans le calme divin des soirs épanouis
Ah! que la vie, ma chère, est une faible chose...

Դարձեալ Թէոդիկի տարեցոյցին մէջ տպագրուած է Կիւրճեանի 1907ին գրուած «Pleurs en la Nuit» («Արցունքներ Գիշերուան Մէջ» - Յ.Մ.) ոտանաւորը, որ նուիրուած է բազմարդիւն դաստիարակ եւ հայկաբան Միհրան Ասքանազի դուստր, ծաղիկ հասակին մահացած օրիորդ Հերմինէ Ասքանազին: Այս քերթուածին մէջ Կիւրճեան կը նշէ կեանքի անզօրութիւնն ու բացակայութիւնը եւ անհուն ու մահաշուք, խորունկ հանգչող Լռութիւնը: Ո՛չ, սակայն, լռութիւնը չի խռովիր, այլ կ՚ունկնդրէ մրմունջն հեռաւոր, վճիտ շատրուանին, որ իր կաթիլները կը ծորէ հնօրեայ աւազանին մէջ:

Բանաստեղծին կը թուի թէ կը լսէ այս խորհրդաւոր ժամուն մենաւոր լռութիւնը, որ կու լայ շիթ առ շիթ անմխիթար հոգիի մը նման՝ կարօտագին գիշերուան մէջ.

Car il me semble entendre,- illusion magique,-
Le Silence esseulé
Qui pleure goutte à goutte en la nuit nostalgique
Comme un inconsolé.

«Հայ Կին» կիսամսեայ հանդէսին մէջ տպագրուած է Կիւրճեանի «La Reine» («Թագուհին» - Ց.Մ.) բանաստեղծութիւնը,[82] որ նուիրուած է ընտրեալին: Կիւրճեան կ'ուզէ իր ընտրեալը՝ իր սիրելին, թագուհի կարգել եւ անոր համար որպէս լուսաւոր պալատ կը տրամադրէ իր երիտասարդ խնկաբոյր հոգին, ուր յաղթական գահին վրայ կ'ուզէ բազմած տեսնել զինքը գիշեր ցերեկ՝ ունենալով բանաստեղծին ամբողջ էութիւնը՝ իշխանութեան համար, ադամանդներով, մարգարիտներով եւ գոհարներով պատրաստուած արքայական զգեստներով, երկնային ու ծովային պայծառ գոյներով նշանուած: Որպէս շքադիր ու պատուադիր տիկիններ կ'առաջարկէ իր խոկումները ու մտածումները, իսկ որպէս արքունական դրանիկներ՝ թագաւորական թիկնապահներ տրամադրելով իր բոլոր ոտանաւորները՝ իբրեւ պահապան զինուորներ: Դուն կը տեսնես իմ սարսռալից բաղձանքները, փափաքները՝ մերթ յանդուգն ու խենթ, մերթ խոհական ու հեզահամբոյր, որոնք կը հետեւին քեզի ամէնուրեք, որպէս ուղեկիցներ:

«Թագուհին» բանաստեղծութիւնը կը սկսի ու կը վերջանայ հետեւեալ տողերով.

Dans mon âme qui vit sans passions ni loi
Dans mon coeur libre ainsi qu'une foule sans roi,
Je voudrais t'installer en Reine, ô Bien-Aimée!

Ինչքա՜ն քնքշութիւն եւ փափկութիւն. ինչքա՜ն նրբութիւն եւ ազնուութիւն կայ այս տողերուն մէջ:

«Ծանթ» կիսամսեայ հանդէսին մէջ տպագրուած է Կիւրճեանի «La Mort mystique» («Խորհրդաւոր Մահը» - Ց.Մ.) չափածոյ գործը,[83] ուր քերթողին բանաստեղծական թռիչքը, խռէալի մը հասնելու փոյթը կը տիրապետէ սկիզբէն մինչեւ վերջ: Արդարեւ, այդ քառատուն ստեղծագործութեան մէջ հեղինակը ազդեցիկ ձեւով, ներգործող եղանակով կ'արտայայտուի: Ան կը խորհրդածէ, կը մտորէ եւ կը շեշտէ սարսափազդու մահուան խորհրդաւորութիւնը՝ նկարագրելով գիշերուան ծանրաքայլ յառաջանալը, մթութեան տիրապետութիւնը, խաղաղութեան յարատեւութիւնը եւ հոգիի յաւիտենականութիւնը: Պոռլէրեան, վէրլէնեան տխրութեան, տրտմութեան, մելամաղձոտութեան բոյրը կը զգացուի այդ տողերուն մէջ, ուր կեանքի ծանր փորձութիւններէն քաղուած եզրակացութիւններու կը յանգի Կիւրճեան՝ բաբախուն սրտատրոփութեամբ:

Ահա այդ քերթուածը:

La Mort Mystique

S'évanouit du jour l'espoir d'azur et d'or...
Le Soir s'aggrave, hélas! comme un mal incurable
Et très mystérieux... En lente et douce Mort,
L'universelle Nuit monte, incommensurable...

O mon âme, voici venir sans bruit
L'heure de lentement mourir avec les choses
Exhalant en secret dans l'unanime Nuit,
Leur âme de lumière et de métamorphoses...

En toi s'apaise enfin le rythme frémissant
Des diurnes émois de la Vie et du Songe.
Pendent qu'occulte et grave, au fond de toi descend
La paix de cette mort qui dure et se prolonge...

Le Temps s'immobilise en une heure infinie,
Plane la solitude immense du néant...
Tu ne vis plus, mon âme, et tu goûtes, ravie,
L'universel bonheur d'être éternellement.

Խորհրդաւոր Մահը

Ցորեկ ատեն կը նուազի յոյսը ոսկեայ եւ կապուտակ...
Որպէս ցաւ մը՝ անբուժելի, Գիշերն աւա՜ղ կը ծանրանայ
Ու չափազանց խորհրդաւոր ... եւ յամրընթաց քաղցր Մահը,
Համընդհանուր խաւար Ցայգը անհամաչափ կը բարձրանայ...:

Օ՜հ, իմ հոգիս ահա կու գայ շատ անշշուկ եւ անաղմուկ
Յամրագնաց ժամը մահուան իրերու հետ անհետանալ
Լուսաճաճանչ իրենց հոգին արձակելով՝ շա՛տ գաղտուկ
Գիշերուան մէջ համախոհուրդ, կերպարանքով այլափոխեալ...

Ապա քու մէջ կը մեղմանայ դաշնակութիւնն սրսըփացող
Ցերեկաթուիչ յուզումները կենցաղական, անըրջական:
Յորժամ ծածուկ, ծանրաքարոյ, քու խորքին մէջ իջեւանող
Խաղաղութիւնն այդ մահուան որ կ'երկարի յար յաւիտեան...

Ժամանակը կ'անշարժանայ ժամի մը մէջ ու անսահման,
Միշտ յղկելով միայնութիւնն անէութեան...
Դուն չես ապրի՛ր, ով իմ հոգիս, ճաշակելով դուն պակուցեալ,
Կ'ուզես ըլլալ՝ բարեբաստիկ, ըլլալ յաւէտ՝ անմահական:
(Թարգմանութիւնը Յ. Մէքէրեանի)

Կիրճեանի ֆրանսերէն գրութիւններուն անդրադառնալու առթիւ պէտք է նշել նաեւ այն հանգամանքը, որ տարբեր ժամանակներ եւ տարբեր տարիներու, ընդհատումներով իր գրած օրագիրներուն եւ ծանօթութիւններու տետրակներուն մէջ եւս կան ֆրանսերէն նշումներ, տպաւորութիւններ եւ Եւրոպա այցելութիւններու օրագրութիւններ, որոնց մէջ կը գտնուին արժէքաւոր գրական դարձուածքներ, նկարագրութիւններ, տեղեկութիւններ, զգացումներու վերարտադրութիւններ: Անոնցմէ ուշադրութեան արժանի են հետեւեալները՝

La nuit marche à pas d'ombre et de silence
(Գիշերը կը քալէ ստուերի եւ լռութեան քայլերով)

կամ՝

Le soleil m'enforce dans l'oeil ses doigts d'or
(Արեւը աչքիս մէջ կը մխրճէ իր ոսկեայ մատերը)

կամ՝

La douceur du ciel fondue dans le lac
(Երկինքի քաղցրութիւնը՝ ձուլուած լիճի մէջ)

Որքա՜ն գեղեցիկ եւ պատկերաւոր է հետեւեալը՝

L'abus fait le moins
(Չեղծութիւնը նուազ կը փախչի)

Կիրճեան ապահովաբար շատ սիրած է իր այս զգացումը եւ մտայղացումը, որովհետեւ զայն ստորագրած է իր անուան եւ ազգանուան սկզբնատառերով:
Օրինակ մը եւս՝

Les anciens Grecs étaient épiques,
les modernes épiciers

(Հին յոյները դիւցազներգակներ էին
Արդիականները՝ նպարավաճառներ)

Հոս Կիւրճեան ցոյց կու տայ ֆրանսերէնով ալ բառախաղի իր ընդունակութիւնը՝ դիւցազներգակ եւ նպարավաճառ բառերու սրամիտ օգտագործումով:

Ահա՛ եւ ուրիշ օրինակ մը՝

Les littérateurs font de peinture
Et les peintres font de la littérature
(Գրագէտները նկարչութիւն կ'ընեն
Եւ նկարիչները գրականութիւն կ'ընեն)

Այս երկտողին մէջ նկատելի են ինչպէս գրագէտներու եւ նկարիչներու բաղդատութիւնը, այնպէս ալ վարպետ հանգաւորումը՝ peinture, litterature:

Կիւրճեան չորս անգամ օդափոխութեան գացած է Եւրոպա՝ 1920ին, 1924ին, 1927ին եւ 1933ին: Չորսին ալ այցելած է Փարիզ: Ըստ օրագրութեան, ամենէն տպաւորիչն ու հաճոյալին եղած է երկրորդ այցելութիւնը, որովհետեւ ֆրանսերէնով կատարած է բազմաթիւ նշումներ, ուր նկարագրած է իր այցելած վայրերը՝ Լիւքսէմպուրկի պարտէզը, Վէրսայլի պալատը, թանգարանը եւ պարտէզը, Փարիզի տեսարժան եւ պատմական վայրերը, Լիւքսէմպուրկի թանգարանը: Ան իր հիացումը յայտնած է Վիքթոր Հիւկոյի թանգարանին մասին, ուր այցելած է յիշատակութեան արժանի օր մը՝ Շաբաթ, 15 Հոկտեմբեր 1927ին.

Les dessins et tableaux de V. Hugo sont choses absolument uniques foudroyantes! Jamais je n'ai été peut être autant secoué...

Mon impression en sortant est celle-ci:

Si Hugo n'avait pas voulu être le plus grand poète lyrique de son siècle et de tous les tempe, il eut été le plus grand peintre-dessinateur des temps modernes, comme Rembrandt moderne! J'amais paintres n'a dessiné et peint comme lui, car jamais peintre n'a été grand poète comme lui.

Je suis sorti de ce musée, titulant, ivre... tout tremblant. La décharge de beauté, de mystère et de sublime avait été trop forte! ...

«Վիքթոր Հիւկոյի գծագրութիւնները եւ նկարները բացարձակապէս անզուգական եւ շանթահարիչ բաներ են: Գուցէ երբեք ես այսչափ ցնցուած չեմ:

Դուրս ելլելու ժամանակ իմ տպաւորութիւնը սա է.

Եթէ Հիւկօ չուզէր ըլլալ իր դարուն եւ բոլոր ժամանակներու

ամենէն մեծ քնարերգակ բանաստեղծը, ան պիտի ըլլար նոր ժամանակներու ամենէն մեծ նկարիչը-գծագրիչը՝ ինչպէս արդի Ռէմպրանտը: Երբեք նկարիչները չեն գծած եւ նկարած իրեն պէս, վասնզի երբեք նկարիչը չէ եղած իրեն պէս մեծ բանաստեղծ:

Ես այս հռչակաւոր թանգարանէն դուրս ելայ արբեցած, գինով... ամբողջովին ցնցուած: Գեղեցկութեան, խորհուրդի եւ վսեմութեան սփոփանքը շատ ուժեղ էր...» (թարգմանութիւնը՝ Յ.Մ.):

Այս ճանապարհորդութեան ժամանակ է որ Կիւրճեան այցելած է Փէր Լաշէզի գերեզմանատունը իր յարգանքը մատուցելու համար շատ սիրած ֆրանսացի բանաստեղծ Ալֆրէտ տը Միւսէի եւ իտալացի հռչակաւոր երգահան Ռոսսինիի շիրիմներուն (1 Հոկտեմբեր 1927ին), ապա աչքէ անցուցած է Լիւքսէմպուրկի թանգարանը (13 Հոկտեմբերին), որուն մասին գրած է. «Les impressionistes m'ont beaucoup impressionné» («Տպաւորապաշտները զիս շատ տպաւորեցին» - Յ.Մ.): Այցելած է նաեւ Լուվրի թանգարանը (14 Հոկտեմբերին), ուր անցուցած է «անմոռանալի օր մը»: Կիւրճեան նաեւ հանդիպումներ ունեցած է ինչպէս հայ ականաւոր դէմքերու (Զօպանեան, Գաբրիէլեան եւ ուրիշներ), այնպէս ալ ֆրանսացի հեղինակաւոր անձնաւորութիւններու հետ (*Nouvelles Litteratures*-ի խմբագիր Fréderic Lefèvre, Pierre Champion, Bourget եւ ուրիշներ): Հակառակ անձրեւային եւ ցուրտ եղանակին, Զօպանեանի հետ մասնակցած է Մոնփառնասի գերեզմանատան մէջ ֆրանսացի գրող Շարլ Պոտլէրի շիրիմին վրայ տեղի ունեցած յիշատակի ու մեծարանքի արարողութեան՝ Կիրակի, 23 Հոկտեմբեր 1927ին, որուն ընթացքին Պոտլէրի մահուան 60ամեակին առիթով Պուրժէ[84] կարդացած է ճառ մը եւ գրողէն արտասանուած են բազմաթիւ քերթուածներ:

Օրագրութիւններու ուրիշ տետրի մը մէջ, նոյնպէս կան ֆրանսերէն նշումներ եւ տպաւորութիւններ, որոնք գրուած են Փարիզ իր չորրորդ այցելութեան մասին՝ 1933ի գարնան, Մայիս-Յունիս ամիսներուն: Սակայն այս անգամ բոլորովին անտրամադիր եւ առանց նախորդ անգամուան ուրախ տրամադրութեան. «Չորրորդ անգամ ըլլալով Փարիզ եմ... սակայն նոյնը չեմ զգար ինքզինքս, ուրախութեան եւ ապրելու մեծ նուազում...»: Պատճառը յստակ չէ իրեն համար. տարի՞ք, աննպաստ ֆիզիքական վիճա՞կ, թէ՞ վերջին երկու տարիներուն պատահած դէպքեր: Թերեւս ալ իր կնոջ ընկերակցութեան բացակայութիւնն է պատճառը, քանի որ անոր ներկայութեան աւելի ուրախ եւ աշխոյժ եղած էր ան 1927ին, միասնաբար զբօսաշրջելու ժամանակ: Իր սէրը ուժեղ եւ կաթոգին էր անոր նկատմամբ եւ ինք աւելի ապահով կը զգար ինքզինք:

Այս չորրորդ այցելութեան ընթացքին եւս Կիւրճեան հանդիպումներ կ'ունենայ գրչեղբայրներու հետ (Տիգրան Կամսարական, Վահան Մալէզեան, Արամ Անտոնեան, Տարիա Կամսարական, Վահան Թէքէեան,

Միքայէլ Ալէմշահ, Գրիգոր Թէլլալեան եւ ուրիշներ), որոնցմէ յատկապէս Կամսարականի եւ Թէքէեանի հետ կը քննարկէ գրական հարցեր, վերջինին կարդալով նաեւ «Ֆրանքօ-Թրքական Պատերազմ»ի շարունակութիւնը՝ մէկ արարնոց կատակերգութիւնը եւ «Ազգայիննին»ի առաջին արարը: Ուշագրաւ է իր մէկ ժամ տեւած հանդիպումը Nouvelles Littéraires-ի խմբագիր Fréderic Lefèvre-ի հետ, որ ծանօթանալով Կիրճեանի ֆրանսերէն գրութիւններուն (Le Rêve de Kiatib, Le Café, Le Vin de l'Hiver, Harem, եւայլն), յատկապէս կը հաւնի «Քեաթիպին Երազը», ըսելով «C'est très jolie, très bien» (շատ գեղեցիկ է եւ շատ լաւ - Յ.Մ.):

Կիրճեանի օրագրին մէջ, 25 Հոկտեմբեր 1907 թուակիր նամակով մը, արձանագրուած է նաեւ Գաճիրէի Անգլօ-Եգիպտական դրամատան հայ պաշտօնեայի մը բարձր գնահատականը հեղինակին «Սրճարանը» գրութեան մասին. «Je ne puis resister au plaisir de venir vous serrer la main et de vous faire mes plus vifs compliments pour l'excellent article "Le Café" que je viens de lire dans "L'Orient" de ce matin» (Չեմ կրնար դիմադրել ձեր ձեռքը սեղմելու հաճոյքին եւ ձեզի յայտնելու իմ ամենաջերմ մեծարանքի ողջոյնները այն սքանչելի «Սրճարանը» յօդուածին համար, զոր կարդացի այս առաւօտուան «Լ'Օրիան»ին մէջ - Յ.Մ.): Այնուհետեւ կը շարունակէ. «Ես կը խորհիմ որ լաւ դպրոց աւարտած ֆրանսացի շատ հեղինակներ պիտի ուզէին ստորագրել այդ տողերը: Զուտ եւ մաքուր ֆրանսերէնով, որ ոչինչ կը ձգէ ցանկալու վայելչութեան, պարզութեան, արդիականութեան տեսակէտէն, այս յօդուածը ինքը միայն պիտի բաւականացնէր ձեզ դասելու անուանի գրողներու ընտրանիին մէջ»: Նամակագիրը նաեւ կը հաստատէ. «Ես ձեզ կը համարեմ որպէս մէկը այն հազուագիւտ հայերէն, որոնք գիտեն լաւագոյնս գործածել Պոլէրի եւ Կի տը Մոփասանի լեզուն»:

Կիրճեանի ֆրանսերէնով գրած նիւթերէն ուրիշ գործեր չունինք մեր տրամադրութեան տակ, բայց այս սակաւաթիւ երկերն անգամ կ'արդարացնեն անոր ֆրանսերէն գրութիւններուն ոճին, լեզուին մասին բարձր գնահատանքները, քանի որ ան իր խստապահանջութեամբ մեծ զգուշաւորութիւն ցուցաբերած է նաեւ ֆրանսերէն երկերուն մէջ՝ անթերի խնամքով վարուելով իւրաքանչիւր բառի, նախադասութեան եւ կէտադրութեան հետ: Կիրճեանի ֆրանսագիտութեան տակաւին առիթ կ'ունենանք անդրադառնալու: Առայժմ կը փափաքինք շեշտել թէ քսաներորդ դարասկիզբին Կիրճեան արդէն կեդրոնական դէմք մըն էր մտաւորական շրջանակներու մէջ եւ հեղինակութիւն կը վայելէր օտար գրական շրջանակներու մէջ եւս:

* * *

Կիրճեան իր վիպակներուն եւ պատմուածքներուն մէջ արտացոլած է ընդհանրապէս պոլսահայ կեանքէն իրական դէմքեր ու դէպքեր: Ան իր յուշերով միշտ կապուած մնացած է իր ծննդավայրին հետ, որ խոր ազդեցութիւն թողած է թէ՛ իր եւ թէ իր ստեղծագործութիւններուն վրայ:

Ծուրջ երկու տասնեակի կը հասնին պոլսահայ տիպերու մասին իր ստեղծագործութիւնները, որոնք իբրեւ ենթախորագիր կը կրեն «Պոլսահայ Բարքեր»ը:

1901ին Գահիրէի «Արշալոյս» օրաթերթին մէջ Դիտակ ծածկանունով լոյս տեսած է Կիւրճեանի «Անունին Գիշերը» պատմուածքը, ուր մերկացուած են սեփականատիրական հասարակութեան վերնախաւին բարքերը: Ստեղծագործութիւնը հարուստ է այդ խաւի ներկայացուցիչ՝ «պզտիկ գեղին մեծ աղայի» ջոջական նիստուկացի նկարագրութիւններով: Այս պատմուածքին մէջ Կիւրճեան նկարագրած է սկիւտարցի նպարավաճառ Սարգիսը: Այս ջոջը «իր անձին նկատմամբ կազմած բարձր համարումով եւ պատշաճ արարողականով» կը նշէ իր անուանակոչութեան օրը բանջարավաճառ Գրիգորի, եազմաճի Յակոբի, հիւսն Խաչիկի, պէրպէր Ալեքսանի, հացագործ Համբարի, կօշկակար Նշանի, մխլայըճի Միհրանի, երկաթագործ Պօղոսի, խահվէճի Լեւոնի եւ խոնարհ դասի ուրիշ արհեստաւորներու հետ՝ բաց սիրտով ու բաց դէմքով մարդիկը հիւրընկալելու մեծ ցոյցով եւ ուրիշներուն պատիւ ընելով ինքզինք պատուած ըլլալու սնափառութեամբ:

Պարոյր Սեւակ Վիգէն Խեչումեանի «Գիրք Պանդխտութեան» ժողովածուին մասին իր գրախօսականին մէջ ճշգրտօրէն կը հաստատէ. «Անհնարին է գրող լինել՝ առանց դիտողականութեան: Միաժամանակ՝ կարելի է շատ սուր աչք ունենալ, բայց գրող չլինել: Հարկաւոր է նկատածը նկատելի դարձնել, տեսածը տեսցնել: Իսկ դրա համար գրողը միայն մի գործիք ունի՝ խօսքը»:[85]

Արդարեւ, Կիւրճեանի կարեւոր յատկանիշներէն մէկն է շատերու տեսողութենէն դուրս մնացած մանրուքները նկատելու եւ խորապէս զգալու դիտողականութիւնը: Ստուգիւ, առանձնայատուկ է նաեւ անոր ազատ ու անկաշկանդ պատմելու, ճշմարտացի մատուցման եւ գեղարուեստականօրէն համակողմանի ներկայացնելու տաղանդը: Այս առումներով ակնառու է «Անունին Գիշերը» պատմուածքը իր կեդրոնական հերոսով՝ սկիւտարցի պախալ Սարգիսով: Իրաւամբ, այդ ժամանակներուն «բարձր» կոչուած դասակարգի՝ ողդենկոտով, ֆրանքով ու պոնժուրով նորելուկ մարդոց հակապատկերն է Սարգիս աղան՝ նախնիներու սովորութեան հետեւող «հինին աւանդապահ անեղծ հայը» իր նահապետական հագուստով:

Հարազատ մնալով իր պատկերաւոր ոճին, Կիւրճեան ինքնատիպ գիծերով կերտած է Սարգիսի կերպարը հետեւեալ նկարագրութեամբ. «Կարելի չէ երեւակայել ճշմարիտ նպարավաճառ մը առանց փորի: «Պախալ»ի մը փորը էն շահեկան, ակնառու եւ խորհրդանշական մասը կը ձեւացնէ իր խանութին, կարելի է ըսել թէ մէկ մարմին կը կազմէ անոր կարգ մը ապրանքներուն հետ, մերձաւոր ազգական կամ խնամի է տիկերուն, տակառներուն, պարկերուն եւ անոնց հետ կը շփոթուի յաճախ...: Պախալի մը փորը կ'երգէ փառքը իր նպարեղէններուն բոլոր այն ճարպոտ, իւղոտ կուռտ ու կլոր, համով հոտով ե՛ւ գոյնով բաներուն զորոնք կը ծախէ, եւ այսու կարելի լաւագոյն ռէքլամն է իր խանութին, կենդանի ազդը, շրջուն մունետիկը»: Կիւրճեան այնուհետեւ կը բնութագրէ Սարգիս աղայի դիմագիծերն ու հագուստները, որոնք աւելի ընդգծուն կը դարձնեն անոր նպարավաճառ ըլլալու անվիճելիութիւնը: Սարգիս աղայի երգիծական կերպարի կողքին, ջերմ տրամադրութեամբ ներկայացուած են արհեստաւոր դասակարգի պարզամիտ թաղեցիները՝ «երջանիկ մարդեր, որոնք հարստութեան տեղ ունին առատ առողջութիւն, որոնք շատ կ'աշխատին, քիչ կը վաստըկին»: Յատկանշական է նաեւ անոնց նիստուկացը. «Իրենց խօսքերը, շարժումները լայն են, ազատ, անկաշկանդ, առանց այն սանձին որ չափ կ'ըսուի կամ ճաշակ: Կը զգաս որ շարժած, խօսած ատենին՝ ոեւէ պատկառանք չեն զգար «քաղաքավարութիւն» ըսուած քարոզիչէն, որեւէ «ամօ՛թ է» ըսուած ոստիկանէ»:

Սարգիս աղայի փառասիրութիւնը եւ ցուցամոլութիւնը քննադատուած է ամբողջ պատմուածքի ընթացքին, սկսելով հանդերձանքէն, *սկամպիլ* խաղալէն, սեղանը ուտելիքներով ու խմիչքով դասաւորելէն, հիւրասիրութենէն մինչեւ հիւրերը ճանապարհ դնելը:

Կիւրճեան շատ գրաւիչ, համարձակ եւ սահուն գրիչով եւ նոյնիսկ քիչ մըն ալ երգիծանքով գեղարուեստօրէն կը ներկայացնէ ուսանողական ու երիտասարդական տարիներուն Պոլսոյ Սկիւտար թաղամասին մէջ իր տեսածն ու ապրածը:

Կիւրճեան իսկական արուեստագէտ է իր լաւագոյն պատմուածքներուն մէջ: Ան գիտէ սկսիլ, շարունակել եւ ճիշդ ժամանակին վերջացնել: Իր դիտողականութիւնը, խորագիտութիւնը, միտքի սրաթափանցութիւնը եւ գրիչի նրբութիւնը կատարելութեան օրինակելի նմոյշներ են՝ գնահատանքի եւ գովասանքի արժանի:

Այս պատմուածքը պերճախօս վկայութիւնն է թէ Կիւրճեան քսաներորդ դարասկիզբին իսկապէս հմտօրէն ձեւաւորուած, լուրջ, հասուն, ինքնատիպ անհատականութիւն մըն էր, գեղարուեստական իր ինքնուրոյն աշխարհով, որ ունէր կայուն չափանիշներ եւ հաստատ սկզբունքներ:

Կիւրճեան իր «Մարտիկ Աղա» վէպով, ինչպէս նաեւ սքանչելի պատմուածքներով, վիպակներով, քրոնիկներով, արձակ ու չափածոյ քերթուածներով մէկ անգամէն հրապարակ իջաւ որպէս հասուն, փորձառու գրող, առանց սկսնակի մոլորուն նախաքայլերու, փորձնական հրապարակումներու եւ նախապատրաստական սկզբնական դեգերումներու, որ իրաւունք եւ հիմք տուած է գրաքննադատ Երուանդ Ազատեանին գրելու՝ «Միքայէլ Կիւրճեան գրական մեծ ԽՈՍՏՈՒՄ մըն էր 19 տարեկանին» շատ բնորոշիչ եւ յատկանշական բնութագիրը՝ «Ո՞վ Պիտի Տնկէ Վառենի Մը...» յօդուածին մէջ, գրուած Կիւրճեանի մահուան առաջին տարելիցին առիթով «Արեւ» օրաթերթի 11 Յուլիս 1966ի թիւին մէջ:[86]

1902ին Գահիրէի «Նոր Օր» լրագրին մէջ Զարմայր Սահակեան ծածկանունով տպագրուած է Կիւրճեանի «Ընտանիք Մը» պատմուածքը, ուր ներկայացուած է կեսարացի վաճառական Սարգիս էֆէնտի Համբարձումեանի քաղքենի կահաւորումով տունը՝ իր ձանձրացուցիչ լռութեամբ: «Անունին Գիշերը» պատմուածքին մէջ հիւրերով լեցուած սենեակի, բարձրաձայն խօսակցութիւններով ժխորալի մթնոլորտի, *սկամպիլի* վրդովալից բացագանչութիւններուն, պարտուողներուն խռովայոյզ արտայայտութիւններուն, երախաներուն ծեծ ու կոծին, երկարատեւ լացի, ծնողներու տփոցով միջամտութեան, սաստումներու, բանավէճերու եւ երբեմն ալ հայհոյանքներու աղմկալից տան փոխարէն, «Ընտանիք Մը» պատմուածքին մէջ նկարագրուած է կատարեալ լռութեամբ ճնշիչ ձմեռ իրիկուն մը: Ամբողջ պատմուածքին մէջ երկար ժամերով սպասման ընթացքին միայն հետեւեալ կարճ խօսքերը կը փոխանակուին կեսուրի եւ հարսի միջեւ՝

- Ժամը քանի՞ն է, Մարի...
- Եօթնուկէս...

....

- Մարի, սըկէ դերձան կուտա՞ս:
- Ծատ աղէկ...

....

- Աս օր ի՞նչ օր է, Մարի:
- Չորեքշաբթի...

....

- Հիմա, ուր որ է նէ զաւակս կուգայ:
- Այո...

....

Սարգիս աղա եւս սակաւախօս է՝
- Աս ի՞նչ ցուրտ է պէ...

....

- Է, ի՞նչ կայ նայինք... ի՞նչ ըրիք այսօր...
- Ինչ պիտի ընէինք... ամէն օրուայ պէս...

....

- Է՛, ճաշ ընենք, Մարկոսին ըսէք, անօթի եմ...

....

Եւ իրարմէ հեռու, ապաշխարող վանականներու պէս լուռ ու մունջ ճաշելէ, գրասեղանին առջեւ նստելէ, գրպանէն թուղթերու խառնաղէզ մը հանելով թղթատելէ, կարդալէ եւ քանի մը թուանշաններ շարելէ ետք, «Ուշ է ատենը, հայտէ երթանք պտոյկինք» ըսելով, կը վերջանայ այս ընտանիքին ամէնօրեայ միատեսակ ու անհետաքրքրական կեանքը: Ծոխ կահաւորուած բնակարանին անշուքն իրերուն նման անշարժ են Սարգիս էֆէնտի եւ իր մայրը, զուրկ՝ նոյնիսկ իրերու շքեղութենէն: Կէս գիշերէն ետք վաճառականին ներս մտնելը ոչ մէկ փոփոխութիւն կը մտցնէ սենեակին ձանձրացուցիչ մթնոլորտին եւ ընտանիքին պաղ ու լուռ միջավայրին մէջ, ուր շրջազգեստը գետինը քսուելու շրշիւնը, դարակի մը բացուելուն եւ գոցուելուն շշուկը, սպասաւորին բան մը շտկելու ձայնը կը խախտեն տիրող գերեզմանային լռութիւնը եւ ժամացոյցի ճօճանին հարուածները կարծես կը թնդան այդ կեանքին վրայ՝ հեգնելով իշխող թմբրանման լռութիւնը:

1902ին «Բիւզանդիոն»ի մէջ լոյս տեսած են պոլսահայ բարքեր շարքէն «Մարտ» եւ «Միսիս Սիսակ» պատմուածքները: Առաջինին մէջ նկարագրուած են խոր ծերութեան հասած Գէորգ աղան եւ իր կինը՝ Թագուկ տուտուն, երկուքն ալ ութսունը անցած, որոնք քսան տարիներէ ի վեր ամէնօրեայ պայքար մը կը մղէին մահուան դէմ՝ ապրելու համար: Տարուէ տարի կ'աճէր, կը սաստկանար իրենց մէջ կարելի եղածին չափ երկար ապրելու մարմաջը, մահաշուք վճարաժամը կարելի եղածին չափ հեռաւոր թուականի մը յետաձգելու տենչը, միշտ վախնալով ձմեռէն, վտանգաւոր եղանակէն, բայց մանաւանդ Մարտ ամիսէն:

«Արեւելքցին այս զգացումը կը թարգմանէ «խենդ» մակդիրով զոր Մարտին գլուխն անցուցած է յիմարանոցի գդակի մը պէս», կը գրէ Կիւրճեան: Տանը վերի յարկը «թախթապոշ» մը ունէին, բաւական ընդարձակ, որ ձորի մը վրայ կը նայէր, բարձրադիր: Մարտ ամիսը չեկած, շաբաթ մը առաջ իրենց սենեակը կը քաշուէին եւ Մարտը երթալէն ետք, հոն կ'ելլային քիչ մը մաքուր օդ շնչելու, «արեւ երես տեսնալու» համար: Ամբողջ Մարտ ամիսը հոն մնալով անդադար կը հարցնէին իրենց զաւակներուն, թոռներուն. «*Տահա* քանի՞ օր կայ, քանի՞ օր մնաց խենդին երթալուն»: Մարտը անցնելէն ետք, կը սպասէին աղուոր օրուան մը, թեւ թեւի, իրարու կռթնելով, զիրար բռնելով, կ'ելլային «թախթապոշ»: Հոն կը ցատկռտէին, ձեռք, ոտք, գլուխ, լեզու կը շարժէին. ինչե՞ր չէին ըներ. ինչե՞ր չէին ըսեր Մարտին դէմ: Այսպէս կը ճամբէին Մարտը: Սակայն վերջապէս կու գայ նաեւ իրենց վերջին Մարտը: Սենեակները քաշուելէն քանի մը օր ետքը երկուքն ալ կ'իյնան գէշ վիճակի մէջ: Ահագին հարբուխ մը կը զգետնէ զիրենք: Կինը առաջ կը մեռնի՝ իր վերջին մտածումն ըլլալով. «Գէորգը մինակը պիտի երթայ թախթապոշ»: Երեք օր ետքը մարդը կը մեռնի, իր ալ վերջին մտածումը «թախթապոշ»ին երթալով. «Թագուկ մինակը պիտի երթայ» մտմտալով:

«Միսիս Սիսակ» պատմուածքին մէջ Կիւրճեան կը քննադատէ «ատ աղջիկը տաս նէ կ'առնեմ առանց թրախոմայի (դրամօժիտի - Յ.Մ.)» ըսելով տունէ տուն պտտող, «հանճարեղութեամբ» փեսացութիւն գործադրող, երիտասարդութեան լաւ օրերը անցընելու համար շատեր խաբող անամօթ Սիսակը: Ընտանիքները իրարու ձեռքէ կը խլէին զայն, կարծելով թէ պիտի յաջողին բռնել զինք: Սակայն Սիսակ անոնց աղջիկներուն վրայ պակասութիւններ գտնելով, ուրիշ մը առնել կ'երթար «առանց թրախոմայի»: Սիսակի փիլիսոփայութիւնն էր «Փեսայ մի' ըլլար առանց երկար ատեն փեսացու ըլլալու» սկզբունքը: Սակայն երեք չորս տարի կին փնտռող եւ չգտնող մարդը ի վերջոյ ստիպուած կ'ըլլայ առնել Չամաշըրճի Նունիկին աղջիկը: Բնականաբար, փեսացուին միտքը ո՛չ թէ Հոռոփն առնել էր «առանց թրախոմայի», այլ՝ հետը իյնալ ելլել: «Անանկ մը ինկաւ սակայն, որ չկրցաւ ոտքի ելլել», կը գրէ Կիւրճեան անպատկառ Սիսակի մասին:

Վերոյիշեալ երկու պատմուածքները շատ հետաքրքրական են իրենց պատկերած թեմաներով եւ դիւրաւ ընթեռնելի, ինչպէս հեղինակէն բազմաթիւ այլ պատմուածքներ, որոնք յափշտակութեամբ կը կարդացուին, որովհետեւ գրուած են շատ պարզ եւ հետաքրքրաշարժ ոճով, առանց երկարաբանութեան եւ ճապաղութեան. ընդհականակը՝ սեղմ եւ անպաճոյճ շարադրանքով, կիւրճեանական բծախնդրութեամբ եւ բարեխղճութեամբ, զգուշօրէն վարուելով եւ գործածելով ամէն մէկ բառ եւ նախադասութիւն, ամէն մէկ կէտադրական նշան:

1903ին, Աղեքսանդրիոյ «Պարտէզ» գրական-մանկավարժական շաբաթաթերթին մէջ տպագրուած է Կիւրճեանի «Ազատամիտ Աղջիկ Մը» պատմուածքը, ուր նկարագրուած է Վերժինի սնափառութիւնը: Ազատախօսութենէ տարուած եւ հաւատալով թէ ինք ազատամիտ է՝ այդպիսին կը հռչակէ ինքզինք, ազատամիտներու իւրայատուկ միջոցներով: Ուսումնականութիւն դրսեւորելու նպատակով՝ իր խօսակցութեան մէջ կ'օգտագործէ *ընդհակառակը, անտարակոյս, անշուշտ, նամանաւանդ, հաւանականաբար, չափազանց, բայց եւ այնպէս, ըստ իս, վերջին աստիճան, ընդհանրապէս, խիկապէս* եւ նմանօրինակ մակբայծ բառեր, ինչպէս նաեւ իր գիտցած քանի մը տասնեակ ֆրանսերէն բառերը՝ *քօմ իլ ֆօ, թուր* մը, *փրօմընատ* մը, *տ'աքոր* ենք, *տիսփոզիսիոն* չունիմ, ի՞նչ *աքանտալ*, եւայլն:

Լկտածութեան հասնող իր շարժուածքը եւ խօսքի անպատկառ համարձակութիւնը ազատամտութիւն համարող, իր ծնողները չհաւնող ու զանոնք «խաւարեալ» անուանող, թաղին բնակիչները արհամարհող եւ ուրիշ աղջիկներ իրմէ նուաստ նկատող օրիորդ Վերժինի Սինեմեան քանի մը սիրահարութիւններ ունենալէ եւ հօրն ու մօրը մահէն ետք առանձին մնացած ըլլալով, կը ստիպուի ապաստանիլ ազգականի մը տունը, ուր «զինքը կը գործածեն իբր ... պատուակալ սպասուհի»:

Կիւրճեան կ'եզրակացնէ. «Ասիկա է՛ն թեթեւն է այն արկածներուն, որոնց զոհ կ'երթան այս տեսակ ազատամիտ աղջիկները»:

Կիւրճեան քաջատեղեակ է աղջիկներու ազատամտութեան, քանի որ «Մարտիկ Աղա» վէպին մէջ ալ լայն տեղ յատկացուցած է յեղափոխական եւ ազատամիտ Զարուհիին՝ նկարագրելով անոր նիստ ու կացը եւ ազատախոհութիւնը զանազան իրադարձութիւններու ընդմէջէն:

«Պոլսահայ Բարքեր» շարքէն են նաեւ «Յետ Մահու» եւ «Բանի Մը Ուժը» պատմուածքները: Առաջինը՝ աղքատ, պարզ ու խեղճուկ սափրիչ Ճանիկ էֆենտի Գրիգորեանի յուղարկաւորութեան առիթով գրուած տպաւորիչ պատմուածք մըն է: Կիրճեան կը նկարագրէ թէ որքան Ճանիկի քրոջ ամուսինը՝ Բեդրակ էֆենտի Մարգարեան յառաջանար առեւտուրի մէջ, այնքան կը բարձրանար ընկերային դասակարգութեան մէջ ու կը փոխէր իր բարքերը, յարաբերութիւնները, միջավայրը՝ աստիճանաբար վերելք ապրելով դէպի «բարձր դաս»: Կինն ալ, Ճանիկ էֆենտիի հարազատ քոյրը ըլլալով հանդերձ, կը սկսի իրմէ շատ վար տեսնել եղբայրը, հակառակ որ նոյն համեստ ծագումն ունէին: Բեդրակ էֆենտիի զզուանքը Ճանիկ էֆենտիէն ատելութեան կը վերածուի: Չհանդուրժելով անոնց վարմունքն ու ատելութեամբ լի արտայայտութիւնները, Ճանիկ կը հեռանայ քրոջ տունէն, կը տեղափոխուի Սկիւտարէն Պալաթ, մինչ «պատուաւոր վաճառական» Բեդրակ էֆենտի աւելի հաստատելով Սկիւտարէն կը փոխադրուի Գատըգիւղ:

Երկու տասնեակ տարի ետք, Ճանիկ էֆենտի իր մահէն առաջ միայն կը յայտնէ թէ ինք Ագապի Մարգարեանի եղբայրն է, ուստի եւ՝ աներձագը Գատըգիւղի ազգային ջոջերէն մէկուն՝ «հարուստ ու պատուաւոր վաճառական», իր քաղաքի խորհուրդի ատենապետ, Պատրիարքարանի մէկ քանի ժողովներու անդամ, պոլսահայութեան հանրածանօթ Բեդրակ էֆենտի Մարգարեանի: Հետեւաբար, այս պարագան նկատի ունենալով, Պալաթի քահանաները կը մերժեն հանգուցեալը ձրի թաղել: Ագապի խորամանկօրէն կը գտնէ այս բարդ դրութենէն ելքը: Ան ամուսնոյն վիզը նետուելով, կ'առաջարկէ եղբօր մարմինը Գատըգիւղ բերել տալ եւ թաղել, ըսելով. «Փառաւոր մեռել մը վերցնել տանք ... ողջութեանը բան մը չըրինք նէ, գոնէ մեռնելէն ետքը ընենք, չեմ ուզեր որ եղբայրս անանկ պանդուխտի պէս ղարիպ տէրտէրով մը թաղեն»:

Այս առաջարկութիւնը իրենց անուան նոր փայլ մը տալու առիթ նկատելով, տասը քահանայով, երեք վարդապետով եւ եպիսկոպոսով մը ազնուաշուք յուղարկաւորութիւն մը կը կատարեն իրենց չսիրած Ճանիկին, որուն մահուան տեղեկացած էին մամուլէն եւ Պալաթի եկեղեցիէն: «Թող չխաբուին մեռնողները: Յաճախ յուղարկաւորութիւնները աւելի ողջ մնացողներուն փառքը կը պատմեն քան մեռնողներունը», կը գրէ Կիրճեան:

«Բանի Մը Ուժը» պատմուածքին մէջ Կիրճեան կը նկարագրէ ոսկերիչ Գաբրիէլ աղային տունը այցելութեան եկած քանի մը շուկացիներ իրենց ընտանիքներով, որոնք ձմեռ իրիկուն մը փառաւոր կրակի մը շուրջ բոլորուած՝ բալի անուշի, բաժակ մը քոնեաքի եւ շագանակի հիւրասիրութենէն ետք, հաճելի ժամանակ անցուցած պահուն, կը խնդրեն որ Կիրճեան խօսակցութեան նիւթ մը ստեղծելով աշխուժացնէ հաւաքոյթին թուլցող խօսակցութիւնը՝ իբրեւ «գրող-կարդացող», «լրագիր եւ վէպ կարդացող» անձ: «Է հայտէ, բան մը զրուցէ *տէ* մտիկ ընենք», կ'ըսեն անոնք: Քիչ մը նազ ընելէ ետք, հազիւ «պատմելիքս լրագրի մը մէջ կարդացեր էի» ըսած, սենեակը տակնուվրայ կը դառնայ լրագիր բառին պատճառով, եւ որպէսզի միջադէպը փակէ, կը դառնայ Սուրբիկ հանըմին տղուն՝ Արշակին, ու կը հարցնէ. «Է, շապիկ պիտի հագնիս հարկաւ, անանկ չէ՞»:

Այս խօսքը պատճառ կը դառնայ որ առաջուան իրարանցումը աւելի սաստիկ կերպով կրկնուի, այս անգամ Սուրբիկի լացով: Երբ Կիւրճեան կը փափաքի պատճառը իմանալ, Սուրբիկ բորբոքած կը պոռթկայ. «*Ղազէթա*ն ալ գետնին տակը անցնի, *ղազէթաճի*ներն ալ, *ղազէթա* կարդացողներն ալ»: Ան կը պատճառաբանէ թէ իր մէկ հատիկ երջանկութիւնն ու խէնդը իր տղան՝ Արշակը տիրացու տեսնելն էր: Կիւրճեան կը դժուարանայ հասկնալ «ղազէթաճի»ներուն կապը Սուրբիկի երջանկութեան հետ: Գաբրիէլ աղա կը բացատրէ թէ լրագրող մը յօդուածի մը մէջ երեք-չորս անգամ տիրացու բառը գործածեր է խլէզ, անփորձ, տղայական իմաստով: Արշակը դիպուածով կարդալով յօդուածը, որոշեր է անգամ մըն ալ շապիկ չհագնիլ:

Սուրբիկ նորէն կը սկսի անիծել *ղազէթաճի*ները: Զգալով գործուած չարիքը, Կիւրճեան ելքը գտնելու համար, ի զարմանս ներկաներուն, կը համբուրէ Սուրբիկի ձեռքը ու կ'ըսէ. «Ինծի նայէ՛, մայրի՛կ, ես քեզի խօսք կու տամ որ տղադ այս Ծնունդին շապիկ պիտի հագնի»: Այս լսելով, Սուրբիկ օրհնութիւններու տարափ մը կը հեղեղէ: Արդարեւ, Կիւրճեան նոյն թերթին մէջ կը հրատարակէ յօդուած մը, ուր քննադատելով միւս յօդուածը եւ խարազանելով անոր հեղինակը, կը շեշտէ թէ տիրացուները յարգանքի ու հիացումի արժանի էակներ են: Անոր հետեւանքը կ'ըլլայ այն, որ Ծնունդի առտուն, Արշակ կը մասնակցի դպրաց դասին, որ ոչ միայն «նորէն կ'ողջունցնէ Սուրբիկ հանըմը, այլ կ'ուրախացնէ նաեւ բոլոր թաղը»: Կիւրճեան պատմուածքը կ'եզրափակէ, գրելով. «Գրիչէն եկած չարիքը գրիչով գացեր էր: Օրհնեա՜լ ըլլայ ուրեմն գրիչը»:

Այս նոյն հարցը արծարծուած է նաեւ Կիւրճեանի «Ինչ Ինչ Խօսքերու Ճակատագրական Դերը Մարդկային Կենցաղի Մէջ» զուարճապատումին մէջ, որ լոյս տեսած է Պոլսոյ «Ծաղիկ» շաբաթաթերթին 7 Փետրուար 1904ի թիւին մէջ Պետրոս Ագաթան ծածկանունին տակ: Հոն հեղինակը կը յիշատակէ խօսքերու վերաբերող երեք դէպքեր, որոնք անխուսափելի եւ վճռական գէշ դեր կը խաղան մարդու կեանքին մէջ: Առաջին դէպքը կը վերաբերի գեղեցիկ աղջկան մը իբրեւ գովեստ յայտնուած «Ծատ մ'ըսէք, *նազար*ի կու գայ» խօսքին: Իրօք, Նազար անունով հարուստ եւ ծայր աստիճան կոշտ ու տգեղ դրսեցիի մը հետ կ'ամուսնացնեն աղջիկը: Երկրորդ պարագային, ամէն ինչի մասին «թիւրիմացութիւն մըն է, եղբայր, եւ ոչ ուրիշ բան» ըսող մարդ մը ուրիշի մը փոխարէն կնակէն կը զարնեն եւ ան կը մեռնի թիւրիմացութեան մը պատճառով: Երրորդ դէպքը կը վերաբերի փարթամ պեխերու տէր հայու մը, որ «աս ասանկ չէ նէ... ես աս պեխերս կ'ածիլեմ» խօսքը միշտ կը վկայակոչէ: Հարուստ անգլիացիի մը քով լաւ պայմաններով կառապանութեան պաշտօնը ստանձնելու համար ան ստիպուած կ'ընդունի անգլիացիին պայմանն ու կ'ածիլէ իր պեխերը՝ ինքզինք զրկելով իր պեխերուն վրայ սովորական խօսքը կրկնելու հիմքէն: Սակայն բուռն յուզումներու ժամանակ, ան կը մոռնար եւ «պեխերս կ'ածիլեմ» ըսելով ներկաներուն քրքջալու առիթ կու տար:

«Նոր Լաթ» պատմուածքը լոյս տեսած է 1905ին Աղեքսանդրիոյ մէջ Կիւրճեանի եւ Թէքէեանի հիմնած ու հրատարակած «Շիրակ» հանդէսին մէջ: Հոն հեղինակը կը նկարագրէ երկաթագործ Մերկերը, որ տղայութենէն ի վեր նոր լաթ հագած չունէր: Իր բնակած գիւղին մէջ թաղային ընտրութիւններու խռովայոյզ շրջանին, Մերկեր իր ժողովրդականութեան պատճառով ձեռքէ ձեռք կը քաշուի հակառակորդ կուսակցութիւններէն: Կուսացկութիւններէն մէկուն պետին երթալով, կ'առաջարկէ ընտրական պայքարին իր աջակցութիւնը բերել «ձեռք մը նոր լաթ»ի փոխարէն: Անսովոր եռանդով կ'աշխատի ու կ'ապահովէ յաղթանակը իր կուսակցութեան, որուն ընտրելիներու ցանկը ամբողջովին կ'անցնի: Ընտրութիւններուն յաջորդ օրը, կուսակցութեան պետը իր խոստումը կը կատարէ եւ իր ուղարկած մարդը Մերկերը կօշկակարի, շապկավաճառի եւ հագուստեղէնի վաճառատուներ տանելով՝ ոտքէն մինչեւ գլուխ կը նորոգէ: Այդ իրիկուն ո՛չ մէկ սրճարան կամ գինետուն երթալէ ետք, յաջորդ օրը նոր լաթերուն մէջ տանջուած մարդու խղճալի երեւոյթով ան կը մտնէ սրճարան: Կիւրճեան կը պատմէ այս կերպարանափոխութեան առիթով ընկերներուն քրքջոտ ծաղրը ի տես ներսով դուրսով այս նոր մարդուն: «Բարով վայելես»ներու, «Նոր լաթ մը հագար *տէյի* հին բարեկամները մոռնալ կ'ըլլա՞յ», «Աստուած մեզի նոր թաղական խորհուրդ շատ տայ... քեզի ալ նոր լաթ» խօսքերու եւ ծիծաղներու տարափին հետեւանքով, Մերկեր յաջորդ իրիկուն ճիշդ սովորական ժամուն գինետուն կը մտնէ իր սկզբնական կերպարանքով ու հին լաթերով: «Ի՞նչ եղան նոր լաթերը» հարցումին ի պատասխան ան բուռ մը ստակ կը թափէ սեղանին վրայ, ըսելով. «Նա՛, նոր լաթերս... ծախեցի, տղա՛ք...: Հարուստ եմ աս գիշեր... ուզածնուդ չափ խմեցէ՛ք, կերէ՛ք»: Յանուն իր նախկին հանգստութեան եւ ազատութեան, ան կը վերադառնայ իր հին զգեստին, ընկերներուն եւ սովորութիւններուն: Այդ օրէն ի վեր Մերկեր հանգիստ կ'ապրի իր հին լաթերուն հետ:

Կիւրճեանի ստեղծագործութիւններուն արժէքը իրականութեան ճշմարիտ ու բազմերանգ վերարտադրութեան մէջ է: Ան կը ցուցաբերէ ոչ միայն զարմանալիօրէն սուր դիտողականութեամբ գրողի կարեւոր յատկանիշը, այլ նաեւ ճշգրիտ եւ պատկերաւոր ներկայացնելու ընդունակութիւնը, հարազատօրէն եւ բազմերանգ վերարտադրելու իր բնածին շնորհը, գրաւոր պատմելու ճարտար բարեմասնութիւնը եւ յատկապէս ճարտար գրելու վարպետութիւնը, ընթերցողը հրապուրելու եւ դիւթելու հմայքը, որովհետեւ լեզուն անարատ արեւմտահայերէն է՝ համեմուած պոլսահայ խօսակցական բարբառի դարձուածքներով:

Տիրան Չրաքեան, որ իբրեւ Կիւրճեանի մանկութեան ընկեր երկար տարիներու նամակագրական կապ ունեցած է «ճշմարիտ գրագէտ»ին հետ, յաճախ անկեղծօրէն անդրադարձած է անոր գրական ստեղծագործութիւններուն, յայտնելով իր հիացումը: Օրինակ, Սկիւտարէն 16/29 Նոյեմբեր 1912 թուակիր նամակի մը մէջ կը գրէ. «Դուն ինծի պէս *տէպիի*ի մը համբակութիւններն ու խակութիւնները ցուցադրած չես երբեք հրապարակի վրայ, եւ առաջին գրութեանդ (Զարմ. Սահակեան ստորագրութեամբ) առթիւ էր որ Եղիա Տէմիրճիպաշեանը Ժընեւի մէջ ըսաւ ինծի թէ արդէն իբրեւ վարպետ մը կը ներկայանայիր: Բախտ ունեցայ *Նոր Կեանք*երուն մէջ *Մարտիկ Աղադ* կարդալու, եւ կը վկայեմ թէ հազիւ քիչ մը նուազ կ'արժէ քան ստորագրութիւնդ կրող մէկ վերջին ոեւէ երկդ, եւ կարծեմ թէ չկայ մեր մէջ ճշմարիտ կարողութեան տէր մէկը որուն գրական կեանքը զերծ ըլլայ, քուկինիդ պէս, իր *զարգացման* պատմութիւնը պարզած ըլլալու տկարութենէն: Գերագոյն հաճոյք մըն էր որ հոստեղի *Ժամանակ* թերթին մէջ Երուանդ Օտեանի իբր թերթօն հրատարակած *Տասներկու Տարի Պոլսէն Դուրսը* տեսայ՝ թէ զքեզ կը յիշէ ներբողալից կերպերով,- հազուագիւտ բան Երուանդ Օտեանի գրչին տակ,- *Մարտիկ Աղայ*իդ յառաջ բերած աղմուկին իրարանցումին պատմութեանը միջոցին, եւ ուրիշ անգամ, *Ազատ Բեմ* թերթին մէջ հրատարակած յօդուածներուդ առթիւ, որոնցմով *արամտութեան հեղեղներ* եւ թափեր (գրեթէ Օտեանին բառերն են ասոնք) թերթին սիւնակներուն մէջ: Վահանէն, որ ունի եղեր թերթին հաւաքածոն, այս օրերս պիտի առնեմ կարդալու համար գրածներդ...»:[87]

Պոլսահայ կեանքի թեմայով գրուած գործերէն է «Ես Ձեզի Չըսի՞» պատմուածքը, ուր յատկապէս ծաղրի ու ծանակի նիւթ դարձած է կանացի սնապարծութիւնը: Հոն Կիւրճեան կը թուէ բազմատեսակ սնապարծներ, որոնց մէջ ամենէն աւելի աչքառու է Պոլսոյ ասիական եզերքի պզտիկ գիւղերէն մէկուն մէջ ապրող վաթսունը անց այրի կին մը՝ Տիկին Փառանձեմ, որ տարիներ առաջ իր գուշակութիւններուն եւ հնարամտութեան շնորհիւ, ինչպէս նաեւ գիւղացիներու դիւրահաւանութեան պատճառով գիւղին մէջ «գուշակող» հռչակուած էր: Սակայն կային նաեւ անձեր, որոնք կը հեգնէին իր մարգարէական յաւակնութիւնները՝ գլխաւորութեամբ ունեւոր վաճառականի մը կնոջ՝ Տիկին Գոհարիկի, որ կը ջղագրգռուէր ամէն անգամ որ Փառանձեմ իր յանկերգը կրկնէր. «Ես ձեզի չըսի՞... ես ըսած չէի՞ ձեզի... չէ՞ք յիշեր...»: Օր մըն ալ, անձ մը հազիւ յայտնած թէ Սիմոնեան մը իր կինը ձգեր է՝ երբ տանտիրուհին կը գոռայ. «Ես ձեզի չըսի՞», Տիկին Գոհարիկ այլեւս չհանդուրժելով, վճռականապէս կը ժխտէ ու գրպանէն տետրակ մը հանելով կը կարդայ Փառանձեմի չիրականացած գուշակութիւններու իր գրառած ցանկը՝ թուականներով: Տանտիրուհին չկրնալով համբերել, ոտքի կ'ելլէ եւ կը պոռայ. «Ես ձեզի չըսի՞ որ աս կնիկը գէշ կնիկ մըն է, չար, նախանձոտ... ըսէ՛ք, ըսած չե՞մ...»: Այդ օրէն ի վեր, կուրքը սկսաւ իր պատուանդանէն վար իջնել, կ'եզրափակէ Կիւրճեան:

Կարելի չէ առանց յուզումի կարդալ ոսկերիչ Գրիգոր աղայի եւ իր որդիին՝ դպրոցական Վահրամի մասին գրուած կարճ, սակայն սրտառուչ պատմուածքը: Յանկարծական ձերբակալութիւններու, խուզարկութիւններու եւ աքսորներու օրերուն, երբ Րաֆֆիի, Խրիմեան Հայրիկի, Խորէն Նար-Պէյի եւ ուրիշ ազգասէր հեղինակներու գիրքերը կամ նոյնիսկ երգարանները «վտանգաւոր» կը նկատուէին, Գրիգոր աղա իր գրադարանին որոշ գիրքերուն հետ կ'ուզէ այրել նաեւ իր որդիին դպրոցական գիրքերէն «ազգային պատմութեան համառօտ դասագիրք մը»: Սակայն շատ կը զարմանայ երբ ի գին սրտաճմլիկ տեսարաններու, լացի ու կոծի, 15 օրուան ժամկէտին վրայ մէկ գիշեր աւելցնելէ ետք ալ, յաջորդ առաւօտ Վահրամ ուրախ եւ յաղթական երեւոյթով գիրքը կը յանձնէ ապշահար հօրը՝ «Ա՛ռ հայրիկ... հիմա կրնաս այրել...» ըսելով: Հօրը համար չլուսաբանուած գաղտնիքը բացայայտելու նպատակով երախային ուղղուած հարցը կը պարզուի, երբ Կիւրճեան կը գրէ. «Գիրքը ամբողջ գո՛ց սորվեցայ, ըսաւ Վահրամ հատիկ հատիկ շեշտելով իւրաքանչիւր վանկը: Գիշերը չքնացայ, կարդացի»: Կիւրճեան «Անջնջելի Մատեանը» վերնագիրն է դրած այս պատմուածքին ո՛չ միայն անոր համար որ «մէջը անանկ աղուոր բաներ, անանկ հրաշալի պատմութիւններ» պարունակող դասագիրքը այրելով հանդերձ անոր բովանդակութիւնը անջնջելի կը մնայ փոքրիկ տղուն ուղեղին մէջ, այլ նաեւ անոր համար որ հեղինակը կ'ուզէ շեշտել թէ հայ ժողովուրդի պատմութիւնն ընդհանրապէս անջնջելի ու յաւերժական է իր կերտողին՝ հայ ժողովուրդին պէս: Այս պատմուածքին փոքրիկ հերոսը իր ազգասիրութեամբ եւ հայրենասիրութեամբ դուրս կու գայ իր նեղ ազգային վիճակէն եւ կը նուաճէ համազգային լայն ընդգրկում: Ուստի, շատ յարմար կը գտնենք որ այս պատմուածքը տեղ գտնէ դասագիրքերու մէջ՝ հայ պատանիներու մէջ զօրացնելու համար ազգասիրութիւնն ու հայրենասիրութիւնը:

Վահան Թէքէեան ալ անդրադարձած է Թուրքիոյ մէջ բռնակալական ու բարբարոսական հալածանքներու եւ ճնշումներու տարիներուն հայ տուներու մէջ գտնուող հայերէն գիրքերու «վտանգ»ին: Զօպանեանի Փարիզ հրատարակուող «Անահիտ» գրական, գեղարուեստական, հասարակական հանդէսի Բ. տարուան 1900 թուականի 9, 10, 11 թիւերուն մէջ լոյս տեսած «Խարոյկը» պատմուածքին մէջ[88] Թէքէեան կը նկարագրէ թէ 1894ի եւ 1895ի դէպքերէն ետք Պոլսոյ մէջ տունը հայերէն գիրք ունենալը ամէնօրեայ մտատանջութեան պատճառ էր: Պատումածքին մէջ, ընտանիքին հայ երիտասարդը իր մօրը պահանջով գիրքերը թիթեղեայ տուփերու մէջ դրած՝

նախ առաստաղի գերաններուն մէջ կը պահէ. ապա, աւելի ապահով ըլլալու համար, զանոնք կը թաղէ պարտէզի մանուշակներու ածուին մօտ եւ յետոյ հոնկէ կը տեղափոխէ նախկին տեղը: Իսկ երբ կը լսէ որ նախորդ գիշեր թուրք ոստիկանները խուզարկեր էին հարեւան տունը եւ ամենափոքրիկ թուղթի կտորն իսկ տարած էին տան երիտասարդին հետ, ի վերջոյ խոհանոցի ծխնելոյզին մէջ կրակ վառելով մէկիկ մէկիկ կ'այրէ զանոնք:

Կիրճեանին յաջողագոյն արձակ ստեղծագործութիւններէն է «Սուտը Իրա՝ Խենդը Խելօք» վիպակը, որ լոյս տեսած է Զմիւռնիոյ «Արեւելեան Մամուլ» շաբաթաթերթին 1903 թուականի Փետրուարի 22-էն 29 Մարտի թիւերուն մէջ Պետրոս Ագաթան ծածկանունով: Հայ կեանքը պատկերող այս գլուխ գործոց վիպակին մէջ սքանչելիօրէն նկարագրուած է Վոսփորի եւրոպական եզերքի գիւղերէն մէկը, ուր կը լեցուին ամառը օդափոխութեան եկող հայ ընտանիքներ: Այդ գիւղը ծնած եւ հոն մեծցած է նաեւ 20-25 տարեկան երեւցող, տասներկու տարեկանէն որբացած խենդ բայց բարի ու աշխատասէր Նասիպը, որ բոլորին կ'օգնէ փայտ կոտրելու, տախտակամած սրբելու, մաքրելու, հորէն ջուր քաշելու եւ այլ գործերու մէջ, փոխարէնը ուտելիք, դրամ, հագուստ առնելով ապրուստը ապահովելով եւ հնչուն դրամները պահելով: Ան, միաժամանակ, գիւղին բնակիչներն ու եկուոր ընտանիքները զուարճացնող միմոսն է՝ իր զաւեշտական ներկայացումներով, կատակներով ու ծամածռութիւններով, «թօհաֆ» ու երկդիմի պատասխաններով: Իր անխնամ հագուածքին պէս կատակերգական է իր հագուստ կապուստը, որուն վսեմագոյն կէտը իր «ուշխուռ»ն էր, պատմական անձի մը չափ հռչակաւոր՝ գիւղին մէջ եւ նոյնիսկ շրջաններէ:

Վիպակին երկրորդ մասին մէջ Կիրճեան կը նկարագրէ Նասիպին տարիներէ ի վեր սիրահարած ըլլալը: Կը պարզուի որ ա՛ն ալ սիրտ մը կը կրէ, գիտէ սիրել, եւ սիրահարած է ձկնորս Պետրոսի աղջկան՝ Հօռօփիկին, որուն հետ մանկութենէն միասին մեծցած է գիւղին մէջ: Այս երկու խոնարհ ու խեղճ արարածներուն բարութեամբ համակուած սէրը աղջկան հօր ընդդիմութեան կը հանդիպի ի զարմանս Նասիպի, որ տարակոյս չունէր թէ պիտի յաջողի: Երրորդ մասին մէջ Կիրճեան կը գրէ թէ յաջորդ ամրան գիւղը նորէն կը լեցուի օդափոխութեան եկողներով, որոնք չեն հաւատար Նասիպի եւ Հօռօփիկի խօսքերուն, թէ մէկը ինքզինք ծովը նետելով պիտի սպաննէ, իսկ միւսը ինքզինք լուցկիով պիտի վառէ:

Նասիպի աղաչանքները մէկ քանի աղաներու եւ հանըմներու,- որ երթան եւ ձկնորսին մօտ բարեխօսեն իրեն համար,- անհետեւանք մնալով, կը պատահի անկարելի ու անհաւատալի թուացող դէպքը.- Նասիպ ծով կը նետուի իր կեանքին վերջ տալու համար: Բարեբախտաբար քանի մը ձկնորսներ նաւակով անցնելու ժամանակ կ'ազատեն զինք: Միմոսի կերպարանքով Նասիպին պէս արարածի մը նման արարքը անըսպասելի վերջաբան մըն էր գիւղին բոլոր եկուորներուն համար, որոնք զաւեշտական արտաքինին տակ չէին նկատեր անոր հոգեկան խորունկ զգայնութիւնն ու լրջութիւնը: Անոր վրայ խնդացողները ապշահար կը մնան կատարուած արարքին մեծութեան առջեւ. ոմանք նոյնիսկ կու լան եւ խղճի խայթ կը զգան իրենց անտարբեր եւ անկարեկիր վերաբերումին համար:

Երկու ամիս ետք, գիւղին եկեղեցիին զանգակը կը ղօղանջէ ու կը հռչակէ Նասիպ Գրիգորեանի ամուսնութիւնը ընդ օրիորդ Հռիփսիմէ Պետրոսեանի, որովհետեւ բնիկ գիւղացիները եւ հանգստանալու եկողները կը յաջողին համոզել աղջկան հայրը՝ խոստանալով միանձնական ջանքերով պատրաստել աղջկան օժիտը, հոգալ հարսանիքին ծախսերը եւ պզտիկ դրամագլուխով փերեզակի խանութ մըն ալ յանձնել Նասիպին:

Նասիպի ոդիսականին նուիրուած այս ստեղծագործութիւնը գրական հիանալի գործ մըն է իր կուռ կառուցուածքով, յղկուած ոճով, պարզ ու խնամուած լեզուով՝ համեմուած պոլսահայ խօսակցութեան տիպական դարձուածքներով: Գիւղին պարկեշտ ու խոնարհ մարդիկը Կիւրճեանի ուշադրութեան առարկայ դարձած են իրենց իսկական գիծերով ու հարազատ յատկանիշներով: Հեղինակը նկարագրած է անոնց կենցաղն ու բարքերը, խոհերն ու իտէալները:

Ինչպէս Կիւրճեանի միւս արձակ ստեղծագործութիւնները, այս վիպակն ալ կը կարդացուի մեծ հետաքրքրութեամբ եւ յափշտակութեամբ, ընթերցողին պարգեւելով հոգեկան վայելք եւ մտային գոհունակութիւն: Ընթերցողը կը ծանօթանայ ժողովուրդի հասարակ մարդոց, որոնք կը վեհանան իրենց մարդկային առաքինութիւններով, դրական յատկանիշներով ու ազնիւ բարեգործութիւններով:

Այս եզակի ստեղծագործութիւնը կ'արժանանայ մեծ ընդունելութեան եւ հեղինակին անունն ու փառքը կ'արձանագրէ հայ մամուլին մէջ:

Գրականագէտ Յովհաննէս Գազանճեան 1904ի սեմին իր «Թրքահայ Գրականութիւնը 1903ին» տարեկան քրոնիկի համարատուութեան մէջ,[89] յետադարձ ակնար մը նետելով անցնող տարուան գրական դէպքերուն վրայ, «Մասիս»ի ընթերցողներուն կը ներկայացնէ իր տպաւորութիւնները: Յիշատակելէ ետք քանի մը նորավէպեր, ան կը գրէ. «Նորավէպէն անցնելով վիպակին ու վէպին՝ նշանակելի է Քասիմի «Կնճռոտ Հանգոյց»ը, Պետրոս Ադամեանի «Սուտը Իրաւ՝ Խենդը Խելօք» վիպակը...»:

Տիրան Չրաքեան Նասիպի արկածալից կեանքին պատմութիւնը կարդալէ վերջ, Մալկարայէն Աղեքսանդրիա Կիւրճեանին ուղղուած 13/26 Ապրիլ 1908 թուակիր նամակով կ'արտայայտէ իր լրջախոհ եւ դրուատալից կարծիքը. «Ինծի կ'ըսես թէ *Ներաշխարհ*ին պէս գործ ունեցած չենք. է՞հ, ուրեմն, նոյնքան ճիշդ է թէ ոչ *Անունին Գիշերը*ին պէս ոչ ալ *Նասիպ*ին պէս գործեր ունեցած ենք. այդ սեռը չկար. ոչ այդքան ազգասիրութիւն ունեցած են մեր տխմար երգերը, ոչ այդքան ուշադիր դիտողութիւն՝ մեր «իրապաշտ»ները, ոչ ալ իրականութեանց ռամկագոյններուն բանաստեղծութիւնը, խորութիւնը, կարելի է ըսել գիտականութիւնը զգացած են մեր «ժողովրդականները»...»: Ինտրա այնքան կը զգացուի պատմուածքին ընթերցումէն, որ կը գրէ. «Բայց ինչ գեղեցիկ էր: Զայն կը կարդայի կոր (խօսքս վերջաբանին մասին է) դասարանին մէջ: Գրեթէ հապճեպով, այնպէս որ զգացած յուզումէս վայրկեաններուն վրայէն ոստումներ ընելով կարդացի Նասիպին հարսնիքը, որ ուրիշ նպաստաւոր պահու մը մէջ ապահովապէս պիտի թրջէր աչքերս»:

Գրականօրէն շատ շահեկան ուրիշ նամակի մը մէջ Չրաքեան կը գրէ. «Նասիպը կարդացի... մարդոց շատը լաւագոյն գործեր պիտի արտադրէր՝ վարպետի գործեր, եթէ գիտնար իւրաքանչիւրը՝ թէ ինչի կարող է, եթէ պարզապէս ինքզինքը ճանչնար: Մեր գրողներուն մէջ քիչեր կան, որ գիտեն ինքզինքնին. օրինակի համար Պէրպէրեանը, Աղեքսանդր Փանոսեանը, Ալփիարը, դուն: Այս գերազանց յատկութիւնը բաւական է տաղանդաւոր գրողի մը, որպէսզի վարպետի գործեր շինէ: Բարեբախտաբար ինքզինքնուն անտեղեակ անմիտները շատ են, եւ վարպետներուն թիւը կը սահմանափակեն ու կը պահծացնեն: Ինչպէս ամէն մարդու՝ Ծանիր Զքեզը օրէնք ըլլալու էր նաեւ գրողներուն: Ինքզինքնին չճանչցող «գրագէտ»ներուն ափեղցփեղ գործերէն կ'երեւայ թէ որքան թերի մշակութեան ու իրականութեան *Սանսի*, դիտողութեան պակասի մը արդիւնք է ինքնագիտութիւնը,- կամ եթէ կ'ուզես, անինքնագիտութիւնը: Արդ անոնցմէ չես դուն. դուն քենէ դուրս բան չես ըներ կոր ցարդ հրատարակածներուդ ամենամեծ մասին մէջ»:

Այնուհետեւ կը շարունակէ. «*Անունին Գիշերը*էն մինչեւ *Սուտը Իրաւ՝ Խենդը Խելօքը* այնքան ճշմարտութիւն կայ պատմածներուդ ու գրականութեանդ մէջ՝ որ իրաւունք ունիս ըլլալու անոնցմէ որ այնքան վարպետ են որքան իրենց եսին բնոյթին հաստատապէս գիտակից, այսինքն, որոնք իրենց սեռերուն վարպետներն են պարզապէս: Որքան յայտնի է թէ մեր գործին կատարելութեանը պայմանն է գիտնալ թէ ինչ գործի կարող ենք: Արդ, Նասիպիդ պատմութիւնը սքանչելի էր, *Անունին Գիշերը*ին պէս, (թէեւ անիկա գերազանց գործ է սա տեսակէտով որ աւելի ճոխ ուսումնասիրութիւն, աւելի գրականութիւն, աւելի կեանք ունի), եւ սա առաւելութիւնն ալ ունէր որ (ինչ որ պզտիկ առաւելութիւն մը չէ՝ ընդհանրապէս աւետիսի մը պէս հռչակելի յատկութիւն մը) վէպն ու *իրականութիւնը*, ստեղծումն ու *պատմութիւնը*, պարզապէս կեդծիքն ու ճշմարտութիւնը կը հաշտեցնէր, կը միատարրէր՝ կարծես սա կանոնը օրինագրելով՝ թէ *վէպ բառը ձեւի անուն մը մնալու է լոկ*, ոչ թէ արուեստի առարկան, թէ *պէտք է իրականութիւնը ստեղծել*: Անշուշտ *Անունին Գիշերը*ն ալ ունէր վերջին գործիդ այդ յատկութիւնը, բայց անիկա վէպի երեւոյթ չունէր, ասիկա ունի, եւ կը ցուցնէ պատմուած բանին վէպութեան սահմանը, այսինքն թէ ինչպէս վէպը պէտք է իրականութեան մէկ արուեստադրական *ֆրիմը*[90] կազմէ»:

Կիրճեան դարձեալ պոլսահայ կեանքէն քաղած է «Տրդատ Եւ Տաճատ» պատմուածքին նիւթը, որ ժողովրդական պատմութիւն մըն է ձկնորս Տրդատի եւ բանջարավաճառ Տաճատի թշնամութեան մասին. Ներհակութիւն մը, որ ծագում առած է Նոյեմզարի հանդէպ երկուքին տածած սէրէն եւ Նոյեմզարի՝ երկուքին ալ տուած սիրոյ երաշխիքէն: Այդ թշնամանքը տեսակ մը յոխորտանք եւ պոռոտախօսութիւն էր, որ ամէնօրեայ մեծբանութիւններով ու գոռոզութիւններով, նախատինքներով եւ աճաբեկիչ խօսքերով, սպառնալիքներով ու մարտահրաւէրներով լեցուն ըլլալով հանդերձ, հակառակորդները իրենց թաղամասերէն դուրս գալով չէին փորձեր հաշիւը կտրուկ միջոցներով փակել: Այդ պայքարը իրականութեան մէջ բանակռիւ մըն էր՝ ուրիշներու միջոցով հաղորդուած: Տեսնելով որ կռիւը վերջ չունի, Նոյեմզար կ'ամուսնանայ երրորդ անձի մը հետ: Ասով հանդերձ, Տրդատի ու Տաճատի թշնամանքը կը շարունակուի երեսուն տարի այսպիսի նախադասութիւններով.-

«Է, ըսի՞ր նայինք երէկ իրիկուն ըսածս»:

«Է՜, ի՞նչ ըսաւ նայինք»:

«Դուն գնա՛, իրեն ըսէ՛ որ»:

Իսկ երբ գիշեր մըն ալ Տաճատ կը մեռնի, յաջորդ օր Տրդատ սեւեր հագած, երեսուն տարուան մէջ առաջին անգամ ըլլալով Սէլամսըզէն Ենիմահալլէ կ'երթայ ու կը մասնակցի յուղարկաւորութեան, նոյնիսկ մինչեւ գերեզմանատուն կ'երթայ սգակիր ազգականի մը պէս, դագաղը փոսը իջեցուելէ առաջ բանալ կու տայ, մեռելը կը պագնէ եւ ականջին բաներ մը կը փսփսայ՝ ի զարմանս բոլոր ներկաներուն, որոնք կարգով ցաւակցութիւն կը յայտնեն իրեն իբրեւ հարազատ սգակիրի:

Սկիւտարի ծերունիներուն պատմած այս հին պատմութիւնը Կիրճեան գրականացուցած է սքանչելիօրէն, ստեղծելով հոգեբանական կերպարներ եւ պատմութեան տալով նոր բովանդակութիւն ու հիմայք: Ուշագրաւ են հեղինակին ստեղծագործական վարպետութիւնը, ժողովրդական պարզ գրելաոճը եւ անսայթաք սահուն լեզուն:

Շատ սիրելով պատմուածքի ժանրը, Կիրճեան գրած է բազմաթիւ պատմուածքներ, որոնց մէջ միշտ հանդէս եկած է իբրեւ իրապաշտ գրող, հաւատարիմ մնալով այն սկզբունքին՝ թէ գրողը միշտ պէտք է ըլլայ իր ժամանակին եւ ապրած տարիներուն վստահելի ականատեսը, ականջալուրը, գրաւոր ապացոյցը եւ կենդանի վկան:

Կիրճեանի դիտողունակութիւնը կարեւոր ազդակ մըն է իր գործերուն յաջողութեան: Ան կը նկատէ այնպիսի մանրուքներ, որոնք դուրս կը մնան յաճախ ուրիշներու տեսադաշտէն:

Կասկածէ վեր է Կիրճեանի իսկական տաղանդով օժտուած անհատականութիւն մը ըլլալը, քանի որ գիտէ իրայատուկ նկարագրութեամբ պատկերել տարբեր բնաւորութիւններու, խառնուածքներու եւ հոգեբանութիւններու տէր մարդիկ՝ տարբեր միջավայրերու եւ հանգամանքներու մէջ. այս բոլորին միացնելով դիւրութեամբ շարադրելու ձիրք մը:

Օրինակ, «Միրիճանը»[91] պատմուածքին մէջ Կիւրճեան կը նկարագրէ մին սրճարանի այն տիպարներէն, որոնք «կը խլեն զքեզ մտածումէդ, ընթերցումէդ, մտերիմի մը հետ շահեկան խօսակցութենէդ», թեթեւ եւ անգոյն խօսքերով գլուխ ցաւցնելով, աստիճանաբար համբերութիւն հատցնելով եւ շուրջիններն քաղաքավարութեան զոհ դարձնելով՝ զանոնք ժամավաճառ ընելով:

«Անդրաշխարհեան Պատմութիւն»[92] զուարճապատում պատմուածքին մէջ ալ ան սրամտօրէն կը հեգնէ Նիկողոս աղան, որ ամբողջ կեանքը թաղականի, հոգաբարձուի, քահանայի խնդիրներով անցուցած՝ մահանալէ ետք Արքայութեան դուռը բաց գտնելով՝ ներս կը մտնէ անկէ: Պետրոս Առաքեալ նկատելով անծանօթ մարդ մը, ամէն կերպ կ՚աշխատի դուրս հանել զինք՝ համոզելով, սպառնալով, աղաչելով, բայց ի զուր: Յանկարծ հանճարեղ գաղափար մը կը փայլատակէ Առաքեալին ուղեղին մէջ: Երթալով հրեշտակներու պետին քով, կ՚առաջարկէ որ քանի մը հարիւր հրեշտակ հաւաքուին Արքայութենէն դուրս եւ մեծ աղմուկով խօսին ու խնդան, իսկ ինք կը վերադառնայ Նիկողոս աղային քով: Յանկարծ ահագին վայնասուն մը կը բրդի դուրսէն: Նիկողոս աղայի զարմացական հարցումին պատասխանելով, Պետրոս Առաքեալ կ՚ըսէ. «Նորէն թաղականի կռիւ ըլլալու է, եա՛ ժամկոչին համար է, եա՛ աւագերէցին»:

Լսելով որ Արքայութեան մէջ արգիլուած է թաղականի կռիւ ընել, այդ կռիւը յետ մահու ալ շարունակելու համար, հոգ չէ թէ դրախտէն դուրս, դուռը կը բանայ ու դրախտէն դուրս կ՚ելլէ, ըսելով. «Քեզի ըլլայ Արքայութիւնդ... բարով վայելես... աչք չունիմ. թաղական, հոգաբարձու չըլլալէն ետքը Արքայութիւնդ քանի՞ փարայի կ՚առնեմ, առաջուընէ չըսէի՞ր, մարդ Աստուծոյ»:

Կիւրճեանի գեղեցիկ պատմուածքներէն է նաեւ «Հրաշքի Մը Պատմութիւնը», որուն մէջ Գաբրիէլ աղա Տէր Սարգիսեան կ՚ուրանայ իր պարտքը, եւ քանի որ ո՛չ գրաւոր, ո՛չ ալ կենդանի վկայութիւն կար, երդումի կը ձգուի խնդիրը եւ խնդրոյ առարկայ կողմերը եկեղեցի երթալով, քահանային ներկայութեան Աւետարանին վրայ կը դնեն իրենց ձեռքերը, մէկը ըսելով «Եթէ այս դրամը առած եմ եւ կ՚ուրանամ կոր, տասնհինգ օր չանցած՝ յանկարծամահ ըլլա՛մ», իսկ միւսը ըսելով. «Եթէ այս դրամը փոխ տուած չեմ եւ անիրաւաբար կը պահանջեմ կոր՝ տասնհինգ օր չանցած, յանկարծամահ ըլլա՛մ»: Ճիշդ տասնհինգ օր ետք Գաբրիէլ աղայի հակառակորդը կաթուածահար կ՚ըլլայ, մինչ Գաբրիէլի համբաւը կ՚աւելնայ՝ զինք հաւցնելով սուրբի բարձունքը: Երկար ժամանակ ետք, Գաբրիէլ աղա քահանայ կ՚ուզէ «խոստովանանքի համար»: Քահանան կ՚այլայլի լսելով որ քառասուն տարի առաջուան դէպքէն ետք կաթուածահար մահացած անոր հակառակորդը ճշմարտութիւնը ըսած էր, մինչ իր գործերուն գէշ վիճակին հետեւանքով չսնանկանալու համար Գաբրիէլ աղա դիմած էր այդ յանդուգն սուտ երդումին, որ հետագային դարմանելու համար ինքզինք բարեգործութեան տուած էր «հարիւրապատիկ վերադարձնելով աղքատներուն ինչ որ անիրաւաբար կորզած էր տարաբախտ հանգուցեալէն»:

Զգայացունց եւ տպաւորիչ է այս պատմուածքը, ուր կերպարները ներկայացուած են իրենց ամբողջ էութեամբ եւ հոգեկան ապրումներով:

«Պարոն Քաղաքագէտը» ստեղծագործութիւնը եւս յաջող գործ մըն է: Պատմուածքին հերոսը՝ Սողոմոն, անգործ ըլլալով, ամէն օր սրճարան կը յաճախէ քաղաքական կնճռոտ հարցեր քննարկելու, լրագիրներու մէջ թաղուելու, խորհասուզուելու եւ կամ՝ ունկնդիրներով շրջապատուելու, քաղաքականութիւն ընելու համար: Կիրճեան իր ազնուազարմ ծաղրով կը քննադատէ եւրոպական ընդարձակ օրաթերթերը ծայրէ ծայր կարդացող եւ գոց սորվող, քաղաքականութիւն քննարկող, երեք կամ չորս տողնոց հեռագրէ մը երկու ժամուան խօսելիք նիւթ գտնող, հմուտ դիւանագէտի յաւակնութիւններով երգիծական կերպարը: Սողոմոն, որ պատերազմ չեղած ժամանակ ալ չէր դադրեր քաղաքագէտի լրատուական եւ մեկնաբանական գրոյցներ վարելու պաշտօնէն, պատերազմի ընթացքին գլուխ քերելու ժամանակ չէր ունենար: Ինք ունկնդիր փնտռելու, գտնելու կամ որսալու փոխարէն, ունկնդիրները իրմէ կը խնդրեն օրուան նորութիւնները յայտնել ու պարզաբանել, ամբողջ օրը սրճարանէ սրճարան քաղաքականութիւն վերլուծել, մեծ պետութիւններու գործունէութիւնները գնահատել կամ քննադատել, առանց երբեք մոռնալու ամէն հարցի մէջ անգլիացիի մատ տեսնելը, որ ըստ իրեն «տիեզերական առանցքն է, որուն վրայ կը դառնայ աշխարհիս քաղաքականութիւնը, Ասիայէն Եւրոպա, Ափրիկէէն Ամերիկա»:

Ցատկանշական է նաեւ «Կաղանդչէք» պատմուածքը, զոր Կիրճեան գրած է 1909ին: Ընդամէնը երեք էջերէ բաղկացած այս պատմուածքը չափազանց խտացուած, կուռ ոճով շարադրուած եւ շատ յուզիչ ու սրտաճմլիկ ստեղծագործութիւն մըն է՝ վրդովիչ հոգեվիճակներու նկարագրութիւններով: Հեղինակը միաժամանակ կը ներկայացնէ հակատիպ երկու տարբեր կեանքերու վիճակը՝ չքաւոր աղքատութիւնը եւ ճոխ հարստութիւնը, խեղճուկրակ թշուառութիւնն ու զեխակենցաղ շռայլութիւնը, տխրութիւնն ու հրճուանքը: Կմախակերպ բարակ մարմնով, հին ու մին պատռուած զգեստներով որբ աղջիկը՝ Մարիամ, Կաղանդի օրը երեկոյեան կը բախէ քիչ մը վեր ապրող տօնախմբութեամբ, ուրախ քրքիջներով, բարձրաձայն ծիծաղով եւ երջանկութեամբ լի իրեն ծանօթ ընտանիքի տան դուռը: Սակայն տաք սենեակի պաղ ընդունելութենէն ցաւատանջ էակը պահ մը կը զգաստանայ ամէնուրեք ցրուած բազմաթիւ նուէրները, խաղալիքները եւ ներկաներուն տօնական հագուստ-կապուստը տեսնելով: Ծտապելով դուրս գալու ընթացքին իր բզքտուած շալով կերպով մը գլուխը ծածկելը տեսնելով, տանտիրուհին կէս հին-կէս նոր շալ մը կը հանէ դարակէն ու կ'ըսէ. «Ա՛ռ, Մարիամ, աս ալ իմ կաղանդչէքս ըլլա՛յ քեզի»: Տեսնելով շալին հնութիւնը ի հակադրութիւն չորս կողմը լեցուած անթիւ նոր ու փայլփլուն խաղալիքներուն, Մարիամ կը հրաժարի «Ծնորհակալ եմ, չեմ ուզեր, ձեզի պահեցէ՛ք» ըսելով, կը հեռանայ: Տանտիրուհին եւ իր ամուսինը կը սկսին փիլիսոփայել աղքատներու հպարտութեան վրայ, առանց խղճի խայթ զգալու, կարծրասիրտ երջանկութեամբ, հաւատացած ըլլալով որ աղքատներուն ներելի չէ հպարտութեամբ նուէր մերժելը: Անոնք հաշուի չեն առներ իրենց անվայել վերաբերումը՝ հին եւ գործածուած շալը նուիրելու անյարմարութիւնն ու անպատշաճութիւնը: Ծատ յուզիչ եւ սրտաշարժ է այս պատմուածքը եւ, միաժամանակ, արգահատելի ու խղճալի, որովհետեւ ընթերցողը կաղանդչէքը վերնագրին տակ կ'ակնկալէ տարբեր բան եւ ոչ թէ ունեւոր մարդոց անգութ, անտարբեր, անմարդկային վերաբերումը աղքատ, չունեւոր ու որբ հայ աղջնակի մը հանդէպ, որ շքեղ, փայլուն ու թանկարժէք խաղալիքները տեսնելէ ետք բնականաբար կը մերժէ ընդունիլ հին ու գործածուած շալ մը որպէս կաղանդչէք:

* * *

Կիւրճեանի գրչին արգասիքն են նաեւ գրական պատկերներ, ինչպէս՝ «Աղբիւրը», «Փախած Ձիեր», «Սրճարանը» եւայլն, որոնք մեր տպաւորապաշտ գործերու լաւագոյններու շարքին կարելի է դասել: Ուշագրաւ է որ յաճախ աննշան բաներէ ներշնչուելով՝ գրողը շնորհիւ իր բանաստեղծական հոգիին եւ արթուն զգայնութեան կրցած է գրականացնել պատկերներ, որոնք իրենց փիլիսոփայականութեամբ եւ հոգեբանութեամբ դուրս կու գան լոկ անհատական, նեղ մարդկային կամ ազգային պարունակէն եւ կ'անցնին ընդհանրական, համամարդկային ստեղծագործութիւններու շարքը՝ նուաճելով համաշխարհային գրականութեան բարձունքները:

Կիւրճեան «Աղբիւրը» պատկերը գրած է ներշնչուելով իր մտերիմ ընկերոջ՝ Տիրան Չրաքեանի մէկ գեղեցիկ գծագրութենէն, որ բանաստեղծը իրեն նուիրած է 1898ին: Նկարը պատկերած է հոյակապ աղբիւր մը, մանկամարդուհի մը, որ ջուրի ամանը կը կարկառէ ծարաւ ու յոգնած ծերունիի մը՝ հեռուէն երեւացող երկնասլաց նոճիներու ենթախորքին վրայ: Կիւրճեան այդ նկարը անմահացուցած է իր գրական պատկերին մէջ, առանձնապէս ընդգծելով աղջկան կենսաւէտ երիտասարդութիւնը եւ կորաքամակ ծերունիին դանդաղաքայլ ընթացքը դէպի թաւուտքը նոճիներու, որոնց շուքին տակ օր մը պիտի տարածէ իր յոգնած մարմինը առ յաւէտ: Ապահովաբար նոյնքան սրտաշարժ ու գեղեցիկ եղած ըլլալու էր Չրաքեանի գծագրութիւնը, որ կրցած է այդքան ոգեւորել ու թրթռացնել Միքայէլի սիրտն ու միտքը, հոգին ու գրիչը:

Անձնական եւ սքանչելի գործեր են «Քեաթիպին Երազը» եւ «Սրճարանը» ստեղծագործութիւնները, որոնք որպէս գրական հրաշալի նմոյշներ ընդ-գրկուած են հայ գրականութեան դասագիրքերու մէջ՝ իրենց լեզուաոճական կատարելութեան համար: Երկուքն ալ որպէս ենթավերնագիր ունին «Արեւելապատում» բնութագրումը, որովհետեւ երկուքն ալ իսկական արեւելեան երկիրներու բնորոշ ստեղծագործութիւններ են:

Առաջինը պատմուածք մըն է տպագրուած «Շիրակ»ի մէջ 1909ին: Հոն, տաղանդաւոր քեաթիպը իր հօրմէն ժառանգութիւն ստացած է քեաթիպութիւնը, զոր կը շարունակէ: Ամբողջ կեանքը ուրիշներու համար նամակներ գրած, ծերացած ու յոգնած քեաթիպը, «թուղթի լեռներ սեւցուցած, մելանի ծովեր հոսեցուցած, գրիչի անտառներ սպառած» բարի, համբերատար, խղճամիտ այդ քեաթիպը գիշեր մը տարօրինակ երազ մը կը տեսնէ, թէ մզկիթի գմբէթին վրայ ելած, որպէս գրիչ մինարէն ձեռքն առած, կապոյտ երկինքն իբրեւ թուղթ գործածելով, աղերսագիր մը կը գրէ Ալլահին՝ այս անգամ ինքը իրե՛ն համար աղերսելով քիչ մը հանգստութիւն: Ստանալով քեաթիպին աղերսագիրը, Ալլահը ընթացք կու տայ անոր աղաչանքին՝ կեանքէն ի մահ անցընելով ու յաւիտենական հանգիստի արժանացնելով զինք: Կիւրճեան յաջողապէս շարադրած է այս համամարդկային թեման, որ աշխարհի բոլոր տքնաջան եւ աշխատասէր էակներուն կը վերաբերի, եւ կրցած է վերարտադրել արեւելեան կեանքը, արեւելքցի մարդոց հոգեբանութիւնն ու անոնց զգացումներն ու երազները, որոնք բոլորովին տարբեր են արեւմտեան քաղաքակրթութենէն եւ սովորութիւններէն:

Շատ գրողներ ու քննադատներ հիացումով արտայայտուած են «Քեաթիպին Երազը»ին մասին, բայց այստեղ կ'ուզենք մէջբերել միայն Ինտրայի կարծիքը. ««Քեաթիպին Երազը» զիս լացուց,- չես հաւատար,- գոհար մըն էր, կատարելութիւնն իսկ: Ինչ որ խորհեցայ այն առթիւ, սա է թէ զուտ մտաւորական մըն ալ (որպէս դուն եղած ես) կրնայ եղեր սիրտ շարժել, յուզումնականի մը արդիւնքներուն հասնիլ՝ շնորհիւ (à force de ...) ճշտութեան,- *վարպետ*ութեան: Եւ ո՞վ մեր մէջէն կրնայ պահանջել իրեն այդ *վարպետ* եւրոպական անունը քան դուն, զոր պատիւ ունեցած եմ *գտնելու, տեսնելու*, եւ խանդավառօրէն ներկայացնելու անոնց որ ինքզինք չեն կրնար տեսնել»:[93]

«Սրճարանը» տպաւորապաշտ պատկերը կը ներկայացնէ շատերու համար անկարեւոր եւ հասարակ վայր մը, որուն Կիւրճեան կրցած է տալ իրայատուկ իմաստ, հոգի եւ բովանդակութիւն, յատկապէս շեշտելով անոր կենդանի մթնոլորտը, հոն տիրող արեւելքի ոգին եւ արեւելեան վարքն ու բարքը: Արեւելեան այդ հաւաքավայրին անկիւնը հեղինակին առիթ տուած է հաւատարմօրէն խորհրդածելու, խոկալու եւ փիլիսոփայելու սրաճարանին անժխտելի մտերմութեան մասին:

«Փախած Ձիերը» եւս տպաւորապաշտ գործ մըն է: Կիրճեան կը նկարագրէ անսանձ ձիերու խելայեղ վազքը, անոնց ազատութիւնն ու ինքնիշխանութիւնը՝ զերծ ուրիշներու հսկողութենէն եւ զսպիչ կապանքներէն: Հեղինակը այդ անկախութիւնը կը բաղդատէ ազգերու ազատութեան հետ, միշտ հիացումով խօսելով մերկ, բաշարձակ ու խօլարշաւ փախած ձիերու անկաշկանդ ազատութեան մասին:

Կիրճեանի գեղարուեստական պատկերներէն յիշատակութեան արժանի է նաեւ իր բարեկամին՝ Սիմոն Սիմոնեանի ձօնուած «Ծնճիները» տպաւորապաշտ գործը, ուր գեղեցիկ առաւօտ մը, արեւածագին, իր գնահատանքին առարկայ կը դարձնէ Լիբանանի վայելուչ բնութիւնը, յատկապէս շոճիները իրենց գեղեցկութեան եւ լռակեցութեան, իսկ ճպուռները իրենց անվերջանալի երգին համար: Մայր բնութեան գիրկին մէջ հանգիստ խոկալու միջոցին, Կիրճեան կարծէք երազի մը մէջ կը լսէ բնութեան ձայնը, որ կ՚ըսէ թէ քաղաքակիրթ աղմկոտ քաղաքներէն յոգնած, մտածումներով, զգացումներով եւ կիրքերով խճողուած մարդիկ չեն զգար ապրելու երջանկութիւնը: Գրողը կեանքի մասին իր ըմբռնումները կը մարմնաւորէ անկրկնելի եղանակով եւ կը թելադրէ «գոհանալ ապրելով»:

Կիրճեան Լիբանանեան պանդոկէ մը տեսած նոր ամուսնացած սիրահարներէ կրած տպաւորութեան տակ գրած է «Երջանիկները» պատկերը, որ կը յիշեցնէ Լաֆոնթէնի «Երկու Աղաւնիներ» առակին հետեւեալ տողերը.

Եղէ՛ք մէկզմէկու համար աշխարհ մը նոր,

Միշտ այլազան, միշտ աղուոր:

Կիրճեանի թէ՛ պատմուածքները, թէ՛ նորավէպերը, թէ՛ պատկերները իրական կեանքէ ստացուած տպաւորութիւններու արդիւնք են, հեռո՛ւ կեանքի լոկ պատճէններ ըլլալէ, որովհետեւ անոնց մէջ ներկայ են հեղինակին անսանձ երեւակայութիւնը, գաղափարներու խորութիւնը, ստեղծագործական գեղարուեստականութիւնը, ինքնուրոյնութեան դրոշմը:

Իմաստասիրական առումով, սրատես խորաթափանցութեամբ եւ համամարդկային զգացումներու վերլուծութեամբ աչքառու է Կիրճեանի ամբողջ ստեղծագործութիւնը, որովհետեւ որպէս խոհուն եւ մարդասէր գրող, ան համաշխարհային հարցերը կը քննարկէ բարեսրտութեամբ եւ անկեղծ զգօնութեամբ: Ահա թէ ինչու զինք կարելի է դասել համաշխարհային խոշորագոյն գրողներու շարքին՝ Կէօթէ եւ Շիլլէր, Հիւկօ եւ Զոլա, Թոլսթոյ եւ Տոսթոեւսկի, եւայլն:

Հայ ժողովուրդի եղեռնն ու տեղահանութիւնը խորապէս յուզած են Միքայէլի դիւրաբեկ ու զգայուն էութիւնը: Օսմանեան թուրքերու անմարդկային, բարբարոսական բռնութիւնները հիմնովին ցնցած են իր հոգին: Թշուառ մայրերու տառապանքը, հալածուած որբերու անմխիթար կացութիւնը, իր ազգակիցներուն զարհուրելի տանջանքներով նահատակութիւնը, հայ ժողովուրդին օրհասական ու տագնապալի վիճակը էապէս յուզած են դեռ երեսունը չբոլորած Կիւրճեանը, որ չէր կրնար լուռ մնալ նման հոգեվիճակի մը մէջ: Ուստի, բացի հրապարակագրական յօդուածներէն, ան իր գեղարուեստական գործերուն մէջ ալ նկարագրած է աճաւոր աղէտը:

«Ինչ Որ Հրեշտակը Տեսաւ»ը իւրօրինակ ստեղծագործութիւն մըն է, ուր վշտահար, այլայլած երեւոյթով Հայկական Ծնունդի Առաւօտը լուսաւորող հրեշտակը օրուան անդրանիկ շողերը արձակելուն պէս՝ անճանաչելի կը գտնէ Հայաստան երկիրը, որուն գիւղերուն ու քաղաքներուն, գեղջուկ տուներուն ու խոնարհ հիւղակներուն փոխարէն ընդարձակ լռութիւն մը, անծայրածիր ամայութիւն մը կը տեսնէ: Շէնքերուն տեղ աւերակներ ու արտերուն տեղ խանձած հողեր նշմարելով, եւ զգալով թէ մինչեւ երեկոյ պիտի չկարենայ մնալ այդ դժոխքին մէջ, լալագին ցաւատանջ կերպարանքով անմիջապէս կը վերադառնայ Տիրոջ մօտ ու կը տեղեկացնէ իր տեսածը.- ամէնուրեք դիակներ, արեան լիճեր, մոխրակոյտեր, կիսամերկ խելայեղ ամբոխներ, որոնք անօթութենէ եւ սարսափէ ոռնալով կը քաշկռտուին դէպի անծանօթ արհաւիրքներ՝ ժանտատեսիլ մարդոց կողմէ հալածուելով: Հրեշտակը անսովոր փայլող աչքերով Յիսուսին կը պատմէ թէ ամբողջ երկիրը կարծես հողեղէն անսահման խաչ մըն էր՝ ամբողջ քրիստոնեայ ժողովուրդ մը վրան գամուած: Տեսարանը Քրիստոսի կը յիշեցնէ Գողգոթայի չարաշուք գագաթը եւ երկար լռութենէ ու անձայն լացէ ետք, Քրիստոս կ'ըսէ. «Ան ալ յարութիւն պիտի առնէ»:

Կիւրճեան այսպիսով Եղեռնի ազգային վիշտն ու տանջանքը կը դարձնէ համամարդկային նիւթ, նկարագրելով կատարուած զարհուրելի եղեռնագործութեան հետքերը եւ, ինչպէս իր բոլոր գործերուն մէջ, լաւատեսօրէն ու վստահօրէն եզրակացնելով թէ ան ալ յարութիւն պիտի առնէ:

«Մոգական Գորգը» պատկերն ալ գրուած է թուրքերու կողմէ հայերու ցեղասպանութեան կսկծալի ներգործութեան տակ: Կիւրճեան ցնորավէպ կ'անուանէ այդ գրուածքը, որուն համառօտ ուրուագծային նկարագրութիւնն իսկ սրտայոյզ է ոեւէ մարդկային էակի համար: Թուրք պատուիրակներ արեւելեան սքանչելի գորգ մը կը նուիրեն արեւելամոլ եւ թրքասէր Բիէր Լօթիին,[94] որպէս մեծարանքի եւ երախտագիտութեան արտայայտութիւն: Լօթի ափիոնով խառն թէմպէքիի ազդեցութեան տակ, թմբիրի ծանր ճնշման ներքեւ, սոսկումով կը տեսնէ թէ անհետացած գորգին տեղ գետինը նստած են խումբ մը աղջիկներ, որոնք կ'ըսեն. «Գորգը որուն վրայ կը զմայլիս դուն՝ իբրեւ արուեստին ու տաղանդին մէկ հրաշակերտին վրայ, մենք գործեցինք... եւ մենք միսիւլման չենք, այլ՝ հայ քրիստոնեաներ»: Այդ ժամանակ նոր ձայն մը կը լեցնէ սենեակը: Այս անգամ Լօթի կը տեսնէ շարժող կմախքներ, որոնք ուրուականներն են այս գորգին տէրերուն, եւ որոնք կը պատմեն թէ թուրքերը մէկ մէկ դեւ կտրած խուժած են իրենց գիւղը, ջարդած բոլոր բնակիչները, յափշտակած, կողոպտած բոլոր գոյքերը, կրակի տուած իրենց պապենական տուները: Իսկ այս գորգը գեղեցկագոյններէն մէկն է իրենց տունէն գողցուած առարկաներուն: Կմախքները ցոյց կու տան գորգին վրայ արեան հետք մը, որ իրենց ընտանիքի անդամներէն մէկունն է, զոր թուրքերը սպաննած են այդ գորգին վրայ: Յանկարծ, Լօթի կը տեսնէ թէ արեան բիծը կը մեծնայ, կը ծաւալի զարհուրելի արագութեամբ, կ'ողողուի արիւնով եւ ինք կը զգայ պղպջող լիճի գաղջ եւ պժգալի գգուանքը իր գալարուող մարմնին վրայ: Ահռելի աղաղակ մը արձակելով, Լօթի կ'իյնայ բազմոցին վրայ ու զոհերուն ծովացած արիւնը կը սպառնայ խեղդել զինք, որ դահիճներուն բարեկամն ու պաշտպանն է եղած:

Այս ստեղծագործութեամբ եւս Կիւրճեան ազգային թեման համամարդկային հարց դարձնելով, բոլոր ժողովուրդներու ուշադրութիւնը կը հրաւիրէ հայկական տառապագին տանջանքներուն վրայ, յիշեցնելով ֆրանսացի թրքասէր գրողին եւ ընթերցասէր հասարակութեան: Պատկերին մէջ իրարու յաջորդող ոգիները եւ ցնորական տեսիլները նահատակուած հայերու ուրուականներն են, որոնք արդարութիւն կը փնտռեն քաղաքակիրթ աշխարհէն՝ գործուած եղեռնին հոգեվիճակէն դուրս գալու համար:

Կիւրճեան ունի ուշադրութեան արժանի ուրիշ գործեր ալ, որոնց մէջ եւս արտացոլուած են պոլսահայ սովորոյթները, տեղական բարքերը, աշխատաւոր դասակարգի խոնարհ մարդիկը, ազգային իշխանութիւններու ինքնայատուկ տիպերը, գաղութահայ կեանքի ինքնատիպ կերպարները, եւայլն: Կիւրճեանի այս եւ այլ արձակ էջերը աչքի կ'իյնան աւարտուն խորութեամբ, սեղմ ոճով, կուռ կառուցուածքով, յստակ եւ խնամուած լեզուով: Ան վարպետ է բնութեան եւ հասարակութեան երեւոյթները, մարդկային ապրումները եւ գեղարուեստական զգացումները վերարտադրելու եւ կենդանիօրէն գեղարուեստական բովանդակութեամբ մատուցելու մէջ: Ան ճարտար վարպետութեամբ կը նկարագրէ բնութեան տեսարանները, հանգամանքները եւ սուր հոգեվիճակները իրեն յատուկ ներշնչանքով, խոհական նրբազգացութեամբ, ինքնատիպ առանձնայատկութեամբ, զգայուն մտայղացումով: Կիւրճեան զուտ փաստագրութիւն չէ որ կը կատարէ եւ իր ձգտումը չի յանգեցներ դէպքերու, իրողութիւններու եւ կերպարներու սովորական արձանագրութեան, այլ կը կատարէ իրականութեան գեղարուեստական իմաստաւորումը՝ իր գործերուն տալով արուեստի կատարելութիւն: Ահա թէ ինչու հայ գրականութեան հպարտութիւններէն է Միքայէլ Կիւրճեան իր տաղանդալի ստեղծագործութիւններով:

Ցաւալի է նշել որ Հայաստանի Գիտութիւններու Ազգային Ակադեմիայի Մանուկ Աբեղեանի անուան Գրականութեան Հիմնարկի «Հայ Գրականութեան Պատմութիւն» հինգ հատորանի ծաւալուն ակադեմական հրատարակութեան մէջ (Երեւան, 1962-1979), ոչ իսկ կարճ ուսումնասիրութիւն կամ փոքր գլուխ մը նուիրուած է Կիւրճեանին: Մինչեւ օրս չկայ նաեւ առանձին հրատարակուած ուսումնասիրութիւն մը անոր ստեղծագործութիւններուն մասին:

Այս անարդար անտեսումը պէտք է ուղղել եւ Կիւրճեանի անունը դասել իր գրչակիցներէն Արփիարեանի, Տէմիրճիպաշեանի, Զօհրապի, Կամսարականի, Սրմաքէշխանլեանի, Չրաքեանի, Օտեանի, Բաշալեանի, Չօպանեանի, Թէքէեանի եւ այլոց շարքին՝ բարձր գնահատելով անոր արձակ եւ չափածոյ ստեղծագործութիւնները, հրապարակագրական ու թարգմանական գործերը, խմբագրական ու թատերագրական երկերը. մէկ խօսքով՝ անոր գրական ու հասարակական գործունէութիւնը:

ՉԱՓԱԾՈՅ ԵՒ ԱՐՁԱԿ ԲՆԱՍՏԵՂԾՈՒԹԻՒՆՆԵՐ ՔԵՐԹՈՂԸ

Կիւրճեան յայտնի է որպէս բանաստեղծ: Անոր բանաստեղծութիւնն ունի ընկերային, քնարական եւ սիրային հնչեղութիւն: Երիտասարդ տարիքէն մինչեւ խոր ծերութիւն իր արձակ եւ չափածոյ քերթուածներուն մէջ ան թուղթին յանձնած է իր յոյզերն ու ապրումները բանաստեղծական շունչով:

Քսաներորդ դարասկիզբի ամենէն արժէքաւոր գրական հանդէսներէն Սան Փեթերսպուրկի «Բաներ Գրականութեան Եւ Արուեստի» պարբերականը, ուր հրատարակուած են ժամանակի յայտնի եւ լաւագոյն գրողներու ստեղծագործութիւնները, տպագրած է նաեւ Կիւրճեանի «Դալկուհի», «Իրիկուն», «Հոգիս Ի Ծով», «Յուշերք», «Գիշեր» եւ «Պատուհանին Քերթուածը» քնարերգական ստեղծագործութիւնները՝ «Վայրկեաններ Եւ Վանկեր» ընդհանուր խորագրին տակ (էջ 138-142): Նոյն հանդէսին 1904 թուականի երկրորդ հատորին մէջ այլոց ստեղծագործութիւններու կողքին կը հանդիպինք Կիւրճեանի «Երկուորեակները» բանաստեղծութեան:

Ֆրանսացի ռոմանթիք բանաստեղծներու ազդեցութեամբ եւ իր ապրած օրերու մռայլ իրականութենէն մղուած՝ Կիւրճեան Ծարլ Պոտլէրը յիշեցնող խոհեր եւ զգացումներ կ'արտայայտէ այդ վաղ շրջանին իր գրած բանաստեղծութիւններուն մէջ, երգելով անփայլ ստուերն ու երաժշտական լռութիւնը, նկարագրելով վերջալոյսի «մութի, լուռի մէջ պլլուած» վհուկ գիշերուան էջքը:

> Մթութեան հոծ քայլերով եւ ձայներով լռութեան
> Լոյսին մահը ողբացող ամբաւ Քայլերգ-Մեռելական
> Կը լսե՞ս մեծ գիշերն յառաջանալ ու ջայլել...
>
> («Գիշեր»)

Գիշերը վերջալոյսի գոյներու հրաշքէն ետք կը գուժէ լոյսին մահը:

Այս քերթուածին շատ համապատասխան է Ծարլ Պոտլէրէն ընտրուած բնաբանը, որ կ'ամփոփէ երկին հիմնական գաղափարը՝

> Entends, ma chère, entends la douce Nuit qui marche
> (Լսէ՛, սիրելիս, լսէ՛ քաղցր գիշերը որ կը քալէ - Յ.Մ.)

Անհաւոր նախազգացումով կը պաշարուի բանաստեղծին երազուն հոգին, որ կը զգայ իրիկուան հիւծիլն ու սարսռալը («Իրիկուն»):

Օրօրուն եւ հիւծախտէ մեռնող երեկոյ մը, որուն անմահութեան ծոցին մէջ «յոգնած հոգիս ալ կ'երազէ, ինչպէս ծով մը կը հանգչի», կը գրէ բանաստեղծը («Դալկուհի»):

Վեհ քնարականութիւն կայ Կիւրճեանի «Երկուորեակները» բանաստեղծութեան մէջ, ուր արտայայտուած են գրողին զգացումները, տպաւորութիւնները եւ խոհը: Բանաստեղծը կ'երգէ փայլ չունեցող աստուերն ու երաժշտական լռութիւնը, որոնք իր երազող պանդուխտ հոգիին որդեգիրները կը նկատէ: Ահա՛ երեք տուներէ բաղկացած խաչաձեւ հանգաւորումով այդ ոտանաւորը.-

Ստուերն անփայլ՝ նման գոյնն է Լռութեան,
Եւ լռութիւնն միգիքն իսկ է Ստուերին...
Իրարու ալ որքան վայել ու նման,
Հէք երկուորեակ կարծես որբեր ըլլային...

Երազողին ընտանիքն են որդեգիր
Այս գաղտնապահ երկուորեակներն որոնց մին
Իր երգեցիկ հոգւոյն կ'ըլլայ ունկնդիր.
Մինչ միւսն իրեն ժպտի դէմքովն իր մթին.

Ինչ հեշտութիւն երբ խռովեալ այս կեանքէն
Հրաժարած՝ երթայ հանգչիլ անոնց քով...
Պանդուխտ հոգին հոն կը սփոփուի քաղցրօրէն
Ընտանեկան մտերմութեան գեղումով...

Տիրան Չրաքեանին ձօնուած «Հոգիս Ի Ծով» բանաստեղծութեան մէջ Կիւրճեան կը մտասուզուի խորունկ խոհերու մէջ՝ լսելով ծովուն հեւքոտ կեանքը գիշեր ժամանակ եւ կը սարսափի ալիքներուն հեծկլտանքէն ու հառաչանքներէն՝

Որովհետեւ կ'զգամ, աւա՜ղ, թէ այս մռայլ ծովուն դիմաց
Հոգիս համակ կը դողայ, ինչպէս որ որսը դողաց,
Ինչպէս որ հէ՜գ, անզօ՜ր, մինա՜կ բան մը խպա՜ռ դողար պիտի
Հրէշի մ'առջեւ անծանօթ, կամ ահարկու մէկ հըսկայի...

Բանաստեղծը պատուհանը կը նմանցնէ խոշոր բացուած երկրեղէն աչքի մը, որ իրականութեամբ շրջանակուած բացուածքէն ներս կը հոսեցնէ խաղաղ յուզումներ՝ թրթռացնելով լուսեղէն զգացումներ («Պատուհանին Քերթուածը»):

Կիւրճեանի երիտասարդական շրջանի բանաստեղծութիւններէն են «Խարոյկը» (1903) եւ «Լաց Գիշերուան Մէջ» (1905) գործերը, որոնցմէ առաջինը գրուած է վաղամեռիկ աղջկան մը յիշատակին: Կիւրճեան անոր հեգ էութիւնը կը նմանցնէ խարոյկի մը, զոր վառ պահելու համար աղջիկը իր բոլոր զգացումներով, յոյսերով ու երազներով անդադար կը սնուցանէ.

Մինչեւ այն օրն ուր թոքերուդ ոյժն հատաւ,
Ու ներսիդիդ վառելիք բան չի մնաց...
Փըլաւ խարոյկն, եղաւ մոխիր ու մոռաց
Զոր ամփոփեց մահն ծոցին մէջ անբաւ:

Երկրորդ բանաստեղծութիւնը նոյնպէս տխուր տրամադրութեամբ գրուած ոտանաւոր մըն է, ուր աւազանին մէջ շիթ առ շիթ կաթկթող ջուրի ձայնը գիշերուան լռութեան մէջ միակ մնացած անվերջ արտասուող լացին կը նմանցնէ՝ նշելով կեանքի բացակայութիւնը խոր գիշերուան մէջ:

Կիւրճեանի չափածոյ ստեղծագործական կարողութիւններու վկաներ են նաեւ «Գեղօն Հայ Տաներուն» ներբողը, «Աղերսագիր» ոտանաւորը եւ «Պիտի Երթայ» ցնծերգը: Առաջինը զրոյց մըն է, ուր հեղինակը դիմելով մեր հայ տուներու հնարիչներուն՝ Մեսրոպին եւ Սահակին, հարց կու տայ թէ արդեօք կը զղջա՞ն տեսնելով «վիժուկ» եւ «անճոռնի» երկերու բուրգը եւ հայատառ թերթերու մէջ մեր նուիրական մայրենի լեզուին եղծանումը եւ աղաւաղումը:

«Աղերսագիր»ին մէջ Կիւրճեան պաղատանքով կը խնդրէ փափկասուն կիներէն որ պչրանք, «նայուածք ու ժպիտ – լոյս, բոց ու ալքոլ» չշռայլեն բարեսրտօրէն ծեր մարդուն, «Որ մերժուած է ըլլալ սիրահար...»:

Բայց ան սիրտ մ'ունի եւ չէ՞ք գիտեր որ
Մինչ կը ծերանայ մարմինն օրէ օր՝
Սիրտը կը մնայ մի՛շտ քսանամեայ
Եւ յիմարաբար, ա՜հ միշտ կը յուսայ:

«Պիտի Երթայ» ցնծերգը Կիւրճեան գրած է վառ լաւատեսութեամբ եւ ազատաշունչ պաթոսով: Ազատութեան այս ցնծերգը ոգեւորութեամբ երգուած է 1909ին Պոլսոյ մէջ, Սկիւտարի հայ օրիորդներու քառաձայն երգչախումբին կատարմամբ, Հայաստանի սովեալներուն ի նպաստ կազմակերպուած նուագահանդէսին: Օսմանեան «ազատութեան» դառն օրերուն անգամ, Կիւրճեան կը տեսնէ հայ ժողովուրդի լուսաւոր ապագան. ա՛յն ժողովուրդին, որ համատարած բանտ ու շիրիմի հին ոստանէն պիտի երթայ դէպի երջանկութիւն: Ահա ոտանաւորին եզրափակիչ տողերը՝

Ան չկասի պիտի բնաւ, այլ անդադար
Աչքերն յառած վաղուան լոյսէ հեռուներուն
Յառաջ, յառաջ պիտի սուրայ դարէ ի դար
Յառաջ, յառաջ պիտի սուրայ դարէ ի դար:[95]

Կիրճեան միշտ լաւատես եղած է հայ ժողովուրդի պայծառ ապագային նկատմամբ եւ յուսացած ու գուշակած է լուսափայլ գալիք:

Ինչպէս «Պատուհանին Քերթուածը» արձակ բանաստեղծութեան մէջ Կիրճեանի հոգին կ'օրօրուի ու կը ժպտի տեսնելով կապոյտ երկինքին վրայ հովէն թրթռացող կանանչ տերեւները՝ զանոնք նմանցնելով իր խաղաղ հոգիին յուզումներուն, կամ ինչպէս «Խարոյկը» ոտանաւորին մէջ ան կը նշէ վաղամեռիկ թշուառ աղջկան խարոյկի պէս քիչ առ քիչ մոխրանալը, այնպէս ալ «Սուրին Երգը» արձակ քնարերգութեան մէջ բանաստեղծը կը փառաբանէ ճշմարտութիւն շողացնող մոգական զէնքը՝ Անդրանիկի սուրը: Այս ստեղծագործութիւնը ներբող մըն է նուիրուած ազգային հերոսի մետաղեայ իրին հաստու էութեան եւ յատկութեան, որուն մահաստեղծ շարժումները «արուեստով կը գեղեցկացնեն մահը»:

«Ձեւի սիրահար մէկու մը համար՝ քենէ զարնուիլը պէտք է ըլլայ հեշտանք մ'ահուելի», կը գրէ հեղինակը, ըստ որուն՝ այդ սուրը «հրաշքով մետաղացած փայլակ մըն է» կամ «յանկարծ սառած խտացած շանթի բեկոր մը»:

Այս ստեղծագործութիւնը գրուած է 1903ին, «Արեւ» օրաթերթի խմբագրութեան նախաձեռնած հանգանակութեամբ եգիպտահայերու կողմէ Անդրանիկին նուիրուած սուրին յանձնումէն տասնեօթ տարի առաջ: Ազգային հերոսը, որ ա՛յդ եւ յաջորդո՛ղ տարիներուն մեծ ժողովրդականութիւն կը վայելէր յատկապէս արեւմտահայութեան մէջ, այդ սուրը հետագային պիտի նուիրէր Հայաստանի պատմութեան թանգարանին:

Դարձեալ 1903ին էր որ Սիամանթօ, Փարիզ գտնուած միջոցին, իր «Անդրանիկ» վերնագրով բանաստեղծութեամբ ջատագոված, մեծարած եւ գովերգած է ազգային հերոսին արիութիւնն ու անյաղթելի քաջութիւնը:

Կիրճեան իր «Սէր» խորագրով յօդուածաշարքին մէջ[96] ընդարձակ, խորաթափանց, մանրազնին կերպով կը քննէ եւ կը խորհրդածէ սիրոյ իմաստին ու էութեան շուրջ:

Ուսումնասիրելով Միւսէի, Պոտլէրի, Լամարթինի ու եւրոպական այլ հեղինակներու սահմանումները սիրոյ մասին, հեղինակը կը պարզէ իր տեսակէտը. «Սէրը տեսակ մը աստուածութիւն է, որուն գործած բարիքը եւ չարիքը, ծնած հեշտանքներն ու տանջանքները, բաշխած պարգեւներն ու պատիժները կը տեսնենք, կը վայելենք եւ կը կրենք, բայց որ յաւէտ անտեսանելի կը մնայ մեզի, անշօշափելի, խորհրդաւոր, ինչպէս ամէն աստուածութիւն զոր մարդիկ պաշտած են»:

Կիրճեան քնարերգուին սէրը աշխարհային է. հեռու՝ միստիկականութենէ, զերծ՝ սենթիմենթալութեան տարրերէ: Բանաստեղծին քնարերգութեան մէջ սէրն ու ատելութիւնը, ուրախութիւնն ու վիշտը, ներկան եւ ապագան միասին հանդէս կու գան, որովհետեւ անոր գեղարուեստական իտէալը հաւասարակշռութեան եւ անհատին բարձրացումն է:

Բանաստեղծը որպէս գերագոյն էութիւն կ'ընդունի միայն բնութիւնը եւ այդ իսկ պատճառով իրապաշտ ու վիպապաշտ պատկերներու իւրայատուկ միաձուլումով կը յայտնուի անոր սիրոյ տառապանքին խոր զգացումը.

Մաքրամաքուր շըքեղութեամբ ձուլանի՝
Մարմինդ, ո՞վ կոյս, սափոր մըն է լուսերփեան
Գըլուխ-գործոց գեղարուեստի մը գաղտնի,
Ելած ձեռքէն արուեստագէտ Բընութեան:

Այսպէս կը գրէ ան «Սափորը»[97] բանաստեղծութեան մէջ: Սափորը երկնահամ ըմպելիքով լեցուն, կնքուած ու գոց պիտի մնայ «Մինչեւ ծագի օրն առաջուց սահմանուած, երբ պիտի գայ մենաշնորհեալ մարդը»:

Վերոյիշեալ «Սէր» յօդուածին մէջ Կիւրճեան կարճ նախադասութեամբ մը կու տայ սիրոյ իսկութիւնը, գրելով. «սէրը տենչանքին քնարերգութիւնն է»:

Կիւրճեանի բանաստեղծութիւնը ձիւսուած է հոգեկան շատ նուրբ թելերէ: Անոր բանաստեղծութիւններուն շունչը հնչեղ է, իսկ գեղարուեստական պատկերները կը բնորոշեն իր ըմբռնումները, միտքի եւ զգացումներու խորութիւնը՝ թեմաներու եւ մօթիւներու, շարժառիթներու եւ բնախորհուրդներու բազմազանութեամբ: Հաւատարիմ մնալով իր բանաստեղծական շնորհին, ան իր քնարերգութեամբ լայն ճանաչում ունի գրական անդաստանին մէջ:

Յատուկ ուշադրութեան արժանի են Կիւրճեանի արձակ բանաստեղծութիւնները: Արձակ քնարերգութեան անուանի հեղինակներ են ռուս Իվան Թուրգենեւը, ֆրանսացի Շարլ Պոտլէրը, հնդիկ Ռապինդրանատ Թակորը, ֆրանսագիր Էմիլ Վերհարնը եւ ուրիշներ: Հայ գրողներէն քիչեր փորձած են գրել արձակ բանաստեղծութիւն, որ իր երեւումը կատարած է քսաներորդ դարասկիզբին: Գրական այս սեռը մշակողներէն յայտնի են Աւետիք Իսահակեանը, Միսաք Մեծարենցը, Վրթանէս Փափազեանը, Ռուբէն Որբերեանը, Ինտրան, Մովսէս Արազին եւ ուրիշներ: Գրականագէտ Թոմաշեւսկիի խմբագրութեամբ 1931ին Թուրգենեւի «Արձակ Բանաստեղծութիւններ»ուն հայերէն հրատարակութեան (Երեւան, 1968) յառաջաբանին մէջ կատարուած է հետեւեալ թելադրութիւնը. «Իմ բարի ընթերցող, այս բանաստեղծութիւնները միանգամից մի կարդա իրար ետեւէ, կը տխրես եւ գիրքն էլ կ'ընկնի ձեռքիցդ: Բայց դրանք կարդա հատ-հատ. այսօր մէկը, վաղը՝ միւսը, եւ դրանցից որեւէ մէկը գուցէ հետք թողնի քո հոգու վրայ»:

Նոյն թելադրութիւնը պէտք է ընել Կիւրճեանի «Ի Խորոց Սրտի Խօսք Ընդ Պաշտելւոյն» (1960, Պէյրութ) գիրքը ընթերցողներուն, որոնք հոն պիտի գտնեն քսաներորդ դարասկիզբէն մինչեւ 1960ական թուականները իրարմէ անջատաբար մամուլի մէջ լոյս տեսած երեսունմէկ արձակ բանաստեղծութիւններ:

Կիւրճեանի քնարերգութեան մէջ անձնական յոյզերն ու ապրումները շաղախուած են խորունկ վիշտով եւ թախիծով, որովհետեւ ան հոգեկան բանաստեղծ է, որուն լիրիքական հերոսը կերտուած է գործողութենէ աւելի՝ հոգեկան ապրումներով: Անոր արձակ քերթուածները իրենց ջերմութեամբ, անմիջականութեամբ եւ անկեղծութեամբ կը խռովեն, կ'ալեկոծեն ընթերցողին միտքն ու հոգին, որովհետեւ հեղինակը նախ եւ առաջ լիրիք, քնարերգակ բանաստեղծ է:

Այս հատորիկը վառ ապացոյցն է սիրով ալեկոծ քերթողի հոգիի անսպառ պոռթկումին, որ ծնունդ կու տայ սրտաբուխ արձակ քերթուած-ներու, որոնք իրենց առանձին հրապոյրներով ամբողջ ժողովածուին կու տան գեղեցիկ ծաղիկներէ կազմուած փունջի մը տպաւորութիւնը:

Ընդհանրապէս քնարական բովանդակութեամբ եւ ոչ տաղաչափեալ արձակ բանաստեղծութեան գրական սեռը խիստ յուզական է: Սիժէն կը բացակայի անկէ եւ դէպքերու ընթացքը կը գծագրուի ու կը մատուցուի առանձին ակնարկներու ձեւով:

«Ի Խորոց...»ի երեսունմէկ արձակ բանաստեղծութիւնները կապուած են իրարու եւ կը կազմեն մէկ ամբողջութիւն՝ իբրեւ խոհա-փիլիսոփայական սքանչելի կտորներով ժողովածու մը: Բանաստեղծը զգացումի եւ միտքի թռիչքներով կրցած է շօշափել կենսա-փիլիսոփայական շատ խնդիրներ, որոնց մէջ սէրը կը տիրապետէ որպէս հիմնահարց եւ որուն յարատեւօրէն կ'անդրադառնայ բանաստեղծը ինքնատիպ արտայայտչական միջոցներով ու տպաւորիչ անկեղծութեամբ: Կիւրճեանին սիրոյ երգերը կը դիւթեն եւ կը հրապուրեն ընթերցողը, որովհետեւ հեղինակը դուրս եկած է ներանձնական մեկուսացումէ եւ բուռն պոռթկումով կը ժայթքի մշտացայտ շատրուանի մը պէս՝ յար թրթռացնելով կարդացողին բաբախուն սիրտը, որովհետեւ սէրը ամենազօր համամարդկային ուժ մըն է:

Սէրէն ծանրօրէն հիւանդացած բանաստեղծը զարմանալիօրէն կը սիրէ իր հիւանդութիւնը եւ չ'ուզեր զայն փոխել աշխարհի բոլոր առողջութիւն-ներուն հետ («Զեմ Ուզեր Բուժուիլ»), քանի որ կ'ընդունի եւ կը խոստովանի. «օրս ամայի էր մինչեւ երեկոյ, կատարեալ անապատ մը, զի շնորհդ բացակայ էր անկէ», կը գրէ Կիւրճեան «Ովասիս» քերթուածին մէջ, քանի որ մինչեւ իր սիրեցեալին հանդիպիլը հոգին կը թափառէր անսպառտակ ամայութեան մէջ, որ ովասիսի մը պէս յանկարծ հրաշքով կը յայտնուի՝ իր տոչորող հոգիին պարգեւելով շուք եւ զովութիւն, զինք կազդուրելով լոյսի եւ մեղրի խառնուրդ ըմպելիով:

Այդ խորհրդաւոր հիւանդութենէն բուժուիլ չուզելը տարօրինակ գտնելով հանդերձ, Կիւրճեան վճռապէս կը գրէ թէ միանգամայն շատ քաղցր եւ հեշտալի է ան եւ իր միակ մաղթանքն ու ընձանքն է «չբուժուիլ բնաւ», չառողջանալ՝ չվերադառնալու համար միօրինակ, անփոյթ, անկենդան կեանքին, զոր կ'ապրէր մինչեւ զինք սիրելը: Հաստատ մնալով իր համոզումին մէջ, ան կը յայտնէ այնուհետեւ. «Ո՛չ միայն չեմ ուզեր բուժուիլ, այլ ամէն ջանք ի գործ կը դնեմ հիւանդութիւնս խորացնելու եւ յաւերժացնելու համար»: Ի վերջոյ ան կ'օրհնէ այն օրը որ բռնուած է այդ վսեմ հիւանդութեանէն, որ կեանքի զգայութիւններով կը զեղու եւ կը յորդի:

«Վարդ Մը Տամ Քեզի» քերթուածին մէջ Կիւրճեան ծաղիկներու թագուհի վարդը կը համեմատէ իր սիրելիին հետ, որովհետեւ երկուքն ալ իրենց արքայական շքեղութեամբ համանման են իրարու՝ բանալով միայն իրենց արտաքին թերթերը, իսկ իրենց արձակած զգլխիչ բոյրը կը պահեն ներքին տերեւներուն խորը, «հոգիին յետին ծալքերուն մէջ»:

Իր շատ սիրած բանաստեղծին՝ Ծարլ Պոտլէրի «Գինովցի՛ր, գինովցիր, գինիով, առաքինութեամբ կամ բանաստեղծութեամբ» պատգամով կը սկսի «Եռամեծ Գինով» քնարերգութիւնը, ուր Կիւրճեան սէրը կը համարէ գինիներու ամենաբարկը, առաքինութիւններուն մեծագոյնը, բանաստեղծութեանց բանաստեղծութիւնը. մէկ խօսքով՝ բոլոր ներշնչումներուն, խանդավառութիւններուն եւ յափշտակութիւններուն անսպառ աղբիւրը, սրտաբուխ անկեղծութեամբ գրելով. «Ես գինով եմ, գի՛նով, պաշտելիս, բայց, ո՛չ գինիով, ո՛չ առաքինութեամբ, ո՛չ ալ բանաստեղծութեամբ, այլ սէրով, քու սէրովդ միայն»: Այսպիսով, ան աստուածաբանական առաքինութիւններու՝ հաւատք, յոյս ու սէր երրորդութեան զուգահեռ կը թուէ առաքինութիւն, բանաստեղծութիւն, սէր երրորդութիւնը:

Անշուշտ սէրը կը բնակի ամէն մարդու մէջ, սակայն տարբեր տարողութեամբ եւ ուժգնութեամբ: Ջերմ, յուզական եւ կրքոտ են Կիւրճեանի սիրոյ քերթուածները, որովհետեւ անոր զգացումներուն ներդաշնակութեամբ հարուստ բանաստեղծական աշխարհը խոր է, տագնապներով լեցուն եւ հոգեբանական դրսեւորումներով յագեցած:

Նոյն «Սէր» յօդուածաշարքին մէջ Կիւրճեան խորհրդածելով «սէր» բառին բնութագրութեան մասին, կը գրէ. «Այս միավանկ բառը ո՞րքան կը նմանի Տէր բառին: Եւ իրա՛ւ սէրը տէրն է մեր կեանքին, մեր հոգիներուն, տէր մը քմահաճ, խստապահանջ եւ բռնաւոր, որ կ'ուզէ բացարձակ հնազանդութիւն, հպատակութիւն եւ զոհաբերութիւն, որ կը ներշնչէ մեզի ամենէն վեհ, ազնիւ, դիւցազնական, ինչպէս ամենէն յիմարական ու եղեռնական խորհուրդներն ու արարքները»:

Պէտք է առանց տարակոյսի ըսել թէ Կիւրճեանի մօտ սէրը հասած է գերագոյն բարձրութեան՝ երկրպագութեան եւ պաշտամունքի: Սակայն անհրաժեշտ է նաեւ նշել, որ հեղինակը իր սիրածին արտաքին ու ներքին առաքինութիւններուն մասին գրելով չի գռեհկանար, այլ քաղաքակիրթ պարկեշտութեամբ, քիւրեղեայ մաքրութեամբ եւ բացառիկ պարզութեամբ կ'արտայայտէ իր տագնապալից հոգիին խռովքը, զգացումներուն նրբութիւնը եւ սիրոյ երանգները: «Կը Մօտենաս, Կը Հեռանաս» բանաստեղծութեան մէջ Կիւրճեան մերթ կը զգայ որ իր պաշտելիին հոգին կը հսկի քնարերգակի հոգիին, մերթ ալ խոյս տալով անմատոյց բարձունքի մը վրայ կը թառի: Ահա այդ բանաստեղծութեան վերջաւորութիւնը՝ հեղինակին պատկերաւոր համեմատութիւններով. «Երկրային լամբար մըն ես, որ երբեմն բարութեամբ պանդուխտ առանձնութիւնս կը լուսաւորէ, երբեմն ալ աստղ մը հեռանշոյլ, որ հոգիիս վերեւ կը պլպլայ ... երբ կը խօսիս ինծի ու կը ժպտիս, պատրանք կ'ունենամ որ մահկանացու էակ մըն ես ինծի պէս, եւ ահա յանկարծ, այն վայրկեանին ուր ձեռքերս կ'երկարին իրականութիւնդ ստուգելու համար, ամպի մը մէջ փաթթուած՝ կ'ամբառնաս եւ աներեւոյթ կ'ըլլաս, դիցուհիի մը նման որ, երկնային քմահաճոյքէ մը ներշնչուած, պահ մը կ'երեւայ մահկանացու աչքերու, եւ զանոնք շլացնելէ յետոյ կը վերադառնայ բնագաւառը անմահներուն»:

Սիրած էակին մազերը համբուրելով, պաշտելիին անուշահոտութիւնը շնչելով, քնարերգուին կը թուի թէ կը հոտոտէ հրաշաբոյս մարմնին անպատում խորհուրդը, քանի որ «Արաբիոյ եւ ուրիշ վայրերուն բոլոր բոյրերը կարծես հաւաքուած, ընդխառնուած եւ խտացած էին մազերուն մէջ», որոնք «թեթեւ, փափուկ բայց միանգամայն ա՛յնքան հզօր [էին], որ պողպատէ հանգոյցներ պիտի չկրնային աւելի ամուր բանտարկել հոգիս իրենց մետաղեայ ցանցին մէջ» («Անկորնչելի Բոյրը»):

Հիմնուելով երեւոյթներու նմանութիւններուն, ընդհանրութիւններուն, ինչպէս նաեւ համեմատուող առարկային բնորոշ յատկութիւններուն վրայ, Կիւրճեան կը կատարէ գեղեցիկ համեմատութիւններ, ինչպէս, օրինակ. «պաշտելիին ներկայութիւնը շքեղ արեգակն է բնութեանս, համակ լոյս եւ ջերմութիւն, իսկ յիշատակը՝ լուսին մըն է տժգոյն, միստիկ պայծառութեամբ մը կ'ողողէ զայն», նոյնիսկ եթէ օր մը արեգակը հեռանայ բանաստեղծին կեանքի հորիզոնէն («Արեւ Եւ Լուսին»):

Կիւրճեանի գործերուն մէջ առանձնակի ուշադրութեան արժանի են նաեւ անոր պատկերաւոր ու տիպական բաղդատութիւնները, որոնք արդիւնք են կեանքէն քերթողին ստացած տպաւորութիւններուն. անոնք հեղինակին լեզուի եւ երեւակայութեան հնարքներն են. մէկ խօսքով՝ գեղարուեստական ոճի արտայայտութիւններ:

«Այսօր չհանդիպեցանք իրարու: Այսօր զրկուեցայ երանութենէն զքեզ տեսնելու, ո՞վ հոյակապ պատկեր որուն նմանը ոչ մէկ թանգարան կրնայ ընծայել ինծի. զքեզ լսելու, ո՞վ զմայլելի երաժշտութիւն՝ որուն նմանը ո՛չ մէկ նուագահանդէսի մէջ կրնամ վայելել», կը գրէ Կիւրճեան նոյն «Արեւ Եւ Լուսին» քերթուածին մէջ, որովհետեւ առանձնութեան մէջ տրտմութիւնը փարատելու ուրիշ միջոց չունի, բացի իր սիրածին վրայ մտածելէ եւ արձակ քերթուածներ գրելէ, որպէսզի մենութիւնը ոգեւորուի «անտեսանելի ներկայութեամբ մը» եւ «անբացատրելի երանութիւն մը» ծաւալի իր հոգւոյն մէջ:

Յոյզով, յոյսով, անապարանքով դէպի իր պաշտելին փութացող սիրահարած բանաստեղծը, որ կ'երթայ գտնելու համար սիրած էակը, Կիւրճեան կը բաղդատէ ա՛յն հեւոին հետ, որ իր նպատակին կ՚ուղղուի. ա՛յն թռչունին հետ, որ դէպի իր բոյնը կը սուրայ. ա՛յն գետին հետ, որ դէպի ծով կը դիմէ («Երջանիկ Գնացքը»):

Կիւրճեան քնարերգուին մօտ փիլիսոփայական եւ խոհուն պարփակումները կը զարգանան գրողին պատկերաւոր խօսքերով: Ան չի սահմանափակուիր լոկ մակդիրներով եւ ածականներով արտայայտելու համար իր զգացումներն ու տպաւորութիւնները, այլ ինքնագիտ համեմատութիւններով կը պատկերէ երեւոյթներու եւ զգացումներու գեղարուեստական բնորոշումները, նկարագրելով յատկանշական գեղարուեստական գիծերը, արտայայտելով իր ինքնուրոյն մտածողութեան ընդգրկումներուն խոհական խորաթափանցութիւնը եւ իմաստասիրական սեփական նրբազգաստ բիւրեղեայ սրամտութիւնը՝ ալեկոծելով, արտակարգ խռովքով համակելով ընթերցողին ներաշխարհը, շարժելով կարդացողի բնածին գիտակցութեան փափուկ ջիղերն ու նրբին լարերը:

Կիւրճեան կը համարէ որ սէրը երջանկութեան կեղծանունն է, այն տաւրօրինակ երջանկութեան, որ կը բաղկանայ հառաչանքներէ եւ արցունքներէ, որոնք կը սարսռացնեն զինք՝ թէ՛ տառապեցնելով իր խեղճ սիրտը եւ թէ՛ խանդավառելով զինք իր սիրածին ամենէն յուզիչ դէմքով, խօսուն աչքերով, փափուկ ու քաղցր ժպիտով, զգլխիչ ձայնով, հրայրքոտ հոգիով («Կը Գովեմ Զքեզ Եւ Ինքզինքս»), որովհետեւ բազմամարդ երկրի մը ինքնակալը, աշխարհի ամենահզօր կայսրն իսկ այնքան սիրուած ու պաշտուած չէ, որքան ամայի կղզիի վեհապետուհին՝ իր պաշտելի թագուհին («Վեհապետուհին Եւ Իր Հպատակը»):

Քնարերգուն կը հաւատայ իր սիրելիին ամենազօրութեանը եւ կը խոստանայ. «Պիտի օրհնեմ քեզ երբ երջանկութիւն պարգեւես: Չպիտի անիծեմ քեզ եթէ ապերջանկութիւն տաս»: Ան պատրաստակամութիւն կը յայտնէ ընդունիլ ամէն բան իր սիրած էակէն, որ կրնայ զինք հաւասարապէս երջանկացնել կամ դժբախտացնել,[98] որովհետեւ կը խոստովանի. «սէրս համակ քաջութիւն է եւ անձնազոհութիւն: Դիւցազն մըն է ան, որ փառքի դափնիներուն կը տենչայ եւ միեւնոյն ատեն միսթիք հաւատացեալ մը, որ պատրաստ է ամէն վայրկեան մարտիրոսութեան փշեղէն պսակը ընդունելու, իր պաշտած աստուածութեան սիրոյն համար («Խոստովանանք»):

Եթերային շղթաներով կապուած կաշկանդուած բնութեան խոնարհ զաւակին՝ բանաստեղծին կը թուի որ Սամփսոնի ոյժն ալ եթէ ունենար՝ պիտի չկարենար խորտակել զանոնք, քանի որ կ՚ընդունի. «կալանաւոր եմ, գիտե՛մ, բայց գերութիւնս չեմ փոխանակեր աշխարհի բոլոր ազատութիւններուն հետ», եւ համոզուած կը գրէ. «գանձ մը կորսնցուցի, ազատութիւնս: Աւելի մեծ գանձ մը շահեցայ, սիրոյ երջանկութիւնս» («Կորուստ Եւ Շահ»):

Պաշտելւոյն կախարդական ներկայութիւնը կ՚ոգեւորէ Կիւրճեանի հոգին, անոր լուսաշող դէմքն է որ կը լուսաւորէ քերթողին օրը, անոր անմահարար շունչն է որ կը կենդանացնէ բանաստեղծին անկենդան օդը, անոր նայուածքներն են որ լոյս կը սփռեն քնարերգուին հոգւոյն մէջ, քանի որ առանց անոր գգուանքներուն ցուրտ կ'ընէ: «Առանց քեզի, աշխարհը անսահման պարապութիւն եւ մեռելութիւն է ինծի համար», կը գրէ սէրէն խոցուած մելամաղձոտ բանահիւսը:

Կիրճեան պահ մը կ'ուզէ նմանիլ Լաթմոսի գեղեցիկ հովիւ Անտիմիոնին, որ ակնարկը յառած ըլլալով Հերային՝ Արամազդի կողմէ կը դատապարտուի յաւիտենական քունի: Ինք եւս կը բաղձայ նման պատիժի արժանանալ, որպէզի յաւիտեան քնանայ՝ երազելով իր սիրած երկրաբնակ աստուածուհին եւ երբեք չուզէ արթննալ այդ հրաշալի երազէն («Անտիմիոն»): Այլուր տիեզերքի չորս տարրերը՝ հողը, օդը, ջուրն ու հուրը ան կը համեմատէ իր փոքրիկ տիեզերքի միայն մէկ տարրէ բաղկացած սիրոյ հետ, որ նոյնքան զօրաւոր է որքան չորս տարրերը միասին («Յաւէտ Եւ Ուրախութենէն Անդին»):

«Կը Յիշե՞ս» քերթուածին մէջ Կիրճեան կը վերյիշէ ամրան այն գիշերը, երբ «խօսակցելով եւ լռակցելով» կը հասնին ծովեզերք՝ իր պաշտելին «անմատոյց դիցուհիոյ մը կերպարանքով» ալիքներու անվախճան երգին գոռ երաժշտութեամբ եւ լուսնին սպիտակ մոգութեամբ, մինչ ինք աղաղակելով իր անբաւ սէրը: Ծարք մը համեմատութիւններէ, բաղդատութիւններէ ետք, հետեւեալ պարբերութեամբ կը վերջացնէ ան բանաստեղծութիւնը. «եւ ինծի թուեցաւ յանկարծ -խուսափու՞կ պատրանքերբ կը խօսէի այսպէս յարաճուն յուզմամբ եւ յափշտակութեամբ, թէ սէրս այդ ծովն էր որ անհուն կիրքի մը անվերջ աղաղակը կը բարձրացնէր դէպի լուսինը եւ դուն, պաշտելիս, այդ լուսինն էիր, վեհանդորր լուսինը, որ բարձրէն իր ճառագայթները կ'առաքէր ծովուն, խորհրդաւոր ժպիտներու պէս»: Ահաւասիկ այսպէս երանգափայլ գունաւորումներով կը մտաբերէ յիշարժան երջանիկ անցեալը՝ բախտաւոր երանելիութեամբ լեցուն անվերադարձ օրերը:

Գիշեր ժամանակ սիրած էակի պատուհանին առջեւ հիբնոսացած քերթողին համար անսահման տիեզերքին մէջ չկայ կէտ մը, որ աւելի լուսաշող, աւելի խորհրդաւոր, աւելի մագնիսող ըլլայ քան այդ լուսաւոր պաստառը՝ պատուհանը, որ բանաստեղծին համար կը թուի ըլլալ խորհրդայեղձ պալատի մը կամ առասպելական *Հազար Ու Մէկ Գիշերներ*ու անձաւի մը մուտքը, լուսաբացուող գանձերու, հրաշալիքներու վրայ («Լոյս Եւ Խորհուրդ»):

Երկու հաւասարազօր բեւեռներու միջեւ անընդհատ տարուբերող հոգին կը տատանի սիրեցեալին ներկայութեան բոցավառութեան եւ բացակայութեան երանութեան միջեւ, որովհետեւ ըլլա՛յ անձը, ըլլա՛յ յիշատակը, մի՛շտ իրեն հետ են, եւ տարբեր ախորժներ կը բերեն պաշտողին, կը գրէ Կիրճեան «Երկու Բեւեռներու Միջեւ» քերթուածին մէջ:

Կարելի է բազմաթիւ այլ մէջբերումներով հաստատել թէ Կիւրճեանի գրելաոճը, հնարամիտ պատկերները, հանճարեղ համեմատութիւնները, ճոխ փոխաբերութիւնները կենդանի վկայութիւն են այն անուրանալի իրողութեան, որ գրագէտը կեանքը կը ճանչնար խոր գիտակցութեամբ, իրականութիւնը կ՚ըմբռնէր լայն իմացողութեամբ, կենցաղային երեւոյթները ու յարաբերութիւնները կը հասկնար աւելի դիւրազգած հասողութեամբ:

Բանաստեղծին ներշնչման հիմնական աղբիւրները են կինն ու բնութիւնը: Ինչպէս պաշտելին զինք կ՚ոգեւորէ ու կը գինովցնէ, այնպէս ալ բնութիւնը իր երեւոյթներով կը յուզէ ու կը խռովէ իր հոգին: Հովը անալեկոծ, խաղաղ, հանդարտ լիճը այնպէս կը խռովէ որ ան իր խաղաղութիւնը կորսնցուցած վիճակը աւելի կը նախընտրէ քան երկրի ու երկինքի բոլոր հանդարտութիւնները: «Հովը կեանքն է լիճին, սէրը հովն է հոգիին», կը գրէ Կիւրճեան «Լիճը Եւ Հովը» կարճ ու սեղմ քերթուածին մէջ, նշելով որ լիճին միակ ցանկութիւնն է որ հովը չդադրի փչելէ, որպէսզի երջանիկ ալիքները երգեն փառքը հովին:

Կիւրճեան չի սիրեր ձանձրալի խելօքութիւնը. ընդհակառակը՝ կը փառաբանէ գինին, քանի որ ինչպէս գինովը աշխարհը վառ ու կենդանի գոյներով կը տեսնէ, այնպէս ալ հանդարտաբարոյ մարդը սիրոյ ազդեցութեամբ աւելի երջանիկ կը զգայ ինքզինքը («Նոյն Բանը Կ՚ըսեմ Տարբեր Ձեւով»):

Օրուան մտածումները ու դէպքերը քունին մէջ եւս շարունակելու, երազելու մասին մտորելով, հեղինակը այդ առեղծուածը կը լուծէ հետեւեալ բացատրութեամբ. «Երազը, բու՛ն, ճշմարի՛տ երազը իմ տուընջեան կեանքս է, իմ հանապազօրեայ կեանքս, ուր շնորհուած է ինծի քեզ տեսնել, հետդ խօսիլ, վրադ մտածել անդադար, ներկայութեամբդ գրաւուիլ եւ յիշատակովդ պաշարուիլ», մինչ անդին քունը կը նմանի տժգոյն իրականութեան, ուր կ՚ապրին կիրքէ զուրկ մարդիկ («Ճշմարիտ Կեանքը»):

Ծով, անապատ, երկինք երեք կատարեալ պատկերներուն մէջ տիրող խորունկ ներդաշնակութիւնը սոսկում կ՚առաջացնէ բանաստեղծին մէջ, որ կը մտորէ թէ յանկարծ եթէ այդ անայլայլ կապոյտէն պատառ մը, անապատին ամայութենէն աւազահատիկ մը, միապաղաղ ծովէն կաթիլ մը իյնան պաշտելիին հոգւոյն մէջ՝ որքան ծանր պիտի ճնշեն բանաստեղծին վրայ այս անտարբերութիւնը, անհոգութիւնը, անզգայութիւնը («Բնութիւն Եւ Կին»):

Բանաստեղծը երկինքի դաշտերուն մէջ յառաջացող ամպերը կը նմանցնէ ոչխարներու հօտի մը, իսկ հովը՝ հովիւի: Ինչպէս երբ յանկարծ հովը կը խենթենայ, հովիւին ոչխարները խառնիխուռն կը վազեն դասալիք զինուորներու պէս, այնպէս ալ սէրը կը սկսի հանդարտ ու մեղմ հովի մը պէս՝ օր մը խենթեցած սաստկանալով քշելու համար հօտը դէպի անծանօթ հորիզոններ: Ինչպիսի՜ պատկերաւոր համեմատութիւն, ուր հովիւը, ոչխարներու հօտը, դասալիք զինուորները կը նմանցուին հովին, կուտակուած ամպերուն, ցիր ու ցան մթնոլորտային պաղած շոգիներուն, որոնք դէպի անորոշ ուղղութեամբ կ'ընթանան («Հովը»):

«Յաղթանակի Երթ» բանաստեղծութեան մէջ Կիւրճեան կը նկարագրէ սիրածին քովէն մեկնելէ ետք անմիջապէս տուն չդառնալը՝ չառանձնանալու, անոր վրայ չմտածելու կամ չգրելու համար: Ի փոխարէն, ան ցատկելու, պարելու, թռչելու չափ թեթեւ եւ ուրախ կը զգայ ինքզինք եւ ժամերով կը քալէ, փափաքելով «օրերով, ամիսներով, տարիներով սիրոյ երջանկութեան անհագինօրէն բեռը շալկած» անվերջ քալել դէպի անմահութիւն:

Կիւրճեանի քերթուածները կ'ընթերցուին հաճելի սահունութեամբ, շնորհիւ իրենց պարզ արտայայտչականութեան, գեղարուեստական ներդաշնակութեան եւ երաժշտականութեան: Կարելի չէ կարդալ զանոնք եւ չհամակուիլ այնպիսի երանութեամբ ու ներքին ալեկոծումով, որոնք միայն իսկական արուեստը կրնայ պարգեւել ընթակային:

Կիւրճեանի համար կարեւորը սիրելն է, սիրոյ երազներուն, անուրջներուն մէջ ապրիլը: Քնարերգակ բանաստեղծի բարդ հոգեվիճակին թափանցելով, կը զգանք անոր խորապէս լաւատես հայեացքը, անսասան հաւատքը եւ փիլիսոփայութիւնը: Տէրեանական վիպապաշտ, երազային նուրբ անուրջներուն նման, այս հատորիկին կենսափիլիսոփայութիւնը քնարերգակին սիրոյ զգացումներուն խտացումն է, քերթողին անվերջանալի տառապանքին ակունքը, լաւատեսական պայծառ ընդհանրացումներուն ազդակը:

«Ի Խորոց Սրտի Խօսք Ընդ Պաշտելոյն» արձակ քերթուածներու ժողովածուին հրատարակութիւնը ցնցեց հայ գրկան աշխարհը: Իր ներածականին մէջ, Զաւէն Վարդապետ Չինչինեան (հետագային Արքեպիսկոպոս) կ'ըսէ. «Ճուրջ երեսուն տարիներ առաջ գրուած այս էջերը ունին 1900ի մեր գեղապաշտ սերունդի գրագէտներէն ոմանց շատ սիրելի եւ այն ատեն ի պատուի եղող արձակ քերթուածի ձեւը, որ քիչ անգամ եւ տաղանդաւորներու գրչին ներքեւ միայն յաջողած սեռ մը եղած է»: Այնուհետեւ նշելով հեղինակին բազմալար տաղանդը եւ սահուն լեզուն, բարձր կը գնահատէ գրքոյկին գրական ու գեղարուեստական արժանիքները. «Սիրոյ թէմային վրայ գրուած շարունակական բանաստեղծութիւններ են, գեղեցիկ ոճով, պերճ լեզուով եւ հաղորդականութեամբ զեղուն, ինչպէս է պարագան ճշմարիտ արուեստով եւ խորունկ ապրումով գրուած գործերուն»:

Գրքոյկը զարմանք պատճառած է տաղանդաւոր գրագիտուհի Վիքթորիա Արշարունիի ընտանիքին, որ Աղեքսանդրիոյ մէջ երկար ժամանակ դրացի ըլլալով հանդերձ Կիւրճեանի, չէ գիտցած թէ «սրամիտ, հեգնող բարեկամը, միշտ պատրաստ բառախաղ մը դարբնելու, որ զուարթութիւն կը սփռէ շուրջը, միեւնոյն ատեն այսքան զգայուն բանաստեղծ մըն է եղեր: Որու՞ն միտքէն կ'անցնէր»: Ապշահար գրագիտուհին իր յափշտակուածութիւնը եւ հիացումը կ'արտայայտէ գովաբանելով խորքով այնքան գեղեցիկ եւ յուզիչ որքան ձեւով կատարեալ սիրային քերթուածները. «Այս քերթուածները նշանաւոր են իրենց անկեղծութեամբը, զգացումի խորութեամբն ու զօրութեամբը եւ իրենց հոգի տուող երիտասարդական ջերմութեամբը: Եւ ինքնատպութիւնը մեծագոյն յատկանիշն է անոնց»:[99]

Հրանդ Բալուեան իր հրատարակած պարբերաթերթին «Գիրքեր, Դէմքեր» բաժնին մէջ ընդարձակ յօդուածով մը բարձր կը գնահատէ Կիւրճեանին գրքոյկը:[100] Ան նա՛խ կը նշէ թէ Կիւրճեանի ծաւալուն բերքը թաղուած կը մնայ ցանուցիր հին պարբերականներու մէջ եւ թէ «ինք երգիծանքէն աւելի մեր գեղեցիկ գրականութեան առաջին գիծի վրայ եկող ներկայացուցիչներէն մէկն է եղած», ապա կը շեշտէ թէ այս գիրքը «հոգիդ կլանող երաժշտութեան մը նման կու տայ պատկերներ, խոստովանութիւններ, մեղմ մրմունջներ, որոնք տպաւորիչ են»: Յօդուածագիրը ընթերցողներուն կը յանձնարարէ փնտռել գրքոյկը եւ անպայման կարդալ զայն, որովհետեւ «այս արտառոյց գեղօնը, գրուած քանի մը տասնեակ տարիներ առաջ, սիրոյ զգացումին աստուածացումն է, զեխ պոռթկումով մը տրուած»:

Հմայեակ Գրանեան 1962ին Պէյրութի մէջ գրախօսական մը նուիրած է այս գրքոյկին, նշելով. «Կիւրճեանը մեր «արուեստաւոր գրականութեան» ամենէն շնորհալիօրէն կատարելագործուած ներկայացուցիչներէն մէկն է»: Գրանեանի կարծիքով «Հայ լեզուն քիչ անգամ իր քնարական գեղեցկութեան պերճութիւնը, իշխանապետութիւնը այնքան մեծավայելչօրէն զգեցած է, որքան Կիւրճեանի գեղագիր գրչին տակ»:

«Արեւ»ի խմբագրապետներէն Յովհաննէս Պօղոսեան իր «Միքայէլ Ս. Կիւրճեան» յօդուածին մէջ[101] ինքզինք բախտաւոր կը համարէ որ վայելած է Կիւրճեանի մտերմութիւնը: Պօղոսեան համառօտակի անդրադառնալով Կիւրճեանի գրական գործունէութեան, կու տայ հետեւեալ բնութագիրը. «Ուշադիր դիտող մըն էր՝ մարդկային ընկերութեան երեւոյթներուն եւ արտայայտութեանց, ու խորաթափանց միտք մը, որ կը սիրէր փիլիսոփայել, վերէն դիտելով դէպքերն ու դէմքերը, իր ծխամորճը սեղմած բերնին ծայրը, իր աշխատասենեակին խաղաղութեան մէջ, ուր հազիւ կրնային լսուիլ դուրսի աղմուկը եւ մօտակայ ծովուն ալիքներուն շառաչիւնը»: Այնուհետեւ խօսելով Կիւրճեանի վերլուծութիւններուն, պերճ արտայայտութիւններուն, լեզուական հմտութեան, հին ժամանակներու դասական ոգիին եւ ոճին մասին, կը գրէ. «Ու իր հասունութեան ծանրախոհ մտածումներուն հետ հաճելի էր իր սրտի բաբախիւնը լսել՝ երիտասարդական աւիւնով, երբ իր «պաշտելի»ին հետ կը խօսէր՝ ի խորոց սրտի»:

Երուանդ Ազատեան Կիւրճեանի սիրային խռովայոյզ արձակ բանաստեղծութիւնները ընդգրկող գրքոյկը կը բնութագրէ որպէս հատոր մը, «ուր ի յայտ կու գար Կիւրճեան իրաւ բանաստեղծին դիմագիծը»: Արդարեւ, ոչ տաղաչափեալ քնարերգութեան գունագեղ ու չքնաղ ստեղծագործութիւններուն զգայացունց ու սրտայոյզ արտայայտութիւններով զեղուն է այդ երկը, որովհետեւ արձակ քերթուածները գրուած են բանաստեղծական անսահման թռիչքով, զգացումներու հրաբխային ժայթքումով եւ մանաւանդ սիրային եռքով ու գրական հրապոյրով:

ՄԻՔԱՅԷԼ ԿԻՐՃԵԱՆ ՀՐԱՊԱՐԱԿԱԳԻՐԸ

Կիրճեան ապրած եւ ստեղծագործած է միջազգային եւ ազգային պատմութեան անհարկու դարաշրջանի մը մէջ՝ քաղաքական-հասարակական չափազանց բարդ ու դժուար, խառն ու հակասական պայմաններու տակ: Ծանր էր հայերու վիճակը թէ՛ արեւելեան եւ թէ՛ արեւմտեան Հայաստանի մէջ: Եւրոպական մեծ տէրութիւնները վեհաժողովէ վեհաժողով փոխադրելով հանդերձ, չէին կրցած լուծել հայկական հարցը եւ այդպիսով շատ աւելի լուրջ ու դժնդակ դարձած էր արեւմտահայերու դրութիւնը: 1890ի Գում Գաբուի արիւնահեղ ցոյցէն յետոյ, Թուրքիոյ մէջ բնակող քրիստոնեաներու եւ մասնաւորապէս հայերու կացութիւնը աւելի վտանգաւոր հանգամանք ստացաւ: Սուլթան Համիտ սաստկացուց իր հայահալած քաղաքականութիւնը: Թուրքիոյ բանտերը լեցուեցան որպէս յեղափոխական ամբաստանւած հազարաւոր հայերով, մտաւորականներով եւ ազգային գործիչներով: 1894ի Սասունի եւ 1895-1896ի հայկական ընդհանուր կոտորածները ցնցեցին ամբողջ բարեկիրթ աշխարհը: 1908 Յուլիս 11ին հեռագիրները համայն աշխարհին «աւետեցին» Թուրքիոյ Սահմանադրութեան հռչակումը, յայտարարելով որ Օսմանեան պետութեան բոլոր քաղաքացիները, ներառեալ Թուրքիոյ բոլոր քրիստոնեաները, հաւասար իրաւունքներ պիտի վայելեն: Սահմանադրութեան յայտարարութենէն տակաւին տարի մը չանցած, 1909 Մարտ 31ին, Իթթիհատականները պետական հարուածով գահազուրկ ըրին Սուլթան Համիտը: Հայրս, Յակոբ Մէքէրեան, որ այդ ժամանակ Պոլիս կը գտնուէր, կը պատմէր թէ անհուն ուրախութեամբ ականատես եղած էր կարմիր դահիճին գահընկէցութեան, երբ պալատէն դուրս կը բերուէր ու փողոցէն հետիոտն գլխիկոր կը տարուէր: Հետագայ ջարդերն ու կոտորածները, կողոպուտներն ու թալանները, աքսորներն ու հալածանքները, սակայն, ցոյց տուին թէ Երիտասարդ «զարգացած» Թուրքերը նոյնքան եւ աւելի ծարաւի էին հայերու արիւնին, նոյնքան եւ աւելի կը տենչային հայոց հարստութեան եւ ունեցուածքներուն, որքան իրենց մոլեռանդ, նախանձոտ ու դաժան ծնողները:

Քաղաքական այսպիսի խառնաշփոթ ու խաբուսիկ իրադրութեան մէջ արտասահման անցած էին Դանիէլ Վարուժան, Ատոմ Եարճանեան (Սիամանթօ), Արփիար Արփիարեան, Երուանդ Օտեան, Վահան Թէքէեան, Լեւոն Բաշալեան, Տիգրան Կամսարական, Միքայէլ Կիրճեան, Արշակ Չօպանեան, Երուանդ Սրմաքէշխանլեան, Սուրէն Պարթեւեան, Լեւոն Շանթ, ապա նաեւ Ռուբէն Զարդարեան, Գրիգոր Զօհրապ, Զապէլ Եսայեան եւ ուրիշներ:

Արփիարեան «Պատմութիւն ԺԹ դարու Թուրքիոյ Հայոց Գրականութեան» (Գահիրէ, 1944) գիրքին մէջ կը գրէ. «Մինչեւ 1880 թուականը ո՛չ հատորին, ո՛չ օրագրին համար կանխարգել գրաքննութիւն օրէնադրուած էր: Մերթ ընդ մերթ հեղինակ մը կամ տպագրիչ մը ձերբակալուելով կը բանտարկուէր, բացորոշ օրէնքի մը դէմ առանց մեղանչած ըլլալու... 1888ին հայ մամուլին վրայ ալ գրաքննութիւն հաստատուեցաւ»:

Այսպիսով, լրագիրը թէեւ կը կորսնցնէ իր անկախութիւնը, բայց եւ այնպէս կը վայելէ որոշ առանձնաշնորհումներ, որոնցմէ զրկուած կը մնար հայ գիրքը, որ աւելի կաշկանդուած վիճակի մէջ կը գտնուէր: Այս պայմաններուն տակ, գրողներն ու հրապարակագիրները աւելի կը համախմբուին հայ մամուլին շուրջ:

Ամերիկա, Եգիպտոս, Պուլկարիա եւ Ռումանիա արդէն կային բաւական հոծ եւ կազմակերպուած հայ գաղութներ, ուր կը հրատարակուէին զանազան պարբերականներ, գլխաւորաբար կուսակցական եւ յեղափոխական նկարագրով: Քաղաքական, ընկերային եւ ազգային հարցերու շուրջ խմբագրականներն ու յօդուածները ուշագրաւ հետաքրքրութեամբ կը կարդացուէին գաղթական թէ բնիկ ընթերցողներու կողմէ: Մամուլը կարեւոր դեր կը կատարէր հայ ժողովուրդը առաջնորդելու, զայն յոյսերով եւ լաւատեսութեամբ ներշնչելու գործին մէջ: Համայն մարդկութեան եւ մասնաւորապէս հայութեան վերաբերեալ բազմազան հարցեր ուշադրութեան առարկան կը դառնային հայ վաստակաւոր հեղինակներու եւ տաղանդաւոր գրչի տէր երիտասարդ գրողներու:

Ինչպէս քաղաքական, տնտեսական եւ հասարակական հարցերը, այնպէս ալ հայ ժողովուրդին, հայրենիքին ու մշակոյթին խնդիրները միշտ յուզած եւ զբաղեցուցած են Կիրճեանի միտքն ու հոգին: Միջազգային եւ ազգային շատ հարցեր Կիրճեանի առոյգ ու համարձակ գրչին տակ յաճախ հնչած են որպէս ամէնօրեայ ղօղանջ՝ իր երիտասարդ օրերէն մինչեւ ծերունազարդ տարիները:

Հայ ժողովուրդը 20րդ դար թեւակոխեց պատմա-քաղաքական եւ ազգային-կուսակցական իրադարձութիւններու խառնաշփոթ պայմաններու տակ: Այդ տարիները ներքին վէճերու եւ կռիւներու, սպառնալիքներու եւ իրարանցումի, խռովութիւններու եւ անհաբեկչութիւններու, պահպանողականներու եւ ազատականներու կամ սահմանադրականներու պայքարի շրջան մըն էին՝ կուսակցութիւններու գործօն մասնակցութեամբ: Այս պայքարին նկատմամբ անտարբեր չէին կրնար մնալ հայ մամուլն ու մտաւորականութիւնը: Տարբեր երկիրներու գաղթօճախներուն մէջ սկսան հրատարակուիլ նոր հայատառ պարբերականներ, որոնք զգաստացնող յօդուածներով խոհեմութիւն կը քարոզէին ժողովուրդին:

Եգիպտոսի մէջ ալ սահմանադրականները սկզբունքային պայքար կը մղէին ապօրէն կերպով կազմուած եւ գործող խնամակալութեան մը դէմ, քանի որ այլեւս յոյս չունէին Պոլսոյ ազգային կեդրոնական վարչութեան վրայ:

Օտեան կը վկայէ թէ Ֆրանսայէն Աղեքսանդրիա հասնելէն քանի մը ամիս ետք երբ կը շարունակէ հրատարակել «Ազատ Խօսք»ը, որուն առաջին երեք տետրերը տպագրուած էին Փարիզ, Տիգրան Կամսարական եւ Միքայէլ Կիւրճեան կը սկսին աշխատակցիլ անոր:

Մինչ այդ, Կիւրճեան արդէն հրապարակագրական եւ գեղարուեստական գրութիւններով կ'աշխատակցէր «Մասիս»ի երբեմնի խմբագրապետ Տիգրան Արփիարի եւ երգիծաբան Յարութիւն Ալփիարի Գահիրէ հրատարակած «Փարոս»ին, Եղիշէ Թորոսեանի «Արշալոյս»ին, որ տասնհինգ տարուան կեանք մը ունեցած է Գահիրէ, եւ «Փիւնիկ» կիսամսեայ հանդէսին, որ 1903ի Յուլիսին օրաթերթի կը վերածուի Աղեքսանդրիոյ մէջ:

Թուրքիոյ ճնշումներէն, հալածանքներէն ու բռնութիւններէն փախչող հայ մտաւորականներ հայկական վարժարաններու մէջ ուսուցչութիւն ընելէ զատ կը սկսին հրատարակել նոր պարբերականներ: Միհրան Ասքանազ Թուրքիայէն Եգիպտոս անցնելէ յետոյ, ուսուցչութեան կողքին կը հրատարակէ «Պարտէզ» գրական, մանկավարժական շաբաթական հանդէսը: Օրիորդ Մարի Պէյլէրեան, որ իր յեղափոխական գործունէութեամբ դարձած էր անուանի, Թուրքիայէն փախչելով Գահիրէ, Գալուստեան Ազգային Վարժարանին մէջ ուսուցչութեան զուգահեռ, 1902-1903 թուականներուն կը հրատարակէ «Արտեմիս» գրական եւ ընտանեկան ամսագիրը: Աւետիս Պալեան 1903ին լոյս կ'ընծայէ «Ժողովուրդ»ը, նա՛խ որպէս ամսաթերթ Գահիրէի մէջ եւ ապա որպէս շաբաթաթերթ Աղեքսանդրիա: Երբ Տիրան Քէլէկեան 1904ին ընտանիքով Եգիպտոս կ'ապաստանի, Գահիրէի մէջ կը վարէ երկու ֆրանսերէն կարեւոր թերթերու խմբագրապետութիւնը՝ Le Journal du Caire եւ La Bourse Egyptienne: Այս ծանր եւ յոգնատանջ աշխատանքին կողքին, ան ժամանակ կը գտնէ հիմնելու նաեւ թրքալեզու «Եէնի Ֆիքիր» ամսաթերթը: Լեւոն Բաշալեան կը ստանձնէ Վերակազմեալ Հնչակեան Կուսակցութեան Լոնտոն հրատարակուող«Նոր Կեանք» ազգային, գրական, քաղաքական հանդէսին խմբագրութիւնը: Օտեան Աղեքսանդրիոյ մէջ կը հրատարակէ «Թերթիկ» օրաթերթը 1906 Յուլիս 11էն Օգոստոս 17, ընդամէնը 28 թիւ:

Տակաւին կարելի է թուել տասնեակ մը այլ պարբերականներ, որոնք քսաներորդ դարասկիզբին լոյս տեսած են Եգիպտոս, ինչպէս՝ Սմբատ Բիւրատի «Նոր Օր»ը (1900-1901), Տիրան Փափազեանի «Հայելի»ն (1903-1904), Վահան Քիւրքճեանի «Լուսաբեր»ը (1904-1908), Սմբատ Բիւրատի եւ Երուանդ Սրմաքէշխանլեանի «Սիսուան»ը (1905), Սիսակ Մուրատեանի «Պիծակ» երգիծական շաբաթաթերթը (1906), եւայլն:

Եգիպտահայ գաղութի այդ ժամանակներու նորահաստատ պարբերականներուն մէջ ուշագրաւ են Օտեանի «Ազատ Խօսք», «Ազատ Բեմ»,

«Թերթիկ», «Արեւ» եւ «Կրակ» թերթերը իրենց երգիծական գրութիւններով, ինչպէս նաեւ Թէքէեանի ու Կիրճեանի միասնաբար հրատարակած «Շիրակ»ը եւ Թէքէեանի առանձնաբար խմբագրած «Նոր Ժամանակներ»ը իրենց գրական ստեղծագործութիւններով:

Կիրճեան իր անսպառ աշխատակցութիւնը բերած է վերոյիշեալ պարբերականներուն գրական եւ հրապարակախօսական գործերով:

Օտեան իր «Տասներկու Տարի Պոլսէն Դուրս» յուշագրութեան մէջ բարձր կը գնահատէ Կիրճեանի աշխատակցութիւնը, նշելով. ««Ազատ Բեմ»ի մէկ տարուան հաւաքածոն, զոր քովս չունիմ ափսո՜ս, կրնամ ըսել որ բաւական ճոխ է եւ կրնայ հայ թերթերու հաւաքածոներուն մէջ պատուաւոր տեղ մը գրաւել: Թերթին մշտական աշխատակիցն էր Միքայէլ Կիրճեան, որ իր անսպառ սրամտութեամբ կ'ողողէր «Ազատ Բեմ»ի էջերը»: Այնուհետեւ Օտեան կը նշէ. ««Ազատ Բեմ»ը մեծ յոգնութիւն չէր տար ինծի, շաբաթը հազիւ քանի մը ժամ կ'երթայի տպարան յօդուած գրելու կամ փորձ սրբագրելու համար: Մնացած ժամանակս կ'անցընէի Միքայէլ Կիրճեանի հաճելի ընկերակցութեամբը: Շատ անգամ ծովեզրը, սրճարան մը նստած, միասին քրոնիկներ կը գրէինք զորս կը ստորագրէինք Ե. Մ. Կիրօտ, այսպէս երկուքնուս անունները իրար խառնելով»: Ահա թէ ինչու երբ Օտեանի եղբայրը Երուանդը իր քով կը հրաւիրէ զինք փոխարինելու համար Պոմպէյի մէջ, Երուանդ անմիջապէս կը համաձայնի Հնդկաստան անցնիլ՝ յարմար կարգադրութիւն մը ընելով: Նա՛խ, այդ միջոցին Աղեքսանդրիոյ Վերակազմեալ Հնչակեանները կ'ուզէին իրենց յատուկ օրկան մը ունենալ եւ անմիջապէս համաձայնութիւն կը կայանայ որ «Ազատ Բեմ»ը իր ունեցած պարտքերովը փոխանցուի անոր, պայմանով որ եթէ Օտեան Հնդկաստանէն վերադառնայ, դարձեալ ինքը ըլլայ խմբագրապետը, որոշեալ ամսականով մը, մինչ իր բացակայութեան խմբագրութիւնը վարէ Միքայէլ Կիրճեանը: Ասիկա ապացոյց մըն է այն մասին թէ Օտեան մեծ վստահութիւն ունէր Կիրճեանի գրական, հրատարակչական եւ խմբագրական կարողութեան վրայ եւ անկեղծօրէն մտերմացած էր անոր հետ:

Ահաւասիկ նոր խմբագրին, Կիրճեանի գրած ֆանթէզիներէն օրինակ մը, «Բաժանորդը» վերանգրով, որ լոյս տեսած է 1904ին «Ազատ Բեմ»ի մէջ, երբ Օտեան կը բացակայէր Եգիպտոսէն: Հեղինակը կը ներկայացնէ երբեք թերթ չմերժող, բաժանորդագրութեան գումարը կանոնաւորաբար վճարող Սենեքերիմ Ղուկասեանի զարմանալի եւ ինքնատիպ կերպարը՝ տաճկախառն հայերէն խօսող, գիտցած ուսումնքը ստորագրութիւն դնել է, երկու տող նամակ գրել է անհին չանցնող, սակայն ազգային դաւանանքով նորօրինակ տիպար մը, որ ազգասիրութեան դիւրին ձեւ մը որդեգրած է.- իր նիւթական կարողութեան չափով ազգին օգնելու համար «ընդունիլ իրեն ղրկուած բոլոր թերթերը, անոնց ամէն մէկուն վճարելով կտոր մը իր ազգասիրութենէն»: Հոգ չէ թէ սեւեակի մը անկիւնը բաց պահարանի մը մէկ քանի դարակներուն վրայ, նոյնիսկ ծրարները չբացուած վիճակով իրարու վրայ դիզուած անձեռնմխելի մնան թերթերը նուիրական բաներու պէս եւ ոչ թէ բացուելու եւ ընթերցուելու համար:

1904ի Դեկտեմբերին, երբ Օտեան Պոլսէն Աղեքսանդրիա կը վերադառնայ, Կիւրճեան ինքնաբերաբար իրեն կը վերադարձնէ «Ազատ Բեմ»ի խմբագրութիւնը, միշտ աշխատակից մնալով թերթին: Օտեան կը վկայէ. ««Ազատ Բեմ»ը իմ բացակայութեանս միջոցին, կանոնաւորապէս շարունակուած էր, խմբագրապետութեամբ Միքայէլ Կիւրճեանի, որուն կ՚օժանդակէր նաեւ քանի մը ամիսէ ի վեր Վահան Թէքէեան, որ Համպուրկէն կամ Մարսէլիայէն Աղեքսանդրիա գալով, հոն հաստատուած էր»:[102] Հետագային, Լեւոն Լարենցի ժամանումով, «Ազատ Բեմ»ը կը դառնայ Հնչակեան Կուսակցութեան օրկան եւ Օտեան, Կիւրճեան ու Թէքէեան կը քաշուին անկէ:

Գրիգոր Նազարէթեան, որ տպարանատէր եւ միանգամայն փորագրիչ էր, տեսնելով որ Օտեանի «Ազատ Խօսք»ը անկանոն պարբերականութեամբ կը հրատարակուի, կ՚առաջարկէ անոր իբրեւ երգիծական պատկերազարդ շաբաթաթերթ կանոնաւոր հրատարակութեան բերել իր մասնակցութիւնը եւ այդպիսով շուրջ մէկ տարի (1906-1907) «Ազատ Խօսք»ը կանոնաւորապէս կը հրատարակուի Աղեքսանդրիա, աշխատակցութեամբը Արփիարեանի, Կիւրճեանի, Թէքէեանի եւ Բարսեղ Ճահպազի, զբաղելով միայն տեղական հարցերով:

Կիւրճեանի խմբագրական գործունէութեան կարեւորագոյն էջը պէտք է համարել «Շիրակ» գրական հանդէսին հրատարակութիւնը 1905ին: Կիւրճեանի եւ Թէքէեանի միասնաբար հիմնադրած «Շիրակ»ին ուղղութիւնը պիտի ըլլար, ըստ թերթին առաջին թիւի առաջնորդողին, «գրագէտներու ընտրելախումբի մը օգնութեամբ աշխատիլ հայ դպրութեան վերականգնումին արտասահմանի մէջ: Անկարելի ըլլալով որ ներկայ ժամուն հայ գրողը չանդրադառնայ հայրենիքին մշտահեծ ցաւերուն, անոնցմէ իր յուզումին արիւնը եւ մտածմանց հիւթը չծծէ՝ «Շիրակ» պիտի ընէ ազգային գրականութիւն մը, առանց մտնելու կուսակցական նկատառումներու եւ մասնաւորութեանց մէջ. լա՛յն պիտի բանայ իր էջերը բոլոր ճշմարիտ ու վաւերական գրագէտներուն առջեւ, ընծայելով այսպէս անոնց գերազանց միջոցը կատարելու իրենց վրայ ծանրացող պարտքն հանդէպ հայ դպրութեանց եւ անով՝ հանդէպ ազգային վերածնումի գործին»:[103]

Պարզ է որ այսպիսի վեհ նպատակներ հետապնդող գրական եւ ընկերային պարբերական մը չէր կրնար չօգնել ազգային զարթօնքին, այդ ծանր եւ դժուարին օրերուն: Արդարեւ, հանդէսին հերթական թիւերուն մէջ յաճախ կը նկարագրուի արեւմտահայութեան անիշխանական կացութիւնը, իսկ արեւմտահայ լաւագոյն գրողները (Արփիարեան, Օտեան, Վրթանէս Փափազեան, Ատոմ Եարճանեան, Տիրան Չրաքեան, Յովհաննէս Սէթեան եւ ուրիշներ) կ'աշխատակցին «Շիրակ»ին՝ արձակ եւ չափածոյ գրական ստեղծագործութիւններով:

Հրատարակութեան առաջին տարուան ընթացքին, Յունուարէն Նոյեմբեր 1905, անոնք կը հրատարակեն տասնմէկ թիւ, ապա քանի մը ամիս դադրելէ ետք, թերթին հրատարակութիւնը կը վստահուի այդ օրերուն Գահիրէ բնակող Արփիար Արփիարեանի, որ 1906-1907 տարիներուն կը հրատարակէ ընդամէնը ինն թիւ: «Շիրակ»ի երկրորդ շրջանի հրատարակութիւնը կը դադրի, երբ Արփիարեան «Լուսաբեր»ի խմբագրապետ կը դառնայ:

«Շիրակ»ը իր հրատարակութեան երրորդ շրջանին լոյս կը տեսնէ իբրեւ գրական եւ քաղաքական շաբաթական հանդէս Պոլսոյ մէջ, այս անգամ միայն Վահան Թէքէեանի խմբագրապետութեամբ: Թէքէեան 1909 Փետրուարէն Օգոստոս ամիսներուն լոյս կ'ընծայէ շաբաթաթերթէն քսանվեց թիւ, որով եւ կ'աւարտի գրական կեանքը այս հետաքրքրական հանդէսին, որ Եգիպտոսի պարբերական հրատարակութիւններուն մէջ կը գրաւէ առաջին տեղը թէ՛ գրական տեսակէտով եւ թէ՛ իր կուռ պարունակութեամբ:

Կիւրճեան քրոնիկներով, ֆանթէզիներով, յօդուածներով, պատմուածքներով, քաղաքական վերլուծութիւններով եւ երգիծական ու գրական ակնարկներով աշխատակցած է նաեւ Յարութիւն Ալփիարի եւ Տիգրան Արփիարի «Փարոս»ին (Գահիրէ), Սմբատ Բիւրատի «Փիւնիկ»ին (Գահիրէ, 1899 եւ Աղեքսանդրիա, 1901-1903), Եղիշէ Թոռոսեանի «Արշալոյս»ին, (Գահիրէ 1899-1914), Մառի Պէյլէրեանի «Արտեմիս»ին (Գահիրէ, 1902-1903), Տիգրան Փափազեանի «Հայելի»ին (Աղեքսանդրիա), Աւետիս Պալեանի «Ժողովուրդ»ին (Գահիրէ, 1903-1904), Վահան Քիւրքճեանի «Լուսաբեր»ին (Գահիրէ, 1904-1908), Միհրան Ասքանազի «Պարտէզ»ին (Աղեքսանդրիա, 1904), Տոքթոր Թէոֆիլի «Փեթակ»ին (Աղեքսանդրիա, 1903), Օտեանի «Թերթիկ»ին (Աղեքսանդրիա, 1906) եւ Պոլիս թէ այլուր հրատարակուող հայ պարբերականներու:

Խորապէս գիտակցելով հրապարակախօսութեան կարեւոր դերին հայ զանգուածներու հոգեկան տրամադրութեան բարձրացման եւ բարոյական կորովի ամրապնդման առումով, Կիւրճեան մարդասիրական գաղափարներով եւ ոգեւորիչ խօսքերով զօրավիգ կը կանգնի հայ ժողովուրդին՝ քաղաքական ու տնտեսական այդ ծանր օրերուն, ընթացիկ կարեւորագոյն հարցերու եւ օրուան անցքերուն շուրջ մեկնաբանութիւններ կատարելով:

Դժբախտաբար Կիւրճեանի, հանոյքով ընթերցուող բազմաթիւ յօդուածներն ու խմբագրականները մինչեւ այսօր կը մնան արեւմտահայ մամուլի էջերուն մէջ ցան ու ցիր:

Օտեանին անդրադառնալով, Սիրունի կը գրէ. «Օտեանի քրոնիկներուն մէջ է որ ցանցնուած է իր ամէնօրեայ հիւմորը, որովհետեւ հազարաւոր սրամիտ էջեր պառկած են այսպէս օրաթերթի հաւաքածուներուն մէջ, ու խնամոտ ձեռքի մը կը սպասեն փունջ կապուելու համար»: Այդպէս ալ Կիւրճեանի օրը օրին եւ հետ ի հետ գրուած ու այդ ժամանակներու պարբերական մամուլին մէջ հրատարակուած նիւթերուն մէջ չեն պակսիր հեգնանքի եւ սրամտութեան բազմաթիւ գլուխ գործոցներ, օգտակար խորհուրդներ, իմաստուն միտքերու, լրջախոհ յորդորներու եւ պիտանի կարծիքներու թելադրական գրութիւններ:

Կիւրճեան իր քրոնիկներուն, լրագրական ժամանակագրութիւններուն, յօդուածներուն եւ հրապարակագրական էջերուն մէջ կ'արծարծէ օրուան հրատապ հարցերը, հասարակական-քաղաքական առօրեայ երեւոյթները պատկերաւոր յուզականութեամբ, գիտա-փիլիսոփայական հարցադրումներով եւ մանաւանդ գեղարուեստական շունչով:

Ինչպէս 1898ին Կիւրճեան իր հռչակաւոր «Մարտիկ Աղա» վէպով մէկ անգամէն իջաւ գրական ասպարէզ, այնպէս ալ հրապարակագրական բնագաւառ մտաւ որպէս հանճարեղ հրապարակագիր «Հէմ Լանք, Հէմ Երթանք» յօդուածով, որ լոյս տեսաւ Ալփիարի «Փարոս»ին մէջ 1900ին: Ընտրուած խորագիրը լիովին կը համապատասխանէ յօդուածին թէ՛ բովանդակութեան եւ թէ՛ ոգիին: Միաժամանակ, ան կը մարմնաւորէ հայուն աննկուն կամքը եւ աւելի փայլուն ապագայի մը յոյսը:

Յօդուածը փիլիսոփայական վերլուծումն է հայկական «Հէմ լանք, հէմ երթանք» ասացուածքին: Կիւրճեան կը բացատրէ թէ հակառակ իրենց կրած դարաւոր չարչարանքներուն, հայերն ունին կեանքին կառչած մնալու հաւատք եւ դիմացկունութիւն, երբեմն արտասուալից, երբեմն արիւնլուայ, բայց միշտ առոյգ, պայքարող եւ առհաւական անդրդուելի բնաւորութեամբ մը յարատեւող:

Արդարեւ, իր բոլոր դժբախտութիւններով հանդերձ, հայը յաջողած է գոյատեւել դարերու ընթացքին՝ թէ՛ լալով եւ թէ՛ քալելով: Կիւրճեանի համոզմամբ, դժբախտութիւնը կրնայ տկարը կործանել, բայց զօրաւորը աւելի կը զօրացնէ՝ տոկունութիւն ներշնչելով անոր. հետեւաբար, «Հէմ լանք, հէմ երթանք» արտայայտութիւնը ողբ մը ըլլալով հանդերձ, քայլերգ մըն է միաժամանակ դարերով տառապած հայուն համար: Գրողը, որ միշտ լաւատես է, վստահ է թէ «պիտի գայ հարկաւ այն օրը, ուր հայութիւնը ապրելու, վերապրելու իր հրաշալի կարողութեան, ազնուական հանճարին վարձքն ու պսակը պիտի ստանայ հասնելով *կեանքի երջանիկ ձեւի* մը, եւ այն օրը վերջապէս պիտի ջնջէ *ողբը* եւ պիտի պահէ միայն նուիրական քայլերգը», քանի որ հին ժամանակներէն մինչեւ այսօր տառապանքն է եղած հայութիւնը պահող ուժը:

1909ին, թրքական յեղափոխութեան վաղորդայնին, ներշնչուած այն միամիտ եւ ազգովին տարածուած յոյսէն թէ նոր րէժիմը մոռնալ պիտի տայ հինին արհաւիրքները եւ «երջանիկ» կեանքի մը բարիքները պարգեւէ Թուրքիոյ հպատակ ցեղերուն, Կիւրճեանի այս յօդուածը կը վերահրատարակուի «Բիւզանդիոն»ի մէջ, վերջաբանի փոքր փոփոխումով մը:

Հայուն խանդավառութիւնն ու լաւատեսութիւնը երկար չտեւեցին: Պայթեցաւ Համաշխարհային Առաջին Պատերազմը եւ հայ ժողովուրդը լացաւ այնպէս, ինչպէս լացած չէր երբեք իր ամբողջ պատմութեան ընթացքին:

Նոյն «Հէմ Լանք, Հէմ Երթանք» յօդուածը Կիրճեան 65 տարիներ ետք վերահրատարակութեան յանձնած է «Արեւ»ի մէջ, ներածական բացատրութեամբ մը, ուր կը շեշտէ թէ հակառակ անոր որ «թրքահայութեան ստուարագոյն մասը բնաջնջուեցաւ անլուր բարբարոսութեամբ, եւ արիւնահեղեղէն մազապուրծ «մնացորդները» այսօր բազում երկիրներու մէջ կը կազմեն առաւել կամ նուազ բարգաւաճ գաղութներ եւ շատոնց կորսնցուցած են այդ մռայլ դիմագծութիւնը, հայ ազգը շատոնց դադրած է լալէ, եւ կը քալէ, կը քալէ յաղթական, եւ պիտի քալէ հասնելու համար իր նպատակին»: Ան կ'աւելցնէ թէ յօդուածին աւարտին բանաձեւուած լաւագոյն ապագայի մը յոյսերը իրականացած են շնորհիւ Հայաստանի գոյութեան եւ հրաշալի բարգաւաճումին:[104]

Տիրան Չրաքեան Սկիւտարէն Կիրճեանին գրած 14/27 Սեպտեմբեր 1909 թուակիրին մէջ կ'ըսէ. ««Հէմ Լանք, Հէմ Երթանք»դ, օրաթերթի մը մէջ միայն մնալու դժբախտութիւնն ունեցող այդ յօդուածդ (թո՛ղ Մեծին Քէչեանի թերթն իսկ եղած ըլլայ ան) գլուխ գործոց մըն էր»:

1906ին Գահիրէի մէջ կը հիմնուի Հայկական Բարեգործական Ընդհանուր Միութիւնը, որ հետագային պիտի դառնար սփիւռքի ամենակենսունակ բարեսիրական կազմակերպութիւնը: Առաջնորդուելով «Միութիւնը զօրութիւն է» բնաբանով, ՀԲԸՄ-ը 1912ին կը սկսի Գահիրէի մէջ հրատարակել «Միութիւն» ամսօրեայ պաշտօնաթերթը, որուն աշխոյժ թղթակիցներէն մին կը դառնայ Կիրճեան: Ան իր գրական ու ընկերաբանական մտային հարուստ շտեմարանը բանալով, նկարագիր կերտող, բնաւորութիւն դարբնող սրամիտ ու դաստիարակիչ յօդուածներ կը հրատարակէ հոն:

«Մեծ Մարդոց Դերը» յօդուածին մէջ սխալ համարելով հռետորական այն կարծիքը թէ «պատմական մեծ րոպէները կը ծնին ճակատագրականօրէն պատմական մարդերը», հրապարակագիրը համոզումով կը գրէ թէ ազգի մը համար բախտաւորութիւն է պատմական ճգնաժամային շրջաններուն իր ծոցին մէջ ունենալ նախախնամական նշանաւոր մարդ մը կամ մարդիկ, որոնք կարողանան ազգին գոյութիւնը պաշտպանել վերահաս վտանգներու դէմ: Կիրճեան իր տեսակէտը հաստատելու համար կը յիշատակէ յոյներու պատմութիւնը: 1896ի ձախող պատերազմէն ետք, տարիներով զինուորապէս տկար եւ անպատրաստ, ներքնապէս պառակտուած եւ անհամաձայն նկարագիր մը պարզելէ ետք, Վէնիզելոս Կրետէէն գալով քանի մը տարուան միջոցին կը յաջողի կերպարանափոխել Յունաստանը՝ «քաղաքային վարչութիւն, բանակ, նաւատորմիղ կանոնաւորուեցան, բարենորոգուեցան, զօրացան. յունական դիւանագիտութիւնը մէկ օրէն միւսը ուժ մը դարձաւ, արթուն, խելացի, գործօն»:

Այս յօդուածով Կիւրճեան ցոյց կու տայ թէ ինչպէս կրետացի նախկին փաստաբանը՝ Վէնիզելոս, բոլոր ընդդիմադիր հոսանքները միաւորելով, կարողացաւ մեծ նուագապետի մը պէս վարել «ազգային մեծ դաշնակաւոր ալէլուն», բոլոր նուագածուները իր ճպոտին տիրական հարուածներուն ենթարկելով:

Եզրակացնելով իր գրութիւնը, ան խորհուրդ կու տայ. «Մենք հայերս լաւ կ'ընենք որ անդրադառնանք այս ճշմարտութիւններուն, որովհետեւ ոչ մէկ ազգ այնքան պէտք ունի նշանաւոր մարդոց որքան որ մենք, այս ճակատագրական պահուն, եւ ո՛չ մէկ ազգ այնքան պարտաւորութիւն ունի թերեւս որքան մենք՝ ճանչնալու եւ գնահատելու այն նշանաւոր մարդիկը կամ մարդը, զոր բախտը պարգեւած է մեզի»:

«Ողջմտութիւն Ու Դիւցազնութիւն» յօդուածին մէջ Կիւրճեան կը նշէ թէ այս երկուքը զիրար լրացնող մարդկային յատկութիւններ են, որոնցմէ առաջինը կը ծառայէ խաղաղութեան ատեն, իսկ երկրորդը՝ վտանգի պահուն: Ապա ան կը հաստատէ. «Մենք ապրելու իրաւունք ունեցող» ազգ մըն ենք, որ «պիտի ապրի ազատ, երջանիկ» իր դիւցազնական ինքնակամ վարմունքով եւ խորունկ ողջմտութեամբ:

Քսաներորդ դարու առաջին տասնամեակին էական խնդիր մըն էր մատաղ սերունդին կրթութեան հարցը: Կիւրճեան «Միութիւն»ի մէջ 1912էն սկսեալ կը հրատարակէ շարք մը յօդուածներ հայկական դպրոցներու կրթական ծրագրերու բարելաւման վերաբերեալ: Ան կը շեշտէ դաստիարակութեան բազմակողմանիութեան, վարժարաններու տեսական ու գործնական դերերու, աշակերտները ֆիզիքապէս եւ բարոյապէս դարբնելու կարեւորութիւնը («Ամբողջական Դաստիարակութիւն»): Կը գրէ. «Վարժարանը պէտք չէ որ ըլլայ արհեստական միջավայր մը, ուր տղաք կեանքին հետ հաղորդակցութեան մէջ ըլլան միմիայն գիրքերուն միջոցով. անիկա պարտի ըլլալ պզտիկ աշխարհ մը, իրական, դրական, որ տղան դնէ այնքան մօտ բնութեան եւ իրականութեան որքան որ կարելի է: Պէտք չէ որ անիկա սորվի լոկ տեսականը, այլ եւ գործնականը, եւ այս երկու տարրերը պէտք է սերտօրէն միացած ըլլան դպրոցին մէջ, ինչպէս որ են մեր շուրջը, որպէսզի կեանքի մէջ մուտք գործած ատեն, երիտասարդը չմտնայ աշխարհի մէջ որուն համար պատրաստուած չէ, եւ ուր մնայ շուարած, ուղեկորոյս»:

Կիւրճեան «Միութիւն»ի ընթերցողներուն կը ներկայացնէ անուանի տնտեսագէտ-ընկերաբան Լը Բլէյի լաւագոյն աշակերտ, ֆրանսացի գիտնական Էտմոն Տէմոլէնի շահեկան տեսակէտները կրթութեան մասին: Տէմոլէն ֆրանսացի ծնողներու համար օրինակ կը բերէ անգլիական դպրոցական դրութիւնը, որ յարմարցուած է կեանքի նորագոյն պայմաններուն եւ շատ աւելի կը յաջողի պատրաստել ձեռներէց, համարձակ ու ինքնաբաւ անհատներ՝ «կարող ինքզինքնին պեճերելու կեանքին ամէն դժուարութեանց եւ կացութեանց մէջ» («Ամբողջական Դաստիարակութիւն»):

Կիրճեան յարատեւ որոնող եւ ընթերցասէր ըլլալով, քաջատեղեակ էր նշանաւոր ընկերաբաններ Իբօլիթ Թէնի, Կիւսթավ Լըպօնի, Էրնըսթ Ռընանի, Վօլթէրի, Թարտի եւ ուրիշ տնտեսագէտներու եւ ընկերաբաններու տեսութիւններուն: Որպէս կրթասէր անձ, ան «Միութիւն»ի թիւերուն մէջ քանիցս անդրադարձած է Տէմօլէնի «A quoi tient la supériorité des Anglo-Saxons» աշխատութեան, յատկապէս շեշտելով թէ անոր գաղափարները շահեկան են հայերու համար ալ: Ըստ հեղինակին, անկլօ-սաքսոն ծնողներ իրենց զաւակները չեն նկատեր իրենց սեփականութիւնը: Ընդհակառակը, զանոնք կը դիտեն իբրեւ էակներ, որոնք սահմանուած են աստիճանաբար անկախանալու իրենց ծնողներէն: Անկլօ-սաքսոն ծնողներ իրենց զաւակներուն հետ կը վարուին իբրեւ խելահաս անձերու, անկախ անհատներու: Ֆրանսացի ծնողներ, ինչպէս հայերը, միշտ տրամադիր են իրենց զաւակները նկատելու տղաներ, նոյնիսկ չափահաս տարիքին: Սաքսոն ծնողներ դաստիարակութեան գործին մէջ նպատակակէտ ունին ապագայ կեանքի կարիքներն ու նոր պայմանները եւ ոչ թէ անցեալը:

Ուրիշ յօդուածի մը մէջ, Կիրճեան կը նշէ թէ ծնողները պէտք է հոգ տանին ո՛չ միայն իրենց զաւակներուն առողջութեան, այլեւ ու մանաւանդ ֆիզիքական ուժին բնականոն ու լիակատար զարգացման: Ան այս առթիւ յատկապէս օրինակ կը բերէ անկլօ-սաքսոն ծնողները, որոնք կանուխէն իրենց զաւակները կը վարժեցնեն նիւթական իրերու եւ ձեռային արհեստներու: Մարզումը եւ ո՛չ թէ ճնշումն ու բռնադատութիւնը պէտք է կազմէ ծնողական դաստիարակութեան մեթոտը: Հարկ է աւելի շատ խրատել, համոզել, թելադրել, քան՝ հրամայել եւ սպառնալ:

Կիրճեան կը շեշտէ. «Ցորչափ ֆիզիքապէս չվերածնինք, չվերանորոգուինք, անկարելի պիտի ըլլայ մեր ցեղին՝ բարոյապէս վերանորոգուիլ» («Ֆիզիքական Կրթութիւն»): Ան կը խորհի թէ ամուր պէտք է պահել կենսօգուտ մարմնամարզի հիւղը, դպրոցականներու ֆիզիքական դաստիարակութիւնը, որովհետեւ անկէ է որ պիտի բարձրանան մեր մտաւոր-բարոյական վերածնութեան ընձիւղները:

Կիրճեան կրթական ծրագրին անհրաժեշտ մաս կը նկատէ դպրոցական տարիքի աշակերտներուն իմացական զարգացումն ու նկարագրի կազմութիւնը: «Բարոյական դաստիարակութիւն ըսելով պէտք է հասկնալ առաւելապէս այն կրթութիւնը, ուղղակի, կենդանի, դրական հետեւաբար մեծազդեցիկ, զոր ուսուցիչը կրնայ եւ պարտի տալ իր աշակերտներուն, իր վարուելակերպովը դպրոցին մէջ եւ դպրոցէն դուրս, իր գործունէութեան, իր շարժումներուն եւ արարքներուն բարբառուն ու տպաւորիչ օրինակովը» («Բարոյական Դաստիարակութիւն»):

Այսպիսի ճիշդ եւ օգտակար խորհուրդներ կան նաեւ «Ինչպէս Կրթելու Ենք Մեր Զաւակները» եւ այլ կրթա-մանկավարժական յօդուածներու մէջ՝ ազգային դաստիարակութեան շուրջ: Ըստ Կիրճեանի, «Մեր դպրոցներէն շրջանաւարտ -շատ անգամ կիսաւարտ- ելլող տղաքները տարապայմանն հակում մը ցոյց կու տան երկու բանի — *գրականութիւն* եւ *քաղաքականութիւն*, երկու ամենէն աւելի «անդրական» բաները որոնք գոյութիւն ունենան աշխարհի երեսը, *երբ հայկական են անոնք*»: Նկատի ունենալով որ «մեր գրասէրներուն եւ *ազգայիններուն* թիւը անհամեմատ մեծ է եւ թէ ժամանակն է որ անդրադառնանք իրերու այս յոռի վիճակին վրայ եւ անհրաժեշտ է միջոցներ մշակել առողջ դրապաշտութեան որովհետեւ կրթութիւն, մամուլ եւ քաղաքականութիւն ա՛յդ մարդոց ձեռքը կը գտնուին, ա՛յդ գէշ պատրաստուած գործիչներուն»: Նկատի ունենալով իր ժամանակի կացութիւնը եւ ապագան, Կիրճեան կը հաստատէ. «ուրիշ ո՛չ մէկ ցեղ մեզի չափ առատօրէն կ'արտադրէ «գրասէր» ու «գրագէտցու»» («Քիչ Մը Դրականութիւն»):

«Հայուն Միտքը» ընդարձակ յօդուածին մէջ Կիրճեան հաստատելով հանդերձ թէ «անվիճելի է որ խելացի, մտաւորական ցեղ մ'ենք, բայց ֆրանսացիին ըսածին պէս, «փայտի տրցակ կայ՝ տրցակ ալ կայ» (Il y a fagots et fagots), այնպէս ալ՝ խելք կայ՝ խելք ալ կայ»: Վկայակոչելով նշանաւոր ընկերաբան Կ. Թարտի տեսութիւնը, թէ ընկերական կեանքի վարիչ ուժերն են «ստեղծումն ու նմանողութիւնը», Կիրճեան անաչառօրէն կը գտնէ թէ մեր քաղաքակրթութիւնը առաւել կամ նուազ յաջող ընդօրինակութիւնն է օտար քաղաքակրթութեան մը, կամ քաղաքակրթութիւններու: Դիցաբանութիւն, կրօնք, գրականութիւն, գեղարուեստ, քաղաքական եւ ընկերական բարքեր, եւայլն փոխ առած ենք մեզ շրջապատող, մեր վրայ տիրող ազգերէ, քաղաքակրթութեամբ օժտուած ցեղերէ: Հայ միտքը իր ընդհանուր եւ էական գիծերուն մէջ, կը ներկայանայ իբրեւ աւելի նմանող քան ստեղծագործող միտք մը, աւելի ընկալուչ քան արտադրող միտք մը, աւելի հասկցող եւ ըմբռնող քան ստեղծող, աւելի տպաւորական քան ներգործող, աւելի վերլուծող քան համադրող: Հայ միտքի գլխաւոր յատկանիշը իւրացումն է: Մեր ցեղին ի սկզբանէ անտի ճակատագրուած գոյութեան աննպաստ պայմաններուն պատճառաւ հայ միտքը չէ կրցած ազատօրէն զարգացնել ու փթթեցնել ստեղծագործ ուժի սերմերը:

Կիրճեան «Միութիւն» ամսօրեայ պաշտօնաթերթի 1910ական թուականներու թիւերուն մէջ իր լոյս տեսած յօդուածները ստորագրած է «Միքայէլ Ս. Կիրճեան» ստորագրութեամբ եւ ոչ թէ մինչ այդ օգտագործած ծածկանուններով:

Սփիւռքահայ մամուլին մէջ ցրուած Կիրճեանի յօդուածները, առաջնորդողները, խմբագրական սիւնակները թելադրելի եւ ուսանելի են ներկայ օրերուն ալ, հակառակ տասնամեակներ առաջ գրուած ըլլալնուն:

«Ինչ Որ Ունինք Եւ Ինչ Որ Կը Պակսի Մեզի» յօդուածին մէջ[105] Կիրճեան կ'ըսէ. «Կրնանք առանց սխալելու երկիւղի ըսել որ միջին կարողութեանց տէր հայ մը շատ աւելի կ'արժէ, մտաւորապէս,- իբր խորհրդածող, հասկցող եւ օգտուող միտք,- քան նոյն աստիճանի ֆրանսացի մը, անգլիացի մը, գերմանացի մը: Ամենէն տգէտ հայը անգամ ունի յատուկ կեանքի փորձառական եւ «աւանդական» իմաստութիւն մը»: Ապա կը յիշատակէ մեծանուն քաղաքագէտ Նուպար Փաշայի համբաւաւոր խօսքը՝ «Մէկ հայ երեք եւրոպացի կ'արժէ», ու կը շարունակէ. «Այո՛, բայց *մտաւորապէս*, այսինքն խելքով, խորամանկութեամբ, բանիմացութեամբ: Իսկ տասը հայ շատ անգամ մէկ եւրոպացի չեն արժեր բարոյապէս, այսինքն նկարագրով, կամքի ուժով: Այս է բուն վէրքը»: Ան կ'ընդգծէ. «մեր ձիրքերը առաւելապէս իմացական, մտաւորական (intellectuel, mental) կարգէ են» եւ կ'եզրափակէ. «Մեր տղաքը դպրոցներուն մէջ շատ բան կը սորվին, նոյնիսկ թերեւս համապատասխան վարժարանէ մը ելլողը անկլօ-սաքսոն ուսանողէ մ'աւելի լեզու գիտէ. բայց չեն սորվիր այն մեծ բանը զոր այս վերջինը խորապէս կը սորվի եւ որ այնքան էական է յաջողութեան տեսակէտով. այն է՝ «ինքզինքը կեանքի մէջ վարել, կառավարել գիտնալ»»:

Ուրիշ յօդուածի մը մէջ ան կը գրէ. «Մեր մէջ, հանրային գործոց խանգարման ու քայքայումին, կամ՝ այլապէս խօսելով՝ հանրային արգաւանդ ու տեւական գործունէութեան մը գրեթէ անկարելիութեան պատճառներէն մին, եւ թերեւս գլխաւորը, ուրիշ բան չէ բայց եթէ անհատական *եսը* կամ կուսակցական *մենքը*, որ անոր խոշորացումն է միայն» («Եսը»): Ի վերջոյ մարդկային *եսը* կը դառնայ ունայնամտութիւն, սնափառութիւն եւ անձնասիրութիւն: Ուստի անհատական եսին տեղը կ'առաջարկէ դնել *հանրային եսը* բոլոր անոնց որոնք կը ստանձնեն ազգային ո՛եւէ պաշտօն, որ զոհողութիւն կը պահանջէ:

Խօսելով մեր անմիաբանութեան եւ միաբանելու անկարողութեան մասին, գրողը կ'առաջարկէ իրագործել համերաշխութիւն, որովհետեւ «երբեք չարիքը այնքան մեծ եղած չէ որքան այդ ժամանակներուն. ապա ուրեմն միութեան պէտքը չէ եղած այնքան մեծ որքան այդ օրերուն» («Վասն Միութեան»):

Կիւրճեան «Միտքին Անբաւականութիւնը Իբրեւ Յաջողութեան Միջոց» յօդուածին մէջ կը գտնէ թէ կեանքի մէջ յաջողելու համար պէտք է գիտնալ գործել, եւ նկարագիր ու կամք ունենալ. «Միտքը շատ բան կրնայ յղանալ, մտածել... բայց գործադրողը՝ մարդուս կամքն է, նկարագիրն է, բնախօսութիւնն է»: Ան որպէս օրինակ կը բերէ Նաբոլէոնի, Ռոքֆելլերի, հռովմայեցիներու ամուր եւ էական յատկութիւնները: Մէջբերելով Բասքալի յայտնի խօսքը. «Մարդս խորհող եղէգ մըն է», ան կը նշէ թէ այդ խօսքը անկատար է: Մարդը ոչ միայն *խորհող եղէգ* է, այլեւ մանաւանդ գործող: «Եղէգ»ը ոչինչ պիտի կրնար ընել, ոչինչ ստեղծել, եթէ միայն խորհող ըլլար:

«*Մտածել* գիտենք, քիչ մըն ալ *գործել* սորվինք» կոչով կը վերջացնէ իր յօդուածը ազգասէր գրողը:

Փոխ առնելով ֆրանսացի մեծ բանաստեղծ Ռասինի ողբերգութեան տիտղոսը, Կիւրճեան իր յօդուածներէն մէկը կոչած է «Թշնամի Եղբայրներ»: Հոն ան կը քննարկէ կազմակերպութեան մարզը եւ անհատապաշտութիւնը. «Հայ ազգը միշտ տառապած է նուագապետի (chef d'orchestre) բացակայութեան չարիքէն», որովհետեւ մեզմէ իւրաքանչիւրը ինքզինք կը կարծէ պետ: «Ամէնքս ալ հրամայել կ'ուզենք. *հնազանդիլը մեր կարողութենէն վեր է.* կամ մեր ... *արժանաւորութենէն շատ վար*»: Նոյն յօդուածին մէջ ան կը գրէ. «Մենք չենք կրնար հանդուրժել որ հայ մը, *ազգային* մը, մեզի հրամայէ. տայ կարգախօսը, ցուցնէ հետեւելիք հասարակաց ուղղութիւնը...: Անհատ անհատի, ընկերութիւն ընկերութեան, կուսակցութիւն կուսակցութեան հանդէպ՝ կարծես յարատեւ եւ անողոք մրցման մէջ ենք»: Ապա նշելով գերմաններու, լատիններու, անկլօ-սաքսոններու, ֆրանսացիներու օրինակը, Կիւրճեան խորհուրդ կու տայ կազմակերպուիլ եւ որդեգրել կարգապահութեան եւ հնազանդութեան խորունկ ոգին՝ յանուն ազգային փոքր կամ մեծ նպատակի հետապնդման, որպէսզի չցրուին մեր ճիգերը, ի զուր չվատնուին ջանքերն ու կորովները եւ ունենանք բեղուն, կանոնաւոր ու տեւական գործունէութիւն:

Հայ մամուլի խիզախ եւ արդարակորով գործիչին մօտ կը նկատուի քաղաքական խորաթափանցութիւն, դէպքերու եւ դէմքերու նկարագրութեան հմտութիւն, միջազգային օտար մամուլի, պատմական ու պետական գործիչներու մասին քաջատեղեակութիւն, գիտելիքներու հարուստ պաշար: Ան մէջբերումներ կ'ընէ Մորիս Պառէսի յօդուածէն, Նուպար Փաշայի խօսքէն, օրինակ կը բերէ Նաբոլէոնը, Զօրավար Ժօֆրը, Լոռիս-Մէլիքօֆը, Այվազովսկին, Էտկար Ծահինը, Տիգրան Երկաթը, Եփրեմ Խանը եւ ուրիշներ, որոնք իրենց արտակարգ տաղանդին ու ձեռներէցութեան շնորհիւ փայլուն դիրքերու եւ միջազգային համբաւի տիրացած են արուեստներու, քաղաքականութեան, վաճառականութեան, զինուորականութեան ու այլ բնագաւառներու մէջ:

Հանրային կեանքի մէջ անհատապաշտ չըլլալու եւ հաւաքապաշտ ըլլալու, ազգովին համերաշխաբար գործելու մասին կարեւոր խորհուրդ կու տայ ան «Մեր Անհատապաշտութիւնը» յօդուածին մէջ:[106]

Զգաստութեան, պարկեշտութեան, անձնական կիրքերու հանդարտութեան, կուսակցական ատելութիւններու եւ կռիւներու դադարեցման կոչով հանդէս կու գայ «Լռութի՜ւն, Պարոննե՛ր, Հոն Կը Մեռնին...» յօդուածին մէջ՝ միտքերը բարձրացնելու եւ սիրտերը հաշտեցնելու համար: Ազգասիրութիւն կը քարոզէ՝ ոգեկոչելով մեր կտրիճ եղբայրները, որոնք կը մեռնին գունդագունդ, իրենց առնացի անձնազոհութեամբը վերահաստատելով հայուն պատիւը աշխարհի առջեւ, յիշեցնելով որ «անդի՜ն, անիծապարտ Տաճկաստանի ոճրաւուն արիւնորոգ հողին վրայ, մեր քամբախտ հայրենակիցները գեհենական տանջանքներու մէջ կը մարտիրոսանան, անօթութենէ տառապելով»: Ան կը յիշեցնէ այդ օրերուն տեղի ունեցող սպանօ-ամերիկեան պատերազմը, երբ ամերիկեան նաւատորմիղը կը ջախջախէր սպանականը, մարտանաւեր կ'ընկղմէին բոցերու, ծուխերու ժայթքումներով եւ որոտագին պայթումներով:

Ընթերցողներու ուշադրութիւնը սեւեռելով պատերազմական նախարարութեան դէմ ֆրանսական խորհրդարանի քանի մը անդամներու քննադատութիւններուն վրայ, Կիւրճեան կ'անդրադառնայ Առաջին Համաշխարհային Պատերազմի ժամանակ պատերազմական նախարար Միլերանի յուզիչ ճառին՝ ուղղուած հրամակիր եւ ընդդիմադիր բոլոր երեսփոխաններուն. «Ի սէ՛ր հայրենիքին միաբան ու համերաշխ մնանք գոնէ՛ մինչեւ յաղթութեան օրը»: Միլերան այդպիսով կը փորձէ դադրեցնել քաղաքական կիրքերն ու ընկերային պայքարները, որովհետեւ թշնամին ֆրանսական հողին վրայ էր եւ վտանգը չէր ելած երկրին սահմաններէն դուրս:

Կիւրճեան իր մտածումը կը դարձնէ մեր պզտիկ ազգին, որուն գլխուն եկած աղէտը, անոր գոյութեան սպառնացող վտանգը աւելի մեծ է, ուստի վերապրելու համար «ամէն ատենուընէ աւելի՝ պէտք է որ *հաւաքապաշտ* ըլլանք, պէտք է *համազգային* ըլլանք, հրաժարինք մեր անհատականութիւններէն ու պատկանինք ցեղին, անոր անսխալական բնազդէն վարուինք, անոր անհուն սիրտովը բաբախենք» յանուն նուիրական հայրենիքի շահին: Հայրենանուէր զգացումով ան կը գոչէ. «Հայե՛ր, միանա՛նք, հայե՛ր, միացած մնանք *գէ՛թ մինչեւ որ անցնի մահուան վտանգը*» («Գոնէ Մինչեւ Յաղթութեան Օրը»):

Կեանքի մէջ ինքնուրոյն ըլլալու, ուրիշ ազգերէ լաւ օրինակներ վերցնելու, ինքզինքէն աւելի ուրիշներու վրայ յոյս չդնելու, սնափառութենէ, օտարամոլութենէ զերծ մնալու, զարգացած եւ կատարելագործուած ազգ մը ըլլալու յորդորով յիշարժան է «Մեր Նկարագիրը» յօդուածը:

1911ին Սուրէն Պարթեւեան կը հաստատուի բուրգերու երկիրը՝ Եգիպտոս, ուր կային կարեւոր թիւով հայ մտաւորականներ, եւ երբ 1912ին կը հրատարակէ «Հոսանք»ը՝ գրագէտ-հրապարակագիրներու հոյլի մը (Տիգրան Կամսարական, Լեւոն Մկրտիչեան, Վահան Մալէզեան, Յովհաննէս Սէթեան, Յովհաննէս Գայայեան, Արտաւազդ Հանըմեան, Աղեքսանդր Ծաքլեան, Գառնիկ Ֆնտգլեան, Մուշեղ Եպիսկոպոս Սերոբեան, Տիրան Քէլէկեան, Վահան Թէքէեան, Տիրան Չրաքեան, Երուանդ Օտեան, Արտաշէս Յարութիւնեան, Օննիկ Չիֆթէ-Սարաֆ, Թլկատինցի, Ռուբէն Որբերեան, Արամ Անտոնեան եւ ուրիշներ) հետ Կիւրճեան եւս կ'աշխատակցի այդ պարբերականին:

«Հոսանք»ի առաջին տարուան՝ 1912ի 1, 3, 8, 12 եւ 18րդ թիւերուն մէջ «Թնդա...Նօթեր»ու շարքով մը ան կ'անդրադառնայ Ազգային Ժողովին, Գրիգոր Զօհրապի ճառերուն, Օսմանեան Երեսփոխանական Ժողովի թեկնածուներուն եւ նիստերուն, սահմանադրական յօդուածի մը շուրջ քննարկումներուն, ճարակաւն կառավարութեան դէմ պայքարը դադրեցնելու անհրաժեշտութեան, ազգային ու միջազգային հարցերու, միշտ հայ ազգին շահերը պաշտպանելու սկզբունքով:

Խօսելով նորաստեղծ քաղաքական հոսանքներու, վարդապետութիւններու, կազմակերպութիւններու եւ կուսակցութիւններու մասին, Կիրճեան օրինակ կը բերէ Ֆրանսայի մէջ կազմութիւնը քաղաքական նոր կուսակցութեան մը, որուն անունը պիտի ըլլայ «Քաղաքական Ապագայապաշտութիւն», որուն գլխաւոր սկզբունքը՝ ապագայապաշտութիւնը, կու գայ գրականութեան եւ արուեստի մէջ արդէն գոյութիւն ունեցող նոյն *ութիւն*ով յորջորջուած դպրոցէն, որ կը դաւանի ուրանալ անցեալը եւ զբաղիլ միայն ապագայով: Այս նոր կուսակցութեան հիմնադիր Լըֆէվր ինքզինք թեկնածու ներկայացուցած է Բարիզի թաղապետական ընտրութեանց, նպատակ ունենալով «Ոսկեդարը» վերադարձնել երկրի վրայ կամ «երկրաւոր դրախտ» մը ստեղծել:

Կիրճեանի հրապարակագրական եւ խմբագրական գործունէութեան մասին խօսելու ժամանակ պէտք է անպայման նշել անոր կատարած դերը «Արեւ» օրաթերթին խմբագրութեան մէջ:

1920-1923 թուականներուն Կիրճեանին վիճակուած էր վարել «Արեւ»ի խմբագրի պաշտօնը: Այդ տարիներուն անոր գրած յօդուածներն ու խմբագրականները կը հանդիսանան իր քաղաքական առաջաւոր հայեացքներուն լաւագոյն արտայայտութիւնները եւ հայրենիքի նկատմամբ տածած հաւատքի ու լաւատեսութեան հիանալի վկայութիւնները:

Կիրճեանի յօդուածներէն եւ խմբագրականներէն մի քանին իրենց շահեկանութեան համար արտատպուած են սփիւռքահայ այլ պարբերականներու մէջ: Օրինակ, «Թէ Ինչո՞ւ Պօղոս Բաշա Նուպար Չստորագրեց Հաշտութեան Դաշնագիրը» խմբագրականը արտատպուած կը տեսնենք Նիւ Եորքի «Կոչնակ Հայաստանի»ի 16 Հոկտեմբեր 1919ի թիւին մէջ (էջ 1346-1347): Այդ խմբագրականով, հեղինակը ընթերցողներու ուշադրութիւնը կը հրաւիրէ այն արժանահաւատ տեղեկութիւններուն վրայ, զորս ինք կը յայտնէ Սավօյ հիւրանոցին մէջ տեղի ունեցած ճաշկերոյթի ընթացքին իր հարցումին ի պատասխան Հայաստանի Հանրապետութեան վարչապետ Ալեքսանդր Խատիսեանի տուած անկեղծ պատասխանին վրայ: Հաշտութեան դաշնագիրը իբրեւ Ազգային Պատուիրակութեան նախագահ ստորագրելու արարողութեան վերջին պահուն, թուրքերը կ'առարկեն թէ Պօղոս Նուպար իրաւունք չունի ստորագրելու զայն: Խատիսեան եւ Աւետիս Ահարոնեան կը խնդրեն որ Նուպար Բաշա տեղի չտայ եւ պնդէ ստորագրելու իր իրաւունքին վրայ:

Դաշնակից կառավարութիւնները ընդունելով որ թրքական առարկութիւնը ունի «օրինական» հիմք, հայկական շահերու տեսակէտէ նախընտրելի կը գտնեն որ Պօղոս Նուպար չստորագրէ դաշնագիրը, որպէսզի ապագային որեւէ պատրուակ հայթայթուած չըլլայ թուրքերուն՝ դաշնագրին դէմ բողոքելու իբրեւ անկանոնութեամբ գործադրուած բանի մը:

«Ն. Վսեմութիւնը, խնդիրը լաւ մը ուսումնասիրելէ, օրէնսգէտ անձնաւորութիւններու եւ հեղինակաւոր հայասէրներու հետ խորհրդակցելէ յետոյ՝ հայրենասիրական հասկնալի խղճահարութեան մը սիրայօժար զոհած է անձնական գոհունակութիւնը, որ պիտի ըլլար իր հայրենասէրի անխոնջ անձնուէր ջանքերուն բարոյական արդար վարձքը իր ստորագրութիւնը դնելու միջազգային դաշնագրի մը ներքեւ որ կը նուիրագործէ ազգին անկախութիւնը, որուն համար բազում տարիներէ ի վեր կ'աշխատի այնքան եռանդով եւ ձեռնհասութեամբ»:

Ան կ'որոշէ չստորագրել ուրիշ նկատառումով մը եւս: Դաշնագիրը ստորագրելով, պաշտօնապէս ընդունած պիտի ըլլար Հայաստանի տրուած ոչ գոհացուցիչ սահմանները: Չստորագրելով, ան կը պահէր «իր բողոքելու եւ գործելու ազատութիւնը յօգուտ հայ ազգին տակաւին չկատարուած բաղձանքներուն իրականացման»:

Արդարեւ, հետագային, 14 Օգոստոս 1920 թուակիր պաշտօնական գրութեամբ Պօղոս Նուպար Դաշնակից Պետութիւններուն իր երախտագիտութիւնը յայտնելով հանդերձ հայկական երկիրներու մէկ մասը ազատագրելու եւ անոնցմով անկախ տէրութիւն մը կազմած ըլլալնուն համար, կը բողոքէ որ Կիլիկիոյ մեծագոյն մասը եւ Խարբերդի նահանգը, որոնք պէտք էին անջատուիլ թուրք կայսրութենէն եւ մաս կազմէին ֆրանսական գօտիին, ձգուած են դարձեալ թրքական տիրապետութեան տակ, իսկ Ատանան՝ Կիլիկիոյ մայրաքաղաքը, Սիսը՝ հայոց կրօնական մայրաքաղաքը, դիւցազնական մարտնչումներու թատերավայր Զէյթունը, որ նոյնիսկ թրքական րէժիմին ներքեւ իր կիսանկախ վիճակով ճանչցուած էր Ֆրանսայի կողմէ կէս դար առաջ, մնացած են թրքական լուծի տակ:

Անկարելի է այստեղ թուել, վերլուծել եւ լուսաբանել Կիւրճեանի բազմաթիւ խմբագրականներն ու յօդուածները, որոնք հատորներ կրնան կազմել. սակայն անհրաժեշտ է որ հաւաքուին եւ առանձին հատորով հրատարակուին անոր լաւագոյն կտորները, որովհետեւ անոնք հարուստ են Կիւրճեանի հասուն մտածողութեան, յստակ եւ պարզ ոճին, լրջախոհ ազգասիրութեան եւ պայծառատես հայրենասիրութեան բարիքներով: Այդ գրութիւններէն իւրաքանչիւրին մէջ կարելի է գտնել ազգին հոգերով տառապող ազնիւ մտաւորականը:

ՀԱՐԱՏԱՏ ԹԱՐԳՄԱՆՈՒԹԻՒՆՆԵՐՈՒ ՎԱՐՊԵՏԸ

Կիրճեան իր աւանդը ունեցած է օտար գրականութենէ թարգմանութիւններով հայ գրականութիւնը հարստացնելու ասպարէզին մէջ:

Թարգմանական արուեստը իր սկզբնաւորութիւնը ունեցած է մեր մէջ հայ գիրերու գիւտէն անմիջապէս ետք, հինգերորդ դարէն սկսեալ, նախ Աստուածաշունչին յունարէնէ եւ ասորերէնէ թարգմանութեամբ եւ ապա հայերէնի վերածումովը հին աշխարհի համբաւաւոր փիլիսոփաներ եւ ականաւոր գիտնականներ Պղատոնի, Արիստոտէլի, Եւկլիդէսի, Եւսեփիոս Կեսարացիի, Աթանաս Աղեքսանդրիացիի, Եպիփանոսի, Եփրեմ Ասորիի, Դիոնիսիոս Թրակիացիի եւ ուրիշներու գործերու:

19րդ դարուն, Պոլսոյ եւ Իզմիրի հայ մտաւորականները սորվելով եւրոպական լեզուները եւ մասնաւորապէս ֆրանսերէնը, ոգեւորութեամբ ձեռնարկած են գեղարուեստական գրականութեան թարգմանութեան գործին: Արփիար Արփիարեան կը վկայէ. «Ֆրանսերէնէ թարգմանութիւնները, գլխաւորապէս վէպերը, ժողովուրդին միտքը սկսան մարզել, թեքել, ու անոր ճաշակը կամաց-կամաց քիչ մը եւրոպականացնել»:[107]

Հայ գրագէտներ օգտակար կը նկատէին օտար հեղինակներու գործերու թարգմանութիւնը՝ իբրեւ միջոց հայ հասարակութեան լուսաւորման եւ զարգացման, ինչպէս նաեւ ժողովուրդներու մշակութային հաղորդակցութեան: Շնորհիւ այս մօտեցման, մեր գրականութիւնը հարստացած է ստուարաթիւ եւ արժէքաւոր թարգմանութիւններով:

Կիրճեանի ստեղծագործութիւնները եւ թարգմանութիւնները պրպտելու ընթացքին աւելի քան յիսուն տարբեր պարբերականներու մէջ, նկատեցինք առկայութիւնը մեծ քանակութեամբ թարգմանական գրականութեան, որ կը կարօտի լուրջ բանասիրական ուսումնասիրութեան: «Թափառական Հրեան», «Թշուառները», «Ռաֆայէլ», «Գաղտնիք Փարիզու», «Երեք Հրացանակիրք», «Խորհրդաւոր Կղզին», «Վերթեր», «Ֆաուստ», «Իւանօէ», «Քսան Տարի Ետք», «Աշխարհի Շրջանը Ութսուն Օրուան Մէջ» գործերը, օրինակ, բազմած են հայ մամուլի էջերուն մէջ:

Հայ թարգմանիչներու նախասիրութիւնը եղած են Վիքթոր Հիւկօ, Էօժէն Սիւ, Ալեքսանտր Տիւմա, Ժիւլ Վեռն, Անաթոլ Ֆրանս, Ալֆոնս Տոտէ, Կիւսթաւ Ֆլոպէր, Ալֆոնս տը Լամարթին, Ժան Ժաք Ռուսսօ, Մոլիէր, Վոլթէր, Միւսէ, Շէյքսպիր, Պայրըն, Շէլլի, Ուոլթըր Սքաթ, Տանիէլ Տէֆօ, Չարլզ Տիքընզ, Կէօթէ, Շիլլէր, Հայնէ, Թասսօ, Էտկար Բօ, Էմիլ Վերհարն, Թոլսթոյ, Փուշքին, Լերմոնթով, Նեքրասով, Քռիլով, Կոկոլ, եւայլն:

Լաւ տիրապետելով իր մայրենի լեզուին, Կիւրճեան չափածոյ եւ արձակ թարգմանութիւններու մէջ կը հնչեցնէ անարատ մայրենին՝ բանաստեղծական գործերու թարգմանութիւնը կատարելով չափածոյ թարգմանութեան սկզբունքներով, իսկ արձակ գործերը հայացնելով ազատ թարգմանական արուեստի սկզբունքներով:

Կիւրճեանի թարգմանութիւններուն մէջ բառացի չոր մեքենականութեան փոխարէն կը հանդիպինք զգացական, ստեղծագործական աշխատանքի: Ան պատահական թարգմանիչ չէ, այլ՝ ստեղծագործող անձ մը, որ մայրենի եւ թարգմանուող երկի լեզուներու տիրապետումը եւ անոնց պատկերաւոր խօսքերու եւ այլաբանութիւններու իմացութիւնը նախապայման կը նկատէ թարգմանական աշխատանքին:

Կիւրճեանի չափածոյ եւ արձակ թարգմանութիւնները, հաւաքուելու եւ հրատարակուելու պարագային, կրնան լեցնել երկու մեծածաւալ հատոր: Թարգմանական ասպարէզին մէջ ան մնաց սիրող: Ան մեզի չներկայացաւ Հայր Արսէն Բագրատունիի, Եդուարդ Հիւրմիւզի եւ Հայր Արսէն Ղազիկեանի կատարած թարգմանութիւններուն պատկառազդու եւ հսկայ ցանկով, ոչ ալ Զօպանեանի նպատակային ծրագրուած գործունէութեամբ. սակայն իր հոյակապ թարգմանութիւններուն որակով ան գլեց անցաւ առատ թարգմանութիւն կատարած շատ ուրիշ հեղինակներ:

Ահաւասիկ Շարլ Պոտլէրէն գողտրիկ բանաստեղծութիւն մը Կիւրճեանի թարգմանութեամբ:

Տարաշխարհիկ Բոյր

Երկու աչքերս երբ փակած, գաղջ երեկոյ մը աշնան,
Ես կը շնչեմ հեշտանքով հոտը ծոցիդ հոլանի,
Ծառուիղը կը տեսնեմ ծովափներու սրխրալի
Զոր կը վառեն բորբ հուրերն արեգակի մ'անխափան:

Եւ կղզի մը կը տեսնեմ ուր բնութիւնը կը ծնի
Բոյսեր, ծառեր տարօրէն եւ պըտուղներ ալ համեղ
Այրեր որոնց մարմինը նրբակազմ է եւ զօրեղ,
Կիներ որոնք համարձակ քեզ կը նային շեշտակի:

Դէպի անդորր կլիմաներ առաջնորդուած քու հոտէդ,
Նաւակայք մը կը տեսնեմ, առագաստներ ու կայմեր,
Որ յոգնաբեկ ալիքներէն հոս կը հանգչին աներեր:

Մինչ՝ ծառերէն արձակուած բուրումները խընկաւէտ
Որ ունգերը շոյելով ջերմ օդին մէջ կը շրջին,
Կը խառնըւին հոգւոյս մէջ նաւազներու խըմբերգէն:

Առանց աղարտելու Պոուլէրի բնագրին ուղղակի իմաստը, Կիրճեան կրցած է ճշդօրէն վերարտադրել բանաստեղծութիւնը՝ պահպանելով եւ գեղարուեստօրէն արտայայտելով Պոուլէրի միտքն ու շունչը, առանց զգացնելու որ թարգմանութիւն է կատարուածը:

Թարգմանութեան մը յաջողութեան նախապայմաններէն մէկն է թարգմանչին սէրն ու հիացումը թարգմանուող հեղինակին եւ անոր ստեղծագործութեան հանդէպ: Կիրճեանի ստեղծագործական ոգին եւ ոճը յարմար ու համապատասխան են Պոուլէրի ոգիին, մտածումներն ու տպաւորութիւնները յայտնելու եղանակին, գրելաձեւին ու ստեղծագործական անհատականութեան:

Կիրճեանի յաջող թարգմանութիւններէն են Փիէր տը Ռոնսարի «Վարդը», Ալֆրէտ Տրուանի «Արեւագալ»ը եւ Շարլ Պոուլէրի «Ծաթած Զանգակը»:

Ֆրանսայի եւ եւրոպական այլ երկիրներու մէջ 17րդ եւ 18րդ դարերուն երեւան եկան եւ զարգացան բանաստեղծութեան համար սահմանուած պայմաններ. սակայն ուրիշ ոչ մէկ տեղ պայմանադրութիւնները այնքան ազդու, կարծր ու խստաբարոյ էին, որքան Ֆրանսայի մէջ:

17րդ դարու ֆրանսացի թատերագիր Ժան Ռասինի բանաստեղծութիւնները, օրինակ, միշտ յանգաւորուած էին եւ իր տաղերը անփոփոխելիօրէն դասաւորուած համաձայն բարդ ու անդրդուելի կանոններու, որոնք կը ցոլացնէին քերականական կառուցուածքը: Նոյն երեւոյթը տեսանելի էր Միլթոնի եւ Շէյքսփիրի մօտ:

Պոուլէր, որոնելով չափածոյ խօսքի կատարեալ ներդաշնակութիւնը, խորապէս զարգացուց քերթողական զգացումը՝ մինչեւ մահ պահպանելով իր միտքի պայծառութիւնը:

Ֆրանսական ոտանաւորը ի սկզբանէ հիմնուած չէ չափական զարկերու թիւին, ինչպէս է պարագան անգլիական ոտանաւորներու, կամ ձայնաւորներու քանակին վրայ, ինչպէս են լատինական ոտանաւորները: Ան կը հիմնուի յանգաւորողի վանկերու թիւին վրայ: Ֆրանսերէն անձայն e-ն որպէս վանկ կը համրուի բաղաձայններու միջեւ եւ երբեմն նկատի չառնուիր կամ չարտասանուիր ձայնաւորէ մը առաջ: Հակառակ ձայնաւոր e-ի ներկայութեան, -es եւ -ent վերջաւորութիւնները երբեմն անձայն են: Կայ նաեւ ձայնաւորներու զուգորդութեան պարագան: Օրինակ՝ i ձայնաւորը ուրիշ ձայնաւորի մը հետ զուգորդուելու պարագային, երկու ձայնաւորները երբեմն կը նկատուին մէկ վանկ, երբեմն ալ՝ երկու:

Կիրճեան այս բոլորը նկատի առնելով կրցած է հարազատօրէն վերարտադրել Պոուլէրի «Ծաթած Զանգակը» քերթուածին ոճն ու բանաստեղծական ոգին, ինչպէս կը պարզուի բնագրին եւ թարգմանութեան բաղդատութենէն:

Ճաթած Զանգակը

Դառն եւ քաղցր է միանգամայն, ձըմրան գիշեր մը երկար,
Մըտիկ ընել կրակին քով, որ ճարճատուն կը մըխայ,
Յիշատակներն հեռաւոր որ կը յառնեն յամրաբար
Ի լուր մէգին մէջ երգող զանգակներուն մերձակայ:

Բի՜ւր երանի զանգակին որու կոկորդն է հըզօր,
Որ հակառակ տարիքին, միշտ քաջառողջ եւ արթուն,
Վըրանին տակ յար հսկող զինուորին պէս ալեւոր,
Իր աղաղակն երկիւղած վեր կ’արձակէ օրն ի բուն:

Հոգիս ճաթած է, աւա՜ղ, եւ երբ կ’ուզէ, վշտահար,
Ոգեւորել երգերովն պաղած օդը գիշերուան,
Կը պատահի շատ յաճախ որ իր խեղճ ձայնը տըկար

Վիրաւորուած զինուորի մը հոնդիւնին նըմանի
Որ դիերու տակ մոռցուած եզրը լիճի մը արեան,
Դանդաղօրէն կը մեռնի չարչարանքով մ’ահռելի:

La Cloche Fêlée

Il est amer et doux, pendant les nuits d'hiver,
D'écouter, près du feu qui palpite et qui fume,
Les souvenirs lointains lentement s'élever
Au bruit des carillons qui chantent dans la brume.

Bienheureuse la cloche au gosier vigoureux
Qui, malgré sa vieillesse, alerte et bien portante,
Jette fidèlement son cri religieux,
Ainsi qu'un vieux soldat qui veille sous la tente!

Moi, mon âme est fêlée, et lorsqu'en ses ennuis
Elle veut de ses chants peupler l'air froid des nuits,
Il arrive souvent que sa voix affaiblie

Semble le râle épais d'un blessé qu'on oublie
Au bord d'un lac de sang, sous un grand tas de morts,
Et qui meurt, sans bouger, dans d'immenses efforts.

Կիւրճեան հիմնուած է ոչ թէ բառերու արտաքին երեւոյթին, այլ անոնց ներքին իմաստին վրայ, որ անտարակոյս աւելի վաւերականօրէն կ'արտայայտէ բնագրին ոգին: Ան նոյնիսկ բնագրին *կը ճարճատէ* (qui palpite) բայը վերածած է ածականի (*ճարճատուն*), կամ յոգնակին վերածած է եզակիի (des nuits – գիշերուան), կամ «Au bruit des carillons qui chantent dans la brume»ը ազատօրէն վերածելով «Ի լուր մէգին մէջ երգող զանգակներուն մերձակայ»ի: Կիւրճեանի վերարտադրութիւնն այնքան յաջող է, որ ընթերցողին կը թուի թէ այս յանգաւոր եւ կշռութաւոր բանաստեղծութիւնը հայերէն ստեղծագործութիւն մըն է եւ ոչ թէ բոնազբօսիկ թարգմանութիւն:

Վերջին տողը՝ «Et qui meurt, sans bouger, dans d'immenses efforts», որ բառացիօրէն պիտի ըլլար՝ «Եւ կը մեռնի, առանց շարժելու, ահաւոր ճիգերու մէջ», Կիւրճեան վանկերու որոշակի խմբաւորումով եւ 4+3+4+3 բանաստեղծական ոտքերու յաջող շեշտով վերածած է հետեւեալին՝ «Դանդաղօրէն կը մեռնի չարչարանքով մ'ահռելի»:

Բաղդատելով այս բանաստեղծութեան հայերէն թարգմանութիւնը անգլերէն թարգմանութեան հետ, մարդ կը համոզուի թէ Կիւրճեան աւելի հարազատ մնացած է բնագրին, իր ստեղծագործական անհատականութեան կնիքը դնելով անոր վրայ:

Ահաւասիկ անգլերէն թարգմանութիւնը:

The Cracked Bell

How bittersweet it is on winter nights
To hear old recollections raise themselves
Around the flickering fire's wisps of light
And through the mist, in voices of the bells.

Blessed is the bell of clear and virile throat
Alert and dignified despite his rust,
Who faithfully repeats religion's notes
As a soldier keeps a watchman's trust.

My spirit, though, is cracked; when as she can
She chants to fill the cool night's emptiness,
Too often can her weakening voice be said

To sound the rattle of a wounded man
Beside a bloody pool, stacked with the dead,
Who cannot budge, and dies in fierce distress![108]

Անգլերէնի թարգմանիչը սահմանափակուած է բառացի թարգմանութեամբ, մինչ Կիւրճեանին թարգմանութիւնը համարժէք է բնագրին եւ ինքնուրոյն ստեղծագործութեան հրապոյրն ունի:

Ինչպէս իր արձակ ստեղծագործութիւններուն, այնպէս ալ չափածոյ թարգմանութիւններուն մէջ Կիւրճեան սիրած է վերջին հպումներով փոփոխութիւններ մտցնել: Օրինակ, «Ծաթած Զանգակը» 22 Յունիս 1963ին «Արեւ»ի մէջ լոյսին տալէ ետք, երբ Պէյրութի «Շիրակ» ամսագրին կը ղրկէ, չորս տարբեր տողերու մէջ *անցեալին*-ը *հեռաւոր*-ի, *պահակին*-ը *զինուորի*, *աւա՜ղ*-ը *ափսո՜ս*-ի եւ *դիակներու*-ն *դիերու* փոխած է: Այս յաջող փոփոխութիւնները աւելի գեղեցկացուցած են բանաստեղծութիւնը:

Թումանեան կ'ըսէ թէ նոյնիսկ լաւ թարգմանութիւն մը ապակիին տակ դրուած վարդ մըն է: Մեծ բանաստեղծը կ'ուզէ շեշտել թէ ձեւը կը տեսնուի, բայց բուրմունքը չզգացուիր: Անոր համոզումով, թարգմանիչին «շնորհք է հարկաւոր, որ ոչ միայն հարազատ ձեւը ցոյց տայ, այլեւ ինքնուրոյն բուրմունքը հաղորդի»:[109]

Ֆրանսական դասական գրականութեան հետաքրքրական էջերու բուրմունքը վայելած եւ զանոնք թարգմանաբար ընթերցող հասարակութեան վարպետօրէն մատուցած են նաեւ արեւելահայ գրագէտներ: Ահաւասիկ «Ծաթած Զանգակը» անոնցմէ Աբրահամ Ալիքեանի թարգմանութեամբ:

Ծաքած Զանգը

Դառն ու անուշ է միշտ, ձմրան գիշերներին,
Լսել մարմանդ վառուող կրակի շուրջ ծխուն,
Թէ ինչպէս են մեղմիկ յառնում յուշերը հին,
Երբ որ ղօղանջները են երգում շամանդաղում:

Բի՜ւր երնէկ կորովի հագագով այն զանգին,
Որ զառամեալ թէպէտ, սակայն առոյգ է դեռ
Եւ հաւատարմօրէն օրհներգում է կրկին,
Ինչպէս վրանի տակ հսկող զինուորը ծեր:

Ծաքա՜ծ է իմ հոգին եւ ձանձրոյթից երբ նա
Ուզում է երգերով լցնել մութը ցրտին,
Պատահում է յաճախ, որ ձայնն իր թուլանայ,

Թուայ դիակոյտում, արեան լճի ափին
Մոռացուած վիրաւոր մարտիկի հնդիւն,
Որ մեռնում է, անշարժ, ճիգերի մէջ անհուն:[110]

Ֆրանսական վիպապաշտութիւնը աւետեց յայտնութիւնը գրականութեան մը, որ հիմնուած էր զգացողութեան վրայ: Գրական այս յեղաշրջումը արդիւնքը չէր քննադատներու քաջագործութեան, այլ՝ մասնաւորապէս բանաստեղծներու, որոնց օրինակին աւելի ուշ հետեւեցան թատերագիրներն ու վիպագիրները:

Ֆրանսական վիպապաշտութիւնը ծնունդ առաւ 1820ին, երբ Ալֆոնս տը Լամարթին հրատարակեց իր «Բանաստեղծական Մտորումներ» հատորը, որուն յաջորդեց, 1823ին, «Նոր Բանաստեղծական Մտորումներ»ը: Այս գիրքերով Լամարթին հռչակուեցաւ հիմնադիրը ֆրանսական վիպապաշտ քնարերգութեան:

1827ին, Վիքթոր Հիւկօ իր «Քրոմուէլ» ողբերգութեան յառաջաբանին մէջ ջատագովելով յեղաշրջական հայեացքները, քննադատեց դասական երեք միութիւններու (գործողութիւն, ժամանակ եւ վայր) տեսութիւնը, որ տարածուն կիրարկութիւն ունէր նախորդ դարերու թատերագիրներուն կողմէ, բացառութեամբ Շէյքսփիրի: Հիւկօ կը յայտարարէ իր դիտաւորութիւնը՝ ողբերգութիւնը փոխարինել նորաձեւ թատերախաղով եւ պատմական ընդարձակ անդրադարձումով. այնպէս որ վիպապաշտութեան յատկանշական գիծերը պէտք է փնտռել բանաստեղծութեան եւ ոչ թէ թատերախաղին մէջ: Վիպապաշտ բանաստեղծը իր անձնական յոյզերը կ'արտայայտէ հաւաքականութեան անունով: Հիւկօ կը գրէ. «Ah! insensé qui crois que je ne suis pas toi» («Ո՜հ, ո՞վ կը հաւատայ թէ ես դուն չեմ»):

Հիւկօ կը յուզէ շարժումը, Լամարթին՝ երաժշտութիւնը, իսկ Վինեի կ'անդամահատէ փիլիսոփայական գաղափարները: Միւսէ կ'երգէ իր սիրային հանդիպումները, Սէնթ-Պէօվ կը նկարէ քաղքենի բնանկարները, մինչդեռ Ներվալ կը պայքարի խորհրդապատկերի դժոխքին մէջ: Ահա թէ ինչու վիպապաշտ բանաստեղծներու երիտասարդ սերունդը ողջունեց Լամարթինը որպէս իր վարպետին, թէեւ ան՝ վիպապաշտ համերգին առաջին ձայնը, պիտի մահանար քիչ մը մոռցուած՝ աղքատութեան մէջ:

Լամարթինի երկերը թարգմանուած եւ բազմիցս հրատարակուած են աշխարհի շատ երկիրներու մէջ, զանազան լեզուներով:

Արեւմտահայ եւ արեւելահայ գրողներ եւ թարգմանիչներ եւս թարգմանած են Լամարթինի բանաստեղծութիւնները: Խորէն Գալֆայեան (Նար-Պէյ) թարգմանած եւ հրատարակած է «Դաշնակք Լամարթինեան» բանաստեղծութիւններու ժողովածուն 1859ին: Հրապարակախօս եւ քաղաքական-հասարակական գործիչ Գրիգոր Օտեան եւ բանաստեղծ ու մշակութային-կրթական գործիչ Մինաս Չերազ եւս թարգմանած են քերթուածներ Լամարթինէն:

Հետագային, անոնց միացած են նաեւ Գրիգոր Չիլինկիրեան, Արշակ Չօպանեան, Եղիշէ Արքեպիսկոպոս Դուրեան, Թորգոմ Արքեպիսկոպոս Գուշակեան, Հայր Արսէն Ղազիկեան, Վահան Թէքէեան, Միքայէլ

Կիւրճեան, Մառի Աթմաճեան, Գուիտոն Լուսինեան (Ամբրոսիոս Գալֆայեան) եւ ուրիշներ:

1811ին, Լամարթինի Իտալիա ճանապարհորդութիւնը զինք կը լուսաւորէ միջերկրական լոյսով եւ իր մէջ կ'արթնցնէ սիրահար սիրտի առաջին յոյզերը: Այնուհետեւ, 1816ին Էքս ջերմաջրային քաղաքը գտնուած միջոցին, կը ծանօթանայ գիտնականի մը կնոջ՝ Տինին Շարլի: Այդ հանդիպումը զինք կ'ալեկոծէ եւ Էլվիր անուան տակ կը գովերգէ զայն: Իր ամենէն յատկանշական բանաստեղծութիւններէն «Լիճը»ին մէջ Լամարթին փիլիսոփայական քանի մը վճռական կերպարանաւորումներով կը ներբողէ իր տարփագին սէրը՝ բանաստեղծական հանճարի զօրաւոր ցայտքերով:

«Լիճը»ին մէջ խտացած եւ ցայտուն արտայայտութիւն գտած են իրականութեան գեղարուեստական արտացոլման այնպիսի կողմեր, ինչպէս՝ կեանքի վերակերտումը ըստ գեղագիտական իտէալի, բացառիկն ու արտասովորը բանաստեղծականացնելու հակումը՝ ի հաշիւ կեանքի առարկայական ու բազմակողմանի պատկերման:

Քերթուածը կառուցուած է նկարագրութեանը վրայ այն լիճին, ուր տարի մը առաջ բանաստեղծը գտնուած է իր սիրեցեալ Նէի հետ: Վերապրելով անցած գեղեցիկ ու շնորհալի օրերու քաղցրաբարոյ յուշերը, հեղինակը կ'ուզէ վայելել աղուոր անցեալը: Ան ժամ ու ժամանակին կոչ կ'ընէ չանապարել, չփախչիլ եւ չսահիլ, որպէսզի ճաշակէ վաղանցուկ, արագասահ եւ հրճուալի բերկրանքները հանճոյալի կեանքի: Յոյզերով զեղուն այս բանաստեղծութիւնը հայերէնի վերածած են Կիւրճեան, Եղիշէ Արք. Դուրեան, Աթմաճեան եւ ուրիշներ:

«Լիճը» քերթուածին հայերէն թարգմանութեան երկու տարբերակ ունինք մեր տրամադրութեան տակ, որոնց վերջաւորութեան գրուած է. «Թարգմ. Միքայէլ Կիւրճեան»: Անոնցմէ մէկը, որ Կիւրճեանի գրչին չի պատկանիր, տպագրուած է Գահիրէի «Կեանք Եւ Գիր» պարբերականի Դ. հատորի Բ. պրակին 25-26-րդ էջերուն վրայ, այսպէս՝

Լճակը

Այսպէս, մղուած միշտ ափունքներ նորանոր,
Անվերադարձ՝ տարուած մութին մէջ անվերջ,
Չպիտի՞ կրնանք խարիսխ նետել գէթ մէկ օր,
Ժամանակի ծովուն մէջ:

Լըճա՜կ, տարին հազիւ ըրած է շրջան,
Ու ափունքիդ, ուր նա կրկին պիտի գար,
Տե՛ս, միայնակ կուգամ նստիլ քարին այն,
Ուր զինքը օր մը տեսար:

Այսօրուան պէս կը մռնչէիր ափդ ի վեր,
Փշրուելով՝ ժայռերուն վրայ պատառուն,
Հովն ալ այսպէս փրփուրներըդ կը նետէր
Իր պաշտելի ոտքերուն:

Իրիկուն մը, կը յիշե՞ս, լո՞ւռ կը սահէր
Նաւակը մեր ջուրերուդ վրայ. երկնից տակ՝
Կը լսուէին թիակներուն միայն մեր
Ծողփիւնները ներդաշնակ,

Երբոր շեշտեր աշխարհին այս՝ անծանօթ,
Ափունքներէդ յանկարծ տուին արձագանգ,
Ու սիրելի ձայն մը անուշ ու թախծոտ,
Սա բառերուն տուաւ կեանք.

«Ո՛վ ժամանակ, մ՛անապարէր, մի փախչիր,
Եւ դո՛ւք ժամեր, մի՛ սահիք.
Թողէ՛ք վայլենք վայրկեաններն, է՛ն քաղցրալիր,
Մեր օրերուն գեղեցիկ:

Թշուառներ ձե՛զ կը պաղատին անդադար,
Անոնց համար սահեցէք.
Առէ՛ք անոնց կեանքն ու ցաւերն անհամար,
Երջանիկները մոռցէք:

Բայց կը հայցեմ ի զո՞ւր քանի մը վայրկեան,
Ժամանակը կը թռչի.
Ի զուր կ՛ըսեմ ես՝ դանդաղէ գիշերուան,
Այգը ահա կը բացուի:

Սիրե՛նք ուրեմն, փախչող ժամերը համայն,
Անապարենք ու ապրինք.
Չունին, մարդը՝ կայան, ու ժամը՝ սահման,
Կը սահի նա ու կ՛անցնինք»:

Կարելի՞ է, ո՞վ ժամանակ անտարբեր,
Որ խելայեղ վայրկեաններն այդ հեշտանքի,
Փախչին մեզմէ այնքան արագ որքան մեր
Օրերը մո՞ւթ արցունքի:

Ուրեմն անոնց հետքն իսկ պահել չէ՞ հընար,
Ուրեմն անոնք գացին անդարձ ու անհետ.
Ժամանակ որ տարիր զանոնք, չե՞ս կրնար,
Տալ վերստին օր մը ետ:

Յաւերժ, անցեալ, անդունդներ մութ ու նըսեմ,
Ի՞նչ ըրիք մեր այդ օրերը գեղեցիկ,
Ըսէ՛ք, պիտի տա՞ք մեզ կրկին այն վսեմ
Յօյզերը զոր՝ խլեցիք:

Լճա՛կ եւ դուք անխօս ժայռեր, անձաւներ,
Որոնց վրայ օրերը չեն թողուր հետք,
Երազային այդ գիշերուան գոնէ մեր,
Յիշատակը պահեցէք:

Թո՛ղ ապրի նա, սիրուն լճակ, անվրդով
Գինջիդ մէջ ու ցասումներուդ կատաղի,
Նոճերուդ մէջ սեւ ու ջրերդ եզերող
Սեպ ժայռերուն մէջ վայրի:

Թո՛ղ մնայ ան, զեփիւռին մէջ սարսըռուն,
Ալեակներուդ յանկերգին մէջ հոգեխռով,
Մահիկին մէջ՝ որ կ՚արծաթէ թրթըռուն
Ջուրերդ, իր նուրբ ցոլքերով:

Թո՛ղ հեծեծող հովերուն ողբն անսահման,
Թո՛ղ բուրաւէտ ափունքներըդ տրտմագին,
Թո՛ղ ամէ՛ն իր, ամէ՛ն բոյր ու ամէ՛ն ձայն,
Ըսեն յաւէտ՝ «սիրեցի՛ն»:

Միւս տարբերակը, որուն հեղինակը իսկապէս Միքայէլ Կիւրճեանն է, կը գտնենք Գահիրէի «Արեւ» օրաթերթի 8 Յունիս 1963ի թիւին մէջ: Անբաղդատելիօրէն յաջող թարգմանութիւն մըն է ան:

Լիճը

Զօն՝ ասմունքող Նորա Իփէքեանին

Դէպի ափեր նորանոր քըշւած այսպէս անդադար,
Յաւերժական ցայգին մէջ տարուած անդարձ եւ անհետ,

Ժամանակաց ծովուն վրայ պիտի չըլլա՞յ մեզ հընար
Խարիսխ նետել օր մը գէթ:

Լիճ սիրեցեալ հազիւ թէ տարի մ'անցաւ եւ ահա
Ալեացըդ մօտ ուր եղանք մենք ժամադիր իրարու՝
Տես, միայնակ եւ տըխուր, կուգամ նստիլ քարին վրայ
Ուր կը նստէր Նէ հերու:

Կը գոռայիր դուն այսպէս խոր ժայռերուն այս ներքեւ
Անոնց պատռած կողերուն զարնըւելով ցաւմամբ լի,
Եւ հովն այսպէս կը նետէր ալեաց փրփուրը թեթեւ
Իր ոտքերուն պաշտելի:

Երեկոյ մը, կը յիշե՞ս, կը նաւէինք մունջ ու լուռ,
Ջուրերուդ վրայ, երկնից տակ, ոչ մէկ շըշունջ թիերուն
Ծողփիւնէն զատ՝ որք չափով կը բախէին դաշնալուր
Կոհակներըդ ծփծըփուն:

Յանկարծ շեշտեր տարօրէն, անծանօթ իմն աշխարհի,
Արձագանգներն յարուցին ըզմայլահար լըճափին.
Ալիքն եղաւ ուշադիր, եւ ձայնը ինձ սիրելի՝
Բացագանչեց տրտմագին.-

«Ով ժամանակ, կեցուր թռիչքդ, եւ դուք, պահեր երջանիկ,
Կասեցուցէք ձեր խօլ չուն.
Թոյլ տուէք մեզ ճաշակել հեշտանքները վաղանցիկ
Մեր էն աղուոր օրերուն:

«Շատ թշուառներ կան յաստիս որ ձեզի միշտ կ'աղերսեն
Անոնց համար շուտ անցէք.
Առէք իրենց կեանքին հետ՝ իրենց ցաւերը ամէն.
Երջանիկները մոռցէք:

«Բայց զուր քանի մը րոպէ ես կը խնդրեմ տակաւին,
Ժամանակը խոյս կու տայ.
Կ'ըսեմ ցայգին՝ «դանդաղէ՛» եւ արշալոյսը լըռին
Կը փարատէ ցայգն ահա:

«Սիրենք ուրեմն, ա՜հ, սիրենք, վայրկեաններն խուսափուկ
Վայելելու ըշտապենք.

Մարդը չունի նաւ'հանգիստ, եւ ժամանակն ալ ափունք.
Ան կը հոսի, կ'անցնինք մենք:»

Նախանձաբեկ ժամանակ, ինչո՞ւ ժամերն անմոռաց
Ուր սէրն արբշիռ կ'ընէ մեզ երանութեամբ մ'անսահման,
Դժբախտութեան եւ սուգի օրերուն պէս սրընթաց
Մեզմէ հեռու կը սուրան:

Պիտի երբեք չըկրնա՞նք պահել անոնց հետքը գէթ.
Ի՞նչ, անցած են առ յաւէտ, ամբողջովին կորուսեալ.
Ժամանակը որ տուաւ, ապա խըլեց, զանոնք ետ
Չըդարձընէ՞ պիտի ալ:

Յաւերժութի՜ւն, կեանք անցեալ, անէութիւն, վիհք ընսեմ,
Ըսէք, օրերն ի՛նչ կ'ընէք զոր կուլ կուտաք անդադար.
Պիտի չըտա՞ք մեզ դարձեալ ըզմայլանքները վըսեմ
Զոր կ'ապշսպէք մեզմէ յար:

Ո՛վ լիճ, ժայռեր, քարանձաւ, ըստուերամած անտառակ,
Դուք որոնց հետ ժամանակն այնքան գութով կը վարուի.
Պահեցէք գէթ, Բընութիւն, անջինջ պահէ յիշատակն
Այդ գիշերուան սխրալի:

Թող անիկա անդորրիդ, մրրիկներուդ մէջ ըլլայ,
Եւ տեսքին մէջ, լիճ չքնաղ, բլրակներուդ բուսառատ,
Եւ եղեւնեաց մէջ մըռայլ ու ժայռերուն ալ հսկայ
Որ կը կախուին քու վրադ.

Թող ան ըլլայ սիւքին մէջ որ կը թեւէ սարսըռուն,
Ծըշուկին մէջ ափերուդ արձագանգուած ափերէդ,
Արծաթափայլ լուսնին մէջ որ կ'ողողէ քեզ համբուն
Պայծառութեամբն հեշտաւէտ.

Թող հովը որ կը հեծէ, թող եղէգը հառաչող,
Թող օդիդ մէջ սփռըւած բուրումները ռետնային,
Ինչ որ տեսանք, լսեցինք եւ շնչեցինք, ըսեն թող
«Այստեղ անոնք սիրեցին»:

Տեղին է նշել թէ «Լիճը»ին առաջին տարբերակին հրատարակութիւնը Կիւրճեանի անունով գրական բարոյականութեան ամենակոպիտ խախտումներէն մէկն է: Կիւրճեան անոր դէմ իր զայրոյթը արտայայտած է «Գրական Առեղծուած Մը Եւ Անձնական Խնդիր Մը» յօդուածով («Արեւ» օրաթերթ, Գահիրէ, 15 Յունիս 1963): Հոն Կիւրճեան բաւականացած է քննադատելով անուանագողութեան տգեղ արարքը որպէս անպատուաբեր վարք ու բարք, առանց բացայայտելու բանագողին անունը:

Կիւրճեանի թարգմանութեամբ Լամարթինի «Լճակը» առաջին անգամ լոյս տեսած է «Արեւ»ի մէջ 1942ին, Վահան Թէքէեանի խմբագրապետութեան ժամանակ:

Թէքէեան իր խմբագրական ծանօթութեան մէջ կը գրէ. «Լամարթինի քերթուածը առ նուազն երկու թարգմանութիւն ունեցած է մեր մէջ: Ասիկա անբաղդատելիօրէն լաւագոյնն է, եւ գեղեցիկ է ինքնին, ինչպէս կը սպասուէր նրբարուեստ Կիւրճեանէն»:

«Լճակը» «Արեւ»ի մէջ հրատարակուած է նաեւ Ազատ Նորենցի փոխադրութեամբ (18 Մայիս 1946): Ահաւասիկ քերթուածին առաջին տունը:

Ainsi, toujours poussés vers de nouveaux rivages,
Dans la nuit éternelle emportés sans retour,
Ne pourrons-nous jamais sur l'océan des âges
Jeter l'ancre un seul jour?

Եղիշէ Դուրեան «Սիոն» ամսագրի Օգոստոս 1932ի 8րդ թիւին մէջ, էջ 243-244, հետեւեալ ձեւով կը թարգմանէ այս տունը:

Այսպէս մղուած միշտ դէ՛պ ափունք մը նորոգ,
Անդարձ քշուած գիշերին մէջ անվախճան,
Պիտ չկրնա՞նք ծով դարերու վրայ արդեօք
Խարիսխ նետել օր մը միայն:

Մանի Աթմաճեան «Պայքար» եռամսեայ հանդէսին 1967ի 26րդ տարուան թիւ 1 (17)ի մէջ նոյն տունը կը թարգմանէ այսպէս:

Արտամղուած մի՛շտ նորանոր ափեր եւ ա՛յլ անդաստան
Ու միշտ տարուած անվերադարձ՝ գիշերին մէջ առ յաւէտ,
Պիտի երբեք չըկարենա՞նք անդունդին վրայ դարերուն՝
Խարիսխ նետել օ՜ր մը գէթ...:

Ինչպէս կը տեսնենք, Դուրեան ոտանաւորին տուներուն առաջին երեք տողերը կը թարգմանէ 4+4+3, իսկ չորրորդը 4+4 եւ երբեմն ալ 4+3 վանկերու բացորոշ շեշտով մը, իսկ Մանի Աթմաճեան առաջին երեք տողերուն համար կ'ընտրէ 4+4+4+3, իսկ չորրորդին համար 4+3 կանոնը:

Կիւրճեան, սակայն, կ'որդեգրէ 4+3+4+3 վանկաճատումը, որ աւելի տպաւորիչ եւ ազդեցիկ է շեշտերու ճնշիւնայնութեամբ:

Ձեռքի տակ ունինք Եղիշէ Դուրեանի, Մառի Աթմաճեանի, Աբրահամ Ալիքեանի եւ Կիւրճեանի (երկու տարբերակով) ստորագրութիւնը կրող թարգմանութիւնները, ինչպէս նաեւ անգլերէն թարգմանութիւն մը, որոնք կը համեմատեմ Լամարթինի բնագրին հետ: Յաջորդական տուներու մէջ, Լամարթին միայնակ նստած կը խօսի լիճին հետ՝ յիշելով կոհակներուն ծփանքները, ջուրերու ճողփիւնները, բնութեան ներդաշնակութիւնը, երբ տարի մը առաջ գտնուած էր նոյն լճափին իր պաշտելիին՝ Նէի հետ:

Դուրեան 2-5րդ տուները կը թարգմանէ այսպէս:

Ով լիճ, ահա լրացաւ շրջանը տարւոյն.
Ծըփանքիդ մօտ՝ ուր պիտի գար վերըստին՝
Տե՛ս, մինակ եմ բազմեր քարին վըրայ նոյն,
Ուր տեսար դուն իր հանգիստին:

Կը մռընչէիր այսպէս խոր ժայռից տակ,
Փըշրըւելով անոնց կողին դէմ հերձոտ,
Ու կը շըքթէր հովը փրփուրդ ըսպիտակ
Իր պաշտելի ոտքերուն մօտ:

Իրիկուն մը լո՞ւռ նաւարկեցինք, չե՞ս յիշեր.
Լոկ կը լսուէր կոհակին վրայ ւ'երկնի տակ՝
Այն ելեւէջը թեւակին՝ որ կ'բախէր
Քու ալիքներըդ ներդաշնակ:

Այն շեշտերուն՝ որ անծանօթ են երկրի,
Դիւթուած ափունքն յանկարծ տըւաւ արձագանգ,
Ուշ դրաւ ալիքն, ու ձայնը ինձ սիրելի
Հոսեց բառերն իր յորդաւանգ:

Նոյն տուները Մառի Աթմաճեան հետեւեալ ձեւով կը թարգմանէ.

Ո՞վ լիճ, տարին նոր աւարտեց եղանակն իր անկայուն,
Երբ պէտք էր Ան ըլլար դեռ հիւրն ալեակներուն լուսածոր,
Աւա՜ղ, այսօր ես առանձի՞ն կուգամ ժայռիդ մեզ ծանօթ՝
Ուր կը նստէր ան անդորր...:

Նո՜յնն ես դուն միշտ, որոտայորդ՝ քառաժայռին յատակին,
Ու միշտ այսպէս ջարդ ու փշուր եղած՝ խութի կողերուն...

Ու միշտ այսպէ՞ս կը վանէր հովն ալեակներդ փրփրադէզ՝
Դէմն իր մանրիկ ոտքերուն...:

Իրիկուն մ'էր, ա՜հ, կը յիշե՞ս, ջուրերուդ վրայ լըռակեաց,
Կը նաւէինք երբ Ան ու ես, կը լսէինք միասին
Հըպանցումը թեւնակներուն, կըշռութաւոր իբր նըւագ,
Երգի մը պէս ցաւագին...:

Իմաստացած շեշտեր յանկարծ, օտարոտի՝ միւսներուն՝
Կը հասնէին լըճափունքէն եւ արձագանգ կուտային...
կոհակները կ'ունկնդրէին այդ համերգին գերագոյն,
Ձայներուն՝ որ կ'ըսէին.-

Այնուհետեւ կուռ կառուցումով ու սեղմ ոճով քերթուածը կը յորդի արտազեղումներով, որոնք սիրոյ վայելքի զեղումներ են եւ բանաստեղծը թախանձագին կոչ կ'ընէ ժամանակին, որ կասեցնէ իր վազքը, կանգ առնէ, որպէսզի երջանիկները իրենց ապրումները ճաշակեն ու սիրոյ դիւթանքը երկար տեւէ: Սակայն քերթողը համոզուած է թէ ժամանակը դադար ու կայան չունի, անհանգրուան է:

Ահա՛ Լամարթինի թախանձանքը:

O temps! suspends ton vol, et vous, heures propices!
Suspendez votre cours:
Laissez-nous savourer les rapides délices
Des plus beaux de nos jours!

Ինչ որ Կիւրճեանի թարգմանութեամբ կը հնչէ այսպէս:

Ով ժամանակ, կեցուր թռիչքդ, եւ դուք, պահեր երջանիկ,
կասեցուցէք ձեր խօլ չուն.
Թոյլ տուէք մեզ ճաշակել հեշտանքները վաղանցիկ
Մեր էն աղուոր օրերուն:

Ա. Լուսինեան եւս թարգմանած է «Լիճը» բանաստեղծութիւնը գրաբարով, Պոլսոյ «Երկրագունտ» շաբաթաթերթին մէջ, 1870ին: Հաւանական է որ ուրիշ թարգմանիչներ եւս փորձած ըլլան այլ գործերու կողքին թարգմանել այս գողտրիկ, անկեղծ եւ պարզ ոճով գրուած ոտանաւորը:

Թէ ինչո՞ւ շատ գրագէտներ սիրած են թարգմանել Լամարթինի ստեղծագործութիւնները եւ յատկապէս «Լիճը» բանաստեղծութիւնը, պատասխանը պարզ է. քանի որ Լամարթին 1820ին իր «Բանաստեղծական

Մտորումներ» գիրքով նորութիւն մտցուց քնարերգութեան մէջ: Այդ մտորումները հեղինակին ձայնին անձնական հնչումն էին, նոր երանգ՝ բաւական համարձակ ու մտերիմ՝ այդ օրերու տափակ արձակին մէջ: «Հաստատակութիւնը,- ինչպէս Լամարթին գրած է աւելի ուշ,- տեսաւ մարդկային էակ մը՝ գիրքի փոխարէն»: Այնպէս որ լեռ, գետ, արեւ, լուսին, ժայռ ու լիճ ներկայացուած են ո՛չ թէ իրենց սիրոյն համար, ինչպէս Ռուշէ կամ Սէն Լամպէր ներկայացուցած էին զանոնք մէկ սերունդ առաջ, այլ միայն գրողին վրայ գործած իրենց ազդեցութեան համար: Լամարթին բանաստեղծը սիրած է մէկը, Նէն: Քերթողը կը վերադառնայ անոր հետ իր հանդիպման վայրը, բայց ան հոն չէ: Առանց անոր՝ ամբողջ բնութիւնը անարժէք է իրեն համար: Այդ վիճակը երբեք հանդարտ ու խաղաղ չէ նկարագրուած: Նէն երբեք չէ անուանուած կամ ստուգիւ նկարագրուած «Լիճը»ին եւ այլ բանաստեղծութիւններու մէջ, բայց եւ այնպէս անոր ներկայութիւնը պայծառօրէն կը զգացուի: Լամարթին կը գրէ ոչ թէ անամոք հակումով, այլ՝ հակակշռուած յօժարութեամբ, միտելով պարզել ու հաստատել անունն ու զարգացումը: Նոյն տպաւորութիւնն ինքնին կ'երեւի տաղաչափութեան մէջ: Իր մելամաղձութիւնը կը գործէ իր բառերաժշտութեան նոխութեան եւ կշռական նմոյշին դէմ: Արդիւնքը՝ հետաքրքրական մետաքսեայ երփնահիւս ներգործութիւն, որ էական յատկանիշներէն մէկն է լամարթինեան հրապուրիչ թովչանքին:

Անձնական խոր զգացումներու եւ հաստատական մտածումներու լամարթինեան խոկումները արեւելեահայ ընթերցողին աւելի հարազատ ու մատչելի դարձնելու համար, այստեղ կը ներկայացնենք Աբրահամ Ալիքեանի թարգմանութիւնը:

Լիճը

Այսպէս, յաւէտ քշուած դէպի տարբեր եզերք,
Անդարձօրէն տարուած գիշերում անվախճան՝
Օրերի ովկիանում մեզ չի՞ տրուի երբեք
Խարիսխ գցել առժամ:

Ո՜վ լիճ, ծիրն իր հազիւ բոլորել է տարին:
Ալիքներիդ մօտ սուրբ, ուր պիտի նա էլ գար,
Տե՛ս, ահա մեն-մենակ նստում եմ այն քարին,
Ուր նստելն իր տեսար:

Այսպէս շաչում էիր այս ժայռերի ծոցում
Ու փշրւում այսպէս նրանց ծուատ կողին,
Այսպէս իր պաշտելի ոտքերին էր գցում
Փրփուրներդ քամին:

Յիշո՞ւմ ես, մի գիշեր նաւում էինք մէկտեղ.
Լռութեան մէջ, հեռւում, միայն երկու թեւնակ
Դաշըն ճողփում էին ջրերիդ մէջ հնչեղ
Ու բաց երկնքի տակ:

Յանկարծ դիւթուած ափին խուլ արձագանգ տուին
Այս աշխարհին անյայտ ելեւէջ ու հնչիւն.
Ալիքը ուշք դրեց ինձ սիրելի ձայնին,
Որ բարբառեց իսկոյն.

«Օ՜, ժամանա՛կ, կանգ առ, ա՜հ, կանգ առէք եւ դուք,
Ժամե՜ր հոգեհմայ,
Թողէք որ ըմբոշխնենք հեշտանքը վաղանցուկ
Մեր լաւագոյն օրուայ:

Ի՜նչ, քի՞չ են դժբախտներ, որ վշտերից կքած,
Հայցում են ձեզ՝ անցէ՛ք.
Անցէք նրա՛նց համար եւ երջանիկ մարդկանց
Մի՛ յիշէք դուք երբեք:

Բայց ես զո՜ւր եմ խնդրում դեռ մի քանի վայրկեան՝
Սլանում է րոպէն:
Ասում են գիշերուան՝ եղիր դանդա՜ղ, սակայն
Ծուտով այգն է արդէն:

Ուստի սիրե՛նք, սիրե՛նք եւ ժամից խուսափուկ
Քաղենք յոյզ եւ հեշտանք:
Մարդը չունի կայան, ժամանակը՝ ափունք,
Անցաւ, ու մենք չկա՜նք»:

Ցա՛նտ ժամանակ, կարո՞ղ է, որ այս վեհ ներկան,
Ուր մեզ սէրն է բաշխում դիւթանքներն իր բոլոր,
Խոյս տայ մեզնից նոյնքա՛ն արագօրէն, ինչքան
Դժբախտութեան մի օր:

Է՛հ, ի՜նչ, չե՜նք դրոշմի գոնէ հետք ու նշան,
Ի՜նչ, չքանա՞լ իսպառ, ի՜նչ, կորչե՞լ առյաւէտ:
Ժամանակն այս, որ միշտ տալիս, կորզում է այն,
Միթէ չի՞ տայ էլ ետ:

Յաւերժութի՛ւն, անցեա՛լ, անէ՛, վիհե՛ր նսեմ,
ի՞նչ էք անում օրերն, որ կլանում էք դուք.
Ասէ՛ք, չէ՞ք տայ մեզ ետ զմայլանքն այս վսեմ,
Որ խլում էք գաղտուկ:

Ո՜վ լիճ, համր ժայռե՛ր, այրե՛ր, մթին անտա՛ռ,
Դուք, որ տեւում էք միշտ կամ վերստին փթթում,
Պահեցէք գէթ մի յո՛ւշ գիշերից այս անճառ,
Պահի՛ր, մա՜յր բնութիւն:

Թող նա, լի՛ճ իմ չքնաղ, մնայ անդորրիդ մէջ,
Մնա՛ քո տարերքում, բլրակներում զուարթ,
Այս սեւ եղեւնուտում եւ ժայռերում այս լերջ,
Որ հակւում են վրադ:

Մնա՛ սիւքիդ մէջ, որ ցանում է հեւք ու դող,
Ձայների մէջ, որ ափերում են զնգում,
Աղօտ պայծառութեամբ ջրերըդ արծաթող
Լուսնակի մէջ դժգոյն:

Եւ ոլորտըդ խնկող մեղմ բոյրերը բազում
Եւ հեծեծող եղէգն ու հառաչող քամին,
Բոլորն, ինչ որ շնչում, տեսնում ենք ու լսում,
Թող ասեն՝ սիրեցի՛ն:[111]

* * *

Հայ գրողներու սիրած հեղինակներէն մին եղած է Ալֆոնս Տոտէ, որուն «Թարասքոնցի Թարթարէն»ը հայերէնի թարգմանած եւ 1891ին առանձին գիրքով Թիֆլիսի մէջ հրատարակած է բժիշկ Թ. Ջաքարեանը: Կիւրճեան ի՛նք ալ թարգմանած է նոյն գործը 1903ին եւ ան սփիւռքահայ մամուլին մէջ լոյս տեսած է երեք անգամ.- Աղեքսանդրիա, Միհրան Ասքանազեանի «Պարտէզ» շաբաթական հանդէսի 1903-1904ի թիւերուն մէջ, ապա Զմիւռնիա, Սուրէն պարթեւեանի «Դաշինք» օրաթերթին մէջ 1912ին, եւ վերջապէս Գահիրէ, «Արեւ» օրաթերթին մէջ 1965ին, միշտ ալ թերթօնի ձեւով:

Տիգրան Կամսարական ալ շատ սիրած է Ալֆոնս Տոտէն եւ հաւանաբար ներշնչուած ալ է անկէ, քանի որ «Մասիս»ի 1893ի թիւերէն մէկուն մէջ կը գրէ. «Տոտէն իմ զգայութեանցս մեծ սրիչն եղաւ, ու տակաւ ինծի համար անբաժան ընկեր մը. բայց խորհրդակից մըն էր մանաւանդ՝ որուն ես բան մը չէի ըսեր, ու ինք ամէն բան կ'ըսէր ինծի...»:

Գաւառական գրականութեան գլխաւոր ներկայացուցիչ Ալֆոնս Տոտէն, որ իր գրական նախաքայլերը՝ ոտանաւորներու «Les amoureuses» ժողովածուն հրատարակած էր 1858ին, քանի մը թատերական գործերէ ետք, իր «Նամակներ Իմ Հողմաղացէն» գլուխ գործոցով 1866ին արդէն հանրածանօթ դարձած եւ 1872-ին հրատարակած էր «Թարասքոնցի Թարթարէն» դիւցազնավէպը:

Տոտէի գրիչը շատ պարզ, բնական եւ անպաճոյճ է: Յատկանշական է Տոտէի յուղարկաւորութեան առթիւ Էմիլ Զոլայի ճառին վերջին հատուածը. «Ալֆոնս Տոտէ բացառութիւն մըն էր, ըլլալով քաղցր եւ բարձր ֆրանսական գրականութեան մէջ: Եզականութիւն մը՝ անուշ բայց ուժեղ, ծնած էր ջղուտ տուեալներով: Այսինքն զգալ եւ արտադրել այնպիսի հարուստ արուեստով մը, որուն ամէն մէկ էջը, քանի մեր լեզուն կ'ապրի, պիտի թարգմանը դառնայ իր հոգեկան ապրումներուն»:

Արկածային գրականութիւնը տեսակներէն մէկն է պատմողական գրականութեան: Արկածային ստեղծագործութիւններու մէջ գործողութիւնները կը յառաջանան արագընթաց պատահարներով լի դէպքերով, յաճախ անհաւանական, պատահական իրադարձութիւններու զուգորդութեամբ: Տոտէի վառ երեւակայութիւնը, նիւթին հետաքրքրական շարժունութիւնը եւ կերպարներու գրաւչութիւնը միացած են «Թարասքոնցի Թարթարէն»ի էական բովանդակութեան հետ: Հեղինակը մանրամասնօրէն նկարագրած է վիպերգութեան հերոս Թարթարէնի արտաքին դիմագիծերը, շարժուձեւը եւ հագուստները, որքանով որ հերոսին դիմանկարը կ'արտայայտէ անոր ներքին էութիւնը:

Նիւթը հետեւեալն է:

Ֆրանսայի հարաւը, Պուշ տիւ Ռոն նահանգի Աւինիոն քաղաքին մօտ, Թարասքոնի մէջ ամէն մարդ որսորդ է: Դիւցազնական բնութեան տէր կրկնապինդ դնդերներով, անվեհեր եւ զգուշաւոր Թարթարէն ամէն Կիրակի առտու կորդոյր որսալու կ'երթար, իսկ մնացած ժամանակը կ'անցնէր ակումբը, շուկայի հրապարակը, Քոսթեքալտ զինագործին խանութը, որսորդներու վէճերը քննելով: Թարթարէն, որ մինչեւ 45 տարեկան դառնալը երբեք քաղաքէն չէր հեռացած, կ'որոշէ Ալճերիա երթալ՝ առիւծ որսալու եւ իր դիւցազնական ծարաւը յագեցնելու համար: Աֆրիկեան մեծ զբօսաշրջիկներու ճամբորդութիւններու պատմութիւնները կարդալէ, անօթութեան, ծարաւի, ամէն տեսակ զրկանքներու տոկալու համար ինքզինք մարզելէ եւ զէնքեր, պահածոյ ուտելիքներու սնտուկներ, դեղերու նախազգուշական տուփեր, գիշերելու ապաստարան-վրան մը ապահովելէ ետք, գլուխէն մինչեւ ոտք ալճերիական տարազով կը հեռանայ Թարասքոնէն: Զինք ճամբու դնելու համար կը հաւաքուին հարիւրապետ Պրավիտա քաջարի հրամանատարը, Լատիվէզ նախագահը, Քոսթեքալտ զինագործը, Պիւզիւքէ դեղագործը, կորդոյրի որսորդները, կառքերը եւ ժողովուրդը, որոնք «Կեցցէ Թարթարէն», «Երթա՜ս բարով, Թարթարէն» կ՚աղաղակեն:

Երեք դրուագներէ բաղկացած դիւցազնավէպին մէջ հեղինակը կը պատմէ Թարթարէնի ճամբորդութեան արկածալից միջադէպերը եւ աղիտալի ձախորդութիւնները՝ երբ նաւուն բեռնակիրները ծովահէններ կարծելով, թուրը բարձրացուցած անոնց վրայ կը յարձակի, կամ գիշերուան մութին մէջ ինքզինք Սահարայի վայրի անապատին մէջ կարծելով, բանջարեղէններու ածուի մը մէջ անցնող առաջին առիւծին վրայ կրակելու համար դարան մտածի տարապայման տենդով՝ ամէն վայրկեան առիւծ երազող Թարթարէն կը կրակէ ամէն շարժումի վրայ զոր կը նկատէ: Լուսաբացին, կը գտնէ թէ իր սպաննածը իշուկ մըն էր, որուն տիրոջմէն տփոց մը կ՚ուտէ եւ խնդիրը կը փակէ 10 ֆրանք արժող իշուկին համար 200 ֆրանք վճարելով:

Այսպէս ձախողութիւններով լի ուղեւորութեան ընթացքին, երբ դրամապանակը խաբէութեամբ կորսնցնելէ ետք ան կ՚արտասուէ մտածկոտ, յանկարծ կը տեսնէ առիւծ մը եւ իսկոյն կրակելով կը սպաննէ զայն, այնուհետեւ ստիպուելով կոյր եւ ընտելացուած առիւծին խափշիկ տէրերուն տալ իր ամբողջ ունեցուածքը: Հակառակ այս բոլորին, թարասքոնցիները զինք կ՚ընդունին փառահեղօրէն իր վերադարձին:

Կիւրճեան վարպետ թարգմանութեամբ այս վէպը հայ ընթերցողին մատչելի դարձուցած է պատկերներու անաղարտ վերարտադրութեամբ եւ հարազատօրէն պահպանելով բնագրին գեղարուեստական ուժն ու հմայքը:

23-24ամեայ թարգմանիչը չէ դժուարացած գտնել քիչ գործածական բառերու հայերէնները, ինչպէս՝ պերեւեթիլ (հագուիլ, սքուիլ), դուզնաքեայ (չնչին, աննշան, հասարակ), կառավար (կառք վարող), խառնակեցիկ (անկարգ վարքով, ցոփ), ձորձ (լաթ, հագուստ, զգեստ), ջրդեղ (ռետնային նիւթերէ ծեփ, որով կը ծածկեն զանազան բանուածքներ՝ անոնց փայլ տալու եւ զանոնք ջուրի եւ օդի ազդեցութեան դէմ պաշտպանելու համար — vernis), վաչ (սայլի ծածք), եւայլն:

Ահա թէ ինչո՛ւ Միհրան Ասքանազ[112] իր «Պարտէզ» շաբաթաթերթին մէջ կը գրէ. «Ալֆոնս Տոտէի երգիծաբանական այս նշանաւոր երկին թարգմանութիւնը, մաս առ մաս, պիտի երեւայ *Պարտէզ*ի մէջ իբր թերթօն: Ֆրանսական մատենագրութեան սոյն չքնաղ գոհարին անմահ հեղինակը անշուշտ բարեբախտ պիտի համարէր ինքզինքը, երբ իմանար անոր հայերէնի թարգմանութիւնը, երկու լեզուներուն ալ հաւասարապէս քաջահմուտ թարգմանիչի մը կողմէն: Եգիպտահայ գաղութին գրագէտնե-րուն Բենիամինը՝ արդարեւ մեծ յաջողութեամբ թարգմանած է զայն, այնչափ շնորհիւ իր լեզուական հմտութեանը, որչափ երկը ինքնին յանկ ու պատշաճ գալով իր երգիծաբանական տաղանդին ու խառնուածքին: Խմբագրութիւնը իր խնդակցութիւնը ու շնորհակալութիւնը կը յայտնէ, սոյն արժանաւոր երկին արժանավայել թարգմանութեանը համար, Տիար Միքայէլ Կիւրճեանի, իր ազնիւ բարեկամին ու անձնուէր աշխատակցին»:

Կիւրճեան արձակ գործերու թարգմանութեան ժամանակ ալ կը ցուցաբերէ լեզուական, ոճական խստապահանջութիւն, բառերու ճշգրիտ օգտագործում եւ՝ ինչ որ իրեն շատ բնորոշ է՝ բառակերտում: Ան չի սիրեր օտար բառերու օգտագործումը. միշտ կը գտնէ հայերէն համապատասխան ճիշդ բառը, իսկ չգտնելու պարագային՝ կը յօրինէ նոր մը:

«Թարասքոնցի Թարթարէն»ը հայ ընթերցողին աւելի մատչելի դարձնելու համար, թարգմանիչը էջատակերուն իր կողմէ դրած է բացատրութիւններ եւ ծանօթութիւններ ֆրանսական յատուկ բառերու եւ դարձուածքներու համար:

Բազմաթիւ հետաքրքրական ծանօթութիւններէն նշենք հետեւեալները:

Թարասք- հրէշատիպ անասուն մը ներկայացնող տեսակ մը խամաճիկ, զոր Հոգեգալստեան եւ Ս. Մարթայի տօներուն առթիւ կը պտտցնէին Գաղղիոյ հարաւային քանի մը քաղաքներուն մէջ, մասնաւորապէս ի Թարասքոն:

Հոռեջարդ- Ֆրանսական յեղափոխութեան ժամանակ, 1792ին, Սեպտեմբեր (հայերէն՝ Հոռի) ամսին երկու, երեք, չորս եւ հինգ օրերուն ֆրանսական բանտերուն մէջ կատարուած ազնուականներուն ջարդը:

Ծիծեռնակ ուտելը մեղք համարող գաղղիական աւելորդապաշտութեան մը ակնարկութիւն:

Ճագար մըն է- Զինուորական ծածկալեզուի բացատրութիւն մը, որ կը նշանակէ քաջ զինուոր:

Չինացի «վագր»- Չինական հետեւակ զինուորի տեսակ մը:

Պատերազմի իրարանցում- *Պլանըր-պա տը քոմպա*, ծովամարտի ժամանակ ծանր քալել: Ակնարկութիւն Խրիմի մէջ, Պալաքլավայի յարձակումին, ուր անգլիական բանակը թշնամիի համասփիւռ կրակին տակ ամենայն հանդարտութեամբ, քայլ առ քայլ յառաջանալով 12,000 հոգի կորսնցուց:

Հիտալկօ- Սպանացի ազնուական:

Քեքիա- Ալճերիական ֆէս:

Միսթրալ- Հիւսիս-արեւմտեան կատաղի հով, Միջերկրականի դրացի երկիրներու յատուկ:

Սփահի- Ալճերիացի հեծելազօրք:

* * *

«Թարասքոնցի Թարթարէն»էն բացի, Կիւրճեան Հայ Սահմանադրական Ռամկավար Կուսակցութեան Աղեքսանդրիոյ ակումբի հանդէսին համար թարգմանած է Լէոբոլտ Լալիւէի «Գարնանը» մէկ արարով կատակերգութիւնը, որ 1912 Մարտին յաջողութեամբ ներկայացուած է՝ Նուագախառն փանթէզիի վերածուած: Կիւրճեան նաեւ թարգմանած է Արմենակ պէյ Կամսարականի հազիւ քսանամեայ դուստր՝ Տարիա Կամսարականի ֆրանսերէն վիպակը «Արիւնի Ճակատագրականութիւնը», որ լոյս տեսած է «Արեւ»ի մէջ:

ԿԻՐՃԵԱՆԻ ԳՐԱԿԱՆ ՔՆՆԱԴԱՏԱԿԱՆ ՀԱՅԵՑԱԿԷՏՆ ՈՒ ԳՐԱԿԱՆԱԳԻՏԱԿԱՆ ԾԵԾՏՈՒԱԾ ՈԳՈՐՈՒՄԸ

Կիրճեանի գրչին կը պատկանին գրաքննադատական յօդուածներ եւ գրախօսականներ, զանազան գիրքերու տեսութիւններ, յառաջաբաններ, գրողներու եւ արուեստագէտներու կենսագրական շարադրանքներ, գեղարուեստական երկերու եւ հեղինակներու ուսումնասիրութիւններ, դիմանկարներ, եւայլն:

Ծնորհիւ յարատեւ ընթերցումներու, գրականագիտութեան եւ գրական քննադատութեան տեսական սկզբունքներուն գիտակ եւ հարուստ գրական պաշարով օժտուած գրագէտը շարունակած է 19րդ դարու արեւմտահայ եւ արեւելահայ գրական գործիչներու՝ Գրիգոր Օտեանի, Ստեփան Ոսկանեանի, Յարութիւն Սվաճեանի, Յակոբ Պարոնեանի, Արփիար Արփիարեանի, Լէոյի, Մանուկ Աբեղեանի, Ալեքսանտր Ծիրվանզադէի եւ ուրիշներու գրաքննադատական գործունէութիւնը՝ նպատակ ունենալով նպաստել գրականութեան գեղարուեստական բովանդակութեան եւ բարոյագիտական էութեան զարգացման՝ հիմնաւոր վերլուծութեամբ, յատկապէս շեշտելով այն տեսակէտը թէ գրականութիւնը պէտք է ունենայ հասարակութիւնը դաստիարակելու եւ կրթելու բնոյթ եւ հանդիսանայ ժողովուրդին բազմակողմանի մտաւոր յառաջդիմութեան կարեւոր ազդակ:

Ան իր երիտասարդական տարիքէն մինչեւ մահ միշտ ալ գրած եւ տպագրութեան յանձնած է բազում գրութիւններ, որոնց մէջ բացայայտած է գրականութեան ստեղծած գեղագիտական արժէքները, ձգտելով սատարել ժողովուրդին իմացական զարգացման:

Ուշագրաւ է Կիրճեանի «Քննադատութեան Կարեւորութիւնը Եւ Անոր Պակասը Մեր Մէջ» ուսումնասիրութիւնը, որ շուրջ մէկ մամուլ ծաւալով լոյս տեսած է «Շիրակ»ի մէջ (Յունիս 1905, թիւ 5, էջ 439-453), բնաբան ունենալով «Քննադատութիւնը արուեստին գիտութիւնն է» սկզբունքը:

Հոն ֆրանսական քննադատական միտքի պատմութեան քաջածանօթ յօդուածագիրը հանգամանօրէն կը խօսի ֆրանսացի անուանի գրող, քննադատ եւ ֆրանսական ակադեմիայի անդամ Նիքոլա Պուալոյի «Բանաստեղծական Արուեստը» (1674) գիրքին քննադատական տեսակէտներուն, ֆրանսացի քննադատ, գրող եւ ֆրանսական ակադեմիայի անդամ Ծարլ-Օկիւսթէն Սէնթ-Պէօվի գիտական հիմքերով քննադատութիւններուն եւ այլոց հայեցակէտերու մասին: Կիրճեան կը գովաբանէ ճշմարիտ քննադատները եւ կը մատնանշէ ձախորդ քննադատներու անխուսափելի վնասարարութիւնը: Այնուհետեւ, խօսելով հայ քննադատութեան մասին, ան կ'ընդգծէ կանոնաւոր քննադատութեան պակասը, կը թուարկէ քանի մը յիշատակութեան արժանի արեւմտահայ քննադատներ, որոնց գործերը յաջող փորձեր ըլլալով հանդերձ, չեն կրնար կանոնաւոր քննադատութիւն նկատուիլ: Կը խոստովանի թէ ինք շատ «դժուարահաճ է գրականութեան մէջ», հետեւաբար շար դժուար է իրեն «բան հաւնեցնելը», մանաւանդ՝ միջակ, ցածորակ կամ անարժէք գրական գործերը:

Կիւրճեանի աչքառու ուսումնասիրութիւններէն պէտք է նկատել Ալեքսանդր Շիրվանզադէին նուիրուած «Նորավէպագիրը» աշխատութիւնը, ուր ան կը դրուատէ Շիրվանզադէի արժանիքները: «Ով որ շատը կրնայ քիչն ալ կրնայ» առածով սկսող յօդուածին մէջ, Կիւրճեան օրինակ բերելով Պալզաքը, Ֆլոպէրը, Տոտէն, Մոբասանը, Տիքընզը, կը նշէ. «Շիրվանզադէն եւս, մեր մեծ թատերագիրն ու վիպասանը, կը յայտնուի ճարտար ու կատարեալ պատմող մը իր կարճ գրութիւններուն մէջ»: Բացի Շիրվանզադէի երկարաշունչ գործերէն, կարդացած ըլլալով անոր «պզտիկ երկերէն» մի քանին ալ, Կիւրճեան կը հետեւցնէ թէ անոնք կը ներկայացնեն «արուեստագէտին ճաշակն ու ճարտարութիւնը»:

Ան հանգամանօրէն կը վերլուծէ «Նորերից Մէկը» հոգեբանական պատկերը, «Շրջանից Արտաքսուածը» հոգեբանական նորավէպը, «Թանկագին Կապանք» գեղեցիկ պատմութիւնը, ընդարձակ մէջբերումներ կատարելով քննարկուող գործերէն: Ան կը գտնէ թէ «Նորերից Մէկը»ին մէջ Քամալեանը «խիստ յաջող մարմնացումն է չարաշուք ազդեցութեան ու արդիւնքներու անմէթոտ կրթութեան մը, որ միայն միտքին կ'ուղղուի, եւ կ'անտեսէ թէ՛ ֆիզիքականը, որ հիմն է շէնքին, եւ թէ՛ նկարագիրը, որ *պսակաւորումն* է անոր»:

«Շրջանից Արտաքսուածը» հոգեբանական նորավէպը քննարկելու ընթացքին, Կիւրճեան Շիրվանզադէն կը բնութագրէ իբրեւ ընկերային բարքերու եւ նախապաշարումներու մեծ դիտող:

«Թանկագին Կապանք»ը մայրական եւ որդիական սիրոյ յուզիչ նկարագրութիւն մըն է: Ամուսինը եւ ուրիշ զաւակ մը կորսնցուցած Հռիփսիմէի միակ սփոփանքը Սմբատն է, որ մօր տեւական հսկողութեան տակ ինքզինք խիստ ճնշուած զգալով, կ'ուզէ արտասահման մեկնիլ: Խեղճ մայրը, որ «Առանց քեզ մի օր չեմ կարող ապրել» կ'ըսէ, ողբալիօրէն կը թախանձէ, կը պաղատի, կու լայ եւ հիւանդագին իր սենեակը կ'առանձնանայ, համոզուած ըլլալով որ իր ցաւին դեղ ու դարման չկայ բժշկութենէն: Կիւրճեան այնքան սրտաշարժ ու հոյակապ կը գտնէ Շիրվանզադէի միտքը, տպաւորութիւնները եւ նկարագրելու վարպետութիւնը, որ կը գրէ. «Հոս ամենագեղեցիկ տեսարան մը կայ զոր ամբողջովին արտագրելու փափաքիս չեմ կրնար դիմադրել», եւ յիսուն տողանի մէջբերում կը կատարէ նորավէպէն:

Մեկնումի վերջին պահուն մօր խելակորոյս, նուաղուն ուշաթափութիւնն ու գետնին փռուիլը, սարսափահար որդւոյն «Մայրի՜կ, մայրի՜կ» աղաղակը, մօր «Մի գնա՛ր, մի գնա՛ր» աղաչանքը եւ Սմբատի «Այս թանկագին շղթան անկարելի է փշրել» խօսքը կ'եզրափակեն այս սրտաճմլիկ պատմութիւնը եւ Կիւրճեան իր գնահատանքը կը բանաձեւէ այսպէս. «Հեղինակի աղուոր խօսք մը որ ամբողջ նիւթը կը խտացնէ ու պատմութեան բարոյականը կը հանէ, գեղեցկագիտօրէն, եւ որ սակայն կեղծ «գրական» չի հնչեր բնաւ, որովհետեւ աղեխարշ նիւթին ընդերքէն իսկ հանուած է, անոր իրականութեամբը համակ թաթաւուն ու տամուկ:

«Որդիական սիրոյ համբուրելի՜ խօսք»:

«Նորավէպագիրը» յօդուածին մէջ Կիւրճեան համոզումով կը վկայէ. «Իր «պատմուածք»ներուն մէջ, Ծիրվանզադէ կը ներկայանայ վիպասանի ու թատերագրի կրկնակ ու կերպիւ իւիք իրարու մէջ ձուլուած յատկութիւններով, ու եթէ իր վիպական ձիրքերը կը կրճատուին հոն՝ հարկաւոր զեղչումովը, յապաւումովը հոգեբանական, վերլուծական, նկարագրական մասերուն,- որոնք վէպի մը ընդարձակ սահմաններուն մէջ միայն կրնան տարածուիլ հեղինակին քմահաճոյքին եւ նիւթին պահանջումներուն համեմատ,- տրամատուրգի (ինչպէս կ'ըսեն մեր ռուսահայ եղբայրները) իր հզօր ձիրքերը մեծապէս կը նպաստաւորեն զինքը: Որովհետեւ նորավէպը, յաճախ կարճ, բայց տպաւորիչ ու կարեւոյզ գործողութեան մը ծաւալումն է, ուր մէկ քանի յատկանշական տեսարաններու եւ կացութիւններու արագ ու ճարտարահիւս յաջորդութիւն մը պէտք է յանգի «ճակատագրական» լուծման (dénouement) մը, զգացումը ուժգնակի ցնցող, կամ մտածումը խորունկէն դղրդող, դրդող վերջաւորութեան մը, զոր հեղինակի խօսք մը,- ինչպէս կ'ըսեն թատրոնի լեզուով,- անակնկալօրէն կը լուսաբանէ, կը լուսաւորէ յաճախ»:[113]

Վրացեան քննադատելով «Ծիրվանզադէ Եւ Իր Գործը» հատորը, որ անոր յոբելեանին առիթով «գրական կոչումք» մըն էր իր թրքահայ եղբայրակիցներէն, «Ազատամարտ»ի մէջ կը գրէ թէ հատորը «*տապանաքար* մըն է զայն կազմող տասնըեօթը գրողներէն տասնըվեցին, ինչպէս եւ ենթակային՝ Ծիրվանզադէի վրայ»:

Վահան Թէքէեան ««Ծիրվանզադէ Եւ Իր Գործը» Եւ Իր Քննադատը» յօդուածին մէջ[114] կ'արդարացնէ յոբելեանական յարգանքի արտայայտութիւն ժողովածուն, որուն տապանաքար համարուիլը սխալ կը նկատէ: Թէքէեան կ'ըսէ. «Երեք ամիս առաջ, Թիֆլիսի մէջ հանդիպեցանք Ծիրվանզադէին, որ գիշեր մը *կլուբ* հրաւիրեց մեզ՝ Չիֆթէ-Սարաֆը եւ զիս: Պէտք է այստեղ յիշեմ, որովհետեւ անոնք ուղղուած են բոլոր այն գրողներուն որ աշխատակցած են իրեն նուիրուած մեծարանքի հատորին, այն խօսքերը որով *Պատւի Համար*ի հեղինակը ուրախութիւն եւ շնորհակալութիւն յայտնեց իր թրքահայ եղբայրներուն, անոնց իրեն ընծայած պատիւին համար, որ, ըսաւ, իր յոբելեանի առթիւ իրեն մատուցուած նուէրներուն ամենէն թանկագինն եղած է իրեն համար»: Այնուհետեւ «Քառս»ի հեղինակը նշած է. «Դուք ինծի համար արիք ա՛յն որ մեր մէջ մինչեւ այժմ ոչ մի գրագէտի համար չէր եղել. դուք հարիւր անգամ աւելին արիք՝ քան ինչ որ իմ ռուսահայ եղբայրակիցներս արին, եւ ես իմ սրտի խորքից շնորհակալ եմ ձեզ»:

Կ'արժէ մէջբերել նաեւ Ծիրվանզադէի Տիգրան Կամսարականին ուղղած նամակէն հետեւեալ նախադասութիւնը. «Եթէ իմ գրական ճակատագիրը որոշող կշիռքի մի թեւի վրայ սկզբից եւեթ ծանրացած էր ռուսահայ մամուլի չկամութիւնը, միւսի վրայ համարձակօրէն բարձրացաւ թրքահայ անկեղծ համակրանքը, եւ այդ մանաւանդ թանկ էր ինձ համար այն պատճառով որ Պոլիսը աւելի մօտիկ է Եւրոպային քան Թիֆլիսը...»:

* * *

Կիրճեան Երուանդ Օտեանի գրութիւնները սկսած է կարդալ եւ ըմբոշխնել դպրոցական գրասեղաններու վրայ աշակերտելու տարիներէն սկսեալ, իսկ Օտեան Կիրճեանի «Մարտիկ Աղա»ն կարդացած է «Նոր Կեանք»ի յաջորդական թիւերուն մէջ առանց գիտնալու Պարոյրին ո՛վ ըլլալը: Անոնք անձամբ իրարու ծանօթացած են 1898ին Աղեքսանդրիա եւ դարձած են սրտակից մտերիմներ, որոնց համագործակցութիւնը տեւած է շուրջ 28 տարի. Կիրճեանի խօսքերով՝ «հետզհետէ աւելի սերտ, տաք, մտերմիկ, գրական աշխատակցութեամբ ամրապնդուած, նուիրագործուած» բարեկամութիւն մը:

Օտեանի մահուան առթիւ «Իր Յիշատակին» յօդուածին մէջ Կիրճեան կ'աւաղէ. «Այսօր անհուն պարապ մը կայ մեր գրականութեան մէջ»: Համբաւաւոր երգիծաբանին հետ իր վերջին հանդիպումը վերյիշելով, ան կը գրէ. «Ստացած էր արդէն վերջին հարուածն այն անողոք ախտին որուն հետ գլուխ պիտի չկրնար ելլել հէգ սիրելի բարեկամս: Ո՞ւր էին, ո՞ւր կորսուեր էին իր անսպառ շէնշողութիւնը, ծիծաղելու եւ ծիծաղեցնելու իր հրաշալի կարողութիւնը, է՛ն մեռած զուարթութիւնն անգամ ողջցնելու կարող իր կատակերգական աւիւնը, իր համով հոտով պատմութիւնները որոնց պաշարը չէր հատներ»:

Ափսոսալով ժպտուն, կենսուրախ, սրտբաց երեւոյթով, սրամտութեամբ ու զուարթութեամբ լի համագաղափարակից մտերիմին կորուստը, թախծալից կսկիծով ու անզուսպ վիշտով Կիրճեան կը վկայէ. «Անմոռանալի բարեկամիս կորստեան ցաւը տակաւին շատ ուժով կը կոտտայ ներսիդիս, որպէս զի կարենամ պաղարեամբ խօսիլ գրագէտին վրայ: Հարկ կա՞յ արդէն: Կա՞յ մեր մէջ Օտեանէն աւելի ճանչցուած, սիրուած, *ժողովրդականացած* հեղինակ մը. բառին լաւագոյն իմաստովը, քանի որ իր անհամար հիացողները կը պատկանին մեր ժողովուրդին բոլոր խաւերուն անխտիր: Թերուս ընթերցողներէն մինչեւ փափկաճաշակ գրասէրը եւ մինչեւ դժուարահաճ գրագէտը, ամէն ոք այսօր կը զգայ թէ ի՜նչ անփոխարինելի կորուստ մըն է որ կ'ընէ մեր գրականութիւնը Օտեանի անհետացումովը: Անշուշտ Օտեանի փառքն ապահովուած, իր անմահութիւնը — ցորքան ապրին հայ ազգն ու լեզուն — երաշխաւորուած է այն բազմաթիւ երկերովն ու մէկէ աւելի գլուխ-գործոցներովը զորս կը ձգէ. իշխանական ժառանգութիւն, մեր աղքատիկ գրականութեան»: Կիրճեան կ'եզրափակէ. «Ան տակաւին կարող էր երկար տարիներ արտադրել, մեր ամենամեծ հաճոյքին եւ հայկական դպրութեան օգտին ու փառքին համար»:

* * *

Հայ գրականութեան մէջ «Փանջունի»ն բացառիկ գործ մըն է, ուր Օտեան ծաղրած ու դատապարտած է ընկերվարական արկածախնդիրներու գործունէութիւնը Արեւմտեան Հայաստանի մէջ: Երգիծանկարիչ Ալեքսանտր Սարուխան, որ Օտեանի եւ Կիրճեանի մտերիմներէն էր, մեծապէս տպաւորուած էր «Փանջունի»ն կարդալով: 1931ին ան գաղափարը յղացած է առանձին հատորով մը վերահրատարակելու «Փանջունի»ն եւ բազմակի ընթերցումներէ ետք իր տպաւորութիւնները երգիծանկարներու վերածելով իր աշխատութիւնը 1934ին աւարտելէ ետք, իր նկարազարդումներով Օտեանի գլուխ-գործոցը լոյսին տուած է 1938ին:[115]

Սարուխանի խնդրանքով, այդ հրատարակութեան ներածականը գրած է Կիրճեան: Ան հանգամանօրէն բնորոշած է երկու ճշմարիտ վարպետներու գործերը՝ ինչպէս Օտեանի երգիծական տաղանդն ու համաշխարհային գրական արժանիքը, այնպէս ալ Սարուխանի բնատուր ձիրքն ու երգիծանկարչական շնորհքը: «Հայ տիրացուին դասական տիպարն է ան, անմահ ընկեր Փանջունին, որ ցեղայատուկ հարազատ գիծեր ունենալով հանդերձ, իր շատ մը կողմերովը կը պատկանի մարդկային մեծ ընտանիքին,- ինչ որ իրաւունք կու տայ իրեն մտնելու հռչակաւոր տիպարներու տիեզերական պատկերասրահին մէջ եւ իր տեղը գրաւելու սպանացի Տօն Քիշօթին, անգլիացի Բիքուիքին եւ ֆրանսացի Թարթարէնին առընթեր»:

Արժեւորելով Սարուխանի գործը, Կիրճեան կ'ըսէ. «Իր գծած պատկերները աւելի պերճախօս են քան ամէն մեկնաբանութիւն» եւ կը հիանայ «հրաշալիօրէն հաւատարիմ, եղբայրական եւ միեւնոյն ատեն հզօրապէս անձնադրոշմ աշխատակցութեան վրայ զոր Սարուխան բերած է Օտեանի գլուխ-գործոցին»:

Հայ տպագիր գիրքի պատմութեան մէջ երկու տաղանդաւոր արուեստագէտներու արգասիքը եղող այս աննախադէպ գործը Կիրճեան կը բնութագրէ հետեւեալ սեղմ նախադասութեամբ. «*Ծաղկվարը* Երուանդ Օտեանի երգիծական գլուխ-գործոցն է, իսկ անոր պատկերազարդումը Ալ. Սարուխանի ծաղրանկարչական գլուխ-գործոցը»:

«Սարուխան ... Ընթերցողի Ակնոցով» յօդուածին մէջ[116] Կիրճեան հանգամանօրէն կը վերլուծէ երգիծանկարչին իմաստնաբար խնդացնելու ձիրքն ու արուեստը, զայն նմանցնելով մեծ կատակերգակ Մոլիէրի. «Սարուխան միշտ առանց տխրութեան, առանց դառնութեան չէ որ կ'երգիծէ, կ'երգիծանկարէ»: Ան նաեւ զինք կը նմանցնէ Պալզաքին, որ «չէ գոհացած նկատելով միայն ծիծաղելի, զզուելի եւ սոսկալի տիպարներ, անոնց քով, անոնց դիմացը կանգնեցուցած է մարդկային էակներ՝ արժանի սիրոյ, գութի եւ սքանչացման»: Նկատի ունենալով բազմատաղանդ Սարուխանի երեք գիրքերը եւ խոհուն հայեցակէտերով հրապարակագրական յօդուածները, ան կը հաստատէ. «Այսօր Սարուխան արժանաւորապէս կը շարունակէ իր մեծ նախորդներուն՝ Պարոնեանի եւ Օտեանի երգիծական գործը, երգիծանկարչութեան կարեւոր յաւելումով»:

Ուշադրութեան արժանի է նաեւ Կիրճեանի «Սարուխան» յօդուածը,[117] ուր ան «մեծատաղանդ» բառին արդարօրէն կ'աւելցնէ «բազմատաղանդ» ածականը՝ «լիովին սահմանելու համար զինքը»: Յօդուածագիրը Սարուխանը կը համարէ «Հայ Տոմիէ[116] մը. այսինքն՝ իշխանը հայ երգիծանկարիչներուն, ինչպէս է Տոմիէն՝ ֆրանսացիներունը»: Այնուհետեւ կը շարունակէ. «Անշուշտ իր ծաղրանկարելու կամ իր նախասիրած բառովը՝ երգիծանկարելու եղանակովը չէ որ Սարուխան կը նմանի ֆրանսացի հսկային, այլ իր ստեղծագործ ուժովը, անսպառ, ապշեցուցիչ բեղմնաւորութեամբ եւ իր գծագրութեան անթերի թեքնիքովը»: Արդարեւ, արուեստագէտի փայլուն ձիրքի տէր, բացառիկ սրատեսութեամբ եւ արտակարգ սրամտութեամբ օժտուած, աշխարհի մեծագոյն երգիծանկարիչներէն մէկն է եղած Սարուխան. գեղարուեստական արժանաւոր ստեղծագործող մը՝ խիզախ գործունէութեամբ, միշտ մտահոգ ու գրիչը հետը կրող՝ իր մտայղացումները անմիջապէս թուղթին յանձնելու եւ մանաւանդ երգիծանկարելու պատրաստ:

* * *

Գրագէտներու եւ արուեստագէտներու մասին Կիրճեանի կենսագրական շարադրանքներէն եւ քննադատական յօդուածներէն ամենաընդարձակը «Օնօրէ տը Պալզաք» յօդուածաշարքն է, որ պարբերաբար լոյս տեսած է «Արեւ»ի 2 Յուլիս 1949էն 3 Սեպտեմբեր 1949ի թիւերուն մէջ:

Կիրճեան հանգամանօրէն կը վերլուծէ տիեզերահռչակ հեղինակին ստեղծագործութիւնները, կ'անդրադառնայ որոշ կենսագրական տուեալներու եւ մասնաւորապէս համաշխարհային գրականութեան զարգացման ու հարստացման մէջ անոր երկերու նշանակութեան, անկեղծօրէն խոստովանելով որ Պալզաքի հետ իր ծանօթացումը եղած է իր «մտաւոր-գրական կեանքի մեծագոյն յայտնութիւններէն մին, միւսները ըլլալով հանդիպումները Շէյքսփիրի, Պոտլէրի եւ մեր համճարեղ, անբաղդատելի Ինտրային (Տ. Չրաքեան) հետ»:

Կիւրճեանի հետաքրքրութիւնը Պալզաքի ստեղծագործութիւններուն նկատմամբ յառաջացած է «Մարդկային Կատակերգութիւն» վէպին մասին քննադատի մը գովեստին հետեւանքով: Հետեւաբար, տասնին կամ քսան տարեկանին, Աղեքսանդրիոյ մէջ, գնած եւ կարդացած է Պալզաքի «Béatrix» վէպը եւ հետեւեալ օրն իսկ գնած է քաղաքը գտնուող պալզաքեան բոլոր վէպերը, մնացեալները ապսպրելով եւ ապա յափշտակութեամբ ընթերցելով մէկէ աւելի անգամ «միշտ նոր բաներ գտնելով, միշտ աւելցնելով խոկումի եւ հիացումի պատճառները»:

Կիւրճեան կը հաւաստէ. «Պալզաք իր ինքնատիպ հանճարով վիպական սեռը բարձրացուց իր արհամարհուած դիրքէն, զայն վերանորոգեց, վերաստեղծեց, գծեց անոր շրջանակը, սահմանները, հաստատեց անոր օրէնքները իր գլուխ-գործոցներովը, ինչպէս որ ըրած էին ԺԷ դարուն Քոռնէյ եւ Ռասին՝ ողբերգութեան եւ Մոլիէր՝ կատակերգութեան համար»: Ան համառօտ ակնարկ մը կը նետէ նախապալզաքեան ֆրանսական վիպական ստեղծագործութիւններու վրայ.- Տիկին տը Լա Ֆայէթի[119] գլուխ-գործոց «La Princesse de Clèves»ը, որով ճանապարհ բացուեցաւ հոգեբանական վէպին (1678), Ապպէ Բռէվոյի[120] «Manon Lescaut» վէպը (1731), որ սիրոյ բուռն կիրքի ճշգրիտ եւ խորաթափանց ուսումնասիրութիւն մըն է, Պէնժամէն Քոնսթանի[121] «Adolphe» (1806) հոգեբանական նշանաւոր վիպակը, ինչպէս նաեւ «Շաթոպրիանի, Հիւկոյի, Վինեիի եւ Լամարթինի ռոմանթիք բանաստեղծական կամ դիւցազներգական վէպերը եւ վիպակները, Ալեքսանդր Տիւմայի եւ Էօժէն Սիւի մշակած եւ այնքան ժողովրդական դարձած թերթօն-վէպը, որ միտքերը կը զուարճացնէր կամ երեւակայութիւնները կը սարսափեցնէր ցնորական պատմութիւններով»:

Կիւրճեան ափսոսանքով կը նշէ թէ մինչեւ 1830 թուականը, այսինքն իր մահուընէն քսան տարի առաջ, Պալզաք զանազան ծածկանուններով գրած է բազմաթիւ վէպեր, ցնորական, մռայլ կամ մելոտրամաթիք պատմութիւններ, որոնք բոլորովին անարժան են իր կոչումին եւ հանճարին, որովհետեւ գրուած են «յոռեճաշակ ոճով» եւ «սանձարձակ երեւակայութեամբ»:

Յայտնի է որ դրամ չունենալուն պատճառով եւ պարտքերէ ձերբազատուելու համար Պալզաք անճապարանքով արտադրած է «անբնական տիպարներով եւ անճշմարտանման դէպքերով լեցուն» հատորներ՝ առանց մտահոգուելու ճաշակի, ոճի, նիւթի եւ ճշմարտութեան «ակադեմական» խնդիրներով:

Վերջապէս, 1830ին, «Les Chouans»[122] վէպով կը սկսի Պալզաքի ճշմարիտ գործունէութիւնը: Իրապաշտ գրողը գիտուն եւ խորհող արուեստագէտ մըն էր, քննական միտքով եւ ստեղծագործ ուղեղով, որ իր դարու գիտական եւ արհեստագիտական ծանօթութիւններու հարուստ պաշարով բեղուն եւ մարդկային բարքերուն հաւատարիմ պատմագրողի ու նկարիչի մը դերը կը կատարէ՝ ցանկալով բարոյախօսել եւ ուղղել ընկերութիւնը:

Կիրճեան կը գրէ. «Ես կը սիրեմ զինքը անուանել արդի ժամանակակից մեծագոյն *վարպետը կեանքի գիտութեանց*», որովհետեւ «Պալզաքի բոլոր վէպերը մտածել կու տան, խոկալ կու տան կեանքին վերաբերեալ, մարդը եւ մարդկային ընկերութիւնը շահագրգռող բոլոր մեծ ու պզտիկ հարցերուն մասին, առանց վնասելու ուշադրութիւնը միշտ գրգռուած, լարուած պահելու, երեւակայութիւնը գրաւելու, յափշտակելու, զգայարանքները տպաւորելու եւ զգայնութիւնը խորապէս յուզելու յատկութիւններուն, որոնք անհրաժեշտ են որպէսզի վէպ մը ըլլայ, եւ ո՛չ թէ կեանքին ջերմութենէն եւ բաբախումէն զուրկ, անմարմին անհոգի բան մը, վարդապետական (didactique) գրուածք մը կամ երկար քարոզ մը»:

Ահա պատմողական գրականութեան ժանրերէն մէկուն՝ վէպին ճշգրիտ բնութագրումը ըստ Կիրճեանի, որ կ'աւելցնէ. «Կարելի չէ Պալզաքի վէպերը կարդալ առանց հարստանալու եւ արգասաւորուելու»:

Կիրճեան համոզումով կը գրէ. «Չկայ, որքան որ գիտեմ, բոլոր ազգերու գրական պատմութեան մէջ ուրիշ օրինակ մեծ գրագէտի մը, որ այնքան գէշ, այնքան ձախող եւ ողբալի սկզբնաւորութիւն մը ունեցած ըլլայ»: Այնուհետեւ իր հիացումը կը յայտնէ. «Չկայ նաեւ գրագէտ մը, որ յանկարծ եւ հրաշիւք իմն հասունցած, իր ճամբան գտած, իր կոչումին բարձրութեանը վրայ կանգնած, այդքան քիչ ատենուան մէջ - հազիւ քսան տարի — արտադրած ըլլայ այդքան ստուար գործ մը եւ այդքան հրաշակերտներ»:

Պալզաքի նիւթին նորութեան ակնարկելով, Կիրճեան կը նշէ. «Առաջին անգամն ըլլալով վիպասան մը կը ձեռնարկէր ներկայացնելու, պատկերացնելու եւ պատմելու, իր յայտնի եւ թագուն ամէն կողմերովը, մարդկային ընկերութեան մը բոլոր խաւերուն կեանքը, մէջն ըլլալով հասարակ ժողովուրդը, գիւղացիութիւնը, պզտիկ եւ միջին քաղքենիութիւնները (bourgeoisie), հարուստ եւ ազնուապետական դասակարգը», մինչդեռ այն ատեն գրուած վէպերուն մէջ ԺԵ. դարէն սկսեալ գլխաւոր անձնաւորութիւնները կը պատկանէին տիրող դասակարգին, հետեւաբար զուրկ էին վիպական շահեկանութենէ եւ հետաքրքրականութենէ, ուստի ընթերցողները շահագրգռող եւ հրապուրող չէին: Կիրճեան յատկապէս կը վկայէ. «Պալզաքի գործը կ'ընդգրկէր, կը պարփակէր ժամանակակից ընկերութիւնը իր բոլոր խաւերովն ու դասակարգերովը, իր բոլոր ներկայացուցչական տիպարներովը, որ իրեն ուսումնասիրութեան նիւթ ընտրած էր անոնց պատմութիւնը, հոգեբանութիւնը, վարքն ու բարքը, նիստն ու կացը, կեանքը եւ հոլովոյթը, որոնք սիրտերը թունդ կը հանէին, երեւակայութիւնները կը յանկուցանէին» եւ որոնք ամենէն կարեւորներն են վիպասանական տեսակէտէ:

Յօդուածաշարքին հեղինակը ցաւով կ՚արձանագրէ թէ Պալզաք իր կենդանութեանը չարժանացաւ այն փառքին, որուն արժանի էր եւ չդասուեցաւ ֆրանսական գրականութեան մէջ այն առաջանակարգ տեղը՝ ամենէն մեծերուն փառաւոր շարքին մէջ, այն ժամանակ, երբ գրական աշխարհին մէջ յաճախ շնորհալից յօդուածով մը մէկ օրէն միւսը հռչակաւոր կը դառնան գրեթէ անծանօթ հեղինակներ, որոնց առջեւ կը բացուի փառքի ճամբան:

Այս հարցին մէջ Կիւրճեան յատկապէս կը մեղադրէ ֆրանսացի քննադատներու իշխան Սէնթ-Պէօվը, որ մեծ հմտութիւն, նուրբ ճաշակ եւ խորաթափանց միտք ունենալով հանդերձ պատասխանատու է ժամանակակից գրագէտներու եւ տիտղոսակիր գրադատներու բիծ ու թերութիւն փնտռող եւ առարկող վերաբերումը չպարսաւելուն համար, անոնց սխալ գաղափարները եւ իրապաշտ վիպասանին համբաւի արժանի գործերը ըստ արժանւոյն չգնահատելուն համար, որովհետեւ Կիւրճեանի համոզումով, գործի մը առաւելութիւնները եւ թերութիւնները մատնանշելու հետ միասին, քննադատութեան դերը պէտք է ըլլայ լուսաւորել եւ առաջնորդել ընթերցողը, անոր ծանօթացնելով գրական ամէն նոր արժէք:

Իր յօդուածաշարքին մէջ Կիւրճեան կը յիշատակէ նաեւ Պալզաքի մասին ֆրանսացի փիլիսոփայ, պատմաբան եւ քննադատ Իփոլիթ Թէնի,[123] ֆրանսացի գրող եւ գրաքննադատ Էտմոն Ժալուի[124] եւ ուրիշներու դրական կարծիքները: Ան յանդուգն վստահութեամբ կը գրէ. «Կը համարձակիմ ըսել որ Պալզաք ֆրանսական գրականութեան համար այն է, ինչ որ է Շէյքսփիր անգլիականին համար», որովհետեւ «ան կը պատկանի այն հանճարներուն, որոնք մէկ հատիկ (unique) են ո՛չ միայն իրենց ազգին, այլ բոլոր միւս ազգերուն դպրութեանց մէջ. այսպէս՝ իտալացի Տանթէն, սպանացի Սէրվանթէսը, անգլիացի Շէյքսփիրը եւ գերմանացի Կէօթէն»:

Կիւրճեան կը մէջբերէ ԺԹ. դարու մեծերու մեծին՝ փառքով յագեցած Վիքթոր Հիւկոյի ափսոսանքը Պալզաքի դագաղին վրայ եղոյթի պահուն. «Աւա՜ղ, այս հուժկու եւ անխոնջ երկասիրողը, այս փիլիսոփան, այս խորհողը, այս բանաստեղծը, այս հանճարը մեր մէջ ապրեցաւ փոթորիկներու, կռիւներու, պայքարներու կեանքովը որ հասարակաց եղած է ամէն ժամանակներու բոլոր մեծ մարդոց»:

Կիւրճեան արդարացիօրէն կը նշէ. «Իրապաշտ եւ բնապաշտ դպրոցները ուղղակի սերած են Պալզաքի գործէն եւ անոր ազդեցութեան անվիճելի ծնունդն են», ինչպէս՝ Ֆլոպէր, Կոնքուրներ, Տոտէ, Մոբասան, Զոլա եւ ուրիշներ, որոնց գործերը համեմատաբար յոգնեցուցիչ եւ ձանձրացուցիչ են, որովհետեւ գրուած են զսպուած երեւակայութեամբ եւ չափաւորուած աւիւնով: Անոնք չեն ստեղծուած Պալզաքի հզօր վրձինով եւ լուսավառ գոյներով. անոնց կը պակսի խորհողի եւ ստեղծագործողի արուեստագիտական պալզաքեան հանճարը:

Ինչպէս տեսանք, Կիրճեան «Օնօրէ տը Պալզաք» յօդուածաշարքին մէջ կը դրսեւորէ գրականագէտի ճարտարամտութիւն, յաջողակ արուեստագէտի հմտութիւն եւ օտար, յատկապէս ֆրանսական գրականութեան խոր գիտակութիւն:

* * *

Կիրճեանի ծանօթութիւնը եւ մտերմութիւնը Վահան Թէքէեանի հետ սկսած է 1903ին, երբ Թէքէեանի զարմիկը՝ գրասէր Բարսեղ Օհանեան, Մարսիլիայէն Եգիպտոս հրաւիրած է բանաստեղծ եւ հրապարակագիր Թէքէեանը: Ի հարկէ անոնք մինչ այդ Պոլսոյ մէջ զիրար տեսնելու առիթ ունեցած են՝ երկուքն ալ ծնած եւ մեծցած ըլլալով Սկիւտար, ապա նաեւ մամուլի մէջ իրենց գրութիւններու ընթերցանութեան միջոցով:

Այդ հարազատ մտերմութեան հիմքը կը կազմեն երկու գրագէտներու նկարագրի, մտածողութեան ու գաղափարներու նմանութիւնը, գրական նախասիրութիւններու ընդհանրութիւնը եւ մանաւանդ բարձրարուեստ գրականութեան պահանջկոտութիւնն ու իքնատիպ ներշնչումներով ստեղծուած արուեստի գործերու պաշտամունքն ու հրայրքը:

Կիրճեան հրապարակագրական յօդուածներով՝ «Վահան Թէքէեանի Կեանքը», «Վերյիշումներ», «Տրտունջք» եւ այլն, յաճախ անդրադարձած է Թէքէեանի կեանքին ու նրբարուեստ ստեղծագործութիւններուն: Դժբախտաբար, երբ 1901ին Փարիզի մէջ Թէքէեան հրատարակած էր իր բանաստեղծութիւններու առաջին ժողովածուն՝ «Հոգեր»ը, Կիրճեան ընդունելով հանդերձ որ «Թէքէեան Եւրոպա գտնուող մեր նորագոյն գրական հեղինակաւոր ներկայացուցիչներէն մէկն է», ունի «բանաստեղծի վաւերական ակներեւ նշանները» եւ «խոստումը ապագայ լաւագոյն երկերու», առանց արգահատանքի կը գրէ չափազանց ժխտական յօդուած մը «Հարբխտ Բանաստեղծ Մը» վերնագրով, քննադատելով Թէքէեանի զգայնոտութիւնը եւ մելամաղձոտութիւնը, որոնց աղբիւրը կը համարէ Պոտլէր, Վերլէն, Լը Քոնթ տը Լիլ, Ռոտենպաք, Ռէմպօ, Մալարմէ, Միրպօ. այլ խօսքով, կը տեսնէ վիպապաշտ եւ խորհրդապաշտ գրողներու ազդեցութիւն մը Թէքէեանի քերթուածներուն վրայ: Կիրճեան ինք ալ շատ կը սիրէր կարդալ այդ գրողներու երկերը, որոնք զինք յոռետեսութեան կը տանէին եւ իր քսանամեայ հաւակին ֆիզիքական ծանր տագնապ մը անցընելէ յետոյ, կը փոխէ իր ապրելակերպը եւ կը սկսի աւելի ուրախ տրամադրութիւն յարուցող գրականութիւն կարդալ: Հաւանաբար Կիրճեանի այս ներքին յեղաշրջումը պատճառ դարձած է երգիծական սուր ոճով գրուած անողոք «Հարբխտ բանաստեղծ Մը» յօդուածին:

Թէքէեան Մարսէյլէն, 2 Նոյեմբեր 1901 թուակիր նամակով մը շատ զուսպ եւ ոչ-վիրաւորական ոճով ազնուօրէն կը հասկցնէ թէ բուռն յարձակման կարիք չկար իր անդրանիկ երկին վրայ: «Ափյափոյ ընթերցումի մը արդիւնքն է այդ անգութ յօդուածը ... վերջէն սխալնիդ պիտի ճանչնաք – թէպէտ ո՛չ ձեր ընթերցողներուն, ո՛չ ինծի պիտի չըսէք զայն», կը գրէ ան:

Արդարեւ, Թէքէեանի մահէն երկու տասնեակ տարի ետք, 30 Յունիս 1965ին, Կիւրճեան կը գրէ «Ինչպէս Ծանօթացայ Վահան Թէքէեանի Հետ» զղջումի յօդուածը, որ «Արեւ»ի մէջ կը հրատարակուի 15 Յուլիս 1965ին, Կիւրճեանի մահէն տասներկու օր ետք: Այսպիսով, Կիւրճեան զղջումով կը քաւէ իր խիստ անգութ ոճով գրած եւ երիտասարդական տարիքին գործած մեղք մը:

Թէքէեանի մահուան առիթով Կիւրճեան կը սգայ իր «ամենասիրելի եւ ամենաթանկագին մտերիմ»ին վախճանը, կ՚ողբայ «Ճկարագրի հազուագիւտ յատկութիւններով օժտուած բանաստեղծի եւ հրապարակագրի» մահը, իր վիշտը կ՚արտայայտէ «ազգին եւ գրականութեան կրած մեծ եւ անդարմանելի կորուստին» համար: Կիւրճեան կ՚ընդգծէ մեծ քերթողին արժանիքները. «Քերթող մը, որ պատիւ պիտի բերէր ոեւէ ազգի գրականութեան»: Ան կը դրուատէ ազնուազգի հրապարակագրին պայծառատեսութիւնը, արդարադատութիւնը, կորովամտութիւնը, կը գնահատէ հանրային գործիչի անշահախնդիր գործունէութիւնը, որուն հետ աւելի քան քառասուն տարի բարեկամ եղած է, գաղափարակից, գրչակից եւ «մտքի եւ սրտի թանկագին, անփոխարինելի» ընկեր:

Թէքէեանի մահուան քառասունքին առիթով Կիւրճեան «Արեւ»ի մէջ լոյս տեսած իր «Տրտունջք» յօդուածով ոգեկոչելով «հայ դպրութեանց եւ հրապարակագրութեան իշխանը», կը գրէ. «Յաւիտենական Թէքէեանն է որ կ՚ապրի այսուհետեւ, պիտի ապրի որքան ատեն որ ապրին հայ ցեղն ու հայ լեզուն»:

Մտքի եւ սրտի անփոխարինելի ընկերոջ մահուան 18րդ տարեդարձին կապակցութեամբ «Արեւ»ի 10 Մայիս 1963ի թիւին մէջ Կիւրճեան կը շեշտէ. «Թէքէեան մեծ ազդեցութիւն ունեցած է մեր գրականութեան երիտասարդներէն ամենէն աւելի սիրուած սեռին՝ բանաստեղծութեան վրայ» եւ համոզում կը յայտնէ. «սփիւռքի մէջ չկայ այսօր քերթող մը որ առաւել կամ նուազ խորութեամբ եւ արդիւնաւորութեամբ կրած չըլլայ ազդեցութիւնը խորքով եւ ձեւով կատարեալ այս քերթողին»: Խօսելով ջերմեռանդութեան եւ հայրենասիրութեան մասին, Կիւրճեան որպէս մտատիպար, ուղեցոյց եւ ներշնչող կը դիտէ «այս անզուգական հայը, այս դիւցազնը, որ իր ամբողջ կեանքը ի սպաս դրաւ գեղեցիկին, որ արուեստն է, բանաստեղծութիւնն է, բարիին որ ազգասիրութիւնն է եւ մարդասիրութիւնը, ճշմարիտին, որ այդ երկուքին պսակումն է» եւ խորհուրդ կու տայ որ բոլոր անոնք որ կը սպասարկեն կամ կ՚ուզեն սպասարկել ազգին խօսքով, գիրով եւ գործով հետեւին Թէքէեանի օրինակին, քանի որ ան ազգասէր եւ ճշմարտասէր էր, ունէր քաղաքացիական արիութիւն եւ մանաւանդ զոհաբերութեան պատրաստակամութիւն եւ անշահամոլ անձնազոհութիւն, ազգին ծառայելու անտրտունջ նուիրում:

«Վահան Թէքէեանի Կեանքը» յօդուածին մէջ[125] Կիւրճեան առանձնապէս կ'անդրադառնայ թէ մօր, քրոջ, կնոջ, սիրուհիի խնամքէ եւ հոգածութենէ զուրկ, երկարատեւ պանդխտութիւն ապրած տաղանդաւոր բանաստեղծը մինչեւ իր կեանքին վերջը բախտաւոր եւ հպարտ կը զգար «ստեղծագործ արուեստագէտի եւ բարեգործ հայրենասէրի» երջանկութեան գիտակցութեամբ ու ազգին ծառայելու խոր գիտութեամբ:

* * *

Գրականագիտութեան եւ քննադատութեան առումով ուշագրաւ է Միքայէլ Կիւրճեանի քննական տեղեկագիրը ուղղուած Սրբոց Թարգմանչաց Դուրեան Յանձնաժողովի նախագահ Երուսաղէմի պատրիարք հօր՝ Յակոբ Օշականի «Արեւմտահայ Գրականութիւնն Ու Վահան Թէքէեան» ուսումնասիրութեան մասին: Այդ տեղեկագրին մէջ Կիւրճեան նշելով հանդերձ թէ մեր գրականութեան մէջ քննադատութիւնը սկիզբէն ի վեր քիչ եւ գէշ մշակուած սեռ մը եղած է, Օշականի աշխատութիւնը եզական, արժէքաւոր եւ աննախընթաց երեւոյթ մը կը նկատէ, որովհետեւ մինչ այդ «Ո՛չ մէկ արեւմտահայ մատենագիր առարկայ եղած է այսքան լիակատար, բազմակողմանի, այսքան հիմնալից ու խորաքնին ուսումնասիրութեան մը», որ կատարուած է ո՛չ Իբրլիթ Թէնի «զուտ առարկայական ծրագրով եւ հակումներով»[126] եւ ո՛չ ալ Ֆերտինանտ Պրիւնըթիէրի[127] «վարդապետական (dogmatique) առաջադրութիւններով», այլ՝ սկզբնական համակրութիւն մը Օշականը լծած է այդ գործին ու արուեստին՝ ժամանակակից տաղանդներու խայտաբղէտ հոյլին մէջէն ընտրելու Թէքէեան քերթողը՝ իբր ամենէն համապատասխանը բանաստեղծի մը մտապատկերին, որ չէ գրաւած մեր դպրութեանց մէջ այն առաջնակարգ դիրքը որուն արժանի կը կացուցանեն զինք՝ իր բանաստեղծի տաղանդն ու իր գործը»:

Տեղեկագրին հեղինակը կը հաստատէ թէ հայ եւ օտար գրականութեան գլխաւոր ներկայացուցիչներու գործերուն եւ գրական տարբեր հոսանքներու գաղափարական սկզբունքներուն քաջատեղեակ, գրող ու քննադատ, արուեստագէտի զգայնութեան եւ արտայայտութեան տէր Յակոբ Օշական «անժխտելիօրէն ունի պէտք եղած գրական ճաշակը, հմտութիւնը եւ ընթերցմանց պաշարը», ընտրած է Վահան Թէքէեան քերթողը՝ սիրով, համակրութեամբ եւ «հաւատարմօրէն ցոլացնելով անոր բոլոր հրապոյրները ու խորհուրդները» բազմաթիւ մէջբերումներով, բաղդատութիւններով, եւ հակադրութիւններով՝ ուրիշ երկերու»:

Կիւրճեան ընդունելով Օշականի այն համոզումը թէ Թէքէեան «իմաստապաշտ» է, կ'եզրակացնէ. «Վահան Թէքէեան մեր ամենէն ազնուական, խորազգաց, անձնական (personnel) եւ *կատարեալ* բանաստեղծն է», որովհետեւ օժտուած է «բոլոր այն վաւերական յատկութիւններով եւ շնորհներով, որոնք յատուկ եւ անհրաժեշտ են բանաստեղծին»:

Մէջբերելով ֆրանսացի քննադատ Էտմոն Ժալուի այն տեսակէտը թէ «ամէն ճշմարիտ բանաստեղծ ռոմանթիք է, ռոմանթիք կը ծնի», Կիւրճեան կը նշէ, որ Թէքէեան իր «խստապահանջութեամբ, ճաշակով, չափի, ժուժկալութեան բնազդով զինքը ամենէն «դասականը» կ'ընէ մեր ռոմանթիքներուն», որովհետեւ զեղծանումէ, հռետորութենէ, ճռոմութենէ, պոռոտութենէ զերծ է եւ ունի խոր, սարսուռն, բայց զուսպ զգայնութիւն՝ առանց աւելորդ շռայլութեան եւ ցուցամոլութեան: Կիւրճեանի խօսքով, «ստուգիւ, Թէքէեան մեր միակ բանաստեղծն է թերեւս որ, բացի իր ազգասիրական կարգ մը քերթուածներէն ուր աստիճան մը արդարանալի է անիկա, զերծ մնացած է հռետորութեան սկզբնական մեղքէն, եւ զոր՝ այս պատճառաւ իսկ կարելի է բաղդատութեան դնել եւրոպական իմաստով ու տարազով «արուեստագէտ» բանաստեղծներու հետ, ինչպէս Պոտլէր, Մալարմէ, Ռէնէիէ, Սամէն, Մոռէաս, Ռոտէնպախ, նոյնիսկ Վէռլէն, նուազ «արուեստագէտ», որ սակայն իր «Արուեստ Քերթողական»ին մէջ զառաջինն պատգամեց նոր Հանգանակը՝ «Prends l'éloquence et tords-lui son cou», այսինքն՝ «Առ ճարտարախօսութիւնը եւ ոլորէ անոր վիզը», կամ՝ «Առ պերճախօսութիւնը եւ գալարէ անոր պարանոցը»»:

Ընդունելով հանդերձ թէ Օշական տաղանդաւոր, ինքնատիպ ու արտայայտութեան մեծ կարողութեամբ օժտուած գրագէտ մըն է, Կիւրճեան տեղեկագիրը կը վերջացնէ քանի մը դիտողութիւններով Օշականի լեզուի խրթնութիւններուն, փակագիծներու եւ միջանկեալներու ծայրայեղ գործածութեան, էջատակի նօթերու ստուարութեան, եւայլնի մասին: Ընդհանուր առմամբ քննադատին դատաստանները անաչառ գտնելով հանդերձ, Կիւրճեան անտեղի կը նկատէ Օշականի չափազանցեալ արհամարհանքը Թովմաս Թէրզեանի մասին եւ անիրաւ՝ Ռէթէոս Պէրպէրեանի «Խոհք Եւ Յուշք» արժէքաւոր գործին նկատմամբ:

* * *

Բազմաթիւ են Կիւրճեանի գրական-քննադատական ու գեղագիտական ասոյթները, որոնք ան արտայայտած է զանազան գրողներու, արուեստագէտներու եւ անոնց ստեղծագործութիւններուն մասին.- Յակոբ Պարոնեան, Եղիա Տէմիրճիպաշեան, Երուանդ Օտեան, Ծիրվանզադէ, Տիրան Չրաքեան, Ռէթէոս Պէրպէրեան, Ալեքսանտր Սարուխան, Վահան Մալէզեան, Տարիա Կամսարական, Հրանդ Անդրանիկեան, եւայլն:

Կիրճեան կը հաստատէ թէ Պարոնեանի կեանքը մշտատեւ պայքար մը եղած է ընդդէմ վատառողջութեան եւ չքաւորութեան: Ան ապրած է կիսաղքատ եւ մահացած՝ թոքախտէ: Սակայն Մոլիէրի պէս ան հաւատարիմ մնացած է իր կոչումին եւ մարդոց պարգեւած է կատակերգութիւն ու զաւեշտ՝ շնորհիւ իր ընդոծին զուարթախոհութեան, խնդալու եւ խնդացնելու իր երջանիկ կարողութեան, որովհետեւ «Թալիան՝ կատակերգութեան մուսան ներշնչած է զինքը մինչեւ իր մահը»:[128]

«Գարունը Ռ. Պէրպէրեանի Եւ Ինտրայի Գրչին Տակ» յօդուածին մէջ[129] Կիրճեան կը գնահատէ Ռէթէոս Պէրպէրեանի արտայայտութեան ձեւը: Ան իր սկզբնական երկերուն մէջ գրաբարախառն հայերէն գործածելէ ետք, հետագային մաքուր, վայելուչ, ներդաշնակ, ճոխ լեզուով եւ մանաւանդ բառերու ճիշդ գործածութեամբ «կրնայ իբր օրինակ եւ յարացոյց ծառայել մերօրեայ գրողներէն շատերուն որոնք իրենց գրելակերպով աղաւաղելով աղճատելու վրայ են այն գեղեցիկ աշխարհաբարը զոր տաղանդաւոր գրագէտներու սերունդներ, 1880էն ի վեր, սկսած եւ շարունակած էին կերտել, ձեւաւորել, եւ գրեթէ կատարելութեան հասցուցած էին»:

Կիրճեան կ'արժեւորէ նաեւ գեղեցկաբան եւ արուեստագէտ Եղիա Տէմիրճիպաշեանի բանաստեղծական արձակի լաւագոյն էջերը եւ բանաստեղծութիւններու ոգեկանութիւնը, որոնք ստեղծուած են քերթողին սիրտի խորերէն սլացած հառաչանքով եւ հոգեկան ապրումներով, ըստ Կիրճեանի՝ «խելայեղ խոյանքով... ներշնչումով, միացյալ աւիւնով եւ ինքնաբուխ յորդութեամբ»:[130]

Կիրճեան զմայլանքով կ'արտայայտուի մեր մեծագոյն արուեստագէտ-բանաստեղծ-խորհող Տիրան Չրաքեանի մասին, որ անբաղդատելի ձիրքերով օժտուած ինքնատիպ հզօրութիւն մըն էր, եւ որուն «Ներաշխարհ»ը «անհաւասարելի գագաթ մըն էր մեր գրականութեան մէջ, յաւերժական փառքով մը լուսաճաճանչ»:

Թէքէեանի փառքին նուիրուած Օշականի այնքան խանդաղատալից եւ ներհուն ուսումնասիրութեան մէջ («Արեւմտահայ Գրականութիւնն Ու Վահան Թէքէեան») Կիրճեան անհանճոյ գտնելով կը քննադատէ անձնական կտրուկ վճիռները Չրաքեանի ստեղծագործութեան մասին: «Ապշեցուցիչ, եւ ընդվզեցուցիչ կերպով անարդար կը գտնեմ զինքը Տիրան Չրաքեանի մասին, որ իմ համոզումովս, եւ ինծի պէս մէկ քանիներու համոզումովը՝ որ ապագայ սերունդներո'ւնը պիտի ըլլայ ապահով, մեր մեծագոյն հանճարն է, եւրոպական իմաստով մեր ամենէն «տիեզերական» հանճարը, մեր մեծագոյն արուեստագէտ-բանաստեղծ-խորհողը»:

Ինչպէս «Ֆաուստ»ի հեղինակը՝ Կէօթէ, փիլիսոփայութիւնը խառնած էր արուեստին, այնպէս ալ Չրաքեան իր «Ներաշխարհ»ին մէջ փիլիսոփայութիւնը խառնած էր արուեստին, կ'ըսէ Կիրճեան, ափսոսալով որ փոխանակ այդպէս շարունակելով «նոր Ոսկեբերան մը, երկրորդ Նարեկացի մը ունենալու, ունեցանք աւա՜ղ, հասարակ *շաքաթապահ* մը, որ, զոհ կրօնքին զոր կը քարոզէր, մեռաւ՝ մեռցնելէ ետք իր մէջ հանճարեղ բանաստեղծը, Ինտրան: Չեմ գիտեր թէ Եհովայի փառքը ի՞նչ շահեցաւ այս զոհաբերումէն, բայց գիտեմ թէ հայկական դպրութիւնները ի՜նչ ահագին եւ անդարմանելի կորուստ մը կրեցին...»:[131]

* * *

Շատ հետաքրքրական եւ շահեկան է Կիւրճեանի «Հրաժարումն Ի Գրականութենէ» յօդուածը, որ լոյս տեսած է նախ «Հայաստանի Կոչնակ»ին եւ ապա «Արեւ»ի մէջ: Յօդուածին դրդապատճառն է ֆրանսական հանդէսի մը մէջ Կիւրճեանի կարդացած հաղորդումը այն մասին, թէ Ճորճ Մուր[132] իր վերջին գիրքին հրատարակութենէն ետք որոշած է հրաժեշտ տալ գրականութեան: Յօդուածագիրը թերահաւատ է: Ան կը տարակուսի թէ Մուր պիտի կարենայ հաստատ մնալ իր որոշումին վրայ: «Ո՛վ որ, ներքին հզօր մղումի մը հնազանդելով, գրիչ շարժել սկսած է, պիտի շարունակէ շարժել, առաւել կամ նուազ կանոնաւորութեամբ, մինչեւ կեանքին վերջը, պիտի շարժէ մերթ նոյն իսկ մահուան ուրուականին դէմ, եթէ ոչ զայն ի բաց վանելու սին յոյսով, գէթ իր գրական անմահութեան հնարաւորութիւնները (chance) աւելցնելու համար...»:

Այս մասին իր տեսակէտը հիմնաւորելու համար, Կիւրճեան կը բերէ փաստացի օրինակ մը, ինչպէս՝ «Պետրոս Դուրեանը, որ իր ամենէն *ներ-շնչուած* քերթուածը, որ՝ առանձին՝ պիտի բաւէր իր անունը յաւերժացնելու հայկական դպրութեանց մէջ» գրած է երբ երիտասարդ հասակին մահուան դուռը հասած է եւ բնական էր որ պէտք էր իր հոգիին «յատակը» գտնուող «փրփուրները» գերագոյն ժայթքով մը դուրս պոռթկային: «Մինչ Ճորճ Մուր տարիքոտ է, արտադրած է բազում գործեր, ըսած է արդէն իր ըսելիքը, ի մի բան՝ յոգնած, յագեցած է գրելէն...»:

Կիւրճեան կը խորհի որ եթէ անգլիացի գրագէտը իսկապէս քաշուի գրական հրապարակէն, եթէ վերջնականապէս կոտրէ իր գրիչը եւ դադրի այլեւս գրելէ, «ատիկա պիտի նշանակէ կենսունակութեան վերջին ծայր նուազումը իր մէջ, տեսակ մը բնախօսական անկարողութիւն, որովհետեւ՝ խորքին մէջ՝ գրելը ուրիշ բան չէ ի ծնէ գրագէտին համար բայց եթէ ապրելու ձեւ մը միայն, կեանքի արտայայտութիւն մը,- ձեւ ու արտայայտութիւն որոնք ամէն բանէ աւելի յարմար եւ սիրելի են իր խառնուածքին, իր բնութեան»:

Կիւրճեան կը թուէ գրականութենէն հրաժարած խիստ սակաւաթիւ դէմքերէն երկու յատկանշական անձերու պարագայ՝ ֆրանսական գրականութեան մէջ Արթիւր Ռէմպօ եւ մեր գրականութեան մէջ՝ Տիրան Չրաքեան, որոնք հանճարեղ եւ խոստմնալից ըլլալով հանդերձ լքած են գրականութիւնը եւ որոնց հոգիներուն մէջէն արուեստի եւ գրականութեան դեւը ելած է. առաջինը քսանամեայ տարիքին դրամ վաստակելու եւ հարստանալու մոլուցքէն տարուած, իսկ երկրորդը՝ «Ներաշխարհ»ի եւ «Նոճաստան»ի պէս բանաստեղծական հոյակապ գլուխ-գործոցներ պարգեւելէ ետք ինքզինք նուիրելով Աստուծոյ Բանին քարոզութեան:

Կիւրճեան կը շեշտէ թէ գրողներ եւ արուեստագէտներ կը ստեղծագործեն իրենց մէջ զգալով զօրաւոր կոչում մը. «Նուիրական հուրը, անգամ մը որ վառեցաւ մարդու մը ներսիդին, կեանքին հետ կը շիջանի»: Իբր ապացոյց ան կը բերէ ֆրանսացի նկարիչ Օկիւսթ Ռընուարի պարագան, որուն մասին կը պատմուի թէ մահուընէն քիչ առաջ, իր անդամալոյծ ձեռքին երանգապնակ մը կապել տալով, փորձած է նկարել:

Տարիա Կամսարականի «Ուղեւորութիւն Ստուերի Մը Հետ» (Voyage avec une ombre) ֆրանսերէն հոգեբանական-վերլուծական վէպին մասին իր գրախօսականին մէջ Կիւրճեան դարձեալ կը հաստատէ ներքին զօրաւոր կոչումի ճշմարտութիւնը, հաւաստելով թէ անուանի արուեստագիտուհին, ինքնատիպ քանդակագործուհին, որ կանուխէն փորձած է արուեստի բոլոր սեռերը,- բանաստեղծութիւն, երաժշտութիւն, նկարչութիւն, արձանագործութիւն,- «իր կապերը չէ խզած երբեք գրականութեան հետ, որ եղած է իր առաջին սէրը ի տղայ տիոց. ան կը սիրէր գրել եւ բոլորովին չէ դադրած գրելէ, ապացոյց ասոր՝ իր առաջին եւ երկրորդ վէպերը, որոնց յաջորդ մը տալ կը պատրաստուի»:

Տիգրան Կամսարականի զարմուհի եւ Արմենակ Կամսարականի դուստր տաղանդաւոր քանդակագործուհի Տարիա Կամսարականը,[133] որ 1937ին Փարիզի միջազգային ցուցահանդէսին արժանացած է ոսկեայ շքանշանի եւ Փարիզի ու Գահիրէի միջազգային ցուցահանդէսներու ընթացքին տիրացած է համբաւի իր «Մերկ Մարդը», «Ճիչը», «Քրիստոսը», «Եւա», «Յաւակնոտը», «Կուժով Կինը», «Լուտասենի», «Տոն Քիշոթ», «Ողջոյն Խաղաղութեան» եւ այլ ինքնատիպ քանդակներու համար, հազիւ քսանամեայ տարիքին գրած է «Արիւնին Ճակատագրականութիւնը» յուզիչ վէպը, որուն հերոսուհին քանդակագործ է: Կիւրճեան թարգմանած եւ «Արեւ»ի մէջ հրատարակութեան յանձնած է այդ գործը, մինչ Զօպանեան իր «Անահիտ»ին մէջ դրուատալից խօսքեր նուիրած է անոր:

* * *

Հրանդ Անդրանիկեանի օրագրի էջերէն ընտրուած մտորումներու եւ հոգեկան ապրումներու գրքոյկին մասին իր յօդուածին մէջ,[134] Կիւրճեան հանգամանօրէն կը վերծանէ օրագրողին խորհրդածութիւնները, որոնք մտատանջած են արուեստագէտը: Հայկական Բարեգործական Ընդհանուր Միութեան հիմնադիրներէն Մկրտիչ Անդրանիկեանի երեք որդիներէն

(Տիգրան, Նուպար եւ Հրանդ) Հրանդ կը տառապէր ֆիզիքական դժբախտութենէ մը, որուն մասին ոչ մէկ ակնարկութիւն կը պարունակէ օրագիրը: Կիւրճեան կը գրէ. «Վերլուծումները զարգացած ներհուն եւ պայծառատես միտքի մը դրոշմը կը կրեն»:

Ընկճուածութեան փոխարէն՝ անվհատութիւն, յոռետեսութեան փոխարէն՝ լաւատեսութիւն, դժգոհութեան փոխարէն՝ հանդուրժողութիւն պարփակող, մէկ խօսքով՝ առաքինութիւններով օժտուած առօրեայ հետաքրքրական խոհերու գրառումներով ճոխ հատորիկը կը բացայայտէ Անդրանիկեանի՝ հոգին դիտողի, խոհուն զննողի, տրամաբանօրէն մեկնաբանողի ներհուն կարողութիւնը եւ զգայուն վերլուծողի ողջախոհութիւնը: Կիւրճեան բազում եւ ընդարձակ մէջբերումներով կը հաստատէ օրագրողին զգաստ մտածումները կեանքի, երջանկութեան, ուրախութեան, տխրութեան, սիրոյ եւ մանաւանդ դժբախտութեան մասին, քանի որ իր ալ ներաշխարհէն կը թելադրուի թէ էականը սիրելն է, իսկ սիրուիլը երկրորդական՝ քանի որ սիրուիլը ուրիշ անձէ կախում ունի: Դժբախտ էակը չսիրուած անձը չէ, այլ այն՝ որ սիրել չի գիտեր, որովհետեւ մարդկային սէրը երջանկութիւն կը պարգեւէ:

* * *

Գրական-գրականագիտական առումով շահեկան է Կիւրճեանի «Խորհրդածութիւններ Պ. Վահան Մալէզեանի «Յուշամատեան»ի Առիթով» յօդուածը, որ հրատարակուած է «Հայաստանի Կոչնակ»ին մէջ: Հոն Կիւրճեան խորունկ խոհերով կ'անդրադառնայ ֆրանսացի հռչակաւոր մատենագիր Մարսէլ Բրուսթի «Ի Խնդիր Կորուսեալ Ժամանակի» (A la recherche du Temps perdu) ընդարձակ վէպի հեղինակին անձնական յիշատակներուն՝ վերլուծելով իր եւ ուրիշներու զգացումները, պատմաբան եւ ժամանակագիր Ֆիլիբ Քոմինի յուշագրութիւնները Ֆրանսայի Շարլ Ը. եւ Լուի ԺԱ. թագաւորներու մասին, Ժան Ժաք Ռուսոյի «Խոստովանութիւններ»ը (Confessions), բանաստեղծ Ալֆրէտ Վինեիի «Օրագրութիւն»ը, Ժոզէֆ Ռընանի «Յիշողութիւններ»ը, Ֆրանսուա Շաթոպրիանի եւ կարգ մը պետական անձնաւորութիւններու, հանրային գործիչներու, կրօնաւորներու, դերասաններու, գրողներու ինքնակենսագրական եւ յուշագրական գործերը, որոնք պատմական եւ գրական արժէք ունին:

Կիւրճեան ցաւով կը գրէ. «Մեր գրականութիւնը մեծ պակաս մը, թերի մը ունեցած է սկիզբէն ի վեր, գրեթէ բոլորովին խոպան ձգուած դաշտ մը: Օտար գրականութեանց նմանողութեամբ, կարգ մը սեռեր առաւել կամ նուազ յաջողութեամբ ու խնամքով մշակուած են մեր մէջ,- բանաստեղծութիւն, երգիծաբանութիւն, վէպ, նորավէպ, նոյն իսկ թատրոն, բայց ողբալիօրէն անտեսուած է *յուշագրութեան* (mémoires) ճիւղը, որ եւրոպական մատենագրութեանց՝ ու մասնաւորաբար ֆրանսականին մէջ այնքան ծաղկած ու պտղաբերած է սկսեալ ԺԳ. եւ ԺԴ. դարերէն»: Այդ պակասին պատճառը փնտռելով ան կը գրէ. «ԺԸ. դարէն ասդին հայ ժողովուրդին կեանքը — մի միայն Թուրքիոյ մէջ — լեցուն եղած է ամենակարեւոր դէպքերով,- մտաւորական վերածնունդի շարժում, յեղափոխական գործունէութիւն, համազգային աղէտներ»: Այնուհետեւ կը յիշատակէ Արփիարեանի անունը որպէս «ճշմարիտ mémorialiste-ի խմորով մեծ գրագէտ»ի, եւ կը թուէ անոր «Օրուան Կեանքը», «Հողվրտիք», «Ժամանակակից Պատմութեան Էջեր» խորագիրներուն տակ տարիներով անոր հրատարակած քրոնիկներն ու յօդուածները, որոնք կը հանդիսանան ժամանակակից շրջանի վաւերագրութիւններ ու ազգային կեանքի վերաբերեալ յուշեր՝ ապագայ պատմաբանին համար իբր օգտագործելի աղբիւր:

Կիւրճեան կը նշէ նաեւ թէ Երուանդ Օտեանի «Տասներկու Տարի Պոլսէն Դուրս»ը գրական արժէքաւոր յուշագրութիւն մըն է՝ շնորհիւ հեղինակին սուր յիշողութեան եւ համով-հոտով պատմելու տաղանդին:

Ցաւալի է որ ինք՝ Միքայէլ Կիւրճեան չէ թողած յուշագրական եւ ինքնակենսագրական գործեր, որոնք հաւանաբար պիտի պարունակէին արժէքաւոր տեղեկութիւններ իր ժամանակակիցներուն մասին:

Գալով Մալէզեանի «Անցած Օրեր - Յուշամատեան Գատը-Քէօյի Գրական Երեկոյթներուն (1892-1894)» հատորին, Կիւրճեան շահեկան կ'որակէ զայն, քանի որ անոր մեծ մասը «յատկացուած է ափ յափոյ յօրինուած էջերուն ընդօրինակութեանը, որոնք այսօր ալ կը կարդացուին հետաքրքրութեամբ եւ շատ հաճոյքով»: Փաստօրէն պոլսահայ գրականութեան եւ մամուլի ներկայացուցիչներու, գրասէրներու եւ մտաւորականներու ընտրանիի գրական երեկոյթներու բնանկարը ու Հարց-Պատասխանի ժամանցի արդիւնքն է որ ընդգրկուած է այդ հատորին մէջ՝ ոտանաւորի յանգաւորումով եւ արձակ գրելաձեւով, ազատ գրուածքով:

Գրող ու բանասէր Կիւրճեանի գրական-քննադատական ժառանգութիւնը հարուստ է գրականագիտական յօդուածներով, գրողներու եւ արուեստագէտներու դիմանկարներով, գրախօսականներով, տեսական բնոյթի աշխատասիրութիւններով, գրական ուսումնասիրութիւններով, որոնց մէջ նկատելի է վարպետ գրականագէտի, ներհուն արուեստագէտի, համաշխարհային գրականութեան քաջատեղեակ անձի ներկայութիւնը՝ ճոխ պաշարով եւ անաչառ քննադատի նուրբ զգացողութեամբ: Գրական-գեղագիտական նոր ու առաջաւոր ըմբռնումներով յագեցած հետախոյզը աշխատած է զարգացնել հայ մշակոյթը, յատկապէս՝ գրականութիւնը, նպատակ ունենալով նպաստել իր ժողովուրդին մտաւոր յառաջդիմութեան:

ՅԱՋՈՂԱԿ ԲԱՌԱԿԱԶՄՈՂՆ ՈՒ ՎԱՐՊԵՏ ԲԱՌԱԿԵՐՏՈՂԸ

Կիւրճեանի ձեռագիր անտիպ գործերը վերծանելու եւ զանոնք հրատարակութեան պատրաստելու դժուարին աշխատանքը կատարելու, բազմաթիւ հայատառ պարբերականներու բազում տարիներու հաւաքածոներուն մէջէն գրագէտին գործերը գտնելու, հաւաքելու, դասդասելու եւ անոնցմէ հատընտիր ժողովածու մը պատրաստելու ժամանակ, նկատած ենք որ ան բծախնդրութիւն ցուցաբերած է հայերէն լեզուի անաղարտութեան, բառերու իմաստային ճշգրիտ նշանակութեան եւ անոնց պատշաճ գործածութեան նկատմամբ:

Կիւրճեան եղած է ոչ միայն հմուտ բառագէտ, այլեւ՝ ճարտար բառակապակցութիւններ ստեղծող, ածանցումով եւ բարդացումով բառակազմութիւններու վարպետ եւ հնարագէտ բառաստեղծ կամ բառակերտող:

Հայ գրականութեան մէջ շատ են գրողներն ու բանաստեղծները, որոնք Ոսկեդարէն մինչեւ միջնադար ու նոր ժամանակներ ստեղծած են երկու արմատէ եւ ածանցէ կազմուած բարդածանց բառեր. սակայն Կիւրճեանին ժամանակակից ոչ մէկ գրող կերտած է այնքան նոր բառ, որքան՝ Կիւրճեան ինք իր ստեղծագործութիւններուն մէջ:

Կիւրճեան, ի հարկէ, բառագիտութեամբ չէ զբաղած: Ան լեզուաբանի նման չէ աշխատած բառապաշարի, բառերու ծագման եւ բառիմաստի ուսումնասիրութեամբ: Սակայն իր բծախնդրութեամբ ուշադիր եւ հետեւողական եղած է բառերու իմաստային ճիշդ ընտրութեան եւ օգտագործման հանդէպ:

«Բառարան Թղթատելով» յօդուածին մէջ[135] Կիւրճեան հռետորական հարցումով կը հաստատէ. «Բառարան թղթատելը սիրական զբաղում մը եղած է ինծի համար. գրողը փառասէր ըլլալէ առաջ պէտք է ... բառասէր ըլլայ, այնպէս չէ՞»: Ան կը նշէ թէ ընթացիկ, շատ գործածական բառերու հետ բառարաններուն մէջ կան փոքրաթիւ բառեր, որոնք շատ օգտակար ըլլալով հանդերձ, վերապահուած են բարձր խօսակցութեան կամ գրականութեան եւ դատապարտուած են բառարաններու խորը մնալու՝ ուշադրութենէ եւ գործածութենէ հեռու: Ան օրինակ կը բերէ *խաբեղայ* բառը, որ ստուգաբանօրէն կեղծ, խաբող աբեղայ կը նշանակէ, եւ կ՚աւելցնէ. «հիանալի բառախաղ մըն է, որ ցոյց կու տայ մեր նախնեաց սրամտութիւնը եւ որ կրնայ խաբեբայ բառին հոմանիշը ըլլալ»:

Նոյն յօդուածին մէջ ան կը թուէ թէ բառարանին մէջ գտած է *կարծէխօս* բառը, որ կը նշանակէ անձ մը, որ կը կարծէ խօսիլ, սակայն կը շատախօսէ: Անոր հետեւողութեամբ, ան կը յօրինէ *կարծէգիր* բառը, այսինքն՝ այն կարծէխօսները, որոնք խօսելու մեղքին վրայ կ'աւելցնեն գրելու մեղքը: «Այս բառն ալ ինձմէ», կը գրէ ան:

Հայերէնը ունի այն մեծ առաւելութիւնը, որ բառահիմքին վրայ ածանցներ աւելցնելով դիւրութեամբ կարելի է բառակազմութիւններ ստեղծել: Այդ առաւելութիւնը մեծապէս նպաստած է հայ գրողներուն եւ բանասէրներուն նոր բառերու կերտումին կամ գործածութեան մէջ: Պէտք է ըսել թէ բառակերտումներ շատ կան գրաբարի, միջին հայերէնի, արեւելահայերէնի եւ արեւմտահայերէնի մէջ եւ ան մեր օրերուն ալ կը շարունակէ նպաստել մեր լեզուին կատարելագործման:

Կիրճեան նոր բառեր կազմելու վարպետ է: Ան նորաբան մըն է, որովհետեւ սիրած է գործածել նոր, ոչ-սովորական բառեր: Օրինակ, հայերէնի մէջ *նոր* բառով շատ բարդ բառեր ունինք՝ *նորաբարբառ*, *նորաբողբոջ*, *նորաբոյս*, *նորագիր*, *նորագիւտ*, *նորաթագ*, *նորածին*, *նորազուարթ*, *նորալուսին*, *նորալուր*, *նորախօս*, *նորածագ*, *նորաստեղծ*, *նորահաւատ*, *նորապսակ*, *նորասէր*, *նորընծայ*, *նորուս*, *նորօրինակ*, եւայլն, բայց Կիրճեան ստեղծած է *նորաստաց* բառը, որ ուրիշ ոչ մէկ գրողի գործին մէջ գտած ենք:

Մեր լեզուին մէջ շատ գործածական է *հրաշէկ* (կրակ դարձած, կասկարմիր) բառը: Կիրճեան նախընտրած է *ատրաշէկը* (կարմիր կրակի պէս), որուն արմատը՝ *ատր*, գրեթէ չի գործածուիր մեր խօսակցական եւ գրական լեզուին մէջ:

Կիրճեանի ստեղծած բառերէն մէկն է *այոյել*՝ այո ըսել, ընդունիլ, հաստատել, վաւերացնել նշանակութեամբ: Այդ բառը ան յաճախ գործածած է իր ստեղծագործութիւններուն մէջ (*Միսիսի Սիսակ*, *Նոր Դպրոցը*, *Մարտիկ Աղա*, եւայլն), սակայն այդ բառը ո՛չ բառարաններու մէջ մտած է եւ ոչ ալ խօսակցական կամ գրական ընթացիկ լեզուի մէջ ընդհանրացած:

Կիրճեան խուսափած է սովորական բառեր գործածելէ: Օրինակ, սեւագրութեան մը մէջ *չարաշուքը* ջնջելով *աղէտաշուք* բառը ստեղծած է:

Պարոյր Սեւակ «Պահպանենք Եւ Հարստացնենք Մայրենին» յօդուածին մէջ խօսելով բառափոխանակութեան մասին, կը նշէ. «Հայոց լեզուն դարեր շարունակ բարգաւաճել է ոչ միայն իր սեփական միջոցներով, այլ հարստացել է անհրաժեշտ փոխառութիւններով»:[136]

«Անլուելի Զանգակատուն»ի հեղինակը բազմաթիւ օրինակներով ապացուցած է որ «Հայերէնը, օրինակ, ունի մի առաւելութիւն, որ աշխարհի քիչ լեզուներ ունեն. բառակազմութեան հեշտութիւնն ու շահաւէտութիւնը: Ու եթէ որեւէ լեզու, հայերէնից նոյնիսկ աւելի հարուստ ու ճկուն մի լեզու, ստիպուած է օտար բառն ընդունել, որովհետեւ բառակազմութեան իր հնարաւորութիւնները սուղ են, ապա հայերէնի պէս մի լեզու պարտաւոր է հայացնել այդ բառը, որովհետեւ օտար բառը, իբրեւ ընդհանուր օրէնք, շատ աւելի քիչ բան է ասում հային, քան մայրենի լեզուի յաջող բառակազմութիւնը»:[137]

Կիւրճեան ինք ալ դէմ եղած է օտարաբանութեան եւ խուսափած է օտար լեզուներէ բառերու փոխառութիւն կատարելէ: Ընդհակառակը, գրելու եւ թարգմանելու ժամանակ երբ օտար բառն է եկած իր միտքը, փնտռած կամ ստեղծած է անոր համապատասխան հայերէնը, անոր քով փակագիծի մէջ դնելով օտար բառը, որպէսզի ընթերցողը ճիշդ հասկնայ նշանակութիւնը:

Սարուխան օգտուելով բառաշինութեան մասին Կիւրճեանի յայտնած տեսակէտներէն, «Արեւ»ի խմբագրատան մէջ կը հարցնէ թէ քանի՞ բառ կերտած է ան: Կիւրճեան տեղւոյն վրայ կը մտաբերէ շուրջ երկու տասնեակ բառ, առիթ տալով Սարուխանի, որ գրէ իր «Միքայէլ Կիւրճեան Տաղանդաւոր Բառակերտ» յօդուածը:[138]

Սարուխան կը թուէ Կիւրճեանի հնարած տասնութ նորակերտ բառերը (այոյել, աջուձախուած, այծուըռտել, եսաբան - եսեմութիւն, թերակատար, թիւրքիմացութիւն, ծծախոտ, կարծէգիր, հայհոյակապ, ներուժեղ, շրթանց, շքերեւոյթ, պոռազան, սիրասովոր, վախճանավրէպ, տօնաւեր, ցցադրել, փարազուն) եւ երեք հատ ալ նախապէս գործածուած եւ իր կողմէ վերակենդանացուած բառեր (լկտի - շլխտի, խաբեղայ - խաբեբայ աբեղայ, կարծէխօս — կարծել թէ բան մը կ'ըսէ կամ կը խօսի):

Երկու վարպետները նպատակադրած են հետագայ հանդիպումներու ընթացքին շարունակել եւ ընդարձակել նորակերտ բառերու ցանկը, բայց Կիւրճեանի անսպասելի արկածին ու մահուան պատճառով անկատար մնացած է այդ ցանկութիւնը:

Բացի նորակերտ բառեր ստեղծելէ, Կիւրճեան սիրած է վերակենդանացնել քիչ գործածական բառերը եւ յաճախ գոյականը վերածած է բայի, ածականը՝ գոյականի կամ մակբայի, պարզ բառը բարդ բառի: Այնպէս որ անոնցմէ շատեր կարելի չէ գտնել բառարաններու մէջ, որոնց շատ անգամ ստիպուած եղած եմ դիմել իր ձեռագիրները վերծանելու ժամանակ:

Ահաւասիկ մաս մը իմ նկատած ու նշած նորաբանութիւններէն:

Ազատախանդ- ազատութենէ խանդավառուած. «ազատախանդ մոլուցքով խօլ արշաւնին կը կեցնեն ձիերը» (*Ձիերը*):

Ալեփառ- ծանօթ *ալեհերի* եւ *ալեւորի* հետեւողութեամբ. «ալեփառ ծերունի» (*Աղբիւրը*):

Ազդուօրէն- ազդեցիկօրէն իմաստով:

Ահարկուօրէն- *ահարկու* ածականէն ստեղծուած մակբայ:

Աղէտակոծ- աղէտաւոր, ցաւալի իմաստով:

Աղէտաշուք- չարաշուք իմաստով:

Անզգալաբար- կամաց-կամաց իմաստով, *անզգալապէս* մակբային փոխարէն (*Մոգական Գորգը*):

Անէանալ- ոչնչանալ իմաստով, *անէութիւն* գոյականէն:
Անծանօթուհի- անգիտակ, ոչ ծանօթ կին:
Անճանացած- անճանաչելի դարձած, ֆրանսերէն méconnaître-ի համազօրը (*Քսան Տարի Ետք*):
Անվերազէն- հայերէնի մէջ ունինք *վերազինել* բայը, բայց չենք ունեցած *վերազէն, անվերազէն*:
Աստեղացան- բազում աստղեր ցանուած իմաստով. «Եգիպտական ճոխօրէն աստեղացան երկնքին տակ» (*Մարտին Աղա*):
Արեւելամոլ- Արեւելքի սիրահար, մոլի իմաստով՝ *ազգայնամոլի*, *հայրենամոլի* նմանողութեամբ:
Բաշարձակ- ձիու բաշերը արձակուած իմաստով (*Ձիերը*):
Բերնպահութիւն- ուտելու ժուժկալութիւն (*Նոր Լաթ*):
Բուրաքսակ- բուրմունքով լեցուն տոպրակ:
Դիւայնօրէն- սատանայական, ճիւաղային իմաստով, դիւային բառէն ստեղծուած (*Մոգական Գորգը*):
Դիւրընկալուիլ- դիւրին ընդունուիլ:
Եսամարտիկ- ինքնիրմով լեցուած եւ ուրիշը արհամարհող եսամոլներու եւ եսասէրներու անձնասիրութիւնը քննադատելու համար ստեղծուած բառ:
Երկնառաք- երկինքէն ղրկուած, *առաքել* բային բարդումով:
Զայրաշունչ- զայրոյթով, *զայրացկոտի*, *զայրագինի* նման:
Զուարճագեղ- բերկրալի, հրճուալի, ուրախալի իմաստով:
Թաւաստեւ- թանձր մազոտ (*Անունին Գիշերը*):
Թերաստուեր- քիչ գործածուած գոյական մը, բո՛ւն ստուերին շուրջ կամ քով մասնակի լուսաւորուած թերի ստուերի իմաստով՝ ֆրանսերէն pénombre-ի համազօրը (*Նոր Դպրոցը*):
Լայնափեռեկ փոսեր- մեծ բացուած փոսեր: Հին բառարաններու մէջ ներկայ *լայնափեռեկ* բառը դուրս մնացած է նոր բառարաններէն:
Լաւէութիւն- լաւատեսութեան տպաւորութիւն, լաւիմացութիւն, լաւատեղեակութիւն. սեփականատէր դառնալէ ետք անձի մը շատ աւելի լաւ, զօրաւոր ու երջանիկ զգալը (*Պարոն Կալուածատէրը*):
Լուսածիր- Լապտերներու ցոլքերովը լուսաւորուած (*Մարտին Աղա*):
Լուսայայտնուիլ- լոյսի պէս երեւալ:
Լուսապաղպաչ- պսպղուն, շողշողուն: Ինքնաստեղծ բառ, որ կը բացակայի բառարաններէն:
Լռակցիլ- *խօսակցիլ*ին հականիշը. «անցնելով գիւղին ամայի փողոցներէն՝ խօսակցելով եւ լռակցելով՝ հասանք ծովեզերք» (*Կը Յիշե՞ս*):
Լռասոյզ- լուռ եւ խորասուզուած:
Խնկաւէտել- ռետնային վերածխութիւններով օդը խունկի հոտով սփռել, բուրել (*Ծռճիները*):
Խոնաւաթուրմ- խոնաւութենէն թրջած (*Միրիճանը*):

Խորհրդաքօղ- խորհուրդը ծածկող, քօղարկող իմաստով:

Խօլապար- խենդ, խելագուրկ, յիմար, անմիտ պար:

Ծաղրողքալի- ողբագին, վշտալից, ծիծաղելի եւ ողբալի:

Ծարաւակէզ- ծարաւէն այրող: *Բոցակէզ*ի եւ *հրակէզ*ի նմանողութեամբ:

Ծարաւահիւծ- ծարաւէն մաշած, հիւծած:

Ծխամոլ- մոլի ծխող: Ստեղծուած է *գինեմոլ*ի նմանողութեամբ, որպէս ածական կամ գոյական գործածուելու համար:

Ծուլարան- ի հակադրութիւն արեւմուտքցիի շարժունութեան՝ արեւելքցիին ծուլութիւնը նկարագրելու համար *արհարան*ին նմանողութեամբ կերտուած բառ (*Արհարանը*):

Կաղանդաւէտ- Կաղանդ բուրող, Կաղանդի տրամադրութիւն ստեղծող. *հոտաւէտի*, *բուրումնաւէտի* նման (*Կաղանդչէքը*):

Կաղընդչէքել- Նոր Տարուան առիթով նուէր տալ:

Կենսատեւ- կեանքի տեւականութիւն, յարատեւութիւն (*Տրդատ Եւ Տանատ*):

Կիրակնափայլ- կիրակնօրեայ փայլով: Կիւրճեանն է յօրինած:

Կլկլուք- կլկլակի (նարգիլակ) ձայնը: Ճիշդ է, ունեցած ենք կլկլալ, կլկլացնել բայերը, սակայն Կիւրճեան օգտագործած է գոյականաբար:

Հաստաբազուկ- ձիերը սանձահարող, զսպող ամուր, ուժեղ թեւ (*Ձիերը*):

Հեգնախառն- հեգնանքով, ծաղրանքով խառնուած:

Հեծիւն- Յաւագին իմաստով: Հեծեծանք, հեկեկանք, հառաչանք, հեծութիւն բառերուն փոխարէն գործածած է հեծիւն գոյականը:

Հեշտօրօրել- հրապուրել, մեղմօրօրել, դիւթել, թովել, կախարդել իմաստով: Կիւրճեան այս բոլոր բառերուն փոխարէն հեշտօրօր ածականը բայի վերածելով կը նկարագրէ Բիէր Լօթիի վիճակը՝ թմրեցուցիչով կլկլակի զգլխիչ ծուխը ծխելու ժամանակ զգացած երանութիւնը (*Մոգական Գորգը*):

Հէգութիւն- հէգ, խեղճ, ողորմելի ածականէն Կիւրճեան գոյականաբար գործածած է հէգութիւն բառը «Նոր Դպրոցը»ին մէջ:

Հնհնալ- տագնապիլ իմաստը արտայայտելու համար: Հայերէնի մէջ հնհնուք (աշխարհաբար ռամիկ լեզուի մէջ գործածուող՝ մտմտուք, մտատանջութիւն իմաստով գոյականը) Կիւրճեան կ'օգտագործէ որպէս բայ:

Հոյաշուք- հոյակապի փոխարէն (*Լոյս Եւ Խորհուրդ* արձակ բանաստեղծութիւն):

Հրաշաբոյս- սիրելիին մարմնէն բուսնող ու բուրող հրաշալի հոտը:

Հրաշիմաստ- հրաշալի իմաստ ունեցող:

Հրատոչոր- քիչ գործածուող բառ՝ կրակով այրած իմաստով (*Սուտը Իրաւ, Խենդը Խելօք*), երբ Հոռոփի հետ Նասիպի ամուսնութեան առաջարկը կը մերժուի աղջկան ձկնորս հօր կողմէ:

Ջենջալուացում- անտարբեր վերաբերմունք (*Մարտիկ Աղա*):

Մանրացնցուղ- մանր կաթիլներով ջուր տեղալ:

Մարդկեղէն- մարդկութեան պատկանող իմաստով: Կիւրճեան նախընտրած է գործածել *մարդկային* սովորական ածականին փոխարէն:
Մենազատ- ստեղծուած է մինակ եւ ազատ բառերէն (*Սուտը Իրաւ...*):
Միւռոնազօծ- միւռոնով օծուած: Միւռոն գոյականէն եւ օծել բայէն Կիւրճեան կազմած է այս բարդ բառը՝ ոսկեզօծի նմանութեամբ:
Մշտածոր- սիրածին գեղեցիկ ձայնին մասին (*Մշտածոր Երաժշտութիւն*): Մշտաբուխի, մշտահոսի, մշտափթիթի նմանութեամբ կերտուած բառ:
Մսազեղ- միսով զեղուն իմաստով: Մսալի, մսոտ բառերուն փոխարէն, Կիւրճեան յօրինած է այս բառը:
Յաղթազանգուած- յաղթ բառարմատով հայերէնի մէջ կան յաղթահասակ, յաղթամարմին, յաղթանդամ, յաղթանիշ, յաղթապանծ, յաղթապսակ, եւայլն: Յաղթազանգուածը Կիւրճեանի կողմէ ստեղծուած բառ մըն է:
Յառաջակարկառ- առջեւ, դուրս ցցուած իմաստով:
Յոռեշրջել- դէպի վատը դարձնել, դէպի գէշը փոխել:
Յոգնադիմի- սաստիկ, շատ յոգնած իմաստով: Յոգնաբեկի, յոգնասպառի փոխարէն:
Նենգաւոյշ- չար եւ քաղցր. «Մարդիկ նենգաւոյշ խօսքերու եւ զգուանքներու յուդայական քաղցրութեամբ կը խաղաղեցնեն ձիերու ամեհի ցասումը» (*Ձիերը*):
Նուագապետ- նուագախումբի ղեկավար, նուագավար, խմբավար:
Շարակնել- Միեւնոյն յանկերգը կրկնել (*Մարտիկ Աղա*):
Շարժկոծիլ- Շարժիլի փոխարէն Կիւրճեան կը գրէ. «կմախքները կը շարժկոծէին դիւայնօրէն» (*Մոգական Գորգը*):
Շլացք- շլացում գոյականին փոխարէն: Շլացքը գոյութիւն չունի բառարաններու մէջ:
Ողնուղղել- մէկու մը ծուած իրանը ուղղել: Ողն բառարմատէն ունինք ողնախտ, ողնաթեք, ողնացաւ, եւայլն (Մարիամի ծուած իրանին մասին):
Ոսկեդրուագել- ունինք ոսկի եւ դրուագ բառերով ստեղծուած ոսկեդրուագ ածականը, որ կը նշանակէ ոսկիով զարդարուած: Կիւրճեան օգտագործած է բայական ձեւը:
Պարտկել- ծածկել, քօղարկել, թաքցնել իմաստով. կերտուած՝ պարտկում գոյականէն (*Կաղանդչէքը*):
Ռետնային- խէժային իմաստով: Հայերէնի մէջ կայ ռետին գոյականը, որ խէժ, խունկ, բալասան կը նշանակէ:
Սիրախանձ- սէրով այրած, սէրով խանձած. սիրաբորբոքի, սիրաբուղխի, սիրազեղի պէս:
Սիրտմոգիկ- սրտանմլիկի, սրտայոյզի փոխարէն:
Սոսկավիթխար- սաստիկ խոշոր իմաստով. «սոսկավիթխար սպառնալիք»:
Վառենի- բոցանմանաչ, հրացայտ, կարմիր շողշողուն ծաղիկներով ծառ (flamboyant):

Վրիպատեսութիւն- սխալ տեսողութիւն:

Տագնապայոյզ- շատ սովորական տագնապալի, տագնապալից, տագնապեցուցիչ բառերուն փոխարէն Կիւրճեան օգտագործած է «տագնապայոյզ ժամանակներ»:

Տեսլահար- կերպարանքէն, տեսիլքէն հարուածուած իմաստով (*Մոգական Գորգը*):

Տիւանդորր- ստեղծուած տիւ (ցերեկ) եւ անդորր (հանգիստ) բառահիմքերէն, ֆրանսերէն sieste-ի համար:

Ցաւակիր- ցաւ կրող: Ցաւ բառարմատէն հայերէնի մէջ ունինք ցաւագին, ցաւալի, ցաւակից, ցաւատանջ եւ նման բառեր: Կիւրճեան այդ բոլորին փոխարէն ստեղծած է ցաւակիր նոր բարդ բառը:

Ցաւահանգիստ- «Սրճարանը» գործին մէջ Կիւրճեան կը գրէ. «Հանգիլ մահուան մեծ ցաւահանգիստը»:

Ցյագ- մինչեւ յագենալը, կշտանալը: Ցայգ, ցայսօր, ցարդ, ցկեանս, ցմահ բառերուն նմանութեամբ հնարուած բառ:

Ցցադրել- ցուցնել, երեւցնել, աչքի առջեւ դնել: Ցուցադրելու հետեւողութեամբ ստեղծուած բառ:

Քեֆարար- հաճոյք ստեղծող, հաճոյալի:

Քրմաբար- քուրմի պէս, քրմօրէն:

Օղեպինդ- միասին օղի խմելով ամրապնդուած. «օղեպինդ յարաբերութիւններ»:

Ահա եւ հայերէնի մէջ քիչ գործածական բառերու նմոյշներ Կիւրճեանի ստեղծագործութիւններէն՝

ապամահ- յետմահու
անշարժացում- քայքայում իմաստով
բազկապահ- թեւը ուրիշի բազուկին մէջ անցուցած
դուզնաքեայ- չնչին, աննշան
խառնակեցիկ- անբարոյական, անառակ, ցոփ
կառավար- կառքը վարող
ձորձ- հագուստ, զգեստ
պաճուճակ- զարդարանք, աւելորդ զարդ
պերեւեթիլ- հագուիլ, սրգուիլ
ջրդեղել- հրաշէկ երկաթը ջուրի մէջ դնել՝ կարծրացնելու համար. պողպատել
սասանում- ուժեղ ցնցում, տակնուվրայ ըլլալը
սռնակ- երկու անիւներ զիրար կապող ձողը
տեսանող- գուշակող
ցնծուհի- պարուհի, աղիճ

եւ դեռ՝ դալարափող, բոլորախորշ, պնդակառք, սահմանաքար, եւայլն:

Որովհետեւ միշտ չէ որ նորաստեղծ բառակազմութիւններն ու բառերը նշած եւ առանձնացուցած ենք մեր ընթերցումներու ընթացքին, վստահ ենք թէ կարելի է համալրել այս ցանկերը եւ Կիրճեանի նորաստեղծ բառերը կրնան առանձին ուսումնասիրութեան առարկայ դառնալ հետագայ ուսումնասիրողներու կողմէ:

Կիրճեան բառերու ճիշդ օգտագործման նպատակով յատուկ բծախնդրութիւն ցուցաբերած է նաեւ թարգմանութիւններ կատարելու ժամանակ, յօրինելով նոր բառեր կամ ածանցումի եւ բարդացումի միջոցով ստեղծելով նոր բառակազմութիւններ: Ահաւասիկ քանի մը օրինակներ՝

բրդակ- ponpon
զգայախաբող- hallucinant
ծաղարարուհի- pâtissière
կարեյոյզ- pathétique
հիանոյշ- admiratrice
ճակատագրազօր- fathédique
մանրաշխարհ- microcosme
նիրհմայուած- hypnotisé
պչրանոյշ- coquette
վառխարան- moxa
վարմունք- comportement
օդահունչ- accordéon

Ինչպէս կը տեսնուի, բացի նորակերտ բառեր ստեղծելէ եւ գործածելէ, Կիրճեան սիրած է քիչ գործածուող բառերը վերակենդանացնել եւ կեանքի կոչել: Ան գոյականը բայի, ածականը գոյականի վերածող եւ մանաւանդ բազում մակբայներու եւ բարդ բառերու ստեղծարար եղած է: Ուստի, շատ կան այնպիսի բառեր, որոնք ինք օգտագործած է իր երկերուն մէջ, բայց որոնք բառարաններու մէջ չկան:

Ոչ յստակ ձեռագրով գրուած դժուարընթեռնելի, խունացած, գունաթափուած ձեռագրերը վերծանելու ժամանակ շատ անգամ ստիպուած եմ եղած դիմել բառարաններու, ինչպէս՝ գրաբար լեզուի հարստութիւնը ամփոփող «Նոր Բառգիրք Հայկազեան Լեզուի»ն (Վենետիկ, 1936) Մկրտիչ Աւգերեանի կազմած համառօտ «Առձեռն Բառարան Հայկազնեան Լեզուի»ի երկրորդ տպագրութիւնը, Վենետիկ, Սուրբ Ղազար, 1965. Սիմոն Գաբամաճեանի «Նոր Բառգիրք Հայերէն Լեզուի»ն (Պոլիս, 1910, պատկերազարդ), Յ. Թ. Գայաեանի «Բառարան-Գանձարան Հայերէն Լեզուի»ն (Գահիրէ, 1938), Արտաշէս Տէր Խաչատուրեանի, Հրանդ Գանգրունիի եւ Փարամազ Տօնիկեանի «Հայոց Լեզուի Նոր Բառարան»ը (Պէյրութ, 1968) եւ ուրիշներ:

ՎԵՐՋԱԲԱՆ

Անձանձիր գրող Միքայէլ Ս. Կիւրճեան իր ութսունվեց տարիներու երկարակեաց կեանքի ընթացքին, պաշտելով իր ժողովուրդը, ընթանալով ժողովրդայնութեան ճանապարհով, սկզբունք ընդունելով գրական նոր ուղղութիւնները, ջատագովելով առաջաւորը արուեստի եւ գրականութեան մէջ, յարելով հայ գրականութեան մէջ ութսունականներու իրապաշտ փաղանգի արժանաւոր ներկայացուցիչներուն, պաշտպանելով իրապաշտ դպրոցի գեղագիտական դրոյթները, հարստացուց հայ գրականութիւնը արժէքաւոր եւ բարձրարուեստ գործերով, միաձուլելով հայկականը համամարդկայինին, առանց խախտելու ազգային ինքնուրոյնութիւնը եւ հաւատարիմ մնալով իրականութեան ճշգրիտ ու համակողմանի արտացոլման սկզբունքներուն:

Կիւրճեան անձնուիրաբար ծառայեց հայ ժողովուրդին ու մշակոյթին, գեղագիտօրէն եւ վարպետօրէն պատկերելով իրական դէմքեր եւ միջավայրեր՝ առանց ծածկելու անոնց տգեղ, անհաճոյ կողմերը: Իրապաշտ գրողը իրը կամ անձը բոլոր կողմերով պատկերելու ձգտող արուեստագէտ մը եղած է:

Հակառակ անոր որ գրողին մի քանի ստեղծագործութիւնները իբրեւ գրական օրինակելի նմոյշներ ընդգրկուած են անցեալ եւ ներկայ արեւմտահայ դասագիրքերու մէջ,[139] ցաւալի է նշել որ ոչ մէկ մենագրութիւն նուիրուած է անոր կեանքին եւ ստեղծագործութեան:

Ուսուցիչ, բանասէր, լեզուաբան եւ գրագէտ Յովհաննէս Գազանճեան իր «Պատմութիւն Հայ Գրականութեան» երկհատոր դասագիրքին մէջ,[140] որ գրուած է Եւդոկիա 1914-1915 թուականներուն, հայ մշակոյթի արժանաւոր դէմքերու շարքին, որոշակի դիմագիծով կը ներկայացնէ նաեւ Կիւրճեանը՝ անոր կեանքին եւ ստեղծագործութեան ուսումնասիրութիւնն ու դասաւանդումը արժանի համարելով հայ դպրոցներուն մէջ:

Անդին, Գուրգէն Մխիթարեան իր «Քառորդ Դար Գրականութիւն» (Գահիրէ, 1946) գիրքին եւ Կ. Սասունի իր «Պատմութիւն Արեւմտահայ Արդի Գրականութեան» (Պէյրութ, 1951) հատորին մէջ չեն իսկ յիշատակած Կիւրճեանի անունը, մինչ Հայր Մեսրոպ Ճանաշեան իր «Հայ Գրականութեան Նոր Շրջանի Համառօտ Պատմութիւն» (Վենետիկ, 1973) գիրքին մէջ անոր անունը յիշատակած է պարզապէս իբրեւ Օտեանի հետ «Հերոսախաղ» թատերգութեան համահեղինակի եւ Թէքէեանի հետ «Շիրակ» ամսաթերթի խմբագրի:

Կիւրճեան չէ ընդգրկուած նաեւ «Հայ Նոր Գրականութեան Պատմութիւն» արժէքաւոր ու ծաւալուն ննգաժատոր ակադեմական ժրատարակութեան մէջ (Երեւան, 1962-1979): Մենք համոզուած ենք որ հայրենի գրականագէտները կ'ուղղեն այս թերացումը եւ Կիւրճեան կը գրաւէ իր արժանավայել տեղը իր գրչակիցներու շարքին:

Կիւրճեան քաջ ծանօթ ըլլալով համաշխարհային եւ յատկապէս ֆրանսական դասական, վիպական, բնապաշտական, խորհրդապաշտական դպրոցներու հեղինակներու գործերուն (Corneille, Molière, Bossuet, Racine, La Fontaine, Boileau, La Bruyère, Voltaire, Chateaubriand, Stendhal, Lamartine, Hugo, Vigny, Musset, Saint-Beuve, George Sand, Balzac, Mérimé, Zola, Baudelaire, Verlaine, Rimbaud, Malarmé), հարստացուց հայ գրականութիւնը ինքնատիպ ստեղծագործութիւններով՝ նորարարական իրապաշտ ուղղութեամբ: Ան կառչած մնաց իրապաշտութեան սկզբունքին՝ առանց ոգեւորուելու քսաներորդ դարու բազմաթիւ կարճատեւ իզմերով (surréalisme, cubisme, existentialisme, unanimisme, fantaisisme, dadisme, lettrisme, modernisme) եւ հետեւելու անոնց:

Կիւրճեանի իրապաշտ մեթոտին հիմքը հանդիսացած է անոր անյողդողդ աշխարհահայեացքը, առանց որուն հնարաւոր չէր ստեղծել այնպիսի անմոռանալի կերպարներ, ինչպէս՝ Մարտիկ Սրմաքէշեանն ու Լեւոն Սուրեանը (*Մարտիկ Աղա*), Իգնատիոս եւ Զարուհի Ռուբինեանները, Անահիտն ու Բարունակ պէյը, Սեդրակ Էլիասեանն ու Պէրպէր Օննիկը (*«Ազգայիննին» Կամ Մեծութիւն Եւ Անկում Պարոն Իգնատիոս Ռուբինեանի*), Գաբրիէլ Թոթվանեանն ու Սուրէն Սրապեանը (*Փրկանքը*), Մէոնսըզ Թումիկն ու Ուղուրսըզ Ճանիկը, Գինեպան Սերչօն ու Տալի Յուսէփը (*Հերոսախաղ*), ալաթուրքա Արթինն ու ալաֆրանկա Եփիմէն (*Ֆրանքօ-Թրքական Պատերազմը Կամ Չարշըլը Արթին Աղա*), Արամը, Սուրբիկ Հանըմը եւ Մաքրուհին (*Տուրքը*), սկիւտարցի ջոջ՝ Պախալ Սարգիսը (*Անունին Գիշերը*), կեսարացի վաճառական Սարգիս էֆէնտի Համբարձումեանը (*Ընտանիք Մը*), իրենց ութսունամեակը բոլորած Գէորգ աղան ու իր կինը՝ Թագուկ տուտուն (*Մարտ*), «Փեսայ մի ըլլաք առանց երկար ատեն փեսացու մնալու» սկզբունքի տէր Միսիսի Սիսակն ու Չամաշըրճի Նունիկի աղջիկը՝ Հոռոփ (*Միսիսի Սիսակ*), ազատախոհ Վիրժինի Սինեմեանը (*Ազատամիտ Աղջիկ Մը*) եւ երկաթագործ Մերկերը (*Նոր Լաթ*), ոսկերիչ Գրիգոր աղան եւ իր որդին՝ դպրոցական Վահրամը (*Անջնջելի Մատեանը*), միմոսի կերպարանքով Նասիպն ու ձկնորս Պետրոսի աղջիկը՝ Հօռօփիկ (*Սուտը Իրաւ՝ Խենդը Խելօք*), ձկնորս Տրդատն ու բանջարավաճառ Տաճատը (*Տրդատ Եւ Տաճատ*), եւ շատ ուրիշ կերպարներ:

Կիւրճեանի ստեղծած բոլոր կերպարները մտացածին չեն. անոնք ժողովուրդին ծոցէն դուրս եկած հասարակ մարդիկ են, որոնք անողոք պայմաններու մէջ շարունակած են գոյատեւել:

Օժտուած ըլլալով դիտելու եւ զննելու մեծ վարպետութեամբ, լաւ ճանչնալով կեանքը եւ խոր ուսումնասիրելով մարդկային յարաբերութիւնները, Կիրճեան գրագէտը յաջողութեամբ բացայայտած է անհատին եւ հասարակութեան, բնաւորութիւններու եւ գործողութիւններու փոխադարձ կապը: Ան ոչ միայն ճշմարտացիօրէն վերարտադրած է կեանքը, այլեւ ստեղծած՝ անհատականացուած եւ տիպականացուած կերպարներ, որոնք իրենց էական ու ընդհանուր յատկանիշներով արտացոլուած են իր ստեղծագործութիւններուն մէջ եւ որոնք ժողովրդականացնող զօրութիւն ունին իրենց մէջ, որովհետեւ Կիրճեանի գրական ժառանգութեան գեղարուեստական ամենագլխաւոր եւ էական յատկանիշն է իրականութեան ճշմարտացի արտացոլումը՝ անձը, իրը, դէպքը կարելի հարազատութեամբ ներկայացնելու եւ գեղարուեստօրէն վերարտադրելու ճարտարութիւնը:

Ճիշդ է որ Կիրճեան չի ներկայանար վիպասան Օնորէ տը Պալզաքի ստեղծած շուրջ 3000 գրական հերոսներու արգասաւորութեամբ, ոչ ալ բնապաշտական դպրոցի ղեկավար Էմիլ Զոլայի «Ռուգոն-Մաքարները» երկտասնեակէ աւելի վիպաշարքին մէջ պարփակուած 1200է աւելի տիպերու ճոխութեամբ, բայց ան հայ գրականութեան պատարագասեղանը կը շնորհազարդէ բազմահարիւր հայ տիպական կերպարներով, իւրաքանչիւրը՝ իր իւրայատուկ բնաւորութեամբ եւ ինքնատիպ յատկանիշներով:

Հաւատարիմ մնալով հայկական հին սովորութիւններուն եւ աւանդոյթներուն, Կիրճեան իր խորապէս ուսումնասիրած կեանքն է պատկերած իր ստեղծագործութիւններուն մէջ եւ այդ իսկ պատճառով իր գործերը դարձած են ժամանակի իրականութեան բազմաթիւ երեւոյթներու իրապաշտ պատկերները, որոնք յառաջ բերած են աշխոյժ հետաքրքրութիւն ընթերցող հասարակութեան ամենալայն խաւերուն մէջ: Հանոյքով ընթերցուող գրող մը եղած է Կիրճեան, որ գիտցած է կեանքը պատկերել պահանջուած բծախնդրութեամբ, դէմքերն ու դէպքերը նկարագրել խորունկ զգացումով, վարպետօրէն արտայայտելով վիշտն ու ծիծաղը, շաղկապելով թախիծն ու խնդուքը, միախառնելով տառապանքն ու զուարթութիւնը:

Կիրճեանի թողած գրական ժառանգութիւնը հրապուրիչ, դաստիարակիչ եւ իւրայատուկ է, որովհետեւ ան համաքայլ ընթացած է միջազգային ու ազգային նորարարական երեւոյթներուն, գրական նոր ու առաջաւոր ուղղութիւններուն հետ: Ինքնատիպ խորաթափանցութեամբ եւ գաղափարական բովանդակութեամբ, նկարագրութիւններու հարազատութեամբ եւ բարքերու վաւերականութեամբ, պատկերաւոր մտածողութեամբ եւ գեղարուեստական բարեմասնութեամբ, բարեմիտ երգիծականութեամբ եւ ինքնատիպ սրամտութեամբ, ոճի պարզութեամբ եւ լեզուի յղկուածութեամբ:

Ընդգրկուն է Կիրճեանի խորաշխարհը: Անոր գրութիւններուն նիւթը եւ խորքը հարազատ ժողովուրդին կեանքն ու ժամանակի հրատապ խնդիրներն են եղած եւ զանոնք ջանասիրաբար արծարծած է իր ստեղծագործութիւններուն մէջ: Իր գործերը ուշագրաւ են եւ թելադրական, շեշտուած են նուրբ ոճով եւ խստապահանջօրէն մշակուած՝ մաքուր ու սահուն լեզուով:

Կիւրճեանի բազմաթիւ թարգմանութիւնները, որոնք ցիր ու ցան հրատարակուած են զանազան պարբերական հրատարակութիւններու մէջ, կը բացայայտեն գեղագիտական նուրբ շնորհով հմուտ թարգմանիչը:

Քաջ գիտակցելով երգիծանքի հասարակական վեհ նշանակութեան, ան վճռական դեր կատարած է գրականութեան ժողովրդականացման եւ իրապաշտ դպրոցի հաստատման գործին մէջ, որով պայմանաւորուած է իր անուան եւ ստեղծագործութիւններուն անմահութիւնը:

Կիւրճեան իրաւունք ունի մեծն Պարոնեանի աւանդութիւնը շարունակողներուն մէջ իր կարեւոր դիրքը գրաւելու՝ առօրեայէն քաղուած խիստ այժմէական հարցերու անդրադարձող գործերով:

Հայ գրականութիւնը եւ գրաքննադատութիւնը պարտաւոր են վառ պահել Կիւրճեանի լուսաւորած ջահը, որովհետեւ բազմաշնորհ գրագէտը օժտուած էր ստեղծագործական անժխտելի տաղանդով, գրական վարպետութեամբ, երգիծական նուրբ ու բնական ձիրքով, գեղագիտական գերազանց ճաշակով:

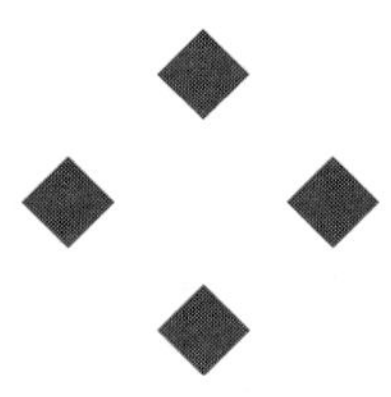

ԾԱՆՕԹԱԳՐՈՒԹԻՒՆՆԵՐ

1 *Արեւ*, 9 Յուլիս 1965:

2 Ակնարկուած թատրերգութիւնը «Փրկանքը» իրապաշտ տրամն է՝ գրուած Միքայէլ Կիւրճեանի հեղինակակցութեամբ:

3 Թէոդիկ, *Ամէնուն Տարեցոյցը*, Կ. Պոլիս, 1910, չորրորդ տարի, էջ 120 (շեղագրումներն իմն են _ Յ.Մ.):

4 Նոյն, Փարիզ, 1928, էջ 468 (շեղագրումներն իմն են _ Յ.Մ.):

5 Վ. Մալէզեան, *Ժամբուս Ծայրը*, Բ. հատոր — *Հնադրոշմ Նամակներ Եւ Գրական Նշխարներ*, Փարիզ, 1955, էջ 59 (շեղագրումներն իմն են _ Յ.Մ.):

6 Գուրգէն Մխիթարեան իր *Քառորդ Դար Գրականութիւն* գիրքին (Գահիրէ, տպագր. Յուսաբեր, 1946) 178րդ էջին վրայ, խօսելով Օշականի պահանջկոտութեան մասին, կը նշէ թէ «իր աչքը նախ՝ ծամածռութիւնները կը տեսնէ, գեղեցկութիւնները փնտռելէ առաջ: Չունի հիացում, ընդհանրապէս.- հիւանդութի՛ւնը մեր դարուն: Չունի բարեկամութիւն.- սակարա՛նը մեր օրերուն: Այս պատճառներով, նախ տխեղծը կը տեսնէ, ապա հաստատելու համար հաստատուն մասը, եթէ գտնէ»:

7 Յակոբ Օշական, *Հայ Գրականութիւն*, Երուսաղէմ, 1942, էջ 565 (շեղագրումներն իմն են _ Յ.Մ.):

8 Ե. Օտեան, *Երկերի Ժողովածու*, Դ. հատոր, Երեւան, 1962, էջ 134:

9 Նոյն, էջ 134 (շեղագրումներն իմն են _ Յ.Մ.):

10 Նոյն, էջ 301 (շեղագրումներն իմն են _ Յ.Մ.):

11 Նոյն, էջ 533 (շեղագրումներն իմն են _ Յ.Մ.):

12 Երուանդ Ազատեան, *Գրական Գեղարուեստական Սեւեռումներ*, Լա Վըրն, Գալիֆորնիա, հրատարակութիւն Ամերիկահայ Միջազգային Գոլէճի, 1988, 333 էջ:

13 Միքայէլ Կիւրճեան, *Քսան Տարի Ետք. Ֆրանքօ-Թրքական Պատերազմը Կը Ծարունակուի Կամ Տիկին Եւփիմէի Յաղթանակը, Պատմուածքներ Եւ Պատկերներ*, Պէյրութ, Հրատարակութիւն Սեւան տպարանի, 1961, 100 էջ:

14 Հայաստանի Գրականութեան եւ Արուեստի Թանգարան, Մ. Ս. Կիւրճեանի արխիւ, *Օրագրութիւն Եւ Նշումներ*, 1903:

15 *Ժամանակ*, Պոլիս, 25-8 Մայիս 1911:

16 Պարթեւեան Սուրէն, *Եգիպտահայ Տարեցոյցը*, 1914, էջ 198:

17 Նոյն:

18 Ռէթէոս Պէրպէրեանի նամակը Մ. Կիւրճեանին, 16 Նոյեմբեր 1904:

19 Պարթեւեան Սուրէն, *Եգիպտահայ Տարեցոյցը*, 1914:

20 Այդ գիրքերը ժառանգ մնացած են Երուանդ Ազատեանի: Անոնց մէկ մասը ղրկուած է Հայաստան, իսկ մնացեալը նուիրուած է Աղեքսանդրիոյ Տիգրան Երկաթ ակումբի գրադարանին:

21 Ազատեան կ'ըսէ. «Կիւրճեանի մահուան առիթով հրատարակած էի «Արեւ»ի մասնաւոր թիւ մը, ուր տպուած էր Կիւրճեանի մեղայականը Թէքէեանին, անոր առաջին հատորին՝ «Հոգեր»ուն հրատարակութեան առիթով խիստ գրախօսականին համար, «Փարոս», 1901: Այնտեղ Կիւրճեան կը նկարագրէ թէ ինչպէս ուզած է նմանիլ Դուրեանին եւ Մեծարենցին՝ լոյսէ եւ արեւէ զրկուելով իր վրայ թոքախտ հրաւիրելով: Օր մըն ալ երբ իր թուքին մէջ արիւն կը գտնէ, կը դիմէ բժիշկին, որ կը յանձնարարէ բաց օդին ելլել եւ երկարօրէն քալել: Այդ ձեւով կեանքին կը վերադառնայ եւ նորադարձի իր բուռն ապրումներուն մէջ հիւանդոտ, «հարբխոտ» բան մը կը տեսնէ Թէքէեանի առաջին հատորին մէջ: «Արեւ»ի ամբողջ այդ թիւը զետեղուած է Աւետիս Սանճեանի հրատարակած «Թէքէեանի Նամականի»ին մէջ:

22 «Միքայէլ Ս. Կիւրճեանի Նամակներէն Տօքթօր Յարութիւն Թիրեաքեանին»: Տես՝ *Պայքար*, Ուոթըրթաուն, 25 Յուլիս 1965:

23 Նոյն:

24 Այս մէջբերումը քաղուած է Մ. Կիւրճեանի 1908 թուականի Նոյեմբեր ամսուն Տօքթօր Յարութիւն Թիրեաքեանին ուղղուած նամակէն, որուն նմանահանութիւնը սիրայօժար ուղարկած է ինծի բժիշկին որդին՝ Միհրդատ Թիրեաքեան, Նիւ Եորքէն:

25 Ֆրանսական քաղաք Փարիզէն 542 քմ հարաւ-արեւելք, նոյնանուն լիճի հիւսիսային ափին:

26 Նահանգամաս, գաւառ Ֆրանսայի հարաւ-արեւելեան կողմը, Ալպեան լեռներու՝ Մօն Պլանի արեւմտեան կողմը:

27 Պուրկոնյի նախկին մայրաքաղաքը, Փարիզէն 309 քմ հարաւ-արեւելք:

28 Ֆրանսացի վիպասան եւ լրագրող (1889-1949): 1917ին գրած է «Ֆրանսական Երիտասարդ Բանաստեղծութեան Մասին» ուսումնասիրութիւնը: Եղած է Les Nouvelles Littéraires-ի գլխաւոր խմբագիր: Լրագրական գործունէութեան զուգահեռ՝ ունի գրական գործեր եւ փիլիսոփայական ուսումնասիրութիւններ:

29 Ֆրանսացի քննադատ եւ վիպասան (1852-1935), որուն անդրանիկ գիրքը՝ «Անհանգիստ Կեանքը» չափածոյ ստեղծագործութիւններու ժողովածուն լոյս տեսած է 1874ին, սակայն առաւել հռչակաւոր դարձած է իր «Ժամանակակից Հոգեբանութեան Նախափորձերը» (1883) աշխատութեամբ, որուն յաջորդեցին «Նորագոյն Սիրոյ Հոգեբանութիւնը» (1890), «Զգացումներ Իտալիայէն» (1891), իսկ 1889ին հրատարակուած «Կարգապահը» հաստատեց իր հռչակն ու համբաւը: Իր բազմաթիւ վէպերէն թուարկենք՝ «Կնոջ Սիրտ Մը» (1902), «Միջօրեայ Դեւը» (1914) եւ «Մեր Գործերը Կը Հետեւին Մեզի» (1927):

30 Ե. Օտեան, *Երկերի Ժողովածու*, Դ. հատոր, Երեւան, 1962, էջ 378:

31 Նոյն, էջ 362:

32 Լեւոնեանի այս աշխատութիւնը, որ կազմուած է իր յիշողութեամբ, բանաւոր գիտելիքներով եւ գրաւոր ծանօթութիւններով, հրատարակուած է յետ մահու լոյս տեսած «Երկեր» ժողովածուին մէջ, Երեւան, 1963:

33 Գ. Լեւոնեան, *Երկեր*, Երեւան, Հայպետհրատ, 1963, էջ 471:

34 Նոյն, էջ 478:

35 Նոյն, էջ 458:

36 Յ. Թ. Գայաեան (Մխիթար Պոնտացի), *Բառարան-Գանձարան Հայերէն Լեզուի*, Գահիրէ, տպագրութիւն Գալֆա, 1938:

37 Ա. Ղազիկեան, *Հայկական Նոր Մատենագիտութիւն Եւ Հանրագիտարան Հայ Կեանքի*, պրակ Բ., Վենետիկ, Ս. Ղազար, 1912, սիւնակ 1319:

38 «Սաւառնակ» երգիծական շաբաթաթերթի խմբագիր Երուանդ Մարլեան ինծի գրած 18 Ապրիլ 1967 թուակիր նամակին մէջ կը յայտնէ որ այդ պատմուածքները «Արեւ»ի մէջ տպագրելու համար պատրաստուած շարուածքէն տպագրուած են եւ թէ միայն գրքոյկին կողքը տպագրուած է Ոսկետառ տպարանին մէջ:

39 Տպագրական վրիպակ պէտք է համարել Սրճեփ Ա.ի փոխարէն *Արճեփ Ա.* սխալագրութիւնը «Սփիւռք»ի մէջ:

40 *Արեւ*, 15 Յուլիս 1965, հրատարակուած յետ մահու:

41 Կիւրճեանի այս նամակին նմանահանութիւնը սիրայօժար ինծի ուղարկած է բժիշկին որդին՝ Միհրդատ Թիրեաքեան, Նիւ Եորքէն:

42 Սահմանադիր Ռամկավար Կուսակցութեան Աղեքսանդրիոյ ակումբի փառատօնին համար Կիւրճեան թարգմանած է Լէոփոլտ Լալիւէի «Գարնանը» մէկ արարով կատակերգութիւնը, որ նուագախառն ֆանթէզիի վերածուած՝ յաջողութեամբ ներկայացուած է Աղեքսանդրիոյ մէջ Մարտ 1912ին:

43 *Ճիրվանզադէ Եւ Իր Գործը*, Պոլիս, 1911, էջ 91-110:

44 «Մշակ»ը լոյս տեսած է 1872-1921 թուականներուն: Հիմնադիրը եւ սկիզբի քսան տարիներու խմբագիրը եղած է հրապարակախօս, քննադատ եւ հասարակական գործիչ Գրիգոր Արծրունին:

45 *Ինքնակենսագրութիւն Եւ Յուշեր*, էջ 5:

46 Պարթեւեան Ս., *Եգիպտահայ Տարեցոյցը*, Գահիրէ, Ա. տարի, 1914, էջ 88-95:

47 Նոյն, էջ 29-32:

48 Նոյն, Բ. տարի, 1915, էջ 64-72:

49 *Նոր Կեանք*, Լոնտոն, Ա. տարի, թիւ 20, 15 Հոկտեմբեր 1898, էջ 308:

50 Նոյն:

51 Նոյն, էջ 309:

52 Նոյն:

53 Նոյն, Բ. տարի, 15 Մարտ 1899, էջ 95:

54 Նոյն, էջ 94:

55 Երուանդ Օտեան, *Երկերի Ժողովածու*, Դ. հատոր, Երեւան, 1962, էջ 132:

56 Նոյն, էջ 134:

57 Ս. Պարթեւեան, *Եգիպտահայ Տարեցոյցը*, Ա. տարի, 1914, Գահիրէ, էջ 211:
58 Երուանդ Օտեան, *Երկրերի Ժողովածու*, Դ. հատոր, Երեւան, 1962, էջ 132:
59 Նոյն, էջ 133:
60 Նոյն, էջ 133-134:
61 Նոյն, էջ 135:
62 *Նոր Կեանք*, Ա. տարի, թիւ 22, 15 Նոյեմբեր 1898, էջ 345:
63 Նոյն, էջ 346:
64 Նոյն:
65 Նոյն, թիւ 23, 1 Դեկտեմբեր 1898, էջ 361:
66 Նոյն, թիւ 20, 15 Հոկտեմբեր 1898, էջ 307:
67 Նոյն, Բ. տարի, թիւ 5, 1 Մարտ 1899, էջ 79:
68 Երուանդ Օտեան, *Երկրերի Ժողովածու*, Դ. հատոր, Երեւան, 1962, էջ 135 (շեղագրումները իմն են - Յ.Մ.):
69 *Արեւ* օրաթերթ, Գահիրէ, 27 Դեկտեմբեր 1963:
70 *Շիրակ*, Կ. Պոլիս, 1909, թիւ 2, էջ 72:
71 *Խարազան*, Ա. տարի, թիւ 4, 28 Փետրուար 1909, էջ 59:
72 Քէօթահեան Ծաhնազար, *Յուշեր Ու Նիշեր*, Լոս Անճելըս, 1990, էջ 165:
73 Մ. Ասլանեանի 7 Ապրիլ 1964 թուակիր նամակը ուղղուած Միքայէլ Կիւրճեանի, «Արեւ», 22 Մայիս 1964:
74 *Հայրենիք ամսագիր*, 1927, Ե. տարի, թիւ 8(56), էջ 45:
75 Երուանդ Օտեան, *Երկրերի Ժողովածու*, Ա. հատոր, Երեւան, 1960, էջ 687:
76 Նոյն, էջ 714:
77 *Արեւ*, Գահիրէ, 27 Դեկտեմբեր 1963:
78 *Շիրակ*, գրական եւ ընկերային ամսաթերթ, Աղեքսանդրիա, 1905, Ա. տարի, թիւ 2, էջ 101-112:
79 *Վահան Թէքէեան, Նամականի*, լոս Անճելըս, 1983, էջ 174:
80 Նոյն, էջ 189:
81 Յակոբ Օշական, *Հայ Գրականութիւն*, Երուսաղէմ, 1942, էջ 404:
82 *Հայ Կին*, կիսամսեայ հանդէս, Գ. տարի, թիւ 6, 16 Յունուար 1922, էջ 867:
83 *Ծանթ*, գրական գեղարուեստական պատկերազարդ կիսամսեայ հանդէս, Ղալաթիա, Ա. տարի, թիւ 14, 1-14 Յունուար 1911, էջ 231:
84 Paul Bourget (1852-1935) ֆրանսացի վիպասան եւ գրաքննադատ:
85 Պարոյր Սեւակ, *Երկերի Ժողովածու*, Ե. հատոր, Երեւան, Հայաստան հրատարակչութիւն, 1974, էջ 52:
86 Երուանդ Ազատեան, *Գրական Գեղարուեստական Սեւեռումներ*, Լա Վըրն, Գալիֆորնիա, 1988, էջ 65-76:
87 *Արեւ* օրաթերթ, Գահիրէ, 9 Յուլիս 1965:
88 Վահան Թէքէեան, *Ամբողջական Երկեր*, Գահիրէ, հատոր 9, էջ 66-71:
89 *Մասիս* պարբերական, Պոլիս, 54րդ տարի, Ե. շրջան, թիւ 2, 10 Յունուար 1904, էջ 19:

90 *Ֆրիմը* (ֆրանսերէն) – կեղծիք, կերպարանութիւն, նկարագրութիւն, պատկերում, կերպարանաւորութիւն:

91 *Խարազան* երգիծական օրաթերթ, Պոլիս, Ա. տարի, թիւ 9, 25 Մարտ 1909, էջ 68-69:

92 *Ծաղիկ* շաբաթաթերթ, Պոլիս, 21 Փետրուար 1904, 17րդ տարի, թիւ 8 (592), էջ 105-106:

93 Տիրան Չրաքեանի նամակը Միքայէլ Կիւրճեանին, գրուած 11/27 Նոյեմբեր 1909ին Սկիւտարէն:

94 Pierre Loti – Ժողովային պաշտօնեայ, եւ ֆրանսացի գրող (1850-1923): Տպաւորապաշտ վիպասան: Ֆրանսական Ակադեմիայի անդամ: Գրած է «Լոթիի Ամուսնութիւնը», «Իմ Եղբայրը՝ Իվ», «Իսլանտայի Ձկնորսը», «Տիկին Քրիզանթէմ», «Անկախարդեալները», «Ռամունչօ» եւ այլ երկեր:

95 Թէոդիկ, *Ամէնուն Տարեցոյցը*, Պոլիս, 1909, Գ. տարի, էջ 278-279:

96 *Արեւ* օրաթերթ, Գահիրէ, 14, 21, 28 Մայիս եւ 4 Յունիս 1949:

97 Վահան Թէքէեանին նուիրուած այս բանաստեղծութիւնը տպագրուած է 1925ին Հ.Բ.Ը.Մ.ի *Յուշարար-Միութիւն* պարբերականին, Թէոդիկի *Ամէնուն Տարեցոյցը*ին եւ այլ հայատառ թերթերու մէջ:

98 Երուանդ Ազատեան կը վկայէ. «Այս հաստատումը տառացիօրէն հաւաստի է եւ ճշգրիտ. որովհետեւ, այն շրջանին երբ Կիւրճեան կը յօրինէր այս տողերը, արդէն իր պաշտելին գտած էր ուրիշ սէր մը՝ Կիւրճեանը առնելով եռոտանիի մը ցանցին մէջ: Տարօրինակ այլասիրութեամբ մը Կիւրճեան երջանիկ էր որ իր սէրը երջանիկ էր ... թէկուզ ուրիշով մը: Դժուար է այս եռանկիւնին սիրային-սեռային խորքին թափանցել՝ եթէ զանց ընենք շրջան ընող գրոյցներն ու բամբասանքները»:

99 *Արեւ* օրաթերթ, Գահիրէ, 4 Նոյեմբեր 1960:

100 *Զուարթնոց* ամսաթերթ գրականութեան եւ արուեստներու, Փարիզ, նոր շրջան, Ե. տարի, թիւ 5-6, էջ 14:

101 *Արեւ* օրաթերթ, Գահիրէ, 21 Օգոստոս 1965:

102 Երուանդ Օտեան, *Երկերի Ժողովածու*, Դ. հատոր, Երեւան, 1962, էջ 362:

103 *Շիրակ* գրական, քաղաքական եւ հասարակական հանդէս, Աղեքսանդրիա, 1905, թիւ 1, էջ 2:

104 *Արեւ* օրաթերթ, Գահիրէ, 23 Յունիս 1965:

105 *Միութիւն* ամսօրեայ պաշտօնաթերթ Հ.Բ.Ը.Մ.ի, Ա. տարի, թիւ 7, Յուլիս 1912, էջ 102:

106 Նոյն, Ա. տարի, թիւ 6, Յունիս 1912:

107 Արփիար Արփիարեան, *Պատմութիւն ԺԹ. Դարու Թուրքիոյ Հայոց Գրականութեան*, Գահիրէ, 1944, էջ 83:

108 *Six French Poets of the Nineteenth Century*, edited with an introduction and notes by E.H. and A.M. Blackmore, Oxford University Press, էջ 165-166:

109 Յովհաննէս Թումանեան, *Երկեր*, Զ. հատոր, Երեւան, էջ 152:

110 *Ծաղկաքաղ Ֆրանսիական Դասական Քնարերգութեան*, Երեւան, 1976, էջ 124:

111 Նոյն, էջ 62-64:

112 Գրաքարագէտ եւ մանկավարժ Միհրան Ասքանազ Պոլսոյ մէջ հրատարակած է «Ծաղիկ Մանկանց» շաբաթական հանդէսը: 1896ին Պոլսէն հարկադրաբար հեռանալէ առաջ, իր բոլոր անտիպ ձեռագրերն ու թուղթերը խնամքով թաղել կու տայ Գատը Քէօյի Ճէվիզլիք թաղի Ֆուատ պէյ անուն թուրքին պարտէզին մէջ: Ապա հայ գաղթականութեան հոսանքին հետ ընտանիքով կ'անցնի Եգիպտոս եւ Աղեքսանդրիոյ Պօղոսեան վարժարանին մէջ կը վարէ ուսուցչական պաշտօն:

113 *Շիրվանզադէ Եւ Իր Գործը*, ժողովածու, Պոլիս, 1911, էջ 93-94:

114 *Շանթ* գրական եւ գեղարուեստական պատկերազարդ կիսամսեայ հանդէս, Ա. տարի, թիւ 19, 15-28 Մարտ 1912, էջ 311-312:

115 Երուանդ Օտեան, *Ընկեր Բ. Փանջունի Ի Ծապլվար Եւ Վասպուրական*. ծաղրանկարեց՝ Ալ. Սարուխան: Գահիրէ, տպարան Սահակ-Մեսրոպ, 1938, 248 էջ:

116 *Արեւ* օրաթերթ, Գահիրէ, 11 Ապրիլ 1962:

117 Նոյն, 4 Ապրիլ 1964:

118 Honoré Daumier (1808-1879) ֆրանսացի անուանի նկարիչ, վիմագրիչ եւ քանդակագործ, որ հռչակաւոր է իր քաղաքական եւ ընկերային երգիծանկարներով:

119 Marie de la Fayette (1634-1693) ֆրանսացի կին գրող, որ ծնած է Փարիզ:

120 Abbé Prévost (1697-1763) ֆրանսացի վիպասան:

121 Benjamin Constant de Rebecque (1767-1830) ֆրանսացի գրող եւ քաղաքական գործիչ:

122 Շուանը անունն է ֆրանսացի Ժան Շուանի գլխաւորած ապստամբներուն, որոնք կը պատերազմէին պուրպոնեան թագաւորներու դէմ:

123 Hippolyte Taine (1828-1893) ֆրանսացի փիլիսոփայ, պատմաբան եւ քննադատ. ֆրանսական ակադեմիայի անդամ:

124 Edmond Jaloux (1878-1949) ֆրանսացի գրող եւ գրաքննադատ:

125 *Արեւ* օրաթերթ, Գահիրէ, 6 Ապրիլ 1946:

126 Թէնի քննադատական տեսութիւնները հիմնուած էին ազգատոհմի, միջավայրի եւ ժամանակի հռչակաւոր եռաքանութեան վրայ:

127 Ferdinand Brunetière (1849-1906) ֆրանսացի գրաքննադատ, որ իր ուսումնասիրութիւններուն մէջ կիրարկած է գրական սեռերու յեղաշրջական տեսութիւնները:

128 Թալիան մէկն է ֆրանսացի քանդակագործ Փիլոնի (1537-1590) «Երեք Դիցուհիները» արձանի երեք դէմքերէն (Aglaé, Thalie, Euphrosyne), որոնք կ'անձնաւորէին գեղեցկութեան մէջ ամենահրապուրիչ բաները:

129 *Արեւ* օրաթերթ, Գահիրէ, 1 եւ 2 Մայիս 1964:

130 «Եղիա Տէմիրճիպաշեանի Մէկ Ձեռագիր Քերթուածին Առթիւ», *Հայ Գրականութիւն*, Զմիւռնիա, Ա. տարի, 1/14 Յունիս 1912, թիւ 12, էջ 11-15, կամ *Հայաստանի Կոչնակ*, ԻԹ. տարի, թիւ 1, 1 Յունուար 1929, էջ 12-14:

131 «Գարունը Ռ. Պէրպէրեանի Եւ Ինտրայի Գրչին Տակ», *Արեւ* օրաթերթ, Գահիրէ, 2 Մայիս 1964:

132 Ուիլիըմ Սամըրսէթ Մոըմ (1874-1965) անգլիացի յայտնի գրող:

133 Տարիա Կամսարական ծնած է 1907ին Աղեքսանդրիա: 1924ին անցած է Փարիզ: Քանդակագործութեամբ սկսած է զբաղիլ ռուս քանդակագործ Կոնստանի հետ, որ Եգիպտոս կը գտնուէր: Փարիզ ան տարիներով աշակերտած է ֆրանսացի հռչակաւոր քանդակագործ Էմիլ-Անթուան Պուտէլի (1861-1929), որ հեղինակն է Զօրավար Ալվէար յիշատակարանի աղեղնաւոր «Հերակլէս» քանդակին:

134 *Արեւ* օրաթերթ, Գահիրէ, 10 եւ 11 Ապրիլ 1964:

135 Նոյն, 19 Մարտ 1963:

136 Պարոյր Սեւակ, *Երկերի Ժողովածու*, հատոր Ե., Երեւան, 1974, էջ 152:

137 Անդ:

138 *Արեւ* օրաթերթ, Գահիրէ, 9 Յուլիս 1965:

139 Կիւրճեանի «Քեաթիպին Երազը» և «Սրճարանը» արևելապատումները լոյս տեսած են Ա. Պիպեռճեանի «Ճաշակ Արդի Հայ Մատենագրութեան» երկի առաջին հատորի չորրորդ բարեփոխուած տպագրութեան մէջ (Պոլիս, 1910, էջ 313-319 և 336-340): «Նոր Լաթ» և «Քեաթիպին Երազը» պատմուածքները ընդգրկուած են Օշականի կազմած «Հայ Գրականութիւն» դասագիրքին մէջ (Երուսաղէմ, 1942), առաջինը որոշ կրճատումներով Ա. հատորի 217-218 էջերուն, իսկ երկրորդը Բ. հատորի 563-565 էջերուն վրայ:

140 Յովհաննէս Գազանճեան, *Պատմութիւն Հայ Գրականութեան*, Բ. հատոր (ԺԹ. դարու կէսերէն մինչև մեր օրերը), Եւդոկիա, 1915, Անթիլիաս, 1970, 214 էջ: